Regulatory Reform and Competitiveness in Europe, I

Regulatory Reform and Competitiveness in Europe, I

Horizontal Issues

Edited by

Giampaolo Galli

Director
Centro Studi Confindustria,
Rome

CONFINDUSTRIA

and

Jacques Pelkmans

Senior Research Fellow
Centre for European Policy
Studies, Brussels

C E
P S

Edward Elgar
Cheltenham, UK • Northampton, MA, USA

Published by
Edward Elgar Publishing Limited
Glensanda House
Montpellier Parade
Cheltenham
Glos GL50 1UA
UK

Edward Elgar Publishing, Inc.
136 West Street
Suite 202
Northampton
Massachusetts 01060
USA

A catalogue record for this book
is available from the British Library

ISBN 1 84064 423 0

Printed and bound in Great Britain by MPG Books Ltd, Bodmin, Cornwall

This project has been undertaken at the initiative and with the main financial support of the Confederation of Italian Industry in close collaboration with the Centre for European Policy Studies. The views expressed in these volumes are those of the authors and do not necessarily reflect the views of the supporting institutions.

This work has been produced with the financial support of the European Commission.

Acknowledgements

The editors wish to thank the authors for sticking to a tight schedule, despite considerable research efforts. The editors would like to acknowledge the contributions of Sandrine Labory (then at CEPS) and Marco Malgarini (CSC) to the success of this large project.

All are grateful for the meticulous technical and linguistic editing (under great time pressure) by Anne Harrington, helped by Isabelle Tenaerts and other colleagues at CEPS. Last but not least, we gratefully acknowledge the financial support provided by DG Enterprise of the European Commission. This support, however, should not be interpreted as an endorsement by the Commission of any particular statement, proposal or analysis contained in these two volumes.

Contents

List of Figures

List of Tables

List of Contributors

Philip Baake is an economist at Humboldt University, Berlin.
Charles Blankart is Professor at Humboldt University, Berlin.
Tito Boeri is Professor at University Bocconi-IGIER, Milan, and CEPR.
Martin Carree is an Economist with the Centre for Advanced Small Business Economics, Faculty of Economics, Erasmus University, Rotterdam.
Alberto Cavaliere is Professor at Universita' di Pavia e Libero Istituto Universitatio C. Cattaneo, Castellanza, Varese.
Peter Clinch is Director of Graduate Studies, Department of Enviromental Studies, University College, Dublin.
Luca Di Mauro is Junior Research Fellow at the Centre for European Policy Studies, Brussels.
Giampaolo Galli is Director of Centro Studi Confindustria (CSC), the research department of the Confederation of Italian Industry in Rome.
George Gelauff is an economist at the CPB Netherlands Bureau for Economic Policy Analysis and Professor at the University of Nijmegen.
Christian Jansen is a Lecturer at Humboldt University, Berlin.
Sandrine Labory is Researcher at the University of Bergamo.
Giandomenico Majone is Professor Emeritus at the European University Institute in Florence.
Marco Malgarini is an Economist at Centro Studi Confindustria, Rome.
Stephen Martin is Professor at the Centre for Industrial Economics, University of Copenhagen.
Giuseppe Nicoletti is an Economist at the OECD in Paris.
Jacques Pelkmans is Senior Research Fellow at the Centre for European Policy Studies, Brussels and Professor of European Economic Integration at Maastricht University.
Marc Pomp is Head of Unit and Economist at the CPB Netherlands Bureau for Economic Policy Analysis.
Pierluigi Sabbatini is at the Italian Antitrust Authority.
Stefano Scarpetta is an Economist at the OECD in Paris.
Francesco Silva is Professor at Libero Istituto Universitario C. Cattaneo, Castellanza, Varese.

Roy Thurik is Professor and associated with the Centre for Advanced Small Business Economics, at the Faculty of Economics, Erasmus University, Rotterdam.

Paola Valbonesi is Professor at the University of Padova.

Patrick Van Cayseele is Professor at the Catholic University at Leuven and is with the Belgian Antitrust Authority.

Wim Van Meerbeeck is a Lecturer at the Catholic University at Leuven.

Ellen Vos is a Lecturer in European Law at Maastricht University.

Preface

Ensuring higher competitiveness standards for firms is a precondition for improving living standards, boosting productivity and increasing employment in Europe. The 1995 UNICE report on regulatory reform already concluded that many aspects of the European regulatory stance reduce the competitiveness of companies in global markets, discourage new entrants, impede the use of new methods of production and inhibit the exit of existing obsolete competitors. As stated in the conclusions of the UNICE report, reforming the regulatory framework is a major task, and responsibilities for successful completion lie with governments at all levels. The role of business and of the academic community may nonetheless be very important in stimulating awareness of the changes needed in order to improve the regulatory framework.

On the occasion of the 90th anniversary of the founding of the Confederation of Italian Industry, the Research Department (CSC) took the initiative to promote an extensive research project on the regulatory stance in the EU, in collaboration with CEPS, an independent research centre based in Brussels. CEPS has a longstanding tradition of research on regulation; CSC has recently promoted major projects on the simplification of the Italian public administration. This new project focuses on Europe as a whole, because in a global world, with 11 European economies now sharing a common currency, the problem of the efficiency of the regulatory framework can no longer be dealt only at the national level. The project was co-financed by the European Commission.

For this project, co-edited by Giampaolo Galli, Director of CSC, and Jacques Pelkmans, Senior Research Fellow at CEPS, a number of well known international experts have been asked to outline the main characteristics of the regulatory regime in their field of research and to lay down concrete policy proposals, aimed at enhancing the growth potential of European economies. The authors have worked in full independence and their opinions do not imply any position of either CSC and CEPS. Thanks to the high quality of the experts involved, the results achieved represent an important contribution to the debate on the regulatory stance in the EU.

xv

The reader will be left with no doubt that the inefficiency of the actual regulatory stance is a major, if not the principal explanation accounting for the poor performance of European economies in the 1990s. Labour markets are still too rigid, protecting the insiders at the expense of outsiders. Competition policies are not implemented in an efficient way. The single market has been a major achievement, but is still incomplete. Protection of the environment and pursuit of consumer safety often cause excessively high compliance costs for firms. In key sectors of the economy, especially in the industries operating in networks and providing public utilities, liberalisation has often been delayed and existing regulation does not guarantee fair competition and discourages competitiveness and growth.

A wave of regulatory reforms, following the suggestions of these two volumes, may therefore dramatically improve the business environment and boost the efficiency of European economies in the years to come.

Guidalberto Guidi
Delegated Advisor to the Research Department, Confindustia
Peter Ludlow
Director, Centre for European Policy Studies

January 2000

1. Introduction: Aims, Structure and Overview

Giampaolo Galli and Jacques Pelkmans

1. WHY STUDY REGULATION AND COMPETITIVENESS IN EUROPE?

Ever since publication of the well known White Paper of December 1993, concerns about European prospects for competitiveness, jobs and growth are on the top of the EU agenda. Regulatory reforms, both at national and EU levels, are widely recognised to be a crucial tool for improving the performance of European economies. The 1995 regulatory report of UNICE[1] already concluded that many aspects of the current regulatory regime in Europe protect the 'status quo' and reduce the competitiveness of European companies in world markets. According to the report, the extensive scope and rigid nature of regulation tend to discourage new entrants, impede the use of new methods of production and inhibit the exit of existing competitors. Such regulation also increases costs, reduces operational flexibility and distorts capital expenditure. Similar conclusions are reached by a number of other studies, prominent among which are the Molitor Report (1995), the Competitiveness Advisory Group Report on Enhancing European Competitiveness (1996), the McKinsey Report on removing barriers to growth and employment in France and Germany (1997) and the European Commission report on the competitiveness of European industry (1998).

CSC, the research department of the Confederation of Italian Industry (Confindustria), and the Centre for European Policy Studies (CEPS), an independent research centre based in Brussels, in close cooperation with the European Commission, have decided to explore in greater depth the concerns expressed in the UNICE and the Commission reports, in a wide-ranging research project on the regulatory stance in the EU. A number of well known independent experts have been asked to outline whether, and to what extent existing regulation is hindering competitiveness in their specific field of research and to formulate policy proposals to release the growth potential of EU countries. Special attention has been devoted to the countries with relatively poor macroeconomic performance in the 1990s, particularly Italy. The analysis has focused both on key 'horizontal' issues (such as environment, consumer protection, labour markets and competition policy) and on no less than nine important sectors. The results presented are a testimony to the variety and complexity of ways in which inappropriate regulation negatively influences competitiveness, through its intermediate effects upon the improper functioning of markets. They leave little doubt about the importance of regulatory reform as a way to overcome the lacklustre average economic performance of the EU in the 1990s.

2. EUROPEAN COMPETITIVENESS: BASIC FACTS AND INTERPRETATION

The performance of the European economy in the 1990s has been rather disappointing: the growth rate of GDP slowed down, unemployment picked up and the attractiveness of the euro area as a recipient of foreign investment declined. Between 1990 and 1998, GDP grew only 1.9 per cent per year in the European Union, slowing down from an average of 2.3 per cent per year in the previous decade; in the same period, GDP grew 2.5 per cent per year in the US. Asymmetries of performance inside Europe have become apparent, with some countries, e.g. Spain, Ireland and the Netherlands, growing at a fast pace, with some of the big economies, such as France, Italy and Germany, lagging well behind. The weak performance of Western Europe relative to the US, and the presence of wide asymmetries inside the EU are also reflected in unemployment data. In the US, the unemployment rate almost halved between 1982 and 1997, falling from 9.7 to 4.9 per cent. In the European Union, it grew from 8.5 per cent to 11.2 per cent, stabilising well above 11 per cent in Italy, Germany and France. Inside the Union, in the same period, the UK and Portugal have been able to reduce unemployment below 6 per cent, and e.g. Austria and Netherlands (in 1999) even to 4 per cent, close to US levels.

One indicator of the relative attractiveness of the EU for business – sometimes termed the 'competitiveness gap' – is the share of FDI inflows into the EU of all OECD FDI inflows: between 1990 and 1997, the share of FDI inflows into the euro area with respect to the OECD total declined from

35 to 24 per cent; in the same period, the share of the US grew from 27 to 35 per cent.

Differences of performance between Europe and the rest of the industrialised world have been explained in terms of differences in the quality of state intervention, but other factors have been considered as well. The two major competing explanations are a lack of aggregate demand and increasing competition from emerging countries with low labour costs. Our view is that these explanations are not fully persuasive and, more importantly, that to the extent that they do play a role, they do so in close interaction with the market rigidities caused by inappropriate regulation.

The aggregate demand story centres around the major fiscal consolidation efforts imposed by the EMU entry conditions, as well as a supposedly too rigid stance of monetary policies. It should however be noted that European growth has continued to lag behind that of the US even in 1998 and especially in 1999, when budgetary policies throughout Europe could no longer be defined as restrictive. As to monetary policy, interest rates have fallen to historical lows and are considerably lower than in the US. The key point however is that the regulatory environment is a key factor shaping the possible trade-offs between inflation and unemployment. Given the protection that Europe grants to the 'insiders' (both workers and firms in the some sectors), the level of unemployment that is consistent with stable and low inflation is much higher than in the US. All empirical estimates of the so-called 'natural rate of unemployment' or 'NAIRU' or related concepts confirm this proposition.[2]

Regulatory reform can hence be seen as a way to improve the trade-off, i.e. to make low inflation compatible with a much lower rate of unemployment. It is possible that a reduction of unemployment in Europe may require a more accommodating monetary policy, but a policy will have to go hand-in-hand with supply-side measures and regulatory reforms. Otherwise, with unchanged structures, a monetary expansion would mainly result in higher inflation.

Similar considerations hold for the problem of competition from LDCs. Such a phenomenon, although rapidly increasing, is not sufficiently large, in terms of actual trade volumes, to explain the problems of Europe. The role of emerging countries in world markets is still rather small and their exports to the EU are only 2.5 per cent of the EU's GDP. The growing competitive pressure may indeed have stimulated cost reductions and innovation, favouring more innovative sectors and penalising mature industries; it does not seem to have had a negative impact on aggregate employment. Available studies show in fact that trade has had a positive effect on aggregate industrial employment;[3] also the impact of foreign direct investment towards developing countries can be shown to have a positive effect on industry's employment at home (see Chapter 3 by Giorgio Barba Navaretti in Volume II). Indeed, the exceptionally deep Asian crisis and its contagion have at most caused a cut of 0.5-1 per cent of the EU's GNP between mid-1998 and mid-1999, after which time the impact disappeared. Now that two-way trade is bouncing back, its advantages work in both directions as well. Therefore, the crux of competitive pressure from developing countries is how to adjust to it and best exploit the opportunities. What matters, therefore, is the regulatory environment and whether it is an obstacle or an incentive to undertake the adjustments necessary to respond to the new world economy. In this respect there is evidence that the US has been far more successful than most European countries. Not only has it adjusted, but by seizing opportunities, the US has also acquired leadership in a number of innovative sectors using highly skilled labour intensively.

In conclusion, it is doubtful whether aggregate demand considerations and competitive pressure from emerging countries may have played a role. If this impact has been negative at all, it is *because of* the inefficiencies of the regulatory environment. There is no point in blaming other countries for problems that are our own and are home-made.

The new international environment is increasingly characterised by the globalisation of markets. The intensification of global competition and the acceleration of technological change induce product differentiation and market fragmentation and call for more flexibility and capacity to adjust to changes. By contrast, European economies are still characterised by rigidities of markets and excessive presence of the state as well as insufficient competition, especially in the services sectors. The regulatory environment should abandon the rigidities of the past and favour flexibility, stimulate R&D intensity and innovation, relax trade barriers, favour financial markets development reducing the cost of financing, and boost productivity in public utilities.

The benefits of regulatory reform are potentially very high. The OECD has shown that regulatory reforms are expected to result in major productivity gains in key sectors such as telecommunications, financial services, road and airlines transport, electricity and retail distribution.[4] Such productivity gains are estimated to increase long-run GDP levels with a minimum of 3.1 per cent to a maximum of 5.6 per cent in the countries considered (namely Japan, Germany, France, the UK, the Netherlands, Spain and Sweden). Similar results are provided in the McKinsey Report.[5] The McKinsey estimates show that existing regulatory barriers in France and

Germany result on average in some 40 and 30 per cent lower output levels respectively than the benchmark countries in selected sectors (automotive, housing construction, telecom, banking, retail and the software industries).

In analytical terms, the OECD study confirms the existence of four types of costs of regulatory failure. First, where regulation shields firms from competition, there are fewer incentives for firms to minimise costs, and stakeholders tend to enjoy rents. Second, regulations may, and often do, prevent firms from exploiting all scale and scope economies, not least in network industries. These first two factors imply that prices in the sector tend to be too high, and that regulatory reform and competitive exposure where possible would yield economy-wide benefits via lower prices and higher productivity. Third, regulations often have disproportionate or unnecessarily high compliance costs for governments themselves, as well as for business or even consumers. Fourth, where inappropriate regulation reduces competition, empirical evidence does not show that the resulting excess profits are ploughed back into higher rates of R&D and innovation. Regulatory failures may also render 'sheltered' firms less capable of adapting to rapid technological or taste changes, let alone responding to consumer needs and preference of high service quality.[6]

Business competitiveness is first of all a function of the company's people, assets and strategy. And governments as well as the EU can facilitate or support competitiveness with a range of instruments other than regulation, such as R&D subsidies, infrastructure and a predictable and reasonable tax climate. However, as McKinsey and the OECD have demonstrated, regulatory reform can make a major difference in Europe, if only because it has been neglected for a long period. Indeed, in the 1993 EC White Paper, regulation is only mentioned in passing and EU regulation is not seen as an issue of competitiveness. Following the pervasive research efforts of the OECD, the present project confirms the actual and potential impact of regulatory reform at EU and member states level, both horizontally and in sectors.

In the following we shall first sketch the origin and significance of regulatory reform in the overall context of the long-run strategy of the EU and its member states, supported by European business and the labour unions, to pursue competitiveness, economic growth and employment. In Section 4 the notion of competitiveness and its interaction with regulatory reform is spelled out and applied to the main challenges for business and European policy-makers alike in the first decade of the new millennium. The key concepts here are the blurring of industry and services, innovation, permanent skill formation in the learning society, flexibility and globalisation. In Section 5 the structure of the book is set out and the selection of topics justified. The remaining parts of this introductory chapter (Sections 6 and 7) give a flavour of the respective contributions in the horizontal and sectoral parts of this project.

3. THE EU STRATEGY FOR GROWTH, COMPETITIVENESS AND EMPLOYMENT

The pursuit of competitive business performance, economic growth and job creation remains at the top of the EU agenda. Government leaders of the member states and the European Commission acknowledge that this priority can only be effectively pursued if there exists a policy consensus about:
- the desirability of accomplishing macroeconomic stability,
- the utility of structural change and adjustment,
- the need to introduce and promote the information society, and
- a commitment to make the most of the greatest asset of the EU: the single market.

Upon the beginning of a new millennium, one can observe considerable progress in following this agenda. All 15 member states have meanwhile demonstrated their commitment to macroeconomic stability. Eleven EU countries have entered Euroland, the final stage of monetary union. This required disinflationary policies and sizeable reductions in budget deficits. The successful pursuit of these measures has created a far healthier macroeconomic environment in the Union than existed only a decade ago. Given the stringent and overriding objective of price stability for the European Central Bank, and the extensive system of macroeconomic policy coordination in the EU as a whole, as well as the Stability and Growth Pact, the macro-climate for business and consumers has become highly favourable. It is stability-oriented and predictable, and has already led to a declining trend in long-term real interest rates.[7] In addition, of course, all kinds of economic transactions in the single market, especially those of a structural character (e.g. long-term supply contracts, direct investments, etc.), can now be expressed in a single, stable currency which is bound to foster such transactions and reduce their costs.

Also the need for structural adjustment on the supply side is now widely recognised. A range of industrial sectors typically recording low or zero growth (such as steel, shipbuilding, coal and leather industries) has undergone considerable rationalisation and restructuring. The European car industry has mended its ways and staged a remarkable revival. However, an overall analysis of the EU's manufacturing industry during the 1990s brings out important weaknesses.[8] An important aspect is the great diversity among member states, with the smaller member states (on average) showing greater economic resilience and ability to adjust. Between industries, those with large investments in intangibles, such as advertising and research-intensive industries grew faster than average. An important policy conclusion from the analysis is that, despite the single market, the business environment in the respective member states still differs so much that it remains a crucial determinant of companies' competitiveness. This inference is one major motivation for the present research project, since a very important reason of these differences is found in regulation.

As to the third element, the EU has begun to accelerate the move into the information society, particularly in the last few years of the 1990s. The liberalisation of telecoms markets, the growth acceleration of the customer base of Internet users and the rapid increase of e-commerce (albeit from a small base) have already influenced both the costs and the ways of doing business in Europe. Radical further change is expected in the first few years of this decade. But the good news should not be exaggerated. The European ICT industry is still quite a way behind its American and Japanese counterparts, both in terms of per capita expenditure on ICT and in terms of ICT per unit of GDP.[9] A rapid shift into the information society will, in and by itself, prompt further restructuring, with a loss of jobs in some sectors and a simultaneous emergence of numerous new companies fuelling a process of job creation in software and ICT services. Convergence between IT, telecoms, audio-visual and media services will induce yet another push for new markets, new approaches to business and new job patterns. The radical changes needed and the growth potential that US restructuring shows can be attained form another set of important arguments for the present project's emphasis on regulation. It is only with adequate and timely regulatory reform that the growth effects of the information society can be reaped.

Where the EU has been least successful in the 1990s is the exploitation of the single market as an asset. Unlike in the 1980s, the culprit is no longer that the internal market is hopelessly fragmented by technical, regulatory and fiscal barriers. Quite the contrary, EC-1992 has been a great success, and some further liberalisation has taken place during the 1990s, especially in network industries and late implementation of measures decided earlier. Also, the opening up towards Central Europe (at least, for industrial products) and the lowering of protection under the WTO obligations from the

Uruguay Round have helped to foster a more competitive European business environment. However, the genuine exploitation of this continental market has turned out to be difficult in actual practice, as the Single Market Review, led by Commissioner Mario Monti has shown in very great detail.[10] There are a number of reasons for that, but a prominent one is no doubt the regulatory climate in the member states. Another query is whether the massive regulation at EU level, which accompanies the EC-1992 programme and some common policies, is appropriate for the proper functioning of markets in the EU. In 1995 the two critical reports of UNICE and the Molitor Group signified a U-turn in the debate about regulation in Europe. Ever since, much more systematic attention, both horizontally and sectorally, has been paid to the regulatory 'burden' of business. In particular the UNICE report made it clear that, more often than not, it is the member states that maintain or introduce restrictive or unnecessarily costly regulation. Or, the problem in markets is caused by the cumulative effects of EU, national and regional/local regulatory requirements. This is not to say that EU regulation is without problems.

4. HOW COMPETITIVENESS IS IMPROVED BY
REGULATORY REFORM

Both competitiveness and regulatory reform are merely labels and not well defined concepts for rigorous economic analysis. Therefore it is indispensable to define them give more precisely and to give an explicit warning against a few misunderstandings that may arise and that should be avoided in any sound policy debate on this topic in Europe (and beyond). The next step is to distinguish regulatory reform from other policy-induced influences on 'competitiveness', in its various meanings. Given these preliminaries, it is possible to provide a basic framework to understand the manifold ways in which regulation and its (appropriate) reforms are likely to impact on business competitiveness and the performance of a national or the EU economy. Keeping the basic framework in mind is crucial because regulatory reform is a long-run (if not, in some sense, permanent) and highly diversified policy process that can easily be derailed in numerous technical instances if the overall perspective is lost.

4.1 Competitiveness

Competitiveness is a straightforward notion for an enterprise. An enterprise is competitive in the short run if its goods and/or services sell well at prevailing prices, such that it can keep or increase market share. It is competitive in the long run if it can remain profitable. Applied to sectors or industries, the notion becomes more elusive. It may refer to the overall strength or performance of the sector, as a collection of enterprises, or to the quality (measured against a benchmark) of its common resources (e.g. skill formation, buyer-supplier relations/co-makership, coordination, R&D networks, quality controls & certification) or its level of rivalry impacting positively on exports or FDI. Applied to countries or the EU economy, the notion of competitiveness becomes problematic, if not controversial. It is meant to express economic performance, without however referring to the 'misery index' of unemployment and inflation. Usually, it incorporates some measures of business performance in *international* markets combined with indicators for the standard of living. Because the former are aggregated (e.g. 'the' share of exports of country A in all OECD or world exports), there is often a confusion with the balance of trade or the current account balance, which depend on exchange rates and other variables. As to the standard of living, this depends almost entirely on domestic productivity, in so far as economic activities measured by GDP are concerned. A richer standard of living concept would include non-market activities (e.g. quantity and quality of leisure: quality of life), but it is not obvious that the 'competitiveness' debate takes this into account).[11]

Just as companies' competitiveness depends, in part, on the corporate environment, of which the regulatory environment is an important part, sectoral performance as well as national (or EU) performance are a function of the regulatory environment. Clearly, this can mean a host of things, and will indeed mean different things to different sectors and to respective countries. Jacquemin and Pench (1997) have convincingly argued that, although a rigorous analytical approach to country/EU competitiveness is impossible, this is not a good reason to reject the competitiveness debate as pointless. They advocate the use of a wide range of economic performance indicators, underpinning an overall view of 'competitiveness' in the pragmatic sense of a set of 'pointers' for reforms, new policies and also business strategies and networking. In this sense, a country is never fully 'competitive' and if it ever would be, the exercise would still be justified in order to make timely adjustments and to anticipate or drive change. A typical competitiveness approach as now practised in many countries worldwide, emphasises the supply side and the international dimension, although often the social dimension comes in too. On the supply side, firm performance is seen as critical for prosperity, and this requires incentives in a market-based environment, facilitating optimal allocation of factors as well as allowing entrepreneurship and innovation.

Competitiveness can then be approached as a triple-layered phenomenon: at the level of the firm, at the level of a sector and its relevant networks, and at the macro level. The macro level should not be understood as relations between economic aggregates (e.g. overall consumption, overall investment, etc.) which are subject to macroeconomic stabilisation policies. It is generally held that predictable macroeconomic stabilisation policies, without disturbing exchange rate misalignments or volatile interest rates, are desirable for business and for the exploitation of the internal market. Thus, in discussing 'competitiveness', sound stabilisation policies are presumed as a prerequisite. Rather, the macro level is viewed from the supply side as the overall endowment of a country's (the EU's) productive factors, including the hard and soft infrastructure needed to induce higher productivity, and the proper functioning of the markets for these factors (mainly, labour, capital and technology).

In this vision, Krugman's (1994) famous criticism about the notion of competitiveness is reduced to a simple warning. He reminded business and politics that countries do not compete in the same sense that firms do, and that international economic intercourse need not be, and usually is not, at the expense of some participants but instead should increase the economic welfare of all. For economists this sounds like a truism, but the language in reports about 'competitiveness' often disregards this truism, when they adopt business strategy parlance to formulate conclusions in terms of rivalry as well as winners and losers. The present project shows that regulatory reform in Europe can greatly boost the performance of the EU economy via its (overall) positive effects upon all three layers of 'competitiveness', but there is no reason to assume that this would work against the US, other OECD economies or developing countries. At the same time, Krugman's point that "competitiveness...turns out to be a funny way of saying 'productivity' " (ibid.) is just semantics, because the whole point is to get policy-makers and business to focus systematically, in all three layers, on ways to improve the supply side so as to generate more value-added, and hence greater productivity.

The present two volumes amount to a comprehensive scrutiny of how regulatory reform can contribute to the better performance of enterprises, of sectors and their networks, and of the factor markets, as well as to man-made improvements of endowments. The international dimension of such an exercise should not be misrepresented as a win-lose race among nations. Rather, the openness of the EU economy in the presence of globalisation has augmented the sensitivity of business performance in the EU to lower input costs elsewhere, to better quality of input elsewhere, to higher performance of inter-firm or intra-industry networks elsewhere, to foregone opportunities here existing elsewhere, to disproportionate constraints (compared to elsewhere) in product, services and factor markets and to better developed infrastructures, both physical and immaterial. Besides prompting possible virtues of international 'benchmarking', inspiring policy changes and reforms at home, such international differences may impact on the competitiveness at the firm level in the EU, precisely because of globalisation. Hence, the confluence of many public interest aspects for EU and national policy-makers with the incessant insistence of European business to improve what can comfortably be labelled as 'competitiveness'.

4.2 Regulatory reform

Regulatory reform refers to the transformation of the regulatory environment with the purpose of making markets function better or accomplishing non-economic objectives at the least cost to society. For the sake of clarity, we exclude fiscal aspects and are interested in subsidies only insofar as they may distort incentives and reduce the proper functioning of the internal market (see Chapter 5 in Volume I on state aids by Stephen Martin and Paola Valbonese).

Regulatory reform is extremely wide-ranging, simply because European countries and the EU (as well as many trade partners in the world) are very active regulators. Before specifying more precisely what regulatory reform is, it is useful to warn the reader what it is not, or not necessarily. First, regulatory reform is not identical to deregulation, if the latter simply refers to the abolition of rules. To be sure, it *can* have that meaning if rules have no other function but to unduly protect certain privileges, with negative effects on market functioning. Such blunt instances, however, are exceptional. In the overwhelming majority of cases matters are more complicated. Thus, regulation may be justified by market failures, but the methods and intrusiveness might be disproportionate (undue regulatory 'burden') or, in the worst case, the costs of regulation may outweigh the cost of market failure (a so-called regulatory failure). In such instances, perhaps less but in any event *better* regulation should be adopted, and this is captured by the term regulatory reform.

Second, regulatory reform is not identical to privatisation. To be sure, in certain situations privatisation – in altering the incentives of managers and in facilitating access to capital markets, inter-firm networks and the market for corporate control e.g. for mergers and acquisitions – will help improve business performance and the functioning of certain markets. However, this critically depends on a) the competitive environment of the erstwhile state-owned company, and b) the way the state exercises its ownership rights. If network industries (former utilities) are privatised and remain monopolies or are exposed only to weak fringe competition, sheltered behind high barriers to entry and exit, the beneficial impact of privatisation will be small and the costs to society may or may not be higher depending on regulation and (tight) supervision. However, if privatisation takes place in highly competitive markets, such as the hotel business, the car industry or the oil sector, it might facilitate the pursuit of competitiveness of these companies. How the state relates to 'its' enterprises, of course, matters too. Under EC law (Art. 295, EC, formerly Art. 222, EC) state-ownership is entirely a matter of the member states. But Community law and case law is clear in that the *exercise* of ownership rights by the state cannot confer any competitive advantage, whether via state aids (direct, or via fiscal treatment, or guarantees, or even via new capital infusion beyond what a private investor would do) public procurement or otherwise.[12] In the case of network industries it is possible, under EC law, to grant exclusive rights, but only if justified as the only effective regulatory solution for a legitimate public interest objective (usually, a universal or public service obligation), and this is independent of the ownership of the network company. It is above all in this area that regulatory reform has been and is still being pursued. And this is so for the twin reasons that state ownership is not in any way essential for the public service tasks (regulation and supervision can deal with this), while, more often than not, exclusive rights are a disproportionately costly option to ensure the public service as they exclude any free movement, free establishment and competition in the internal market.

Third, some regulatory 'reforms' however may go against the public interest. In actual practice, equity considerations or protectionism may cause 'reforms' to take the form of changes in regulations rather than visible direct subsidies. The hidden costs to society *beyond* 'implicit' subsidies, captured via the impact of the rules on wages or prices, render such approaches inappropriate. In certain markets (e.g. labour or agriculture), it is not difficult to observe 'reforms' that blend appropriate and inappropriate elements in an attempt to obtain political and social acceptance of compromises.

Regulatory reform in these two volumes focuses on finding proper solutions to overcome market failures, thereby reducing static and dynamic costs to enterprises, or more broadly to facilitate market functioning (e.g. incentives to innovate, to enter, to start a business, etc.). Where equity considerations are crucial, reforms will go in the direction of letting markets do what they do best (price signals, market clearing, cost minimisation pressures, pressures to innovate, free entry, etc.) while addressing equity issues directly via whatever combination of taxes, tax credits and subsidies that is most suitable.

However, attention is also paid to the political economy of such reforms. Both on theoretical and empirical grounds, it is widely accepted that the very process of getting reform proposals formulated, let alone adopted, is fraught with difficulties, causing the final reforms to be sub-optimal or infeasible. Instances are known from the empirical literature where the actual details of implementation or supervision were so manifestly in the interests of regulatees that the public interest was jeopardised. And this is not only the case in network industries or labour markets. In 1968, the architect of the common agricultural policy, Commissioner Sicco Mansholt, proposed a reform emphasising structural change reducing the pressures on open-ended price support, only four (!!!) years after the first CAP season for grains. The main reason was that the political economy of Council decision-making threatened to turn the CAP into an open-ended subsidy scheme for efficient (read: large) farmers while doing little to shake-out the inefficient ones via free intra-EU trade (because prices were set too high). But this outcome was the result of political economy, and not of the original ideas.

Therefore, reform proposals and processes have to be explicit in pre-empting special interests from hijacking the process of formulation or implementation of the details. In actual practice, at country or EU level, lobbying based on doomsday scenarios of short-run adjustment may thwart the formation of coalitions to see reform through. In this respect the laboratory function of the Union is very helpful, because the blockage of reform in country A may eventually be undone because the empirical evidence of actual reform in country B undermines the credibility of doomsday scenarios or convinces policy-makers of the benefits.

Regulatory reform may affect horizontal and sectoral aspects of the economy. Horizontal aspects can be general and more specific. The former include a general trend of economic openness (although, in effect, negotiated or decided on a piecemeal basis), the (general) implementation of the free movement in the internal market and free establishment, and the (general) application of competition policy vis-à-vis firms and states (as to state aid).

More specific horizontal regulatory reforms include, among other things, the use of self-regulation under pro-market laws with careful principles to ensure results in the public interest (example: voluntary standards, serving safety objectives), so-called economic instruments (example: product liability), least-cost approaches (including economic instruments) to environmental regulation and horizontal approaches across the regulatory and administrative spectrum to facilitate firm creation and entrepreneurship. Still more specific are factor market regulatory reforms. Sectoral regulatory reforms are concerned with the best way to overcome market failures. Such sectors will of course include the network industries and other traditionally regulated sectors, notably services, e.g. banking, insurance and various modes of transport. However, even casual inspection reveals that many product markets are also regulated, be it heavily, moderately or lightly, for reasons of health and safety of products or environmental properties or consumer protection aspects of the goods. Moreover, occupational health and safety (called 'at the workplace', in the EU) tends to be regulated in great detail.

One could easily stretch the notion of regulatory reform to encompass administrative reform as this may well be required before some types of regulatory reform can work.

Despite this enormous potential reform agenda, several other important influences on competitiveness exist which the firm itself cannot control. They include taxation and its reform, national (or EU) innovation systems, subsidies, the quality of business services, higher education and skill formation, not to speak of infrastructure, the efficiency of the public administration and political stability. This mere listing goes to show that there are manifold outside influences on the competitiveness of companies and it is exceedingly difficult to establish hard-and-fast inferences about the impact of regulatory reform on competitiveness (while, ideally, holding everything else constant). Knowing the wide range of regulatory reforms needed, it takes painstaking and detailed analysis – as these two volumes testify – before one can arrive at conclusions with a degree of firmness.

4.3 A basic framework for regulatory reform

A basic framework relating the triple-layered approach to competitiveness to regulation is summarised in Table 1.1. The layered structure of the table as well as most of the specifications in the central competitiveness entries are adopted, with some changes, from Jacquemin and Pench (1997, pp.16-17). The changes are motivated by our focus on regulation and regulatory reform. The right -hand column forms the application to regulation and regulatory

Table 1.1 The basic framework for regulatory reform

Layers	Competitiveness		Regulation
Macro level			
Production factors	Endowments - Population/labour force	Man-made factors of production - Productive capital - Infrastructure physical - Skills/immaterial infrastructure - Research + technology	- General regulatory climate (FDI) - Public procurement rules - Labour market regulation & vocational training - IPR regulation
Factor markets		Capital markets Labour markets	- Securities regulation - (Free) movement of capital - Financial services - regulation - Prudential supervision - Corporate governance rules - Entry/exit of labour rules - Wage/non-wage conditions - Social insurance
Industry level			
	Competitive environment - Internal & external competition - Degree of openness - Degree of industrial rivalry Efficiency of inter-firm networks - Buyer/suppliers - Coordination/alliances - Business services/certification Innovation Demand conditions		- Competition policy - Trade policy - Regulatory reform of network industries - Retail regulation - SHEC regulation/standards (products & services)
Firm level			
	Organisational flexibility Innovation Cost minimisation		- Product market regulation - Services market regulation - Labour market regulation/occupational health safety - IPR regulation

reform. At this stage no distinction is made between EU and national regulation. The concentration on regulation does not mean that there are no other policies promoting competitiveness in the three layers. As noted, beyond the prerequisite of sound and predictable macroeconomic policies, a host of other policies should be considered, including those enhancing man-made endowments (accumulation; e.g. infrastructure policy; education policy and its connection to labour market needs; basic research and technology policies), tax policies and subsidies in the framework of various policies (e.g. industrial policy, even if horizontal).

The most striking aspect of Table 1.1 is that competitiveness is influenced by regulations, and hence regulatory reforms, related to all three layers. If one employs the concept of competitiveness only at the firm level, there is a risk that the reform agenda would merely include regulations of immediate importance to production, sales and in-house innovation. Such an agenda is potentially still very wide indeed as numerous product and services markets are regulated in different degrees, and occupational health and safety often includes sector-specific regulation. But it is well known that intra-sectoral, domestic (or intra-EU) and global competition exerts powerful effects on intra-firm determinants of competitiveness such as organisational flexibility, cost minimisation and the rate of innovation. In other words, horizontal competition and trade policies – both with a strong dose of regulation – in the second layer are indispensable for competitiveness at the firm level. This may directly affect the conditions in final markets but fierce competition will also, in different degrees, impact on inter-firm networks and how they compete, on input prices and qualities and on demand conditions. Final markets will also be influenced by retail regulation and the vast domain of regulation and standards justified by SHEC, that is, safety, health, environment and consumer protection (quantitatively, by far the most sizeable segment of regulation in modern economies). Inputs will, furthermore, be influenced by regulatory reform in network industries such as air transport, telecoms, postal, gas and electricity, rail (especially cargo) and broadcasting.

However, the macro layer of factor markets and accumulation is no less crucial. Table 1.1 specifies five key elements of capital markets and three key elements of labour markets, all potential targets for regulatory reform. Besides, regulatory aspects of man-made additions to an economy's endowment ought to be considered, e.g. overall intellectual property rights (IPR) regulation, the way skill formation before and during employment ties in with the needs of the labour market and its rules, public procurement rules (e.g. do they effectively promote competitive bidding, and, where relevant, encourage innovation?) and the perception of the regulatory and administrative climate by worldwide business, as a determinant for inward FDI.

Table 1.1 represents a framework, leaving considerable discretion for regulatory options to national and/or EU decision-makers. This is important for several reasons. First, although the economics of regulation are much better understood today, it would be unwise to suggest that regulatory reform can be conducted according to a manual or a recipe. There may be different but roughly equivalent options for the pursuit of the same objective, or there may be institutional, historical or legal reasons why distinct approaches are followed in different countries. Second, preferences and objectives may differ even in Europe. Third, risk-taking may differ between countries and this may influence perceptions about the public interest, reflected in regulation. Thus, should workers have no say in the degree of risk-exposure in occupational health and safety? Should bankruptcy unduly restrain future risk-taking in a new venture? Should product liability partly and if so, to what extent, substitute for safety regulation? These are important regulatory questions, the answers to which cannot be universal but which do generate disparities in performance.

4.4 Responding to new competitiveness concerns

Regulatory reforms tend to be regarded as the search for a better solution to existing and well known market failures or specific non-economic concerned. And indeed they often are. Not seldomly – as the sectoral chapters of Volume II and some horizontal papers show – this leads to complicated analyses, requiring detailed expertise of the sector or the market failure involved. Improvements are rarely spectacular – except in some network industries –and the overall gain for the economy only becomes interesting if such reforms are pursued in a broad strategy, tackling analogue market failures in many sectors. Some such reforms may be horizontal, such as the introduction of 'economic instruments', public procurement or prudential supervision in several financial services sectors.

This perspective, useful as it is, does not capture today's urgency of regulatory reform for competitiveness. Approaches to regulation have to be revisited more fundamentally than merely 'bettering' existing regulatory solutions for a given problem. What matters nowadays for European business cannot adequately be reflected in Table 1.1, although the table is consistent with it. At least three characteristics of today's economic dynamism render a static view or review of regulation dangerously insufficient. These characteristics are rapid technological change in products, production processes and services; the blurring between traditional manufacturing industry and services; and globalisation of information, financial markets, telecoms and audio-visual, and – more and more – production, input and trade networks of products, increasingly even distribution and advertising.

Competitiveness is not sustainable in many cases if company, sectoral and factor market responses would be incremental. From Europe's competitiveness debate one can derive at least three responses that go beyond incrementalism, altering the nature and quality of factors of products, the way in which stakeholders in a company as well as in business alliances work together, and the strategies for the long run. These three responses are summed up in the labels: permanent skill formation in what is rapidly becoming a 'learning' society; flexibility in work, living, location or otherwise; and determined and permanent efforts to innovate.

In such a dynamic environment, regulation may become obsolete more rapidly. Prevailing rules may become obstacles to innovation or flexibility. Different perceptions on risk-taking may develop or, as for instance in venture capital, new needs might emerge. What might have been thought at one time to give security to workers may nowadays develop into a rigidity causing lay-offs to some, or less rewarding or monotonous work without much affinity to the quality of output, or the enterprise as a whole, to others. What might have been 'orderly' regulation of securities markets three decades ago is nowadays a recipe for failure. What public service price and quality might have been tolerable a few decades ago, might no longer be consistent with the need to acquire competitive inputs in companies subjected to global competition.

Regulatory reform, in short, should be pursued without too much fixation on narrow, short-run sectoral problems or legalistic puzzles in a given regulatory setting. Rather, it ought to be driven by today's and tomorrow's concerns for competitiveness and performance. This is a powerful argument to design overall regulatory reform strategies, aiming to develop an overall vision on competitiveness, in the sense employed in this project, while making sure that the implementation is and remains in the public interest. Such strategies must develop frameworks, which adequately reflect the responses to the new concern, before formulating the painstaking specifics.

5. THE STRUCTURE OF THE BOOKS

Section 4 strongly suggests that the convenient label 'regulatory reform' may well imply pervasive and sustained efforts in many areas and with great complexity. This impression is confirmed by the magnitude and scope of the OECD work in this area. Therefore, the editors, as designers of the present project, realised from the start that it would be exceedingly difficult to achieve the optimum balance between coverage and depth, on the one hand, and readability and other size constraints on the other. One extra complication when studying European regulation is that, nowadays, it is found at least two levels, national and European, and both exhibit considerable reform activity.

A principal consideration for the project is that the economic effects of regulation or its reform are mainly realised via the impact on market functioning. Whereas taxation or subsidies will target factors, companies or consumers directly, more often than not, regulation corrects or pre-empts market failures, and its impact on competitiveness is a derived one. As a rule the latter impact on companies or market participants more broadly will tend to be felt more directly, the more (sector) specific and detailed regulation is, due to risks of health and safety, the typical asymmetries of information in a particular market, the environmental risk, the threat of anti-competitive structures and/or conduct, the systemic risk (in the case of prudential regulation and supervision) or the potential or actual disparity of (negotiation) power and skills in the case of labour. In horizontal forms of regulation, such 'sectoral' effects will usually be absent, and more general economic considerations on market functioning prevail. The project has thus distinguished a horizontal and a sectoral approach. How important this distinction is becomes clear when reading the ten sectoral chapters in Volume II. To do justice to the characteristics of such markets, broad-brush economic generalisations will simply not be sufficient for designing credible and economically justified reforms.

Nevertheless, the differences between the horizontal and sectoral chapters are a matter of degree. Practically all sectoral chapters reflect the impact of a more competitive climate and the importance of the horizontal strategy of completing the EC internal market. Volume I, on the other hand, comprises horizontal chapters which nonetheless can be quite specific, e.g. for labour and environment.

The volume begins with the economic fundamentals, derived from economic theory as it stands today, about the relation between regulation and economic growth, followed by a closer scrutiny of business complaints about regulation in Europe. Is the regulatory 'burden' justified, given the design and purpose of rules, or do we find costly regulatory failures? These two chapters provide complementary frameworks for analysis, which can be used to assess all other contributions. Of course there is recognition in Europe that regulatory reforms are beneficial. Indeed, Volume I ends with a comprehensive assessment of the reform initiatives at EU level during the 1990s. A survey of regulatory reform strategies of the respective member states could not be undertaken as this would have stretched the limited resources of the present project too much. However, examples of national regulatory reforms can be found in the chapters on national competition policies, state aids and Dutch labour market reforms (and a comparison with the UK, Germany and Italy), as well as the chapter on national product regulation in the EU.

Choices had to be made. Since the competitive environment is so crucial for competitiveness, two chapters are devoted to aspects of competition policies. We decided not to include a chapter on EU-level competition policy as this is very well known and the need for reform is minor as confirmed by the recent reforms undertaken. Opting for national competition policies is justified as they represent a significant change for the better during the last 10 to 15 years. State aids policy also warrants closer evaluation because the EU member states remain typical 'subsidisers' in comparison to the US and Japan for instance. Levels of state aids have come down only slowly and their distortive capacity is reason for concern.

Product markets are regulated in so many ways and instances that we had to be very selective in order to do meaningful work. Environmental regulation is an obvious case to include both because the scope and intensity of this field of regulation tends to increase everywhere in the OECD and beyond, and because it is a unique area where two contrasting regulatory approaches – command-and-control versus so-called economic instruments – are in a contest. The editors also opted for a study of product liability in the EU, an 'economic instrument' outside the environmental area, which yet is little noticed or perhaps even understood by economists in Europe. The third chapter is a horizontal study of whether and how the regulatory constraints of the internal market – approximation and, above all, mutual recognition – have disciplined the member states in their product regulation output. The EU constraints are unique in the world, yet it seems doubtful whether even they can moderate the national regulatory machines. These choices imply that other horizontal options had to be dropped, for instance an assessment of standardisation and conformity assessment or more specialist research on classical consumer protection regulation.

With respect to the macro-level, priority was given to labour market reform, almost certainly the EU's most difficult regulatory reform issue. Besides George Gelauff and Marc Pomp's chapter on the Dutch experience in a comparative perspective, a pathbreaking analysis of the impact of regulation (*both* in product and labour markets) on labour market performance, based on a highly comprehensive set of data stylising regulation from all OECD countries, is included as well. Rather than commissioning studies of capital markets or of regulation of technology (e.g. IPR rules), work on new and small firms and their entrepreneurship propelling growth and employment was chosen. Regulation and administrative requirements often have a discouraging impact on entrepreneurship in Europe and this may well impede growth.

Amongst the many possibilities for vertical studies, choices were equally necessary. We have opted for more sizeable sectors in all nine instances. Of the nine selected ones, only one is lightly regulated – textiles and clothing – but here very detailed trade protection is the culprit. Because of the significant liberalisation in sectors other than agriculture, Volume I does not deal with trade regulation. Textiles and clothing is a (dying) exception because quota protection will be removed by the end of 2004. Of the other eight sectors, only two are producing goods in a competitive environment (cars and chemicals). The other ones are either services (retail, road transport and banking) or network industries (telecoms, electricity and scheduled air transport).

Other than pharmaceuticals, food and precision measuring equipment, no goods markets are subject to more regulation than chemicals and cars. The chapters leave no doubt about the scope and pervasiveness of regulation, and hence about the great importance for competitiveness to undertake reform where costs are disproportionate or otherwise unjustified. Europe's even greater reform needs, however, are widely suspected to be in services and network industries. Volume II includes retail trade as this is little studied from an overall perspective of regulatory reform This sector is usually regarded as a local or regional issue whilst rivalry as well as numerous sellers are not suggestive of reform needs. Luca Pellegrini's analysis, by contrast, finds negative effects everywhere in Europe, with cases (such as in Italy) where consumers are deprived of very large potential gains. Road transport and banking are in the process of adjusting to regulatory reforms in a liberalising direction, mainly driven by EC-1992. The very considerable impact of liberalisation on these services sectors confirms the economic potential that can be released by reforms in services.

This effect is even more pronounced in network industries. The fascination with the liberalisation of network industries is so great in Europe that the term 'regulatory reforms' is, not seldomly, narrowly applied to network industries only. Even though this is a major error, as our project amply illustrates, experiments by early liberalisers have provided empirical evidence of impressive productivity gains, with a considerable part passed on to consumers (and, indeed, often more to business users). The gains from liberalisation in telecoms have not petered out, yet are already appreciable. In air transport liberalisation is 'complete' in the EU but the 'cash-cow' intercontinental markets are still restrictively regulated, reducing the pro-competitive effects of the internal market and limiting actual entry. In electricity liberalisation has just begun and early empirical evidence shows up major gains. Regulatory reform in those sectors is clearly promising and supportive of the better economic performance at the macro level while directly reducing input costs for business. Similar efforts in rail, postal and gas may augment these beneficial effects.

The structure of the books is designed in such a way that they touch upon many elements specified in Table 1.1. Yet, a glance at that table reveals that even a project as large as at this one cannot hope to cover the entire spectrum. Thus, IPR, occupational health and safety, public procurement, corporate governance and trade policy are not explicitly covered. Neither is the sectoral scope more than a (wide) selection, nor has it proved feasible to enter the countless regulations in SHEC-driven product and service markets, with a few exceptions.

These limitations of what is a major research effort by some 40 authors underscore the importance of paying greater and incessant attention to the proper design and implementation of regulatory reform, in the European public interest and to the benefit of the competitiveness of European business.

6. REGULATORY REFORM IN THE EU: HORIZONTAL PERSPECTIVES

In concluding this introductory chapter we first zoom in on the horizontal subjects and issues of Volume I.

The nature of the theoretical and empirical relationship between growth and regulation is much debated in economic literature. In Chapter 2 of Volume I, Charles Blankart, Philip Baake and Christian Jansen present the different approaches to aggregate economic growth theory, focusing in particular on endogenous growth models based on technological progress. In this context, growth is positively correlated with the accumulation of augmentable inputs; therefore, regulation is growth-enhancing when it favours either physical or human capital accumulation. Competition policies and policies favouring market entry are found to stimulate R&D intensity and enhance growth, while the relationship between growth on the one hand and trade and patent protection on the other is ambiguous and depends on the critical assumptions made on the characteristics of the industries considered. Allowing capital market imperfections, tax reforms lowering the tax burden and capital market regulation reducing the costs of external financing favour innovation and growth. Empirical findings on the relation between regulation and growth are presented in the third part of the chapter. Regression analysis allows us to consider the effects on growth of different variables linked to regulation, such as R&D expenditure, product market regulation, trade policy, financial development, human capital, public infrastructure spending and the definition of property rights. The authors show that there is a well established positive link between R&D activities, appropriately defined property rights and growth. On the other hand, a negative correlation is found between a high degree of regulation of product and labour markets and growth; in this respect, Italy and Greece appear to be the heaviest regulated countries in the euro area. Empirical analysis is also able to detect a positive relation between growth and such key variables as trade openness, the level of financial markets development and school attainment.

The definition of regulatory quality is the object of Chapter 3, by Sandrine Labory and Marco Malgarini. The authors provide an in-depth analysis of the economic theory on regulation, according to which the quality of regulation is found to depend on its effectiveness in correcting for market failures. The chapter identifies three types of regulatory failure: regulation fails when it is indeed effective in reaching its goal of correcting the market failure, but achieves this objective at too high a cost for the society, i.e. regulation is effective but inefficient. Secondly, regulation fails if it produces net benefits, but does not correct or only imperfectly corrects for market failure: here regulation is efficient but ineffective. Thirdly, regulation can be and often is both ineffective and inefficient. An example of the first type of regulatory failure is a product standard that reduces health risks for consumers, but imposes costs on the producers that are disproportionate to the benefits achieved. The second type of regulatory failure is exemplified by a minimum standard that produces a net benefit but does not significantly reduce a risk or environmental damage. As for the third type of regulatory failure, regulatory capture may generate regulation that is both ineffective and inefficient. Thus defined, regulatory failures may be triggered by a lack of analysis of the regulatory issue, problems and contrasts in the regulatory process and lack of implementation and enforcement of regulation. The peculiar dual-level regulatory framework of the EU area (national and European) can generate poor regulatory quality, because of differences in national interests; also, implementation and enforcement are peculiar problems of EU legislation. Empirical findings on the existence of regulatory failures in Europe, in particular, existing business surveys, emphasise that European countries appear to be badly regulated in comparison to the US, New Zealand and other OECD countries. There is also a high degree of diversity in the quality of economic, administrative and social regulation diversity in the euro area. For Italy, an ad-hoc survey conducted by the authors at the beginning of 1999 indicates that the main problem can be traced to a very difficult, costly and time-consuming relationship between the private sector and the public administration.

In the rest of Volume I, more specific issues concerning the regulatory environment are analysed, starting from the consideration of national and EU competition policies. Chapter 4 by Patrick Van Cayseele, Pierluigi Sabbatini and Wim Van Meerbeeck analyses the functioning and degree of homogeneity of existing national antitrust regulation in the EU area. The authors provide very useful synoptic tables, comparing the existing antitrust regulation in Belgium, the Netherlands, Germany and Italy. A number of general criteria for the economic evaluation of antitrust institutions are provided, such as the general design of antitrust laws, their implementation, the independence of the antitrust authorities and the applicability of antitrust laws. The main conclusion is that although member states have developed competition policies in line with the EC Treaties, national antitrust regulation is not a copy of EU antitrust regulation. Antitrust authorities remain under the control of political authorities; more importantly, the triggers for an antitrust case differ. For instance the threshold for action on mergers and acquisitions is relatively low in some countries. Furthermore some mergers may be accepted in large countries but not in others, because market shares differ. Also the definition of anti-competitive behaviour and the allowed exemptions are different in the countries considered. However, harmonisation should not be the ultimate goal: competition policy may have to tackle different problems in different countries. For example, countries as similar as Belgium and the Netherlands present relevant differences in the average level of price cost margins; because of that, according to the authors, they should be treated differently when applying competition policies. The European Commission should provide guidelines for the national authorities, based on sound industrial economic analysis, aimed at guaranteeing effective competition in the EU. The concrete steps suggested for reforms are: first, horizontal separation, making antitrust authorities more independent; second, the shift from action ex post to ex ante should continue; third, vertical separation between the EU and national levels of action should be made more precise, since there are inconsistencies.

One of the key aspects of competition policy and the single market in the EU is the long-standing problem of state aids. In Chapter 5, Stephen Martin and Paola Valbonesi review the economic rationale for state aids, stressing that they tend to favour inefficient firms, damage the efficient ones, often camouflaging operating aids to specific unsound firms. In this sense, state aids may be potentially distortionary of competition and disruptive of the single market. The authors show however a downward trend of the aids in the period 1990-97, which is attributable mainly to a reduction in horizontal and sectoral aids that offset an increase in regional aids. The decrease in state aids was particularly sharp in Greece, Italy, Belgium, Portugal and Luxembourg. However, overall state aids are still on average well above the EU average in Greece and Italy in the period 1995-97, especially for regional policy. Rapid phasing out of such aids has taken place since.

Chapter 6 by Peter Clinch is concerned with European environmental regulation. Environmental protection has been one of the fastest growing areas of regulation in the last quarter of a century and has imposed very high costs on the business sector. However, a recent survey (European Commission, 1997) contains tentative empirical evidence that business performance is only marginally affected negatively by environmental regulation, and that it may actually spur the pursuit of efficiency and innovation, subject to sectoral differences. Work on environmental compliance is ongoing. Peter Clinch exhaustively reviews policies and measures, as well as various rationales for environmental regulation. The major trend outlined is the shift from command-and-control instruments to more voluntary and market-based approaches, providing market participants with the proper incentives to reduce pollution. Overall, however, this shift often appears to be more rhetorical than being effectively put into practice: both the European Commission and national governments publicly advocate the use of market-based instruments, but empirical evidence shows that command-and-control are still the main instruments used. Given the cost-effectiveness of such instruments, the major policy reform to suggest is the effective and practical shift to economic instruments. At the EU level such a shift has begun to take shape. At national level, however, the progress varies from country to country. Of course, market-based instruments are not always the most cost-effective: for example, for particularly high health and environmental dangers it might be more effective to enforce a law banning dangerous substances.

Jacques Pelkmans, Ellen Vos and Luca Di Mauro (Chapter 7) address regulatory reform in EU product markets. The paper was prompted by the paradox that considerable liberalisation and regulatory reform in the EU since the 1980s has led to a major debate which, surprisingly at first sight, culminated in greater and more insistent demands for further regulatory reforms. The paradox is the greatest for product markets because it was precisely there that the reform and liberalisation efforts were initially concentrated. The paper first inspects four reform tracks in EU product markets: mutual recognition, the prevention of new regulatory barriers, the new approach to approximation and competitive conformity assessment under the global approach. The conclusion is that EU reforms have been significant for the better functioning of the internal product market, yet the economic gains have remained far below their potential.

Two weaknesses in the EC product regime may account for the reduction of actual gains: the difficulties in making mutual recognition work, and the steadily increasing flow of new national product regulation, outside the realm of EC directives. The authors outline the practical problems with mutual recognition at some length, and recommend that the Commission should pursue a much more aggressive, and non-legalistic, information campaign with business and trade, whilst intensifying the 'cooperative federalism' in this area with the member states. The steady increase of national product regulation is empirically shown with the help of a unique data set. Various explanations, some based on the data, some more conjectural, can at best only partially account for the trend increase, especially because a trend *decline* should have been expected (other things equal). The hypothesis that this increase is due to the lack of 'federal' pressures and disciplines at the member state level (unlike the EU itself, which is subjected to such pressures) cannot be rejected. The upward trend is also worrying from a quantitative point of view. Even a constant rate of notifications (extending the annual rate of the late 1990s) would yield no less than 6,000 notifications in the decade to 2010. If a weak trend increase would continue, this could easily double. Such decentralised regulatory pressures cannot possibly be expected to take into account the EC-wide cumulative problems for e.g. business having to operate in the entire internal market. It amounts to a strong case to pay more attention to the Community-wide economic impact of national regulatory activities.

Product liability is one of the few economic instruments used for consumer protection. Little seems to be known about the actual functioning of the EC product liability directive and its national application (a legal report was published years ago, and a new Green Paper was published by the Commission just before these two volumes went to the press). The scope to increase the economic significance of product liability and in this way to better combine market incentives and regulatory goods is examined in Chapter 8 by Francesco Silva and Alberto Cavaliere on the economic impact of product liability. The chapter examines and compares two forms of product safety regulation, namely product liability and safety standards.

Starting from theoretical results on the efficiency of product liability regimes, the authors compare the economic impact of strict liability in the US and in the EU. In the US product liability has expanded both because it has been conceived as a social insurance mechanism and the legal system provides easy access to justice. The liability failures predicted by theory, e.g. due to asymmetric information, have characterised the American experience, both for the market for liability insurance and for many product markets. Despite the presumption of a trade-off between strict liability and product innovation, the evidence shows that liability can foster process innovation, except at very high liability levels. In the EU, no liability expansion has taken place since the introduction of the EC Directive 85/374, in spite of the increasing concern of consumers for product safety. This may be due to the cost of access to justice. But compensation for accidents provided by the welfare state and deterrence by safety regulation also explain the scarce appeal of tort law in Europe. We analyse then the institutional interactions between product liability and safety regulation with particular reference to the EC directive on general product safety and its relationship with quality control inside firms. Some results about the impact of this directive on the Italian insurance markets and the vulnerability of firms to product liability are also presented. A shift from detailed regulation to a voluntary programme of safety certification seems to characterise the recent European experience in the field of product safety control.

The next two chapters focus on the widely debated issue of labour market reforms. In the economic literature, the issue of the interactions between product and labour market regulation and labour market performance has been seldomly analysed, mostly because of a lack of relevant indicators. Chapter 9 by Tito Boeri, Giuseppe Nicoletti and Stefano Scarpetta fills this gap, providing an impressively large data set of cross-country indicators collected by the OECD, covering both labour market (LM) and product market (PM) regulation. In particular, the considered LM indicators measure the level of employment protection legislation (EPL), while PM regulation indicators are concerned with the level of direct state control on economic activities and the existence of barriers to private entrepreneurial activity and to international trade and investment. After reviewing the theoretical evidence of the effects of LM and PM regulation on labour market performances, a first relevant result is that in OECD countries restrictive PM regulations usually appear to be matched by analogous EPL restrictions. Clustering OECD countries according to the strictness of regulation, southern European countries (France, Italy, Greece and Spain) are the most strictly regulated, while common-law countries (US, UK, Canada, Ireland, Australia and New Zealand) are characterised by a relatively liberal approach both to the labour and product market. The authors are then able to show a relevant bivariate negative correlation between PM and LM regulation indicators and the level and composition of employment. To validate this result, they also present an innovative model of employment in which, besides the regulatory indicators, a number of structural variables are considered. It emerges that even in this case EPL regulation appears to have negative effects on employment. Some evidence of a negative correlation between PM regulation and labour market performance is found as well. The authors show that regulation and institutions in EU countries are indeed changing, but the pace of change is still slow.

Chapter 10 by George Gelauff and Marc Pomp analyses the Dutch experience in reforming the labour market, focusing on the role of social partners. After reviewing the economic rationale for labour market flexibility, the authors present a case study of the Dutch reforms since 1982. The main lesson drawn is that the resistance of the social partners protecting the position of insiders delayed reforms. In fact, reforms started only when the serious economic crisis at the beginning of the 1980s called for a new interpretation of existing institutions. The most important result of the reforms was the move towards a stronger separation of responsibilities between the government and the social partners: social partners concentrated on wage negotiations, while the government had the primary responsibility for macroeconomic policies. Separation of responsibilities also implied a change of the 'consultation economy', with a shift from binding central agreements towards broad guidelines implemented in a flexible manner at a sectoral level. The authors then compare the Dutch labour market and social security reform with analogous experiences of four other European countries (UK, Italy, Germany and Austria). It emerges that in Europe social partners virtually never cooperate in reforms that diminish the power of insiders; it is also apparent that, as in the Dutch case, serious reforms, mostly by informal institutional changes, were only undertaken during an economic crisis. The main conclusion of the chapter is that it is pointless for the government to try to lure social partners into cooperating with reforms that reduce the role of insiders. This is particularly true with respect to reform of the social security system. In the view of the editors of this book, Gelauff and Pomp have made a convincing case on the issue of separation between the responsibilities of governments and social partners, compatible with different institutional settings, ranging from the UK model of the 1980s to the so-called neo-corporatist models of Holland and Italy.

A central issue in Europe is whether the regulatory framework promotes or is an obstacle to entrepreneurship. In Chapter 11, Martin Carree and Roy Thurik point out that in recent years market economies have been characterised by a shift away from a 'managed economy', characterised by large corporations, towards an 'entrepreneurial economy', in which small firms tend to predominate. The change could be explained by the intensification of global competition, and by the nature of technological change, both phenomena favouring market fragmentation and product differentiation. In this context, the flexibility and capacity to adjust to ever-changing markets of small firms can contribute to explain their success. The next step of the analysis is to correlate firm dimension and growth. Focusing on non-agricultural sectors, the authors find evidence of a negative correlation between firm size and growth in 13 industrial countries. The authors also find that a move from large to small firms is positively correlated with GDP growth in the period 1990-94. The results appear to be quite robust to model specification; Italy, characterised by a large number of small firms, and by unsatisfactory macroeconomic performance, is an outlier. This may be due to the fact that rapidly growing, newborn SMEs which employ high-skilled workers, as in the US case, may indeed take advantage of globalisation and foster economic activity, while the presence of small and slow-growing firms specialised in traditional sectors (e.g. Italy), may be an obstacle to change. In any case, it is essential that the regulatory environment tends to promote entrepreneurship and firm creation, as well as stimulates growth of newly created firms.

After the extensive liberalisation during EC-1992 and the regulation it required to overcome market failures, the European debate in the 1990s began to emphasise the justification and proper nature of EU regulation in the single market. In Chapter 12, Pelkmans, Sandrine Labory and Giandominico Majone focus on regulatory quality at EU level, measured precisely against the criteria of regulation being justified (by rectifying market failures) and properly drafted, implemented and enforced. Ultimately, regulatory quality is a matter of the credibility of intervention in the (European) public interest. The EU debate, having emerged from the EC-1992 process, began in earnest in 1995 with several widely published reports, deploring the high costs of EU regulation, due to insufficient quality.

The authors distil an emerging EU vision of (five elements to address) regulatory quality. Attention is paid to the application of the subsidiarity and proportionality principles to EU regulation, cost/benefit analysis and the Business Test Panel, and the legislative quality of EC regulation. A critical, detailed analysis of the SLIM (simplification) programme is also included. The conclusion from all this is essentially that, despite the merits of these reforms, they have remained unimpressive if not – at times – 'virtual', having failed to impact noticeably on market functioning and competitiveness.

A series of suggestions is provided for deeper reforms, in addition to the emphasis on an agreed parallelism between reforms at the EU and the member state level. All the suggestions are inspired by the objective to strengthen the disciplines and incentives for all those involved in (making or influencing) EU regulation to raise quality. The suggestions include greater regulatory competition between the member states (under conditions of equivalence of objectives where justified), more EU regulation by information (via special networks), an EU analogue of the US state implementation plan, a central EU regulatory unit with the Commission president, an EU 'regulatory budget' based on systematic (compliance) cost/benefit assessment and the appropriate use of autonomous or independent agencies as a way to raise regulatory credibility, without losing accountability, given the increasing politicisation of the relationship between the Commission and the European Parliament.

7. REGULATORY REFORM IN THE EU: SECTORAL PERSPECTIVES

Giuseppe Volpato (Chapter 2 of Volume II) examines how European regulation affects the European automobile industry's competitiveness, especially with respect to American and Japanese producers. The economic analysis of competitiveness in the European car industry is complicated by the considerable difference between short-run and long-run effects of regulation, the fragmentation of the internal market for cars and the appreciable diversity in Europe's industry, rendering an estimate of aggregate impact difficult.

After outlining the importance of the car industry in terms of its contribution to employment, GDP and trade balances in major European countries, Volpato sets out the different types of regulation. His definition of regulation is very large, and includes taxation and R&D subsidies, labour market regulation, environmental regulation and antitrust regulation. The differences in taxation systems across Europe has induced car makers in different countries to adopt different specialisation. In terms of R&D subsidies, it is claimed that the American and Japanese carmakers benefit from more efficient and substantial help, putting Europe at a competitive disadvantage. As for labour market regulation, the cost of rigidities are outlined and the case for reform that would make labour market regulation more employment-friendly is made. The new orientation of European environmental regulation towards cost-effectiveness and the increasing use of market instruments is seen as positive. Rather than adding new standards on vehicles, it is claimed that measures to favour the renewal of cars or to avoid congestion in cities are essential. Finally, the regulation of car distribution via the block exemption under Art. 81.3 EC, which allows vertical restrictions in the European car distribution system, is discussed. Such regulations are found in all Triad countries (the EU, Japan and the US), so that eliminating it in one market would put producers at a disadvantage relative to others. The problem in Europe is that the exemption causes price discrimination to consumers from different member states. The author ends with a discussion of consumer protection, which is argued to be tougher in the US and Japan than in Europe. Overall, the impact of regulation on the car industry is complex to assess, because it is made of different types of regulation which are decided separately, without taking account of possible interactions between the different types of regulation.

One of the leading explanations of the decline of European industry is competition from low-cost, emerging countries. This preoccupation is particularly strong in textiles, which is sometimes considered as a sector that is doomed to be abandoned in industrial countries. In Chapter 3 of Volume II, Giorgio Barba Navaretti checks this widespread opinion. The innovative contribution of the chapter is the use of a panel of medium-to-large Italian and French textile companies instead of the more usual aggregate or sectoral data. After reviewing the changes in trade regulations that occurred in the 1990s, with the creation of the single market in 1992, the gradual phasing out of the Multifibre Arrangement (MFA) since 1994 and the liberalisation of trade with Mediterranean and Central European countries, the author shows that regulatory reform in the sector has been accompanied by a decline of employment. Empirical analysis suggests that the decline in employment is only partially attributable to the effect of liberalisation; labour-market rigidities, labour-saving technical progress and the organisation of production at the firm level share the burden of guilt. More importantly, trade liberalisation is often deemed to have negative effects on employment in an indirect way, via stimulating direct foreign investment in cheap labour countries. The empirical analysis on a sample of textile companies suggests, on the contrary, that foreign investment in cheap labour countries helps to preserve rather than destroy employment at home. Internationalisation appears to be a strategic move for textile and clothing firms facing competition in global markets.

The impact of regulatory reform in the retail sector has seldom been analysed, perhaps because this is usually considered as less strategic than others. In Chapter 4, Luca Pellegrini takes the opposite point of view, considering the importance of the interactions between retail trade and the rest of the economy and its impact on the welfare of households. The author argues that existing regulation is having a strong negative effect on the industry, depriving consumers of some potentially very large welfare gains. This seems to be true especially for Italy, where the industry is characterised by a low presence of supermarkets and hypermarkets in comparison to other European countries such as France or the UK. The insufficient development of the sector in Italy is linked to stricter regulations than those in other European countries. The costs of restrictive retail regulation are then estimated in terms of price differentials between hypermarkets in France and smaller shops in Italy.

Vittorio Maglia and Cristina Rapisardo Sassoon study regulatory reform in the chemical industry, a sector where firms' behaviour remains deeply affected by regulation. Moreover, the chemical industry plays an important role in the EU panorama of industries, at least (but not only) in quantitative terms, accounting for 30 per cent of world production and being the largest producer (before the US, at 28 per cent of total worldwide production).

The first part of the paper describes the very complex set of regulatory norms that have to be complied with by chemical producers: chemical substances regulations, classification and packaging regulations, water protection regulations and waste regulations. This major regulatory burden is justified by overriding objectives of health, safety and environment. For the European chemical industry, the cost/benefit assessment of such multiple layers of regulation is vital to its competitiveness.

The second part of the paper outlines the competitive performance of the EU chemical industry, comparing it with the US industry. The difference in competitiveness between the EU and the US does not lie in large differences in labour costs, but rather in differences in capital-intensity, human capital structure and the ability to exploit scale economies.

However, there are also a number of regulatory factors that influence competitiveness, and that make the US a more dynamic environment for chemical producers. European regulation has a negative effect on competitiveness, it is argued, because it is too complex, inconsistent among member states, and too burdensome in administrative terms. However, lack of data and the difficulty of developing a rigorous, yet suitable theoretical framework make it difficult to draw any definitive conclusions. Policy-makers are advised to improve the efficiency of environmental regulation in Europe, reducing compliance costs and simplifying the present legislation.

Regulatory reform in the EU's road transport industry consists of liberalisation in terms of entry to the sector, intra-EU free movement of services (and free establishment) by abolishing bilateral quotas, liberalisation of transport tariffs and some approximation of basic professional conditions, social aspects and EU directives on environmental and safety issues. Marco Ponti, in collaboration with Maria Agata Cappiello, studies the impact of this combination of liberalisation and new regulation on the competitiveness of the Italian road haulier industry. Both for structural and policy reasons the average firm size of Italian road transport is very small and foreign hauliers have considerable market share for long-distance and high-quality services. The authors show that the long delays in implementing EU liberalisation and repeated attempts to provided indirect (fiscal and other) aid have actually worsened competitiveness in Italy. New requirements for competitiveness such as integrated logistics and high-quality services in well developed EU-wide networks have not been responded to in Italy, because of the fundamental weaknesses of the sector. Now that environmental rules are tightened at EU level and road pricing will be used to fully internalise external costs, the Italian hauliers will experience yet another burden, which they can barely absorb. A radical restructuring should be expected, with numerous small providers only surviving as external partners to a logistic or a multi-modal firm. The authors underline the importance of timely adjustment to justified regulatory reform by brief comparisons with France, Germany, the UK and the US, all better or far better prepared by now to compete with the new level of commercial and regulatory requirements.

Ugo Inzerillo, Pierluigi Morelli and Giovanni Pittaluga assess the major changes in regulation and market structure which have affected the banking industry over the last ten years, comparing the European situation with that in America. Three main factors explain the dramatic changes that have occurred. First, deregulation, consisting of the abolition of controls on capital flows, the EC Banking Directives and national relaxing or elimination of restrictions on banking activities; second, technological innovation; and third, the increasing diversification of financial assets.

Relative to the US, diversification of investment instruments is still at an early stage in Europe. American banks have chosen to widen the range of services offered to clients and the types of customer claims, and to use off-balance sheet financing sources such as securitisations, loan sales, etc. In short, they have adopted an aggressive strategy. Instead, European banks have adopted a defensive strategy, continuing to place importance on traditional services, in particular, deposits. American return-on-equity and return-on-assets have tended to rise in the US over the last ten years, and to fall in Europe over the same period. The declining performance of European banking is due to several factors. First, some large savers have turned to asset management; second, deregulation and the construction of a single financial market has led to growing contestability of banking markets. Third, major technological innovations, especially those regarding payment systems, have reduced the degree of monopoly related to geographical localisation. The authors demonstrate that such increased competition has had beneficial effects on the industry, because the elimination of market segmentation enables more efficient banks to grow; because it has allowed scale and scope economies; and because of a disciplinary effect. Productivity has also increased.

The increased competition has led to a consolidation process but one that has been slower in Europe. The authors argue that such a slow pace is due to the large amount of state ownership in the banking sector (despite privatisations), leading to some inefficiencies, and the dominant model of corporate governance which makes takeovers difficult. Besides, in many cases, labour market rigidities prevent banks from reducing excess staffing levels.

Policy recommendations include a more careful definition of the relevant market in antitrust, and closer scrutiny of the subtle obstacles to enter other domestic markets due to various controls on the ownership of banks and the undue resistance to foreign investors. Therefore the authors propose the creation of a Euro-area supervisor, whose role would be to stimulate the integration of the European banking market.

Martin Cave and Tommaso Valletti provide an up-to-date survey of the main regulatory issues in the very dynamic European telecoms sector. Until the 1980s and even the 1990s, the industry in Europe consisted of public monopolies, and the need for different and evolving regulation has been strongly felt since early liberalisation. The authors explore how the regulatory framework had to change, and keeps on changing, depending on the (relative) maturity of the industry, the radical transformation of its structure and the convergence with information technology and multi-media and other content service sectors.

The fast-paced developments that have characterised the telecoms market are caused by the rapid evolution of communications technologies. At the same time, the basic features of these technologies represent the main reason for regulation: telecoms is a network industry, and thus the final product is made of interconnected components that are supplied at different points and at different times. This, together with the network externalities which are caused by it, make some of the points of the supply chain more crucial than others, and the cost associated with their functioning higher than that associated with others. Cave and Valletti explain what the different role of regulators has to be in such an industry, through time and through the supply chain: through time, from control on a monopolist's activities through price control, to price caps in the case of a duopoly, to RPI-X regulation of the incumbent in a competitive environment. Through the supply chain, there is (at least) the need for price control at the retail level, for access pricing at any interconnection level (and especially at the local loop level), and a more generic need for maintaining universal service obligations through distribution of the costs that this implies. The paper investigates in more detail the development of the industry in six countries which have been liberalising at different times and at different paces (the UK, Sweden, France, Italy, the US and Australia), as well as the regulatory approach followed by each of them. The main issues arising from mobile and fixed telephony integration and from convergence are addressed at the end of the paper, together with an assessment of what type of regulation, or institutional regulators, can be envisaged in the near future.

The paper by Christoph Riechmann and Walter Schulz examines thoroughly and rigorously economic and regulatory issues arising in the European electricity industry, but mainly through a national perspective. Regulatory reform in European countries has followed different routes, but with a common denominator in the specific features of the industry: electricity remains distinct from other sectors for social (need to maintain universal service obligation), environmental and security considerations (dependency of one nation upon a primary energy source). The authors outline the economics of the industry, and identify the segments where competition, and hence regulation, can improve efficiency (generation and trade), distinguishing them from the network-based activities which present natural monopoly characteristics (transmission and distribution). The issues of network access and the organisation and economics of the markets for generation and retail are then examined at great length. Riechmann and Schulz argue that regulatory reform has surely induced considerable improvements in early liberalising countries, in particular with respect to productivity. However its being far from complete means that further improvements could still be achieved. The authors look at regulatory reform in a number of countries on a comparative basis, empirically assessing industry performance in considerable detail. They conclude that electricity generation, price control, and information management and distribution are all issues that need to be addressed more consistently, Such 'deeper' reforms are likely to lead to substantial gains for those (captive) customers that have been only indirectly affected by the reform.

In a complementary paper by Luigi Prosperetti (Chapter 10), the emphasis in liberalising the European electricity market is laid on a fully fledged and competitive internal market for electricity. The author sets out why the 1996 electricity directive cannot achieve more than partial liberalisation and why the resulting internal market will remain heavily distorted. It is also important to consider that the vested interests in imposing liberalisation are deep and widespread, encompassing both the equipment industry and the labour unions. The distortions in the emerging, although incomplete internal market are likely to be exacerbated by existing excess capacity in France and Germany and the great latitude in the directive about grid access and its pricing and about very strategic bottlenecks, especially for cross-border trade. The author deplores that the directive does not require a fully independent regulator in every member state. Indeed, the distortions and opportunities for strategic behaviour are so serious that he finds it worthwhile to consider the competition approach rather than the current highly imperfect regulatory approach to liberalisation.

The thrust of Chapter 11 by Francis McGowan is that the EU's regulatory reform in (scheduled) air transport has been liberalising and yielded moderate, positive economic gains for the industry and the consumers. However, for reasons of bottlenecks (above all, slot allocation in many congested airports), as well as the partial nature of the liberalisation (namely, only inside the EU, plus a few adjacent countries, but not for inter-continental traffic), the full potential of economic gains cannot be and has not been reaped. As a result, the European economic gains are significantly lower than those obtained following US air transport 'deregulation'. Prof. McGowan proposes what he calls a 'refocusing' of economic regulation – particularly the application of antitrust rules to prevent collusion, predation and other anti-competitive practices – although there might be some scope for replacing regulation with market mechanisms (e.g. for overcoming bottlenecks).

In scheduled air transport inside the EU (plus Norway and Switzerland), there has been active entry and exit, with the overall number of airlines increasing to 134 in 1997. This initial effect is similar in kind to that experienced in the US. It is bound to be followed by consolidation – hopefully consolidation under competitive conditions. Flag-carrier dominance has decreased, both across borders and domestically. Competition on the densest routes has gone up. However, the new low-cost-no-frills airlines often avoid full confrontation with the former flag carriers, and head-to-head competition between flag carriers is rare.

A major issue in the 1990s has been the vigilance and credibility of EU competition policy. The assessment of strategic alliances turned out to be a difficult balancing act because the advantages of (intercontinental) network effects for consumers has to be weighted against the reduction of competition or selected routes. The political problem of state aids constituted in the once-and-no-more nature of the aid, which was, in some cases, rejected at the cost of credibility. A final key issue is of course to liberalise the mercantilistic bilateral-based multilateral air transport system. Here, a major conflict has developed between the member states and the Commission – the latter of which is trying to fight the fragmentation of the internal market caused by bilateral 'open-skies' agreements between the US *and member states* denying intra-EU free establishment with equal rights(!) – on the transatlantic aviation space. This deadlock hinders further restructuring, and new entry at the same time favours US airlines above EU airlines in terms of network advantages.

Once these major issues have been resolved, the benefits of EU liberalisation will further increase.

NOTES

1. UNICE (1995).
2. See on this Debelle and Laxton (1996) and Malgarini and Paternò (1997).
3. See De Nardis and Paternò (1997). See also Brenton and Pelkmans (1999) for a range of recent studies on the case for the EU and a literature survey.
4. OECD (1997).
5. McKinsey Global Institute (1997).

6. See also on this OECD (1994), UNICE (1999) and European Commission (1999a).
7. See, for example, European Central Bank (1999).
8. See, for instance, European Commission (1999a and 1999b).
9. See European Commission (1998), Chapter 2 (especially pp. 24-25).
10. See European Economy (1996), Monti et al. (1996) and European Commission (1997b and 1998b).
11. For an approach that incorporates both environmental and social cohesion aspects, see European Commission (1999a).
12. This implies that the only possible advantage of state ownership is the impossibility of a hostile takeover.

REFERENCES

Brenton, P. and J. Pelkmans (eds) (1999), *Global trade and European workers*, London: Macmillan and New York: St. Martin Press.

Competitiveness Advisory Group (CAG) (1997), 'Four reports on Enhanching European Competitiveness', in A. Jacquemin and L. Pench (eds), *Europe competing in the global economy*, Cheltenham, UK: Edward Elgar.

Debelle, G. and L. Laxton (1996), *Is the Philips Curve really a curve? Some evidence for Canada, the UK and the US*, IMF Working Papers.

De Nardis, S. and F. Paternò (1997), "Commercio estero e occupazione nell 'industria italiana'", in S. De Nardis and G. Galli (eds), *La disoccupazione italiana*, Il Mulino: Bologna.

European Central Bank (1999), 'Stability-oriented policies and developments in long-term real interest rates in the 1990s', *ECB Monthly Bulletin*, November, pp. 31-40.

European Commission (1993), *Growth, competitiveness, employment,* White Paper, 2 volumes, Luxembourg, OOPEC.

European Commission (1997a), *The competitiveness of European industry,* Luxembourg, OOPEC.

European Commission (1997b), *The Single Market Review Series,* Luxembourg, OOPEC.

European Commission (1998a), *The competitiveness of European industry,* Luxembourg, OOPEC.

European Commission (1998b), *The Single Market Review Series,* Luxembourg, OOPEC.

European Commission (1999a), *The competitiveness of European industry*, Luxembourg, OOPEC.

European Commission (1999b), *Structural change and adjustment in European manufacturing* COM (1999)465 of 5 October.

European Economy (1996), *Economic evaluation of the internal market*, No. 4 (Reports and Studies).

Jacquemin, A. and L. Pench (1997), 'What competitiveness for Europe? An Introduction, in A. Jacquemin and L. Pench, (eds) (1997), *Europe competing in the global economy*, Cheltenham, UK: Edward Elgar.

Krugman, P. (1994), Competitiveness, a dangerous obsession, *Foreign Affairs*, Vol. 73, No. 5.

Malgarini, M. and F. Paterno (1997), 'Politiche macroeconomiche e disoccupazione', in De Nardis and Galli (eds*), La disoccupazione italiana*, Il Mulino: Bologna.

McKinsey Global Institute (1997), *Removing barriers to growth and employment in France and Germany*, McKinsey, Frankfurt, Paris and Washington, D.C.

Molitor Report (1995), *Report of the Group of Independent Experts on Legislative and Administrative Simplification*, COM (95) 288 of 21 May, Brussels.

Monti, M. et al. (1996), *The single market and tomorrow's Europe*, Luxembourg: OOPEC.

OECD (1994*), The OECD Jobs Study*, Paris.

OECD (1997), *The OECD report on regulatory reform*, 2 volumes, Paris.

UNICE (1995), *Releasing Europe's Potential: Through Targeted Regulatory Reform*, Brussels, November.

UNICE (1999), *Fostering entrepreneurship in Europe* (the UNICE benchmarking report, 1999), Brussels.

2. Growth and Regulation

Charles Blankart, Philip Baake and Christian Jansen

I. INTRODUCTION

This paper discusses the relation between growth and economic regulation on both theoretical and empirical grounds. The theoretical part is intended to provide the basic link between growth measured on an aggregate level and regulation concerning government intervention into specific industries or markets. The empirical part of the paper considers recent studies concerning the quantitative effects of different policy measures on growth.

We start with a short presentation of different theoretical approaches to analysing aggregate economic growth. After discussing models in which growth is either determined exogenously or in which it is entirely based on factor accumulation, we turn to endogenous growth models based on technological progress. The underlying reasoning of these models implies that regulation is growth-enhancing whenever it stimulates investment in research and development and yields higher incentives for the accumulation of either physical or human capital. Applying this result to specific regulations, it turns out that growth is positively correlated with product market regulation that promotes innovation by fostering competition given a certain technology standard and by stimulating market entry of new firms. Trade liberalisation, capital market regulation that reduces the costs of external financing and tax reforms targeted at lowering taxes on factor incomes are also shown to have positive effects on growth. Finally, growth is positively affected by government expenditures on public infrastructure.

These results are largely confirmed by the empirical findings that are presented in the third part of the paper. We first present the general framework applied in empirical studies and then discuss specific results regarding variables that are theoretically supposed to affect economic growth. The last part of the paper concludes.

II. GROWTH THEORY

According to Romer (1994), any comprehensive theory on economic growth must be able to incorporate the following stylised observations: i) in any market economy there are many firms and consumers, ii) physical capital, such as machineries, buildings etc., can be replicated, iii) technological advances are the result of intended research activities or investment decisions of individuals or firms, iv) discoveries or newly generated knowledge can potentially be used by many people at the same time, and v) individuals or firms may have market power and may be able to earn monopoly rents on discoveries or new technological knowledge.

Taken together these observations point to a theory that builds on individual decisions of consumers and firms. Consumption, output and investment in any kind of capital, either physical or human capital, and investment in generating new knowledge, i.e. research and development (R&D), should be taken as an outcome of individual decisions. R&D should be motivated by monopoly rents which can be earned in the case of successful innovations. Additionally, the process of generating new knowledge should incorporate the potential spillover effects which are due to the non-rival character of knowledge. Finally, output and investment decisions of firms without any monopoly power should be analysed in markets with a competitive market structure.

Of course, combining these characteristics in an analytical framework yields a rather complex theory. We therefore continue with a more detailed description of models which cover some of the above-mentioned observations. In Section 1 we start with a simple neoclassical model with perfect competition. While technological progress is assumed to be exogenous, it is the only source of continuous growth measured by output per worker. Next, we turn to an augmented neoclassical model with human capital (Mankiw et al., 1992) (henceforth MRW). While the model has proved to be largely consistent with main empirical observations, the predicted growth rate is ultimately determined by technological progress which again is assumed to be exogenous. This assumption is relaxed in endogenous growth models. Here, the growth rate depends on the underlying production technology as well as the preferences of consumers. In Section 2 we briefly discuss models with convex technologies. In these models growth is generated by ongoing accumulation of augmentable input factors whereas the production technology is constant over time. Furthermore, markets are still assumed to be competitive. In Section 3 we turn to models where technological progress is the outcome of intended R&D. Competition in markets with ongoing research is assumed to be imperfect allowing successful innovators to earn strictly positive profits. We analyse the model of Aghion and Howitt (1998a) in some detail and discuss several variations and extensions of the basic model. In the last section of this part we use the general reasoning underlying the endogenous growth models based on technological progress to evaluate several policy instruments.

1. Exogenous growth: neoclassical theory

Neoclassical models of growth are essentially based on perfect competition in all markets and exogenous technological progress. While capital accumulation is determined endogenously by the equilibrium interest rate, the assumption of perfect competition rules out any individual investment in R&D. Hence, any long-run growth can only be traced to exogenous technological progress. In order to clarify these statements we begin with a short discussion of the basic model based on Solow (1956). In the next subsection we present an augmented model where both physical and human capital are taken into account. Both models show that the ultimate source of growth has to be technological progress.

1.1 The basic neoclassical model
Let us first consider the simplest neoclassical model with exogenous technological progress (see, Solow, 1956 and Cass, 1965). Aggregate output is produced with labour and capital. The production function exhibits constant returns to scale but diminishing marginal products of each factor. Technological progress is assumed to be labour-augmenting, i.e. technological progress shifts the supply of effective labour upwards. Finally, consumption and saving decisions of households are determined by utility maximisation and all markets are perfectly competitive.[1]

Solving for the long-run growth rate of output per capita, it turns out that the growth rate is only determined by the rate of technological progress. Without technological progress, continuous growth is impossible, and the economy will converge to an equilibrium with constant output per capita. This result, which is fundamental for all neoclassical models is due to the observation that long-run growth can be reached only if the marginal product of some augmentable input, in our case capital, is kept from falling too low. To see this more clearly, assume that the production technology is constant over time. Then the capital stock of the economy will rise/fall until accumulated savings equal accumulated capital depreciation. Once this condition is met the economy is in a stationary equilibrium and output per capita will remain constant over time. Further increasing the capital stock would decrease the marginal product of capital below the rate of time preference of households. Therefore, in order for continuous growth to be possible the marginal productivity of capital must rise ceteris paribus, that is, technological knowledge must grow.

1.2 The augmented neoclassical model

Mankiw et al. (1992) (MRW) proposed to augment the neoclassical model by introducing human capital as an additional input factor. Human capital is analysed in the same fashion as physical capital. Both, physical and human capital, are subject to depreciation and both can be produced according to the same production function.

Concerning the steady-state growth rate, the model predicts the same result as the simple model: along a balanced growth path output per capita grows with the same rate as technological knowledge. Hence, while the model is able to capture the role of human capital as an input factor and is largely consistent with main empirical findings, it suffers from the same theoretical limitation as the simple model.[2] Within the framework of perfect competition, intended R&D undertaken by individual firms to gain monopoly rents from product or process innovations cannot be explained. Thus, technological progress has to be taken as exogenous.

2. Endogenous growth: convex technology

The discussion above has shown that continuous growth is possible only if the marginal product of some augmentable production factor is kept from falling too low. Contrary to the neoclassical model, the endogenous growth models we consider now are based on an aggregate production function which is convex in some augmentable input factor. In the simplest case final output is given by a production function where the marginal product of capital is constant and bounded away from zero. Thus, according to the same arguments as above, the long-run growth rate can be positive even if the technology is constant over time. Furthermore, the growth rate is determined endogenously. It depends positively on the saving behaviour of households as well as the rate of return received by private investors.[3] This result is due to the fact that growth is positively correlated with the accumulation of capital, which in turn depends on the equilibrium rate of interest.

While the general structure of convex models is quite restrictive inasmuch as the production function is constant over time, they have been widely extended to study several aspects of economic growth. Lucas (1988) argues that positive spillover effects of human capital accumulation rather than exogenous technological progress (as in the neoclassical growth model) are the main source of growth.[4] Consequently, in the model of Lucas the aggregate production function is convex in human capital. Alternatively, capital can be analysed as a function of different input factors. Along this modification Barro (1990) shows the potentially positive impact of productivity-enhancing government activities on growth. Similar reasoning implies that any tax policy that lowers the rate of return received by private investors has a negative impact on growth (see King and Rebelo (1990) and Section 4.6 for a more detailed discussion of taxes).

To summarise, models with convex technologies allow for continuous growth even without exogenous technological progress. The growth rate ultimately depends on the level at which investment in augmentable inputs takes place. Since investment decisions are correlated with private incentives, the predicted growth rate is endogenous. However, the models mainly rely on perfect competition and do not allow for private rewards to technological progress.

3. Endogenous growth: technological progress

The general idea of endogenous growth theory based on technological progress goes back to Schumpeter's notion of growth through destructive competition: With imperfect competition firms are able to earn monopoly rents from successful innovations. These rents stimulate firms to invest in costly research activities augmenting technological knowledge. By reverse engineering, studying blueprints or reading scientific publications, new knowledge is, however, also available to other researchers or firms. Hence, subsequent innovators can use an augmented stock of knowledge for their own research. Ultimately, the cumulative process of ongoing research and knowledge accumulation yields technological progress.

The key element for continuous technological progress is that any new knowledge created by research can conceptually be split into a specific and a general component. The specific component enables an innovator to produce a particular new good or to use a new, low-cost production process. Additionally, this component is thought to be protected either by patent laws, imperfections in reverse engineering, or by specific individual knowledge of innovators. The second component is general knowledge. Due to the just mentioned possibilities of learning from successful innovations the general part of new knowledge is also available to other innovators, enhancing their ability of further research (see Griliches, 1992, Coe and Helpman, 1995 and the discussion below on R&D spillovers).

In the following we will first describe the way the general idea can be formalised in more detail; see Aghion and Howitt (1998a) (henceforth AH). It turns out that both capital accumulation and R&D investment influence not only the level of output per capita but also the growth rate. More specifically, the model predicts that capital accumulation and R&D investment are complements for growth. In the second subsection we will discuss variations and extensions of the basic model.

3.1 Innovations and capital accumulation
The AH model combines the structure of the simple neoclassical growth model with technological progress which takes place through R&D investments. In order to introduce imperfect competition, final output is assumed to be produced with labour and different intermediate goods. While the labour market, the capital market, as well as the market for final output are competitive, the intermediate goods sector is characterised by monopolistic competition. More specifically, successful research in each intermediate sector enables a firm to monopolise the corresponding market by producing an intermediate good with higher quality, i.e. an intermediate good with a higher productivity in the production of final output.

To capture the property that research is based on some common technological knowledge, successful research in every intermediate sector is simply assumed to yield the same leading-edge quality.[5] Furthermore, this leading edge quality evolves according to the aggregate rate of successful research projects. That is, each successful research project implies positive spillover effects by increasing the highest possible quality in any other sector.

Solving for the optimal output decisions of firms in the intermediate sector and the optimal investments in R&D, it turns out that the aggregate production has the same properties as in the neoclassical model. Aggregate output is determined by labour, capital and the average quality of all intermediate goods. Moreover, the average quality influences aggregate output exactly as technological knowledge influences output in the neoclassical model. Hence, simply defining average quality as technological knowledge, the long-run growth rate is again equal to the growth rate of technological knowledge. However, technological progress and, therefore, the growth rate are endogenous. Both depend on aggregate research investment determined by the monopoly rents innovators can earn. Finally, without any R&D investments, the marginal product of capital would fall too low and growth would ultimately cease.

Furthermore, similar to growth models with convex technologies, the AH model also predicts that the growth rate positively correlates with the rate of capital accumulation. To see why, consider a subsidy to capital income. This subsidy yields a lower interest rate and hence a higher discounted profit of research investments. Additionally, as long as capital is used in the production of intermediate goods, a decrease in the interest rate also lowers the capital costs in the intermediate good sector. Both effects obviously imply that the expected profits from successful innovations rise. R&D investment increase and the economy will consequently end up with a higher growth rate. Note, however, that although the growth rate is determined by aggregate R&D expenditures, capital accumulation is necessary for long-run growth.[6]

Although the model is based on restrictive assumptions, we think that the intuition of the results is quite convincing. First of all, technological progress is endogenously determined by intended research activities. Second, the assumption that sector-specific research is based on common technological knowledge and that the evolution of this knowledge depends on aggregate research investment reflects the notion of spillover effects generated by any research activity. Finally, the result that capital accumulation and research are complements with respect to growth does not rely on the specific functional forms assumed. Indeed, as long as research is based on some augmentable input, any increase in the expected profits of innovation should yield a higher research intensity and therefore a higher growth rate.[7]

3.2 Variations and extensions

In the AH model technological progress is governed by firms that invest in order to produce intermediate goods with higher productivity in the final goods production. Innovations are assumed to be drastic so that the successful innovator replaces the old supplier. Yet, the literature on endogenous growth theory emphasises several other aspects of technological progress which we now briefly discuss. We begin with modifications concerning the kind of innovations. We first discuss innovations that yield a wider range of different products and innovations targeted at consumer goods. We also consider how the size of innovations can be analysed endogenously. Second, we incorporate learning by doing into the model.

3.2.1 Product variety, consumer goods and endogenous size of innovations.
The most obvious alternative to the above-mentioned model is to assume that research focuses on new goods rather than on improving the productivity of existing goods. Formally, this modification can be easily captured by analysing the intermediate goods sector as being horizontally differentiated.

Innovations would then yield a wider range of different input goods. Similarly, research can be thought of as providing technological progress in consumer goods. In this case, innovations result in either higher qualities of consumer goods or a wider range of these goods. Finally, in order to endogenise the size of innovations one can augment the model by assuming a negative correlation between the probability of success and the size of the resulting productivity improvement. Firms have to decide on both the amount to invest in research and the improvement at which research is targeted.

While the formal details would change for all of these variations, the main conclusions regarding technological progress and growth would remain valid (for the formal details see Grossman and Helpman 1991, Chaps. 3 and 4) and Aghion and Howitt (1992).

3.2.2 Learning by doing. One source of productivity-enhancing technological progress mentioned in the literature is learning by doing (see Arrow, 1962 and for a more recent treatment Young, 1993). The basic idea is that during the production process workers get more experience which enables them either to produce with lower costs or to make further quality improvements. Hence, the current technological standard depends also on output accumulated over time. Technological progress is therefore determined by two sources: investment in research as well as the current level of output. Using the framework given above, these assumptions can be incorporated by assuming that the maximal productivity of an intermediate good is still determined by the date it was invented but that its actual productivity is increasing with its accumulated output. The long-run growth rate of the economy will then depend on investment in research yielding potentially higher productivity, and on the rate at which learning by doing improves actual productivity (see Aghion and Howitt, 1998b, Chapter 6).

4. Regulation and growth

Despite their different assumptions concerning the kind of innovations, the underlying production functions or the number of final and intermediate goods, endogenous growth models emphasise that growth rates are positively correlated with the incentives of firms to undertake costly R&D and with the accumulation of augmentable inputs. Consequently, regulation is growth-enhancing whenever it stimulates R&D and/or the accumulation of either physical or human capital.

In the following we use this general statement to evaluate some specific policy instruments. First, we consider the impact of competition and industrial policy on growth. For simplicity, we define competition policy as promoting competition on the basis of a given technology. Industrial policy is assumed to be directed towards the protection of incumbent firms. It turns out that while competition policy tends to reduce monopoly rents from innovations, it can nevertheless have positive effects on innovation and growth. Second, we turn to a more detailed analysis of the relation between the innovation process and the protection of intellectual property rights by patent laws. Again, while extensive patent protection yields higher monopoly rents (regarding a cumulative innovation process), the optimal patent design has to take dynamic considerations into account as well. In Section 4.3, we discuss the impact of trade liberalisation on growth. While free trade may have negative effects on national growth rates inasmuch as economies may specialise on low-technology products, empirical evidence suggests that international technological spillovers and specialisation according to comparative advantages yield an overall positive effect of trade liberalisation on growth. Capital markets and human capital are considered in Sections 4.4 and 4.5, respectively. Since theoretical arguments imply a positive correlation between growth and both physical and human capital, growth-enhancing policies should concentrate on facilitating the accumulation of both kinds of capital. Finally, we consider tax policies and government expenditures.

4.1 Competition and industrial policy

The first natural suggestion is that since competition in product markets tends to reduce monopoly rents, competition must be detrimental to investment in R&D and growth. This simplistic view, however, is in contrast both to empirical studies, which point to a positive correlation between competition and growth (see Part III), and to theoretical results regarding R&D decisions and firms' performance. We first analyse how competition affects R&D decisions. We then turn to a more detailed analysis of firms' performance. We concentrate on managerial slack and show that more intense competition can increase growth by mitigating managerial slack.

4.1.1 R&D intensity and competition. While R&D investment is obviously driven by expected monopoly rents, Arrow (1962) already pointed out that the incentives for a monopolist to innovate may be lower than for a potential entrant. For example, if the monopolist supplies new goods, he may lose parts of his former monopoly rent. On the other hand, the profit of a new entrant is equal to the total monopoly rent earned from new products. Hence, preventing competition by excluding further market entry has a potentially negative effect on R&D investments and therefore a negative impact on growth.

Similarly, Aghion, Harris and Vickers (1997) emphasise that R&D investment is determined by the relative advantage a firm gets through innovations. They modify the AH model by analysing a step-by-step innovation process where technologically inferior firms must reach the current state-of the-art technology before they can try to become the technological leaders. Since competition turns out to be most intense between firms operating at the same technological level, the relative advantage of successful innovators is highest in markets where firms use the same technology. Hence, firms competing on the same technological level will choose the highest R&D investment.[8] Promoting competition at the level of the current state-of the-art technology can increase both the research intensity and the growth rate.

4.1.2 Firms' performance. Until now we have analysed firms as profit maximisers. The implicit assumption underlying this view is that managers are perfectly controlled by the firms' owners who are only interested in the value of their assets. We now turn to an analysis that is probably more realistic, where due to imperfect information managers have some possibilities to maximise their own utility. In particular, we concentrate on the case where innovations require managerial effort.[9]

Aghion, Dewatripont and Rey (1997) assume that managers try to minimise their effort subject to keeping their private benefits from control over the firm. The manager will lose control once the financial value of the firm is negative. Furthermore, the financial value is positively correlated with the relative technological standard that the firm uses. In order to upgrade the technological standard, however, the manager must invest effort. The intuitive result of this simple model is that a manager will delay innovations as much as possible. While he is forced to innovate by technological progress in other sectors of the economy, he will choose to adopt new technologies such that the financial value of the firm remains positive. Now, if competition is intensified – for example by allowing other firms to produce closer substitutes – the manager is forced to speed up innovation. Since more competition implies a lower financial value of a firm that uses a relatively old technology, the manager has to reduce slack in order to maintain control over the firm. Conversely, industrial policy targeted at protecting the incumbent firm will increase its financial value and will therefore delay the adoption of new technologies.

To summarise, once competition between firms using the same

technology and managerial slack are taken into account, the relation between competition and innovation becomes more complex than the simplistic view suggests. Competition policy can have positive effects on innovation and growth by increasing the incentives to invest in R&D and by reducing managerial slack. Moreover, these results are in accordance with the main arguments stated in the recent debate on deregulation. Concerning network industries Blankart and Knieps (1995) argue that breaking up vertically integrated monopolies and allowing market entry for downstream firms foster not only static efficiency but also innovation. Winston (1998) considers recent US deregulation policies and shows that enhanced competition caused improvements in sector-specific industry efficiency and higher innovation rates. Grandville (1989) shows that relative price declines in input prices yield higher positive effects on growth the higher the elasticities of substitution in the production sectors. Intuitively, higher elasticities of substitution allow for greater adjustments in the production process, thereby causing a higher decrease in production costs. Following this approach Cronin et al. (1997) consider the relative decline in US prices for telecommunication services and conclude that the absolute increase in telecommunication services implied considerable economy-wide resource savings and growth effects. Qualitatively, these findings fit well with the general reasoning of endogenous growth models suggesting a positive correlation between competition-enhancing deregulation and growth. However, the case of network industries also clarifies that regulatory reforms should take into account potential sources of market failures. While competition between firms using a given physical network can imply substantial efficiency gains and incentives for innovations, allowing competition between different physical networks would raise the danger of wasteful resource spending.

4.2 Intellectual property rights and patent policy

In the previous section we discussed the effects of competition concerning entry of new firms. In order to allow entry we implicitly relaxed the assumption that innovations are perfectly protected by patent laws. Now, we turn to a more detailed analysis of this issue.

In general, patent protection leads to ambiguous effects on R&D similar to those of competition policy. Strong patent protection in terms of either the duration and breadth of patents or patentability requirements obviously increases the expected monopoly rents from successful innovations. For example, increasing patentability requirements implies that subsequent innovations must be more sophisticated in order not to infringe on an existing patent. Hence, competing innovations will be either delayed or they will become less likely. Additionally, considering cumulative innovation processes, strong patent protection allows early innovators to charge strictly positive license fees even if subsequent inventions make substantial improvements on initial innovations. Both observations point to a positive effect on R&D investment. On the other hand, strong patent protection will obviously increase the costs of subsequent innovators. Therefore, whether increasing patent protection can enhance growth depends on the relative magnitude of several opposing effects.

Hunt (1995) shows that the positive effect of high patentability requirements is more likely to dominate in industries with rapid innovations. In this case, weak patent protection implies that the expected time until the next successful innovation is fairly short. Hence, increasing patent protection has an overall positive effect on investment in R&D and on growth. Similar results are obtained by O'Donoghue et al. (1995). Analysing situations with frequent innovations they derive the same positive correlation between patent breadth and growth. However, they also emphasise that early innovators are more likely to agree on license contracts the higher the license fee they can charge, i.e. the higher the improvements that are made possible by later inventions. Therefore, increasing patent breadth may have a negative effect on growth by reducing subsequent innovation which only leads to moderate improvements. Focusing on positive spillover effects of basic innovations, Chang (1995) argues that basic innovations should get strong patent protection especially if their stand-alone value is relatively low. Here, strong patent protection and license agreements serve as a simple mechanism to internalise positive externalities and therefore tend to increase basic research.

These results imply a quite complex and ambiguous relation between patent protection and growth. The dynamic aspects of cumulative innovation processes point to positive effects of strong patent protection on growth when innovations are rapid and when innovations have strong spillover effects. On the other hand, in industries with research based on some well known technology and with innovations targeted at rather modest improvements, strong patent protection is more likely to decrease growth.

4.3 Free trade

Concerning the influence of trade on growth one has to analyse how the international flow of final and intermediate goods, of capital (both physical and human capital) and technological knowledge affects the national economy. To put it most generally, the products and activities on which national economies will specialise depend on their comparative advantage, that is, their relative factor endowments as well as their initial technological knowledge. Furthermore, in endogenous growth models, the predicted patterns of trade and growth are also determined by the diffusion of new technologies. Whether new knowledge is available only in the economy where it was generated or whether there are international spillover effects heavily affects the predicted growth rates.

Grossman and Helpman (1991, Chapter 7) assume international spillover effects and show that the main results of traditional trade theory hold for endogenous growth models. More specifically, the equilibrium is fully determined by the relative factor endowments, and an economy will specialise on research activities and high technology products as long as the factors needed for these activities are relatively abundant in this economy. Moreover, the growth rates in different countries will converge with unambiguously positive effects on welfare. In contrast, Young (1991) concentrates on spillover effects limited to national levels and emphasises the notion of dynamic comparative advantage. In particular, he shows that an economy with a low initial stock of technological knowledge may suffer from trade because it specialises on low-technology products implying a continuous fall in its growth rate. Grossman and Helpman (1991, Chapter 8) and Lucas (1993) use similar arguments to highlight the potential positive effects of trade policies and industrial policies.[10]

Overall, the theoretical results point to ambiguous effects of trade on national growth rates. However, empirical evidence suggests that trade has positive effects on growth and convergence (see Part III).

4.4 Capital markets

A common assumption in all models we have presented until now was that capital markets are perfect. While this assumption does not affect the general conclusion in the neoclassical models, with endogenous growth imperfections in capital markets have more significant consequences.[11] Intuitively, since interest payments are part of the cost of private investors and since the growth rate depends on the accumulation of both capital and new knowledge, high interest rates either due to capital market imperfections or due to capital market regulations have a negative influence on the growth rate.

Levine (1997) points out that more sophisticated financial systems affect capital accumulation and R&D investments by lowering informational and monitoring costs, by facilitating risk diversification, and by increasing the amount of available capital. Hubbard (1998) argues that informational asymmetries tend in particular to raise the costs of external financing of R&D

investment. Consequently, R&D investment positively depends on the ability of internal financing.[12] King and Levine (1993) introduce agency costs for evaluating research projects and show that the growth rate depends negatively on these agency costs. Acemoglu and Zilibotti (1997) show that the amount of available capital does not only enhance growth but also influences the variability of the growth rate. They assume sunk costs for research projects and argue that higher total savings allow for a higher number of research projects and therefore for better risk diversification. Hence, the amount of available capital does not only enhance growth but also influences the variability of the growth rate.

These results suggest growth-stimulating effects of capital market policies especially targeted at lowering the costs of external financing and allowing for a better risk diversification for investors. Current policy examples regarding these aspects are the institutions of new stock markets especially designed for technology-oriented small enterprises.[13]

4.5 Human capital
The models of Mankiw, Romer and Weil and Lucas (mentioned in Sections 1.2 and 2, respectively) analyse human capital as an input factor with the same features as physical capital. In contrast, Nelson and Phelps (1966) stress the idea that human capital raises an individual's capacity to learn and to create new technologies. Workers with a good education, i.e. a high stock of human capital, are thought to be more productive in either adapting new technologies or in doing R&D. The first characteristic lowers the cost of implementing new technologies, the second characteristic lowers the cost of research. Obviously, both effects imply that the incentive to invest in research is higher the higher the stock of human capital in the economy. Redding (1996) additionally emphasises that high education and high technological standards are complements in production and shows that this complementarity can lead to low-development traps. Furthermore, assuming imperfect capital markets and human capital investment based on different income levels implies that educational policies that subsidise human capital accumulation can have a positive impact on growth (see Lee and Roemer, 1998.

Despite these general conclusions, however, the question of how the educational sector should be regulated is largely unsolved. While Rothschild and White (1995) argue that with perfect information competition between universities leads to an efficient quality diversification as well as to an efficient allocation of students, Winston (1999) emphasises that imperfect information is likely to imply sub-optimal market allocations.[14] He stresses the positive external effects of recruiting the most talented students and concludes that competition forces universities to offer especially low tuition fees for top students. Since this implies higher prices for other students or cutbacks in socially motivated subsidies, competition may easily yield an average level of aggregate education which is below the optimum. Aghion and Howitt (1998b, Chapter 10) use similar arguments and conclude that common schools for children of parents endowed with different levels of human capital (and therefore with different incomes) may in fact raise the long-run level of average human capital. Hence, the segregation effect of competition between schools may decrease the long-run growth rate.

To summarise the different arguments, the Nelson and Phelps approach suggests the same complementarity between the stock of human capital and growth as between physical capital and growth. Therefore, as long as capital markets are imperfect, subsidising human capital accumulation is likely to enhance growth. Whether competition between schools or universities leads to an efficient allocation and how the educational sector should be regulated are more subtle questions. While the diversification incentives implied by competition may have positive effects on specialised high-level education, competition seems to imply negative effects as far as elementary education is concerned.

4.6 Taxes and government expenditures

The obvious way to analyse taxes and government expenditures is to trace out their effects on growth-enhancing activities. We start with a discussion of taxes on consumption and on production factors, respectively. Finally, we briefly consider public expenditures for consumption and investment in productive capital.

4.6.1 Taxes. Consider first a simple linear consumption tax. This tax does not alter the relative prices of current and future consumption. Hence, with inelastic labour supply the primary effects are income effects on saving and on investment in human capital. Obviously, if these effects are rather low and if the tax revenue is spent in the final goods sector, the effect of a consumption tax on the growth rate is rather low. On the other hand, taxes on factor incomes – either income from physical capital or total labour income – directly decrease the factor supply and distort factor accumulation. Whether these distortions have a high or low effect on growth depends on the elasticities of substitution in the production functions and the elasticity of intertemporal substitution in the utility function of households (see Stokey and Rebelo, 1995). For example, taxes on physical capital income will tend to increase the equilibrium interest rate more the lower the elasticities of substitution in the production functions of final goods. But as long as physical capital is also used as an input for R&D, a higher interest rate implies a negative effect on R&D investment and therefore on the growth rate. On the other hand, if physical capital can be easily substituted or if R&D is mainly based on human capital, taxes on physical capital will have more moderate effects on growth. Similarly, taxes on total labour income tend to have higher negative effects on the growth rate the more elastic the supply of human capital and the more R&D relies on human capital. Additionally, if human capital is the main input in the production of human capital the wage rate for high-skilled workers tends to increase not only because of the reduced incentives to accumulate human capital but also because of increased investment costs. Both effects will obviously increase the costs for R&D and will therefore lower the growth rate.

This analysis points out that taxation is more growth-decreasing the higher the distorting effects regarding factor accumulation. While the exact quantitative effects of different taxes depend inter alia on the properties of the production functions in different sectors, the qualitative analysis confirms the general conclusion that taxes on production factors lead to larger negative effects on growth than consumption taxes. Moreover, taking international factor mobility into account, national taxes on production factors will have additional negative effects on national growth rates.

4.6.2 Government expenditures. In order to analyse the growth effects of different kinds of public expenditures, Cassou and Lansing (1999) distinguish between public expenditures for pure consumption and for productive public capital. While pure consumption (financed by distortionary taxation) is shown to have negative effects on growth, a decline of the ratio between public and private capital may imply considerable slowdowns in the growth rate. Morrison and Schwartz (1996) model firms technology and behaviour explicitly. Analysing US manufacturing industries they show that investment in physical infrastructure yield significant positive effects on productivity and growth. Similar results are obtained by Nadiri and Mamuneas (1994). They also consider public expenditures for R&D and suggest relatively high cost-saving effects of both infrastructure as well as R&D expenditures. Aghion and Schankermann (1999) analyse productive public capital as comprising a broad range of physical and institutional infrastructure. In addition to direct cost savings, public infrastructure is shown to generate considerable indirect effects by reducing both transaction costs and the costs of market entry.

These results support the hypothesis that investment in productive public capital – defined in an appropriate manner – can have positive impacts on growth. While it is quite obvious that public infrastructure may imply cost reductions for private firms, applying a dynamic analysis points to additional growth-enhancing effects. By lowering the capital requirements for private firms public capital can foster market entry and competition which ultimately results in higher innovation rates and growth. On the other hand, public consumption financed by distortionary taxation has a clear negative impact on growth.

III.   EMPIRICAL FINDINGS ON REGULATION AND ECONOMIC GROWTH

This part presents empirical findings on various links between regulation and economic growth. Although the sources of economic growth have recently been subject of intensive empirical research,[15] surprisingly little has been published about the ties between regulation and economic growth directly. For that reason, we will stress the influence of regulation on economic growth by considering the affiliation between various examined determinants of economic growth and regulation.

The remaining sections are organised as follows. Section 5 gives a brief description of the predominant empirical methodologies. Section 6 summarises the main findings with respect to potential sources of growth.

5. Empirical methodology

Most empirical work on the determinants of economic growth uses *regression analysis* of the form: [16]

$$\gamma = \alpha + \beta_1 x_1 + \beta_2 x_2 + ... + \beta_n x_n + \varepsilon$$

where γ typically represents a vector of rates of economic growth, and x_1 to x_n are vectors of explanatory variables, representing various factors that are supposed to affect economic growth. The coefficients β_1 to β_n are measures of the specific effect of each explanatory variable on the rate of growth. This statistically estimated influence can be either positive or negative, strong or weak, and significant or not at a certain level of confidence.

Before we turn to distinct applications of this general framework, we want to emphasise some limitations of this methodology, which will be useful to consider when assessing the findings of the empirical literature. Most important is the problem of causality: A statistical correlation does not necessarily document a causal link. For instance, the question whether growth leads to increased investment or investment increases growth cannot be answered with a simple statistical correlation.[17] Another problem is that the specification of a regression equation always implies assumptions that have to be taken into account to interpret the results accurately. For example, cross-country regressions assume that the sources of economic growth are largely the same across countries. Third, measurement errors, outliers, and lack of data are issues that may limit the explanatory power of empirical results.

The distinct approaches of regression analysis differ mainly with respect to the information – concerning the time dimension and the observed units – they use.

The *time-series* approach uses data on a single country over a period of time. This approach is advantageous if the researcher seeks to avoid problems of heterogeneity or simply concentrates on one country. Heterogeneity refers to the fact that countries differ e.g. in their cultural, political and social attributes, and hence there may be little reason why they should have the same sources of economic growth.

However, most regressions are performed as a comparison between different countries, regions or states at one point in time. This procedure, called *cross-sectional* analysis, is predominant for three reasons. First, a cross-country comparison of economic performance generates more data for analysis than a single country study, and hence provides a superior basis for empirical research. Second, it can be beneficial to compare the specific influence of different parameters that affect growth at one point in time, inasmuch as parameters themselves may change over time. Third, many empirical studies on economic growth focus on the investigation of differences of rates of economic growth between countries, e.g. between developing and developed countries.

More recently, the *panel data* approach is increasingly used. Panel data combine time-series and cross-sectional analysis. This has the advantage of expanding the sample information considerably, since the evidence comes from cross-sectional variation between countries as well as from the time dimension. Therefore, it is possible to detect influences of country-specific characteristics, such as institutional settings. Hence, this procedure abates the problem of heterogeneity. Further, the time series dimension allows us to study dynamic adjustments, such as how regulation and growth change over time. The main disadvantage of this approach is that, until recently, only a few countries recorded adequate data, so that the time series dimension is quite limited.

Apart from the described regression analysis approaches, we will also present a study that provides a worldwide *questioning* on institutional obstacles for doing business to supplement the main research lines of the empirical literature. For our purpose, we suggest using the distinct empirical methods as complementary. Hence, we will stress their common results concerning the connections between regulation and economic growth in the following subsection.

6. Sources of growth

As stated above, most empirical work on growth relies on regression analysis, where the set of explanatory variables represents the specific set of presumed influences on economic growth.

In the following, we present variables that affect economic growth and are themselves linked to regulation, such as: research and development, overall product market regulation, the definition of property rights, trade policy, financial development, human capital, public infrastructure spending and government consumption.

For each of these variables we consider the principle measures that have been used to operationalise them for empirical investigation, and the findings concerning direction and significance of this relationship. Moreover, we briefly present some additional variables that affect growth through a broader political context.

Before we turn to these single variables, however, let us first take a look at the role of technological progress in relation to overall economic growth.

6.1 Technological progress
One common way to investigate the contribution of technological progress to overall economic growth is to consider relative contributions of growth in inputs and growth in efficiency. In other words, it is necessary to separate growth in inputs – typically (human) capital and labour – and the residual total factor productivity (TFP) growth. TFP growth rates can be measured by subtracting the weighted input growth rates from the overall rate of economic growth as shown in Table 2.1.

The column 'TFP growth rate' shows in parentheses the percentage of GDP growth rate that is explained by TFP growth. As can be seen, a fundamental influence of technological progress on growth is reported, but this holds also for factor accumulation. In the period between 1947 and 1973, TFP growth accounts for more than one-third of GDP growth in all countries, ranging from 33.6 per cent for the United States to 63.5 per cent for Italy. Although the period from 1960 to 1990 still shows substantial efficiency improvements, TFP growth clearly accounts for less growth in this period.

It is, however, important to emphasise that such growth accounting – being just a mechanical decomposition of growth rates – does not attempt to explain how growth in inputs and technological progress is tied to factors such as general government policies and regulatory reform (Barro and Sala-i-Martin, 1995). Therefore, we consider variables that are theoretically supposed to affect R&D investment and factor accumulation in the following sections.

Table 2.1 Development of total factor productivity (TFP)

Country	Growth rate of real GDP	Contribution from capital	Contribution from labour	TFP growth rate
		1947-73		
France	0.0542	0.0225	0.0021	0.0296 (54.5%)
Germany	0.0661	0.0269	0.0018	0.0374 (56.6%)
Italy	0.0527	0.0180	0.0011	0.0337 (63.5%)
UK	0.0373	0.0176	0.0003	0.0193 (51.9%)
US	0.0402	0.0171	0.0095	0.0135 (33.6%)
Canada	0.0517	0.0254	0.0088	0.0175 (33.9%)
Japan	0.0951	0.0328	0.0221	0.0402 (42.3%)
		1960-90		
France	0.0350	0.0203	0.0002	0.0145 (41.4%)
Germany	0.0320	0.0188	-0.0025	0.0158 (49.4%)
Italy	0.0410	0.0202	0.0011	0.0197 (47.9%)
UK	0.0249	0.0131	-0.0010	0.0130 (51.9%)
US	0.0310	0.0140	0.0129	0.0041 (13.2%)
Canada	0.0410	0.0229	0.0135	0.0046 (11.3%)
Japan	0.0681	0.0387	0.0097	0.0196 (28.8%)

Source: Barro and Sala-i-Martin (1995).

6.2 Research and development

A bulk of studies has extended the growth-accounting approach to include R&D activities as an additional input. They suggest a strong relationship between R&D activities and economic growth.[18] Usually, researchers derive estimates of TFP growth, and then regress these estimates on various measures of innovation, such as an index that represents R&D spending or patenting.

Frequently, some lag function of past R&D investments is used to represent the level of knowledge in the economy. This proxy – also called R&D capital stock – allows us to estimate output elasticities which measure the output effect of an increase of the R&D capital stock. Table 2.2 gives a flavour of empirical results concerning such output elasticities for the firm, industry and country level.

Table 2.2 Estimates of the output elasticity of R&D

Study	Elasticity	Level	Country
Griliches (1980)	0.06	Firm	US
Mairesse and Cuneo (1985)	0.09-0.26	Firm	France
Englander et al. (1988)	0.00-0.50	Industry	G5
Nadiri and Prucha (1990)	0.24	Industry	US
Coe and Helpman (1993)	0.23	Total economy	G7
Patel and Soete (1988)	0.21	Total economy	West Germany

Source: Cameron (1996).

The results suggest that an increase in the R&D capital stock has a positive impact on total output, although they differ considerably in the magnitude of the estimated effect. For example, Griliches (1980) finds that a 1 per cent increase in the R&D capital stock leads to a 0.06 per cent rise in output, while Englander et al. (1988) find a rise in output of up to 0.50 per cent.[19]

Another widely used variable is the flow of R&D spending as a share of output (typically R&D/sales). If TFP growth is regressed on these R&D-output ratios, rates of return on R&D spending can be estimated. Since the benefits caused by R&D are at least in part public, empirical work often distinguishes between private and social returns to R&D investment.[20] Empirical results indicate that there are significant spillovers from R&D spending on productivity growth at the industry and country level. Table 2.3 shows related evidence for the industry level.

The results show that the rates of return of R&D spending are considerably high if only the industries own spending is included (see in column "Own"), and even higher if the R&D investment of other industries is additionally considered in the regression analysis. The large magnitude of rates of total rates of return appears to support the idea that there is too little private investment in R&D. These rates of return well above the competitive level can possibly persist due to financial market imperfections, which can occur with respect to R&D activities.

Studies concerning the effect of academic and government spending on R&D suggest that spillovers play a role here, too. Nevertheless, these spillovers are found to be smaller than those between firms, as has been shown by Griliches and Lichtenberg (1984b). Another interesting result from empirical research is that basic R&D typically yields higher returns than applied R&D (see e.g. Griliches, 1986).

Table 2.3 Estimates of social rates of return to R&D

Study	Own	Other	Total
Griliches/Lichtenberg (1984a)	0.30	0.41	0.71
Griliches/Lichtenberg (1984b)	0.34	-	-
Hall (1995)	0.33	-	-
Scherer (1982)	0.29	0.74	1.03
Sveikauskas (1981)	0.17	-	-
Terleckyj (1980)	0.25	0.82	1.07

Note: The column 'Own' indicates that only R&D in one´s own industry is included, while 'Other' represents the additional effect of R&D in an upstream industry on own productivity. 'Total' is the sum of the two other columns.

Source: Jones and Williams (1998).

It is well known that the various proxies of technical progress have their drawbacks. For example, the provided data often neglect R&D activities of small firms do not include software developments, and patent statistics differ across countries. But remarkably, whatever proxy is deployed, a strong relationship between R&D and economic growth is reported.

One possible conclusion concerning R&D is that defining the R&D playing field is an important area of political action. One of the key determinants of such a playing field is the design and enforcement of property rights in order to protect rents from innovation. Torstensson (1994) and Sachs and Warner (1995) present results that indicate a positive relationship between broadly defined property rights and economic growth. Park and Ginarte (1997) study this matter in greater detail, concentrating solely on the definition of intellectual property rights (IPRs). On the basis of the national patent law of 60 countries they construct an index that reflects, besides other criteria, the duration of patent protection and the enforcement level of patent law. Using a panel data approach, they find that IPRs matter for R&D activities and growth in developed countries and conclude that R&D is more likely to take place under conditions in which IPRs are well protected and enforced.

Summarising, empirical evidence suggests that R&D activities, especially in the field of basic R&D, are quite fruitful with respect to economic growth. The same holds for appropriately defined intellectual property rights.

6.3 Market opening

The first variable we consider in the context of market opening is product market regulation. Koedijk and Kremers (1996) analysis deals directly with market opening and economic growth. They use data on the degree of regulation of both labour and product markets in 11 EU member countries.[21] To measure the degree of product market regulation, Koedijk and Kremers construct an unweighted index, which takes the following factors into account: the degree of business establishment regulation, competition policy, public ownership, industry specific support, shopping hours, and the extent of implementation of the EU single market programme on a national level. The index indicates that the United Kingdom and Ireland are especially lightly regulated, while Italy and Greece are ranked as relatively highly regulated.

Koedijk and Kremers regress real output growth rates in the market sector (1981-93) on the index of product market regulation and find a negative and significant relationship across countries.

Additionally, they run cross-country regressions considering average (1980-94) TFP growth, labour productivity growth, and capital productivity growth. Here, they detect a significant negative relationship between TFP growth, labour productivity growth and product market regulation. Figure 2.1 illustrates these results, by depicting the ranking of TFP growth and the ranking of product market regulation for the observed countries.

Taken at face value, the results seem to indicate that product market regulation has a strong negative effect on growth. However, these results should be taken with caution. As Röller (1996) argues, many larger firms compete in various countries and hence are affected by diverse product market regulation regimes. Further, Koedijk and Kremers do not refer to institutional changes within the observed period, although the years between 1980 and the early 1990s have seen fundamental changes in European regulatory frameworks. Instead they constructed their index of regulation with data from the late 1980s. Another crucial point is that they neglect the fact that regulation has also a quality dimension. For instance, in the case of telecommunications regulation it is not clear that less regulation concerning bottlenecks alone necessarily implies more efficient competition as has been demonstrated by the light-handed regulation approach in New Zealand.[22]

Figure 2.1 Productivity and product market regulation

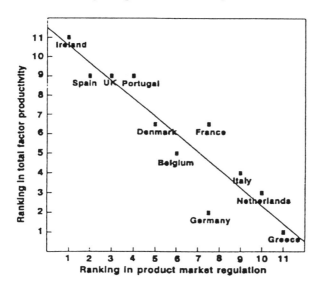

Source: Koedlijk and Kremers (1996), p. 454.

Another possible way to measure the effects of liberalisation is to relate the level of competition to economic growth. Examples are provided by Green and Mayes (1991) or Caves and Barton (1990). They focus on the comparison of technical efficiency across countries by linking stochastically estimated production functions with competition variables such as the number of entrants in the industry. Another approach is to concentrate directly on the performance of individual firms as done by Nickell et al.

(1997) or Blundell et al. (1995). Similarly, Geroski (1989) considers the relationship between entry, innovation and growth for a sample of 79 UK firms from 1976-79. He found that 30 per cent of TFP growth is due to the effect of entry, while 50 per cent is driven by innovation. Altogether, the empirical evidence unambiguously suggests a strong positive relationship between the level of competition and economic performance.

A more direct approach was chosen by Brunetti et al. (1997a and b). They present results from a questionnaire: more than 3,600 entrepreneurs in 69 countries were asked about their perceptions of issues such as predictability of laws and policies, various regulations and the security of property rights. This procedure has the advantage that it produces a transparent quantitative data set on different aspects of institutional problems across countries as actually perceived by entrepreneurs. Furthermore, in contrast to indicators from commercial companies that sell data on specific country risks to international investors, their data cover the problems of domestic firms. This is of importance, since foreign investors are often treated differently from domestic investors. For our purpose the data may be viewed as an indicator of what really matters to business people and possibly provides a hint about policy recommendations. One question addressed various regulations directly. Entrepreneurs were asked to judge different regulations on a scale ranging from 1 ('no obstacle') to 6 ('very strong obstacle'). The average rankings for each obstacle in the sub-sample 'developed countries'[23] indicates that entrepreneurs feel that their activity is negatively influenced by various regulations, most importantly: high taxes, labour regulations (average over 4.0 points) and safety/environmental and financing regulations (average over 3.5 points).

However, whether this perception is coupled with less economic growth may not be answered fully without further investigation, although it appears quite plausible.

6.4 Free trade
The influence of trade policy on economic performance has always been a source of lively debate among economists. Numerous studies on trade claim to have found a positive and significant effect of open trade policy on economic growth. A choice of them is presented in Table 2.4.

Despite these unambiguous empirical results, prominent economists such as Krugman (1994) are sceptical about the influence of openness on economic growth. One of the main problems of the empirical work on trade liberalisation and economic growth is that the studies suffer from proper measurement of trade liberalisation. Besides data problems this is mainly due to the large number of policy instruments – tariffs, quotas, licenses, exchange rate controls, non-tariff barriers – affecting international trade, that are often mixed together more or less arbitrarily in one single index.

Table 2.4 Findings on the relation between trade policy and economic growth

Explanatory variable	Reference	Finding
Leamer index*	Levine and Renelt (1992)	negative
Openness (change)	Harrison (1995)	positive, significant
Tariffs	Barro and Lee (1994)	negative
Years open (1950-90)	Sala-i-Martin (1997)	positive, significant

*Leamer (1998) uses a trade model to estimate trade intensities and uses the differences between predicted and actual intensity as indicators of trade barriers

Source: Durlauf and Quah (1998).

Considering this problem, Edwards (1997) analyses the influence of trade policy on economic growth using nine alternative openness indexes to overcome the single indicators.[24] Furthermore, he uses a new data set, various estimation techniques, and different time periods and growth regression specifications.

The evidence generated by this comprehensive procedure supports previous results and suggests clearly that more open countries have experienced faster productivity growth.

6.5 Capital markets

The relation between financial development and economic growth was, until recently, a fairly neglected part of empirical economic research. Presently, a growing body of work investigates the banking system's impact on growth.[25]

Goldsmith (1969) provides the seminal empirical work in this area. He measures the development of the financial system for 35 countries in a period of 103 years and finds a strong positive relationship between financial and economic development.[26]

Later, studies such as King and Levine (1993) used four additional indicators to measure the level of financial development and find that all four indicators exhibit a strong positive relationship with economic growth.[27]

Similarly, Levine and Zervos (1996) study a measure of the relative volume of financial market transactions in relation to GDP and find this explanatory variable to be positively and significantly connected with growth. Easterly (1993) presents a measure of financial repression and shows that it is negatively connected with growth.

Overall, the level of financial development clearly seems to be one of the factors that foster growth.

6.6 Human capital

Human capital is one of the most frequently used explanatory variables in regression analyses concerning economic growth.[28] For instance, Barro (1997) uses three different variables – average years of male attainment in secondary and higher schools, life expectancy and an interaction between GDP and school attainment – to get a proxy for the level of human capital. The studies on the role of human capital suggest that overall education, health and male education have a positive impact on growth, while female education has no effect and primary school attainment has a negative impact on economic growth.

In contrast, Caselli et al. (1996) find that female rather than male education matters. Temple (1999) states in a recent contribution that although school enrolment rates as measures of human capital were initially regarded as robust and satisfactory variables, it would be of value to remember that they are afflicted with many empirical problems, e.g. training is often completely left out of the analysis and school enrolment rates rarely correspond well with human capital variables in theoretical models.

Summarising, the evidence suggests a positive relationship between human capital and economic growth, although there seems to be a need for further investigations on the basis of more precise data.

6.7 Taxes and government expenditures

Government action may have countervailing effects on growth. On the one hand taxation and the implied distortions of private decisions may lead to less growth, while on the other hand some government spending may raise growth rates, e.g. through providing police services or fostering R&D.

Some early studies on the effects of government spending (e.g. Kormendi and Meguire, 1985) found no significant relation between economic rates of growth and government consumption measured as a ratio of real government consumption to GDP. But, as Barro (1990) argues, this could be a consequence of the definition of government consumption in these studies. Therefore, he modified the previously used data by subtracting the share of government spending on defence and education from general government consumption to obtain a measure of government outlays that do not increase productivity. In this, and in more recent studies, e.g. Barro and Sala-i-Martin (1995) and Barro (1997), it is concluded that this measure of government consumption and its counterpart taxation have a significantly negative effect on growth. Figure 2.2 depicts this effect.

Focusing more directly on the distortionary effects of taxation, Easterly (1993) constructed a measure of the variance of relative prices between commodities to estimate the overall distortion of price systems for a sample of 57 countries and 157 commodities. The argument behind this is that taxing and subsidising goods widens the spread of prices, hence the variance of prices gives a proxy for these influences. He finds that variations in consumption goods prices do not matter, while the mean and variance of input prices (education, health, buildings, equipment investment) affect growth rates significantly negatively. Therefore, distortions of relative input prices can have large negative effects on growth.

Another, more widely used proxy for government induced distortions is the ratio of the official to parallel exchange rate, which is called black-market premium and measures the premium people must pay, relative to the official exchange rate, to exchange the domestic currency for dollars in the black market. The main advantage of this measure is its availability, but on the other hand one could argue that one particular price distortion is not appropriate to serve as a proxy for governmental distortions of markets in general. Nevertheless, many studies document significantly negative effects for this variable (see among others Easterly, 1993, and Barro and Sala-i-Martin, 1995).

Recapitulating the evidence so far in brief, non-productive government consumption as well as taxation of input goods including financial capital seems to be harmful for growth.

But what about public spending on infrastructure? Conventional wisdom suggests that public spending on infrastructure supports economic growth by providing public goods. The connection between economic growth and investment has been included in a variety of studies, but it has proven to be quite difficult to measure the effects of public investment empirically. This is mainly due to a lack of data, e.g. international accounting systems record just the sum of public and private investment and some developing countries do not provide any data. Furthermore, the concept of the public sector is not consistent across countries, and a systematic collection of data started often as late as in the early 1970s.

Nevertheless, Barro and Sala-i-Martin (1995) measure the effect of public investment with the available data and find that public investment is not significantly related to economic growth. However, measures of telecommunications development as well as the share of public investment in transport and communications (see e.g. Easterly and Rebelo, 1993) have been found to have a positive impact on economic growth.

Figure 2.2 Growth rate versus government consumption

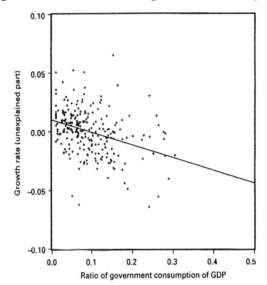

Note: Each dot represents one country

Source: Barro (1997), p. 27.

Hence, one may conclude that there is a positive effect from providing public infrastructure. On the other hand it is worth mentioning that some researchers claim the problem of causality could play a significant role here.

6.8 Additional variables

On a more general level the effects of the social and political environment on economic growth have also been tested in great variety. Variables such as the degree of the rule of law, democracy, political instability or even capitalism as such have been widely used in the literature. The central idea behind such variables is to gauge the general investment climate in a country. Table 2.5 gives a short summary of the findings.

These variables are often measured by using data from political science or commercial agencies that provide data for international investors. For instance, Barro uses an international index of political rights and civil liberties to measure the degree of democracy and takes data from the 'International Country Risk Guide'. Of course, these measures are arbitrary, but in regard to the 'International Country Risk Guide', one argument for their reliability is that clients pay substantial fees for them.

Overall, the findings seem not very surprising: political instability is bad for growth, while the enforcement of law and order, the level of democracy and capitalism have a positive influence.

Table 2.5 Diverse variables and economic growth

Explanatory variable	Reference	Finding
Capitalism (level)	Sala-i-Martin (1997)	positive, significant
Democracy		
Some	Barro (1996, 1997)	positive, significant
More	Barro (1996, 1997)	positive, significant
Overall	Alesina et al. (1996)	?
Political instability	Alesina et al. (1996)	negative, significant
	Barro (1991)	negative, significant
	Barro/Lee (1994)	negative, significant
	Caselli et al. (1996)	negative, significant
	Levine/Renelt (1992)	negative
	Sala-i-Martin (1997)	negative
Rule of law	Barro (1997)	positive, significant

Source: Durlauf and Quah (1998).

IV. CONCLUSIONS

Some policy recommendations are straightforward from our analysis: First, the overall degree of regulation appears to have a negative impact on economic performance. Theoretical results as well as the empirical findings and recent experiences in the US indicate that further deregulation and competition-enhancing policies in product markets are likely to increase growth. Providing open network access in network industries, lightening business establishment regulations and reducing shopping hours restrictions are examples of such policies. Additionally, free trade has proved to have a substantial effect on growth. Second, fostering the development of capital markets seems to be one of the key issues to encourage economic growth. New stock markets like the German Neuer Markt do not only lower the cost of external financing for small firms, by facilitating risk diversification they also provide additional capital for R&D investments. Third, since the accumulation of human capital turned out to have significant positive effects on growth, educational policies should concentrate on both the achievement of a high average stock of human capital as well as the creation of institutions providing highly specialised education.

Nevertheless, concerning competition-enhancing deregulation potential market failures should be taken into account as well. Most obviously, by financing highly non-rival goods such as public infrastructure and basic research, the government can not only enhance static efficiency but it can also lower the costs of market entry by new and innovative firms. Similar reasoning applies to network industries where regulation should take care of an efficient provision of the underlying physical network structure. More subtle problems arise with respect to the question of optimal patent protection. For instance, we have shown that patent protection should be strong if innovations are rapid and when innovations have strong spillover effects. However, in industries with research based on well known technology and with innovations targeted at rather modest improvements, weaker patent protection is more likely to increase growth. Potential market failures due to externalities should also be considered with respect to the educational sector. While competition between schools and universities may yield a relatively high degree of well educated and specialised workers, common education of children with different levels of human capital can raise the long-run level of average human capital and therefore the long-run growth rate.

Finally, concerning the impact of the tax system on growth consumption, taxes should be preferred to taxes on factor incomes from either physical or human capital. Again, the intuition is that in order to increase growth one has to increase the incentives for innovation and capital accumulation.

Overall, we would like to suggest that policy measures may raise rates of economic growth only a small amount, but as Barro (1997, p. 47) puts it: 'increases in growth rates by a few tenths of a percentage point matter a lot in the long-run and are surely worth the trouble'.

NOTES

1. Each household is assumed to have an inter-temporal additive utility function with a constant rate of time preferences and constant elasticities of marginal utility.
2. Specifically, the cross-country regression run by MRW yields estimated coefficients of the production function which are largely consistent with the observed factor shares.
3. The same qualitative results follow from convex models where consumption goods and capital are produced according to different production functions (see Jones and Manuelli, 1994).
4. For a similar approach, see also Romer (1986).
5. The probability of success in R&D is determined by a Poisson process and is proportional to the amount spent on R&D.
6. If capital per worker would be held constant, technological progress would imply a decrease in capital per effective worker. But since capital is assumed to be necessary for production, expected profits in the intermediate goods sector would fall to zero. Long-run growth would be impossible.
7. For a detailed discussion see Aghion and Howitt (1998a), pp. 119-120.
8. See also Harris and Vickers (1987).
9. For a general analysis of incentive problems within firms see Holmstrom and Milgrom (1994).
10. See also Leahy and Neary (1994) for a detailed discussion of a similar infant industry argument in terms of strategic trade policy.
11. In the neoclassical models, a tax on interest income would alter the level of output per capita but not the long-run growth rate.
12. For empirical evidence see Himmelberg and Petersen, (1994).
13. For a discussion of the Neuer Markt in Germany and the NASDAQ in the US, see Theissen (1998). Edey and Hviding (1995) provide a general overview of capital market developments in OECD countries.
14. See also Salop and White (1991) for a discussion of competition and efficiency.
15. For an outline see Temple (1999).
16. See Sala-i-Martin (1997).
17. Therefore, the set of explanatory variables should be in line with economic theory. Furthermore, sophisticated statistical methods can be applied to clarify causality problems, if adequate data are available.
18. Excellent summaries are provided by Cohen and Levin (1991) and Griliches (1992).
19. One reason for such differences is that the definition of the R&D

capital stock varies between studies.
20. Since each firm benefits from its own as well as from other firms' investment in R&D.
21. Since labour market regulations are addressed in a separate contribution to this volume, we will present solely product market considerations here.
22. See Woroch (1995).
23. The sample includes Austria, Canada, France, Germany, Ireland, Italy, Portugal, Spain, Switzerland, the United Kingdom and the United States.
24. These indicators include the World Development Report Outward Orientation Index, Leamer's Openness Index and others.
25. See Levine (1997) for an overview.
26. The indicator he uses is constructed by calculating the fraction of the value of financial intermediary assets of GNP.
27. These indicators are: the relation of financial intermediaries and equal liquid liabilities to GDP, the degree to which the central bank vs. commercial banks are allocating credit, and the ratio of credit given to private enterprises in relation to total domestic credit and GDP.
28. See e.g. Knowles and Owen (1995), Barro and Lee (1994), Forbes (1997) and Levine and Renelt (1992).

REFERENCES

Acemoglu, D. and F. Zilibotti (1997), 'Was Prometheus Unbound by Chance? Risk, Diversification, and Growth', *Journal of Political Economy*, 105 (4), pp. 709-751.

Aghion, P. and P. Howitt (1992), 'A Model of Growth ghrough Creative Destruction', *Econometrica*, 60(2), pp. 323-51.

Aghion, P. and P. Howitt (1998a), "Capital Accumulation and Innovation as Complementary Factors in Long-Run Growth", *Journal of Economic Growth*, 3, pp. 111-130.

Aghion, P. and P. Howitt (1998b), *Endogenous Growth Theory*, Cambridge, MA: MIT Press.

Aghion, P. and M. Schankermann (1999), 'Competition, Entry and the Social Returns to Infrastructure in Transition Economics', *Economics of Transition*, 7 (1), pp. 79-101.

Aghion, P., M. Dewatripont and P. Rey (1997), Corporate Governance, Competition Policy and Industrial Policy, *European Economic Review*,

41, pp. 797-805.

Aghion, P., C. Harris, and J. Vickers (1997), 'Competition and Growth with Step-by-Step Innovation: An Example', *European-Economic-Review*; 41(3-5), pp. 771-82.

Alesina, A. and D. Rodrik (1994), 'Distributive politics and economic growt/h', *Quarterly Journal of Economics*, 109(2), pp. 465-490.

Alesina, A. and Summers (1993), 'Central bank independence and macroeconomic performance: some comparative evidence', *Journal of Money, Credit, and Banking*, 25, pp. 155-173.

Alesina, A., S. Ozler,, N. Roubini. and P. Schwagel (1996), 'Political instability and economic growth', *Journal of Economic Growth*, 1(2), pp. 189-211.

Arrow, K.J. (1962), 'The Economic Implications of Learning by Doing', *Review of Economic Studies*, 29 (1), pp. 155-173.

Azariadis, C. and A. Drazen (1990), 'Threshold externalities in economic development', *Quarterly Journal of Economics*, 105(2), pp. 501-526.

Barro, R.J. (1990), 'Government spending in a simple model of endogenous growth', *Journal of Political Economy*, 98(5), Part 2, pp. 103-125.

Barro, R.J. (1991), 'Economic growth in a cross-section of countries', *Quarterly Journal of Economics*, 106(2), pp. 407-443.

Barro, R.J. (1996), 'Democracy and Growth',' *Journal of Economic Growth*, 1(1), pp. 1-27.

Barro, R.J. (1997), *Determinants of economic growth: a cross-country empirical study*, Cambridge, MA: MIT Press.

Barro, R.J. and J.W. Lee (1994), *Sources of economic growth*, Carnegie-Rochester Conference Series on Public Policy, 40, pp. 1-57.

Barro, R.J. and X. Sala-i-Martin (1995), *Economic growth*, New York: McGraw-Hill.

Blankart, C.B. (1998), Outputfinanzierung von Hochschulen. *Hamburger Jahrbuch für Wirtschafts- und Gesellschatspolitik*, 43. Jahr, pp. 9-30.

Blankart, C.B. and G. Knieps (1995), 'Market-Oriented Open Network Provision', *Information-Economics-and-Policy*, 7(3), pp. 283-96.

Blomstrom, M., R.E. Lipsey, and M. Zejan (1996), 'Is fixed investment the key to economic growth?' *Quarterly Journal of Economics*, 111(1), pp. 269-276.

Blundell, R., R. Griffiths, and J. van Reenen (1995), 'Dynamic count data model of technological innovations', *The Economic Journal*, 105, pp. 333-344.

Brunetti, A., K. Gregory, and B. Weder (1997a), *Economic growth with 'incredible' rules: evidence from a world wide private sector survey*,

Washington, D.C.: The World Bank.

Brunetti, A., K. Gregory, and B. Weder (1997b), *Institutional obstacles for doing business: data description and methodology of a world wide private sector survey*, Washington, D.C.: The World Bank.

Cameron, G. (1996), *Innovation and economic growth*. Centre for Economic Performance Discussion Paper No. 277.

Caselli, F., G. Esquivel, and F. Lefort (1996), 'Reopening the convergence debate: a new look at cross-country growth empirics.' *Journal of Economic Growth*, 1(3), pp. 363-389.

Cass, D (1965), 'Optimum Growth in an Aggregative Model of Capital Accumulation', *Review of Economic Studies*, 32, pp. 233-240.

Cassou, S.P. and K.J. Lansing (1999), 'Fiscal Policy and Productivity Growth in the OECD', Kansas State University, mimeo.

Caves, R.E. and D.R. Barton (1990), *Efficiency in US manufacturing industries*. Cambridge, MA: MIT Press.

Chang, H.F. (1995), 'Patent Scope, Antitrust Policy, and Cumulative Innovation', *Rand Journal of Economics*, 26 (1), pp. 34-57.

Coe, D.T. and E. Helpman (1993), *International R&D Spillovers*, CEPR Discussion Paper, No. 840.

Coe, D.T. and E. Helpman (1995), 'International R&D Spillovers', *European Economic Review*, 39 (5), pp. 859-887.

Cohen, W.M. and R.C. Levin (1991), 'Empirical studies of innovation and market structure', in Schmalensee, R. and Willig, R.D. (eds), *Handbook of Industrial Organization*, Elsevier Science Publishers, Chapter 18.

Cronin, F.J., E. Colleran, and M. Gold (1997), 'Telecommunications, Factor Substitution and Economic Growth', *Contemporary Economic Policy*, 15, pp. 21-31.

Cukierman, A. (1992), *Central bank strategy, credibility, and independence*. Cambridge, MA: MIT Press.

DeLong, J.B., and L.H. Summers (1998), 'How strongly do developing economies benefit from equipment investment', *Journal of Monetary Economics*, 32(3), pp. 395-415.

Durlauf, S.N. and D.T. Quah (1998), *The new empirics of economic growth*, Centre For Economic Performance Discussion Paper No. 384.

Easterly, W. (1993), 'How much do distortions affect growth?', *Journal of Monetary Economics*, 32(2), pp. 187-212.

Easterly, W., M. Kremer, L. Pritchett, and L.H. Summers (1993), 'Good policy or good luck? Country growth performance and temporary shocks', *Journal of Monetary Economics*, 32(3), pp. 459-483.

Easterly, W. and S. Rebelo (1993), 'Fiscal policy and economic growth: an empirical investigation', *Journal of Monetary Economics*, 32(3), pp. 417-458.

Edey, M. and K. Hviding (1995), *An Assessment of Financial Reform in OECD Countries*, OECD Economics Department, Working Paper No.154.

Edwards, S. (1993), 'Openness, trade liberalisation, and growth in developing countries. Journal of Economic Literature', 31(3), pp. 1358-1393.

Edwards, S. (1997), *Openness, productivity and growth: What do we really know?*, Working Paper 5978, NBER, Cambridge, MA.

Englander, A., R. Evenson, and M. Hanazaki (1988*), R&D, innovation and the total factor productivity slowdown*. OECD Economic Studies, No. 11, Paris.

Forbes, K. (1997), *Back to the basics: The positive effect of inequality on growth*, Working Paper, MIT, Cambridge, MA.

Geroski, P. (1989), 'Entry, innovation and productivity growth'. *Review of Economics and Statistics*, 71(4), pp. 572-578.

Goldsmith R.W. (1969), *Financial structure and development*, New Haven, CT: Yale University Press.

Grandville, Olivier De La (1989), 'In Quest of the Slutsky Diamond', *American Economic Review*, 79 (3), pp. 468-481.

Green, A. and D.G. Mayes (1991), 'Technical efficiency in manufacturing industries', *The Economic Journal*, 101, pp. 523-538.

Griliches, Z. (1980), 'Returns to R&D expenditures in the private sector', in K.W. Kendrick and B. Vaccara (eds), *New developments in productivity measurement*, Chicago: Chicago University Press.

Griliches, Z. (1986), 'Productivity, R&D and basic research at the firm level in the 1970s', *American Economic Review,* 76, pp. 141-154.

Griliches, Z. (1992), 'The search for R&D spillovers', *Scandinavian Journal of Economics*, 94, pp. 29-47.

Griliches, Z. and F. Lichtenberg (1984a), 'Inter-industry technology flows and productivity growth: a re-examination', *Review of Economics and Statistics*, 66, pp. 324-329.

Griliches, Z. and F. Lichtenberg (1984b), 'R&D and productivity growth at the industry level: is there still a relationship?' in Z. Griliches (ed.), *Patents and Productivity*, Chicago: University of Chicago Press, pp. 465-496.

Grossman, G.M. and E. Helpman, (1991), *Innovation and Growth*, Cambridge, MA: MIT Press.

Hall, B.H. (1995), 'The private and social returns to research and development: what have we learned?' mimeo.

Hall, R.E. and C.I. Jones (1997), 'Levels of economic activity across countries', *American Economic Review* , 87(2), pp. 173-177.

Hall, R.E. and C.I. Jones (1998), *Why do some countries produce so much more output than others?* NBER Working Paper 6564. Cambridge, MA.

Harris, C. and J. Vickers (1987), 'Racing with Uncertainty', *Review of Economic Studies*, 54 (1), pp. 1-21.

Harrison, A. (1995), *Openness and growth: A time-series, cross-country analysis for developing countries.* Working Paper 5221, NBER, Cambridge, MA.

Himmelberg, C.P. and B.C. Petersen, (1994), 'R&D and Internal Finance: A Panel Study of Small Firms in High-Tech Industries', *Review of Economics and Statistics*, 76 (1), pp. 38-51.

Holmstrom, B. and P. Milgrom (1994), 'The Firm as an Incentive System', *American Economic Review*; 84 (4), pp. 972-91.

Hubbard, R. G. (1998), 'Capital-Market Imperfections and Investment', *Journal of Economic Literature*, XXXVI, pp. 193-225.

Hunt, R.M. (1995), 'Nonobviousness and the Incentive to Innovate: An Economic Analysis of Intellectual Property Reform', mimeo.

Johnson, B.T., K.R. Holmes, and M. Kirkpatrick (1999), *1999 Index of economic freedom,* The Heritage Foundation and Dow Jones & Company Inc., Washington, D.C.

Jones, C.I. (1995), 'Time series tests of endogenous growth models', *Quarterly Journal of Economics*, 110(2), pp. 495-525.

Jones, C.I. and J.C. Williams (1998), 'Measuring the social return to R&D', *Quarterly Journal of Economics*, 113(4), pp. 1119-1135.

Jones, L.E. and R.E. Manuelli (1994), *The Sources of Growth*, SSRI Working Paper 9428, University of Wisconsin.

Jones, L.E. and R.E. Manuelli (1997), 'The sources of growth', *Journal of Economic Dynamics and Control*, 21, pp. 75-114.

Jones, L.E., R.E. Manuelli, and P.E. Rossi (1993), 'Optimal taxation in models of endogenous growth', *Journal of Political Economy*, 101(3), pp. 485-517.

Joskow, P.L. and N.L. Rose (1989), 'The effect of economic regulation', in R. Schmalensee and R.D. Willig (eds) (1989), *Handbook of Industrial Organization,* Vol. II, pp. 1449-1506.

Kelly, T. (1997), 'Public investment and growth: testing the non-linearity hypothesis', *International Review of Applied Economics*, 11(2), pp. 249-262.

King, R. and R. Levine (1993), 'Financial intermediation and economic development', in *Financial intermediation in the construction of Europe,* C. Mayer and X. Vives, London: Centre for Economic Policy Research, pp. 156-189.

King, R. and S. Rebelo (1990), 'Public policy and economic growth: Developing neoclassical implications', *Journal of Political Economy,* 98(5), Part 2, pp. 126-150.

King, R.G. and R. Levine (1993), 'Finance, Entrepeneurship and Growth: Theory and Evidence', *Journal of Monetary Economics,* 32, pp. 513-542.

Knowles, S. and P.D. Owen (1995), 'Health capital and cross-country variation in income per capita in the Menkiw-Romer-Weil Model', *Economics Letters,* 48(1), pp. 99-106.

Koedijk K. and J. Kremers (1996), 'Market opening, regulation and growth in Europe', *Economic Policy: A European Forum,* 23, pp. 445-460.

Kormendi, R.C. and P.G. Meguire (1985), 'Macroeconomic determinants of growth', *Journal of Monetary Economics ,* 16(2), pp. 141-163.

Krugman, P. (1994), 'The myth of Asia's miracle', *Foreign Affairs,* pp. 62-78.

Leahy, D. and J.P. Neary (1994), 'Learning by Doing, Precommitment and Infant-Industry Protection', University College Dublin, mimeo.

Leamer, E. (1988), 'Measures of openness', In: Baldwin, R. (ed.), *Trade policy and empirical analysis,* Chicago: Chicago University Press.

Lee, W. and J.E. Roemer (1998), 'Income Distribution, Redistributive Politics, and Economic Growth', *Journal of Economic Growth,* 3, pp. 217-240.

Levine, R. (1997), 'Financial development and economic growth: views and agenda', *Journal of Economic Literature,* 35(2), pp. 688-726.

Levine, R. and D. Renelt (1992), 'A sensitivity analysis of cross-country growth regressions', *American Economic Review,* 82(4), pp. 942-963.

Levine, R. and S. Zervos (1996), *Stock markets, banks, and economic growth,* World Bank Policy Research Working Paper No. 1690.

Lucas, R. E. (1988), 'On the Mechanics of Economic Development', *Journal of Monetary Economics,* 22 (1), pp. 3-42.

Lucas, R.E. (1990), 'Supply-side economics: an analytical review', *Oxford Economic Papers* 42, pp. 293-316.

Lucas, R.E. (1993), 'Making a Miracle', *Econometrica,* 61(2), pp. 251-272.

Mankiw, N.G., D. Romer, and D.N. Weil (1992), 'A contribution to the empirics of economic growth', *Quarterly Journal of Economics,* 107(2), pp. 407-437.

Mansfield, E. (1988), 'Industrial R&D in Japan and the United States: a comparative study', *American Economic Review,* 78, pp. 223-238.

Mairesse, J. and P. Cuneo (1985), 'Recherche-developpement et performances des enterprises: une etude econometrique sur donees individuelles', *Revue Economique*, 36, pp. 1001-1046.

Morrison, C. and A.E. Schwartz (1996), 'State Infrastructure and Productive Performance', *American Economic Review*, 86 (5), pp. 1095-1111.

Nadiri, M. and G. Bitros (1980), 'Research and development expenditures and labour productivity at the firm level', in J. Kendrick and B. Vaccara, (eds), *Studies in income and wealth*, 44, Chicago: University of Chicago Press.

Nadiri, M. and T. Mamuneas (1994), 'The Effects of Public Infrastructure and R&D Capital on the Cost Structure and Performance of US Manufacturing Industries', *Review of Economics and Statistics*, 76 (1), pp. 22-37.

Nadiri, M. and I. Pruchna (1990), 'Comparison and analysis of productivity growth and R&D investment in the electrical machinery industries of the United States and Japan', in C. Hulten and R. Norsworthy, (eds), *Productivity growth in Japan and the United States*, Chicago: University of Chicago Press.

Nelson, R. and E. Phelps (1966), 'Investment in Humans, Technological Diffusion, and Economic Growth', *American Economic Review*, 61, pp. 69-75.

Nickell, S., D. Nicolitsas, and N. Dryden (1997), 'What makes firms perform well?', *European Economic Review*, 41, pp. 783-796.

O'Donoghue, T., S. Scotchmer, and J.F. Thisse (1995), *Patent Breadth, Patent Life and the Pace of Technological Improvement*, University of California, Berkeley, Working Paper in Economics 95/242.

Park, W.G. and J.C. Ginarte (1997), 'Intellectual property rights and economic performance', *Contemporary Economic Policy*, 15, pp. 51-61.

Patel, P. and L. Soete (1988), 'L'évaluation des effets économique de la technologie', *STI Review*, 4, pp. 133-183.

Persson, T. and G. Tabellini (1994), Is inequality harmful for growth?', *American Economic Review*, 84(3), pp. 600-621.

Prescott, E.C. (1998), 'Needed: A theory of total factor productivity', Lawrence R. Klein Lecture 1997. *International Economic Review*, 39(3), pp. 525-551.

Quah, D.T. (1992), *Empirical cross-section dynamics in economic growth*, LSE Working Paper, London.

Razin, A. and C.-W. Yuen (1994), 'Convergence in growth rates: a quantitative assessment of the role of capital mobility and international taxation', in L. Leiderman and A. Razin (eds), *Capital mobility: the impact on consumption, investment and growth*, Cambridge, pp. 237-257.

Rebelo, S. (1991), 'Long-Run Policy Analysis and Long-Run Growth', *Journal of Political Economy*, 99 (3), pp. 500-521.

Redding, S. (1996), 'The Low-Skill, Low-Quality Trap: Strategic Complementarities between Human Capital and R&D', *Economic Journal*, 106(435), pp. 458-70.

Röller, L.-H. (1996), 'Market opening, regulation and growth in Europe – Comment', *Economic Policy: A European Forum*, 23, pp. 461-462.

Romer, P. (1986), 'Increasing Returns and Long-Run Growth', *Journal of Political Economy*, 94 (5), pp. 1002-1037.

Romer, P. (1994), 'The Origins of Endogenous Growth', *Journal of Economic Perspectives*, 8 (1), pp. 3-22.

Rothschild, M. and L.J. White (1995), 'The Analytics of the Pricing of Higher Education and Other Services in which the Customers are Inputs', *Journal of Political Economy*, 103 (3), pp. 573-586.

Sachs, J.D. and A.M. Warner (1987), 'Fundamental sources of long-run growth', *American Economic Review*, 87(2), pp. 184-188.

Sachs, J.D. and A.M. Warner (1995), 'Economic reform and the process of global integration', *Brooking Papers on Economic Activity*, 1, pp. 1-95.

Sala-i-Martin, X. (1997), 'I just ran two million regressions', *American Economic Review*, 87(2), pp. 178-183.

Salop, S.C. and L.J. White (1991), 'Antitrust Goes to College', *Journal of Economic Perspectives*, 5 (3), pp. 193-202.

Sau-Him Paul Lau and Sin Chor-Yiu (1997), 'Public infrastructure and economic growth: Time-series properties and evidence', *The Economic Record*, 221(73), pp. 125-135.

Scherer, F. (1982), 'Interindustry technology flows and productivity growth', *Review of Economics and Statistics*, 64, pp. 627-634.

Solow, R. M. (1956): A Contribution to the Theory of Economic Growth, Quarterly Journal of Economics, 70 (1), 65-94

Solow, R.M. (1957), 'Technical change and the aggregate production function', *Review of Economics and Statistics*, 39, pp. 312-320.

Stokey, N.L. and S. Rebelo (1995), 'Growth effects of flat-rate taxes', *Journal of Political Economy*, 103(3), pp. 519-550.

Sveikauskas, L. (1981), 'Technological inputs and multifactor productivity growth', *Review of Economics and Statistics*, pp. 275-282.

Temple, J. (1999), 'The new growth evidence', *Journal of Economic Literature*, 37(1), pp. 112-156.

Terleckyj, N. (1980), 'Direct and indirect effects of industrial research and development on productivity growth of industries', in Kendrick, K.W.

and B. Vaccara (eds), *New developments in productivity measurement*, Chicago: University Press.

Theissen, E. (1998), 'Der Neue Markt. Eine Bestandsaufnahme', *Zeitschrift für Wirtschafts- und Sozialwissenschaften*, 118 (4), pp. 623-652.

Torstensson, J. (1994), 'Property rights and economic growth: an empirical study', *Kyklos*, 47(2), pp. 231-247.

Winston, C. (1998), 'US Industry Adjustment to Economic Deregulation', *Journal of Economic Perspectives*, 12 (3), pp. 89-110.

Winston, C. (1999), 'Subsidies, Hierarchy, and Peers: The Awkward Economics of Higher Education', *Journal of Economic Perspectives*, 13 (1), pp. 13-36.

Woroch, G. A. (1995), 'Finishing The Job Of Telecommunications Reform In New Zealand. Comments on Commerce-Treasury's Discussion Paper'. Berkeley.

Young, A. (1991), Learning by Doing and the Dynamic Effects of International Trade, *Quarterly Journal of Economics*, 106 (2), pp. 369-406.

Young, A. (1993), 'Invention and Bounded Learning by Doing', *Journal of Political Economy*, 101 (3), 443-472.

3. Regulation in Europe: Justified Burden or Costly Failure?

Sandrine Labory and Marco Malgarini

INTRODUCTION

In recent decades, European countries as a whole have showed a relatively poor performance with respect to the US, Japan and other OECD countries, in terms of growth, employment, productivity and more generally, competitiveness of the business sector. Entrepreneurial activity has been lower in European countries than in other major industrialised economies. Moreover, within the European area there has been a high dispersion of indicators of competitiveness around the European average. Differences in performance between Europe and the rest of the industrialised world and within European countries have often been explained in terms of differences in the quality of state intervention. Thus the recent UNICE report (1999) emphasises that barriers to entrepreneurial activity and poor macroeconomic performances may be considered as a result of the high tax burden and of high labour and input costs in the EU area; according to the 1992 McKinsey Report on service sector productivity, there is evidence that European countries generally have a poorer regulatory environment compared to other industrialised countries. Therefore, the potential gains from a thorough process of regulatory reforms are high: in a recent OECD study, the impact of reforms in the public utilities and the distribution sector on long-run GDP levels has been estimated in a range varying from 3.6 percentage points in the case of the UK to 5.8 percentage points in Germany and France.[1]

Nevertheless, these studies provide no precise account of why state intervention may hinder the proper functioning of markets, resulting in lower performance of Europe relative to some other countries. One exception is the OECD Survey, to which the general introduction to this volume refers. Chapters 1 and 2 of this volume provided evidence of the effect of regulation on market performance. Negative effects arise when regulation is of poor quality. The next important question is: what does regulatory quality mean? This is the main issue addressed in this chapter. We define regulatory quality and analyse its principal determinants. This allows us to derive an important indicator of regulatory quality: regulatory credibility. We indeed show that poor-quality regulation translates into regulation that lacks credibility, and we provide empirical evidence of this lack of credibility of European regulation, based on survey data. This analysis differs from previous studies such as the OECD Survey in that it considers all European regulation, i.e. both at national and EU level; secondly, it provides a new definition of regulatory quality and outlines both empirically and theoretically the main symptom of low-quality regulation, namely a lack of credibility.

The chapter is organised as follows. The first section examines the performance of the European market with respect to the rest of the world, leading to an outline of the 'competitiveness gap' between Europe and other countries. Section 2 defines and examines the causes of regulatory quality, and gives concrete examples of different levels of regulatory quality. Section 3 focuses on the regulatory quality of the EU regulatory framework. It is shown that a lack of analysis of the regulatory problem and problems in the regulatory process are major causes of poor-quality regulation. In such cases, regulation results are not credible, yielding net costs to society and justified complaints from economic actors (especially business). Section 4 completes the analysis by providing empirical evidence of regulatory quality in Europe. The major indicator used is credibility, which is derived from business surveys conducted at the EU level. A preliminary assessment of the need for reform, both at a national and EU level, concludes the chapter.

1. REGULATORY FAILURES AND COMPETITIVENESS IN EUROPE

The previous chapter showed the extent to which regulation affects market functioning. If the market is not functioning well, one may ask whether it is not due to 'bad' regulation, i.e. poor-quality regulation. Before analysing regulatory quality, we first look at how precisely the EU market is functioning relative to other OECD countries, particularly the US, using a number of indicators.

First, GDP growth (Table 3.1). The US grew by 2.5 per cent per year on average in the period 1990-98, much faster than Europe or Japan (1.9 and 1.8 per cent, respectively), where a marked slowdown in growth rates

Table 3.1 Indicators of countries performance and competitiveness

	GDP growth (%)		Growth in GDP per capita (%)		Unemployment (%)			Shares in world exports (%)			FDI inflow ($ millions)		
	1980-89	1990-98	1981-89	1990-98	1982	1990	1997	1980	1990	1997	1990	1993	1997
Japan	3.8	1.8	3.3	1.5	2.4	2.1	3.4	7.9	8.5	7.6	1806	210	3224
US	2.7	2.5	2.1	1.5	9.7	5.6	4.9	11.7	11.6	12.4	48422	50663	90748
France	2.3	1.7	1.8	1.2	8.0	8.9	12.4	6.0	6.4	5.2	15609	16439	23178
Germany	2.0	1.9	1.7	1.2	6.4	6.2	11.4	10.0	12.1	9.2	2492	1915	-188
Italy	2.4	1.3	2.2	1.1	6.9	9.1	12.3	4.1	5.0	4.3	6344	3746	3779
Netherlands	1.9	2.8	1.4	2.1	8.5	6.0	5.5	4.4	3.9	3.5	12165	8561	8678
Ireland	3.1	6.7	2.7	5.9	11.0	12.9	9.1	0.4	0.7	1.0	258	850	1676
Portugal	3.2	2.6	2.9	2.6	7.5	4.7	5.1	0.2	0.5	0.5	2608	1550	1728
Spain	2.8	2.2	2.5	2.1	15.9	15.7	19.1	1.1	1.6	1.9	13839	8073	5540
EU-11	2.3	1.8	2.0	1.2	8.3	8.6	12.4	31.3	35.6	32.2	62973	54581	61873
UK	2.4	1.9	2.7	1.5	10.4	5.9	6.9	5.7	5.5	5.1	32889	15468	36972
EU-15	2.3	1.9	2.1	1.4	8.5	7.9	11.2	39.8	44.1	39.9	100050	78156	115065
Australia	3.4	3.1			7.1	7.0	8.6	1.1	1.2	1.1	6513	3007	9346
Canada	2.9	1.8	1.9	0.6	11.1	8.2	9.2	3.5	3.8	3.9	7562	4748	8217
Korea	8.1	5.9			4.4	2.4	2.6	0.9	1.9	2.5	789	588	2341
OECD					7.6	5.9	7.2	65.3	74.6	71.7	177699	150748	256574

Sources: OECD (1998) and IMF (1998).

83

occurred during the 1990s. Within Europe, performance was rather different for countries such as France and Italy, which grew at a slow pace during the decade, and the Netherlands and Ireland on the other side. Germany grew at a relatively fast pace (1.9 per cent per year), mainly due to re-unification. Europe is lagging well behind the US and Japan in terms of per capita GDP growth expressed in purchasing power parity (PPP), which is considered as a good indicator of living standards. In the late 1990s, average living standards measured by GDP levels in PPP are still some 50 per cent higher in the US than in the EU; EU living standards also lag behind those of Japan (see Figure 3.1).

Figure 3.1 Real Growth in GDP per capita

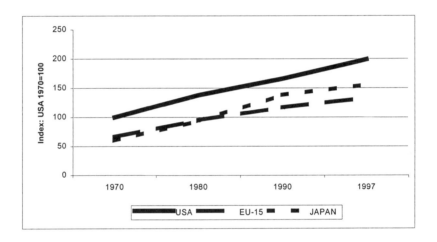

Second, the good performance of the US relative to Europe, and of the Netherlands within Europe, also emerges from an analysis of unemployment data. In the US, the unemployment rate was almost halved between 1982 and 1997, falling from 9.7 to 4.9 per cent. Meanwhile, unemployment grew from 8.5 to 11.2 per cent in the EU-15, and from 8.3 to 12.4 per cent for the euro area. Among the countries participating in monetary union, Italian, German and French unemployment rates stabilised well above 11 per cent. An increase in unemployment also occurred in Spain, reaching 19.1 per cent in 1997. By contrast, the Netherlands and Portugal have been able to reduce unemployment below 6 per cent, on a level not too far from the US; a sharp reduction in unemployment also occurred in the United Kingdom. In Japan, unemployment remained very low, although it increased from 2.1 to 3.4 per cent between 1990 and 1997, and is still rising due to the recessive cycle of the Japanese economy.

Third, the competitive position of European economies also deteriorated in terms of the countries' share in world exports. On average, the EU's share of world exports rose in the 1980s from 39.8 to 44.1 per cent, falling again to 39.9 per cent in 1996. In 1997, the US reached a peak, accounting for 12.4 per cent of total world exports; Japan's share fell from 7.9 to 7.6 per cent. The rise in the US share was the prime contribution to the expansion of the OECD countries' share from 65.3 per cent in 1980 to 71.7 per cent in 1997. In terms of FDI inflows, the European area accounted in 1997 for almost 45 per cent of the total flow of foreign direct investment in OECD countries; the European share deteriorated by almost 10 percentage points from the beginning of the 1990s. In the same period, the US share of total FDI inflows from OECD countries grew from 27 to 35 per cent, confirming the growing attractiveness of the US for business and investments.

The unsatisfactory performance of European economies could be related to the existence of barriers and impediments to entrepreneurial activity, although this is a difficult concept to measure directly. Evidence in this sense comes from the recent UNICE report on fostering entrepreneurship in Europe (see Table 3.2).

Indicators considered in the UNICE report are related to innovation activity in the business sector (high-tech activity, R&D expenditures, investments, use of computers and mobile phones) and creation of new firms (new firms as a share of existing companies, costs sustained, capital and time needed for new companies formation).

European countries, except for the Netherlands and the UK, show 'high-tech' business activity[2] lower on average than that of the US or Japan. Moreover, penetration of new Information and Communications Technologies (ITC) is much lower in Europe than in the US and other industrialised countries, in terms of the number of computers, internet hosts and mobile phones per 1,000 population. This indicates a narrow scope for the developments of these new 'high-tech' markets in the European area. Also for business sector R&D expenditures, Europe is lagging behind other major industrial countries. However, business investment as a share of GDP was higher in Europe than in the US in the period 1992-97, but lower than in Japan, Australia and Canada. As for the rate of creation of new companies as a percentage of existing companies, again the EU lags behind the US, probably due to the high cost, long length of time and high minimum capital needed for new company formation. In this respect, however, Europe is performing much better than Japan (comparable data for other industrial

Table 3.2 Measures of entrepreneurial activity

	High-tech business 1997[a]	Business R&D exp. 1997[b]	Business investment 1992-97[c]	Use of computers 1997/98[d]	Mobile phones 1997[e]	Internet hosts 1997-98[f]	Rate of new companies 1988-94[g]	Time and cost for new company[h]		Minimum[i] start-up capital
								Time	Cost	
US	16.4	456	9.8	450	204	29	11.4	1.5	500	0
Japan	14.7	369	17.8	228	304	11	4.6	3	4000	20000
Austria		142	15.9	246	143	16	8.6			
Belgium		178	11.9	249	96	15	7.2			
Denmark	7.5	235		349	275	36	9.8			
Finland	9.9	303	9.4	354	456	100	5.8			
France	12	233	10.4	234	98	7	11.1	6	3400	8000
Germany	9.5	283	12	231	99	14	11.7	16	1400	25000
Greece		11	10.1	73	86	4	9			18500
Ireland		134	9.2	263	144	13	11.7			
Italy	6.1	94	9.8	158	205	6	5.8	10	2200	10000
Netherlands	13.3	181	11.6	292	108	33	10	12	1000	19000
Portugal		12	14.7	103	154	5	10.8			
Spain	7.1	52	12.5	127	109	6	11.6	24	330	3000
Sweden	10.8	391	9.3	353	358	43	5.6	3	1130	12000
UK	14.5	184	11.4	283	143	21	13.2	1	420	0
EU-15	10	175	11.2	215	129	11	9.9	11 (EU-7)	1600 (EU-7)	11456 (EU-8)
Australia	6.5	133	13.7	366	260	41		1	340	0
Canada	10.5	186	10	364	141	34				
New Zealand	4.5	35	11.5	320	131	49				

Notes: a) Value added from 'high-tech' companies as percentage of total manufacturing. b) Euro at current PPP per capita. c)% of GDP. d) Number of computers per 1000 population.
e) Number of mobile phones per 1000 population. f) Number of Internet hosts per 1000 population. g) New companies as % of existing companies.
h) Time in weeks and cost in euro to set up a private limited liabilities company (1996). i) Minimum charter capital required in euro to form a private limited liability company (1996).

Source: UNICE (1999).

countries are not available). Barriers to entrepreneurial activity and poor macroeconomic performance may be considered as a result of the high tax burden and of high labour and input costs in the EU area. Costs of critical inputs such as new patents, road freight transport, electricity, long distance and mobile phones in 1997-98 were indeed much higher in the EU-15 area than in the US benchmark (see Figure 3.2). Also wage and non-wage costs in the manufacturing sector and the tax wedge on wage increases are higher in Europe than in other industrialised countries (Table 3.3).

Figure 3.2 EU input costs with respect to the US (US=100)

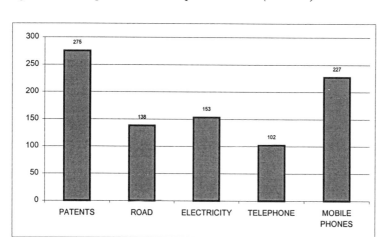

Overall, the data provided show that there is evidence of a performance gap between Europe and mainly the US. The European market base is indeed still too fragmented, which inhibits European firms from rationalising activities (production, marketing, etc.) at European level and, among other things, prevents them from truly benefiting from economies of scale. Although progress has been made towards integration and improvement of the functioning of the European market, there is a perception that this is not sufficient. In Europe, a business survey of the single market conducted by the European Commission (1998b) shows that differences in national regulations form a substantial part of the technical barriers to trade within the EU. Such technical barriers impose requirements for either the use of technical specifications or standards defining some technical aspects of the product, or testing and certification of products or suppliers. The business survey in *The Single Market Review* also shows that the application of the mutual recognition principle is problematic. In particular, the principle works best when there is either a formal mutual recognition arrangement or a mutually recognised standard developed for instance by CENELEC or another European standards body.

Table 3.3 Labour costs and the tax wedge

	Labour costs in manufacturing[a]			Marginal tax wedge[b]	
	Total costs	Wage costs	Non-wage costs	Excl. tax on goods and services	Incl. tax on goods and services
	(euro)			(per cent)	
US	16.18	11.61	4.57	34.9	39
Japan	17.78	10.38	7.4	35.9	40.4
Austria	19.79	10.01	9.78	55.6	64.9
Belgium	20.34	10.64	9.69	68.6	74.5
Denmark	20.71	16.58	4.13	50.1	65.2
Finland	19.78	10.85	8.93	58.5	69
France	16.28	8.45	7.84	51.5	61
Germany	24.36	13.4	10.96	63.9	70.2
Greece	8.04	4.81	3.23	44.5	54.3
Ireland	12.61	9.03	3.58	57.8	68
Italy	15.23	7.5	7.72	59.2	66.3
Netherlands	18.62	10.49	8.13	48.2	58.4
Portugal	5.63	3.16	2.46	40.6	53.5
Spain	12.71	6.96	5.74	44.9	53.2
Sweden	20.04	11.79	8.25	52.2	62.4
UK	14.55	10.38	4.16	39.1	50.6
EU-15	17.57	9.87	7.7	54.3	62.8
Australia	14.04	10.15	3.86	39.4	47.7
Canada	14.84	10.72	4.12	46.7	54.7
NZ				24.2	38.5

a Cost per hour in the manufacturing industry (including non-wage costs such as social security charges) in euro at current exchange rates – 1997.
b Percentage of wage increases that will be paid in taxes; taxes include income taxes and social security contributions but exclude taxes on goods and services.

Source: UNICE (1999).

Overall, 79 per cent of intra-EU trade in products is affected by regulatory barriers (including those sectors where the single market barriers have already been removed by harmonisation). *The Single Market Review,* however, does not report on the cost of such regulatory barriers; it only outlines the improvements made in removing regulatory barriers within the EU. Measures have been successfully implemented for products comprising 64 per cent of EU trade, while cases where measures have been adopted but are experiencing problems in implementation cover about 16 per cent of products (for instance, machinery and construction products). In addition, businesses mention a number of drawbacks, such as the lack of consistent enforcement of some directives (in particular the New Approach directives, which leave it to the member states to develop detailed specifications); the general lack of information available to enterprises and the poor understanding of the needs of the new directives, which causes unnecessary costs; and the sometimes prohibitive costs of attestation.

The 1998(a) report on European competitiveness concludes its analysis of the competitiveness of European industry with some policy recommendations, the first of which is the elimination of institutional and regulatory barriers to the functioning of markets: 'A prime policy target is the elimination of institutional and regulatory barriers to the creative and flexible management of change. Such rigidities can be found in financial, labour and product markets, in particular in basic services, as well as in the highly disparate nature of European innovation systems'.

Hence there are signs that there is some concern for poor regulatory quality. However, regulation is a vast concept, including products, labour, competition, environment, health and safety, and it uses a large number of instruments. Moreover, markets are usually affected by more than one form of regulation. Therefore, regulatory quality is bound to have different levels and causes, leading to regulation that ranges from a justified burden to a costly failure. The next section defines and analyses regulatory quality in more detail and then offers evidence on the actual quality of regulation in Europe.

2. REGULATORY QUALITY: DEFINITION AND DETERMINANTS

We define regulation in its wide sense of governmental intervention in markets in order to correct for market failure. Spulber, a specialist of regulation, defines it as public actions which 'interfere directly in markets' allocation mechanisms, or indirectly by changing supply and demand decisions from producers and consumers' (Spulber, 1989, p. 37). Government intervention takes a variety of different forms in terms of the rationale, the chosen actions and instruments, the means to control the impact of intervention, etc. Hence before analysing regulatory quality and assessing whether and what concrete steps need to be taken in order to improve regulatory quality, this section examines the various rationales, types and effects of regulation. First and foremost, the economic rationale for regulation is recalled in what follows.

2.1 Defining Regulatory Quality

The traditional rationale for regulation is to prevent market failures, i.e. the improper functioning of the market resulting in welfare losses. There are four types of market failures: internalities, externalities, market power and public goods.

Internalities are market failures resulting from information asymmetries within a transaction between agents (individuals, organisations, etc.). The proper functioning of the market requires that all agents have access to all information relevant for the transactions. If one of the agents holds some information that the others do not know and do not learn, then the informed agent can exploit his information advantage at the expense of the others. For example, the average consumer is not informed about the content and effects of medicines. It would be too time-consuming, too costly (and beyond his competence) to enquire, say, about the biotechnology behind a particular medicine. The consumer may end-up buying a medicine that has side-effects of which he is ignorant and that causes a negative[3] internality (the side-effect he did not know would happen). In some cases, regulation might be needed to prevent the occurrence of this kind of internality: product regulations are justified mainly by this type of market failure. Another example of internalities arises in wage contracts, where a worker may accept a contract, containing a wage he finds fair, but later discovers once on the job that the working conditions are poor and pose a risk to his health. Such a health risk not accounted for in the job contract is an internality.

While internalities refer to effects on transacting or contracting parties that are not taken into account in the transaction or contract signed between the parties, *externalities* arise when a party who is not part of a transaction incurs cost (or gains a benefit) from the transaction. When the third party incurs a cost we have a negative externality, and when the third party incurs a benefit, a positive externality. Negative externalities arise in health (contaminating disease), safety (accidents causing injuries to others) and the environment (pollution). The solution to the market failure is to 'internalise' the externality, i.e. induce agents to the transactions to take account in their decisions of the externality they cause on other agents. For instance, a pollution tax induces the polluter to invest in pollution-reducing technologies in order to pay less tax. Regulation (with instruments such as command-and-control, taxes, subsidies, etc.) is one solution, but there might be cases where market solutions can be found. One example of a market solution is the emissions trading markets that are being introduced in the US and may be used in climate change policy.[4]

Market power refers to the possibility of setting prices much higher than costs, to the detriment of consumers and market efficiency. High prices may arise in two particular cases. First, they may result from strategic behaviour of producers aimed at reducing competition, e.g. abuse of dominant position, implicit agreements among producers, price discrimination, product differentiation, and so on. Second, they may result from structural characteristics of the market, such as a natural monopoly in which the cost and production characteristics of the market are such that it is more efficient for one firm to supply the whole market. An example is an essential facility that is costly to build and maintain, or not replicable, and which all market operators have to use in order to perform their activities, such as gas pipelines, an electricity grid, etc. Competition policy or regulation is aimed at tackling such market failures. Generally competition authorities watch markets in order to avoid any abuse of dominant position. If such behaviour is found, authorities act ex post to condemn the illegal behaviour and fine the company (see Chapter 4 of this volume for more details). Generally, natural monopolies are regulated. The chapters in Volume II dealing with network industries, such as telecommunications, electricity and transport, examine the regulatory trends in these sectors and the impact of regulation on market functioning. The major trend is pro-competitive regulatory reform, which aims at introducing competition wherever possible (generally upstream and downstream of the essential facility), and regulating the natural monopoly part (i.e. access to the essential facility[5]).

The fourth market failure results from the presence of *public goods*. These are particular goods which, once produced, can be enjoyed by all citizens and the consumption of the good by one citizen does not reduce the extent to which another citizen can enjoy it. Examples include roads, bridges and defence. The problem is that if left to itself, the market will not produce such goods since free-riding would be too strong: once a lighthouse is constructed, it is difficult to prevent ships from benefiting from it, but it is also difficult to charge all the ships passing by the lighthouse.

This (traditional, neo-classical) economic analysis of the reasons for regulation assumes that governments or regulators always take good decisions, being perfectly informed of the characteristics of markets, acting in the interests of the whole society (benevolent) and being concerned only with efficiency. Thus, for instance, they know all the possible instruments and their effects, and can choose the most appropriate one(s). Since the 1970s, however, public intervention to remedy market failures has been increasingly under debate. One objection to the traditional theory is that the administrative process is ignored and regulatory choices are analysed independently of the institutions that are in charge of implementing these choices. Other objections include the claim that alternative solutions to public intervention do exist, and that there are also government failures. Thus, some economists, and primarily Stigler (1971), recommend that governments do not regulate at all, since regulation is always imperfect: regulators are improperly influenced in their decisions or 'captured' by lobbying groups which pressure for their interests to be served.

Stigler makes a number of hypotheses and generates predictions on the industries that should be regulated, and the form that the regulations should take. His first hypothesis is that the main resource of government is its coercive power and second, that agents maximise their well-being. His main conclusion is that regulation is offered in response to the demands of interest groups, which act in order to maximise their revenues. The reason is that regulators' decisions are guided by their willingness to preserve their jobs, their well-being therefore depending on electoral support, and interest groups offer political support in exchange for favourable legislation.

Without going into detail, there are two major problems with Stigler's approach. First, interest groups cannot always control legislators, and a better approach might be to assume negotiation between interest groups, regulators and legislators. Secondly, his theory is not systematically confirmed by empirical evidence. Thus, for instance in the US, road transport deregulation has not been influenced by lobbies, because their interests have not been served by the measure; the revenue of both owners and workers in that industry have declined as a result of deregulation.

A third theory worth considering is the incentive theory of regulation, with Laffont and Tirole (1993) as important contributors. The latter authors argue that regulatory constraints and instruments should be taken into account in the analysis of regulation. Three such constraints are defined. First, informational constraints, which result from information asymmetries held by the different actors of the regulatory process (mainly, the regulators and the regulatees). These constraints limit the efficiency of regulation. The major information problems are moral hazard and adverse selection. Moral hazard regards some action taken by the regulatee, which the regulator can observe only imperfectly. Take for instance environmental regulation. If the regulator cannot verify cost information, the firm might under-invest in clean technologies and overstate its true costs. Adverse selection arises when some actors have some information that other actors do not have. The regulated firm, e.g. can possess information on some exogenous variable, such as technology or costs, that the regulator does not have and cannot directly observe. The consequence is that the regulatee can extract an informational rent, by manipulating the information it provides to the regulator in order to obtain favourable regulatory measures. This is a weak form of 'capture' of the regulator (a stronger form would be the case where there is no information asymmetry and the regulator willingly serves the firm's interest).

Second, transactional constraints refer to transaction costs arising in the regulatory process. An example is that future events are difficult to foresee and it is therefore difficult to account for all future contingencies in the regulatory decision-making process. Therefore, a regulation decided at a certain point in time may become inefficient or ineffective at a future point in time because of some unforeseen event. Third, administrative and political constraints limit the number of instruments available in the definition of the appropriate regulation.

Regulatory quality depends on these constraints. Box 1 formally illustrates the maximisation of regulatory quality when such constraints exist.

Regulatory maximisation depends to a large extent on the relevance of the instruments used. For instance, 'incentive-based regulation' has been recently advocated by many economists and regulatory actors as the instrument to adopt in order to ensure a good level of regulatory quality. Such instruments have been shown by economists to maximise regulatory quality when there are information constraints.[6] However, one important point which is often forgotten by many advocates of incentive-based instruments is that such instruments do indeed maximise regulatory quality, but under some conditions only. In other words, incentive-based instruments are not always the best instruments to use.

In economic theory, the property of quality maximisation of incentive-based instruments is derived as follows. Regulation is formalised by considering the relationship between the regulator and the regulatee as an agency relationship, where the regulator (the principal) tries to induce the regulatee (the agent) to take appropriate actions, that is, actions that serve society's interests. There is a conflict of interest between the regulator and the regulatee since the regulator maximises social welfare and the regulatee maximises his profit. Besides this, the regulatee generally holds information

Box 1. Maximising Regulatory Quality

High-quality regulation is obtained by maximising the net benefits given
some constraints. For the sake of illustration, consider the figure below. Let
the regulator consider a regulation that may correct a market failure. If the
regulator is perfectly informed, he would evaluate the costs and benefits of
the regulation as shown in the curves B and C. The regulation that maximises
the net benefits to society then is the one that maximises the distance between
the two curves, that is, at the point 'Max' indicated on the curve. However,
the consideration of regulatory constraints may change the result. For
instance, information asymmetry, whereby firms overstate their costs in order
to try and reduce the strictness of regulation will lead to an evaluation of
costs at C1 instead of C, if the regulator cannot verify the information
provided by firms. The regulatory decision will then be at 'Constr.', where
net benefits are lower than at 'Max'. Hence regulatory constraints lead to
'second best' decision: given the information available, the regulator takes
the best possible decision ('Constr.'), but this is not the optimal (which is
'Max'). Similarly, if the regulator is preoccupied primarily by short-term
benefits, say, because his career prospects improve if the results of his
decisions are seen more quickly, his estimation of benefits may end up being
B1 instead of B. The decision will be 'Constr.' instead of 'Max'.

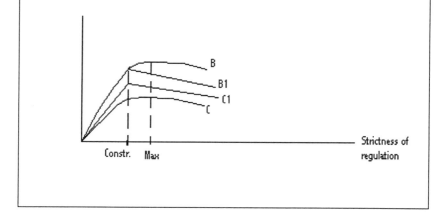

that the regulator cannot either observe or verify, and therefore there is an
information asymmetry (information constraint). Hence the regulator's
problem is to design regulation (price controls, quality standards, etc.) that
maximise social welfare, subject to some constraints. In addition to the above
constraints, another constraint is that the regulatee must find it in its interest

to comply with the regulation. An extreme example of the latter constraint is that the regulation must not result in the firm preferring to declare bankruptcy rather than to continue its activities.

Such regulation is an incentive mechanism: it provides the firm (the regulatee) with the incentives to act in society's interests. For example, a maximum price imposed on a natural monopoly induces the firm to charge low prices and to reduce its costs; a pollution tax induces a polluter to invest in pollution-reducing technologies. Such incentive-based instruments (also called market-based instruments, because they act through the market mechanism, or economic instruments) have been increasingly advocated because they are less rigid than command-and-control instruments, which impose a standard of behaviour without leaving room for the regulatee to choose the best means to comply with the regulatory requirement. Besides this, incentive-based instruments have been shown in economics to be more efficient than those based on command-and-control. Thus Laffont and Tirole (1993) show both the incentive properties and the efficiency of those instruments. Given asymmetrical information, some optimal regulation can be designed. In some cases, however, such as particularly acute informational problems, capture of the regulator, or conflicts between multiple jurisdictions, only the 'second best' may be achieved, which is something in between the optimal and the no-regulation case. In case of regulator's capture, some solutions may be adopted, such as increased monitoring of the activities of the regulator or nomination of different regulators.

The following chapters provide examples of incentive-based regulation and of its increasing use by governments (regulators). For example, throughout the 1990s, the European Commission has become increasingly committed to using such instruments. This is particularly true in the case of environmental regulation (see Chapter 6), although there seems to be a gap between announced principles and implementation, since command-and-control thus far remains the most widely used instrument. Another example is that of EU product safety regulation (Chapter 8), where, given the diversity of national legislative systems, the product liability directive is concerned with wide product classes. This feature, together with the adoption of ISO quality standards, has tended to induce voluntary certification. Such a regulatory system has been shown to be cost-effective, and even resulting in improved sales and productivity for businesses.

However, incentive-based regulation is not always the best solution, that is, the solution (regulation) that maximises net benefits to society. Generally, when information problems are limited, command-and-control is efficient. For example, a standard imposing a maximum level of a certain substance in some product will be efficient if the regulator knows the technology used to manufacture the product and monitoring and enforcement costs are low (it is easy to measure the content of the product). In such a case, the regulator is able to define an optimal standard. Another situation is where compliance costs are fairly high (it is costly for manufacturers to develop a technology to alter the product's content). If such costs are evenly distributed in the industry (homogeneous costs), command-and-control instruments will be efficient. In the case of environmental regulation, such reasoning concludes that when the abatement technology is not known perfectly, command-and-control should not be used, because it will be difficult to assess whether the (pollution) standard is met. Among incentive-based instruments, a tax will be inefficient because the information imperfection will make it difficult to set the tax level. Pollution permits or voluntary agreements may be efficient in some conditions. It is important to stress that incentive-based (or economic) instruments are not inevitably more efficient than command-and-control regulation. Why would command-and-control have been used for such a long time if it had been so inefficient?

The above discussion points to the importance of considering the historical, technological and institutional context in which the regulation is chosen. In fact, most economic instruments are implemented within command-and-control regimes: taxes, subsidies, etc., are implemented within command-and-control (e.g. legislation on targets), and the cost of implementing them without this framework might be extremely high. The historical and institutional context in which instruments are applied has to be accounted for. When the government can easily determine both the pollution source and the technologies available to reduce pollution (low abatement costs and high enforcement and monitoring costs), a command-and-control measure imposing the technology appears to be more efficient. When the government does not know the technologies available to reduce pollution and the institutional context of the policy is unclear (which is the case in the current debate over the implementation of the Kyoto Protocol[7]), both abatement costs and enforcement costs are high, and incentive-based instruments are generally preferred.

3.2 Determinants of Regulatory Quality

Given the above discussion, it can be concluded that poor-quality regulation refers to any regulation for which the wrong instruments are chosen, that is, they are either more costly than other options without offering extra benefits, or yield additional benefits at disproportional costs. If institutions creating, applying and enforcing regulation are not subjected to controls in order to verify the justification of objectives and methods, to generate transparency, to check for consistency or possible duplication and possibly to advise against, the quality of resulting regulation be will very low, and one can even speak of 'regulatory failure', in contrast to the economic concept of market failures. Such failures may have two aspects. First, ineffectiveness, that is, failure to reach the regulatory goal: the goal is the correction of a market failure, answering the question *'why regulate*?'. Second, inefficiency, that is the failure to regulate in a cost-minimising way (maximising net benefits), that is the *'how to regulate*?' question. Regulatory failure can be classified according to these two questions, related to the effectiveness and efficiency questions respectively. Table 3.4 shows the typology.

Table 3.4 Regulatory success/failure

Market failure: Intervention leads to:	Corrected (regulation is effective)	Not corrected (regulation is not effective)
Net benefits (efficient regulation)	Regulatory success	Regulatory failure (Type II)
Net costs (inefficient regulation)	Regulatory failure (Type I)	Regulatory failure (Type III)

Type-I regulatory failure occurs when the regulation is effective in reaching its goal of correction for regulatory failure, but is inefficient, that is, is achieved at too high of cost to society. One example is a product standard that would reduce health risks for consumers but would require investments that would be disproportionate relative to the benefits achieved. Another example is that of a market failure that would be corrected by creating another market failure (e.g. a regulation on waste management systems that reduce land pollution by imposing a new recycling system, but this new recycling system results in pollutant gas emissions, i.e. air pollution). A regulation that would be both efficient and effective when evaluated at a national level, but that would have negative trade effects or spillover effects on other countries, is another case of such regulatory failure.

Regulatory burden enters into this type-I category because bureaucracy and red tape may create high costs for those who have to comply with the regulation. If such costs are so high that the regulation produces net costs to society, there is a 'regulatory failure'. As shown in the surveys reviewed in the previous sections, examples of regulatory burden include lengthy procedures in the certification of products or standards, technocratic government services or other regulating bodies, regulatory inflation (new regulations constantly being added to new ones instead of replacing old ones, leading to inconsistencies), and lack of transparency. An example of the lack of transparency is in public procurement or public tenders, where it is not clear what criteria are followed to select the candidate. The particular case of public procurement in the EU is discussed in Section 3.

The other two types of regulatory failure concern ineffective regulatory options. Type II is a case where the regulation produces net benefits, but does not correct or only imperfectly corrects for the market failure. For instance, a minimum standard produces net benefits but does not eliminate a risk or an environmental damage. Lack of implementation and/or enforcement, or mistakes on the part of the enacting legislature, also leads to ineffective regulation, that is, type-II regulatory failure. Worse, type-III regulatory failures are both ineffective and inefficient. Not only do they generate net costs, but they also do not meet the regulatory objective. For instance, a limitation on the content of a substance in a product to reduce a given risk, when new scientific evidence shows that it is not that substance causing the risk. Generally, the use of obsolete regulatory instruments implies type-III regulatory failures.

The 'capture' of regulators typically leads to type-III regulatory failures. Regulations that are implemented as a response to the pressures of interest groups are likely to be both ineffective and inefficient. Ineffective, because the regulation reaches goals of the interest groups and not societies' goals. Inefficient, because social costs are likely to be ignored or understated and therefore the measure will not be sufficient for the market failure to be fully eliminated, i.e for the benefits to be large enough. Therefore, regulations will tend to be ineffective and unnecessarily restrict market mechanisms, bringing about static and dynamic inefficiencies.

3.3 Regulatory quality in practice

In practice, regulation may be of poor quality, but total failure is unlikely. Regulatory processes contain (possibly imperfect) safeguards that constrain regulators in their decision-making and provide transparency, in order to avoid capture or the pursuit of self-interest on the part of the regulator. In fact, regulators should aim at maximising regulatory quality, i.e. adopting the most effective and most efficient regulation, by adopting the regulations that maximise the net benefits to society. Regulators should consider all the costs and benefits of different regulatory options, in order to choose the regulation that generates the highest net benefits. Such behaviour would be a quality-maximising one. Benefits should include reaching the regulatory goal, i.e. the correction of the market failure at hand. In this case, efficiency (maximising net benefits) implies effectiveness. This optimisation process should obviously take account of the constraints in the regulatory process: available instruments, quality of information and so on.

From the above we can derive the determinants of regulatory quality: sound analysis of the regulatory problem and a transparent regulatory process. Turning the problem upside down, regulatory failures or poor-quality regulation will result from a lack of analysis of the regulatory problem and from problems in the regulatory process, that is, problems at both the decision-making stage and the implementation and enforcement stages. These three factors which reduce regulatory quality are discussed below, in the light of actual regulatory practice in Europe.

a. Lack of analysis of the regulatory problem
If the regulatory problem is not properly analysed, that is, if all the possible solutions (instruments or mix of instruments available) have not been identified and if the costs and benefits of each solution are not evaluated, etc., the regulation will end up being either ineffective or inefficient, or both. The OECD report (1997b) has recognised this problem and proposed systematic regulatory impact analyses to avoid that source of regulatory failure. In the EU, the 18th Declaration of the Member States recommends the use of cost-benefit analyses before making any regulatory decision. Regulatory impact analysis is equivalent to cost-benefit analysis applied to regulations. Pelkmans and Labory (1998) provide a methodological guide to cost-benefit analysis applied to EU regulation. The regulatory analysis is made up of a number of key questions to address, as described below.

Why regulate? At this stage the market failure(s) should be identified and its (their) major consequences outlined.

At what level of government? In the EU, answering this question means applying a subsidiarity test. The Maastricht Treaty restricts the application of subsidiarity to public economic functions where competencies are shared between the member states and the EU. Any action taken by the Community must fulfil two conditions. First, in areas of concurrent competence, the Community must demonstrate a 'need to act', as given by the existence of either economies-of-scale or cross-border externalities. Second, any action must be proportional to the objective. Thus, when deciding whether to enact binding or non-binding measures, the EU level must justify the need for non-discrimination and legal certainty before considering uniformity in measures. Even then, the EU should demonstrate the costs of differentiation before opting for a high degree of uniformity. Besides, the EU must demonstrate that cooperation of member states (rather than supranational action) would not be credible.

In member states, the appropriate level of intervention can be national, regional or local.

What instruments are available? The main instruments available are not only the legal, command-and-control, ones (law, decree, etc.), but also the new instruments (the market-based instrument of Section 2.1) such as information disclosure, economic incentives, tradable property rights, voluntary agreements, self-regulation, risk-based liability, persuasion, performance-based approaches, among others. All these 'new instruments' have been shown theoretically to be efficient and effective in some cases, and have started only recently to be put into practice. In short, command-and-control and market-based instruments can be respectively described as:

- prescriptive, stipulating requirements with or without reference to standards; and
- instruments that affect decisions made by economic actors in markets, such as taxes, subsidies, charges, tradable (pollution) permits and so on; self-regulation, i.e. the idea of such instruments is to let the market find a solution, for instance with the signing of a voluntary agreement (under certain conditions such as feasible and not-too-costly monitoring of compliance).

The appropriate instrument or mix of instruments will vary according to the particular regulatory problem, and according to the constraints of the regulating body. For instance at the EU level taxes are not among the instruments available, and constraints include the different national preferences. In environmental regulation some member states have traditionally preferred voluntary approaches, while others prefer command-and-control approaches. Some states (especially the Scandinavian ones) prefer strict environmental regulation and high environmental standards, while others are less strict. More generally, an important constraint in environmental regulation is the threat of decline and job losses in polluting industries, leading to a dilemma between reduced pollution and higher unemployment (a problem that is addressed in Chapter 6).

Note that the cumulative and interactive effects of different instruments, especially past instruments relative to new ones, must be taken into account in the regulatory impact or cost-benefit analyses because they can reduce regulatory quality. Thus a regulation might be adopted because it is shown, ceteris paribus, to produce net benefits to the economy. However, once the ceteris paribus assumption is relaxed and the regulation is implemented, the effect of the regulation will combine with past regulations or regulations for other market failures but still affecting the sectors, and there might no longer be any net benefits.

Identify the least-cost regulation. The impact (effectiveness) of each instrument or set of instruments on the market failure as well as other side-effects have to be analysed and their costs and benefits (efficiency) evaluated.

Adopt the regulation that maximises net benefits. Following all these steps should lead to regulatory quality maximisation, unless the problem lies in the regulatory framework itself or in the implementation and enforcement phases, both of which are other sources of regulatory failures.[8]

Evidence from Pelkmans and Labory (1998) and from the following chapters shows that both at the EU and the national levels, regulatory problems are generally not well analysed. The following chapters show that although regulators may undertake to perform such analyses (for instance, the commitment of the European Commission to carry out cost-benefit analysis in environmental regulation), the actual practice is imperfect. Chapter 6 recognises the difficulties of carrying out cost-benefit analysis in the case of environmental regulation, especially due to the difficulty of evaluating non-market items such as the benefits of health improvement, of deaths avoided, or of preserving endangered species. However, some methodologies can partly solve such problems (reviewed in Pelkmans and Labory, 1998).

Overall, regulators do not seem to systematically collect data on the costs and benefits of regulation. At the EU level this is increasingly being done, but it is difficult to trace documents on cost-benefit analyses actually performed within the Commission. At the national level, the OECD Survey and its more recent follow-ups express regret of the lack of systematic collection of data and of cost-benefit analyses (OECD, 1997a and 1998). If costs and benefits are not at all or not well assessed, interest groups are likely to lobby more effectively for less stringent regulation, exaggerating the costs of some regulatory options. Worse, the lack of systematic analysis will result in the ignorance of some effects of the regulation. In particular, the combined effects of different instruments and the combined effects of different regulations on some particular sectors or on the overall economy will not be taken into account.

The studies provided in Volume I of this project point to the lack of analysis of such combined effects. For instance, Boeri et al. show that it is likely that both product market and labour regulations interact and affect the functioning of markets. A strict employment protection regulation may raise labour costs, leading to the impossibility for the firm to operate at a minimum efficient scale and therefore to make the investment necessary to develop product features that comply with product safety regulations. Chapters in Volume II which examine the effect of regulation on the competitiveness of particular sectors, also point to a lack of consideration being given to the combined effects of different instruments and to different regulations. This appears to be particularly true in the chemical and automobile sectors, where the combined effect of labour market, environment and product safety regulations are insufficiently accounted for in the regulatory decision-making process (see Chapters 2 and 5 of Volume II).

b. Problems in the regulatory process
The regulatory process is generally a hierarchical structure. Simplifying, one can define three levels of such a hierarchy: the political power, the regulator (public agency in charge of implementing the regulation) and the firm (the regulatee). In principle, the political power defends the interests of voters and delegates responsibility for implementation and enforcement to the regulator. The latter controls the actions of the regulatee, in order to eliminate market failures. In fact, an appropriate definition of the 'regulatees' may be all the groups affected by the market failure and the regulation, which play a role in the regulatory decision-making process. Such a role is both direct, through organised interest groups, and indirect, since the political power is supposed to represent the interest of the consumers (citizens).

Problems in the regulatory process may arise in three cases. The first case is that of a lack of separation between the regulator and the political power. The following chapters provide some evidence of such failures. At the national level, political powers tend to control regulators, leading to a tendency to favour national interests to the detriment of foreign interests, hence to the single European market, or to inefficient regulation (as was the case in the UK regulation of utilities until recently). This appears to be the case also in competition policy and state aids, and in specific sectors, especially textiles and clothing, retail, banking and air transport. Thus, one conclusion of the analysis of competition policy in four European countries (Belgium, the Netherlands, Italy and Germany) by Van Cayseele et al. is that national antitrust authorities are not sufficiently independent of the political power. In other words, there is a certain lack of horizontal separation, leading to inefficiencies in the implementation of antitrust (the empirical evidence of Section 2 of the chapter points to such a problem in Italy). The evidence provided by Martin and Valbonesi (Chapter 5) on state aids is that 'various policies favour national firms relative to firms based in other member states, such as state aids, the nature and enforcement of competition policy, labour market institutions, environmental regulation, consumer protection rules, the tax burden, and the nature of education systems'. The chapter on banking provides evidence of a number of 'regulatory failures': restrictions to entry implying the fragmentation of markets and lack of economies of scale and scope; state ownership implying the favouring of political interests rather than efficiency and profit maximisation motives, leading to both static and dynamic inefficiencies. Thus, the deregulation and setting up of the European financial market has led to some increase in the degree of competition and to consolidation. However, the chapter argues that problems in the regulatory process are preventing the market from becoming truly European (banks are focused primarily on their national markets): political worries persist about the fact that foreigners can purchase national financial institutions.

One reason for the political power to control regulators is 'myopia'. Regulation or regulatory reform is a long-term process, from which society continues to reap benefits as economic actors continue to adjust their behaviour (e.g. as both producers and consumers take increasing care about the environment, pollution levels continues to be reduced). Politicians, however, often take a more myopic view and place a greater weight on minimising disruptions to the public (immediate costs of investing in clean technologies for producers, or of changing products or habits of consumers) than maximising economic efficiency. Impatience may be another related reason. When regulatory reform fails to produce sufficient immediate benefits to their constituents, they may be tempted to re-regulate or to stop further deregulation.

Second, the regulatory framework may be such that regulators are closely controlled so that they may have scope to pursue their own interests (career prospects, etc.) rather than that of the whole society. However, there is little evidence to substantiate this problem. The European Commission has often been accused of being a bureaucratic machine pursuing its own interests, but Chapter 12 shows that this is not a real problem in the EU regulatory framework. The main reason is that the member states and the European Parliament are the real legislators of the EU regulatory framework. As shown in Box 2, in Section 3 below, the Commission proposes and only the member states and the European Parliament adopt.

Third, the regulator may be 'captured' by interest groups. In the EU, the general tendency of member states to favour national firms relative to firms based in other member states may be the result of conscious favouring of national interests or of the capture of national regulators by national industrial lobbies. The latter case of pure capture may arise because of information asymmetry. Regulators generally rely on data from the industry in order to decide on the regulatory options. If no other data sources exist, the industry might over- or understate some data in order to induce the adoption of favourable measures. This was the case in the cost-effectiveness analysis performed for the European Commission in connection with its decision on measures to reduce air polluting emissions by cars. However, the European Commission claimed that it was aware of such data problems in taking its decision.[9]

Problems in the regulatory process may also arise when regulators use the regulatory measure for other purposes than just correcting the particular market failure. For instance, regulation of network industries, namely in the telecommunications, energy and transport sectors, has been used for redistributive purposes. Using regulation for equity considerations need not be wrong per se, but it has to be taken explicitly into account in the analysis of the regulatory problem, because equity adds an objective to the regulatory measure, and therefore adequate instruments also change. The failure is not in adding other objectives to the regulatory purpose, but in not taking it into account in the regulatory analysis, i.e. in the determination of the most appropriate policy.

Another problem may arise when the regulatory process has different levels of application. Thus the EU regulatory process is characterised by both European (supranational) and national levels. The principle of subsidiarity ensures consistency between the two levels, in terms of defining clearly the roles of each level. However, there is evidence of inconsistencies, in particular regarding competition policy, as shown in the study by Van Cayseele et al. in Chapter 4 of this volume. The particular case of the EU regulatory framework will be analysed in more detail in Section 2.4 below.

Such problems in the regulatory process are particularly acute since they may lead to a vicious circle of reducing quality. The reason is that problems in the regulatory process undermine the credibility of regulation (for instance, concerns for capture of the regulator will induce economic actors to think that the regulation adopted does not maximise the net benefits to society), implying that the objectives of the regulation will not be met: economic actors who do not believe in the adequacy of the regulation adopted will not have strong incentives to implement it. Therefore, regulatory quality is reduced due to problems in the regulatory process, and perceptions of problems in the regulatory process (lack of credibility) lead to further reduction in quality. In such a case, one could even speak of regulatory failure, and even 'systematic' regulatory failure.

c. Lack of implementation and enforcement

Bad implementation and compliance constitute another important, and often overlooked regulatory failure. As in point (b), this is a problem in the regulatory process. However, we consider lack of implementation and enforcement separately, because of its significant negative impact on regulatory quality. Lack of implementation and compliance is costly, in terms of market failure that goes uncorrected and waste of regulatory resources (the regulatory decision-making process having spent time and resources to find an appropriate solution). Poor implementation and enforcement may generate the particular problem of 'over-regulation'. Governments may judge that some regulatory instruments are insufficient to solve the regulatory problem, when in fact the poor result is due to improper implementation and enforcement. Hence additional regulation may be decided. The regulatory problem will persist, however, given that the true problem is not addressed. Such a 'vicious circle' of falling regulatory quality will lead to 'systematic' regulatory failures. Of course, we found no empirical evidence of such systematic regulatory failures. However, such reasoning shows that implementation and enforcement should not be ignored in the regulatory reform process.

Incomplete enforcement can originate from various sources. The regulatee may adopt an evasive behaviour (Viscusi and Zeckhauser, 1979), in which case the penalty for non-compliance has to be well defined for firms to find more benefits from complying than from evading (in other words, for firms to have incentives to comply). Administrative and enforcement costs may be too high,[10] due for instance to excessive red tape involved in complying with the regulation, and result in low enforcement quality. Low enforcement may also result from a divergence of interests between the agency deciding on the regulatory measure to adopt and the agency ensuring implementation and compliance. Such problems in the government hierarchy constitutes a regulatory failure. Lastly, poor enforcement may result from asymmetric information. Thus the regulator is likely to hold imperfect information on the firms' technology and costs, so that firms may under-report costs or under-invest in technology relative to what would be required by the regulation. If the regulator lacks data with which to evaluate the degree of enforcement, such behaviour by firms may not be detected.

Implementation and compliance may require the use of incentive-based approaches, rather than a simple reliance on sanctioning and penalty. Incentive-based approaches make it in the interest of the regulatee to comply with the regulation, while command-and-control approaches force the regulatee to comply, with the threat of sanctions and penalties in case of non-compliance. Under some conditions (easy and not-too-costly measurement and monitoring of compliance, impossibility to hide information, etc.), the former approach may be more effective and efficient, inducing regulatees to voluntarily comply. In contrast, the command-and-control approach might be inefficient, that is, both costly (monitoring costs to control the regulatee) and ineffective (non-compliance might not be easy to detect, or may take time to be detected, so that effective implementation and enforcement never takes place). One example of the incentive-based approach is voluntary agreement: under certain conditions (such as an easy and not-too-costly monitoring system), both the regulatee (business) and the government agree to a plan that eliminates the market failures, and since the regulatee(s) has (have) agreed to that plan, they comply with it. Such an approach is now favoured by the European Commission concerning regulations to improve air quality: a voluntary agreement has recently been signed with the ACEA, the European association of car manufacturers.[11] This trend towards incentive-based approaches in environmental regulation at both the EU and national levels is outlined in Chapter 6 of this volume. The following section shows that this problem of implementation and enforcement is particularly acute in the EU regulatory framework.

3.   A CLOSER LOOK AT EU REGULATORY FAILURES

The European Union is more than just an association of countries, which would have in common only certain elements not affecting their sovereignty. A peculiarity of the EU is that certain competencies are assigned exclusively to the European level and that the treaties establish a common Court of Justice whose rulings can override national laws or rulings. Box 2 summarises the main features of the EU regulatory process.

The EU regulatory framework is therefore unique in the world since it lies between federations and pure national systems. It is characterised by different levels of actions, mainly national (and also regional) and supranational (EU level), with different roles. The EU level is characterised by a peculiar regulatory goal: the goal is both to correct market failures and to prevent adverse effects of some national measures on other member states.

The two-level regulatory framework of the EU generates two particular sources of poor regulatory quality. First, strategic behaviour by national regulators. For instance, a regulation on a product consumed only locally may create trade barriers if the regulation specifies the use of factors of production that exist only locally. This is a type-I regulatory failure, since it is effective (correcting the market failure), but inefficient (it creates costs to

---

Box 2. Main Features of the EU Regulatory Framework

The European Commission has the power of initiative in the legislative process of the European Community. It also has to monitor the application of legislation, being the 'Guardian of the Treaties' and has executive powers in some common policy domains, such as competition policy. The European regulatory framework is therefore characterised by multiple-level government. The European Council has no legislative power but has political power. The Council of Ministers has legislative power. The European Parliament has recently been given co-decision powers, but only had a consultative role previously. The legal instruments of the EC are:

1. Regulations: EC laws which apply to all legal persons directly.
2. Directives: EC laws to be transposed into national regulations; when doing this, the objectives and effects of the directive must be ensured.
3. Framework Directives: General objectives and approaches must be implemented and enforced; such directives are followed by more specific directives.
4. Decisions: EC laws specifically directed to a firm or a member state.
5. Recommendations: Consisting of resolutions (of Council or Parliament), communications, Green and White Papers of the Commission, and of opinions, which can have significant influence, but are not binding.

The regulatory instruments available at the EU level are therefore limited. The European Commission can mainly use legal instruments, and command-and-control in particular. This may explain the current gap between the announced intention to implement market-based instruments and actual practice, for instance in the field of environmental regulation. Clinch in Chapter 6 mentions the debate about the use of European green taxes to reduce pollution in the EU. Another constraint in the EU regulatory process is in the definition of its competence, which is defined in the subsidiarity principle, mentioned previously. On the basis of this principle, the EU regulatory framework is hierarchical. The European level is guided by different rules that constitute the single market and the common policies. The free movement principle is crucial as a condition for the establishment of the single market, and constrains member state actions which the Community can override if they hinder free movement within the single market.

Member states regulate in three cases. First, they regulate purely national activities. For instance, the regulation of shop opening hours is decided nationally. Second, member states can regulate, in addition to Community regulation, if this does not hinder the principle of free movement. The reason for this is the principle of mutual recognition. Consider that a European regulation imposes a minimum quality standard on a product, while a national regulation imposes a higher standard. Before 1985, this resulted in a fragmentation of the single market. A foreign product had to comply with the national regulation, leading to a higher cost for the foreign producer. The Community therefore always adopted the strictest standard in the EU, even if the market failure in question did not justify such a 'severity'. The result was either 'over-regulation' or no solution. The famous Cassis de Dijon case led to the definition of the principle of mutual recognition: a product that complies with the country of origin's regulation must be recognised in any other member states where it might be imported, if the objective or effects of the regulation are 'equivalent'. Third, member states can regulate when derogation to the free movement is commonly accepted. This third case is rare; one example is the gas market, which is being partially liberalised, and where 'emergent markets' such as Greece are not required to implement the whole directive while infrastructure is developed in the country, and until the market becomes mature.

foreign business due to the trade barrier). This may lead to an oversupply of regulations: national businesses may press for more regulations that result in increased regulatory barriers and more difficult access by foreign producers to the national market. Evidence exists that, although the European Commission has attempted to improve law-making and regulatory decisions at the EU level (both qualitatively and quantitatively: Ciavarini-Azzi (1998) reports on the sharp decline of proposals for new EU legislation), member state legislative output remains substantial and complex. Second, international agreement might not be credible. One example is when monitoring of implementation is imperfect due to, say, measurement uncertainties, national regulatees may expect their governments not to comply rigorously with the international agreement (or EU regulation), especially when costs are easier to see than benefits. The regulation will end-up being ineffective (type-II regulatory failure).

Implementation is a particular problem of EU regulation, both in terms of speed and quality. In legal terms, implementation effectiveness means the degree to which both the formal transposition and the practical application of supranational measures at the national level correspond to the objectives and effects specified by the European legislation. In fact, the Commission can monitor compliance and only puts cases to the European Court of Justice after long delays. For example, the Commission put a case to ECJ against countries not complying with the liberalising telecommunications directives, one year after day one of the liberalised market). The problem is due to the deficiencies in the EU control of implementation. If the European Commission's means of action against a non-complying member state were quicker, implementation would certainly be improved.

The failure of member states to implement the directives agreed by the Council and the Parliament in a timely fashion, the so-called 'transposition deficit', has been a concern to the European Commission, in particular since the Internal Market Action Plan of June 1997. The transposition deficit is both quantitative and qualitative. In quantitative terms, the situation is improving: the percentage of directives not yet implemented is reducing, e.g. from 35 per cent in June 1997 to 18 per cent on 1 May 1998. In qualitative terms, improvements need to be made so that directives translate into clear and understandable rules (European Commission, 1998b).

The flexibility provided by the directives as an instrument of EU regulation may be source of the implementation and enforcement problem. The majority of EU regulation takes the form of Council directives. These must be implemented in national legislation after they have been adopted by the Council of Ministers. The obligation is to satisfy the objectives set out in the directive, not to reproduce the Council and EP directive word for word in national legislation. Art. 189 (EEC) specifies that 'a Directive shall be binding, as to the result to be achieved, upon each member state to which it is addressed, but shall leave to the national authorities the choice of form and methods'. Such flexibility provided by the use of directives, as opposed to regulations in which common provisions apply directly in all member states, is intended to provide scope for different national traditions and laws. However, this also leaves scope for improper implementation of the provisions. It is difficult to compare the effects of the some 2,000 pieces of implementing legislation in the nine official languages of the EU.

Implementation is poor in some areas because national governments have not adopted implementing legislation or passed national legislation compatible with the objectives set out in the directives. This is the case in areas such as public procurement, insurance, intellectual property and pharmaceuticals. Public procurement is a particular case of EU regulatory failure. The opening of the European public procurement markets date back to 1971, when two directives were approved concerning both public works and goods sold to public agencies.[12] However, in the mid-1980s, only 2 per cent of public procurement was supplied by firms from other member states (public procurement represented about 9 per cent of the EC's GNP). Hence a series of directives was adopted in the late 1980s and early 1990s: for instance Directive 89/440 which introduces competitive norms on public tendering, and the 1991 recommendations of the European Commission on the approximation of requirements and procedures for public auctions.

However, the evidence is that the common market for public procurement is not yet there: the regulatory quality scoreboard derived in Section 1 showed that member states perform poorly in terms of transparency of public procurement. The Cardiff II report[13] also underlines the lack of integration of the public procurement markets (and considers this as one of the problem areas). Besides this, Dewatripont et al. (1997) report that in 1996, 86 per cent of the national transpositions required to implement the eight directives adopted after 1988, had been notified to the European Commission, but only 78 per cent had been carried out properly. Consequently, none of the eight directives had been properly put into effect in the member states. Obviously there is a problem of implementation, probably coupled with a political failure, due to a preference given by national states to national firms. The Cardiff II report states that implementation of EU regulation is poor not only in public procurement, but also in telecommunications, transport and intellectual and industrial property rights. Italy, Portugal and Luxembourg have the worst transposition records. The number of infringement proceedings opened by the Commission against member states for alleged failure to apply single market rules continues to grow.

After implementation, directives must be enforced. Differences in the rigour of enforcement may result in regulatory inefficiencies. For example, if one country fails to ensure that its industries comply with costly minimum standards, it would provide a competitive advantage to the national business. Besides this, the concept of mutual recognition would be undermined, since there would be no confidence that products originating in the country concerned met the minimum requirements. There is diversity in national approaches to enforcement. In some cases the bodies responsible for enforcement are at the national level and in others at the regional level. For example, in metrology (the measurement and calibration of measuring equipment), the responsibility is shared between central and regional bodies in France, Italy and Spain, between central and local governments in the UK and Denmark, and is assigned to the private sector in the Netherlands.

Therefore, it appears that strategic behaviour by member states, and problems of implementation and enforcement are the major problems affecting EU regulation, resulting in insufficient quality. However, Chapter 12 of this volume expresses further concerns over EU regulatory quality. It argues that credibility is a major problem of the EU regulatory process, and that 'politicisation' (the parliamentarisation of the European Commission), although good for democratic legitimacy, raises credibility concerns that should be addressed immediately. Besides, it argues that 'among the major shortcomings of the EC regulatory system are the lack of rational procedures for selecting regulatory priorities, the absence of central coordination and oversight leading to serious inconsistencies across and within regulatory programmes, and the insufficient attention paid to cost-effectivenes of individual rules'.

As a conclusion to this section, regulatory quality can be defined as efficient and effective regulation, resulting from proper analysis of the regulatory problem and proper functioning of – that is, transparent and credibile – regulatory processes. Poor-quality regulation is not credible, and as a result economic actors will not commit to its implementation and enforcement. This may further reduce regulatory quality. Credibility can be argued to be the major indicator of regulatory quality: if business, consumers and other groups in society concerned with regulation perceive it to be of good quality, regulation will be credible, and hence effective and efficient. The next section provides empirical evidence of the credibility of regulation in Europe.

4. EVIDENCE OF REGULATORY FAILURES IN EUROPE: THE IMD AND EIU SURVEYS

A proper analysis of the efficiency and effectiveness of existing regulation should be based on regulatory costs and benefits data. Yet, cost-benefit analysis is difficult to perform because of the lack of available data. In what follows, an overview of the regulatory practices which directly affect competitiveness is provided, using supporting evidence coming from business surveys, conducted both at a national and European level with multinational firms and economic experts. In particular, we used the results of two recent surveys conducted by the management school IMD and the Economist Intelligence Unit (EIU). In addition to these existing surveys, supporting evidence has been gathered from a series of ad hoc interviews conducted in the first months of 1999 with executives of multinational firms operating in Italy. The interviews conducted with Italian-based multinationals concentrated on the regulatory framework, taking as given the other factors considered in the previous analysis.

Evidence derived from this kind of survey consists of perceptions of business operators; in other words, the surveys provide subjective indications about how business operators judge the quality of the economic environment in which they operate. In fact, these perceptions could be heavily influenced by factors different from the 'true' quality of regulation, as the cyclical developments of a country or a sector, or by the general 'image' of a country as provided by the media. However, we think that such surveys are a good indicator of regulatory credibility, because they show what business feels about regulation. Perception of poor-quality regulation means that regulation lacks credibility, which has been shown to be evidence of either lack of regulatory problem analysis or problems in the regulatory process, i.e. true problems of quality of regulation.

The two surveys considered are very detailed in terms of the criteria used to assess the general level of regulatory quality. This detail minimises the risk that survey results could be biased by general factors different from a careful consideration of the regulatory environment.

The IMD and the EIU reports provide a ranking of 46 and 60 countries worldwide, respectively, based on both macro- and microeconomic data and on the results of surveys on the economic attractiveness of countries. In particular, both the IMD and EIU surveys are based on questionnaires returned by business executives (over 4,000 in the case of the IMD survey) worldwide. For reasons of clarity and simplicity, the results are presented using the classification defined by the OECD (1997) which broke regulation down into three categories: economic, social and administrative. In brief, economic regulation refers to public intervention to preserve or develop competition in markets or ensure fair prices. This category includes all the regulations concerned with market entry and exit, the functioning of markets, pricing, competition, the role of regulatory authorities and qualitative standards for products and services. Social regulation refers to regulation of health, safety and the environment, including all the regulations concerning the labour market and human capital formation. Administrative regulation refers to public bureaucracies and red tape that economic actors and business in particular have to deal with to perform their activities. Regulatory failures may stem in this case from inefficiency of government intervention and may result in regulatory growth (both in terms of paperwork needed and time consumed), insufficient transparency of procedures, corruption and compliance costs. Such a breakdown allows us to construct a 'regulatory quality scoreboard', as perceived by business operators, which is straightforward and easy to use.

As already mentioned, both surveys provide detailed information about the criteria used to assess the general rankings. The rankings are based on eight (IMD) and ten (EIU) broad indicators[14] of a country's performance, each indicator being composed of single quantitative and qualitative criteria. The qualitative data could be expressed in scores ranging from 0 (very poor regulation) to 10 (optimum regulation). The methodology used in this chapter (see Table 3.5) was to select and re-aggregate qualitative criteria

Table 3.5 The selected criteria

Indicator 1. Economic regulation	
The IMD survey	The EIU survey
Openness of the internal market	*Openness of the internal market*
National protectionism	Foreign investors regulation
Openness of public sector contracts	Openness of national culture
Investment Protections to foreign investors	Expropriation risks
Incentives for foreign investment	Investor protection
Freedom of foreigners to acquire domestic liabilities	Capital liberalisation
Freedom of cross-border ventures	Tariff and non-tariff protection
Access to local capital markets to foreigners	Openness of trade
Access to foreign capital markets to locals	
Access of foreign financial institutions to domestic market	
Exchange rate policy	
Product markets regulation	*Product markets regulation*
Product liability legislation	Protecion of private property
Price controls	Freedom to compete
Competition laws	Competition policy
Protection of intellectual properties	Protection of intellectual property
Regulation for developing technologies	Price control
	Lobbying
	State control
Indicator 2. Social regulation	
The IMD survey	The EIU survey
Immigration laws	Restrictive labour laws
Environment laws	Hiring foreign nationals
Labour regulation	Labour flexibility
Industrial relations	Industrial relations
Cooperation between companies and universities	Wage regulation
Teaching of science in school	Schooling
Availability of skilled workers	
Efficacy of education	
Equal opportunity regulation	

Indicator 3. Administrative regulation	
The IMD survey	The EIU survey
Improvement of management of public finances	Government policy
Efficacy of economic policies	Government efficacy
Efficiency of the legal framework	Red tape bureaucracy
Efficacy of legislative activity	Legal system
Transparency of government	Corruption
Efficacy of the political system	Crime
Independence of the public service	
Efficiency of the bureaucracy	
Implementing government decisions	
Customs administration	
Administration of justice	
Corruption and bribery	
Protection of property and persons	
Central bank efficacy	

from both surveys, and from these, to construct three broad indicators of economic, social and administrative regulatory quality.

The average score of the criteria included in each indicator gives the score for the indicator; the sum of the score of the three indicators gives the total score for a country, on the basis of which a 'regulatory quality scoreboard' is constructed. In the case of the IMD survey, 53 qualitative criteria of the total 223 were selected and used to build the global ranking; therefore, the sub-sample of information used accounts for almost 20 per cent of the total information used to assess a country's ranking.[15] In the case of the EIU survey, 30 out of 69 criteria were used to construct the global ranking; in this case, the sub-sample of information accounts for almost 45 per cent of the total information used to calculate a country's ranking.

Figures 3.3 and 3.4 show the 'regulatory quality scoreboards', based respectively on the IMD and the EIU surveys, for 28 countries.[16] On the basis of the Spearman index, the two rankings are highly correlated[17]. The UK, Denmark, the Netherlands and Ireland rank in both cases in the 'top 10'. Finland is also performing well according to both surveys. Germany ranks 9th and 14th in the EIU and IMD surveys, respectively, standing in between the top-scoring and lagging countries. In contrast, Spain, France and Italy are lagging behind, Spain being 19th and 15th, France 15th and 19th, and Italy 20th and 23rd, respectively, in the two surveys. Outside Europe, Canada, the

Figure 3.3 The regulatory quality scoreboard

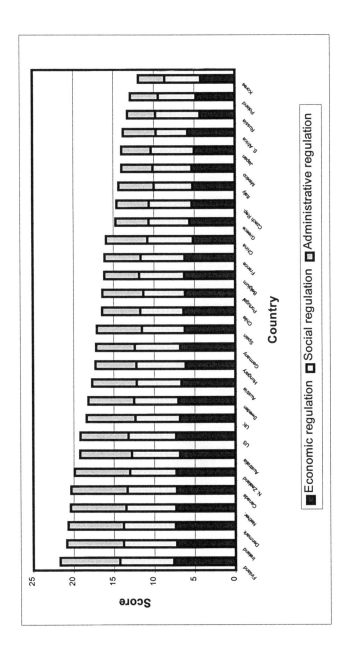

Figure 3.4 The regulatory quality scoreboard – EIU survey

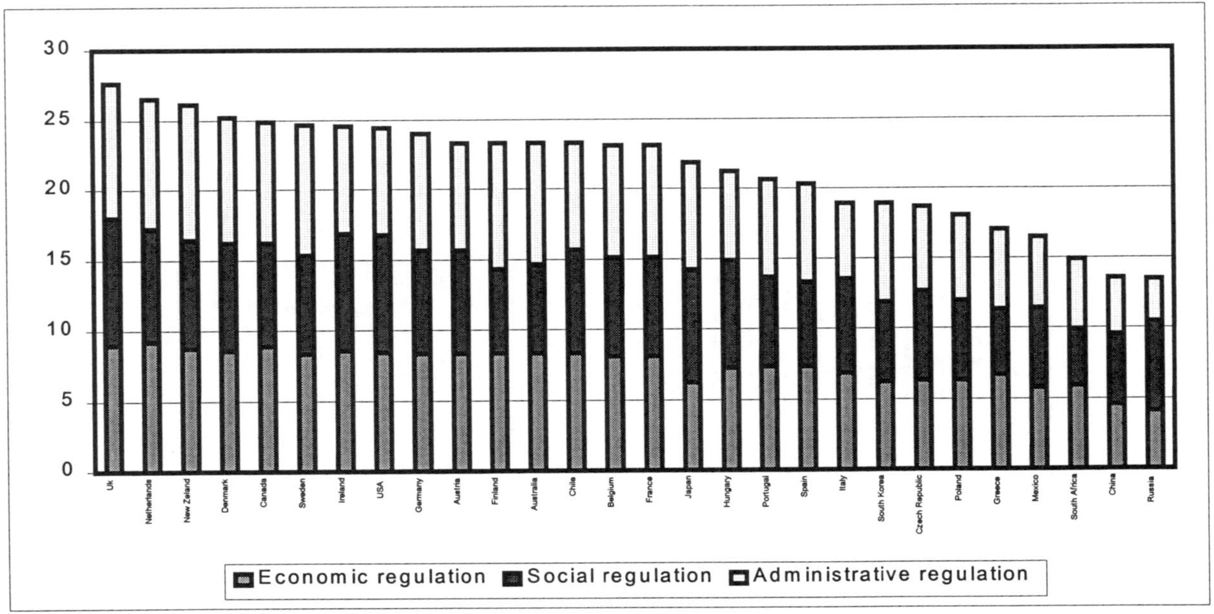

□ Economic regulation ■ Social regulation □ Administrative regulation

Russia, China, South Africa, Mexico, Greece, Poland, Czech Republic, South Korea, Italy, Spain, Portugal, Hungary, Japan, France, Belgium, Chile, Australia, Finland, Austria, Germany, USA, Ireland, Sweden, Canada, Denmark, New Zealand, Netherlands, UK

30 25 20 15 10 5 0

US and New Zealand rank on top of the score in both cases, whereas regulatory quality results are very poor in the East European countries (Russia, Poland and the Czech Republic), Mexico, Japan, Korea and South Africa. It appears therefore that among EU countries, Spain, France and Italy are experiencing particular problems of regulatory quality, since they all rank low in the regulatory quality scoreboards; Germany stands in the middle of both rankings, and the other EU countries have higher regulatory quality. We now turn to the determinants of these results in order to examine whether such poor quality is due to regulatory failures.

The overall results for Germany, according to the IMD survey, are especially related to a poor score in the administrative regulation indicator. According to the survey, this is particularly due to inefficiencies in the management of economic policy, of the legal framework and of legislative activity, which results in a non-transparency of government and inefficacy of bureaucracy. Both surveys also indicate a lack of fiscal incentives to foreign investment and regulatory failures in the administration of the corporate and personal tax system (Indicator 1, economic regulation). As for Indicator 2, (social regulation), it appears that labour, wage and environmental regulations hinder competition in the German market.

Spain ranks 15th, immediately after Germany in the IMD scoreboard, and 19th in the EIU scoreboard. The administrative regulation indicator performs well according to both surveys, while evidence of regulatory failure appears in both the economic and social regulation indicators. As for economic regulation, the main determinants of poor regulatory quality in Spain seem to be both non-competitive public procurement, public sector contracts being insufficiently open to foreign investors, and excessive presence of state control in the market economy. In addition, financial markets are claimed to be inefficiently regulated, with a lack of definition of rights and responsibilities of the shareholders. The quality of social regulation is also poor, due primarily to the low performance of labour market regulation, industrial relations (many industrial disputes) and lack of cooperation between companies and universities.

France ranks 19th and 15th respectively in the IMD and EIU surveys. An efficient economic regulatory framework does not completely offset regulatory failures in social and administrative regulation. In particular, respondents in both surveys perceive labour market regulation and industrial relations as an obstacle to the competitiveness of the country. France is also the only European country, together with Belgium, with poor equal opportunity regulation.[18] In addition, the effectiveness of the various government bodies (parliament, central government, political system, central bank, bureaucracy) is perceived to be insufficient. A lack of independence of the public service from external pressures is also mentioned.

Italy ranks in the last position in both surveys, that is, Italian regulatory quality is poorest not only in EU-11 (the euro zone, which is the focus of the EIU survey), but also in EU-15 (IMD survey). Among EU countries, Italy is followed only by Greece, according to the EIU survey. Regulatory quality is particularly poor in terms of the third indicator, that is, administrative regulation. Poor administration of justice, giving way to corruption and bribery in the system, inefficiency of the bureaucracy (red tape) and of the political system and lack of independence of the public service from external pressures are the major problems in this respect. The other two indicators also provide evidence of regulatory failures. In particular, failures in economic regulation translate into a lack of openness of public contracts to foreign bidders and insufficient incentives in general for foreign investors; ineffective and inefficient regulation of financial institutions and the stock market (definition of rights and responsibilities of shareholders); inefficiency of the distribution system and of the water distribution regulation. Concerning social regulation, Italy, like Germany and France, experiences failures in labour market and wage regulations and industrial relations, not to mention inefficiencies of the educational system.

The regulatory quality scoreboards are useful in highlighting the major regulatory failures affecting the competitiveness of a country, and may hence serve as primary targets of reform. The case of Italy is particularly interesting since it appears as the least efficiently and/or effectively regulated country in Europe. Additional evidence of regulatory failure in Italy is provided below, drawn from interviews carried out in 1998-99 with executives of multinational firms based in Italy. The results obtained are not systematic: the sample is small and it is not possible to generalise evidence from them. Nevertheless, such interviews confirm that business does perceive a lack of quality of regulation. The conclusion is that either business is right and it is high time to reform regulation to make it effective and efficient; or, even if business exaggerates the bad state of regulation, such perceptions show the lack of credibility of the government's commitment to provide a good business environment.

Interview results are synthesised in Table 3.6 and classified according to three categories of regulation, namely economic, social and administrative. For each of these, examples of weaknesses in the Italian regulatory system are provided, ranging from the general (i.e. scarce flexibility of the labour market) to very specific aspects of regulation (i.e. the role of ruling in the tax system). The poor quality of Italian administrative regulation is confirmed.

Table 3.6 Evidence of regulatory failures in Italy drawn from interviews with corporate executives

Type of regulation	Strengths	Weaknesses
Economic	Consumer protection	Development of electronic commerce
	Openness to production	Protection of intellectual property
	for third parties (Pharmaceuticals) Authorisation regime	Competition policies
	for new pharmaceuticals	Tax regulation − IRAP for multinational firms in general, efficiency − No possibility of ruling − Fiscal treatment of dividends − Fiscal treatment of holdings
		Price controls (Pharm.)
		Product standards: − Late to apply EC regulation − No proposals in EC tables
Social	High quality of skills	Time-consuming procedures for CFL
	Environmental regulation	Labour agencies
		Too long scholarship
		Protected categories
		Minimal wage
	Flexibility of labour market (for high skilled)	Labour market regulation (in and out)
		Flexibiity of labour market (low skill)
Administrative		Relationship companies/universities
		Continuing education (on the job)
		Bureaucracy, in particular:
		− Excessive number of financing laws − Excessive number of government bodies − Compliance costs − Irresponsibility of the bureaucrats' application of new laws
		Efficacy of justice
		Political effectiveness and stability
		Opening new plant

Interviewees have generally indicated that the relationship with public administration is very difficult, costly and time-consuming. Regulatory uncertainty is high, in particular due to rapid changes in laws resulting from political instability. The lack of responsibility (and incentives) of bureaucrats partly explains the inefficiency of bureaucracy. Such a lack of responsibility also contributes to another regulatory failure, the lack of implementation of new laws that simplify and enhance the quality of public administration.[19] In the managers' view, giving new responsibilities (and incentives) to public employees could help solve this regulatory failure.

The most sensitive aspect of economic regulation is the one regarding the tax system, which in general is perceived as being highly inefficient and hindering the development of the Italian economy. In this case, interview results could be biased by the consideration of the high level of Italian taxation. However, particular aspects of the tax system concerning multinational firms are also indicated, such as fiscal treatment of dividends and holdings. An interesting example of regulatory failure that emerges from the interviews is the impossibility of obtaining a 'ruling' in the Italian tax system that has a legal value with tax bureaucrats on particular aspects of tax regulation. The ruling criterion gives certainty to firms and simplifies the. relationship with public administration. Other critical aspects of economic regulation in Italy are weak intellectual property rights and inefficient competition policies, especially for the excessive role of authorities and the regulation of product standards. The strengths of Italian economic regulation include efficient and effective consumer protection and some new regulations such as the recently approved regulation in the pharmaceutical sector which introduces the possibility to produce for third parties and the opening of the authorisation regime for new pharmaceutical products. As for social regulation, the interviewees indicated that labour market regulation is still not favourable to the competitiveness of the Italian market, even if it has improved in recent years. In particular, the weak aspects of labour market regulation are minimal wages, which would benefit from local and sectoral differentiation; rigidities in the regulation of protected categories and the state monopoly of the employment agencies.

5. CONCLUSIONS: THE NEED FOR REFORM

The previous chapters have shown that regulation affects the functioning of markets, and hence competitiveness, growth and employment. If well done, regulation contributes to good functioning of markets. This chapter has shown, however, that regulatory quality is quite poor in Europe and might be a reason for the 'competitiveness gap' outlined at the beginning. Business concerns over the adverse effects of regulation on their activities seem to be well founded since there is evidence of insufficient regulatory quality. Our regulatory quality scoreboard shows that the major European countries (Germany, France, Italy and Spain) rank in a low position, with particular problems in administrative and social regulation, i.e. the functioning of public administrations and of the welfare state. At the EU level, although some effort has been made towards reform, three major problems remain. First, strategic behaviour by member states which tend to continue to favour national interests at the expense of foreign ones. Second, implementation and enforcement of EU regulation are poor. Third, the EU regulatory process is complex and lacks credibility.

Maximising regulatory quality means maximising the net benefits to society. All the potential benefits and costs of different regulatory options should be evaluated and compared in order to choose the highest quality regulation. In order for regulation to reach the maximum feasible level of quality, regulatory design should take account of a number of constraints in the regulatory process: history, institutions and information. Problems in the regulatory process, such as a lack of separation between the regulatory and political authorities, capture of regulators, myopia or impatience, substantially reduce regulatory quality. Hence, the importance of credibility and transparency in the regulatory process. In particular, actors in the regulatory process should not only announce their intentions but should credibly commit to regulatory quality, by making clear the criteria for regulatory choice, ensuring compliance and measuring the effects of regulation. Poor quality ranges from a justified burden to costly failures and governments should commit to regulatory quality maximisation in order to avoid adverse effects on markets.

In particular, three major factors have been shown to determine regulatory quality:

1. *Good analysis of the regulatory problem*, and in particular the consideration of combined effects (in the sense of cumulative and interactive). Such combined effects concern joint effects of different instruments for the same regulatory problem and joint effects of different regulations on particular markets. An example of the first joint effect is taking account of some incentive-based instruments when deciding on product standards. The second joint effect is for instance the combined effect of product and labour market regulations in a particular industry or in the overall economy.

2. *Transparency and commitment in the regulatory process.* Insufficient separation between the regulators and the political power, capture by the regulator by interest groups, or lack of control by the regulator are examples of problems in the regulatory process that adversely affect regulatory quality. In the EU, a problem is the strategic behaviour of national governments, resulting in national regulations that favour national business at the expense of business from other member states, or a lack of (or improper) implementation of EU regulation. This problem is particularly acute for the EU, since it impedes the establishment and proper functioning of the single market.

3. *Implementation and enforcement.* This is crucial for the effectiveness of regulations. However, evidence gathered in this chapter is that both implementation and enforcement of regulations are problematic in Europe.

Hence reform should address these three aspects. Concerning the first point above, the use of cost-benefit analysis (following the checklist of questions suggested in this paper) may be a solution. This requires systematic collection of data on the part of national governments and of the European Commission, going through all the right questions, going beyond 'consultation' to a serious attempt to serve the EU's public interest. Regarding the second point above, namely the problems in the regulatory process, reform might be difficult, because it would mean changing some features of the regulatory process. The OECD (1997a) has already recommended the modernisation of the 'regulatory state', but little progress has been made in this sense so far. Establishing a clear separation between regulators and the political power, defining clearly the role of each regulator (to avoid inconsistencies as between the EU and national antitrust authorities), and involving all interest groups in the regulatory decision-making process in a transparent way so that influence of one group or another may be detected are among the needed reforms. Such reforms would enhance the credibility of the regulatory process, and hence ensure better acceptance by business, which is the group primarily affected by regulation. In the EU, a particular problem is the lack of commitment of national authorities to the single market. There is a need for credible domestic authorities and close ties between them and the EU to maintain consistency and enforcement. Member states should also collaborate more effectively in order to avoid the harmful competition in the zero-sum game that tends to exist between them, whereby national business is favoured at the expense of firms from other member states.

In short, there is a need for governments to go beyond the mere announcement or declaration on effective maximisation of regulatory quality. Examples of such declarations are numerous: the 18th Declaration of Member States on the use of cost-benefit analysis for regulatory decision-making or the commitment by the Italian government to improve administrative procedures and the legislative system. This chapter, however, together with the evidence provided in subsequent chapters, shows that there is a gap between such 'promises' and concrete steps. Some reforms have been undertaken, but they do not go far enough. Concrete measures are needed to show that regulators are truly and credibly committed to regulatory quality maximisation. Otherwise, the proper functioning of markets, and of the European single market in particular, will continue to be hindered.

NOTES

1. Blondal and Pilat (1997); an extension of sectoral results for the case of Italy is in Jacobs and Malgarini (1998).
2. In this definition, high-tech includes pharmaceuticals, office and computing equipment, radio, TV and communications equipment, and aircraft.
3. Internalities might be positive, if the unforeseen effect is positive.
4. See Egenhofer and Labory (1998).
5. Notice that regulation is not the only solution to third party access: negotiated access may be allowed, which permits firms perform transactions, while the competition authorities watch that there is no abuse of dominant position on the part of the owner of the essential facility.
6. Incentive-based instruments originate in works of Mirrlees (1971), Green and Laffont (1979), Loeb and Magat (1979), Sappington (1982), and Baron and Myerson (1982).
7. See Egenhofer and Labory (1998).
8. The issue of equity is not explicitly considered in this chapter. The costs of a regulation may unfairly and disproportionately fall on particular groups of society, either business or consumers, and this may be regarded as a regulatory failure. Alternatively, a regulatory measure may be adopted because it enables an even redistribution of some benefits, although the net benefits of the measure are lower than another regulatory

measure. This issue of equity is very difficult indeed. The following chapters will analyse deeper regulatory failures in particular cases, and will provide more insight on the issue. At this stage, we can only note that taken as a methodology rather than an accounting framework, CBA analysis makes the consideration of equity possible: the analysis should identify all costs and benefits and the societal groups on which they fall. A decision-maker may reject a regulation because costs fall disproportionately on one group, without compensation. The three criteria of effectiveness, efficiency and equity may be reconciled by putting weights on costs and benefits.

9. See Pelkmans and Labory (1998, Annex I) for a case study.
10. See Chung-Huang (1996) for a review.
11. See Egenhofer and Labory (1998).
12. Directives 71/304 and 71/305.
13. COM(1999)61 final.
14. The indicators for the IMD are: domestic economy, internationalisation, government, finance, infrastructure, management, science and technology and people. In the EIU survey, the indicators are: political environment, economic stability, market opportunities, policy towards private enterprises, FDI policy, foreign trade and exchange rates, tax regime, financing, labour market, and infrastructure.
15. In fact, each qualitative criteria has an average weight of 0.8 in the IMD report.
16. Countries considered are EU-14 (Luxembourg is not included).
17. Spearman index is equal to 0.82; a value of 1 indicates exact correlation.
18. Encompassing differences in race, gender and family background.
19. On this see also Cassese and Galli (1998).

REFERENCES

Baron, D. and R. Myerson (1982), 'Regulating a Monopolist with Unknown Costs', *Econometrica*, 50, 911-30.

Blondal, S. and D. Pilat (1997), *The economy-wide effects of regulatory reform*, The OECD Report on Regulatory Reform, Vol. II: Thematic Studies, Paris.

Cassese, S. and G.P. Galli (eds) (1998), *L'Italia de semplificare: Vol. I. Le istituzioni*, Bologna: Il Mulino.

Chung-Huang, Huang (1996), 'Effectiveness of Environmental Regulations under Imperfect Enforcement and Firm's Avoidance Behaviour', *Environmental and Resource Economics*, 8, 183-204.

Ciavarini-Azzi, G. (1998), 'Better Lawmaking: The Experience and the View of the European Commission', *Columbia Journal of European Law*, Vol. 4-3, 617-28.

Deighton-Smith, R. (1998), 'Indicators of regulatory capacities in OECD countries: preliminary analysis', OECD, PUMA/REG(98)3, June.

Dewatripont, M., F. Giavazzi, J. Von Hagen, I. Harden, T. Persson, G. Roland, H. Rosenthal, A. Sapir. and G. Tabellini. (1997), 'Implementation and Enforcement in the Single Market', revised version of Chapter 5 in *Flexible Integration: Towards a More Effective and Democratic Europe, Monitoring European Integration*, CEPR, November 1995, revised in March 1997.

Economist Intelligence Unit (1998), *Business environment rankings*, 1st Quarter 1999, December.

Egenhofer, C. and S. Labory (1998), *Climate Change after Kyoto*, CEPS Working Party Report No. 15, Centre for European Policy Studies, Brussels.

European Commission (1997), *Making Single Market rules more effective*, Communication to the European Parliament and the Council, COM(98)296, final, 4 June.

European Commission (1998a), *The Competitiveness of European Industry*, 1998 Report, DG III.

European Commission (1998b), *The Single Market Review*, Subseries III, Volume 1, Office for Official Publications of the European Communities, Kogan Page, Earthscan, 1998.

Green, J. and J-J. Laffont (1979), *Incentives in Public Decision-Making*, Amsterdam: North Holland.

IMD (1998), *The World Competitiveness Yearbook*, IMD International.

IMF (1998), *International Financial Statistics Yearbook*, Washington, D.C.

Jacobs, S., R. Deighton Smith, H. Huigen and R. Buchwitz (1997), *Regulatory quality and public sector reform, The OECD Report on Regulatory Reform*, Vol. II: Thematic Studies, Paris.

Jacobs, S. and M. Malgarini (1998), *A decade of regulatory reform in OECD countries: Progress and lessons learned*, CSC Working Paper No. 14, March.

Laffont, J-J and J. Tirole (1993), *A Theory of Incentives in Procurement and Regulation*, Cambridge, MA: MIT Press.

Loeb, M. and W. Magat (1979), 'A Decentralised Method of Utility Regulation', *Journal of Law and Economics*, 22, 399-404.

McKinsey & Company (1992), *Service Sector Productivity*, McKinsey Global Institute, Washington, D.C., October.

J. Mirrlees (1971), 'An Exploration of the Theory of Optimal Income Taxation', *Review of Economic Studies*, 38, 175-208.

OECD (1994), *Assessing Structural Reform: Lessons for the Future*, Paris.

OECD (1997a), *The OECD Report on Regulatory Reform*, Volumes I and II, Paris.

OECD (1997b), *Regulatory Impact Analysis: Best Practices in OECD Countries*, Paris.

OECD (1998), *Financial Market Trends*, No. 71, November, Paris.

Pelkmans, J. and S. Labory (1998), *European Regulation and Cost-Benefit Analysis: A Methodology for Non-Specialists*, Report for DGIII of the European Commission.

Sappington, D. (1983), 'Optimal Regulation of a Multiproduct Monopoly with Unknown Technological Capabilities', *Bell Journal of Economics*, 14, 453-63.

Spence, M. and R. Zeckhauser (1971) 'Insurance, Information and Individual Actions', *American Economic Review*, 61, 380-87.

Spulber, D.F. (1989), *Regulation and Markets*, Cambridge, MA: MIT Press.

Stigler, G.J. (1971), 'The Theory of Economic Regulation', *Bell Journal of Economics*, 2, 3-21.

UNICE (1999), *Fostering Entrepreneurship in Europe – The UNICE Benchmarking Report 1999*, forthcoming.

Viscusi, W.K. and R.J. Zeckhauser (1979), 'Optimal Standards with Incomplete Enforcement', *Public Policy*, 27, 437-56.

4. National Competition Policies

Patrick Van Cayseele, Pierluigi Sabbatini and Wim Van Meerbeeck[1]

1. INTRODUCTION

With the Sherman Act of 1870, antitrust policies aimed at keeping markets competitive made their entry into the world of economic policy. While economists in those days were not all convinced of the usefulness of such policies, see Shughart and Tollison (1998) on this matter, antitrust policies gradually gained widespread acceptance for their salutary effects. Stigler (1964) reported that the effects of antitrust action in his view were meager, but nonetheless present. Nowadays, more than 60 per cent of the relevant profession, i.e. industrial economists, either agree completely or agree with the following statement: 'Antitrust laws should be used vigorously to reduce monopoly power from its current level'. (23 per cent disagrees and 17 per cent is indifferent.) See Aiginger et al. (1998). Moreover, in the same survey, more than 73 per cent disagrees with the statement that 'International competition has made the regulation of monopolies an outdated policy'. These propositions are among those with the highest degree of consensus, out of a group of 44 propositions, with answers given by 114 respondents.

But now it is equally well known among economists that these antitrust policies can have a serious impact on the future development of any industry. Arguments have been given to point out that the implementation of antitrust action in one direction or another will provide the incentives of firms in industry to develop in one direction or another. In some cases, antitrust policies might give disincentives to firm growth. Overall, the consensus is that it will not. For instance, regarding competition against Asian countries, more than 50 per cent disagrees with the proposition that 'A tough competition policy could hinder US and European firms in the global competitive race against Japanese Keiretsus or against firms in the managed economies of the Tiger States'. But, in any event, the *differential* impact of antitrust policy in a country could interfere with the long-term competitiveness of that economy in much the same way that other elements of the legal and institutional framework in a country determine the evolution of an economy. See Barro and Sala-i-Martin (1995) for the impact of political-institutional elements on growth.

The impact of competition policies became altogether even more important as 'subsidiarity' developments in Europe induced all countries to install a competition law and antitrust authorities, whereas some countries didn't have them before. Therefore, in general, antitrust enforcement is becoming more pronounced in the European Community, with possible discrepancies between those countries who moved from laissez-faire to particular forms of antitrust laws vis-à-vis those who moved from laissez-faire to other forms of antitrust policy. These differences of course already existed between the countries that already had implemented antitrust policies.

In this paper, we briefly investigate in what directions antitrust policy can interfere with the future development of an economy. In order to do this, we borrow from related works to sketch the rationale and hence intentions of antitrust policies (Section 2). We then proceed in a third section by presenting a framework to analyse the working of antitrust policies. Here we rely on the general insights regarding antitrust policy of Section 2, but complement them by referring to general standards for comparing institutions on an economic basis. This enables us to identify relevant economic criteria for analysing antitrust legislation and in particular the policies of four countries in the European Community.

In a fourth section, we then enter the material for each of the four countries selected. The format chosen here is that of a synoptical table, strongly enhancing the possibility to engage in a cross-country comparison. However, the particular elements, relating to the *finesses* of the situation in each country are important too, and don't become clear from a synoptical table. Therefore, the additional elements that also relate to the particular implementation of certain features are discussed in the fifth section. They are equally important for reaching a proper judgement.

In a sixth section, we reflect on the way in which antitrust policies, especially divergent ones, have an impact on competitiveness, growth and ultimately employment. Finally, in a seventh section, we present our conclusions and suggest topics for policy reform.

2. THE ECONOMICS OF ANTITRUST POLICIES

In this section, we start by briefly sketching the idea of antitrust policies. We continue by pointing to the implications these policies can have, thereby already identifying the importance of criteria such as having for instance an efficiency defence clause. We conclude this section by identifying still other criteria to use when investigating antitrust policies.

2.1 Antitrust policy: origins and general ideas

This section is deliberately kept short. It is based on Van Cayseele and Van den Bergh (1999), which can be consulted for further reference. The perspective is an historical one: we start with the antecedents and then try to crystallise the important messages in the subsequent schools.

As mentioned already in the Introduction, at the time the Sherman Act came about, certainly not a majority of the profession was in favour of antitrust action. On the other hand, there certainly were important advocates for competition watchdogs among the classical economists. The important ideas that emerged were the following: healthy competition implies reciprocal rivalry and no government restrictions such as exclusive privileges. This last issue is quite important in view of the many 'national champions' in European countries that are exempt from antitrust legislation, on grounds that they are 'regulated' by a (captured) authority.

Neo-classical economics continued along these lines and clarified what could be considered to be a perfectly competitive market, hence introducing a yardstick that antitrust authorities could use to evaluate market structures in reality. For some time, failures were seen to be sufficient reasons for intervention, but this view quickly changed. Instead, only if government failures were to fall short of market failures would we have grounds for some action. While in many areas of social and economic policy, government failures will almost invariably be larger than market failures, antitrust action is of the policy type where one expects a priori not a lot of capture (see De Bondt and Van Cayseele, 1985). The reason is that antitrust is removed from redistributive policies and tends to have a permanent character.[2] Still, it raises criticism (see Bork, 1978).

Within the neoclassical paradigm, many openings towards and foundations of oligopoly theory were laid. At the same time, the first game theoretic models emerged. Most of these early game theoretical work was merely extending the framework of von Neumann and Morgenstern, more in particular elementary discussions of the Prisoner's Dilemma, while serious applications of the theory to industrial organisation only followed later.[3]

Before that, and starting in 1949 with Mason, the Structure-Conduct-Performance paradigm was developed. The followers of the S-C-P paradigm proclaimed that the performance of an industry uniquely followed from its conduct, which in turn was caused by its structure. Moreover, a set of structural criteria could be identified that would tell everything for each and every industry. As applied game theoretical work became more popular in the last half of the 1970s, it became clear that industry-specific features could not be left out of the equation. Yet, for the practical implementation of antitrust policy, at the present, we only find sectoral specialisation in the German Bundeskartellamt, although a trend towards this kind of specialisation nowadays also exists in other countries (see below).

The S-C-P paradigm was fiercely criticised by the Chicago School. Further elaboration resulted in a critical analysis of the barriers to entry doctrine introduced by Bain. When in practice the antitrust authorities had to distinguish between fixed costs and barriers to entry, erroneous judgement was bound to happen. This led to the contestability theory developed by Baumol, Panzar and Willig (1982), which, should it work, would be highly relevant for the European antitrust scene where the threat of import competition always has been seen as a substitute for monitoring domestic market structure. The Chicago School was also influential on many other issues, too numerous to discuss here. In subsequent revisions of the US Merger Guidelines, core ideas of the school strongly crowded out the older S-C-P views.

As we know, contestability theory is simply a high-tech version of the Bertrand duopoly model with standardised products. Few, if any real-world industries have ever been found to be contestable. Even the flagship example of the contestability theorists, passenger airlines, has been conclusively shown by empirical work not to be contestable. Theoretical work shows that even mild departures from the assumptions of perfect contestability lead to large departures from perfectly contestable performance, and hence robustness is weak (see also Van Cayseele and Furth, 1996).

Finally, the New Industrial Economics has integrated many criticisms by the Chicago School of the S-C-P paradigm within a new framework which is called the Bounds approach, see Sutton (1991 and 1998). Van Cayseele has argued elsewhere, see van Bergeijk et al. (1997), in view of the creation of the new Dutch Antitrust Authority, that an integration of the old I.O. (the S-C-P) and the new I.O. which is explicitly game theoretically founded is inevitable, unless many more means can be devoted to conduct New

Empirical Industrial Organisation exercises (e.g. Gasmi, et al., 1992) than are available at present. Therefore, the bounds approach which does not claim to tell what precisely will happen with the Lerner index after the merger, but rather in general gives an indication, is the first and most necessary step in any antitrust action. Only when serious concerns emerge from that initial analysis can a detailed sectoral study be conducted. Things of course look differently if an econometric analysis is available, but this will not often be the case. Further developments on the economics of antitrust are related amongst other things to localised competition, and can be found in Baker (1999).

2.2 Antitrust policy: dynamic aspects

The enforcement of antitrust laws interferes with the future development of firms in an industry. This has been known for some time in general, but only recently has an effort been made to document precisely what could happen as a result of too-tough antitrust action in a country.

In general, at least since Schumpeter (1934), it has been conjectured that firms operating in more concentrated industries and big firms tout court are more innovative. While Schumpeter was less outspoken and sometimes only mentions that there was no association between competition and innovation, see for instance Capitalism, Socialism and Democracy (1975), the current literature attributes these claims to him. More in particular, Tirole (1988) in his leading textbook classifies them as respectively the first and second Schumpeterian assumptions. For a detailed survey of the literature up to the 1990s, see Reinganum (1989). For a survey to date, see Van Cayseele (1998).

Hence, policies interfering with market structure or firm size will have effects on the growth of a country. While the evidence on this matter is inconclusive, it raises at least the question which group(s) of agents does it aim at? Or what welfare criterion is used? This can be answered in different ways, viz. (static) consumer surplus, consumer and producer surplus, consumer surplus of both current and future consumers, etc.

If for example the broadest definition is chosen, i.e. that in which welfare includes the surplus of both current and future consumers and producers, efficiency defence rules normally will show up in the legislation. Such rules allow the defendants to show that although their operations may harm consumers, the operation is beneficial overall, for instance, because of important cost reductions or serious technological progress that will benefit future generations of consumers.

At the European level, such efficiency defence rules are not always present, but they do apply when an agreement is under examination according to paragraph 3 of Art. 85. This article in principle forbids agreements, but there can be exceptions if these agreements contribute to productive or distribution efficiencies, or economic or technological progress.

At the 'national' level, efficiency defence rules are often present. This has the far-reaching implication that the 'one-stop-shop principle' does not mean that merely a division of the workload according to the size of the operation is established by the subsidiarity principle. On the contrary, it means that a division of powers has been achieved which can be far better explained by asymmetries in information (for instance regarding operating costs) and regulatory capture or other political-economic reasons, as shown by Smets and Van Cayseele (1995), where common agency theory was used to model firms that have to respond to either a national or a supranational authority.

2.3 Antitrust policy: further issues

Besides the just-mentioned identification of the targets: static consumer surplus, sum of consumer and producer surplus (welfare) or static and dynamic welfare, any antitrust policy also will have to answer the following questions:
a) market behaviour and/or market structure; and
b) ex ante or ex post.

Regarding a), competition policies mostly target at interfering with anti-competitive behaviour, which is hard to define but related to practices such as cartel agreements, price discrimination, tie-in-sales, etc.

Nowadays, most competition policies in addition control market structure and can contest the creation of monopolies or 'too strong positions', because the power exists to object to operations (mergers, acquisitions) that lead to these positions. It can be argued that merger control is not neutral. This is shown in the article by Bittlingmayer (1985). If agreements tend to be strictly forbidden, along the lines of Art. 85, but there is no control on mergers, then of course it is clear that in order to cooperate, firms should not attempt to reach an agreement but should rather directly merge. This phenomenon was empirically documented for both the UK (see Swann et al., 1974) and the US where it is said that a strict enforcement of the Sherman Act has triggered a merger wave. Therefore, the presence of merger control needs to be documented explicitly, also for other reasons to be mentioned below.

Moreover, the covering of this item should be in-depth, also focusing on the precise implementation of merger control, because there exists still another channel through which antitrust policies interfere with the long-run growth of a firm in industry, which is even more subtle and barely documented. We briefly expose it here.

If merger controls define the relevant antitrust market very narrowly, diversification will be easier than in the case that the market is defined more broadly. This might re-direct R&D towards broader applicability: if the competition laws do not oppose acquisitions in related industries, which nonetheless allow for a substantial strengthening of the firm's position, then these conglomerates will arise. This in turn will have a feedback effect on innovative activity, for if the second Schumpeterian hypothesis stating that there is a positive relationship between firm size and innovative success is true, these conglomerates will out-perform their single industry rivals who couldn't grow through diversification due to excessively tough antitrust policies in their country.

This conclusion however changes if the firms need to cooperate in R&D in order to achieve innovation. The risk that this cooperation will be forbidden under antitrust laws is higher as markets are defined more narrowly, raising serious concerns among researchers (see for example Gilbert and Sunshine, 1995 or Langenfeld and Scheffman, 1989).

Up to 1990, European Competition Law focused exclusively on anti-competitive behaviour. Art. 85 of the Treaty of Rome forbids cartel agreements while Art. 86 of the same Treaty permits the punishment of abuses of a dominant position. Starting in 1990, however, a new ruling (more in particular the EC merger control regulation 4064/89) opened the way for interfering with the market structure.

Regarding b), ex ante or ex post, Arts. 85 and 86 involve an ex post control, whereas the 1990 regulation involves a control ex ante. At first sight, the distinction between ex ante and ex post might seem not all that important. This view however is not quite accurate, certainly not if taken into consideration from an economic point of view. Ex ante policies indeed involve operations or agreements to be cleared in advance, which points to regulation that has to be passed, and hence analysed in terms of effectiveness and efficiency, but in addition, it involves a sufficient belief in the economics of industrial organisation. This is often problematic if the laws have to be implemented by people who lack sufficient training in this field, especially since it is in quick evolution. This for instance becomes clear in the US when the Merger Control Guidelines are revised. In the 1968 version, the viewpoint was very 'structuralistic'. If the C4 concentration ratios would exceed a particular value, mergers between firms each owning a market share of 5 per cent would be opposed. Also giving problems would be mergers of a firm having 10 per cent of the market with one having [4] per cent, etc.

In the 1984 version of these US Merger Guidelines, the structuralist view was still very present; only the concentration ratio had changed. More in particular, a merger in an industry with an Hirschman-Herfindahl concentration ratio (HHI) below 1000 would not pose many problems. While it is well known that there exists a relationship between the HHI and the Lerner index, a measure of static welfare, it is equally well known that this relationship also depends on a number of assumptions that have been challenged. It was therefore not until the 1992 version that the novel theories of industrial organisation were seriously reflected in the Merger Guidelines, notwithstanding the fact that much of the antitrust litigation triggered by the 1984 guidelines turned out to be without grounds (see Van Cayseele and Van den Bergh, 1999).

Therefore, unless we have reliable models of the link between market structure and performance, or of the link between certain behavioural practices and agreements (exclusive dealing, tie-in sales, strategic export cartels) and performance, and in addition can rely on experts in the matter to join antitrust authorities, ex ante antitrust policy will imply:

- regulatory costs to industry in order to comply ex ante, and
- uncertainty regarding the benefits of antitrust action.

Is all of this so different for the ex post actions? In addition to the economic insights, which also will have to be present here, there is the possibility of getting caught red-handed. i.e. documents can be confiscated, the evolution of market shares, or prices will show some trends, etc. Therefore, successful enforcement ex post is likely to be less dependent on the presence of expertise than ex ante enforcement is. This of course does not imply that ex ante enforcement should be abandoned in favour of ex post enforcement, for detecting collusion from the data can be as hard as simulating the effects on performance resulting from a structural change.

2.4 Conclusions

There are at least three items following from the economics of antitrust law to keep in mind when evaluating antitrust policies:
a) Which goals does antitrust law aim at?
b) Does it try to achieve these goals by interfering with certain forms of conduct, or does it also operate on market structure?

c)   Does it operate ex ante or ex post?

In our economic analysis, we found that a) has implications in terms of whether the possibility of an efficiency defence should be present or not. Item b) implies we have to check whether there are merger controls and how in fact they are decided. Finally, fact c) will lead us to ask whether experts are involved or not. In the analysis we perform regarding the operation of antitrust policies, the reader also will see this reflected in the questions we try to answer.

3. AN ANALYTICAL FRAMEWORK FOR COMPARING ANTITRUST LEGISLATION

In this section, we complement the particular items to investigate in antitrust policies obtained from the previous section with a few general viewpoints pertaining to economic policy in general. This leads to a list of criteria which is put forward by means of a table in the second subsection, and filled up in the next section.

3.1 General criteria for the economic evaluation of institutions

In analysing both legislation and the operation of an environmental regulator, an antitrust authority or a central bank, etc., economists have devised criteria according to their knowledge mainly in the domain of the New Institutional Economics. As such, it seems relevant to ask what authorities are involved, whether these authorities operate independently or under (direct or indirect) political control. Related is the question whether decisions have to be motivated in one direction or another, whether this motivation is made public and whether appeal is possible. Also, to some extent, how the authority is organised. In addition, as argued in the Introduction, antitrust at the national level is a fairly novel matter for a number of European countries. Hence, the availability of expertise but certainly the 'culture' will be influenced by the laws – if any – that preceded the current antitrust law.

Much of these criteria are 'qualitative', for example it might be the case that antitrust officials are appointed by a minister. It could nevertheless be the case that they operate quite independently. Therefore, we will also try to develop 'quantitative' criteria. By this we mean the 'triggers' that activate antitrust action. These triggers are most obvious in the case of merger controls since operations above a certain threshold will imply ex ante investigation. But certain types of conduct might equally well trigger antitrust action, and therefore it is worthwhile to describe as objectively and clearly as possible whether there are explicit rules regarding certain types of conduct.

Last but not least, antitrust policy is not likely to be effective when all the sectors where it could matter remain outside the reach of the law. Therefore we need to document the exceptions, or in this case, the exemptions. These could be on merger control or on anti-competitive conduct, i.e. relating to the matter of competition policy. But they could also exclude sectors at large (the government sector with all the public companies) or very specific industries (telecommunications, banking, insurance etc.) Sometimes, there also could be exemptions for very small companies or export cartels. These elements complete the overall picture we want to have when reaching a judgement on competition policy.

A final remark regards the choice of countries. All that has been said up to now is related to the rows, but how are the columns selected? Our motivation mainly is 'data driven' in that we have chosen the countries with which we are the mostly closely acquainted. But there is more in that our choice has singled out two small countries (on which we also have performed extensive empirical analysis on which we will report) and two large ones. This allows us to make a comparison between antitrust in small and large countries and hence to detect size-driven differences, if any. A priori, one should be conscious that these distinctions might be strongly present in that small countries can rely more heavily on import competition to discipline anti-competitive agreements.

3.2 A synoptical table

Bringing together all the criteria discussed in the previous section, we can produce a synoptical table in which we made five broad categories. In order to facilitate the comparison, we have also indicated for each criterion the section of the text in which this criterion is discussed. In the next section, we will attempt to systematically complete this table.

Table 4.1 A synoptical table

	Belgium	The Netherlands	Germany	Italy
Description of the law				
General	4.1.1.1	4.1.1.2	4.1.1.3	4.1.1.4
Scope	4.1.2.1	4.1.2.2	4.1.2.3	4.1.2.4
Authorities involved?	4.1.3.1	4.1.3.2	4.1.3.3	4.1.3.4
Where to appeal?	4.1.4.1	4.1.4.2	4.1.4.3	4.1.4.4
Implementation of the law				
Who decides?	4.2.1.1	4.2.1.2	4.2.1.3	4.2.1.4
Experts involved?	4.2.2.1	4.2.2.2	4.2.2.3	4.2.2.4
Motivation required?	4.2.3.1	4.2.3.2	4.2.3.3	4.2.3.4
Qualitative analysis				
Decisive authority Politically appointed?	4.3.1.1	4.3.1.2	4.3.1.3	4.3.1.4
Decisive authority Temporarily appointed?	4.3.2.1	4.3.2.2	4.3.2.3	4.3.2.4
Advisory authority Politically appointed?	4.3.3.1	4.3.3.2	4.3.3.3	4.3.3.4
Advisory authority Temporarily appointed? *Quantitative analysis*	4.3.4.1	4.3.4.2	4.3.4.3	4.3.4.4
Description of triggers	4.4.1.1	4.4.1.2	4.4.1.3	4.4.1.4
Analysis of triggers	4.4.2.1	4.4.2.2	4.4.2.3	4.4.2.4
Exemptions				
Anti-competitive behaviour	4.5.1.1	4.5.1.2	4.5.1.3	4.5.1.4
Merger control (sectors, government)	4.5.2.1	4.5.2.2	4.5.2.3	4.5.2.4

3.3 Conclusions

Antitrust legislation and competition policy can be judged on both particular criteria regarding the aims of this policy and general criteria related to all sorts of economic policies. By bringing together both of these angles, we will attempt to detect fundamental differences in the laws of the different countries. Without jumping to the conclusions, we already can state that such differences exist. Contrary to those who have taken the easy approach, arguing that every national law is some copy of the European Treaty, we find clear-cut differences that have economic implications. However, before pointing these out, we use the framework put forward in this section to document the situation in the different countries at hand.

4. A COMPARISON OF ANTITRUST LAWS IN FOUR EUROPEAN COUNTRIES

The evidence is presented by category, sequentially skimming each country under investigation. Each category briefly reviews the critical information it wants to present and the reason why it is important.

4.1 Description of the law

Whereas this title could be used for nearly all the following subsections as well, since they all describe antitrust legislation, we use the title here in the very strict sense: we give an account of the legislation regarding antitrust.[4] Specifically we ask:

- Since when is it effective and are there antecedents (4.1.1 General)?
- What does it target (4.1.2 Scope)?
- Which authorities are involved (4.1.3)?
- Where to appeal (4.1.4)?

4.1.1 General description

4.1.1.1 Belgium
- Law of 5 August 1991 to protect economic competition ('Wet tot bescherming van de Economische Mededinging'). Completed with a series of Royal Decrees. Operational since 1 April 1993.
- Replacing an ineffective law of 1960 ('Wet tegen het misbruik van een dominante positie'), mostly concerned about trade practices, implemented by regular courts, and a system of generalised price controls that persisted until the 1990s (See Sleuwaegen and Van Cayseele, 1998).

4.1.1.2 The Netherlands
- Law of 1 January 1998 ('Mededingingswet')
- Replacing a very permissive law dating 13 November 1958, which permitted anti-competitive agreements, cartels and dominant positions unless it was explicitly shown that harm was done to the general interest.

4.1.1.3 Germany

- The latest version of the German Act against Restraints on Competition ('Gesetz gegen Wettbewerbsbeschränkungen', hereafter GWB) is operational since 1 January 1999.
- The original GWB dates back to 1957 and was only concerned with restricting anti-competitive behaviour. There have been several amendments of the GWB as a response to the various shortcomings that became visible over the years. The control of concentrations became an objective in 1973 while the amendment of 1980 defined the concept of a dominant position. Currently, the 6th amended version of the GWB is operative.

4.1.1.4 Italy

The Italian competition law (no. 287/90) is relatively recent (10 October 1990) and it resembles very strictly the analogous European Community law (Arts. 85 and 86 of the Treaty of Rome). It is based on the same architecture: a) Art. 2 (analogous to the Art. 85 of the Treaty) is about agreements that substantially restrict competition; b) Art. 3 (like the Art. 86 of the Treaty) is against abuses of dominant position; c) Art. 4 (like the Art. 85, para. 3 of the Treaty) provides a temporary exemption under very strict circumstances for restrictive agreements; d) Arts. 5-6 deal with the ex ante merger control. In Art. 1, it is clearly stated that the competition law 'shall be interpreted in accordance with the principles of the European Community competition law'.

4.1.2 Scope

4.1.2.1 Belgium

- Forbids all agreements or factual joint behaviour that limit competition. An explicit mentioning of some of this behaviour is given, see 4.4.1.1 'Triggers/Belgium' below.
- Forbids the abuse of a dominant position, where again this is explicit.
- Requires mergers above certain thresholds to be cleared in advance.

4.1.2.2 The Netherlands

- Forbids all cartel agreements that limit competition.
- Requires mergers above certain thresholds to be cleared in advance.

4.1.2.3 Germany

- Forbids all types of vertical and/or horizontal behaviour that limits competition.
- Forbids the abuse of a dominant position, as defined by the GWB.
- Requires mergers above certain thresholds to be cleared in advance.

4.1.2.4 Italy
- The aim of the law is to enlarge the role of the market economy 'protecting and guaranteeing the right of free enterprise'. It has to be stressed that the Italian economy until the last decade was substantially influenced by the state through public utilities and state-owned companies, not to mention the very intrusive regulation in almost all industrial and service sectors. The competition law and the large programme of privatisation, implemented in the past years, have produced a significant change in this framework. The recent establishment of regulation agencies (the so-called Authorities), not dependent on the government, is an important element of this new scenario.

4.1.3 Authorities involved

4.1.3.1 Belgium
- Council for Competition ('Raad voor de Mededinging') is an Independent Administrative Legal College taking all the decisions, composed of 12 experts and 12 judges).
- Service for Competition ('Dienst voor de Mededinging') (Under the responsibility of the Minister of Economic Affairs, prepares all the decisions, and investigates), composed of civil servants.

4.1.3.2 The Netherlands
- Dutch Competition Authority ('Nederlandse Mededingingsautoriteit', or NMa for short), with the Head of the Department taking decisions. It is divided into three operational sections:
  - OTO: Research, Implementation and Exemptions which looks after cartels and treats exemptions;
  - CoCo: Control of Concentrations: treats mergers and acquisitions;
  - BBB: Contestation and Appeal: treating appeal and determines sanctions.

4.1.3.3 Germany
- The Federal Cartel Office ('Bundeskartellamt') is an independent Federal High Authority. It is responsible for most of the antitrust enforcement in Germany. The Federal Cartel Office has a divisional structure, decisions are taken by one of the ten divisions. Each division has jurisdiction for specific sectors or for certain types of contracts.[5]
- The Federal Minister of the Economy ('Bundesminister für Wirtschaft') has limited responsibilities.

- The State Cartel Offices ('Oberste Landesbehörde'), who are a part of the Ministry for Economic Affairs, are responsible for cases with a regional dimension.
- The Monopoly Commission ('Monopolkommission') studies the development of market concentration and monopoly power in the German markets; it has an advisory role.

4.1.3.4 Italy

- The competition policy is enforced by the Autorità Garante della Concorrenza e del Mercato (Authority Guaranteeing Competition and Market, hereafter Competition Authority), a body formed by a Chairman and other four members. The Competition Authority is appointed jointly by the Presidents of the two houses of Parliament. This agency has the right to open an investigation to ascertain whether a firm is abusing a dominant position or a merger creates (or strengthens) a dominant position and, finally, whether an agreement restricts competition. At the end of the procedure, which allows all involved parties to express their opinions (also submitting reports), the Competition Authority takes the decision.

4.1.4 Appeal

4.1.4.1 Belgium

- Court of Appeal in Brussels, this is the regular court, also treating appeal to other 'economic' legislation, composed of high-level magistrates ('Raadsheren'). No other authority (e.g. the Minister of Economic Affairs) can overrule decisions taken by the Council for Competition.

4.1.4.2 The Netherlands

- Court in Rotterdam.

4.1.4.3 Germany

- Appeals can be made by any party involved in a case, to the Court of Appeal ('Oberlandesgerichte') of the district in which the Federal Cartel Office is located.
- Against decisions of the Court of Appeal, an appeal on points of law can be filed with the Federal Supreme Court ('Bundesgerichtshof').

4.1.4.4 Italy

- Appeals against the decisions of the Competition Authority must be filed before the Latium Region Administrative Court.

- A second-degree appeal has to be filed before the Supreme Administrative Court ('Council of State').

4.1.5 Conclusions

From the general description of the antitrust laws in different countries, it already becomes clear that there exist marked differences in many respects. While most countries have had competition legislation in some format or action for a few decades, most countries have only recently designed the appropriate infrastructure to implement the national antitrust laws that followed the Maastricht Treaty. Here also some marked differences emerge. Some countries have kept the authority under political control, while others such as Belgium have chosen to embed it in the legal order. At the present, we don't wish to judge which system is the best, but certainly in the perspective of tackling the implementation of the law in the next section, these differences have to be kept in the back of our mind.

4.2 Implementation of the law

This section is a follow-up to the previous section. Besides the formal elements, we answer a number of questions on the focus of the decision centre (4.2.1 Who decides?) and the economic expertise involved (4.2.2 Experts involved?). Also, how 'open' is the decision-making process (4.2.3 Motivation required?)

4.2.1 Who decides?

4.2.1.1 Belgium
- The Council for Competition. The Service, after investigation, proposes a decision, a hearing with the parties involved is fixed within a delay of 30 days.

4.2.1.2 The Netherlands
- The Dutch antitrust authority.
- Regarding mergers, the head of the NMa decides, but in case of refusal the Minister of Economic Affairs can overrule if it is shown that the merger is in the general interest.

4.2.1.3 Germany
- The appropriate division of the Federal Cartel Office decides in cases regarding anti-competitive behaviour (vertical and horizontal agreements).
- For concentrations the decision of the (division of the) Federal Cartel Office can be overruled by the Minister of Economic Affairs for reasons of public interest, after consulting the Monopoly Commission.
- The Minister of Economic Affairs has the power to allow cartels, if he judges that the existence of such a cartel is beneficial for the public.

4.2.1.4 Italy
- Usually the Authority takes the decision to open an investigation as a consequence of complaints on conduct deemed to be in violation of the competition law. The Authority can also start a formal procedure without having received any complaints if it suspects some violation of the law. The investigation is carried on by the Directorate[6] responsible for the inquiry phase. After the final hearing, the Authority takes the decision (by a majority vote) in a separate meeting.

4.2.2 Experts involved?

4.2.2.1 Belgium
- Except for a few experts, the Council was composed of individuals with little previous experience or knowledge of antitrust policy.
- Also the Service had no prior knowledge of competition policy and consisted of civil servants who were transferred from the price control service. No training sessions were organised the first years. The Service was seriously understaffed.

4.2.2.2 The Netherlands
- The Dutch antitrust authority is over the three operational services which taken together comprise more than 100 well trained economists and lawyers. Prior to implementation, many training sessions with both academic and non-academic experts, both in the country and abroad, have been organised.

4.2.2.3 Germany
- The Federal Cartel Office has about 250 employees, approximately 110 of whom are senior officials and employees with degrees in law or economics.

- The Monopolies Commission consists of five expert members, who have special knowledge and experience in the fields of economics, business administration, social policy, technology or commercial law.

4.2.2.4 Italy
- The staff of the Competition Authority is formed by highly skilled economists and lawyers. Therefore external technical assistance is not often needed.
- It has also to be considered that, up to now, following the European approach, quantitative analysis, which could require econometric advice, was exceptionally applied. In few circumstances when a very technical sector was under examination following the proposal of the competent Directorate, the Authority took the decision to be supported by external technical assistance, which was usually provided through a written report. This document could be seen by the parties involved in the procedure. Also the parties could provide reports prepared by their own experts.

4.2.3 Motivation required?

4.2.3.1 Belgium
- The Council publishes its decision in the official State Gazette (Belgisch Staatsblad). These decisions include both facts (as long as they don't violate business secrets – parties concerned have the right to indicate what they consider to be business secrets – and the analysis through which the decision was reached.
- Third parties concerned have the right to ask to be heard in the hearing.

4.2.3.2 The Netherlands
- The Dutch antitrust authority has its most important decisions on an internet site.[7] The decisions of the antitrust authority are also published in the Official Newspaper (Staatscourant). Further the Dutch antitrust authority prepares a yearly activity report. This report is, together with the comments of the Minister of Economic Affairs, discussed and approved by the Members of Parliament.

4.2.3.3 Germany
- The decisions of the cartel authorities are published in the Federal Gazette. If the decision is made by a State Cartel Office, it will also be published in a gazette of the respective land.
- The cartel authority shall state the reasons of its decisions.

4.2.3.4 Italy

- Like every other administrative decision, the ones taken by the Competition Authority have to have a motivation. Every decision is published in the weekly Bulletin of the Authority.[8] The motivations for the merger cases that do not request any further investigations, and therefore are not contested by the Authority, are not very detailed. Conversely, the final decision of an investigation is usually reported in very elaborate documents. In particular, all the main constituent parts of an antitrust case are carefully presented. Special attention is paid to the market definition analysis, to the detection of a dominant position and to the analysis of the object and the effects of the infringement of the competition. Separate motivation is required if a fine has to be inflicted. Deficiency of motivation on some constituent part of the decision is a sufficient reason to obtain its rejection by appealing before Regional Administrative Court.

4.2.4 Conclusions

As to be expected, countries that were quick to adopt the competition policy suggested by the Maastricht Treaty, as did Belgium, had to start in a very amateurish way. While a lot of expertise has been acquired in the meantime, serious problems have been encountered, which potentially could jeopardise the future of antitrust policy. New legal developments however indicate that a 'division of powers' in favour of an independent administrative body. Together with some budgetary autonomy, this position is one closely mimicking the American model, and unique on the European continent.

In the Netherlands, implementation of the law was less haphazard. As in the best of Dutch tradition regarding expertise of civil servants, the NMa was started with well trained economists and lawyers. Still, the authority remains under the political supervision of the Minister of Economic Affairs.

Regarding the transparency of decision-making, all countries have adopted strict rules of disclosing the elements that have influenced the decision-making, so as to safeguard the rights of the defence.

4.3 Qualitative analysis

The previous two sections mostly described the different national antitrust policies; the present section enters into analysis. More in particular, qualitative analysis, by which we mean policy elements that hardly can be expressed in data, the matter mostly being the influence of politics on decision-making, both instantaneously or after some time when the decisive authority needs to be appointed.

4.3.1 Decisive Authority politically appointed?

4.3.1.1 Belgium
- The Minister of Economic Affairs proposes the Members of the Council for Competition, which have to be selected according to the law for their expertise in the matter, or have to belong to the legal order.

4.3.1.2 The Netherlands
- The members of the Dutch competition policy are civil servants.

4.3.1.3 Germany
- The Chairman and the members of the divisions of the Federal Cartel Office are civil servants. They must be qualified for holding judicial office or for senior rank in the civil service; the Chairman shall be qualified for holding judicial office. The GWB stipulates further that the members of the Federal Cartel Office must not be owners, chairmen, or members of the board of management or the supervisory board, of any enterprise, cartel or trade and industry association of professional organisation.

4.3.1.4 Italy
- The Competition Authority is one of the so-called Independent Authorities. Independence means that the Competition Authority takes its decisions without being influenced by political power. More specifically, the Authority is appointed by the Speakers of the Chamber of Deputies and the Senate. This mechanism of election, which requires a very broad consensus, limits the influence of a specific party. Moreover, the government cannot exert any direct influence on this process of selection. Secondly, independence is also related to the eligibility criteria. In particular, the Chairman has to be politically independent and he is chosen from a list of persons who have already held a very important institutional responsibility. Also the other four members have to be independent and they are chosen among university professors, judges of the Supreme Court of Appeals, Council of State and the Court of Auditors.
- Therefore we can conclude that the Authority is not dependent on political parties and, in particular, not on the government. This independence is apparent in the numerous notifications sent by the Competition Authority to the Parliament or to the government referring

to existing or draft legislative acts that introduce some restrictions on competition.

- There are only two exceptions to the principle of absence of political influence on competition policy. According to Art. 25 ('Provisions of Government powers over concentrations'), para. 1, of the law no. 287/90, a concentration, which would be prohibited in normal circumstances, could on the contrary be allowed when major general interests related to the process of European integration are involved. This possibility has to be regulated by general criteria laid down by the Council of Ministers. Up to now the government has not yet fixed those criteria. Para. 2 of the same section allows the Prime Minister to prohibit a concentration in the case of one of the involved undertakings having its headquarters in a country applying discriminatory measures against mergers involving Italian firms.

- While law no. 287/90 provides for independence from political power, the code of conduct of the Italian Competition Authority prevents the staff from being influenced by undertakings involved or which could be involved in a procedure (Art. 6 on conflict of interest and Art. 9 on gifts).

4.3.2 Decisive Authority temporarily appointed?

4.3.2.1 Belgium
- Appointment of Members of the Council is for a period of six years. Since appointments are not full time, both the experts and the magistrates have other appointments, often lifetime, and as such don't depend even indirectly on political goodwill. The Council also doesn't offer career opportunities.

4.3.2.2 The Netherlands
- As civil servants, the officials working in the NMa have lifetime employment. They do not depend on the political order for promotion.

4.3.2.3 Germany
- The GWB stipulates that members and chairmen of the divisions of the Federal Cartel Office will be appointed for life.

4.3.2.4 Italy
- The members of the Competition Authority are appointed for a non-renewable period of seven years.

4.3.3 Advisory Authority politically appointed?

4.3.3.1 Belgium

- There is only one advisory authority, the Commission for Competition. The advice is concerning general changes in legislation and policy, for example, the thresholds for merger control, but not regarding particular cases. This Commission is composed by representatives of the social partners, who have advised on many other aspects of economic, social and environmental policy.
- There is no 'Merger Task Force' that analyses the decisions taken by the Council in a systematic way, as is done with decision-making at the level of the European Community.

4.3.3.2 The Netherlands

- To our knowledge, there is no advisory authority, but there is a section 'marktwerking' operating within the Central Planning Bureau (CPB, also under the responsibility of the Minister of Economic Affairs). This section is engaged in analysing sectors and industries, independently of the cases at hand. Members of CPB are also civil servants.

4.3.3.3 Germany

- In general there is no advisory authority. Only in the case that the Minister of Economic Affairs want to overrule a decision of the Federal Cartel Office, the Monopoly Commission acts as an advisory authority. Members of the Monopoly Commission are also civil servants.

4.3.3.4 Italy

- In the framework of the Italian competition policy there is no general advisory authority. In three specific sectors, namely banking, insurance and telecommunications, a consultative procedure has to be implemented before the final decision is taken. In the banking sector, where the competition policy is enforced by the Bank of Italy, the decision is taken after having heard the opinion of the Competition Authority. Conversely, in the insurance and telecommunications sectors, the Competition Authority takes the final decision after hearing the regulators of the two sectors (ISVAP and Autorità per le garanzie delle telecomunicazioni, respectively). This institutional mechanism should preserve the balance of the several public interests involved in an antitrust decision.

4.3.4 Advisory Authority temporarily appointed?

4.3.4.1 Belgium
- Appointments in the Commission are also appointed for six years.

4.3.4.2 The Netherlands
- CPB officials have lifetime employment.

4.3.4.3 Germany
- The members of the Monopolies Commission are appointed for a term of four years by the Federal President after a proposal by the Federal Government. Members can be re-appointed.

4.3.4.4 Italy
- In general there is no advisory authority.

4.3.5 Conclusions

In most national systems of competition policy, a judicious balance of powers can be detected, although the particular format is quite different. Completely independent of any political influence, the Belgian Council for Competition can decide autonomously on mergers, abuse of market power, investigate industries, etc. Belonging to the legal order, it has prosecution authority and can impose fines. For the material support, it however depends on a Service, which has to answer to the Minister. Regarding general advice concerning legislation and policy, the Council is matched with a Commission, which is composed by representatives of the social partners.

The Dutch model achieves the balance of powers in quite a different set-up. The decision-making is not strictly independent of politics since decisions are taken by government officials for which the Minister ultimately resumes the responsibility. The checks and balances however are built in by among other things an independent advisory unit, which can look into the decisions taken and is able to investigate sectors.

4.4 Quantitative analysis

This section continues to characterise the operation of antitrust policy but tries to give a quantitative assessment. Regarding merger control for instance, the thresholds themselves can be quite telling. This can be complemented by data regarding the number of cases dealt with. Also regarding the abuse of dominant positions, the enumeration of what is mentioned explicitly in the law to be considered as a conviction is telling. Here, also the number of cases investigated provides additional statistical information.

Therefore, we will first go into what we have called the 'triggers', both in respect to merger control, abuse of dominant positions or any other element that is considered in violation of keeping markets competitive. In short, triggers are the causes by which the authorities are alerted and antitrust action is to follow. Then we will analyse these triggers and quantitatively assess the impact of competition policy.

4.4.1 Description of triggers

4.4.1.1 Belgium

- Regarding merger control, any operation with a combined market share of 25 per cent of the relevant antitrust market is reached has to be cleared in advance, if also the merging firms jointly realise (worldwide) sales of approximately 3 billion BEF. (74 million euro).
- Regarding agreements and abuse of dominant positions, the law explicitly prohibits all agreements or coordinated behaviour that limits competition. More explicitly is mentioned those agreements that:
  - directly or indirectly determine prices or other terms of contract;
  - limit or control production, technological development or investment;
  - divide the market; and
  - discriminate (in price or otherwise).

Abuse of dominant position is defined as using a dominant position to achieve any of the above.

4.4.1.2. The Netherlands

- Merger control has any operation in which the firms together reach sales above 250 million guilders (113 million euro) and two of them having 30 million guilders (13.6 million euro) in the Netherlands to be cleared in advance.
- Regarding agreements and abuse of dominant positions, the following is mentioned: It is forbidden to engage in collective vertical-pricing agreements, exclusive dealing and geographical market division. Also considered abusive is any form of predatory pricing.

4.4.1.3 Germany

- The merging of enterprises shall be notified to the Federal Cartel Office, if during the completed business year preceding the merger the participating enterprises recorded an aggregate worldwide turnover of more than 1 billion DM, and if the domestic turnover of at least one participating undertaking was above 50 million DM. All concentrating shall be notified to the Federal Cartel Office prior to being put into effect.

- The GBW states that all agreements and decisions made by enterprises or associations of enterprises will have no effect if they are likely to influence, by restraining competition, production and market conditions. Also the abuse of a dominant position ('Misbrauch einer marktbeherrschenden Stellung') is forbidden.

4.4.1.4 Italy

- Turnover thresholds are established in relation to the duty to notify a concentration to the Competition Authority. In particular, at the present time, a merger has to be notified in advance if the combined domestic turnover of the involved undertakings is higher than It. L. 710 billion (euro 367 million) or the turnover of the undertaking which is to be acquired is more than It.L.71 billion (euro 37 million). These two thresholds change every year according to the inflation rate. Only the notified mergers are subject to prohibition if a dominant position is created or strengthened.

- It has to be emphasised that, contrary to the European merger regulation, the two thresholds are both individually qualified for notification duty: therefore if a large firm wants to buy a very small economic activity (even a simple shop) it has to present in advance a formal notification. On the other hand, also mergers not completely insignificant but realised by undertakings that jointly do not have a significant economic dimension have to be notified. Many qualified experts observe that this system based on two recursive thresholds puts an excessive and unnecessary stress both on firms and on the Competition Authority. The argument appears self-evident when we consider the number of notifications and the number of procedures started by the Authority in the presupposition of a creation of a dominant position (345 and 2, respectively, in 1998).

- In the early stage of the application of the merger control, mergers also involving undertakings belonging to the same group were notified to the Authority. Since 1995, following a clarification of the Competition Authority, these concentrations are no longer notified. Therefore, only mergers between independent undertakings are now notified.

4.4.2 Analysis of triggers

4.4.2.1 Belgium

Quite particular for the Belgian case is the prevalence of two triggers: market share and sales volume. This is quite different from the EC level and other countries but reminiscent of earlier versions of the US Department of Justice Merger Guidelines, and has raised problems in the past. Those companies that do not meet the sales threshold often try to redefine the relevant market as broadly as possible, so as to argue that they haven't reached a market share of 25 per cent. However, by doing so, that they often forget that they create a precedent that implies that future operations although having a more diversified nature, will also be considered to be mergers. A notable example was a small producer of soft drinks who bought another brand of soft drinks with local distribution. The firm argued that the relevant market included all non-alcoholic drinks, such as coffee and tea. A year or two later, the firm in its strategy of growth found it a good idea to acquire the distribution of a brand of tea. Since it had argued that the relevant market included tea and coffee as well as soft drinks, it had to justify that it wasn't building up a dominant position in this market. While defining the market very broadly in order not to face merger control, there thus comes negative feedback from possible future operations. On the other hand, by defining the market very broadly, once accepted, rivals who plan a diversification in any of the submarkets that are grouped together as the relevant market will have also to pass merger control. Again this opens the way to misuse of the antitrust law, and the erection of barriers to entry.

The market share criterion therefore has been heavily debated. Another critique is that by using it, one mixes up two phases. In a first stage it is said, the only purpose is to verify whether an investigation has to proceed. If a company is big, the operation has to be checked. In this second stage, market shares can be used to decide whether an excessively strong position is being created.

We don't tend to follow this argument against the market share criterion. The reason is that in small countries (such as Belgium), the sales criterion alone is not sufficient in that monopolies can be created in certain markets even with the sales criterion not being met – unless the sales criterion is then placed at a very low level - at which nearly all the companies that are engaged in some form of export would be involved. This cannot be the purpose either. The new proposal to abolish the market share criterion thus can only be backed with the first (entry barrier) type of argument. One should consider in addition also local sales criteria, as is the case in the Netherlands.

Since the thresholds initially were much lower (1 billion BEF in sales and a market share of 20 per cent), most activity of the Belgian antitrust authority has been regarding mergers, hence less experience has been accumulated regarding the infringement of the cartel agreement prohibition or the abuse of dominant positions. Nonetheless, a few complaints regarding the abuse of market power have been treated with great expertise, leading to a more competitive market structure. In some other cases, the law mainly has served to solve disputes among members of professional orders, notably lawyers.

Finally, regarding agreements, in a few cases a group of small firms has asked an exemption, mainly for investing in higher performing logistics, sometimes in view of strengthening an international position.

4.4.2.2 The Netherlands
As already mentioned, the merger control threshold also is two-fold here, focusing on both worldwide and national sales. Since the law is very recent and only mergers for which there exists a presumption that they might be anti-competitive need to obtain a licence, up to now very few cases needed investigation. The same holds for violations of the prohibition to reach cartel agreements.

The few cases that have been dealt with do not seem to have been problematic. In general, a deep analysis seems to proceed decision-making.

4.4.2.3 Germany
The German law is quite similar to the European insofar that it is the combined turnover triggers of the companies involved in a concentration that prompts an investigation. Notification is mandatory if a concentration satisfies the turnover criterion.

Once the actual investigation starts a number of other factors, including the market share, are taken into account. Much as in regulation 4064/89 the GWB specifies when a concentration will create or strengthen a dominant position.

Merger control was introduced as an objective of the cartel authorities in 1973. In the period 1973-98, the German cartel authorities have stopped 127 concentrations in total. Since the end of the 1980s the yearly number of notified concentrations has been around 1,500. In most of these cases a large company is acquiring a small or very small enterprise. Concentrations between big firms are usually controlled at a European level. In 1998 a total of 1,888 concentrations were examined, of which 12 were stopped. In most of these 12 cases the federal cartel authorities judged that the concentrations would lead to the strengthening of an existing dominant position.[9]

4.4.2.4 Italy

Market share analysis plays a much more crucial role with respect to all three possible antitrust actions (merger control, abuse of dominant position and agreement control). When a procedure related to a merger or to an abuse of dominant procedure has been started, the market share is the first step of the inquiry. Usually market share higher than 35-40 per cent is an important piece of evidence. In normal circumstances a market share higher than 60 per cent represents strong evidence of dominant position (those ratios are not reported in the 287/90 law but emerge from the application of antitrust policy). Also when analysing restrictive agreements the share of the market comes into play because the violation of the law depends on the relevance of the agreement (mainly measured in terms of the market share). Usually a *de minimis* argument applies: therefore, following the European approach (see Commission Communication on the minor agreements), the agreement has been considered relevant by the Authority if the involved undertakings have a cumulative market share higher than 5 per cent.

In defining market thresholds, the Competition Authority has always kept in mind the final justification of this operational step. Therefore when agreements were concerned, the analysis always focused on detecting the restriction on competition. If it emerges clearly that the agreement under examination was restricting the freedom of competition, the market definition analysis played a minor role and was strongly influenced by the nature of the restriction.,

As to the merger procedure, in which the market definition plays a decisive role, sometimes the conclusion was reached by observing not only the substitution among products but also the strategies adopted by the undertakings (e.g. Centrale del latte di Roma-Cirio). In a merger procedure, the analysis of barriers to entry was also considered crucial in deciding if the concentration will create a dominant position on a lasting basis, an essential factual element for prohibiting the merger. When an abuse of dominant position was under examination, the definition of the market thresholds has been conducted keeping in mind the possibility that the eventual dominant position had already produced such an increase in the prices so as to make the relevant market closer to the neighbouring markets, implying the adoption of more strict criteria of analysis for market definition.

When facing innovative products, the Competition Authority has adopted rather narrow standards considering these products belong to specific markets that are different from the markets of ordinary goods. The example of the mobile telephone is paramount. When the digital mobile telephone was introduced, the Authority considered this market separate from the analogue one. After several years, as the digital mobile telephone developed very quickly in combination with a reduced role of the analogue system, the Authority declared that there were no longer any reasons to consider these two products belonging to different markets. This conclusion was also strongly influenced by the factual observation that the utilisation abroad of the pan-European digital mobile telephone, one of the most emphasised characteristics of this product, was in fact very rare. This example shows very clearly how difficult the market definition analysis can be when it cannot be driven by consolidated consumer habits because the new product is not yet traded extensively.

A minor point has to be stressed. In Italian competition law, restrictive agreements or abuses of dominant positions are prohibited only if they concern a national market or a substantial part of it. In the application of the law, the Competition Authority has always considered local markets (the region and also town areas) as a substantial part of the national markets.

4.4.3 Conclusions

Quantitatively, substantial differences exist between the triggers that cause antitrust authorities to come in action. In some countries, the thresholds for merger control are really low, causing many operations to fall under scrutiny by the relevant authorities. For example, for the period 1993-97, the Belgian Council of Competition has looked into more than 225 cases investigated by the Service, or on average, 45 cases a year. The Dutch Authority has, in its first year of existence, been confronted with a much larger number of cases than had been expected. In total, 154 concentration cases were examined; for 6 of those cases a thorough investigation was necessary. In the end the Dutch Authority stopped one concentration while the parties involved in two other cases withdrew from the concentration under investigation.[10]

There are also differences regarding behaviour that is deemed explicitly as non-competitive by some countries, yet not explicitly forbidden by others. Therefore, certain mergers of multinational companies that had to clear in all member states have been approved without much delay by some authorities but not by others. This is of course not abnormal, since the market positions are different in each and every country. If company A has a market share of 10 per cent in country 1 and a market share of 25 per cent in country 2, and it wishes to merge with company B that has a market share of 5 per cent in country 1 and 35 per cent in country 2, then the post-merger market structure will look entirely different in country 2 vis-à-vis what it achieves in country 1. This is the whole idea of having national merger policies and different treatment therefore is not necessary caused by different legislation. Two countries having exactly the same antitrust laws could easily reach different conclusions regarding a merger. This implies that the 'Home-country-control' type of arguments, which are often advanced by companies, make no sense. In a recent case in Belgium, this was one of the arguments of the defence. The Bundeskartellamt, the NMa and the OFT hadn't seen any problems. In those countries, however, there existed many more competitors than in Belgium.

Nonetheless, the differences in legislation exist and therefore also the other case is conceivable. That is, an operation that establishes exactly the same competitive conditions in the market in country 1 as in country 2 could be forbidden in one country while being allowed in another. This of course raises questions but can be justified by the vision on antitrust held by a particular country, as documented in the very beginning, see Section 2.2 above.

4.5 Exemptions

A final element with which to judge antitrust policy is related to what is extracted from the rule. If tough rules are laid down, but they only can be applied to a minority of cases, not much is to be expected from the tough rule. Therefore, we document whether certain anti-competitive actions are exempted (4.5.1). Also, we investigate whether different rules apply for entire sectors (4.5.2).

4.5.1 Anti-competitive behaviour that is exempted

4.5.1.1 Belgium
Exemptions can be given in view of the positive economic development of small and medium enterprises.

4.5.1.2 The Netherlands
- The Dutch law de facto exempts certain types of anti-competitive behaviour. An exhaustive list of this behaviour is given in Arts. 7 to 16 of the law, including:
  - types of agreements that are exempted by the European legislation, and
  - agreements that have a limited impact (small cases).
- On a case-by-case basis, the director general may grant dispensation for certain types of anti-competitive behaviour that contribute to improving the production or distribution or to promoting technical or economic

progress, while allowing consumers a fair share of the resulting benefits (Art. 17).

- The NMa may, on request, declare Art. 24 (abuse of a dominant position) inapplicable to a specifically defined practice if, without this exemption the provision of a service of general economic interest, entrusted to an undertaking by law or by an administrative agency, would be prevented.

4.5.1.3 Germany

- The GWB provides for the exemption of certain specific types of horizontal or vertical agreements. Under certain conditions, horizontal and/or vertical agreements between small and medium-sized enterprises are exempted. Further the Federal Cartel Office will in principle not intervene in agreements between a restricted number of small and medium-sized enterprises as long as their combined market share does not exceed 5 per cent.

4.5.1.4 Italy

- Art. 8 (para. 1) of the law no. 287/90 states very clearly that provisions of competition policy apply also to public undertakings and to those firms in which the state is the majority shareholder.
- According to the same article (para. 2), as in Art. 90 of the Treaty of Rome, the undertakings entrusted by the law with the operation of services of general economic interests are exempted by provisions of competition law. This exception has to be interpreted in a very restrictive way. No wonder that in the extensively regulated Italian framework the Competition Authority has been engaged in several fierce battles to avoid unnecessary protections with respect to antitrust provisions. The activity of the Authority was two-fold. On one side, while taking a decision at the end of a procedure, the Authority was only considering the regulation by the law, rejecting a defence based on second-level regulation (by administrative bodies or by self-regulating associations of undertakings). The examples are numerous and are related to many sectors (e.g. agricultural products, insurance, professions and transport services). On the other hand, the Authority used reporting powers, entrusted by the Arts. 21 and 22 of the law no. 287/90, to notify the Parliament and/or the government sections of existing or draft laws that impose an unnecessary restriction on competition. These notifications have been able to influence the final political decision when they were endorsed by same related European deregulating measures. Therefore the European directives have represented a powerful instrument to

enhance the competition in several important sectors (e.g. telecommunications, energy and insurance), with the only exception being agriculture where it is the pervasive European regulation that limits the application of antitrust provisions also at the national level.

4.5.2 Sectors that are exempt

4.5.2.1 Belgium
No sectors in Belgium are exempt, but the threshold criteria for financial institutions are defined differently. Also, public companies are exempt.

4.5.2.2 The Netherlands
In the Netherlands, for the first two years, concentrations in the banking industry are falling under the authority of the central bank (De Nederlandsche Bank), whereas concentrations in the insurance industry are controlled by the regulator (De Verzekeringskamer).

4.5.2.3. Germany
The GWB exempts certain types of institutions from its application, e.g. the GWB does not apply to the Bundesbank.[11] Further agreements made by associations of agricultural producers and by credit and insurance companies are outside of the GWB.

4.5.2.4 Italy
The Authority has the power (Art. 4 of the law 287/90) to exempt, for a limited period, agreements restrictive of competition which improve the conditions of supply with substantial benefit for consumers. This section allows an efficiency defence when a procedure related to a restrictive agreement is concerned. Efficiency considerations were in fact the most frequent reasons recalled in the cases in which an individual exemption was granted. In the early stage of the application of competition policy, the Antitrust Authority adopted a very strict approach when evaluating the conditions for an exemption. This conduct was also motivated by the warning that an extensive utilisation of the individual exemption could transform the Antitrust Authority into a regulating agency. Up to now no block exemption has been granted.

The last category of exemption is the one represented by the European block exemptions. The strong link between the national and the European competition laws implies that the provisions of national competition law do not apply if a specific agreement is protected by a European block exemption. However the limited practical effect of these protections has to be stressed, keeping in mind that the national Authority adopts the same principles as the European Commission. Therefore an agreement protected by a European block exemption in any case would be granted with an individual exemption from the national Authority.

4.5.3 Conclusions

In the countries under investigation, the trend seems to be to include all of the relevant sectors in the economy into the realm of antitrust analysis. Historically, some sectors in particular countries have been able to get exempted, at least for still a few years to come. The fact that they often are 'key' sectors to the economy implies that these exemptions are not unimportant. The frequency of cases in Belgium in which the previous public monopoly in telecommunications is involved is striking. Yet in the logic of this company getting pushed to diversify into other activities by government itself, stating that the telecom monopoly should do this in view of the opening of the market.

5. ANTITRUST POLICIES: ADDITIONAL ELEMENTS

Some particular features of antitrust policy are 'idiosyncratic' in that they are not 'comparable' across countries. Nonetheless they can be important. In this section, we highlight these elements by country.

5.1 Belgium

The design of the law in Belgium was in the hands of several academic experts. A few past presidents of E.A.R.I.E. (European Association for Research in Industrial Economics) held the pen. A professor in law and economics while working in the cabinet of the Minister of Economic Affairs also contributed, while in the decision-making authority. Several academics in the field of industrial organisation have been appointed. As such, we have a good policy, on paper.

In reality, a few drawbacks exist due to the way in which the law has been implemented. Mainly for budgetary motives, the Service (which investigates and proposes a decision) was seriously understaffed. Also the very brief delay between the announcement of a merger and a decision by the Service, namely four weeks, made it hard to always conduct the appropriate analysis. Nonetheless, most of the decisions published were of a high quality in their motivation, although in a few cases the decision was too much framed in legal terms, missing seriously a reference to the economics of the case.

5.2 The Netherlands

At a recent conference, 'One Year NMa' at CentER, Tilburg University, economists and lawyers discussed with NMa officials the first operational year. A few complaints were voiced on the excessive legal formalism that motivated decisions, often suffocating the economic arguments, if they were present at all.

5.3 Germany

Germany probably has the longest tradition in antitrust policy of all the countries discussed in this chapter. Not only is the current German antitrust law (the GWB) the result of a process of continuous improvements and updates that started with the original GWB in 1957. German cartel policy has its origins even earlier in 1897.[12] While at first focussing on cartel behaviour the scope of German law has widened over time.

As opposed to the other antitrust authorities discussed here, the Bundeskartellamt does not have a hierarchic structure. Instead, decisions are made by one of the ten divisions. Each division has jurisdiction for a number of specific sectors of the economy.

Because of the fact that Germany is a federal state, it is the case that apart from the Bundeskartellamt each Land (region) has its own competition authority. It is responsible for proceedings against infringements of competition that have effect in its Land. As previously mentioned, merger control is the exclusive responsibility of the Bundeskartellamt.

5.4 Italy

In its first period of activity, the Autorità Garante della Concorrenza e del Mercato (the Italian antitrust agency) has focused its intervention on public services sectors characterised by extensive entry regulation or self-regulation (e.g. insurance, distribution and pharmaceutical sectors as well as professions). In the period 1991-98, 31 out of 37 cases of abuses of dominant position (detected by the agency), can be related to public firms or to undertakings protected by some public regulation. In the same period, 34 cases out of 64 agreements restricting freedom of competition, involved associations or large and well known consortia of companies whose self-regulating activity turned out to be partially an infringement of the competition law.

In an environment, such as Italy's, where public intervention and public-owned companies if not to say the entire corporatist economy, which encompasses professions and many guild-style associations of companies, still play a very important role, the Italian antitrust agency has been mainly concerned with enlarging the extension of the free-market economy. The more orthodox antitrust intervention against restrictive practices of private firms not protected by any regulation or self-regulation has played a comparatively minor role: exceptions are the frequent interventions in the cement and derivative products industry, where 13 restrictive competition agreements have been detected.

This characteristic of Italian antitrust activity is explained not only by the specific policy choice adopted by the antitrust agency but also by the absence, until recently, of regulating agencies. In this period voices against monopolies and widespread entry regulation could be addressed only to the antitrust agency. It is easily predictable that as new regulating agencies (the energy regulating agency and the telecommunications regulating agency) are now in action and as the economic role of the state has become less intrusive, the Italian antitrust activity will be similar to that in the other Western countries.

The composition of the instruments used by the Italian antitrust agency was strictly connected to the specific activity performed in this first period: in particular, up to now ex ante control has played a very minor role. Conversely, the advisory activity with respect to the present or future legislation has been impressive: notifications to the Parliament or to the government about laws causing distortions to competition have increased very quickly (see Table 4.2).

Table 4.2 Number of notifications to the parliament or to the government (annual average)

1991-92	1993-94	1995-96	1997-98
3	13	21	40

This activity was aimed at combating the lobbying pressures to protect – with specific legislation lacking any public interest justification – consolidated interests from competition. We have already stressed that the successes obtained in this field by the antitrust agency were almost always related to Italy's adoption of a general system of European laws characterised by a strong anti-regulation flavour (to accomplish the Common Market purpose).

The ex ante control of mergers and acquisitions has been virtually absent: in the period 1991-98, only four concentrations out of 31 where a specific administrative procedure were started, have been stopped. The value of these concentrations (the turnover of the undertakings that should have been acquired) totalled It.L. 263 billion: in the case of two of these concentrations, whose total value was It.L. 219 billion, the buying firm was the public telecommunications monopoly. When in the course of the procedure the undertakings realised that the concentration ran the risk of being prohibited, sometimes (in five cases) they preferred to modify the original design of the operation in order to remove the obstacles to competition. More often (in ten cases), the antitrust agency imposed structural or behavioural measures when clearing the concentration.

The soft approach to ex ante control has several explanations. First, the national industrial environment is still rather fragmented so a concentration rarely poses a relevant problem to competition. There are few big firms, some of them still owned by the state. During the last ten years, the public firms, constrained by strict public budget policies, virtually did not make any acquisitions and, if privatised, they always obtained clearance by the antitrust authority.

The second explanation for the soft approach has to do with the caution shown by the antitrust agency in its first period of activity. This attitude could be explained by the natural reluctance to adopt tough measures, such as prohibitions to concentrations, without a consolidated experience. This behaviour has been fostered on one side by the parsimony in using quantitative analysis. As we have already shown in the first part of this paper, ex ante intervention demands, more than the other antitrust activities, recourse to economic analysis which, in some circumstances, can only be implemented with the support of quantitative analysis. In contrast to US antitrust experience, where econometric methods are currently employed before the courts, the approach adopted in Europe, mainly by the Commission, is very cautious about those methods. Following the Commission's example, the Italian antitrust agency, with very few exceptions, also has not employed quantitative analysis in the course of a formal procedure on concentrations.

Unlike concentration control, ex post intervention, concerning abuses of dominant positions and restricting competition agreements, has been rather intense. As already recalled, this activity has been focused in the direction of reducing the influence of legal monopolies and narrowing the network of corporative agreements which stiffen the activity of several economic sectors.

Under the first sort of action, the antitrust agency has prevented firms in a dominant position from spreading their market power, often obtained with some sort of public regulation, to neighbouring sectors. In this field, application of the competition policy (in particular the Art. No. 3 of the Law No. 287/90, which prohibits the abuse of dominant positions) has allowed the creation and the consolidation of new and dynamic markets. Among others, the example of mobile telecommunications is striking. At the beginning the only operator in mobile telecommunications was the public monopolist in fixed telecommunications. The antitrust agency opened three formal investigations detecting an abusive activity of the public monopolist that deterred entry and compressed the competition in the mobile telecommunications market. The antitrust procedural activity was combined with several notifications to the Parliament or to the government asking for a lessening of normative obstacles to enter this market. Nobody can dispute that the antitrust agency has played a crucial role in developing not only the competition but also the market itself. In 1992 well known experts criticised the activity of the antitrust agency under the belief that competition in mobile telecommunications could not allow the exploitation of scale economies. At that time there were approximately 500,000 subscribers and the mobile telephone was a sort of a luxury service. Thanks to competition, the Italian market grew at exponential rates, becoming, with more than 20 million subscribers, the most important European market. Similar activity has been carried out in other sectors such as ports and airport services, airline, railways and motorway transportation, energy, gas, business firm data storage as well as other sectors characterised by intrusive public intervention.

Taking into consideration the vigorous privatisation process, the European deregulation trend and the results obtained by the application of competition policy, we can expect a considerable shift towards the control of monopoly power. In particular, the focus of this intervention will change from public or strongly regulated firms to private and softly regulated firms whose dominant position has been obtained only with the help of economic supremacy. For this new task better economic analysis is required in order to ascertain the dominant position (which no longer depends on the regulation) and to detect abusive behaviour.

With regard to corporatist remainders that can be found in the Italian economy, the antitrust agency has carried out numerous interventions involving, in particular, professions and associations or consortia of companies. Generally all these bodies carry out an important economic role which is endorsed by primary or derivative legislation. On the other side, sometimes they are the vehicle for agreements among the firms of one market to limit or abolish reciprocal (quantity or price) competition or to pose obstacles to new entrants. In such cases the antitrust law has been applied with the aim of preventing the de facto extension of the exempt zone, established by the ruling laws, where competition policy does not apply. In performing this duty the antitrust agency occasionally addressed specific notifications to the Parliament or to the government about laws unreasonably restricting competition. This sort of activity did not demand great skill in economic analysis to the antitrust agency staff, as the restrictive nature of the agreement was self-evident: the main difficulty, purely legal, was often related from the discrimination from cases where the agreement was a part of a broader design of the ruling legislation (in which case it did not violate the competition law) and the cases where the agreements were freely decided and implemented by the firms.

6. THE IMPACT OF ANTITRUST POLICIES ON COMPETITIVENESS

After having made an inventory and analysis of both antitrust legislation and the implementation of competition policies in four countries in the previous sections, it now is appropriate to ask what the impact is on competitiveness. If competitiveness is defined as the possibility to maintain if not expand a business position *relative* to one's competitors, it is clear that if for some reason these competitors can grow large by merging with other firms more easily, a competitive disadvantage could emerge.

For instance, if the Schumpeterian hypotheses hold and concentrated sectors or big firms are better in developing new products, competitors that are allowed to merge into big firms will own more patents and expand faster in high-tech world markets. Since the evidence in favour of the Schumpeterian hypotheses is far from conclusive, it is worthwhile to mention in detail the work by John Sutton (1998), who has engaged in an attempt to reconcile all the mixed findings in this area, but even more important presents us with a case study of antitrust policies having harmed the development of a particular industry in a particular country.

The industry is the film industry, where the advent of colour film implied that in order to survive, a serious increase in R&D outlays turned out to be necessary. This is relevant for industries that are prone to 'escalation', meaning that by outspending a rival on R&D, a firm will gain market share. Since the market leader, Kodak, substantially increased its R&D spending to a level unseen before, it was hard for the others to follow, and the chances of ever meeting the demanding quality standards set by Kodak were small. Consolidation resulted: Agfa merged with Gevaert, subsequently absorbing Perutz, while in the UK, ICI and CIBA acquired Ilford. Agfa-Gevaert increased its R&D spending to come up with a colour film that could be processed in the same way the Kodak film was, thereby avoiding that small photo shops (mini-labs) would have to invest in other equipment than the one already in use to process the Kodak film. Ilford on the other hand tried to solve the problem in a different way. They sold the film 'processing included', which meant that the customer was to send the film to the Ilford laboratories which would process it and mail it back. This led to a complaint with the OFT who referred the matter to the Monopolies and Mergers Commission, see Sutton (1998), pp. 117-126. The Commission found this tying of selling and processing film to be anti-competitive, greatly increasing Ilford's problems to keep a foot even in the UK market. This led Ilford to withdraw entirely from the colour film market, remaining a (specialised) producer of black and white.

While nowadays most antitrust economists would not advise the Monopolies and Merger Commission to take the same decision, since tying only is prohibited in relation to market power and at the time Ilford was small vis-à-vis Kodak, it illustrates that antitrust authorities seriously can affect the future of a company. If they had allowed in favour of the tying practice, although maybe detrimental in the short run, they would probably have kept Ilford in the running, thereby establishing fiercer competition in the long run. In any event, the example points to the need for an efficiency defence, allowing Ilford to explain why it was necessary to engage for some time in the anti-competitive practice of tying. All countries surveyed have this provision.

While it is clear that a faulty implementation of antitrust laws can endanger the competitive position of a firm, the reverse claim sometimes is also made. Michael Porter, in his book entitled *The Competitive Advantage of Nations* (Porter, 1990), argues that a competitive home market provides the best training for engaging in global competition. In general, to our knowledge there is no systematic empirical evidence in favour of or against the claim that antitrust policies are good or bad for the competitiveness (dynamic performance) of a firm, industry or country.

From the most recent developments in the theory of industrial organisation, we moreover know that the effect of antitrust policy will depend on the sector involved. If an industry is 'in escalation', meaning that R&D expenditures need to increase very fast in order to keep up with the competition, prohibiting mergers that raise the necessary funds to finance R&D might be bad policy. It will imply that the domestic industry cannot keep up with the speed of development elsewhere. For other industries where 'escalation' is not an issue, competition policies can not harm the long-run competitiveness of the economy.

Systematic empirical evidence regarding the static effects (that is on consumer and producer surplus) of antitrust policies is anly recently starting to be available. Since it is unclear what the dynamic effect on competitiveness is, it is even more appropriate to ask whether competition policy is effective in its primary goal: protecting consumers from the adverse effects of firms exploiting market power. In a recent contribution, Konings, Van Cayseele and Warzynski (1999) have investigated this issue for Belgium and the Netherlands. We elaborate on these findings here in more detail, and supplement them with evidence we found for Italy.

In general, and to place it methodologically, the Head of the Danish Competition Authority has described this approach as 'Competition Policy with a Coasian Prior', see Hylleberg and Overgaard (1998). It means that 'competition in itself should not be the aim of competition policy; the promotion of competition is warranted only to the extent that competition improves the incentives of agents to use scarce resources efficiently'.

In practice, according to Konings, Van Cayseele and Warzynski (1998), this implies that with or without an antitrust policy there will be pressure on price cost margins. Antitrust enforcement will then either increase this pressure, for instance by forbidding a merger with a potential entrant, or decrease it, for instance by forbidding mergers that are necessary to create a substansive rival in the future. Or to what extent are price cost margins under pressure when antitrust policy is active? A unique experiment to answer these questions occurs in countries that previously had no antitrust enforcement beyond the one at the EU level and that have now recently have implemented such policies.

For Dutch and Belgian manufacturing industry from 1992 to 1997, Konings, Van Cayseele and Warzynski estimate mark-up ratios according to the techniques developed by Hall (1986 and 1988) and Domowitz et al. (1988). (A more recent exercise applies the methodology to 1998. We will report the results of both studies here.) The findings are remarkable. First, we find higher mark-ups in the Netherlands in the manufacturing industry as a whole and in most 2-digit industries. Second, there is no significant effect on mark-ups in Belgium due to the introduction of a competition policy in April 1993. There is an effect of the policy in the Netherlands, where as of January 1998, pressure on mark-ups results from the antitrust authority. Third, in

Belgium, the threat of import competition decreases mark-ups whereas in the Netherlands, we find no effect, or even a slightly positive one.

These findings show that for two comparable countries the roles of competition policy and import competition are completely different. In Belgium, with low mark-ups, to start with, the role of antitrust seems to be minimal. There were seemingly no strong cartels to fight and the competition policy could consist of keeping the market open, especially for competition from abroad, and preventing strong positions from emerging. Without going into detail, this is precisely what happened. Out of the less than 1 percent of the operations that were forbidden, the idea was to block increasingly dominant positions that already existed in e.g. the food and drink industry, as well as to be aware of predatory practices that would drive out small independent distributors.

In the Netherlands, it was known that a few strong cartels existed. Also the 'bargaining' model that often implements escalator clauses in which increased wages can be passed on to consumers by firms that remain sheltered from import competition by all kinds of quality and environmental regulations can explain why the mark-ups were and still are higher than in Belgium. Competition policy nowadays puts them under pressure.

While very similar in many respects, the Dutch and Belgian economies also have some differences, not only at the institutional level. One such a difference which can explain both the difference in mark-ups and the different impact of import competition, is the intra-sectoral composition of manufacturing goods. Whereas the Belgian economy mostly exports semi-finished goods and components into competitive world markets, the Dutch economy is known to export more finished goods that are registered trade-marks or patented high-tech products, through a few global trading companies with Dutch origins. These products command higher margins, while the import competition variable in our regressions here might mean a low imput price for a concern that adds value and exports the finished products.

In any event, these results point to a few conclusions. First, the layman's view that antitrust policies only make sense for large closed economies such as the US or the EU trading bloc does not hold. Small open economies such as Belgium and the Netherlands also are in need of such competition policies. This is in line with the most recent views regarding the economics of antitrust, see Baker (1999). There it also is argued that the 'local' effect of a merger, that is the impact on subsets of consumers, has its own rights. Moreover, as shown by our regression analysis, the role it needs to play can be quite distinct, ranging from a gatekeeper (keeping the market open for import) in Belgium, to an active challenger of existing cartels in the Netherlands.

And what about the larger countries analysed here, that is, Germany and Italy? For Germany, we could not find a similar research project, but for Italy we are fortunate to have the recent study by Bottasso and Sembenelli (1999). Using essentially the same methodology on an unbalanced panel of Italian firms over the period 1982-93, they investigate the impact of the EU Single Market programme on price-cost margins. This programme can be seen to have a double effect. In much the same way as argued above, the first effect of this programme is to reduce barriers to trade and hence barriers to entry, and therefore to rely on import competition to contest too high price-cost margins. The other effect is a productivity gain that firms have when they can produce at lower costs by hiring cheaper/better factors of production.

The findings of Bottasso and Sembenelli on the role of import competition go in the same direction as those found by Konings, Van Cayseele and Warzynski for Belgium.[13] In some cases, a reduction of the price-cost margin by nearly 50 per cent resulted from 'opening up' the market. The evidence of a further price decrease through productivity gains for Italian firms was less clear. Also the effects of Italian competition policy has not been investigated explicitly. But it is quite clear that also here there is a role for competition policy, since the sample split effectuated by Bottasso and Sembenelli indicate that the Single Market programme only affected the 'most sensitive' firms, in the sense of firms operating in the 'open' sector. Other subsamples either remain unaffected or show no clear pattern of opening-up. To date, we are not able to tell why this is the case, but other barriers to entry together with cartel-like behaviour could be an explanation, justifying a national competition policy. As such, the efforts of the Autorità in telecommunications as documented in the previous section will certainly have an effect on future mergers.

Another particularity of Italian antitrust, having economic implications is the absence in the merger control of an efficiency defence clause. We want to stress that the absence thereof could paradoxically have caused a softer application of the ex ante concentration control. This sort of defence has to focus on the efficiency consequences of a concentration process. If the analysis can show that they are insignificant, by contrast the eventual lessening of competition might ask for a more strict approach.

In this first period of application of the Italian competition law, secret agreements restricting the competition among the interested companies have also been detected. These agreements, even if secret, were covered very badly: in fact the firms, because of the novelty of competition law, were not prepared to face antitrust action. Very explicit written evidence of these agreements was found in the headquarters of the firms during inspection activities. Also in those cases the utilisation of sophisticated economic analysis was almost redundant.

This initial stage of Italian antitrust activity is inevitably coming to an end. On the one hand, the results obtained by the competition policy have narrowed the set of explicit restrictive agreements of a corporatist nature. On the other hand, the agreements that restrict competition are carried out in a less compromising way and are more carefully kept secret. In legal terms, the number of accords will decrease and the one of concerted practices will rise. We can therefore presume that the inspection activity, even if done with more sophisticated techniques, will inevitably play a minor role. In contrast, economic (and probably econometric), analysis will become crucial in evaluating future antitrust cases.

We cannot end this short reconsideration of the Italian competition law without observing that the specific intervention carried out in this first period of application of the Law No. 287/90 has required, as a necessary condition, an agency that is independent of political power and interests groups. Recent experience shows that this independence became stronger because it was founded on a law that is in effect European. The judgement on the independence of Italian competition policy should not be modified even when considering the whole control system based on the administrative Courts (Latium Region Administrative Court and Council of State). Some experts have noticed, however, that the extremely technical nature of antitrust decisions should suggest, for the appeal procedure, recourse to a specialised court also able to manage complex economic problems.

To sum up, we have shown in this section that antitrust policies either are needed in an active sense, that is, fighting cartels, or in a more passive role, that is, as a watchdog. This justifies competition policy also in smaller countries. We however started this section with an example of the detrimental effect of antitrust action on the competitiveness of a firm that otherwise likely would have grown into a global player. Therefore, together with the conclusion that emerged at the end of the previous section, viz. that there exist pronounced differences between the national competition policies, it is likely that a differential impact and hence competitive advantages and disadvantages will result. One then can take two approaches to these differences. The first is to harmonise national competition policies so as to create a 'level playing field'. Given the different needs and roles competition policies must play in reality, however, this does not seem the appropriate response. Rather, the possibility to show that the action taken is not anti-competitive but induced by the aim to stay in the race and survive as a serious competitor, is more important. This calls for an efficiency defence, which is not included in all the national policies. The Belgian experience however shows it is not often used in practice. Out of a few hundred merger clearances, only in about five cases was explicit reference made to the potential advantages of the merger in terms of dynamic competitiveness. Perhaps as firms discover that competitors succeed in getting done abroad what they cannot do in their own country, this avenue will be taken more seriously. This will also imply that national antitrust authorities will be confronted more with 'fake' efficiency defences, and therefore that they should be better document the impact of their actions on innovation, competitiveness and the growth of firms.

7. CONCLUSIONS AND TOPICS FOR POLICY REFORM

In the present paper, we have documented in detail the similarities and differences that exist between the antitrust policies in four European countries. Up to now, the colloquial approach was to take the easy way and state that the national laws merely were copies of the European antitrust policy. This has clearly emerged to be false. How far does this divergence go? Quite far, as it turns out. There are not even 'typologies' of antitrust policy. For example, there is not a laissez-faire approach relying on foreign competition within the context of the contestability paradigm in the typically smaller countries.

On the other hand, competition policy, if based on sound economic analysis, cannot be conducted in 20 different ways. As such, it is not remarkable that we also were able to detect similarities in the actions taken by the different countries. We however cannot avoid concluding that a few pronounced differences dominate the overall picture.

Together with the knowledge that competition policy may interfere with the competitiveness of a firm, this leaves us with a potentially harmful situation. If for some reason competition policy is enforced too toughly in one situation, the company might not have the same avenues for growth as its competitors. If for some reason, in another situation, competition policy is not enforced, the firm might lack the competitive experience to survive in a global world.

The obvious policy recommendation then seems to be a call for harmonisation. Yet even with the same antitrust legislation, we explained that one country might approve of a merger while another might block it, because of a difficult situation regarding for instance the number of competitors. Moreover, we pointed to the possibility that competition policies, even in very similar countries, need to tackle quite different problems. We then gave empirical evidence, showing that indeed quite similar countries must have a different implementation of their competition policies, given a quite distinct outcome on price cost margins. It therefore is useless and counterproductive to work towards harmonisation in this context. In order to avoid mistakes, however, the possibility of efficiency defence should always be open to companies. In order to avoid misuses, the European Commission should issue guidelines based on sound industrial economic analysis of the evolution of competitiveness in each industry. These guidelines should be kept in mind when deciding at the national level, without being binding, in much the same way the US merger guidelines provide a point of reference for the courts.

Since we have a mutual stake that everything goes well in terms of both consumer protection against dominant positions and the competitiveness of firms, the above-mentioned guidelines should be followed by the national authorities whenever possible. They will provide a serious guarantee that we avoid a situation in which one country tolerates every operation in a certain sector because it wouldn't remain viable otherwise, while in another country simply nothing is tolerated because the players are foreign.

In drafting these guidelines, it should be clear that there is interaction between past policies and novel industrial economic insights, in much the same way that the US Merger Guidelines have changed over the last years. Being very structuralistic in the beginning, they evolved toward the inclusion of many of the most recent industrial economic theories. A good start for the European guidelines would be to aim at singling out industries where the efficiency defence should be able to play, with parties trying to show how increased concentration is the result of an escalation process, as documented in Sutton (1998).

Further, the present exercise of horizontal comparison, contrasting antitrust practices in different countries, should be continued. The reason is simple: antitrust enforcement is not a static issue. Policies will change, if not only by the fact that market structures have changed as the result of antitrust action itself. These continued horizontal comparisons will not lead to harmonisation, which as we argued should not be an ultimate goal, but they certainly will lead to convergence of policy practices regarding the same issues, so as to avoid policy reforms in certain countries as the result of interest group actions. Here, the European Commission could take an initiative to create a network similar to the European Corporate Governance Network started in 1996. The framework to do the analysis could be easily copied from the present contribution, but should be extended to include other major countries.

NOTES

1. Comments by our discussant, S. Martin, are gratefully acknowledged. Also the remarks by G. Galli, G. Gerlauff, J. Pelkmans, L. Sleuwagen and R. Thurik have been appreciated.
2. See however Lande (1982) for a somewhat different view.
3. Early contributions applying game theoretical insights to industrial economics, such as Mayberry et al. (1953) or Shubik (1959) did not receive the attention they deserved by industrial economists at the time, keeping the Structure-Conduct-Performance paradigm as the dominant theory.
4. Maitland-Walker (1995) provides a comparison of the legislation in most European countries.
5. More information can be found on the official website: www.bundeskartelamt.de.
6. There are three Directorates (A, B and C) responsible for the enquiry phase, according to the sector involved.
7. The site of the Dutch Antitrust Authority can be found at www.Nma-org.nl.
8. A database containing all the decisions adopted by the Competition Authority can be consulted at www.agcm.it.
9. For more detailed information see Bundeskartellamt (1999).
10. See Nederlandse Mededingindsautoriteit (1999).
11. An exhaustive list of exempted institutions and industries can be found in Maitland-Walker (1995), pp. 180-181, as well as in the GWB the German antitrust law).
12. von Neumann (1998) for extensive coverage of the evolution of German cartel policy.
13. In addition to the evidence concerning the effect of import competition in Belgium, the Netherlands and Italy discussed here, Barry and O'Toole (1998) argue that also in the case of Ireland relying on import competition is not enough to ascertain competitive markets.

REFERENCES

Aiginger, K.D. Mueller and C. Weiss (1998), 'Objectives, Topics and Methods in Industrial Organization during the Nineties: Results from a Survey', *International Journal of Industrial Organization,* 16(6), pp. 799-830.

Bain, J. (1956), *Barriers to New Competition,* Cambridge, MA: Harvard University Press.

Baker, J. (1999), 'Policy Watch Developments in Antitrust Economics', *Journal of Economic Perspectives,* 13(1), pp. 181-194.

Barro, R. and X. Sala-i-Martin (1995), *Economic Growth,* Advanced Series in Economics, New York, London and Montreal: McGraw-Hill.

Barry, F. and F. O' Toole (1998), 'Irish Competition Policy', Chapter 11 in S. Martin (ed.) (1998), *Competition Policies in Europe,* Amsterdam: Elsevier, pp. 229-250.

Baumol, W., J. Panzar and R. Willig (1982), *Contestable Markets and the Theory of Industry Structure,* New York: Harcourt, Brace and Jovanovich.

Bittlingmayer, G. (1985), 'Did Antitrust Policy Cause the Great Merger Wave?', *Journal of Law and Economics,* 28(1) , pp. 77-127.

Bork, H. (1978), *The Antitrust Paradox: A Policy at War with Itself,* New York: Basic Books.

Bottasso, A. and A. Sembenelli (1999), *Market Power, Productivity and the EU Single Market Program: Evidence From a Panel of Italian Firms.*

Bundeskartellamt (1999), *Tätigkeitsbericht 1997/98,* Berlin: Bundeskartellamt.

De Bondt, R. and P. Van Cayseele (1985), 'Innovatie en overheidsbeleid' in *Innoveren en Ondernemen,* Referaten 17e Vlaams Wetenschappelijk Economisch Congres, Brussel, Vereniging voor Economie.

Domowitz, I.R. Hubbard and B. Petersen (1988), 'Market Structure and Cyclical Fluctuations in US Manufacturing', *Review of Economics and Statistics,* Vol. 70 (1), pp. 55-66.

Gasmi, F., J. Laffont and O. Vuong (1992), 'Econometric analysis of collusive behaviour in a soft drink market', *Journal of Economics and Management Strategy,* 1(2), pp. 277-311.

Gilbert, R. and S. Sunshine (1995), 'Incorporating Dynamic Efficiency Concerning Merger Analysis: The Use of Innovation Markets', *Antitrust Law Journal,* 63, pp. 569-601.

Hall, R. (1986), 'Market Structure and Macroeconomic Fluctuations', *Brookings Papers on Economic Activity,* Vol. 2, pp. 285-322.

Hall, R. (1988), 'The Relation between Price and Marginal Cost in US Industry', *Journal of Political Economy*, Vol. 96 (5), pp. 921-947.

Hylleberg, S. and P. Overgaard (1998), *Competition Policy With a Coasian Prior?*, University of Aarhus, Department of Economics Working Paper No. 1998-17.

Konings, J. , P. Van Cayseele and F. Warzynski (1999), 'The Dynamics of Industrial Mark-ups Using Firm-Level Panel Data in Two Small Open Economies: An Empirical Analysis Whether Competition Policies Play a Role', *International Journal of Industrial Organisation*, forthcoming.

Langenfeld, J. and D. Scheffman (1989), 'Innovation and US Competition Policy', *Antitrust-Bulletin*, 34(1), pp. 1-63.

Lande, R. (1982), 'Wealth Transfers as the Original and Primary Concern of Antitrust: The Efficiency Interpretation Challenged', *Hastings Law Journal*, 43, pp. 67-151.

Maitland-Walker, J. (ed.) (1995), *Competition Laws of Europe*, London: Butterworths.

Mayberry, J., J. Nash and M. Shubik (1953), 'A comparison of treatments of a duopoly situation', *Econometrica*, 21(1), pp. 141-154.

Nederlandse Mededingingsauthoriteit (1999), *Jaarverslag NMa* 1998, Den Haag: Nma.

Neumann, M. (1998), 'The Evolution of Cartel Policy in Germany', Chapter 3 in S. Martin, *Competition Policies in Europe*, Amsterdam. Elsevier Science Publishers, 1998, pp. 41-53.

Porter, M. (1990), *The Competitive Advantage of Nations*, Basingstoke: Macmillan.

Reinganum, J. (1989), 'The Timing of Innovation: Research, Development and Diffusion', in R. Schmalensee and R. Willig (1989), *Handbook of Industrial Organisation,* Vol. 1, Amsterdam: North-Holland, pp. 849-908.

Schumpeter, J. (1934), *The Theory of Economic Development*, Cambridge, MA: Harvard University Press.

Schumpeter, J. (1975), *Capitalism, Socialism and Democracy*, New York: Harper and Row.

Shubik, M. (1959), *Strategy and Market Structure*, New York: John Wiley & Sons.

Shughart, W. and R. Tollison (1998), 'Collusion, Profits, and Rational Antitrust', *Antitrust Bulletin*, 43(2), pp. 365-74.

Sleuwaegen, L. and P. Van Cayseele (1998), 'Competition Policy in Belgium', Chapter 9 in S. Martin, *Competition Policy in Europe*, Amsterdam: Elsevier Science Publishers, pp. 185-204.

Smets, H. and P. Van Cayseele (1995*), '*Competing Merger Policies in a Common Agency Framework', *International Review of Law and Economics*, 15(4), pp. 425-41.

Stigler, J. (1964), 'A Theory of Oligopoly', *Journal of Political Economy*, 72, pp. 44-61.

Sutton, J. (1991), *Sunk Costs and Market Structure: Price Competition, Advertising, and the Evolution of Concentration* , Cambridge, MA: MIT Press.

Sutton, J. (1998), *Technology and Market Structure: Theory and History,* Cambridge, MA: MIT Press

Swann, D., D. O'Brien, W. Mzunder and W. Howe (1974*), Competition in British Industry; Restrictive Practices Legislation in Theory and Practice*, London: Allen & Unwin.

Tirole, J. (1988), *The Theory of Industrial Organisation*, Cambridge MA: MIT Press.

Van Bergeijk, P., L. Bovenberg, E. van Damme and J. van Sinderen (1997), *Economic Science: Art or Asset?,* Rotterdam: OCFEB.

Van Cayseele, P. and D. Furth (1996), 'Bertrand Edgeworth Duopoly with Buyouts or First Refusal Contracts', *Games and Economic Behaviour*, 16(2), pp. 153-80.

Van Cayseele, P. and R. Van den Bergh (1999), 'The Law and Economics of Antitrust', in B. Bouckaert and G. De Geest (eds.), *Encyclopedia in Law and Economics*, Aldershot: Edward Elgar, (forthcoming 1999).

Van Cayseele, P. (1998), 'Market Structure and Innovation: A Survey of the Last Twenty Years', *De Economist*, 146(3), pp. 391-417.

Von Neumann, J. and O. Morgenstern (1944), *Theory of Games and Economic Behaviour*, Princeton, NJ: Princeton University Press.

5. State Aid in Context

Stephen Martin and Paola Valbonesi[1]

I. INTRODUCTION

EU competition policy is unique in its control of state aid along with the more traditional elements of competition policy, such as the policing of collusion and of abuses of a dominant position. The rationale for control of state aid is to safeguard the original engine of EU integration, market integration, by protecting against the possibilities that less efficient firms which receive state aid will prosper at the expense of more efficient firms that do not and that more rich member states will systematically give their firms competitive advantages over firms from less rich member states.

The essential elements of EU state aid policy were foreseen in the Spaak Report (1956). European Community control of aid by the member states was justified by the need to ensure the perceived fairness of the competitive process (1956, p. 57):

> Une des garanties essentielles qui doivent être données aux entreprises, c'est que le jeu ne risque pas d'être faussé par les avantages artificiels dont bénéficieraient leurs concurrents.

Despite a history that predates the Treaty of Rome,[2] state aid and state aid policy remain controversial. The trend in the level of state aid seems to be downward, although there are substantial fluctuations around this trend. State aid to business overlaps with regional aid; certain sectors (shipbuilding, steel and transport among others) are the subjects of specific policy measures. As (in general) the share of publicly owned business in economic activity shrinks throughout the EU, aid to privatised or privatising firms continues to cause concern. At the same time, EU regulation of aid granted by the member states needs to be coordinated with the aid that the EU grants through the Structural Funds and the Cohesion Fund.

Furthermore, state aid is but one of a multitude of member state policies that affect the competitiveness of national firms vis-à-vis firms based in other member states. Other such policies include (but are not limited to) the nature and enforcement of national competition policy, labour market institutions, environmental regulations, consumer protection rules, the magnitude of the tax burden (direct and through social charges) that falls on business, physical infrastructure and the nature of the educational system. For some sectors, public procurement policy is an important factor. Effective policy towards state aid must take into account how state aid fits into this broader menu of policies that, like state aid, affect business competitiveness and afford member states the opportunity to deliver competitive advantages to their own firms.

We begin by outlining the formal structure of EU state aid policy (Section 2) and present statistics on the magnitude of and trends in state aid (Section 3). This is followed by an overview of the economic analysis of state aid (Section 4) and a discussion of the relation of state aid policy towards other policies that affect competitiveness (Section 5). Section 6 concludes.

2. INSTITUTIONAL FRAMEWORK

Like the more traditional aspects of EU competition policy, the basis of EU state aid policy is constitutional, contained in Arts. 87 to 89 of the Treaty Establishing the European Community.[3] The framework laid out in these Arts. includes a basic prohibition of state aid that distorts competition and affects trade (Art. 87(1)), with some mandatory exceptions (Art. 87(2)),[4] and discretionary exceptions (Art. 87(3)).

The provision for discretionary exceptions to the Art. 87(1) prohibition makes it possible for the Commission to permit:

- regional aid (87(3)(a) and (c));
- aid to combat unemployment (87(a));
- aid to advance important EU goals (87(b));
- aid to specific economic activities (92(c));
- aid to deal with serious economic disturbances (87(b)); and
- other aid, with authorisation of the Council.

This broad range of discretionary exceptions gives the Commission the flexibility to fashion a policy that allows some types of state aid, even if the result is distortion of competition, provided there is an overriding EU interest (Evans and Martin, 1991).

EU control of state aid bumps up against other aspects of EU law that are on the same level as Arts. 87-89. Art. 295 of the Treaty Establishing the European Community[5] guarantees the right of member states to public ownership of enterprise, from which it follows that such ownership does not in and of itself violate Art. 87[6]. Art. 86 makes public enterprise subject to EC competition policy: public enterprise is not to use state resources to compete with private enterprise. But Art. 16 emphasises that EU competition policy does not infringe the ability of member states to operate services of general economic interest (European Commission, 1998a, p. 47).

Art. 36 of the treaty indicates that the provisions for control of state aid will apply to agriculture only to the extent specified by the Council. Control of state aid to agriculture is part of the administration of the common agricultural policy.

Art. 73 makes aid to the transportation sector 'compatible with the Treaty' if it meets the 'needs of coordination of transport' or if it 'represent[s] reimbursement for the discharge of certain obligations inherent in the concept of a public service.' Art. 76 gives to the Commission the power to authorise support of this industry by a member state; Art. 154 provides for Community support of trans-European networks.

Commission and Council decisions and practice have erected an administrative superstructure on top of this constitutional foundation. This superstructure includes guidelines governing aid to specific sectors (discussed in more detail below). General practice is codified and strengthened in the 1999 Regulation on State aid procedures.[7]

On the surface, the principles that govern state aid are straightforward and reasonable. State aid is present when public policy directly or indirectly gives a firm an economic advantage it would not otherwise have (Morch, 1995). Member states are obliged to notify the Commission in advance of aid projects. Aid projects are not to be put into effect unless and until approved by the Commission. Aid that is not notified to the Commission cannot benefit from the possibility of exemption under Art. 92(3), and aid that is granted without receiving an exemption is to be recovered.

Beneath the surface, the situation is less serene. The 1999 Regulation stiffens the Commission's investigatory powers and establishes that legal appeals before national courts are not to delay recovery of aid that has been denied an exemption. But there are clear signals that member states honour state aid rules more in the breach than in the observance. member states have persistently failed to notify the Commission of grants of aid; 21 per cent of 1997 aid cases were not notified to the Commission (Sinnaeve, 1998, p. 80). In many instances firms have retained aid after a finding that it was incompatible with the common market: 'Nearly 10 per cent of the recovery decisions are not executed *10 years* after they have been taken, in the majority of cases because of pending procedures before national courts' (Sinnaeve, 1998, p. 80; emphasis in original).

In a market system, the generic economic justification for the granting of state aid is the existence of market failure. Analytically, market failures fall in several categories, and different types of market failure call for different types of corrective measures. Aid measures aimed at different types of market failure promise different benefits (which may justify exemption under Art. 87(3)) and carry the threat of different types of policy failure (which may render the net effect of the policy measure negative as far as overall welfare is concerned). The existence of market failure does not automatically justify corrective measures; the cure may be worse than the disease.

Table 5.1 outlines three broad categories of state aid measures. *Horizontal aid* targets market failures that affect firms without regard to location or sector. Most market failures in this category involve an externality of one kind or another — a social cost created by business activity that is not reflected in business cost or revenue and not, therefore, taken into account by the business when it makes decisions. The Community benefit that is seen as flowing from the aid — and justifying an exemption under Art. 87(3), when such an exemption is forthcoming — is that the aid will reduce or eliminate the harm flowing from the externality. All these horizontal measures carry with them the danger that what is portrayed as aid to accomplish a desired EU goal will in fact deliver operating aid to the recipient firm, aid to cover normal and routine expenses of operation. Operating aid falsifies market processes in exactly the way foreseen by the Spaak Report.

Member state *regional aid* aims to promote development of disadvantaged regions. The EU's commitment in principle to such development has been reinforced by the Single European Act and the Treaty on European Union, with its emphasis on social and economic cohesion.

This commitment does not, however, translate into an open-door policy for regional aid. One long-standing source of concern has been the possibility of bidding wars, in which member states grant businesses competing subsidies that cancel each other out, benefiting firms but leaving investment decisions unchanged (European Commission, 1972, p. 116):

> Part of the aid granted at present only achieves reciprocal neutralisation with unjustified profits for the benefiting enterprises as the only counterpart. In fact, this process of outbidding cannot appreciably affect the aggregate flow of investments, which, at the Community level, can be mobilised for the purpose of regional investment.

Table 5.1 A taxonomy of state aid

Aid type	Potential benefit	Potential distortion
Horizontal		
Employment	Reduce labour market imperfections	Camouflage operating aid
Environment	Increase environmental quality	Camouflage operating aid
R&D	Promote innovation	Camouflage operating aid
Rescue & restructuring	Facilitate survival of fundamentally sound firms	Preserve Fundamentally unsound firms
Small & medium sized enterprise	Ameliorate financial and other market failures that differently affect small firms; promote job creation	Create or preserve fundamentally unsound firms
Regional		
	Promote development of peripheral regions	Aid wars; channel more aid to least developed regions of wealthiest member states than to least developed regions of less wealthy member states
Sectoral		
Declining or consolidating industries	Ease labour market transitions; facilitate restructuring; share adjustment costs	Delay inevitable reorganisation; favour firms from richer member states; less efficient firms survive, more efficient firms exit
Privatising Industries	Increase share of economy guided by market forces	Artificial advantage for former public firm

The Commission has also been concerned to concentrate regional aid in areas that are most disadvantaged from an EU perspective, seeking to avoid situations in which some regions of the wealthiest member states receive greater levels of aid than regions of less developed member states, even though the least developed regions of wealthy member states are not underdeveloped from the point of view of the EU as a whole.

Sectoral aid falls in two broad categories. The first is aid to declining sectors. EU rules for this type of aid are contained in sector-specific codes, such as those for coal,[8] steel,[9] shipbuilding[10] and synthetic fibres.[11] The rationale for this type of aid is to spread the social costs of adjustment and, where feasible, enable reorganised firms to continue operations on a stand-alone basis.

Historically, EU competition authorities maintained strict controls on restructuring aid, requiring that the following Conditions are met (European Commission, 1995, p. 172):[12]

- aid to be part of a realistic plan for restructuring that will be completed after a limited period of time;
- minimising harm to competitors and reducing capacity (in sectors afflicted by structural over-capacity);
- aid be limited to the minimum amounts necessary to obtain the perceived benefits to the Community; and
- with the implementation of the restructuring plan to be monitored by the Commission.

The Commission's attitude towards operating aid has been hostile, although this position has been relaxed somewhat in the context of aid to severely depressed regions (European Commission, 1989, p.147; 1996; 1998b). The administration of sectoral aid is thus influenced by regional considerations.

A second type of sectoral aid targets firms in sectors that are newly exposed to the full forces of market competition, such as banking, air transport,[13] shipping,[14] and motor vehicles.[15] Here too the rationale is to facilitate adjustment to an exogenous, and putatively one-time, shift in market circumstances. But for declining industries, the danger is that aid which is intended to be limited to an adjustment period becomes open-ended operating aid, simply delaying unavoidable adjustments.

Table 5.2 State aid to manufacturing sector in the Community 1990-97, annual values (million ECU) in constant prices (1996)

	1990	1991	1992	1993	1994	1995	1996	1997
EU-12						40622	36594	35823
EU-15	44652	40623	42020	44766	41332	39328	35367	34400

Note: Figures for 1997 exclude 391 Meuro.

Source: Fifth and Seventh Survey on State Aid; 1990/1991/1992, our own calculations from data in the Fifth Survey.

Table 5.3 State aid to the manufacturing sector in the Community, 1990-97

	1990	1991	1992	1993	1994	1995	1996	1997
% of value-added EU-15						3.1	2.8	2.5
% of value-added EU-12	4	3.6	3.2	3.8	3.5	3.2	2.9	2.6
Euro per person employed, EU-15						1341	1231	1209
Euro per person employed, EU-12	1149	1067	1136	1540	1457	1385	1269	1236

Source: Fifth Survey and Survey on State Aid; 1990/91/92, are our elaboration on data from the Fifth Survey.

Note: Annual values 1990-97, at 1996 constant prices, 1997 slightly underestimated.

3. STATE AID: MAGNITUDE AND TRENDS

3.1 General trends

The manufacturing sector received 40 per cent of member state aid to manufacturing, agriculture, fisheries, coal, transport and financial services over the period 1990-97, and is the sector that received the largest share of member state aid. Aid to manufacturing shows a downward trend from 1990 to 1997, with an upward blip in 1993 that appears, in retrospect, to be a one-time exception (see Table 5.2). 1997 aid for the EU-12 is 23 per cent lower than the 1990 value, and sharp decreases were recorded in 1990-91 and 1995-96.

The generally downward trend of state aid is confirmed by the figures for state aid as a per cent of value-added and by the annual values in euro per person employed (see Table 5.3). In 1996, member state aid fell below 3 per cent of EU value-added for the first time in memory.

The lower figures for the EU-15 in the period from 1995 to 1997 in terms of value-added and per person employed reflect on the one hand the declining aid trend in the Community and on the other the fact that the aid levels recorded for the three new Member states are below the EU average.

The value of state aid to manufacturing in proportion to intra-Community manufacturing trade is a good indicator of the potential distortion of competition produced by the aid itself. We can observe in Table 5.4 that this proportion peaks in 1993 for the EU-12 and declines sharply with the expansion of the EU to 15 member states.

Table 5.4 State aid to the manufacturing sector, EU-12 and EU-15

1992	1993	1994	1995	1996
5.7	7.0	5.7	4.8	4.4

Note: Figures show percentage of intra-Community trade in manufacturing, at 1995 constant prices.

Source: Sixth Survey on State Aid.

Considering trends in aid on a state-by-state basis (Table 5.4), decreases have occurred in particular for Greece,[16] Italy, Belgium, Portugal and Luxembourg. Greece (5.6 per cent) and Italy (5.3 per cent) remain noticeably above the EU average for the period 1995-97, followed by Germany (3.1 per cent), Spain (3.0 per cent) and Denmark (3.0 per cent). Over the same period, the lowest levels of state aid are recorded for Finland (1.6 per cent), Austria (1.5 per cent), the Netherlands (1.2 per cent) Sweden (1.0 per cent), and the United Kingdom (0.9 per cent).

Comparing the periods 1995-97 and 1993-95, aid as a per cent of value-added rose in seven member states and fell in five member states (Table 5.5). The overall reduction in state aid in the Community appears to be driven by the decrease in German aid, which is essentially a reduction in aid to the New Bundesländer, and to a lesser extent by reductions in Italian aid.[17]

Table 5.5 State aid to the manufacturing sector in the Community, as a percent of value-added, moving averages, 1990-97

	1990-92	1992-94	1993-95	1994-96	1995-97
Austria				1.3	1.5
Belgium	7.9	2.5	2.5	3	2.4
Denmark	1.9	2.5	2.7	2.9	3
Germany	3.5	4.4	4.4	3.8	3.1
Greece	12.5	6.5	5.2	6.3	5.6
Spain	2.1	1.8	2.1	2.7	3
Finland				1.6	1.6
France	2.7	2.4	2.1	1.8	2
Ireland	2.7	1.7	2.4	1.5	2.2
Italy	8.9	6.4	6.1	5.8	5.3
Luxembourg	3.5	2.6	2.2	2.3	2.3
Netherlands	2.5	1.5	1.1	1.4	1.2
Portugal	4.6	2.5	2.7	1.9	2.8
Sweden				0.8	1
United Kingdom	1.4	0.9	0.8	0.9	0.9
EU-12	3.8	3.5	3.5		2.9
EU-15				3	2.8

Sources: Fifth, Sixth and Seventh Survey on State Aid.

Martin and Valbonesi

Given the reduction in aid by Germany and Italy, the absolute levels of state aid to manufacturing among the four large countries (Germany, UK, France and Italy) show a trend towards convergence, despite the fact that Italian aid in proportion to value-added is more than twice that of France and five times higher that of the United Kingdom.

The Sixth and Seventh State Aid Surveys show that the share of the four largest countries in total aid is declining, while the share of the four cohesion countries – Spain, Ireland, Portugal and Greece – is increasing. State aid declined from 85.3 per cent in the period 1994-96 to 80.3 per cent in the period 1995-97, whilst the share of the four cohesion countries is increased respectively from 9.0 per cent to 10.7 per cent (see Table 5.6). Moreover, it is interesting to stress the magnitude in terms of total aid: Greece has the highest share of state aid in terms of value-added but a low position in terms of total aid, while Italy and Germany hold high positions in both rankings (see Tables 5.5 and 5.6[18]).

Within the manufacturing sector, shipbuilding continues to receive substantial amounts of aid. Community average aid to shipbuilding fell from 34 per cent of sectoral value-added in 1988-90 to 24 per cent in 1990-92, then stabilised at around 25 per cent in 1992-94 and 1994-96. In the period 1995-97, aid granted to shipbuilding dropped for the first time since 1990-92 to some 20 per cent of sectoral value-added (European Commission, 1999, p. 11).

In the steel sector aid had been phased out by the end of 1992. Restructuring and capacity reductions mandated by decisions taken under Art. 95 of the ECSC Treaty were undertaken in the new German Länder, Spain, Italy, Portugal, Ireland and Austria during the period 1994-96. The changes in the sector are confirmed by the low level of aid in 1995-97, which amounted to an annual average of around 113 billion euros[19] a decrease of over 30 per cent compared with the period 1993-95.

In contrast with the recent declining trends in state aid granted to shipbuilding and steel, aid to the motor vehicle industry shows a 24 per cent increase in the period 1995-97 when compared with the previous period 1993-95. This is not related to any specific scheme; the aid is mainly made up of regional and rescue and restructuring aid.

Increasing use of state aid in the form of government support measures to foreign direct investment carried out by small- and medium-sized enterprises are also evident. In 1997, the total amount of this form of state aid has been about 30 million euro, granted mostly through guarantees (28 million euro; European Commission, 1999, p. 15).

Table 5.6 Share of member state's aid in total state aid to the manufacturing sector in the Community

	1981-86 (EU-10)	1986-88 (EU-12)	1988-90 (EU-15)	1990-92	1994-96	1995-97
Germany	16.8	22.7	22.1	47.9	44.3	35.9
Italy	31	28.4	31.1	24.9	26	27.7
France	18.7	16.8	17.1	11.9	10	11.4
Spain	-	8.7	7	3.2	5.6	6.6
UK	12.4	10.6	8.8	3.5	4	4.3
Belgium	3.4	3.1	3.4	2.2	3.1	2.5
Netherlands	2.5	3.2	3.5	1.7	1.8	1.8
Denmark	0.8	0.8	0.9	1.3	1.8	1.9
Greece	3.2	3.1	3	1.7	1.8	1.7
Austria	-	-	-	-	1.2	1.4
Portugal	-	1.4	1.7	1.1	1	1.4
Finland	-	-	-	-	1	1
Sweden	-	-	-	-	0.8	1
Ireland	1.2	1.2	1	0.5	0.6	1
Luxembourg	0.2	0.1	0.1	0.1	0.1	0.1

Source: Sixth and Seventh Survey on State Aid.

3.2 Types of Aid

Comprehensive grants and tax exemptions are the most common types of member state aid. In the period 1995-97, grants were more than twice as large as tax exemptions (see Table 5.7). The share of grants in total aid rose from 1992-94 (48 per cent of the total) to 1995-97 (57 per cent), while the share of tax exemptions decreased (from 26 per cent to 24 per cent).[20] This shift in the form of aid is related to the fact that grants are more easily adopted by governments than tax exemptions, since the latter require changes in tax laws.

Table 5.7 Breakdown according to type of aid, 1992-94 and 1995-97 (per cent)

	92-97 A1	95-97 A1	92-94 A2	95-97 A2	92-94 B	95-97 B	92-94 C1	95-97 C1	92-94 C2	95-97 C2	92-94 D	95-97 D
Germany	41	53	25	14	0	1	21	24	1	2	11	5
Italy	42	50	38	41	14	5	5	4	0	0	0	0
France	46	30	19	40	12	14	5	10	2	1	15	5
Spain	86	88	0	0	0	3	12	9	0	0	2	0
UK	87	89	6	5	0	0	2	1	1	1	4	4
Belgium	37	57	45	33	1	1	9	4	0	0	8	4
Netherlands	78	70	13	23	0	0	2	4	0	0	7	2
Denmark	94	84	2	9	0	0	3	6	0	0	1	1
Greece	54	96	20	0	0	0	13	4	0	0	13	0
Austria	-	79	-	0	-	0	-	15	-	0	-	7
Portugal	72	41	21	56	0	0	1	3	0	0	5	0
Finland	-	83	-	3	-	0	-	13	-	0	-	1
Sweden	-	66	-	16	-	2	-	16	-	0	-	0
Ireland	79	93	6	0	8	0	3	1	0	0	3	5
Luxembourg	93	92	0	6	0	0	7	2	0	0	0	0
EU-12	48		26		6		12		1		8	
EU-15		57		23		3		13		1		4

Notes: Group A: A1=direct grants; A2=tax exemptions; Group B: B=equity participation; Group C: C1=Soft Loans; C2=tax deferrals; Group D: D=guarantees.

Source: Sixth and Seventh Survey on State Aid.

Aid in form of state equity participation is limited, except for France with 14 per cent in 1995-97. The share of equity participation aid in total aid fell from 6 per cent in 1992-94 to 4 per cent in 1995-97.

Soft loans are a relatively small share of aid (about 13 per cent in both the periods compared here), since they place heavy burdens on the state budget. They are important for Germany, Sweden, Spain and Austria. Tax deferral is the least used form of aid in the Community: it is adopted only by Germany, France and the UK and it represents a very small share of total aid.

Guarantees are mainly used to help in rescue and restructuring operations and to foster the development of small- and medium-sized enterprises. The calculation of the magnitude of aid conveyed by guarantees, as with equity participation, is very difficult; thus it remain a very non-transparent form of state aid. Guarantees are a relatively important form of aid for Austria, France, Germany and Ireland.

In terms of type of aid granted, the four cohesion countries have very similar patterns, concentrating almost the whole amount on grants and tax exemptions, whilst the four largest countries are much more differentiated in terms of aid categories and quantities of aid allocated.

Collecting these forms of aid instruments according to the mode of financing, we find that since 1992 most of the member states have granted aid by means of *budgetary expenditures* – grants, equity participation, soft loans, guarantees – rather than by means of tax *expenditure* – tax rebates, tax deferrals. Aid by means of *tax expenditure* is particularly employed in Portugal, Italy, France, Belgium and Ireland.

3.3 Objectives of Aid

There is often an arbitrary element in defining the primary objective for which aid is granted. With this qualification in mind, aid classified as regional represented over half of the total granted in the EU over the period 1990-97, aid classified as sectoral about 12 per cent, and aid classified as horizontal aid about 30 per cent. The share of regional aid has tended to increase (from 50 per cent in 1990 to 58 per cent in the 1997), while the shares of horizontal aid (from 35 per cent in 1990 to 31 per cent in 1997) and sectoral aid (from 15 per cent in 1990 to 12 per cent in 1997) have tended to fall.

Aid to research and development accounts for about one-third of horizontal aid. Regional aid granted under Art. 88(3) accounts for more than 80 per cent of all regional aid. Aid to shipbuilding accounts for about one-third of the sectoral aid.

In the period 1990-97, France, Denmark, Belgium, the Netherlands, Finland, and Austria granted the largest part of their aid to horizontal objectives; Germany, Italy, Ireland, UK, Luxembourg, Sweden and Greece mostly for regional objectives, and Portugal and Spain mostly to sectoral objectives (see Tables 5.8, 5.9, 5.10). Considering member states where regional aid predominates, there has been a reduction in the share of regional aid in total state aid for Germany, Ireland, and Sweden, some increase for Italy (57 per cent in 1990-92, 69 per cent in 1995-97), substantial increases for the United Kingdom (31 per cent to 63 per cent) and Greece (29 per cent to 100 per cent), with the share of regional aid in total aid essentially constant for Luxembourg.

Table 5.8 Horizontal objective (per cent)

	1990-92	1992-94	1993-95	1994-96	1995-97
Germany	16	14	16	19	24
Italy	25	35	26	31	24
France	66	70	67	51	57
Spain	39	38	29	24	22
UK	50	32	24	22	24
Belgium	62	56	46	46	47
Netherlands	73	76	70	74	75
Denmark	67	73	77	84	85
Greece	61	53	27	31	0
Austria	-	-	-	74	68
Portugal	57	23	23	24	20
Finland	-	-	-	74	71
Sweden	-	-	-	34	29
Ireland	31	36	22	37	26
Luxembourg	30	29	29	33	27
EU-12	35	31	27		
EU-15				30	31

Source: Fifth, Sixth and Seventh Survey of State Aid.

Table 5.9 Particular sectors (per cent)

	1990-92	1992-94	1993-95	1994-96	1995-97
Germany	3	6	7	7	5
Italy	18	12	13	11	6
France	17	11	11	15	9
Spain	39	43	54	63	65
UK	18	16	11	19	13
Belgium	29	19	29	29	22
Netherlands	10	5	8	10	11
Denmark	31	26	21	14	13
Greece	10	20	16	3	0
Austria	-	-	-	13	-
Portugal	33	36	40	52	22
Finland	-	-	-	2	9
Sweden	-	-	-	4	18
Ireland	0	0	46	7	39
Luxembourg	0	0	2	2	2
EU-12	15	11	13		
EU-15				13	12

Source: Fifth, Sixth and Seventh Survey on State Aid.

Table 5.10 Regional objective (per cent)

	1990-92	1992-94	1993-95	1994-96	1995-97
Germany	81	80	77	74	71
Italy	57	53	61	58	69
France	17	19	22	34	34
Spain	12	19	17	13	13
UK	31	53	65	59	63
Belgium	9	26	25	25	30
Netherlands	17	19	22	17	14
Denmark	2	1	1	2	2
Greece	29	27	57	66	100
Austria	-	-	-	-	24
Portugal	10	41	37	24	58
Finland	-	-	-	23	20
Sweden	-	-	-	61	53
Ireland	69	63	32	56	35
Luxembourg	70	70	69	65	71
EU-12	50	58	60		
EU-15				56	57

Sources: Fifth, Sixth and Seventh Survey of State Aid.

3.4 Aid to sectors other than manufacturing

In the Seventh Survey data on aid to agriculture are presented as annual average budget outlays; in the previous Surveys many gaps are recorded or closed by extrapolations. This makes it difficult to compare aid to agriculture over time and to interpret the trend of state aid in the agriculture sector, notwithstanding the high amount of aid granted to the sector. The Commission's goal of establishing transparency of the amount of state aid has not been met for agriculture.

State aid to fisheries represents a small proportion of total aid and shows a decrease for the period 1995-97.[21]

Aid to coal mining fell by more than 20 per cent from 1993-95 to 1995-97. However, it remains high in an absolute sense, considering the fact that it involves mainly a few member states (Belgium, Germany, Spain, France, Portugal and the United Kingdom).

There is a high level of public intervention in the transportation sector, which makes control of state aid to transportation a complex and politically sensitive matter. A gradual reduction in overall aid to transportation can be observed from the 1993-95 to 1995-1997 period.

Aid granted to financial services sector is relatively small and involves only France, Ireland, Italy and Portugal. However, this type of aid shows a continued increased in recent years (see Table 5.11).

Table 5.11 Overall national aid in the Community, 1993-95 and 1995-97 (millions of euro)

	1993-95 EU-12	1995-97 EU-12	1995-97 EU-15
Overall national aid of which:	101,464	88,466	95,064
Manufacturing sector[d]	42,882	36,365	37,680
Agriculture	10,772	9,658	13,129
Fisheries	333	240[a]	252
Coal mining	11,487[c]	7,646[b]	7,646
Transport	34,843	31,855	33,655
Financial Services	1,147	2,702	2,702

a 1997 total estimated.

b 1997 data for French coal mining not included.

c Including an annual average of 2,900 million euro for social welfare programmes.

d Figures do not include ICT.

Source: Seventh Survey on State Aid.

4. ECONOMIC ANALYSIS OF STATE AID

4.1 Horizontal aid

4.1.1 Camouflaged operating aid

There is a simplistic element to the argument that externalities justify public subsidies to external costs, such as labour market adjustment costs, or the cost of adapting production techniques in an environmentally friendly way. The simplistic element is that such costs are viewed as being external to the firm only because they have traditionally been defined as such by prevailing legal systems. In principle, the option is always open to change the legal system so that such costs become internal to the firm.

If production methods employed in an industrial sector have always generated pollution, and a political decision is made to reduce or stop such pollution, one way to achieve that goal is to grant subsidies to businesses that operate in the sector, subsidies that are conditioned on changes in production methods. This approach views the costs that polluting imposes on society as external to the firm.

Another way to induce a change in production techniques is to pass a law requiring that firms stop polluting, and to subject them to substantial fines if they do not adhere to the law. This second approach makes the cost of pollution internal to the firm.

In the absence of informational imperfections, either approach – subsidy or internalisation – could be put into effect. If there is imperfect and impacted information, so that enforcement agencies could not effectively monitor compliance with pollution-regulating laws, subsidies might be justified as a way of eliciting the cooperation of the business sector. More generally, the granting of subsidies would seem to require the political decision that the cost being subsidised has a sufficient social character to justify spreading the cost over all of society.

But just as it may be difficult to monitor pollution-regulating laws because firms have more information than government agencies, so it may be difficult to monitor the use to which subsidies are put. Subsidies that are intended for other purposes but are diverted by recipient firms to cover normal operating costs present at least three dangers for market performance and, more generally, for the legitimacy of the market mechanism.

A subsidy is an artificial reduction in a firm's cost of production. Whether or not a subsidy is socially beneficial (from the point of view of the country granting the subsidy) typically depends on details of oligopolistic interaction in the market supplied by the subsidised firm.[22] But a subsidy typically increases the profitability of the subsidised firm at the expense of its rivals, generating an artificial competitive advantage and falsifying the market process.

In an integrating market, if one member state subsidises its firms, it will typically benefit those firms and harm firms based in other member states. If several member states each subsidise their own firms, and if those subsidies are financed by distortionary taxation (Collie, 1999), the result can be a prisoner's dilemma outcome in which subsidies neutralise each other, so that funds are transferred from the rest of society to firms, leaving recipient firms better off in an absolute sense but without altering the relative position of any one firm vis-à-vis others.

4.1.2 Research and development

A market system is likely to lead to under investment in research and development, justifying public support for innovation. In some sectors, where the form of market failure that generates private under investment in innovation stems from the high cost and risks of R&D, subsidies may be an appropriate policy response. Semiconductors and the aerospace industry are examples of such sectors, although even here R&D subsidies are affected by a high degree of uncertainty, which relates at least to three factors (Aghion and Howitt, 1998):

- difficulty of measuring the spillover effects from innovation;
- the unpredictable output produced by the R&D activities; and finally
- informational asymmetries between the government granting the aid and the beneficiaries with respect to the measurement of R&D inputs and the additionality of R&D subsidies.

In other sectors, however, subsidies are likely to be ineffective in promoting innovation. In high-technology industries where new SMEs are the most common vehicles for development of new products (the software industry, for example), the critical handicap is the inability of SMEs to obtain funding. Rather than subsidising businesses directly, it may be efficient to subsidise financial capital markets, deepening venture capital markets and channelling funds to start up SMEs indirectly, while taking advantage of the monitoring abilities of venture capitalists (Martin and Scott, 1999).

In agriculture and light industry, innovation often takes the form of applying new products or techniques that are developed in other sectors of the economy. Publicly supported networks (extension services) serve as repositories of state-of-the-art information and its use in the field will promote innovation more than direct subsidies. In areas such as biotechnology and pharmaceuticals, university-industry industrial parts will promote awareness of frontier research and promote innovation in a way that subsidies would not.

A strong case can be made for public support of private innovation. But the nature of public support should be tailored to the specific factors that restrict innovation, and state aid subsidies will be suitable only in specific circumstances.

4.2 Regional aid

It would be difficult to quarrel with the stated goals of EU regional policy (1996, p. 1):

> Regional aid is designed to develop the less-favoured regions by supporting investment and job creation in a sustainable context. It promotes the expansion, modernisation and diversification of the activities of establishments located in those regions and encourages new firms to settle there.

Certain themes appear repeatedly in the EU policy debate on regional aid, some of which were noted in the *First Report on Competition Policy* quoted below (European Commission, 1972, pp. 116-117). These include the danger of outbidding as member states implement regional aid programmes that cancel each other out, the need to concentrate regional aid on the most disadvantaged regions of the Community, and the desirability of minimising sectoral distortions that flow from regional aid programs.[23]

> National initiatives for regional development are becoming more and more costly. Part of the aid granted at present only achieves reciprocal neutralisation with unjustified profits for the benefiting enterprises as the only counterpart. In fact, this process of outbidding cannot appreciably affect the aggregate flow of investments, which, at the Community level, can be mobilised for the purpose of regional investment.
>
> The rate of aid and the means employed no longer correspond to the relative seriousness of the situation in the various regions when assessed at Community level. The choice of the location of investments tends to be made at the expense of the less-favoured regions and against the distribution of activities required by the common interest.
>
> In order to attract investments, the advantages offered often exceed the compensation for material inconvenience imposed on the

benefiting enterprises as a result of the particular choice of location it is hoped to bring about. Under cover of worthwhile regional objectives, artificial sectoral development can be brought into being.

Many of these same themes appear in the 1996 *Guidelines* and in a 1998 Commission Communication emphasising the importance of concentrating aid on the neediest regions. Recent policy statements also emphasise the need to coordinate EU control of state aid with the operations of the EU's own Structural Funds.

The analytical basis for regional aid has received a substantial boost by the work of 'new economic geographers', who argue that in the presence of congestion externalities and increasing returns to scale, the location decisions of private firms may be sub-optimal from a social point of view. Regional aid then serves a pump-priming function that induces private investment and starts a virtuous development cycle.

The new economic geography has been criticised both in general (Martin, 1999) and for the extent to which it provides a justification for regional state aid (Beasley and Seabright, 1999). In applications, governments may lack the information and analytical ability to identify regions that can benefit from 'pump-priming' regional aid; governments of more developed member states may channel aid to the least developed of their regions, although those regions may not be underdeveloped from an EU perspective; firms may collect regional subsidies without putting in place investments that trigger enduring development. Further, to the extent that regional aid induces private firms to shift investment from one region to another *within the EU*, the net benefit of the aid is the incremental development in the aided region, less any reduction in development that would have taken place elsewhere in the EU without aid. The new economic geography demonstrates the possibility that this difference may be positive. It does not establish that the difference is in fact positive in specific cases.

4.3 Sectoral Aid

Our discussion of operating aid took market structure – loosely, the number of firms – as given. Another factor comes into play in declining industries and for integrating markets where the fixed cost of production is large.

Some sectors of the EU economy – coal; steel; synthetic fibres – are characterised by severe excess capacity. Adjustment to equilibrium market structures requires a substantial reduction in the number of firms, often accompanied by a reorientation of production towards specific segments of the market. State aid to retrain workers that have been made redundant, or to facilitate restructuring, may be justified on social grounds, although there is a sense in which adapting business operations to changing market conditions is part of normal business operations.

Economic efficiency requires that resources be transferred out of declining industries and into sectors where they can find productive use. There is always the danger that subsidies granted with the intention of easing the transfer of resources out of a declining sector will instead be used to delay the socially desirable adjustment.

Even in the absence of a secular trend of declining demand, market integration in and of itself will normally imply a reduction in the equilibrium number of firms, particularly if the fixed cost of operating a business is large. Such a reduction is a major source of gains from market integration, as surviving firms exploit economies of scale and reduce the average cost of production, while the assets of exiting firms are transferred to some other industry. In such markets, one cannot speak of a secular decline in demand; the reduction in the equilibrium number of firms is a one-time change due to market integration itself. To realise the greatest gains from market integration, it should be the most efficient firms that stay in the market, while less efficient firms exit. Subsidies, especially competing subsidies granted by different member states, can distort the triage function of the market by allowing less efficient but subsidised firms to survive while more efficient firms that are not subsidised exit.

The risk of sectoral aid is that in circumstances when increased concentration on the supply side of the market is inevitable and a source of efficiency gains from the formation of a single market, state aid can allow less efficient firms to survive at the expense of more efficient firms, reducing the gains from completion of the single market for all concerned.

5. IS THE PLAYING FIELD LEVEL?

At the same time that it regulates aid by the member states, the EU administers its own aid programmes through the Structural Funds (the European Social Fund, the EAGGF[24] and the European Regional Development Fund) and the Cohesion Fund (originally set up to promote adaptation of Greece, Ireland, Portugal and Spain to the Single Market).

European Commission analysis suggests that aid from the EU funds contributes to raising income per capita in target regions, over and above the changes that would come simply from completion of the single market (Smith, 1999). Independent research on the same question is, on balance, more sceptical about the contribution of the Structural Funds (Neven and

Gouyette, 1995; Canova and Marcet, 1995). There is also evidence that member states cannot effectively utilise available funds (Van Eeckhout, 1999; Di Stefano, 1999).

Distributions through these programs are comparable in magnitude to aid by the member states (Table 5.12), as are expenditures for agricultural aid. Spending under the Common Agricultural Policy and funding for the Structural Funds were vigorously defended at the EU's March 1999 Berlin summit, at which efforts to initiate reform and control such spending met with some success, but also less than had been hoped for in some quarters.

Thus control of state aid seeks to regulate one source of competitive inequality in the European Union, while two other (if anything, larger) potential sources of distortion are determined by the workings of the political process.

Table 5.12 Appropriations for commitments, billions of euro at 1999 prices

	Agriculture	Structural operations
2000	40.9	32.0
2001	42.8	31.5
2002	43.9	30.9
2003	43.8	30.3
2004	42.8	29.6
2005	41.9	29.6
2006	41.6	29.2

Source: EU Presidency, Norman (1999).

To agricultural subsidies and aid from the Structural Funds, one may also add differences in member state labour laws, tax laws, environmental regulation and the like. The impact of such differences is highlighted for the member states that have adopted the euro as a single currency. Table 5.13, for example, reports substantial differences among 12 member states in hourly labour costs. Labour leaders in various member states have expressed concern about a 'race to the bottom' in EU wage rates as governments of high labour-cost states seek to avoid an envisaged flight of capital (for example, Burt, 1999). Governments of some member states have called for harmonisation of a broad range of policy measures that determine the environment within which firms compete (Forfás, Section 4.3.2):

> The key words here are 'social dumping.' For the last decade it has been a constant complaint from France and Germany, with highly regulated labour markets and (consequently) higher than necessary

unit labour costs, that their competitive position is being undermined by the access to their markets of goods produced in member states with lower labour costs based on a less regulated and lower social security taxed market.

Differences in tax rates also create differences in competitivity. Just as labour leaders have pressed for labour market harmonisation, so business leaders (in some sectors, at least) have pressed for excise tax harmonisation (Willman, 1999, quoting a statement of the UK Brewers and Licensed Retailers Association):

> A single market cannot work without looking at excise duty. Duty rates are the single biggest cause of price differentials between member states – VAT rates have converged and differences in corporation tax levels have little effect on pricing.

That institutional factors of this kind create irregularities in the 'level playing field' is undeniable, although the magnitude of the effects is difficult to gauge. Differences in cost are far from transparent, particularly when one considers that although firms in high-wage, high-cost states have higher operating costs on that account, they may have lower costs, in other dimensions, for the same reason. Firms that pay high taxes in part to support an elaborate system of public education, for example, will be able to draw on a highly qualified workforce.

But the same constitutional authority that gives the European Union the responsibility to control aid by the member states guarantees to member states the right to maintain diversity in general policy measures (Art. 95 of the Treaty Establishing the European Community).[25] Even if one accepts for the sake of argument that 'social dumping' could be defined in a sensible way,[26] the political consensus that supports control of state aid does not exist to harmonise general policy measures.

However, evolutionary processes now underway suggest that such diversity will shrink over time, as will the distortions in market competition that it creates. Fiscal pressures on the member states associated with the single currency and on the EU associated with the prospect of expansion to the East mean there will be less and less flexibility for member states and the EU to implement policies that distort competition. These pressures do not have as their purpose the bolstering of a level playing field for business rivalry with the European Community, but that will be one of their consequences.

6. CONCLUSIONS

EU control of business and regional aid by the member states has a long and checkered history. From its foundation, the entity that has become the EU has defended the principle that state aid is incompatible with the common market and permitted only on an exceptional basis. There is, however, an equally long history that member states do not notify the Commission of grants of aid for which notification is required, appeal strenuously against negative decisions regarding such aid, and in many cases do not recover aid that has been declared incompatible with the common market. The principle that incompatible aid is to be recovered was only established in a specific regulation in March 1999.

Over the period 1990-97, a reduction in horizontal and sectoral aid was neutralised by an increase in regional aid; there is at best a modest overall decline.

The economic analysis of state aid suggests that its effects on market integration are largely negative, that it either delays inevitable structural adjustments or traps member states in a negative-sum subsidy game that benefits firms but not the rest of society. Regional development aid may indeed be effective in narrowing geographic income differentials, but this is by no means a certain result, and such aid should not be open-ended.

NOTES

1. We are grateful to Ioannis Ganoulis for comments on a previous draft. All responsibility for any errors, however, is our own.
2. The Treaty of Paris (1951) bans state aid outright for the coal and steel sectors, but these provisions have been superseded by specific sectoral guidelines.
3. These are the paragraph numbers established by the Treaty of Amsterdam. Under the numbering system of the Treaty of Rome, these are paragraphs 92 to 94.
4. It is the Merger Regulation (Council Regulation (EEC) No. 4064/89 OJ 395/1 30 November 1989) that underlies EU competition policy control of market structure. See also note 2.
5. The mandatory exceptions are for some social aid, for aid related to natural or other disasters, and (now of historical interest only) for aid related to the post-war division of Germany.
6. Art. 222 of the Treaty of Rome.
7. Art. 90 of the Treaty of Rome.

8. Council Regulation (EC) No. 659/1999 of 22 March 1999 OJ L 83/1.
9. OJ L 329/12 30 December 1993.
10. OJ L 338/32 28 December 1996.
11. OJ L 332/1 30 December 1995.
12. OJ C 94 30 March 1996.
13. See also European Commission (1997).
14. OJ C 205 5 July 1997.
15. OJ 94/C 350/07.
16. JO C 279/1 15 September 1997.
17. Data for Greece are of doubtful quality, so this indication should be treated with caution.
18. See the Seventh Survey, p. 8.
19. In Tables 5.5 and 5.6, the moving averages for the periods 1991-93 and 1993-95, respectively, are absent.
20. This figure does not include aid granted to the steel sector supporting objectives such as R&D, regional development and environmental protection.
21. Comparison between the two periods should take account of the change in the number of member states (EU-12 and EU-15) and that the three new member states have levels of state aid below than the Community average.
22. See the Seventh Survey on State Aid.
23. This is a standard result of the strategic trade policy literature; see, for example, Krugman (1988).
24. In the *27th Report*, the Commission indicated its intention to integrate sectoral and regional aid (1998a, p. 77): The Commission's broader objective of ultimately putting an end to the various existing sectoral rules on State aid with a view to adopting a single approach to major awards under regional aid schemes regardless of the sector involved, except in the case of coal and steel, which will remain subject to the ECSC Treaty until July 2002.
25. Guidance Section of the European Agricultural Guidance and Guarantee Fund.
26. Art. 100a of the Treaty of Rome.
27. The overwhelming consensus among economists is that 'dumping' as that term is used in the international trade literature cannot be sensibly defined, and there is good reason to think that 'social dumping' is a similarly vacuous concept.

REFERENCES

Aghion, Philippe and Peter Howitt (1998), *Endogenous Growth Theory,* Cambridge and London: MIT Press.

Beasley, Timothy and Paul Seabright (1999), 'The effects and policy implications of state aids to industry: An economic analysis,' *Economic Policy* 28, April, pp. 15-53.

Burt, Tim (1999), "Call for probe into corporate exodus,' *Financial Times,* 13 January 1999, p. 3.

Canova, Fabio and Albert Marcet (1995), *The poor stay poor: Non-convergence across countries and regions,* CEPR Discussion Paper No. 1265, November.

Collie, David R. (1999), 'State aid in the European Union,' *International Journal of Industrial Organization,* forthcoming.

Comité Intergouvermental créé par la Conférence de Messine (1956), *Rapport des Chefs de Délégation aux Ministères des Affaires Etrangères* (Spaak Report), Bruxelles, 21 avril.

Di Stefano, Andrea (1999), 'Fondi Ue, Ciampi bacchetta Ronchi,' *La Repubblica* 15 aprile.

European Commission (1972), *First Report on Competition Policy,* Brussels.

— (1989), *Eighteenth Report on Competition Policy,* Brussels.

— (1995), *XXIVth Report on Competition Policy 1994,* Brussels-Luxembourg.

— (1996), *Guidelines on National Regional Aid,* 16 December.

— (1997a), *Guidelines on States aid for rescuing and restructuring firms in difficulty,* OJ C 283, 19.09.

— (1997b), *Fifth Survey on State Aid in the European Union in the manufacturing and certain other sectors,* COM 97/170.

— (1998a), *XXVIIth Report on Competition Policy 1997* Brussels-Luxembourg.

— (1998b), *Guidelines on National Regional Aid,* OJ C74/9 of 10 March.

— (1998c), *Communication from the Commission to the Member States on the links between regional and competition policy reinforcing concentration and mutual consistency,* 26 March.

— (1998d), *Sixth Survey on State Aid in the European Union in the Manufacturing Sector and Certain Other Sectors,* COM (98) 417.

— (1998e), *9th Annual Report of the Structural Funds 1997.*

— (1999), *Seventh Survey on State Aid in the European Union in the Manufacturing Sector and Certain Other Sectors,* SEC (99) 148.

Evans, Andrew and Stephen Martin (1991), 'Socially acceptable distortion of competition: EC policy on state aid', *European Law Review*, Vol. 16, No. 2, April, pp. 79-111.

Forfás (1999), 'Regulatory issues in Ireland: an overview,' mimeo, July.

Krugman, Paul R. (ed.) (1988), *Strategic Trade Policy and the New International Economics,* Cambridge, MA: MIT Press.

— (1995), *Development, Geography and Economic Theory,* Cambridge, MA: MIT Press.

Martin, Ron (1999), "The new 'geographical turn' in economics: Some critical reflections," *Cambridge Journal of Economics,* Vol. 23, No. 1, January, pp. 65-91.

Martin, Stephen and John T. Scott (1999), 'The nature of innovation market failure and the design of public support for private innovation', *Research Policy* (forthcoming).

Morch, Henrik (1995), 'Summary of the most important recent developments,' *Competition Policy Newsletter,* Spring 1995, pp. 47-51.

Neven, Damien and Claudine Gouyette (1995), 'Regional convergence in the European Community,' *Journal of Common Market Studies,* Vol. 33, No. 1, March, pp. 47-65.

Norman, Peter (1999), 'Twenty-hour talk marathon ends in compromise,' *Financial Times,* 27-28 March, p. 2.

Sinnaeve, Adinda (1998), 'The Commission's proposal for a Regulation on State Aid procedures,' *Competition Policy Newsletter,* June, pp. 79-82.

Smith, Michael (1999), 'Brussels says aid does help regions," *Financial Times,* 3 February, p. 2.

Van Eeckhout, Laetitia (1999), 'Les collectivités territoriales sous-utilisent les aides communautaires,' *Le Monde Economie,* 12 janvier, p. IV.

Vinocur, John and John Schmid (1999), 'Counting out the euros in wages and jobs,' *International Herald Tribune,* 29 January, p. 1.

Willman, John (1999), 'Brewers to lobby Brussels on beer taxes,' *Financial Times,* 8 February, p. 8.

6. Environmental Policy Reform in the EU

Peter Clinch[1]

INTRODUCTION

The driving force behind regulatory reform in the context of the European Union's environmental policy is the increased prominence of sustainable development and environmental protection in EU legislation and the shift in emphasis from regulatory environmental policy instruments to what are known as economic instruments. This paper examines the development of EU environmental policy, the environmental policy instruments in use, and how a shift from regulation to economic instruments in the EU can result in a more effective protection of the environment while contributing to the better functioning of markets in Europe and thereby contribute to competitiveness, growth and employment.

The history of EU environmental policy is first outlined. Environmental policy instruments in use at EU and member-state level are briefly examined. There follows an explanation of the alternative policy instruments available to environmental policy-makers and an assessment of their economic efficiency and environmental implications with examples presented. The impact of environmental policy on competitiveness and employment is examined and the likely impact of regulatory reform is assessed. The use of techniques for assessing the benefits and costs of environmental policy is explored. Finally, conclusions are drawn with particular regard being paid to issues for the future in relation to reform of environmental policy and its impact on markets. The paper does not discuss explicitly the environmental issues facing the EU as this can be found in an excellent recent report by the European Environment Agency (1999).

EU ENVIRONMENTAL POLICY

Legal basis

The Treaty of Rome (1957) which established the European Economic Community made no reference to the environment. It was not until the Single European Act was introduced in 1987 that a legal basis for EU environmental policy was provided. The act included the following environmental objectives:

- Preserve, protect and improve the quality of the environment;
- Protect human health; and
- Ensure a prudent and rational utilisation of natural resources.

In 1992, in addition to the above, the Treaty of the European Union (the Maastricht Treaty) included the following objectives of EU environmental policy:

- Article 2: Economic development must be sustainable respecting the environment and
- Article 130 R:
  - Integration of environmental protection into the definition and implementation of other EC policies;
  - Promoting measures at international level to deal with regional or worldwide environmental problems;
  - Achievement of a high level of protection taking into account the diversity of situations in the various regions;
  - It shall be based on the precautionary principle;
  - Preventative action should be taken;
  - Environmental damage should be seen as a priority and rectified at source;
  - The polluter should pay; and
  - The potential benefits and costs of action or lack of action must be taken into account in the preparation of policy on the environment.

Another important feature of the Maastricht Treaty was that it replaced unanimity with qualified majority voting between member states for most environmental measures and the principle of subsidiarity was introduced (Lévêque, 1996). This principle proposes collective solutions within the EU only when the solutions cannot be reached at national level.

Article 1 of the Amsterdam Treaty amends the Treaty of the European Union and, in doing so, gives environmental considerations greater prominence:

Amended seventh recital: promotion of economic and social progress taking into account the principle of sustainable development and within the context of the accomplishment of the internal market and of reinforced cohesion and environmental protection, and to implement policies ensuring that advances in economic integration are accompanied by parallel progress in other fields.

In addition, the treaty devolves more power to the European Parliament.

The vehicle for EU environmental policy

Probably the most significant development in EU environmental policy took place well before the Single European Act was signed. In 1972 at the Paris Summit, Heads of State of the EU agreed that the Commission of the European Communities would develop an Environmental Action Programme. These action programmes outline the Commission's intentions and recommendations regarding environmental policy. Since the first was published in 1973, there has been a further four. Ultimately these programmes are translated into regulations, directives, recommendations and non-biding opinions (Artis and Lee, 1997). Regulations are binding as to the results achieved and the method of achieving them. Directives are the most common instruments of EU environmental policy. These are binding as to the results but not the method of achieving them. Once an environmental action programme is adopted, its regulations and directives must be translated into national legislation.

The Fifth and most recent Environmental Action Programme, covering 1992 to 2000, outlines the main policy issues facing the EU and the policy instruments available. However, from the point of view of regulatory reform and its impact on markets, the main importance of the programme is its emphasis on the integration of the economy and the environment. The programme states that its strategy 'is to create a new interplay between the main group of actors (government, enterprise and public) and the principal economic sectors (industry, energy, transport, agriculture, tourism) through the use of an extended and integrated range of instruments' (European Environment Agency, 1999). In this regard it places particular emphasis on the use of so-called market-based instruments.

Summary

In summary, two key observations can be made regarding the development of EU environmental policy:

1. Sustainable development and environmental protection have been given greater prominence in EU legislation. Increasingly the emphasis has been on improving the consideration of environmental matters in all decision-making at EU level and in the integration of EU economies.
2. There has been a change in emphasis regarding the policy instruments recommended. In particular, the emphasis has switched from traditional regulatory instruments to the use of market-based instruments. The rationale for this is that market approaches are more effective and less costly in their achievement of the integration of the environment in the advancement of economic integration.

ENVIRONMENTAL POLICY INSTRUMENTS AT EU AND MEMBER-STATE LEVEL

The extent of involvement of the EU in environmental policy-making has increased rapidly when measured by the amount of environmental legislation adopted (see Lévêque, 1996). Since 1992 there has been a broadening of the range of policy instruments with a greater use of taxes, environmental agreements and information (European Environment Agency, 1999). Most EU-level environmental policy-making is executed through directives. According to the European Environment Agency (1999) from which most of this section is taken, there are about 315 environmental directives (Table 6.1) relating mostly to industry, agriculture and transport but there are a growing number in the energy and household sectors (Table 6.2). It is estimated that about 91 per cent of the directives have been transposed into the legislation of member states.

At member state level, the progress in introducing environmental taxes has been disappointing with little change since 1992. However, the progress varies considerably between countries. Figure 6.1 shows that most progress is being made in the Nordic countries. However, it is important to note that the number of taxes is a poor indicator of progress in the use of such instruments. Progress at EU level has been slow. The mineral oils directive, which sets a minimum level of excise duty on motor fuels in all member states, was adopted in 1992. However, the 1992 proposal for an EU-wide carbon/energy tax failed to be approved but such an instrument is back on the agenda in the light of the Kyoto Protocol.

Table 6.1 Progress at EU and member state level in introducing environmental policy instruments

Instrument	EU level initiatives	Member state initiatives
Regulations	Approx. 315 directives	Approx. 90% of EU directives translated into national legislation
Environmental taxation	Mineral oils directive (1992) Proposal for VAT on energy to be harmonised and discussion of pesticide tax	Growth in environmental taxation in Nordic countries leading the way. €6 billion raised in pollution taxes in EU in 1996, a 100% increase since 1990
Voluntary agreements	Agreements on energy efficiency in washing machines and TVs and CO_2 emissions with auto industry	More than 300 voluntary agreements agreed from 1990-96, mostly for industry, with about 100 in Germany and 100 in the Netherlands
Emissions trading	CO_2 trading being discussed in relation to implementation of the Kyoto Protocol	CO_2 trading being discussed in many member states. Germany in process of introducing a trading scheme for VOCs from small industry.
Subsidy reform	Reform of CAP, Common Fisheries Policy, Structural Funds, Cohesion Fund, European Investment Bank	Reform of domestic energy and industrial subsidies underway
Environmental impact assessment	Directive on EIA in 1985 (revised in 1997)	Approx. 7,000 EIAs per annum conducted across the EU
Environmental management systems	Eco-Management and Audit Scheme (EMAS) from 1993	Approx. 1,500 sites registered with EMAS by 1998
Research and development	Funding in 5th Framework Programme will be €2 billion for the environment	Support for clean technology in many member states

Source: Adapted from European Environment Agency (1999).

Table 6.2 Summary of use of instruments in sectors within the EU (%)

	Agriculture	Industry	Energy	Transport	Households
Regulations (315 directives)	30	40	5	14	9
Environmental taxes (134)	3	9	18	54	16
Voluntary agreements (305)	3	88	5	4	-
EIAs per annum (7,000)	16	26	8	30	20 (waste)
Environ. Management Systems (1,714 sites)	-	88	4	8	-

Source: European Environment Agency, 1999.

All countries have voluntary agreements relating to the environment with the Netherlands and Germany being at the forefront in their use (Figure 6.1). The agreements are mostly with industry (Table 6.2). At the EU level, there has been a move to increase the use of such agreements. The first EU-level agreement, which agreed an improvement in the energy efficiency of washing machines, TVs and video recorders, was introduced in 1997. In 1998, the European auto industry agreed to cut emissions from cars by 25 per cent between 1996 and 2008, and there are discussions between the European Commission and the pulp and airline industries, which may result in new agreements.

The correction of government failure via subsidy reform has made some progress. At EU level, while there has been reform of the Common Agricultural Policy, subsidies to agriculture are still high (Table 6.1). There has been a move to increase subsidies for farming that provides environmental benefits. The Environmental Impact Assessment Directive has resulted in about 7,000 EIAs per year being carried out within the EU.

Figure 6.1 Environmental taxes and agreements in EU countries, 1996

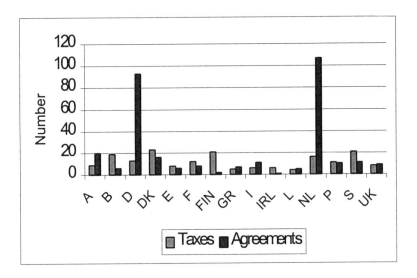

Sources: OECD (1997) and European Environment Agency (1997).

REGULATION VS. ECONOMIC INSTRUMENTS IN ENVIRONMENTAL POLICY[2]

Integration of the economy and the environment is the central objective of the Fifth Environmental Action Programme (European Environment Agency, 1999), and it is clear that there has been a move to increase the range of instruments in use, particularly those that try to mobilise the power of the market. The extended use of voluntary agreements at both EU and member state level is a clear example of a shift towards the use of so-called economic instruments. While there is considerable variation across member states, there is also an increased use of environmental taxation, which is also an economic instrument. The question arises as to why is there such a shift in emphasis and how such instruments work. This is explored below.

Market failure in relation to the environment

The environment can be defined as those parts of our physical and psychological endowment which we somehow share, which are 'open access' (Clinch and Convery, 1999). It is precisely this shared nature of many environmental endowments that threaten their quality and character. In a market system, goods are allocated by the price mechanism. In a free market, the price of a good is determined by the demand for, and supply of, the good. Price is therefore a reflection of society's willingness to pay for, or the valuation it places on, the good in question. However, the shared nature of many environmental assets such as air, the atmosphere and water resources means that they are not owned and so do not have a price. When goods are seen as free they are overused. Thus, the market fails to protect environmental assets adequately.

This failure of the market can be best demonstrated with a simple example: If a chemical factory pollutes a river and the pollution imposes a cost on the fishing industry downstream, this cost will not be reflected in the cost of producing chemicals. Thus, the price of the chemicals will not reflect the true cost to society of producing chemicals. In this case, the economy will produce more chemicals and use more of the environmental asset than is socially efficient. When a cost is imposed upon those other than the person or business that produces the cost, this is known as an external cost. Unless some mechanism is found to 'internalise' an externality, it will cause a misuse of society's scarce resources. This provides the basis for government intervention in the market.

Command-and-control vs. market-based instruments

The emphasis of environmental policy in the 1970s and 1980s was on the management of environmental resources by the imposition of institutional measures aimed at directing the environmental performance of firms. This approach is known as regulation or command and control. An ambient standard is set such that firms are permitted to produce a certain level of pollution. Non-compliance results in penalties usually in the form of legal action and/or fines or liability for correction of environmental damage. In the 1980s and 1990s, policy-makers became interested in what are known as market-based, economic, or fiscal instruments to control pollution such as are recommended in the Fifth Environmental Action Programme of the EU (see Box 1).

Market-based approaches harness the power of incentives to encourage individuals acting more-or-less in their own best interests to interact with the environment in a way that is in the best interests of society. Economists had noticed as far back as the 1920s that the market fails because there is no price to reflect the value of the environment and so it is overused. Their prescription was to create a set of surrogate prices, e.g. through taxation or direct charges per unit of pollution, such that individuals and firms pay for the pollution they produce. This is known as the polluter-pays principle.

Those who pollute less are rewarded financially since they avoid having to pay for their use of the environment. Thus, economic instruments shift the property right from the polluter to the victim.

Box 1. EU position on market-based instruments

The Fifth Environmental Action Programme states: 'in order to get prices right and to create market-based incentives for environmentally friendly economic behaviour, the use of economic and fiscal instruments will have to constitute an increasingly important part of the overall approach'.

The Communication on *Economic Growth and the Environment* (1994) states: 'In our economy, economic decisions are to a large extent taken on the basis of price signals. As customers adjust their purchase decisions to price changes and companies determine product design, technological development and the organisation of their production processes to a large degree as a function of market prices, it is essential that these prices correctly reflect the full costs and benefits to individuals and to society... Environmental taxes will prove to be one of the more effective policy responses in a significant number of cases'.

The Delors White Paper on Growth, Competitiveness and Employment (1993) advocates the replacement of taxes on labour with environmental taxation to benefit from the 'double dividend'. The correction of government failure via subsidy reform has made some progress. At EU level, while there has been reform of the Common Agricultural Policy, subsidies to agriculture are still high (Table 6.1). There has been a move to increase subsidies for farming that provides environmental benefits. The Environmental Impact Assessment Directive has resulted in about 7,000 EIAs per year being carried out within the EU.

Source: European Environment Agency, 1996.

Policy-makers became sympathetic to this approach for a number of reasons. Firstly, regulation had not been as effective as imagined. It was costly to bring firms to court and, in some cases, the probability of prosecution and the level of the fine were not sufficient to encourage compliance. In the free-market era of Reagan and Thatcher, the use of decentralised market-oriented approaches became more acceptable. In addition, policy-makers became more open to alternatives to regulation. The strongest argument for the use of economic instruments is that they minimise the cost to society of reducing environmental damage. With an economic instrument such as a charge on emissions, the firm or individual can decide upon the level of pollution they produce. A firm with a very high cost of abatement will pollute relatively more as it is cheaper than paying the charge while a firm with a relatively low cost of abatement will pollute relatively less as abatement is less costly than paying the charge. Under regulation, each firm pollutes the same amount. Therefore, there is no incentive for the firm facing lower costs of abatement to undertake more of the clean-up, so the reduction in emissions is made at a greater cost to society. Thus, economic instruments are cost-minimising while regulation generally is not (see Table 6.3).

Table 6.3 The gains from least-cost air pollution control

Study	Pollutants covered	Area of the US	Command-and-control policy benchmark	Ratio of CAC cost to least-cost policy
Atkinson and Lewis (1974)	Particulates	St Louis	State Implementation Plan (SIP) regulations	6.00
Roach et al. (1981)	Sulphur dioxide	Four Corners: Utah, Col., Arizona, New Mexico	State Implementation Plan (SIP) regulations	4.25
Hahn and Noll (1982)	Sulphates standards	Los Angeles	California emission standards	1.07
Krupnick (1986)	Nitrogen dioxide regulations	Baltimore	Proposed RACT (technology requirements)	5.96
Seskin et al. (1983)	Nitrogen dioxide regulations	Chicago	Proposed RACT (technology requirements)	14.40
McGartland (1984)	Particulates	Baltimore	State Implementation Plan (SIP) regulations	4.18
Spofford (1984)	Sulphur Dioxide Particulates	Lower Delaware Valley	Uniform percentage reductions	1.78 22.00
Harrison (1983)	Airport Noise	US	Mandatory Refit	1.72
Maloney and Yandle (1984)	Hydrocarbons	US DuPont plants	Uniform percentage reductions	4.15
Palmer et al. (1980)	CFC emissions ex. aerosols	US	Proposed emissions standards	1.96

Source: Tietenberg, 1990.

Market-based instruments also provide an incentive for firms to abate more than required by law. Under a regulation, firms will abate only as much as the standard set by the authorities. A further advantage of some economic instruments is that they are revenue-generating. It is sometimes suggested that the revenues can be used to reduce other taxes that are distortionary (see below).

Box 2. Why market-based instruments are favoured where implementation is feasible

Market-based instruments tend to be favoured by most economists over other instruments, especially over command-and-control, because:

1. Lower cost of compliance – improved efficiency: They allow the choice of strategy mix (change of product, change of inputs, change of process, change of treatment) to the polluter, and therefore are likely to yield the *least cost mix* of control strategies. There is a growing body of evidence that, if these instruments are applied properly, there will be very substantial cost savings to the economy as a whole. The cost issue is important for a number of reasons, not least because the costs of compliance with ever-tightening standards is becoming very large. Annual abatement expenditures for pollution control are estimated to amount to 1.3 to 1.5 per cent of GDP in the US, Germany, the UK and the Netherlands (Nicolaisen, Dean and Hoeller, 1991).

2. Reduced bureaucracy – improved efficiency in administration and implementation: Markets are more or less automatic in their effects, thereby minimising 'bureaucratic interference'. However, there may be substantial set-up costs involved. Command-and-control systems already have a bureaucracy in place, while some forms of market-based systems will require that a new bureaucracy be created.

3. Incentives to improve over time – dynamic efficiency: They create continuing incentives to innovate and to improve environmental performance. This is so because there is a direct benefit from improvement no matter what the level of existing performance. The command-and-control approach tends to impose a level of performance; once achieved, there is little incentive to improve.

4. Improved environmental performance: There is evidence that environmental performance is improved.

5. Generator (under certain conditions) of funds: The application of charges for emissions to water in France, the Netherlands and Germany has been used for decades to help finance watershed management and the provision and operation of collective treatment facilities. Where governments or public agencies are short of cash, this is perceived to be a potentially significant advantage, when compared with command-and-control and subsidy approaches, which are typically a drain on public funds.

Source: Convery (1998).

A summary of why market-based instruments are often thought to more favourable than traditional regulatory instruments is provided in Box 2. It is important to note that while regulatory reform in terms of environmental policy can provide the vehicle for replacing regulatory instruments with market-based instruments, these new instruments will generally require a regulatory framework in order to be effective. For example, in the case of environmental taxes, property rights must be assigned such that the polluter must pay for environmental damage and a law is required to ensure that polluters are made to pay the taxes.

Forms of market-based instruments

Interventions that seek to correct these failures of market economies to protect the environment include:
- removal of environmentally damaging subsidies
- assignment of property rights, including tradable pollution permits and development rights
- environmental taxation
- subsidies
- voluntary approaches
- improvement of information provision.

Removal of environmentally destructive subsidies

In terms of reducing environmental degradation, the first place to start is to reverse what is often called 'government failure'. Most governments provide fiscal incentives (soft loans, tax allowances) and some combination of price and grant support to develop particular assets. The results can be both economically inefficient and environmentally destructive. This may apply in cases such as the provision of incentives to promote otherwise uncompetitive domestic industry and/or to attract mobile capital.

The 'simple' solution to the subsidisation of environmentally damaging activity is to eliminate the subsidy. However, these subsidies have created powerful advocates for their retention, especially (but not exclusively) amongst the beneficiaries. The short-term social and economic implications for affected regions of their removal can be very painful, and countries will feel that their competitiveness will be threatened if they are precluded from competing with subsidies for the growth sectors of the global economy. Another issue is the fact that there may be large losses incurred by a country or region, which unilaterally reduces or eliminates subsidies which attracts mobile investment.

Box 3. EU agricultural policy

Agricultural policy has been the most heavily subsidised sectoral policy supported by the European Union. The environmentally relevant support has been of two types – price protection and subsidies for intensification, e.g. grants to drain or otherwise clear land for intensification of production, headage payments. These policies have had a number of negative environmental effects:

- *Intensification*: increased output per unit area: this has resulted in nutrient run-off and enrichment of fresh waters; nitrification of ground water; increased waste storage and disposal; increased abstraction of water for irrigation and other uses; and greater use of pesticides.
- *Extensification*: cultivation of areas for grassland, wine, olive and forest production of semi-wild areas, wetlands, scrub woodlands, rough grazing land, uplands, which would not otherwise have been brought into production, with resulting losses in terms of erosion and biodiversity.

In the MacSharry reforms of the CAP in 1992, a number of changes were introduced which diminished some of these perverse incentives. Price support was reduced, subsidies for development were reduced, while direct income support, unrelated to output, was increased. A series of accompanying *environmental protection* measures were introduced, to promote the use of farming practices which reduce pollution, support extensification, protection of landscape and countryside, provision of public access and leisure activities, education and training of farmers in environmental protection and upkeep of the countryside. Building on these reforms, Agenda 2000 proposes a 20 per cent cut in the intervention price of cereals in 2000, coupled with an area payment, and a 30 per cent cut in the price guarantee for beef by between 2000 and 2002 compensated by direct income payments. A similar approach has been put forward for the dairy sector involving a 10 per cent cut in average support prices by 2006. The objective is to improve the competitiveness of the EU, to provide stable incomes and a fair standard of living for the agricultural community, and to make agricultural production more compatible with the environment.

Source: Clinch et al. (1999).

Assignment of property rights

For economic instruments to work, property rights must first be established, i.e. does the victim of pollution have a right to a clean environment (the polluter-pays principle, PPP) or does the polluter have a right to pollute (the victim-pays principle, VPP). In the cases below, the PPP is assumed to hold given that this is the principle adopted in EU legislation (see above).

No interference in the market required?

There is one case where explicit intervention by policy-makers is not required even if pollution exists. Nobel laureate Ronald Coase suggested that government intervention would not be needed if property rights are assigned and the perpetrators and victims of pollution can negotiate. If property rights are assigned to the perpetrator, the victim will pay the perpetrator not to pollute so long as the benefits of abatement outweigh the costs; otherwise the victim will put up with the pollution. If the victim has the property right such that the polluter-pays principle is in force, the polluter will pay the victim compensation so long as the costs of abatement are greater than the benefits to the victim; otherwise the perpetrator will abate. In this way, the most efficient outcome is achieved without intervention. A simple example is the case of a polluting chemical factory located upstream from a food factory on a river. If the pollution coming down the river imposes a cost of €1 million per annum on the food factory and the cost to clean up the pollution at source is only €0.5 million, gains from negotiation exist. If property rights are assigned and negotiation can take place, then a solution can be reached:

Case 1:   The chemical factory is entitled to pollute (VPP) – the food factory can pay the chemical factory half €0.5 million to clean up the pollution and thus save a further €0.5 million.

Case 2:   The food plant is entitled to clean water (PPP) – the chemical plant will spend €0.5 million to clean up. This is because the food plant will not accept in payment anything less than €1 million to put up with the pollution since the pollution imposes a cost of €1 million on the food factory.

The Coasian solution is generally the exception. Even if property rights can be assigned, transaction costs may act as a wedge. This happens frequently in practice. Most environmental problems involve many polluters and/or many victims. The costs of negotiation can sometimes be overcome by the use of representative organisations such as residents' associations. In addition, there may be a free-rider problem. Taking the case of noise from a factory (where the factory has the right to pollute), there is an incentive for a villager affected not to contribute to a collection for a muffler to reduce the noise since if the other villagers contribute he or she will benefit from the reduced noise for free.

Transferable development rights

The key to channelling development in an efficient and equitable fashion seems to lie in separating the market for the right to develop from the right to use land. Transferable development rights (TDRs) work as follows: in a certain jurisdiction, e.g. a county or region, areas where development should be limited or prohibited are identified according to some criteria (e.g. landscape uniqueness, species protection, conservation of ecosystem processes, role in flood control, conservation of farmland); these are called sending areas. Also identified are areas where development is to be facilitated and encouraged; these are called receiving areas. Development rights are identified as follows: the land owners in the sending areas are given development units, designated per unit area, e.g. one residential unit of a certain size per 10 acres, but these can only be exercised in the receiving zone. If developers in the receiving zone wish to exceed the standard densities (or other norms to be defined) in the receiving zone, then they must purchase the right to do so in the development rights market. The legal instrument developed to transfer development rights in the US is an easement document and a deed of transfer, which are recorded and approved by the Planning Board. (Banach and Canavan, 1989). Two areas in the US – Montgomery County, Maryland, and the Pinelands, New Jersey – have successfully implemented a transferable development rights programme.

Box 4. A property rights approach from California: the 1991 water bank

In most countries and regions where a large proportion of the water supply is used for irrigation, the following difficulty arises. The water is nominally owned by the State, but the farmers have rights to traditional allocations, which gives them a sort of de facto property entitlement. They receive the water free or at substantially below the price that the water would fetch on the open market. Because they have free or very low-cost water, they use it at the margin in uses that yield very low value. Such was the situation in California, when a Water Bank was established, operated by the State Department of Water Resources. In February 1991, purchases from sellers of water were negotiated at a fixed price of $100/1000 m^3. Purchases ceased in April 1991.

Thirty per cent of the transferred water was needed for carriage water to provide salt protection in the Sacramento Delta. At this price, plus the transportation cost from the Delta, the bank sold 488 million m^3. Three-quarters of the water was sold to urban agencies at a cost, including transportation, of over $185/m^3. The water was purchased mainly from farmers – 50 per cent from irrigation water which they would otherwise have consumed, 33 per cent in the form of exchanging their surface water rights for ground water rights and selling the surface water to the bank.

The demand was obtained from a committee representing urban and agricultural purchasers. There were far fewer purchasers than suppliers, but the fixed-price approach eliminated the potential market power of purchasers. The estimated critical needs dropped from 769 million m^3 before the water bank was fully operational to 601 million m³ after, indicating how responsive to price such needs can be. The transfers generated an estimated net income and employment gain for the economy – as a result of transferring from lower to higher value uses – of $106 million and 3,741 jobs respectively. Note however that jobs did move out of the water-exporting regions, but the gain in the importing regions more than compensated for such losses.

Source: Howitt (1994).

Emissions trading

In a tradable permit system, permits to emit a specified volume of pollution are traded in the marketplace. The total amount issued is set such that the environmental objective will be achieved. Trades can take place within a plant, within firms (bubbling) or among different firms (offsetting). Earned credits can sometimes be saved for later use, known as banking. The ability to trade in the marketplace has the following advantages: the price of the permits expresses the scarcity value of the assimilative capacity being used; those firms with high marginal costs of control can 'buy' reductions from those for whom reductions are cheaper; promoting cost-savings and innovation. New entrants can then come into the area by 'buying out' enough permits to meet their requirements. Sorrell and Skea (1998) specify the conditions that should be met if trading is to fully fulfil its potential (see Box 5 below).

Box 5. Tradable permits - preconditions for success

Simplicity: Minimal restrictions on trade and streamlined administration and enforcement procedures.

Permit allocation: The most intractable issue. The system should be simple, based in part on historical data (grandfathering), with at least a small amount auctioned, and it should be perceived as fair.

Data: Accurate data on the baseline for permit allocation and reliable systems for emission-monitoring and permit-accounting.

Certainty: Protected from confiscation or arbitrary modification, and stability over a reasonable period of time.

Banking: Allow permits to be banked. This runs the risk of emissions exceeding a limit in a given year, but it enhances system performance considerably.

Enforcement: Strong penalties for evasion, and high probability of detection.

Compatibility: With existing regulatory systems. These should not inhibit trade.

Commitment: Strong political support, and commitment from key stakeholders, including the affected parties, non-governmental organisations and the implementing agency.

Source: Sorrell and Skea (1998).

A key issue in the design of emissions trading systems is the initial allocation of permits. Firms, as would be expected, favour grandfathering whereby, initially, pollution permits are allocated free-of-charge to existing firms. However, this follows the victim-pay principle since the firms are not paying for the pollution they produce. Rather, there is an opportunity cost in terms of the revenue foregone by the exchequer, which could be used to reduce a distortionary tax such as a tax on labour. In addition, the allocation of permits in this way may result in barriers to entry to the industry in question as new firms entering the market will have to buy permits from existing firms who received them free and therefore have lower costs of production. Grandfathering, however, has the advantage that the shock to the industry in question is less severe and it is more politically acceptable. A free allocation of permits is therefore simply an industrial subsidy from the government in question although, if the quantity restriction set by the number of permits grandfathered is less than would allow the firms to emit the same level of pollution as before, the firms will be absorbing a greater cost. In addition to the avoidance of the opportunity cost of the funds foregone, auctioning off of at least a portion of the permits has the advantage that the regulatory authority can use the funds in future years to 'buy out' some of the permits in order to reduce the overall level of emissions.

Box 6. The US acid rain programme

A tradable permit scheme was introduced to apply to sulphur-emitting electricity generating plants – based on tonnes of SO_2 emitted – in the US. When trading started in early 1993, the price per tonne of SO_2 was about $175 per tonne, and the volume of trading was very modest; trading on a serious scale did not begin until early 1995. As the volume of trading increased, the price per tonne traded declined, falling to as low as $75 in February 1996, but has since shown recovery, to reach $100 in February 1997. Most of the trading is done privately, but the US EPA still sells a small quantity at auction.

Reduction in emissions attributable to trading amounted to 3.88 million tonnes, from a total emission level pre-1995 of approximately 9 million tonnes. The marginal costs per tonne removed increased at an increasing rate as the reduction achieved approached 4 million tonnes.

The costs were substantially less than expected, in part because a parallel de-regulation of the rail system connecting the low sulphur coal-producing area in Utah (Powder River Basin) with the eastern electricity generating plants substantially reduced the costs of purchasing low sulphur coal.

Source: Ellerman (1997).

Most of the experience with tradable permits comes from the US (Box 4). However, there is some European experience with tradable permits, notably the use of trades to achieve reductions in the production of ozone-depleting substances – CFCs and halons. It enabled the chemical companies to concentrate production and shift to substitutes (Klaassen, 1997). Høibye (1997) reports on the design for a scheme of SO_2 trading in Norway. The main incentive 'driving' the Norwegian proposal is the quid pro quo of abolition of the existing SO_2 tax on mineral oil. Bohm (1997) reported on an experiment in the Nordic countries where the costs of unilateral compliance by the year 2000 with the CO_2 target are compared with the costs of achieving the same by allowing trades between Denmark, Finland, Norway and Sweden. Joint implementation would succeed in reducing compliance costs by 50 per cent.

Emissions trading has become of particular interest in the light of the UN Conference on Global Warming in Kyoto in 1997, when an international system of emissions trading in greenhouse gases was agreed upon.[3] Prior to this meeting, EU countries agreed in Luxembourg to make reductions in greenhouse gas emissions based on a 'burden-sharing' arrangement whereby most countries must make reductions in emissions by 2010, but the Cohesion countries and Sweden will be allowed increases.

In the light of the Kyoto agreement, Norway has devised an internal greenhouse gas emissions trading system which will link to the international system. EU countries are also examining such schemes to reduce the costs of meeting their targets set in the Luxembourg Agreement.

Environmental taxation

An environmental tax imposes an obligation on users to pay for the use of environmental resources. Charges and taxes in environmental policy bring the costs of pollution and of using environmental resources into the prices of goods and services produced by economic activities. As with other economic instruments, environmental taxes and charges provide an incentive for the cheapest means of preventing pollution to be implemented first and therefore offer the prospect of meeting environmental objectives more cost-effectively than total reliance on regulation.

The European Environment Agency's (1996) report on environmental taxes both documents the range of measures – including fiscal environmental taxes, incentive charges, cost-covering charges, and earmarked charges – which apply across the world, and their effectiveness. The European Environment Agency (1996) suggests that the taxes evaluated exhibited environmental benefits and appeared to be cost-effective; NOx charges and tax differentiation schemes for vehicle fuels in Sweden.

Subsidies

Another approach to reducing pollution is to give subsidies to firms if they do not pollute. Understandably, this is often advocated by the polluters. The difficulty with this approach is that, while an individual firm may pollute less, the availability of subsidies may attract firms into the industry and thereby increase industry pollution. Although the theory would suggest this, it may not be the case in practice. In addition, it may encourage firms to increase pollution prior to assessment so that they can take advantage of a higher subsidy. The use of subsidies in this manner does not comply with EU legislation, which stipulates that the polluter must pay.

Box 7. Examples of emissions and waste-related charges

1. The *Swedish sulphur tax* came into force in 1991, and is levied on coal, peat and oil, at a rate of 3,500 ecu per tonne of sulphur emitted.
Some results: Tax revenue of 34 million generated, sulphur content of heavy fuel oil decreased from 0.65 per cent to 0.50 per cent, sulphur emissions reduced by 6,000 tonnes annually, efficiency of sulphur removal improved at some coal and peat installations.

2. The *Swedish nitrogen oxide tax* was introduced in 1990, and came into force in 1992. It is charged on large and medium-sized boilers, at a rate of 4,500 per tonne of NOx emitted. The charge is assessed directly on emissions, and monitoring costs are high (35,000 ecu per plant per annum). The charges are refunded to the plants that pay it, in proportion to the amount of useful energy they produce, thus creating an incentive to not waste energy.
Some results: In the plants concerned, average emissions have dropped from approx. 150 mg NOx/MJ in 1990 to approximately 99 mg NOx/MJ fuel in 1992, and emissions in total have dropped from 24,000 tonnes in 1990 to about 15,300 tonnes in 1992.

3. *Waste charge in Denmark,* designed to reduce waste generation and increase recycling and re-use.
Some results: Re-used fraction of demolition waste increased from 12 per cent to 82 per cent, and waste re-use and recycling generally increased by 20-30 per cent from 1985-93.
The UK has also introduced a landfill tax, and reduction in waste volumes and increased recycling and re-use are being reported.

Sources: Bergman et al. (1993) and European Environment Agency (1996).

Voluntary agreements

Voluntary agreements (VAs) are agreements whereby an individual firm or group of firms make a commitment to operate in a certain way, and/or achieve certain qualitative or quantitative objectives such that environmental performance is improved. The use of the term 'voluntary' is perhaps misleading as there tends to be a 'stick' being waved by the regulator who must provide a credible threat of an alternative instrument being imposed on firms, e.g. a regulatory instrument. It is believed that firms participate in such agreements because they believe that they can achieve an environmental target at lower costs than they would have to endure if the regulation were imposed. This also suits the rest of society since the cost of achieving a particular level of environmental quality is minimised.

The number of such agreements has been increasing at EU, national and sub-national levels. This idea has had its most complete expression in Japan, where thousands of agreements have been made between local communities and their local factories, where the latter have agreed to achieve particular objectives, often with the local government acting as mediator and guarantor. In Europe, there has been considerable development of the approach in the Netherlands and Germany. They tend to be used more often in countries where environmental polices have matured and where there is a tradition of consensus-building, negotiation and decentralisation, which usually found where pollution occurs the most. Because voluntary agreements have been presented by various lobbies as an alternative to charges or taxes, there is considerable suspicion that they are favoured precisely because they are likely to be more symbolic than real in effect.

Storey (1996) recognises four categories of VAs, namely, those that are: target-based – required to meet a quantified target; performance-based – required to meet certain operating standards; cooperative R&D to meet environmental objectives; and monitoring and reporting – agreement to provide particular monitoring and ensuing data.

Such agreements appear to be most useful as complements to other policy instruments such as regulations and fiscal instruments, where they make a valuable contribution in terms of their ability to raise awareness, create consensus and provide a forum for information-sharing among parties. The absence of monitoring and reporting restrictions damages credibility of the instruments and denies accountability. This also makes ex-post studies of effectiveness difficult, as does the variations in the agreements examined in terms of their objectives and approaches, and variations in cultural, political, economic and environmental contexts in which they operate. Ideally, effectiveness should be judged against an alternative policy scenario or a business-as-usual scenario. This can often be speculative due to the absence of data. Evaluation of such agreements is also difficult as they are new, and relevant empirical and theoretical analysis is scarce.

The European Environment Agency (1997) concludes that, in relation to the environmental effectiveness of voluntary agreements, there is a need for the setting of clear targets, for greater transparency during negotiation, for more implementation and evaluation of EAs and for the introduction of reliable monitoring and reporting arrangements. Few evaluations of EAs, whether ex-ante or ex-post, have been made and there is a little literature available on their use. As a result, it is in most cases not possible to make a quantitative assessment of the environmental effectiveness of the agreements due to the lack of reliable monitoring data and consistent reporting. This prevents comparisons being made between the current situation and what is most likely to have happened if no agreement had been concluded. Some wider benefits are found, including environmental improvements on the situation prior to the agreements, and the encouragement of environmental management in business.

The use and effectiveness of voluntary approaches is linked to the use of information as a policy instrument, especially in the US, where, for example the 30/50 programme invites companies who are reporting toxic releases under the Toxics Release Inventory (TRI) to commit to substantial percentage reduction in emissions. In Europe, the Eco-Management and Auditing Scheme (EMAS) provides a voluntary register whereby firms must establish an environmental policy, conduct an environmental review of sites, set and implement environmental improvement programmes and an environmental management system, and have its policy and sites reviewed and its improvement and management system examined to verify that they meet the requirements.

Box 8. Voluntary approaches – The Rhine contract

The Rhine contract, between the Municipality of Rotterdam and a number of polluters of the Rhine, including the German Association of Chemical Industries (VCI – representing 600 firms), Duisburger Kupferhütte, Berzelius, Deutsch Giessdraht, and Ara Pro Rheno, to meet certain reductions in toxic emissions by 2010. The base line was established in 1985 by the Amsterdam-based International Centre of Water Studies, and agreed by industry. Cooperation was facilitated by the finding in 1988 by the Netherlands Supreme Court ('Hoge Raad') against the MDPA (French Potassium Mines) in a case taken by Dutch nursery firms on the basis that MDPA's emissions of chloride to the Rhine in Alsace, France – which reached a peak of 22 million tonnes – was contributing to damaging salt water pollution in the Netherlands. After 14 years of litigation, the Dutch court made a judgement against MDPA, in spite of the fact that the French company had a valid license to emit from the French authorities. This case established the principle that trans-frontier polluters could be sued successfully across frontiers, notwithstanding their compliance with the law in their own jurisdiction (van Dunné, 1996). The contracts negotiated between Amsterdam and the parties are in many respects confidential. The essential characteristic is the waiver of claims by Rotterdam for damages if the contracts – aimed at an overall reduction of 70 to 90 per cent in toxic emissions – are fulfilled. The modes of dispute resolution in the contract vary. There are indications – based on periodic monitoring – that the objectives specified will be reached.

Source: van Dunné (1996).

Liability systems and performance bonds

The following are examples of liability systems: legal liability for environmental damages is facilitated, e.g. the costs of fully restoring a fishery would be payable if the polluter(s) which damaged the same were identified; private or citizen enforcement actions are facilitated, whereby an individual can bring private enforcement actions against a polluter; in the US, 'Superfund' legislation attempts to levy funds for the clean-up of 'vintage' toxic waste damages. Examples of performance-bond-type instruments include: funds which are independently held, are set aside by resource extraction companies to make good any damages imposed as a result of ore extraction; provision of refunds for users of bottles and cans, or for cars to be scrapped, on their return to the supplier or other intermediary.

The law in most countries is moving to increase liability for damage, and to facilitate court action in this regard. Mining firms in many jurisdictions are being required to post performance bonds pending satisfactory environment and related performance. A number of countries, including Belgium, Canada, Finland, Norway, Portugal and Sweden have levied taxes on containers which are not part of a refund system or are not reusable.

Information

Approaches such as education, information and training change the perception and priorities within an agent's decision-making framework. This internalises environmental awareness/responsibility into individual decisions by applying pressure indirectly or otherwise. Tietenberg (1997) identifies the elements of an information strategy as follows:

- Environmental risks must be identified – amount emitted, degree of exposure, sensitivity to exposure.
- Reliable information must be assured, with penalties for misleading reporting.
- The information must be disseminated, in a form which can be used by the community, and to which the community has access, in a timely fashion.
- What can be done with information must be defined, which in the case of a polluting firm could include: a switch by consumers away from environmentally damaging products, selling – or not buying – stock in the relevant companies, difficulties in hiring very skilled and mobile labour, legal action by individuals or citizen groups, legislative change and private enforcement actions.

There is a literature that assesses the performance implications of specific information transmission schemes. The Toxics Release Inventory (TRI) has been implemented in the US, whereby companies must file annual reports based on a consistent and readily understood format as to the volume and character of specific categories of emissions.

The European Environment Agency has been established specifically to provide the Community and the member states with objective, reliable and comparable information at European level enabling them to take the requisite measures to protect the environment, to assess the results of such measures and to ensure that the public is properly informed about the state of the environment. (Art. 1.1, Regulation 1210/90).

There is also a Directive on Freedom of Access to Information on the Environment, (90/313/EEC) which: shall ensure that public authorities are required to make available information relating to the environment to any natural or legal person at his request, and without having to prove an interest. (Art. 3.1) Member states are required to implement mechanisms for ensuring public access to environmental data.

The Council Directive concerning integrated pollution prevention and control (96/61/EC*).* requires the issuing of a permit detailing the pollution limits and control procedures for emissions to all media for a wide range of industrial and related activities. In regard to information, under Article 15:

> Member States shall take the necessary measures to ensure that applications for permits for new installations or for substantial changes are made available for an appropriate period of time to the public, to enable it to comment on them before the competent authority reaches its decision...
>
> The results of monitoring of releases...must be made available to the public. An inventory of the principal emissions and sources responsible shall be published every three years by the Commission on the basis of the data supplied by the Member States. The Commission shall establish the format and particulars needed for the transmission of information in accordance with procedures laid down in Article 19.

Information on environmental performance also has the potential to either help or hinder commercial success. This is the principle behind the EMAS and eco-label schemes at EU level, whereby an imprimatur in regard to the quality of environmental management and environmental products respectively is provided to companies, on the principle that such may give them a commercial edge in some markets.

Choosing the appropriate policy Instrument

Sterner (1998) points out that policy selection and development is an art in itself and policies should not be picked 'off the shelf'. Neither should it necessarily be left to the environmentalists or others who propose a policy or are lobbying for certain improvement. Policy selection should instead be undertaken as a serious and difficult but not impossible profession. He says that, often, the range of policies is much broader than might at first be apparent. He also recommends that policy-makers should not focus too much on double dividends (see below) as they might not exist and will inevitably lead to long discussions. The environmental gains are real and many issues are so serious that they are more than sufficient cause to use policy instruments. Policies must be designed carefully if improvements are to be achieved at least cost and without conflict.

Sterner also suggests that the criteria that are the most relevant and important for the case at hand must be decided upon, as must the key features of the technology, economics and ecology under consideration. If efficiency is a key criterion and there are many agents with different cost structures, then economic instruments are strongly superior. If political acceptability is important, he states that attention will need to be paid to the issue of distribution of costs and that this depends very much on the type of policy used and can be a crucial way of gathering support and avoiding opposition from key groups.

A physical regulation may sound more definite and exact than an economic instrument but this need not be so. Sometimes bans or regulations just have perverse effects. On the other hand, there are other cases when economic instruments also have perverse effects. Sterner suggests that expertise in environmental economics is needed to judge the cases and to design instruments together with policy-makers and other advisors.

ENVIRONMENTAL POLICY, COMPETITIVENESS AND EMPLOYMENT

While environmental policy is designed to improve environmental performance, a key characteristic of an effective environmental policy must be that the costs it imposes on the rest of the economy should be minimised. The principal concerns in this regard relate to the impact of environmental policy on competitiveness and employment.

Competitiveness

In general, concerns about competitiveness and environmental policy relate to how domestic or regional (e.g. EU) policies affect the competitiveness of firms within the region vis-à-vis firms outside the region. Much of the research in this area centres around a one-page article by Michael Porter in *Scientific American*. The Porter hypothesis states that "strict environmental regulations do not inevitably hinder competitive advantage; indeed they often enhance it" (Porter, 1991).

There have been numerous articles using various methodologies to test this hypothesis; e.g. by examining trade patterns, Tobey (1990) found that environmental regulations imposed by most industrialised countries in the late 1960s and early 1970s did not measurably affect trade patterns and that there was no evidence to suggest that strict environmental regulations had pushed industry out of the US. Meanwhile Bartik (1988) showed there to be no statistically significant effects of environmental regulation on business location decisions. In one of the exceptions to the majority of the papers in this area which tend to concur with the above studies, Gray (1997) concluded that there is a significant relationship between the strictness of environmental regulation and the number of manufacturing plants in an area. He suggests that environmental regulation is as significant a factor in location decisions as such things as the rate of unionisation.

In general, however, the results suggest that, for existing industry, environmental regulation does not have a significant impact on competitiveness. Barker and Köhler (1998a) believe that the evidence does not support fears of adverse effects from environmental policy and this is supported by the OECD (1996) which states that the trade and investment impacts that have been measured empirically are almost negligible. However, Jaffe et al. (1995) suggest that the data available for such studies may have hindered their ability to measure the effects properly. There is little evidence to suggest environmental regulations can cause firms to relocate. The evidence regarding the initial location of new firms is less strong. The rationale behind the 'good news' is that the magnitude of environmental expenditures is small relative to other considerations.

The latter part of the Porter hypothesis is more controversial. It claims that competitive advantage rests not on static efficiency nor on optimising within fixed constraints, but rather on the capacity for innovation that shifts the constraints (Porter and van der Linde, 1995). This argument is based on the idea of firms having a first-mover advantage in their response to environmental regulation and that the adoption of cleaner technology often reduces costs of production. However, authors such as Palmer, Oates and Portney (1995) are of the view that, while there are exceptions, industry is unlikely to profit from stricter environmental regulation. However, Barker and Kohler (1998a) point to another benefit of strict environmental regulation, that is, that it may improve competitiveness in the long run by making a locality or country more attractive for mobile capital and labour; if environmental policy is part of an overall drive to modernise, improve standards and reduce waste, competitiveness may be enhanced.

Clinch et al. (1999) in their case-study approach of four industries conclude that environmental regulation has not had an adverse effect on competitiveness due to the identification of cost savings when improved management systems were put in place and as a result of consumer demand for better standards. However, this is not generalisable to all industries. In industries that compete worldwide, such as textiles, standards vary considerably and so the costs of higher standards in these industries are greater than in an industry such as dairy products where trade tends to be within Europe.

In conclusion, the evidence regarding this hypothesis can be grouped around the following questions with this author's suggestion as to the answer:

Q1:   Are established firms in a region with strict environmental regulation at a competitive disadvantage against firms in a region with lax regulation?

A1:   Not generally.

Q2:   Do stricter environmental regulations actually improve the competitiveness of existing firms?

A2:   Not generally.

Q3:   Will firms move in response to stricter environmental regulation?
A3:   Not generally.

Q4:   Is the extent of environmental regulation a significant influence on the location decisions of a new plant?

A4:   Possibly.

The competitiveness of nation states in the future

In terms of relative competitiveness within the EU, the harmonisation of environmental policy should reduce any competitive advantages that exist merely as a result of environmental policy. However, where regulations regarding ambient standards are set, countries with higher assimilative capacities will find it cheaper to comply all else being equal.

At a more global level, Barker and Köhler (1998a) state that future competitiveness has already been improved by environmental regulation in some areas e.g. the environmental protection industry that has sprung up at least partly as a result of environmental regulation is now a major arena for international competition in its own right. By 1991 this sector was valued at DM 26 billion alone and was estimated to be among the fastest growing sectors in OECD countries. Those countries which are major net exporters in this sector, the US and Germany (countries that have been characterised by high environmental standards for many years) may be considered to have gained in national competitiveness from it.

However, Barker and Köhler (1998a) suggest that the fact that environmental policy in the past does not seem to have affected national competitiveness does not mean that it will not do so in the future for several reasons, including:

- increasing globalisation with ever fiercer international competition may make environmental policy more disadvantageous than before;
- environmental policy is becoming more strict; and
- there is a cost of cleaning up past environmental damage (e.g. the US faces clean up costs of $750 billion for hazardous waste sites and $200 billion for nuclear weapons manufacturing). They suggest that such clean-up problems face all industrial countries to some extent and may well not yield 'win-win' gains of the kind hypothesised by Porter.

Employment

The effect of environmental policy on employment relates directly to its effect on competitiveness, the fear being that should firms become less competitive this will result in job losses. Thus, the conclusions presented above regarding competitiveness hold for employment with studies such as OECD (1997) and Robson (1997) indicating that the net effect on employment of environmental measures already taken is likely to be modest. Therefore, this section concentrates on whether regulatory reform in terms of a move away from command-and-control type approaches to market-based instruments will have any effect on employment.

Clinch et al. (1999) show that, in regard to the employment implications of taxes and charges, the empirical evidence from the past is modest, because these instruments have not been long in use, and such evidence as there is, is 'masked' by a wide variety of other factors. There is a more extensive literature focused on the future, using models, both econometric and general equilibrium, to assess the likely impact on employment of applying taxes and charges. This work was stimulated by a number of coincident forces, including the European Commission's proposal to apply a carbon energy tax, and recycle the proceeds in the form of reduced payroll taxes, the rising unemployment in the Union, and the linking of employment and sustainability in the Delors White Paper. The suggestion is that the revenue from an environmental tax be used to reduce labour taxes, thereby attaining the double-dividend of improved environment and higher employment. With this in mind, Koopman (1994) examines the economic effects for the EU of a 1 per cent of GDP general reduction in social security contribution rates financed in a budget-neutral manner by a carbon tax. His results suggest the impacts on private consumption, GDP and employment are all modest but positive.

There is now an extensive literature which examines the issues of a double-dividend in a partial or general equilibrium context, and which draws conclusions based both on theoretical models and quantitative analysis. The most complete rendering of such work in Europe was provided in 13 papers presented at the International Workshop on Environmental Taxation, Revenue Recycling and Unemployment, at the Fondazione Eni Enrico Mattei, Milan; this work has been summarised by Brunello (1995). These papers demonstrate that the outcome of such analyses depends on the assumptions made, in particular the assumptions as to how labour markets work. If the market for labour is reasonably competitive, in the sense that entry and exit are easy, and monopoly power by suppliers and demanders is limited, then the labour market will 'clear', and the economy should tend anyway towards full employment. These conditions are presumed to be approximated in the US, where unemployment in recent years has been much lower than in Europe, and where the 'double dividend' debate is not on the policy or intellectual agenda. If it is assumed that the labour market is perfectly competitive, then the double dividend is a chimera. But if there are rigidities (as is certainly the case in parts of Europe), then it seems likely that, in the short run, there will be an employment dividend as a result of a recycled carbon/energy tax. But in the long run, such rigidities become less relevant, as real wages adjust to the 'gain' represented by the fiscal transfer from environment to labour. The short run is not explicitly defined, but for the unemployed worker, the short run can seem very long indeed; it is clear that, in Europe, the linkage between environmental taxation, overall tax policy and employment is an important policy concern. In addition to the pan-European work, there are a number of country reports. Examples include Norway (Norwegian Green Tax Commission, 1996), Sweden (Swedish Green Tax Commission, 1997) and Nordic Council of Ministers (1996).

It is important to note that with the introduction of a carbon tax, losses tend to be concentrated in a few key sectors and regions, with a few large firms, while the winners are more diffuse (see Ekins and Speck, 1998).

Summary

In terms of regulatory reform and environmental policy, one thing is clear: the evidence suggests that effects on competitiveness and employment are relatively small. In addition, the replacement of command-and-control approaches with market-based instruments will have a beneficial effect due to their cost-minimising characteristics. However, it should be stressed again that the impact of environmental policy on competitiveness is highly industry-specific. The policy challenge is to design effective and efficient policies in these sectors.

ASSESSING THE BENEFITS AND COSTS OF ENVIRONMENTAL POLICIES

The Treaty of the European Union (1992) stipulates that the potential benefits and costs of action or lack of action must be taken into account in the preparation of policy on the environment. This suggests that environmental projects and policies should be subjected to a cost-benefit analysis. However, as discussed at the outset, environmental assets tend not to be mediated through markets and so do not have a price, which can be, used to reflect their value. To help ensure that non-market goods and services in general and environmental goods and services in particular, can command the requisite degree of attention and resources, a wide range of techniques has been developed to generate so-called non-market values. There are two broad categories of non-market valuation methods: revealed preference methods and stated preference methods (Clinch, 1999).

Revealed preference studies use data from actual behaviour to derive values for environmental assets. Suppose the value of a marketed good depends in part upon an environmental good. These methods try to isolate the value of the environmental good from the overall value of the marketed good. Such techniques include the following:

- Hedonic pricing: The value of a house depends, in part, on its surrounding environment. This method examines the determinants of the house's value and then isolates the effect that the environmental feature (e.g. a nearby park) has on the house. This is used as an estimate of the value of the environmental asset in question.
- Travel cost method: The value of the park can be estimated by the willingness to pay by people to attend the park in terms of costs of travel and entrance to the park.

- Production function approaches: These value a decrease (increase) in environmental quality as a result of some activity by the loss of (addition to) the value of production due to that activity e.g. the cost of pollution in a river to a fishery can be measured by the lost output of fish (dose-response functions), the cost of restoring the damage (replacement cost) or the cost of defensive expenditures e.g. a water filter.

Stated preference methods are direct valuation methods which ask people in a survey to place a value on the environmental asset in question either by rating (contingent valuation), ranking (contingent ranking) or choosing trade-offs between various policy alternatives (choice procedures). These direct methods via questionnaires are the only approaches that can estimate existence value. The best known and most controversial of these methods is contingent valuation.

Ideally environmental valuation would be used to calibrate market-based instruments. An environmental tax is like a price imposed on an activity for using the environment. It should be based on the costs of the environmental damage caused by the activity and the benefits of the products and services produced with pollution as a by-product. Put more clearly, we should weigh up the costs and benefits of abatement in order to calculate the appropriate tax. In reality few economic instruments are actually based on such cost-benefit analyses, an exception being the original UK landfill tax. Research on so-called target-setting using environmental valuation is still at a preliminary stage.

CONCLUSIONS AND POLICY RECOMMENDATIONS

The key vehicles for regulatory reform in regard to environmental policy are the increased prominence of sustainable development and environmental protection in EU legislation and the shift in emphasis from traditional regulatory or command-and-control type instruments to market-based instruments. The latter have been shown in many cases to be more environmentally effective. In addition, they minimise the cost of achieving environmental targets and in some cases provide revenue that can be used to reduce other taxes. The focus of EU environmental policy has reflected this knowledge with the Fifth and latest Environmental Action Programme recommending the adoption of market-based instruments as a vehicle for sustainable growth and environmental protection in the move to further economic integration while maintaining or improving competitiveness and employment. However, while the EU has championed the move, the progress varies quite remarkably from country to country (see OECD, 1997). Initially the idea that there was an acceptable level of pollution and that people could 'pay' to pollute meant that governments were slow to introduce market-based instruments. However, with the increasing sophistication of policy-makers the reasons for command-and-control continuing to be the predominant instrument for addressing environmental problems in many countries as outlined by Convery (1998) seems to be some combination of the following (re-ordered here):

- Familiarity breeds affection: those being controlled regard it as 'tolerable' while an alternative approach might not be so.
- There is a comfort factor for the public, administrators and politicians in knowing that each individual plant or facility is 'controlled'; the necessary institutions – courts, government agencies, business associations – are in place with sufficient credibility and adequately trained staff to implement the regulations to some minimum degree of competence.
- There is a cultural dimension whereby in societies where there is a respect for the law, where the reflex is to obey the law, to comply, the command and control approach is likely to be more feasible than where such respect does not exist.
- In some cases, it is the most effective means of achieving the relevant objective. For example, in the case of radon (a naturally occurring carcinogenic gas) which can be emitted in households, a regulation requiring the relevant protection and other measures be installed in all new houses ensures that the remedial action is taken at a time when it is only a fraction of the cost of retrofitting measures to deal with the problem.
- There are pollution categories where even small emissions are thought to be so toxic that a policy instrument is needed where there is no margin for error, where thresholds must be met at all times.
- Political barriers to implementation including perceived impact on competitiveness, perceived impact on low income groups.

In addition, Europe finds itself in a difficult position in regard to the use of taxes and charges as there is an inability to apply Europe-wide fiscal measures for the environment, as a result of the unanimity rule, and Single Market imperatives make it very difficult to apply such measures at member state level. Within countries, also, there is an interesting 'geography of opposition' to environmental taxation. Green Tax Commissions which have reported on their experiences state that much of the political difficulties arise, not from a fear of uncompetitiveness in general, but from specific instances of a small number of financially vulnerable plants in isolated regions with limited or no alternative employment opportunities which would be adversely affected by a carbon or other type tax.

However, despite the difficulties, there is still more scope for the use of economic instruments in almost all EU countries. The challenge is to determine from existing application where economic instruments work best and where they do not.

Clinch et al. (1999) recommend the following:

- Research in the area needs to focus more on the basis for the level of environmental taxes, i.e. target-setting using environmental valuation. The basis for environmental taxes and charges tends to be based on a second-best 'two-step' approach, i.e. an ambient standard is set and then taxes and charges are used to meet this standard. While this is usually more efficient than using regulation, it would be preferable to base charges on the costs and benefits of pollution control, the basis for so doing is provided in the Treaty of the European Union.

- Fears about the negative effects of market-based instruments on competitiveness are largely unfounded in many industries. These fears could be reduced by better information provision by government.

- While hypothecation (earmarking of funds) is not generally a good idea, the raising of revenue through environmental taxes could justify more funding for information provision. Fears about the effect of such instruments on competitiveness will also be allayed if taxes are introduced at EU level and if special attention is paid to those industries that compete with firms outside Europe.

- The introduction of EU-wide taxes is complicated by sovereignty issues. Efforts to harmonise taxes across Europe may have the positive effect of easing firms' concerns about their competitiveness. However, the harmonising of 'green' taxes is not necessarily efficient. A tax on pollution should be based on the damage it does to the environment and the costs of control. This may vary by country and, if so, a uniform tax rate while perhaps more acceptable will not be optimal.

- Guidelines on the evaluation of economic instruments, in terms of effectiveness and efficiency, should be built into the policy process.

- The implications of the broadening of the tax base through the introduction of environmental taxes should be explored. In particular, efforts should be made to avoid double taxation. If the public sees environmental taxes being introduced without a consequent reduction elsewhere, the taxes will be seen as revenue-generating rather than distortion-correcting. This is likely to lead to opposition.

- Distributional issues need to be examined before any environmental tax is introduced. There are 'fair' and 'unfair' ways of introducing such taxes. Distributional issues should not be used as an excuse to avoid the implementation of economic instruments. Distributional issues also arise when using regulation.

In summary, regulatory reform in terms of increased consideration of the environment in EU and member-state actions and policies is to be welcomed as is the increased focus on the use of alternative instruments to traditional regulation. However, in regard to the latter, the progress in individual member states is highly variable. It is important that greater progress be made in terms of the adoption of market-based instruments. The appropriate application of such instruments would result in more effective protection of the environment at a lower cost, thereby contributing to the better functioning of markets in Europe.

NOTES

1. The author would like to thank Frank Convery for helpful comments. The comments received from Cristina Sassoon (the discussant) and the other participants at the Regulatory Reform conference at CEPS in June 1999 are also greatly appreciated.
2. This section relies heavily on Clinch et al. (1999).
3. Further discussion of the details and issues of this agreement can be found in Bohm (1999).

REFERENCES

Artis, M.J. and N. Lee (eds) (1997), *The Economics of the European Union*, Oxford and New York: Oxford University Press.
Banach, M. and D. Canavan (1989), 'Montgomery County, Maryland: A Transfer of Development Rights Success Story,' in H. Hiemstra and N. Byshwick (eds), *Plowing the Urban Fringe: An Assessment of Alternative Approaches to Farmyard Preservation,* Joint Center for Environmental and Urban Problems, Monograph Number 88-2, Fort Lauderdale: Florida Atlantic University.

Barker, T. and J. Köhler (1998a), *Environmental Policy and Competitiveness*, Policy Brief Number 6, Environmental Policy Research Series, Dublin: Environmental Institute, University College Dublin.

Barker, T. and J. Köhler (1998b), *International Competitiveness and Environmental Policies*, International Studies in Environmental Policy Making, Cheltenham, UK: Edward Elgar.

Bartik, T.J. (1998), 'The Effects of Environmental Regulation on Business Location in the US,' *Growth and Change*, Vol. 19, No. 1.

Bergman, H., O. Jörnstedt and K. Löfgren (1993), *Five Economic Instruments in Swedish Environmental Policy*, Stockholm: Swedish Environmental Policy Agency.

Bohm, P. (1997), 'An Emissions Quota Trade among Four Nordic Countries', in S. Sorrell, and J. Skea (eds*), Pollution for sale: Emissions Trading and Joint Implementation*, Cheltenham, UK and Northampton, MA: Edward Elgar.

Brunello, G. (1995), 'Is the Double-Dividend Hypothesis a Cure for European Unemployment', *FEEM Newsletter,* No. 1.

Clinch, J.P. (1999), 'Why should we value the environment and how can we do it?', in S. Blau (ed.), *Economic Evaluation Methods of Environmental Measures*, Brussels: European Environment Bureau.

Clinch, J.P. and F.J. Convery (1999), 'Evaluation and the Environment', in M. Mulreany (ed.), *Economic and Financial Evaluation*, Institute for Public Administration, Dublin.

Clinch, J.P., F.J. Convery, E. Fitzgerald and S. Rooney (1999), *Economic Instruments for Sustainable Development: Improving the External and Working Environments*, Luxembourg: Office of Official Publications of the European Communities.

Convery, F.J. (1998), 'The Types and Roles of Market Mechanisms in Environmental Regulation', paper presented at the Conference Board Europe Brussels Forum, Brussels, January 28.

Ekins, P. and S. Speck (1998), 'The Impacts of Environmental Policy on Competitiveness: Theory and Evidence,' in T. Barker and J. Köhler (eds), *International Competitiveness and Environmental Policies,* International Studies in Environmental Policy Making, Cheltenham, UK: Edward Elgar.

Ellerman, A.D. (1997), 'Assessment of Compliance and Allowance Trading in the US Acid Rain Programme', paper presented at a Workshop on Tradable Permits, University of Sussex, Brighton, April 9 and 10.

European Environment Agency (1996), *Environmental Taxes: Implementation and Environmental Effectiveness,* Environmental Issues Series, No. 1, Copenhagen: EEA.

European Environment Agency (1997), *Environmental Agreements, Environmental Issues Series*, No. 3, Vol. 1, Copenhagen: EEA.

European Environment Agency (1999), *Environment in the European Union at the Turn of the Century*, Luxembourg: Office of Official Publications of the European Communities.

Gray, W.B. (1997*), Manufacturing Plant Location: Does State Pollution Regulation Matter*, NBER Working Paper No. 5880, January.

Høibye, G. (1999), 'Designing a scheme for SO_2 Trading in Norway', Sorell S. and J. Skea (eds) (1999), *Pollution for sale: Emissions trading and Joint Implementation,* Cheltenham, UK and Northampton, MA: Edward Elgar.

Howitt, R. (1994), 'Empirical Analysis of Water Market Institutions: The 1991 California Water Market, *Resource and Energy Economics*, 16.

Jaffe, A.B., S.R. Peterson, P.R. Portney, and R.N. Stavins, (1995), 'Environmental Regulation and the Competitiveness of US Manufacturing: What does the evidence tells us?', *Journal of Economic Literature*, Vol. XXXIII.

Klaassen, G. (1999), 'Emissions Trading in the European Union: Practice and Prospects', in Sorell S; and J. Skea (eds) (1999*), Pollution for sale: Emissions trading and Joint Implementation*, Cheltenham and Northampton: Edgar Elgar.

Koopman, G.J. (1994), 'Eco-taxes and Employment in Europe: Under which Conditions Can an Employment Benefit from Green Fiscal Reform be Expected?', paper presented at the Fourth European Round Table on Cooperation and the Role of the Social Partners in the Environment, hosted by the European Foundation for the Improvement of Living and Working Conditions, Dublin, 21-22 September, 1994.

Lévêque, F. (ed.) (1996), *Environmental Policy in Europe*, Cheltenham, UK and Northampton, MA: Edward Elgar.

Nicolaisen, J., A. Dean and P. Hoeller (1991), 'Economics and the Environment: A Survey of Issues and Policy Options', *OECD Economic Studies,* No. 16, Spring.

Nordic Council of Ministers (1996), 'Environmental Protection and Employment in Nordic Countries', Copenhagen.

Norwegian Green Tax Commission (1996), *Policies for a Better Environment and High Employment,* Oslo: Norwegian Green Tax Commission.

OECD (1996), *Implementation Strategies for Environmental Taxes*, Paris: OECD.

OECD (1997), *Evaluating Economic Instruments for Environmental Policy*, Paris: OECD.

Palmer, W. Oates and S.R. Portney (1995), 'Tightening Environmental Standards', *Journal of Economic Perspectives*, Vol. 9, No. 2.

Porter, M. (1991), 'America's Green Strategy', *Scientific American*, Vol. 264, No. 4, p. 168.

Porter, M. and C. van der Linde (1995), 'Towards a New Conception of the Environment – Competitiveness Relationship', *Journal of Economic Perspectives*, Vol. 9, No. 4.

Robson, C. (1997), *Employment and Sustainability*, Dublin: European Foundation for the Improvement of Living and Working Conditions.

Sorrell, S. and J. Skea (eds) (1999), *Pollution for Sale, Emissions Trading and Joint Implementation,* Cheltenham, UK and Northampton, MA: Edward Elgar.

Sterner, T. (1998), *Environmental Implications of Market-Based Policy Instruments*, Policy Brief Number 7, Environmental Policy Research Series, Dublin: Environmental Institute, University College Dublin.

Storey, M. (1996), 'Voluntary Agreements with Industry', paper presented at a workshop on *The Economics and Law of Voluntary Approaches in Environmental Policy,* Fondazione ENI Enrico Mattei and Cerna, Ecole des Mines, Paris, Venice, November 18 and 19.

Swedish Green Tax Commission (1997), *Taxation, Environment, and Employment*, Stockholm: Ministry of Finance.

Tietenberg, T.H. (1990), 'Economic Instruments for Environmental Regulation', *Oxford Review of Economic Policy*, Vol. 6, No. 1.

Tietenberg, T.H. (1997), 'Disclosure Strategies for Pollution Control', paper presented at the Annual Conference of the European Association of Environmental and Resource Economists (EAERE), Tilburg, June.

Tobey, J.A. (1990), 'The Effects of Domestic Environmental Policies on Patterns of World Trade: An Empirical Test', *Kyklos*, Vol. 43, No. 2.

van Dunné, Jan M. (1996), 'The Use of Environmental Covenants and Contracts in the Case of River Pollution in the Netherlands', paper presented at a workshop on *The Economics and Law of Voluntary Approaches in Environmental Policy*, Fondazione ENI Enrico Mattei and Cerna, Ecole des Mines, Paris, Venice, November 18 and 19.

7. Reforming Product Regulation in the EU: A Painstaking, Iterative Two-Level Game

Jacques Pelkmans, Ellen Vos and Luca Di Mauro

1. INTRODUCTION

Over the last 15 years or more, a paradox has emerged in the EU's product markets. In the early 1980s, prompted by stagflation, Eurosclerosis, stalemate in the Community and a loss of global market shares, it became clear to European business and governments that market reforms were indispensable. Over more than one and a half decades, reforms have been implemented both at EU and national levels. In product markets, the EU has realised much greater external openness (other than agriculture) and liberalised the internal market drastically in its '1992' programme.[1] Competition policy has become stricter, too. At national level, privatisation has been pursued in different degrees by different member states during the 1980s, and became widespread and similar between all the member states in the course of the 1990s. Regulatory reform has taken place at both levels, often directly linked with domestic, intra-EU or external liberalisation.

After so much reform effort, surely, one would not expect a major debate on the urgent need for regulatory reform, because product markets in Europe do not function properly? Paradoxically, this is exactly what has happened since the mid-1990s. The UNICE and Molitor pleas for regulatory reforms in 1995 were mainly about product markets.[2] The 1996-97 Single Market Review by the Commission found the overall economic gains from EC-1992 ('Completing the internal market') to be positive but far lower than the potential gains indicated in the Cecchini report on the basis of simulation.[3]

Since the June 1998 European Council meeting in Cardiff, economic reform issues – with product markets taking a prominent place, at both EU and national level – have become part of the Broad Economic Guidelines.[4] And although the important recent work of the OECD[5] and the McKinsey Global Institute[6] is mainly concerned with regulatory reform in services markets, product markets are included selectively and in the aggregate analysis. For the UK, McKinsey[7] is even more straightforward: 'The major culprit [of low- labour productivity] is product market regulation'. Was not the UK a front-runner in privatisation, liberalisation and regulatory reform, and has it not retained its commitment to regulatory reform?

The present paper is prompted by this apparent paradox. How much 'deeper' and wider in scope should product market reforms be before they yield the dynamism that benchmarking (e.g. with the US) and different simulations show is potentially feasible?

In trying to understand why so much reform effort has yielded only modest economic gain to the EU, we shall have to delve deeply into the intricacies of a highly complex two-level game, played between the EU level and the member states. On the premise (supported above) that product market reforms in the EU should be more effective in making markets more competitive, we examine the main avenues of regulatory reform which would, in the words of the Commission, 'make the most of the internal market.'[8] Having sketched the economic context of regulatory reforms and possible reasons why economic gains from reforms of product regulation have remained fairly modest (Section 2), we explore the nature and effectiveness of these reforms at both EU and national level. At the EU level, we survey reforms carried out in the single product market and point to the difficulties in rendering them effective for business conduct and competitive exposure. Four main tracks of product regulatory reforms are identified and their merits and weaknesses assessed (Section 3). Subsequently, we examine some of the remaining difficulties and barriers to economic effectiveness and regulatory reforms, including mutual recognition (Section 4). We also observe that, despite EU regulatory reform and approximation which would suggest (ceteris paribus) a decline of member states regulatory activity, a worrying secular trend of ever increasing regulation takes place at the national level. We attempt to underpin these observations with empirical data on the actual flow of the activities of the member states on product regulation over the past 11 years. Although some justification for this trend cannot be rejected a priori without detailed research, national data suggest that the EU reforms are apparently 'rowing against the tide' of strong regulatory pressures on both national and Community authorities. There is room for doubt whether these pressures, especially at the national level, are subjected to the required scrutiny in terms of costs and justification. If not, the internal market will suffer and with it the competitiveness of European business. In conclusion, we advance some suggestions for improvement (Section 5).

2. THE ECONOMIC CONTEXT OF PRODUCT REGULATORY REFORMS

We briefly remind the reader of the requirement, from an economic point of view, to regulate only when justified, and to do this properly. As is well known, this public-interest-driven prescription might not actually be followed in the regulatory process, because incentives, lack of discipline on the part of decision-makers and regulators as well as their private interests may lead to quite different results. We will argue that, other things being equal, member states' regulatory processes provide more scope for regulatory failure than the EU regulatory process does today. We will also sketch a few possible economic reasons why the economic gains from product market reforms in the EU have remained below potential.

2.1 The need for effective reforms: two hypotheses

The purpose of product-market reforms should be clear. If product regulations have not been properly designed or implemented, they may be less effective or even ineffective in overcoming market failures, while distorting markets unnecessarily. Such distortions are likely to be costly, in a static and dynamic sense, and hence reduce the competitiveness, growth and employment potential that markets could otherwise generate. Such costs can take many forms. There is broad agreement[9] that inefficiencies could include the following:

- Less incentive to economise on resources (cost minimisation or X-efficiency); they may take the form of employing too many factors (labour, capital, hence lower productivity), not least because competitive pressure to move to best-practice internal organisation is lacking.
- (Insofar as distorted markets allow excess rents) higher profits and/or wages, which have no basis in productivity levels; in the longer run, wages would almost certainly capture a considerable share of those rents, creating rigidities and resistance to change; they might also reduce competitiveness, hence growth and eventually lower the return on investment, dimming further the prospects for dynamism.

- Less responsiveness of firms sheltered by excessive regulation to market signals to change the product mix, improve product quality (as defined by the consumer/user) and to engage in innovation and targeted R&D.
- Delay in restructuring for reasons of scale, networking, engaging in mergers and acquisitions, and shedding relatively inefficient non-core business.

Against this backdrop, regulatory reforms should be governed by the following dictum: 'regulation should overcome market failure at minimal costs, without introducing regulatory failure'. Assuming that the reader is familiar with this terminology (see for details, Labory and Malgarini, elsewhere in this volume), we shall briefly sketch the two components of this dictum.

The first component is the standard result of the public interest approach to regulation. It implies that regulation can only be justified economically by market failures.[10] However, regulation always has a cost; the ideal regulation minimises these costs to all market agents while fully overcoming the market failure. In actual practice, even if regulation is properly justified, it turns out to be very difficult to achieve 'regulatory quality'. That is, maximising the net benefit of overcoming the market failure with the minimum of costs, including uncertainty, compliance costs, etc. (for the problems of regulatory quality at EU level, see Pelkmans, Labory and Majone elsewhere in this volume). Regulation-at-maximum-net-benefits is extremely demanding, even in a public-interest perspective. It requires a great many pre-conditions, and discipline and effort in the process of drafting, adopting, implementing and enforcing regulation. Moreover, 'good' regulation will deteriorate in quality, if not turn into 'bad' regulation, if private interests can influence the regulatory process.

The second component introduces regulatory failure. Regulatory failure can be generally defined as an excess of regulatory cost over benefits. It makes matters worse; accepting the market failure without regulating would actually be better. Regulatory failure may occur because rules are ineffective in overcoming the market failure (no benefits) while imposing positive costs. Or the regulation may be excessively costly, not worth the benefits. Regulatory failure is an extreme form of regulatory burden, i.e. situations in which the benefits are lower than possible and/or the costs are higher than necessary.[11]

The explanation of regulatory failure can sometimes be ad hoc. But severe or systematic regulatory failure calls for a more fundamental explanation. The private-interests approach views regulation as a principal-agent problem, in the presence of complexity (of sectors, and of techniques) and asymmetries of information. Without incentives and discipline and the appropriate institutional requirements, those directly involved in the regulatory process will perceive some scope for pursuing private-interests, which may be magnified by the lobbying process. Well organised groups, whether they be businesses (or segments of business), regions, environmentalists, consumer groups, labour unions, or others, may succeed in exercising an undue influence on those preparing, adopting, or implementing regulation. In extreme cases, particularly in sectoral issues where asymmetry of information and expertise play a great role, it is possible that regulatees might even 'capture' regulators or ministers or the specialist civil servants or the relevant parliamentary committee.

It is neither possible nor necessary to develop this theory here in detail. Its extreme versions[12] are somewhat controversial, particularly after the waves of regulatory reform in network industries in the entire OECD. But the approach might well have practical applicability in weaker versions, where different mixtures of private and public interests could give a more realistic flavour to the theory. Insofar as one may distinguish institutions that produce or enforce regulation, from actors who decide on regulation or who influence drafters and legislators, the following might be hypothesised. The institutions can be argued to have a pro-regulation bias and will be less interested or uninterested in the costs of regulation, except insofar as they are constrained by principles, instructions and case law. The actors have various roles, and all kinds of conflicting interests will play a part. This leads us to formulate a *first hypothesis*. Unless a powerful set of disincentives, controls and basic principles is adopted, which cannot be altered easily in day-to-day politics, one should expect *the quantity of regulation to be insufficiently constrained, the scope too large, and the quality (with respect to proper market functioning) sub-optimal*. Reforms will fail to generate the potential gains in actual practice if these basic requirements are not sufficiently fulfilled.

A second hypothesis relates to problems of national regulation arising from the two-tier structure of the EU. In the aftermath of the Single Act, the expansion of the regulatory acquis at EU level gave rise to fears of excessive centralisation, especially amongst the member states. This fear has prompted the emergence of a regulatory vision at EU level, which has had the effect of disciplining the EU regulatory machine to some extent, and of raising the quality of regulation via improvements in the regulatory process. The incentives behind this process are strong and permanent: the member states' actors involved in regulation will be keen to preserve the scope and powers of national regulation, unless case law, conflicts between member states or strong joint interests override this preference.

However, *member states themselves are not subject to similar pressures and disciplines*. For the sake of the single market and given the exposure to world competition, their regulatory autonomy has surely decreased. But such exposure factors similarly play a role at the EU level. Other things being equal, member states are not subject to typical 'federal' discipline as the EU level has increasingly come to experience. The *second hypothesis* is that, ceteris paribus, member states will use the remaining regulatory autonomy in an enthusiastic fashion, constrained by the single market and globalisation but sheltered by 'subsidiarity' in many other ways. The upshot will be fewer and weaker mechanisms that check the quantity and improve the quality of national regulation.

Of course, 'other things' need not be equal. Member states may come to recognise the long-run costs of excessive regulation, in terms of both quantity and quality, and initiate reforms. But without permanent discipline, national reform 'fatigue' and 'deeper' problems in the public administration as well as the impact of sophisticated lobbying might make it extremely difficult to sustain reforms over long periods of time. This would lead one to expect strong regulatory output even in countries that are more predisposed to undertake reform. If this were correct, it would – in the long run – exert a negative impact on the performance of the single market, as the manifold complexities and the compliance costs would, at some point, begin to discourage investments, initiative and innovation.

2.2 Non-regulatory reasons reducing gains from reforms

This paper focuses on regulatory reasons for difference between the actual and the potential gain from reforms, as expressed in the two hypotheses. It would be simplistic, however, to seek the explanation for the limited economic gains from product market reforms in the EU only within the regulatory realm. Some economic reasons suggest themselves, too, and this should be kept in mind, both in this context and in Section 4.

A first reason is that the potential gains could be overestimated. The problem is in the methodology. This does not apply to product markets only. In the Cecchini report (Emerson et al., 1988), Single Market Review (European Economy, 1996, Chapter 7) and the OECD report (1997), the micro-macro link is performed by exogenous shocks to large macro models. The approximate size of those shocks is derived from microeconomic field and desk research. As Nieuwenhuis (1997) has argued (and simulated), it is not correct to give simultaneous shocks by exogenous shifts in prices, wages, and productivity. This will involve double-counting, and hence the expected potential from the reforms will be lower.[13]

Second, the impact of product market reforms may be limited because of strong linkages with other markets. One-fifth of EU industry's inputs came from services in 1985,[14] and this share might well be higher today. Without reforms in services (especially in network industries like telecoms and postal, as well as road transport, air transport and logistics), the impact of reforms on competitiveness in product markets will be somewhat limited. The link with the labour market is perhaps even more important. With relatively inflexible real wages (downwards), the adjustment to greater competitive exposure will be almost entirely a quantity response – labour shedding and lower new demand. To the extent this painful adjustment will be avoided or delayed, especially given high unemployment in most of the member states, reforms in product markets will fail to generate more than marginal gains. Ironically, some of the existing unemployment is already a consequence of undue regulatory 'shelter': if prices are high and allow high mark-ups, this will increase wage pressure in shielded sectors and wages may come to exceed market-clearing levels, causing unemployment. In other words, the two-way interaction between product and labour markets may have the unfortunate effect of mitigating the expected potential of product market reforms. For an intensive theoretical and empirical analysis of this link, see Boeri, Nicoletti and Scarpetta, Chapter 9 of this volume.

Third, the impact of product market reforms may be limited because of interdependencies between product markets themselves. Despite the considerable reforms undertaken there are still product markets in Europe with relatively weak competition, and high prices, which supply inputs to other production. Examples include energy markets,[15] automotive parts and agriculture. Clearly, this reduces the scope for price competition, especially in product markets that use such inputs heavily. It is quite possible that, if competitive pressure in final goods markets is fierce enough, these markets will be eventually forced into competition, if not via direct price negotiation, then perhaps via mounting pressures on governments to extend regulatory reforms to those sectors as well. But this spread effect may take a long time.

Thus, economic analysis would seem to indicate that spreading reforms over all relevant markets may significantly boost the dynamic performance of the EU economy. In that sense, it supports the quest for further regulatory reform. This has been recognised in the Cardiff process (since 1999) where structural reforms are advocated for purposes of improving the overall performance of the European economy (see Pelkmans, Labory and Majone, in this volume, Section 2.2 for details).

3. REGULATORY REFORMS BY THE EU

3.1 From 1979 to 1999: 20 years of product regulation reforms

During the least two decades the Community has engaged in pervasive reforms of product regulation. These reforms have followed different – in part, complementary – tracks and it is far from easy to obtain a comprehensive picture, let alone to grasp their overall economic meaning. This section aims to provide the main features of the reforms and to highlight their qualitative economic significance for the internal market of the EU. We may observe four main tracks of regulatory reforms (see Figure 7.1). These reforms are primarily driven by the commitment to realise the free movement of goods in the internal market without addressing the economic justification of product regulation directly. It has only been in the 1990s that the quality of the EU regulatory activities has become an issue of concern.[16]

Figure 7.1 shows four reform tracks since 1979, driven by the completion of the internal market. Two tracks emanate from EU disciplines on national regulatory activities, which (may) fragment the single market. A distinction should be made between existing and new draft regulation: the former has become subject to mutual recognition via innovative case-law (the 1979 *Cassis de Dijon* ruling and its follow-up), and the latter has been subordinated to EU-level scrutiny in an exhaustive and powerful notification procedure, jointly exercised by the member states and the Commission.[17] The other two tracks concern regulation at EU level, in fact mainly approximation,[18] the bulk of the 'acquis' of the internal product market. First, approximation directives no longer apply total harmonisation with exhaustive specifications, but, in a 'new approach', concentrate on the objective(s), with a standards system backing this up where possible. Second, the entire field of compulsory conformity assessment has been rationalised and made transparent, by setting clear and objective criteria for assessment requirements, including for the bodies who provide these services, with mutual recognition of conformity assessment and hence EU-wide competition for these services, without a 'race to the bottom'. Below, we discuss the main features of these avenues.[19]

Figure 7.1 Reform tracks of EU product regulation

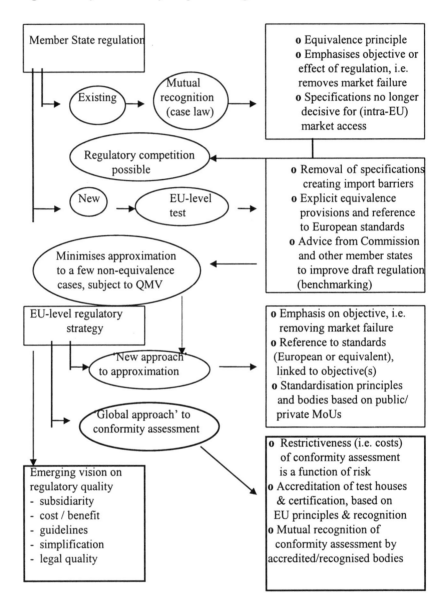

3.2 Mutual recognition of product regulation

The principle of mutual recognition has been developed by the European Court of Justice (ECJ) in its case-law. In its famous *Cassis de Dijon* case, the ECJ held that, in principle, a member state must allow a product lawfully produced and marketed in another member state into its own market, unless a prohibition of this product is justified by mandatory requirements, such as health and safety protection (see below).[20] This means that member states cannot apply certain specific details of national regulation to intra-EC imports of goods, if the objective or effect of the relevant law in other member states is equivalent to that of the importing country. The idea behind mutual recognition is that all member states care for their citizens and cannot be assumed to produce, for instance, unsafe or unhealthy products, merely because technical specifications differ somewhat. Hence, the principle of mutual recognition plays a pivotal role in the internal market since it ensures free movement of goods (and services) without making it necessary to harmonise national legislation. Since free movement of goods is essential to the internal market, it is not surprising that the burden of proof of 'non-equivalence' of objectives is on the member state which is unwilling to allow the import of the products concerned. Where the regulatory activities are not equivalent, free movement can be impeded. In such cases, however, the Treaty offers a remedy to the free movement by allowing for the approximation of precisely those objectives or effects under Art. 95 EC (ex Art. 100a EC).

In order to grasp fully the role and significance of mutual recognition one needs to understand how liberalisation (free movement), mutual recognition and approximation link together. This interrelationship is summarised in Table 7.1. As is shown in the table, the Treaty provides instruments for both liberalisation (mutual recognition) and approximation. Art. 28 EC gives expression to the general principle of free movement of goods by prohibiting the member states from imposing quantitative restrictions on imports or measures having an equivalent effect. This prohibition is a means of dismantling national barriers in order to allow for the free movement of goods throughout the Community market. Quantitative import (or export) restrictions include all legislative or administrative rules restricting the importation (or exportation) of one or more products according to quantitative norms. In *Dassonville*, the ECJ removed all uncertainties about the interpretation of the concept of 'measures having equivalent effect' by declaring that trading rules enacted by member states which are capable of hindering, directly or indirectly, actually or potentially, intra-Community

Table 7.1 Interaction between liberalisation, mutual recognition and approximation

Article	Nature	Main features
28 EC (ex 30 EC)	Liberalisation	• Prohibition of quantitative restrictions on imports or measures having an equivalent effect (regulatory barriers)
	Extended: (ground work for mutual recognition)	• Dassonville Ruling of 1974: widening of prohibition to all regulatory barriers: '[a]ll trading rules enacted by Member States which are capable of hindering, directly or indirectly, actually or potentially, intra-Community trade are to be considered as measures having an effect equivalent to quantitative restrictions' • Enhances liberalisation
28 EC (ex 30 EC)	Mutual recognition	• Cassis de Dijon Ruling of 1979: further refinement of the principle of equivalence • Member states must allow a product lawfully produced and marketed in another member state into their own market, unless a prohibition of this product is justified by mandatory requirements (see Derogations below) • If regulatory objectives or effects such as Safety, Health, Environment and Consumer protection (SHEC) are equivalent member states must mutually recognise each other's legislation • Obligation to include a mutual recognition clause in national legislation (Foie Gras Ruling and Dir. 98/34) • If not equivalent, then approximate (see Approximation below) • Enhances liberalisation even more

Table 7.1 continued

30 EC (ex 36 EC) and 28 EC (ex 30 EC)	Derogations to liberalisation and Mutual recognition	• All grounds mentioned in Art. 30 EC, which are restrictively interpreted and • Other 'mandatory requirements' developed in the ECJ's case-law, notably the Cassis de Dijon Ruling ('rule of reason') • All derogations are subject to a proportionality test
95 EC (ex 100a EC)	Approximation 'New Approach' (broad and/or horizontal)	• Where national (SHEC) objectives are *not* equivalent, approximation unifies those objectives • Wide sectors covered (e.g. machines) • Or horizontal issues covered (e.g. directives on food additives or general product safety)
95 EC (ex 100a EC) only if not applicable: 94 EC (ex 100 EC)	Approximation 'Old Approach' (specific and/or vertical)	• All other (product) approximation; for instance: ⇒ Involving high risk (chemicals, cars) ⇒ Precision in rules required (measuring instruments) ⇒ Specifying certain product compositions, such as jam and marmalade and cocoa and chocolate)

trade are to be considered as measures having an effect equivalent to quantitative restrictions.[21]

This interpretation paved the way for a very broad interpretation of measures of equivalent effect.[22] In its famous *Cassis de Dijon* ruling, the ECJ further refined the principle of equivalence and ruled that products lawfully produced and marketed in one member state must be admitted by another member state, save where refusal is justified by virtue of mandatory requirements.[23] The Commission eagerly concluded from this judgement that many obstacles to trade could simply be eliminated by strictly applying the prohibition contained in Art. 28 EC (ex Art. 30 EC), since whenever an imported product 'suitably and satisfactorily' satisfied the legitimate objective of a member state's rules (such as SHEC objectives), the importing country could no longer justify prohibitions on its sale by claiming that it fulfilled the legitimate objective in a different manner from domestic products.[24] Hence, in its 1985 White Paper on the Completion of the Internal Market (European Commission, 1985), the Commission adopted the principle of mutual recognition as its main strategy to achieve the internal market. In addition, it proclaimed its intention to concentrate its approximation activities mainly in areas where trade barriers were justified according to the criteria determined by the Court.

The principle of mutual recognition thus implies that member states, when drawing up commercial or technical rules liable to affect the free movement of goods, may *not* take an exclusively national viewpoint and take account only of requirements confined to domestic products. The proper functioning of the common market demands that each member state also give consideration to the legitimate requirements of the other member states. In this way, mutual recognition case-law boils down to regulatory reform because exposure to competition from elsewhere in the Union is enhanced, without compromising the purpose of regulation, namely, overcoming SHEC-type market failures. According to the ECJ's case-law, member states are moreover required to include in their national legislation a so-called mutual recognition clause, in order to allow the acceptance on their territory of products which are in conformity with the legislation of another member state.[25] This requirement stems from the implementation of the notification procedure laid down in Information Directive (98/34/EC, see below).

In emphasising the objective(s), rather than the detailed specifications, in a national product law or decree, the national regulation as well as the regulation of member states where the imported product comes from are *forced to concentrate on overcoming the market failure*. This will tend to make regulatory failure unattractive. At the same time, however, it assumes that the grounds in Art. 30 EC (ex Art. 36 EC) represent market failures. If one includes the so-called 'rule of reason' of Art. 28 EC (ex Art. 30 EC) which justifies national regulation involving environment and consumer protection, and observes that almost all the relevant product regulation related to Art. 30 EC (ex Art. 36 EC) is about health and safety protection, this assumption is broadly correct.

Another matter altogether is whether the market failure is overcome *at least cost*. Two aspects must be mentioned in this regard. On the one hand, mutual recognition greatly reduces the importance of product specifications in the law (as long as the objective or effect of regulation under which the imported product is produced is 'equivalent'). This is *cost-reducing* because disproportional or unnecessary requirements can be avoided, at least for imported products; it will also facilitate wider choice and product innovation as more flexibility is allowed. On the other hand, one should consider the question of whether domestic regulation is altered once mutual recognition leads to greater import competition. Such strategic alteration of domestic regulation is called 'regulatory competition.' As long as the new regulation succeeds in overcoming the market failure, regulatory competition will tend to reduce regulatory costs, without a loss of benefit. Mutual recognition may induce regulatory competition under the constraint of 'equivalence', but whether it actually does this effectively is doubtful (see Section 4.2.3). *Mutual recognition does not ensure a genuine cost/benefit test of national regulation*, since this is not necessary for the achievement of free movement of goods. All that one can say is that mutual recognition serves, under EC law, as a prerequisite for a proportionality test of *national* product regulation (e.g. labelling instead of an import ban).

3.3 Disciplining national regulation

There are three ways by means of which the EU can discipline national regulation or interventions in product markets: 1) infringement procedures under Art. 226 EC (ex Art. 169 EC); 2) the notification procedure under the Directive 98/34 (better known as 83/189, as it was referred to before its consolidation in 1998);[26] and 3) the notification – derogations to free movement procedure under Decision 3052/95.[27]

The first means of disciplining national regulation are infringement procedures. These procedures, which the Commission has at its disposal to supervise the application of Community law by the national authorities, are important instruments for ensuring the free movement of goods. Yet they are very time-consuming and costly, work only after the fact and respond only in an ad hoc fashion. Although the mere existence of these procedures exercises a disciplinary effect, and the ensuing case-law establishes authoritative interpretation, they are insufficient. And in no way can these procedures prevent the *creation* of trade barriers. For the purpose of our paper we shall therefore focus on the two other means of disciplining national regulation, which have been used as preventive instruments.

There was a need for a general mechanism to discipline the *preparation* of national regulatory activities. Hence, to allow the Commission to closely monitor national legislative proposals, an information system was set up in 1984 that obliged the member states to notify all their draft technical regulations. This system, originally laid down in Directive 83/189 and currently in 98/34, has as its leading objective the *prevention* of new regulatory barriers. Revolutionary at the time it was adopted, this system is arguably the most important reform since the *Cassis de Dijon* ruling (for more detail see Section 4.3.1). Directive 98/34, the so-called Mutual Information Directive, obliges member states to notify of all draft product regulation which they intend to adopt unless these relate merely to a full transposition of an international or European legal requirement (e.g. EU directives). In practice, this means that *all national regulation has to pass an EU test*. This test includes an assessment by the Commission of the impact of the proposed national legislation on the free movement of goods. The Commission concentrates on the removal or amendment of provisions considered likely to create barriers to free movement, and on the explicit insertion of 'equivalence' and of reference to European standards (rather than national, or other specifications). The damage to the functioning (indeed, the credibility) of the internal product market would undoubtedly have been enormous without this strict test. The difficulty of measuring the benefits of preventing would-be barriers should not lead one to underestimate the significance of this daring reform. Daring, because national legislative procedures are blocked (the so-called 'stand-still' period) for anything between three months and 18 months, essentially on the grounds of the expected benefit to the internal market. The test does not, however, comprise an assessment of whether the national regulation (in draft) actually overcomes a market failure at least-cost or whether the benefits are worth the expected costs to market participants (and the government). What matters for the Commission is safeguarding free movement, if possible by facilitating mutual recognition, but not interfering in national regulatory autonomy otherwise. This is viewed as contrary to the subsidiarity principle. Where cost-raising specifications are not contrary to EC law, the Commission and the other member states might provide 'comments' of an advisory nature, about whether the specifications are disproportional (i.e. too costly) and indeed necessary for achieving the objective.

A third instrument for disciplining national regulatory activity is the notification-of-derogations procedure laid down in Decision 3052/95. As will be explained into more detail below (see Section 4.3.2), this Decision establishes a 'procedure for the exchange of information on national measures derogating from the principle of the free movement of goods within the Community.' It develops a mechanism for making derogations of free movement transparent (here: of mutual recognition) in 'non-harmonised sectors' and requires member states to notify the cases in which they want to prevent, on ground of non-conformity with their own national rules, the free movement or placing on the market of goods lawfully produced or marketed in another member state.

3.4 Approximation under the 'New Approach'

Where mutual recognition fails, the EU can decide to take up regulation approximating national legislative provisions in order to ensure the free movement of goods. In an attempt to overcome the drawbacks of the 'old approach' to the abolition of technical barriers to trade followed by the Council since 1969,[28] the Commission launched in 1985 its 'New Approach to Harmonisation and Technical Standards,' focusing on the reduction of the Council's workload and on accelerated decision-making procedures. This approach restricts legislative approximation to stipulating essential health and safety requirements, whilst the specification of these requirements in technical standards is left to the European standardisation bodies (CEN and CENELEC). The distinction between the essential safety requirements and technical specifications constitutes the main characteristic of the New Approach. The 'New Approach' thereby absorbs the common national dichotomy between law and technical norms. Under it, products which are manufactured according to the harmonised standards are presumed to meet the essential safety requirements, although the technical specifications maintain their status of voluntary standards.

From an economic perspective the 'New Approach' can be assessed in two complementary ways. The usual evaluation compares it to the 'old' approach of exhaustive and total 'harmonisation'. Since the latter violates the criteria for optimal regulation of product markets, such as least-cost and proportionality, and possibly implies 'regulatory failure' in some cases, it is clear that the 'New Approach' is a major step in helping product markets in the EU to function better. The launch of the 'New Approach' coincided with the introduction and systematic application of qualified majority voting (QMV) by the Single European Act for harmonisation directives under Art. 95 EC (ex Art. 100a EC). Hence, QMV (the White Paper's institutional corollary) provided the necessary means to accelerate decision-making. Admittedly, application of the QMV would also have made the 'old approach' more attractive and would have facilitated decision-making, removing the threat of veto by the member states. Yet it must be noted that application of QMV under the 'New Approach' differs in that it is much easier to reach consensus in the Council on, for instance, health or safety objectives than on each and every specification of a specific product, or even on its testing and certification. In fact, the introduction of qualified majority voting in Art. 100a (now 95) has proved particularly significant for the adoption of product regulation. The threat of being outvoted has made member states more willing to negotiate, which has resulted in compromise solutions in fields where, for many years, no decision had been possible.[29]

The second manner of assessment is to compare the 'New Approach' to mutual recognition and regulatory competition. Approximation suggests that there is no prior equivalence between objectives of national regulation, otherwise mutual recognition should apply. A lack of equivalence could be due to the fact that some member states have barrier-prone regulation and others have not, or, that the objectives of all existing national regulation of a product differ 'too much.' Under the 'New Approach', approximation can be viewed as a written agreement in Council on equivalence. In actual practice, it turns out to be far more complex, because the 'New Approach' defines the objectives over wide product groups. As soon as the objectives have to be operationalised in mandates for European standardisation, differentiation and precision are often required, hence directives have to go further than mere equivalence of objectives. Some economists have attempted to show that regulatory competition between member states driven by free movement under mutual recognition can be (economically) superior to approximation. Given the equivalence, 'the market' (rather than civil servants and ministers) would reveal consumer and user preferences, and in this way the desired specifications could be 'discovered,' which can then be codified in directives to facilitate trade. Although this might possibly be correct in comparison with the 'old' approach, it is unlikely to be superior to the 'New Approach' (Sun and Pelkmans, 1995). Moreover, where the 'New Approach' fails because no qualified majority on objectives (or effects) can be found, regulatory competition fails as well, because free movement would be blocked.

The Achilles heel of the 'New Approach' is the availability and the quality of European standards. To be sure, the European standardisation community has adopted useful principles and is now more closely linked to world standard bodies and therefore attune to global standards, where possible. By mandate, the European standards relevant to regulation are linked to the regulatory objectives in directives. All these elements should improve standardisation and hence help markets function better. Nevertheless, a number of problems in standard setting are still evident. The most difficult economic problem is that it is next to impossible to judge the quality of standards from the point of view of market functioning, which is, nevertheless, their very purpose. From a legal perspective, the division of labour between the Community institutions laying down the general safety requirements and the standardisation organisations translating these requirements into standards has been ardently debated. In general, this public/private dichotomy has been viewed as problematic if not illegal as it would amount to a delegation of powers to private standardisation bodies.[30]

3.5 Competitive conformity assessment between accredited bodies

Yet another reform was needed in testing and certification or, more widely, conformity assessment (including also inspection, etc.). A product from country A offered in country B under the 'New Approach' might be refused if the testing methods used to verify compliance with the standard differ between A and B, or if the intensity of conformity assessment differs (e.g. type approval versus regular samples of batches versus product-by-product approval versus a mere manufacturer's declaration based on in-house conformance procedures).

The so-called 'global approach'[31] of the Community has greatly improved matters in this respect by defining seven modules of conformity assessment, ranging from relatively low-cost and flexible (module A, manufacturers declaration of conformity) to module G (EC unit verification), dependent on risk assessment, plus a module on quality systems for designs. Moreover, for mandatory conformity assessment (under EC directives), so-called Notified Bodies have been identified in all member states, subject to ISO quality standards for conformity assessment bodies. With European standards, modules and quality level of conformity assessment all equivalent, not only do arbitrary barriers – in this respect – in the internal market disappear, but mutual recognition has been introduced as well. In other words, between accredited test houses and between Notified Bodies, conformity assessment valid for the entire single market has become competitive, without lowering the level of trust. For industry, this means that production can take place in member state C and conformity assessment in D, with subsequent sales being EC- wide. It goes without saying that this has reduced direct costs for any given level of requirements, and has greatly reduced associated costs of uncertainty, waiting lists, etc. An additional advantage is that *voluntary* conformity assessment (for quality, guarantees, liability, etc.), which is a major 'industry' in the EU, has begun to organise itself Europe-wide and to align procedures and quality, with similar beneficial effects (see e.g. Machado, 1995). One extra benefit for industry is that economies of scope can be reaped in numerous cases where collocation of voluntary and compulsory conformity assessment takes place.

In turn, this has fostered a well defined external policy for the conclusion of mutual-recognition-agreements (MRAs), as foreseen in the TBT

Agreement in the WTO. Under such MRAs, now concluded with, e.g. the US, Canada and Australia, the quality of conformity assessment in Europe is trusted by trading partners, even when such European assessors verify standards or technical requirements of the trading partners themselves.

Once again, this significant improvement, though reducing costs compared to the past, is not rigorously based on cost-benefit analysis, as the primary purpose is to accomplish free movement in the single market.

4. WHY MORE POTENTIAL IS NOT RELEASED

From the preceding sections it can be concluded that *EU reforms have been significant for the functioning of the product markets and are commendable steps in the direction of making the internal market function better.* Exactly how effective the reforms are in achieving a better market is exceedingly difficult to assess. Not only is the empirical economic incidence of such complex and long-run reforms almost impossible to establish with confidence, important pieces of the puzzle are resistant to economic analysis (such as economic optimality of several thousand standards, linked to regulatory objectives. All one can say is that the principles promote flexible outcomes, e.g. performance rather than design standards, and are market-driven – without collusion).

However, the four tracks of EC reforms do not 'make the most of the internal market.' Remaining weaknesses, for instance, result from insufficient depth of reforms and, in selected cases, a moderate degree of avoidable EC regulatory burden.

This section will concentrate on two weaknesses in the EC product regime that prevent the efficient and effective functioning of the internal market: the considerable practical problems of *making mutual recognition work*, and the consequent weakening of competitive pressures; and the *steadily increasing flow of new national product regulation.*

4.1 The problematic application of mutual recognition

Mutual recognition has rightly been praised as an important innovation, allowing member states to retain limited regulatory autonomy and avoid centralised regulation, while potentially generating some of the benefits of regulatory reform. Over the years, however, mutual recognition has not had the practical success that the Commission envisaged in its 1985 White Paper.

4.1.1 Practical problems of mutual recognition

Obviously, it would be impractical to measure the actual application of mutual recognition for many thousands of products. It is easier to establish when mutual recognition is not implemented. In general, four information sources on the denial of mutual recognition exist: a) the notifications of draft technical regulations and standards by the member states under the Information Directive and other Community acts; b) information obtained by the Commission from private organisations contracted by the Commission to detect breaches of the notification obligation; c) complaints on the refusal to recognise and hence eliminate existing trade barriers, filed by individual economic actors and/or citizens with the Commission; and (d) individual enforcement and infringement proceedings before the European Court of Justice.

On the basis of the information thus obtained, the voluntary application of mutual recognition has been judged disappointing, faltering, inter alia, in the face of the member states' unwillingness simply to accept each other's products, and unable to address the health and safety regulatory concerns of national authorities. Particularly in fields of health and safety, where consumers cannot evaluate the cost-safety trade-offs in relation to certain products, member states have often refused to accept the products from other member states and national authorities have continued to adopt legislative provisions to provide additional protection. For instance, with respect to medicinal products, a field where politically sensitive decisions on 'risky' medicines are taken, member states have often been very distrustful towards other administrative authorities and have insisted on compliance with their own regulations, refusing entry to imported goods and forcing the Community to set up authorisation procedures for medicinal products and to set up a European Agency for the Evaluation of Medicinal Products.[32] The lack of mutual trust, has often led national authorities to prefer to undergo the full Art. 226 EC (ex 169 EC) procedure or to confront actions brought by interested parties in national courts before eventually being forced to accept mutual recognition by the EJC (in the latter case by virtue of Art. 234 EC (ex 177 EC). In view of the time and energy which such procedures entail, mutual recognition has therefore demonstrated its inadequacy as a regulatory instrument in overcoming the differences in national legislative provisions.

Moreover, as the ECJ's case law shows, mutual recognition also has its shortcomings where the objectives of national legislation diverge or where there is no agreement on the means of achieving regulatory equivalence.[33] Such cases require approximation by the EU. Seen in this way, the new Commission strategy has to some extent resulted in a re-regulatory operation at the Community level in areas such as consumer and environmental protection, policies largely based on Art. 95 EC (ex 100a EC).[34] It has led to the re-organisation of traditional legislative techniques and the establishment of comprehensive mechanisms for health and safety regulation within the internal market.[35] At the same time, however, the Commission has never lost faith in mutual recognition. Faced with disappointing results so far, the Commission has concentrated on making mutual recognition work.[36] It has attempted to tackle one of the major problems, namely the lack of mutual trust between administrative authorities, by promoting administrative co-operation between national administrations,[37] which would enhance mutual confidence between them.[38] These initiatives have, however, proved insufficient, and the lack of confidence and other administrative attitudes still form one of the main obstacles for the application of mutual recognition.[39] It is precisely these administrative attitudes that make mutual recognition less attractive from a trader's perspective, who may doubt its practical application by public authorities. Mutual recognition may simply lack the predictability required to encourage traders to construct cross-border commercial strategies.[40]

4.1.2 Does mutual recognition work for business?

The foregoing makes clear that it is important to ask how mutual recognition works for business. This section will therefore examine how European business experiences mutual recognition in everyday practice in the single market, largely drawing on a recent empirical study carried out by Atkins (1997).[41] The study carried out by Atkins is instructive in showing how far removed from actual market practice the regulatory approach might be. Mutual recognition has been examined in seven cases (electric cables, cement, pesticides, structural steel, carpets, fortified food & drinks, and water pipe fittings).

Table 7.2 provides a summary of the findings in shorthand. In pesticides, carpets and fortified (or 'enriched') food and drinks, mutual recognition does not work well. But the reasons are different in the three sectors. In pesticides, the detailed approximation accomplished should lead one to expect mutual recognition 'beyond' the approximated objectives. However, the 'effects' of pesticides on health (plant, animal, human) and environment are so sensitive that effect-based disparities between member states' laws persist. In carpets, some regulatory barriers linger but private disparities (e.g. in classification and environmental labels) persist, which have only recently begun to be tackled by private mutual recognition agreements. Barriers may therefore be reduced. In fortified drinks, preferences differ sharply between member

Table 7.2 The functioning of mutual recognition in seven product sectors

Electric cables	• Some common standards and a private mutual-recognition agreement between certification bodies, which reduces competition • Barriers are weak and compliance costs low
Cement	• Regulatory and non-regulatory barriers, and little trade • One Art. 28 EC case, successful but with little practical effect • Some voluntary harmonisation has begun, and cement will come under the Construction Product Directive
Pesticides	• Strong technical barriers and high costs of compliance • Mutual recognition does not work and detailed harmonisation has not yet been effective
Structural steel	• Voluntary common standards: some non-regulatory barriers remain • Mutual recognition functions without infringement procedures
Carpets	• Regulatory (fire testing) and non-regulatory (use classification and environmental labels) barriers • High compliance costs • Mutual recognition does not work, but embryonic private mutual recognition agreements exist
Fortified food and drinks	• Strong regulatory barriers and costly conformity requirements • Mutual recognition does not work (but some notable successes in accomplishing mutual recognition and in opening specific markets)
Water pipe fittings	• No regulatory barriers reported, but there are diverse customer specifications

Source: Atkins (1997).

states; complete bans exist next to much greater discretion and – sometimes – mandatory 'fortification' (e.g. margarine). One reason is that scientific evidence on 'fortification' is unclear (which suggests that the ECJ will give derogations the benefit of the doubt, as indeed it did in 1983). The situation can perhaps best be described as caught in a dilemma between insufficient approximation (which would remove barriers) and insufficient functioning of mutual recognition.

Three other cases – cement, structural steel and waterpipe fittings – are examples of mutual recognition functioning more or less satisfactorily. The lesson here is that this is no automatic guarantee of successful market penetration, despite the mutual recognition achieved. Cement, for example, falls under the Construction Product Directive, which is far from fully operational. For the time being, mutual recognition applies. However, until late 1996, the mandate for transforming a pre-standard (ENV-197-1) into a formal EN standard, later to become mandatory under the directive, had not yet been issued by the Commission.[42] Meanwhile, the testing procedures for cement (which previously were very different in member states) have now been agreed in a CEN standard EN 196, which has greatly reduced complications and costs of testing.

The current main problems include: 1) the lack of *factual* mutual recognition of laboratories (e.g. quality) and of certificates, 2) the lack of mutual recognition agreements in the (private) conformity assessment fields outside Benelux and Germany and outside the bilateral relationship between Belgium and France, 3) public procurement requirements (these are now formally adjusted to European standards, but since the product and testing standards do not yet exist, this means little, and disparities in building codes and architect traditions linger on), 4) insurance requirements for certain buildings (again, an area for private mutual recognition), and 5) a general reticence to penetrate one another's 'national' markets.[43] Step-by-step, these problems are being overcome, so mutual recognition can really work in cross-border intra-EC trade. By that point the standards and the Global Approach (all in relation to the directive) will give the final boost to establishing a true single cement market.

In structural steel, standards and mutual recognition work much better, even though these products also fall under the construction product directive. One reason is a slow but steady standardisation process (ECISS) going on under the Coal and Steel Treaty since 1953. For heavy beams, etc., there are lingering problems (e.g. welding certification). Overall, however, trade is relatively unproblematic.

Finally, the case of electrical cables is interesting because of its history and special characteristics. Like structural steel and cement (also subject to the construction product directive), electrical cables can be characterised as 'partially harmonised' because there is a basic directive: the 1973 Low Voltage Directive. A range of CENELEC standards have been adopted over the years. The problem is found rather in the mutual recognition of conformity assessment. The market itself is competitive, margins are rather low, and entry into the sector is not too difficult, since it is a mature industry (except e.g. for optical fibre.)

The particular solution is the HAR agreement, predating the Global Approach *and* the EOTC (EU-wide private, non-compulsory conformity assessment) by many years. Today, the EOTC does not recognise the HAR agreement, and for good reasons: rather than opening for accreditation all laboratories and certification bodies which pass the quality test (e.g. EN 45000), HAR restricts the agreement to one assigned body in each of the 16 countries[44] to the agreement. The HAR agreement confirms mutual recognition between the 16 based on uniform test methods, but under restrictive residence requirements: no certification outside one's own country (except for non-HAR countries). The two restrictions together are probably inconsistent with Art. 81 EC (ex Art. 85 EC) as a cartel-like restriction of competition in conformance services. All this does not mean that HAR works badly – in fact it works well, and intra-EC trade is greatly facilitated by it. Nevertheless, once the quality requirements (which EOTC sets) are fulfilled, there is no reason why this system should not be opened up.

4.1.3 Faint regulatory competition

Regulatory competition between member states would seem to be a natural consequence of mutual recognition, under free movement obligations, if one takes judicial mutual recognition as the starting point. It will expose national regulation to the forces of arbitrage: consumers may choose between products produced under domestic regulation or that of any other member state by importing the relevant products or services. To the extent that production factors find it profitable to respond to regulatory differences, mutual recognition and free movement may induce cross-border factor flows. All this should improve welfare on account of greater variety and additional output in the EU. But, since mutual recognition is a static notion, no more than a one-time adjustment would take place.

Regulatory competition is dynamic and takes this process further. It is defined as the alteration of national regulation in response to the actual or expected impact of cross-border mobility of goods or services on national economic activity (Sun and Pelkmans, 1995). Behind this alteration are complex business-government interactions. Jurisdictions with costly regulations may find businesses pressing for reductions in their regulatory burden when faced with import competition from jurisdictions with 'light' regimes. Alternatively, local businesses and governments may agree on strategic de-regulation so as to boost certain activities in the internal market. Since this may also be practised, or responded to, by other member states, iterative processes of regulatory competition may develop. Where member states would maintain ambitious regulation, the costs will fall on that member state's economy; this can be interpreted as meaning that the local benefits of satisfying these preferences are more than worth the local costs. Quality or other non-price determinants induced by this regulation would make products from other jurisdictions poor substitutes, and hence would protect local business from suffering too much from import competition. When factor mobility is at issue, location benefits would apparently outweigh the benefits of relocation at the margin. The upshot would be that where regulatory differences remain large, despite exposure to arbitrage, this would be economically justified.

As a rule, however, one would expect a process of regulatory competition to induce a 'market-driven' regulatory convergence in the EC. The condition is that this should not be allowed where negative externalities produce the relevant market failure as this would lead to fragmentation of the internal market or too low regulation (exposing the environment, for example, or failing to deal with discriminatory measures), but it would be suitable if information asymmetries or other 'internalities' are the problem. At the end of a process of regulatory competition, the market-driven convergence could be codified in essential requirements in EC approximation. This economic 'model' of regulatory competition can be shown to be of some but not great practical relevance in the EU (with respect, for example, to equivalence). There is also little empirical evidence that intra-EC regulatory competition does take place (e.g. Neven, 1996).

Initial fears in the Community that regulatory competition would create a 'regulatory gap' (Bourgoignie, 1987, pp. 171-172) or a race to the bottom have not been borne out. This is indeed what a proper understanding of mutual recognition – a prerequisite of regulatory competition – would lead one to expect. After all, mutual recognition only applies if the objectives or effects of regulations in different member states are equivalent. A race to the bottom, removing regulation justified by market failure would clearly violate the equivalence test. Perhaps it may well work the other way, at times, as Vogel (1995, 1997) and Genschel and Pluemper (1997) attempt to show, namely pushing regulation 'upwards,' especially in environment and food law. This 'trading up' prompts the question whether it indicates a regulatory failure, ex-post, or a failure to tackle a market failure, ex ante. If the political economy is not disciplined by regulatory quality requirements, there is a risk that regulatory failure may occur.

4.1.4 Compulsory mutual recognition?

Certainly, when faced with an unwillingness by member states to apply the mutual recognition principle voluntarily, the Community might have decided to impose mutual recognition by a decision of the Community institutions, either under the normal decision-making procedure of Art. 95 EC (ex Art. 100a EC) or under Art. 100b (deleted by the Amsterdam Treaty). However, imposing mutual recognition would be undesirable since such a move would once again raise the spectre of the regulatory 'race to the bottom.' Indeed, in practice, the Commission has opted to enhance transparency and strengthen mutual confidence.[45] This is achieved by, for instance, the notification of derogation to the free movement of goods procedure laid down in Decision 3052/95/EC (see, for more detail, Section 4.3.2).[46]

4.2 The steady increase of new national product regulation

It is puzzling that despite the prohibition on creating new trade barriers, despite mutual recognition, and despite approximation and joint regulation in a number of product markets, which pre-empts similar national regulation, member states continue to adopt a great number of technically complex national product regulations. It is puzzling because, other things being equal, these three elements would lead one to expect a drastic *decline* in national product regulation. Not only are there no signs of decline, empirical evidence points to a secular *increase* in national product regulation, notwithstanding the smaller 'regulatory space' available. As set forth above, it is exactly this type of regulatory behaviour that the EU wants to supervise by means of the information and notification system set up under the Information Directive. Study of national regulations has led the Commission to express continually its concern about their impact on the internal market.[47] In the UNICE 1995 report, the problem of overregulation was attributed to 'cumulation': EU, national, regional and local. This section will therefore examine the functioning of the Information Directive and its impact on national regulatory activities. We shall also consider the notifications of derogations of mutual recognition. We shall then turn to the data on eleven years of national product regulation, describe the upward trend, formulate possible reasons for this trend, and draw inferences about the second hypothesis, formulated in Section 2.1. Some statistical underpinning on the trends of notifications of draft legislation by the member states will also be provided.

4.2.1 The Information Directive and its impact

In Section 3.2, we observed that EU reforms do not comprise a test of the quality (justification and least-cost, or cost-benefit) of national product regulation. A limited test for new draft national legislation has been established by the Information Directive, although this is only to facilitate mutual recognition, not to raise quality, other than by voluntary 'comments'. But no text exists for the prevailing stock of national regulation. The Information Directive establishes a procedure requiring the member states to notify all draft technical regulations they intend to adopt. In addition, there is a parallel information requirement for (voluntary) draft standards; this requirement falls outside of the scope of this paper. The directive enables the Commission to monitor regulatory activities of the member states and installs a preventive mechanism to detect the possible creation of trade barriers at an early stage. At the same time, it also gives member states the opportunity to supervise each other's legislative proposals.

Over the years, the notification procedure has been developed and improved by various amendments. The main requirements of the procedure are laid down in Arts. 8-10 of the directive and can be briefly summarised as follows (see Table 7.3). Member states are required to notify the Commission (and through the Commission, the other member states) of their draft technical rules (in the language of the Directive: technical specifications and other requirements) which they intend to adopt. Having notified their legislation, member states are barred from adopting these rules during at least the three following months (the so-called 'stand-still period'). This allows both the Commission and the other member states to react to the notification and, where desired, to consult a Committee composed of national representatives, set up by the directive (the 98/34 Committee). The course of the subsequent procedure depends on these reactions.

As a general rule, the notifying member state may adopt its draft legislation upon expiry of the three months standstill period. During this period, the Commission and/or other member states may make 'comments' on the draft legislation, suggesting improvements to the notifying member state, which can be interpreted as a kind of 'bench-marking.' These 'comments' need not be followed but should be taken into account 'as far as possible.' Since these comments may come from different member states and from the Commission, and since this happens routinely, in hundreds of cases per year, the long-run impact of such 'peer review' may well be a steady improvement in the quality of national product regulation in the EU over time. It goes without saying that an empirical underpinning of this conclusion is extremely difficult to establish.

Table 7.3 Operation of the notification system under the Information Directive (98/34) for technical regulations

Key aspects	Main characteristics and procedures
1. Benefits	• Preventive nature; national drafts can still be altered • Gets around the taboo of Art. 227 EC (ex 170 EC); Member States examine and discuss one another's draft laws routinely in atmosphere of dialogue, cooperation and increasing trust • Approximation can be proposed before barriers arise • Supports mutual recognition • Obligation to include a mutual recognition (and/or 'equivalence') clause in national laws of this kind (e.g. Foie Gras ruling of 1998)
2. Scope	

Type of measures:	• Technical specifications:
	  ⇒ Technical product requirements (in a wide sense)
	  ⇒ Production methods and processes
	• Other requirements:
	  ⇒ Especially recycling systems or reusable packaging
	• Technical regulations: technical specification and other requirements, including de facto and de jure relevant administrative provisions
	  ⇒ Professional codes, codes of practice or, e.g. insurance polices referring to technical specifications, and inducing compliance
	  ⇒ Voluntary agreements, if and only if the State is a signatory party (e.g. against pollution)
	  ⇒ Fiscal or financial measures affecting the consumption of products by promoting compliance with technical specifications or other requirements (e.g. 'clean' cars)

Type of products:	• All industrially manufactured and agricultural products (including cosmetics, medicines, foodstuffs) • Information Society product and services (Dir. 98/48)

Table 7.3 continued

3. Notification and reporting obligation of the member states	• Any draft technical rule (see point 2) • Statement of the grounds for the draft law, etc. • Text of basic regulatory provisions, directly concerned and necessary to understand the notification • Extra notification requirements if marketing or use of product will be limited (grounds: public health, protection of consumers, environment), e.g. detailed data, including substitutes, effect and risk analyses (especially for chemicals) • New notification is compulsory, if draft laws are altered in ways significant for potential barriers (often, e.g. changes in their technical annexes, e.g. on equipment, etc.) • Information supplied is not confidential unless requested • Communication of final text without delay
4. Exemptions to the notification obligation	Legislative provisions which: • Comply with binding Community acts • Meet the obligations arising out of international agreements • Concern safeguard clauses provided for in binding Community acts • Apply the emergency procedure under Art. 8 (1) of the General Product Safety Directive • Implement a ECJ judgement • Amend a technical regulation upon the Commission's request to remove a trade barrier
5. Consequences of failure to notify	• Infringement of EC law (see case-law) • Non-notified laws are unenforceable inasmuch as they hinder the use or marketing of a product not in conformity therewith (see CIA-Security Ruling of 1996) • However the use of a product which is in conformity with non-notified regulations are not rendered unlawful; e.g. the use of a breath test product as evidence in criminal proceedings (see Lemmens Ruling of 1998)

Table 7.3 continued

6. Postpone-ment of national legislation ('standstill' obligation)	• Automatic postponement of 3 months • 4 months in case of 'detailed opinions' on 'voluntary agreements' (see point 7) • 6 months in case of 'detailed opinions' (on any other draft regulations) (see point 7) • 12 months, the so-called 'blockage', when the Commission has proposed or intends to propose a Community act on the matter covered by the notified draft regulation • 18 months in case of a 'common position' by the Council on a proposed directive • Urgency exception: no postponement for urgent reasons caused by unforeseeable circumstances relating to the protection of human and animal health and safety and the environment; e.g. natural disasters, epidemics, nuclear accidents
7. Reactions by the Commission and member states	• 'Comments', advisory in nature, must be taken into account by the notifying member states 'as far as possible' • 'Detailed opinions'; on the grounds that the notified regulation will cause trade barriers in the sense of Art. 28 EC; notifying member state must report to the Commission the action it intends to take on the detailed opinion, and the Commission must comment on this reaction
8. 98/34 Committee	• Composed of representatives of the member states • Chaired by a representative of the Commission • May be consulted by the Commission on notified draft regulation • Acts as forum for practical problem-solving and management of the system • Enhances administrative cooperation

The definitive text of the legislation must be communicated by the member state concerned to the Commission without delay. The standstill period is, however, extended when the Commission and/or other member states intervene. For instance, the standstill period is extended to four months when the draft technical regulations are voluntary agreements; six months if the Commission or another member state delivers a reasoned opinion holding that the draft legislation entails a trade barrier; to 12 months if the Commission announces that the draft legislation concerns an issue covered by a proposal for a Community act; and 18 months if the Council adopts a common position. In a few cases, member states are exempted from the notification obligation (see Table 7.3).

The Information Directive ensures a permanent protection against the erosion or practical inapplicability of mutual recognition. Since national implementation of EC directives falls outside the scope of 98/34, the overwhelming majority of draft laws submitted for notification are in the area of 'non-harmonised sectors.' An important role in the functioning of the notification procedure is played by the 98/34 Committee. This Committee was set up in 1984 by the former Directive 83/189. It is composed of the national representatives and is chaired by a Commission representative. Although it is not compulsory to do so, in practice the Commission always consults this Committee on draft technical regulations. The Commission reports that the Committee allows systematic monitoring of member states responses to comments and detailed opinions. The regular meetings of the Committee (in principle, every two months)[48] allow both the Commission and the member states to discuss and exchange views on general issues or on specific issues concerning specific parties. In this way, the Committee has helped to remedy the lack of efficient communication and is regarded as a key forum for practical problem-solving and more generally for the management of the system set up by the Directive.[49] Through the Committee, the notification system can nourish a cooperative network with dialogue prevailing over confrontation.[50]

Directive 98/34 thus functions as an 'early warning' system and institutes dynamic co-operation between the national and Community authorities. It envisages a kind of 'learning process': by means of information exchange, both the Commission and other national authorities can learn of national activities in advance of their adoption to verify their compatibility with the provision on the free movement of goods, whilst on the other hand national initiatives may serve as a potential basis for the introduction of regulatory requirements at Community level. Hence the directive not only offers an intense framework of cooperation to improve the process of internal market building, but can also serve as a source of innovation through sharing and learning. In this way, the directive has been described as a device of 'cooperative federalism'.[51]

Although it is true that over time member states have become more active in notifying, this is not to say that they have been very enthusiastic about the EU disciplining their regulatory activities. Member states have regularly failed to notify all their draft legislation or have invoked the urgency exception after the adoption of the legislation in question. Faced with this practice, the Commission has decided, for instance, to contract an external organisation to detect national regulations adopted in breach of the Directive.[52] Over the years the Commission has not grown tired of repeating the need for stricter supervision of the notification requirement and its intention to initiate as a matter of course the Art. 226 procedure (ex Art. 169 EC) where a failure to notify has been identified.[53] Recent case-law on the Information Directive has offered the Commission a helping hand. In cases in the early 1990s, concerning Italian, German and Dutch instances of non-notification, the ECJ confirmed that non-notification is an infringement of Community law, thus giving the procedure considerably more weight.[54] In 1996, the ECJ went even further and declared that the failure to notify national laws under the Information Directive meant that such laws were unenforceable. Suddenly, member states were under pressure to review their intra-and inter-ministerial procedures thoroughly so as to be more certain that their notification of all kinds of special decrees, or amendments of technical annexes, is indeed complete. Consequently, the fear of being saddled with non-enforceable laws, at least as far as equipment or other technical aspects are concerned, which would cause regulatory crises, has led several member states into new notification action (see Box 1 on the Netherlands). It is possible that this contributes to explaining the rise in the number of notifications during recent years (see Section 4.3.3).

This case law is no doubt likely to induce member states to notify. Although the risk remains that, within the framework of the Council, hostile member states might reduce the detail required by information systems in order to avoid the non-enforceability sanction for non-notified laws, the costs of disclosure paid by a member state are probably far outweighed by the benefits of access to information about practices in other states.[55] On the other hand, following this ruling, similar cases were bound to come before the ECJ. Indeed, the ECJ was soon asked a preliminary question involving the applicability of non-notified Dutch decrees on alcohol level tests. The ECJ clarified that the failure to notify technical regulations renders such regulations only inapplicable where they hinder the use or marketing of a product that is not in conformity with them. Hence, non-notification did not make unlawful the use of a product that was in conformity with non-notified rules.

Box 1. Non-notification and the Dutch regulatory crisis

Ten years after the Commission had formally expressed the view that non-notification under the Information Directive would automatically mean that the relevant laws or decrees would be unenforceable ('direct effect'), the ECJ confirmed this position in the *CIA Security* case on 30 April 1996 (Case C-194/94 [1996] ECR I-2201). Soon it appeared that this ruling had important consequences for the Netherlands, resulting in a true regulatory crisis. Following discussions in the 98/34 Committee on the *Security* case (in the meetings of July and December) and a so-called 'package meeting' (dealing with the entire spectrum of national implementation problems of the single market, between the Commission and a member state) with the Netherlands in October 1996, the Dutch administration faced the task of scrutinising many recently adopted laws, secondary decrees and amendments of technical annexes of existing rules: had they been notified, and, if not, was there reason to suspect that they should have been?

In early June 1997, rumours about a huge list of 400 'unenforceable' laws and decrees were leaked to the press, and the Dutch Parliament held an emergency debate. Fearing severe judicial consequences and dramatic legislative embarrassment – not to speak of the embarrassment in the 98/34 Committee – the government kept the list secret. Forced by an interim judgement of a Dutch court, however, the government published the list on 22 July 1997; and although the government lost face and was heavily criticised, the two responsible ministers retained their positions.

With hindsight, one can explain the length of the list for two reasons. First, the Dutch administration had always refused to accept 'direct-effect' of the Information Directive; it adhered to this position even after the ECJ had condemned it for non-notification of three decrees in 1994 (Case C-93/61 [1994] ECR I-3607). The Dutch government felt that withdrawal of the acts and a new submission to parliament, followed by notification to the Commission, was superfluous as long as traders from other member states did not complain about the existence of trade barriers for non-implementation of mutual recognition. Once that this position became untenable, a major 'catch-up exercise' became necessary. Secondly, the Dutch 'regulatory style' requires a combination of formal transparency and precision. This practice seems indeed to be confirmed by the fairly high number of notifications that the Netherlands actually makes (despite its failure to notify all): from 1992 to 1994, it notified 102 measures, higher than seven other member states; in 1996 it notified 62 measures, the third highest number.

Eventually, the Dutch 'catch-up exercise' was resolved thanks to the co-operative attitude of the other member states, which recognised the special nature and broad scope of the problem. In 230 cases, notification proved to be necessary, 60 instances of which led to detailed opinions, prompting the Dutch authorities to amend the relevant laws or annexes.

This 'happy ending' was, however, overshadowed by criminal proceedings pending before a Dutch court, in which the applicability of Dutch non-notified legislation on the conduct of tests to determine the alcohol level of breath analysis for drivers was challenged. Could the evidence obtained by means of a breath analysis apparatus authorised in accordance with the non-notified legislation be relied upon against Mr. Lemmens, charged with driving while under the influence of alcohol? In its preliminary ruling the ECJ, nevertheless, carefully considered that the failure to notify technical regulations renders such regulations only inapplicable where they hinder the use or marketing of a product which is not in conformity with them. It subsequently considered that non-notification did not make unlawful the use of a product which is in conformity with non-notified rules. The ECJ thus saved the Dutch regulatory system (Case C-226/97, *Lemmens* [1998] ECR I-3711).

4.2.2 The notification procedure of free movement derogations

Committed to its aim of strictly supervising the effective application of existing rules, the Commission has also been eager to create a broader system of notification. A perfect occasion presented itself after the drawing up of an inventory of national laws that fell under Art. 95 EC (ex Art. 100a EC),[56] as required by the former Art. 100b EC. Faced with the somewhat disappointing results of the inventory,[57] the Commission decided to develop a mechanism which would reveal derogations of free movement (of mutual recognition) in 'non-harmonised sectors.' This would allow for the identification of the cases in which a member state intended to prevent, on grounds of non-conformity with its own national rules, the free movement or placing on the market of goods lawfully produced or marketed in another member state. It would thus identify negative decisions pursuant to technical regulations, the drafts of which had been notified under the Information Directive. This mechanism was laid down in Decision 3052/95 and entered into force on 1 January 1997.[58]

The logic of mutual recognition implies that only non-equivalence can justifiably lead to derogations. Decision 3052/95 therefore does not apply to: a) aspects of products subject to approximation; and b) derogations not based on Art. 30 EC (ex Art. 36 EC) grounds or on the 'mandatory requirements' recognised by the Court under Art. 28 EC (ex Art. 30 EC). Both would amount to infringement, and the Commission should deal with them. Also, the notification procedure should not duplicate notification or information procedures provided by other Community measures, especially the Information Directive and Arts. 7 and 8 of the General Product Safety Directive.[59]

The Decision requires member states to notify the Commission of a general ban on the goods in question, a refusal to allow the products to be placed on the market, the modification of the model or type of products, or the withdrawal of the products from the market. The notification requirement applies to measures taken by the competent authorities, with the exception of judicial decisions. That the decision intends to be complementary to the Information Directive can be clearly seen from the reference to the 98/34 Committee and the Commission's obligation to keep that Committee, and where necessary other sectoral committees, informed of the functioning of the procedure laid down in the decision.

In 1997, the mechanism was apparently still functioning unsatisfactorily, presumably for practical reasons and lack of awareness. A specific issue is the concern about a failure to notify measures such as a refusal to register vehicles, a refusal to authorise and/or permit imports of foodstuffs, whether enriched or not, and a refusal to permit parallel imports of pesticides. Although not many notifications are expected, given the exceptional nature of the derogations, notification was unsatisfactory: only France (26x), Finland (3x) and Germany (4x) notified. In 1998, 69 notifications were made but this doubling was mainly due to Greece with 43 notifications. Eleven member states did not notify at all. The EEA now uses the procedure but, in 1998, no notifications were received from non-EC EEA countries.[60] Therefore, the awareness of the problems of derogation for the proper functioning of the single market is grossly insufficient. The economic importance of the issue is probably not great, but there is no evidence on this.

4.2.3 National product regulation: trends, rationales and inferences
Trends in national product regulation are rarely discussed in general terms, simply because it is exceedingly difficult, if not impossible, to grasp the developments in many special areas at the same time. When general suggestions are made at all, they tend to be qualitative and impressionistic. 'Measuring' regulatory trends is impossible until a proper methodology is developed[61] and the data is available. For these reasons, some primitive volume indicators such as the annual number of pages published in the US Federal Register or comparable outlets in other countries are employed to underpin suggestions about the quantity of regulation (be it stock or flow).

A unique opportunity to derive trend data now presents itself in the EU. The Mutual Information Directive 98/34 (formerly 83/189) has generated a highly developed notification system for new draft legislation of member states. As explained before, national administrations have to be properly organised to fulfil the reporting requirements under the directive. This has gradually been improved due to a) the compulsory nature of notifications, b) the Court's view that non-notification is a treaty infringement, and c) the Court's ruling that non-notified new laws are unenforceable in some respects (see Section 4.2.1). Therefore, a data set about national product regulation has gradually been built up which is unique in the world. Although from a

purely statistical point of view, the quality of the data is still below standard
– see below – it does allow a number of conclusions about the regulatory
activity of member states in product markets. For the purpose of the present
paper, such conclusions can help us to draw empirical inferences about the
second hypothesis (Section 2.1). In turn, this might allow some conclusions
about the assertion, often made in business circles, that the secular rise in
regulation is, invisibly yet incessantly, imposing more and more difficulties
and costs on doing business as well as narrowing the scope of initiative,
innovation and entrepreneurship. The context of the second hypothesis
narrows this general assertion to the following one: is there empirical
evidence of a steady rise in national product regulation, gradually making it
more difficult to exploit the potential of the internal product market, given
that federal-type disciplines at the EU-level do not or hardly apply at the
member states level?

Consider Figure 7.2. It shows the total of notifications for eleven years
(1988-1998 inclusive). A secular upward trend is clear. The regression line
shows that the average annual increase over the period is around 20 per cent.
In 1997, the Dutch regulatory crisis (see Box 1) inflated the number of
notifications, but a secular increase is still found when this incidence is
removed from the 1997 data. The reader ought to note what exactly this trend
reflects. Figure 7.2 (and the following ones) report all national product
regulation, which is *not* purely the result of the transposition of EC
directives. So, it results either from purely national initiative or from the so-
called 'gold-plating' of EC directives with all kinds of extra requirements.

Before jumping to conclusions, however, there are several qualifications
to consider. In 1995, Austria, Sweden and Finland joined the EU and,
inevitably, this increased the total number of notifications. Thus, the trend
increase between 1988 and 1994 was weaker, but once the three new member
states were in, the trend increase picked up again and more strongly so (even
without the 'extra' Dutch 1997 notifications).

Second, the underlying sectoral coverage of the data was not constant, but
has widened since 1988. Directive 88/182 amended the Mutual Information
Directive by extending the scope of the reporting requirements to agricultural
products, foodstuffs, medical products and cosmetics. Thus, we shall have to
verify whether, and to what extent, the trend (as of 1989) in these sectors
explains the overall trend increase. Third, an inevitable drawback of the data
is that the unit of measurement is not precisely given. Every notification
enters as one 'unit.' Obviously, this may vary from a comprehensive law
with many requirements in an economically important product market, all the
way to an amendment of a technical annex of a secondary law or statute on,

say, the safety of ladders for painters. There is no practical way of verifying the importance of this drawback. However, we submit that this objection loses much of its force, the longer the trend and the larger the annual flows. The grand total of Figure 7.2 is some 5000 notifications over eleven years – this is so large that such discrepancies will tend to average out.

Figure 7.2 Trend in total number of notifications

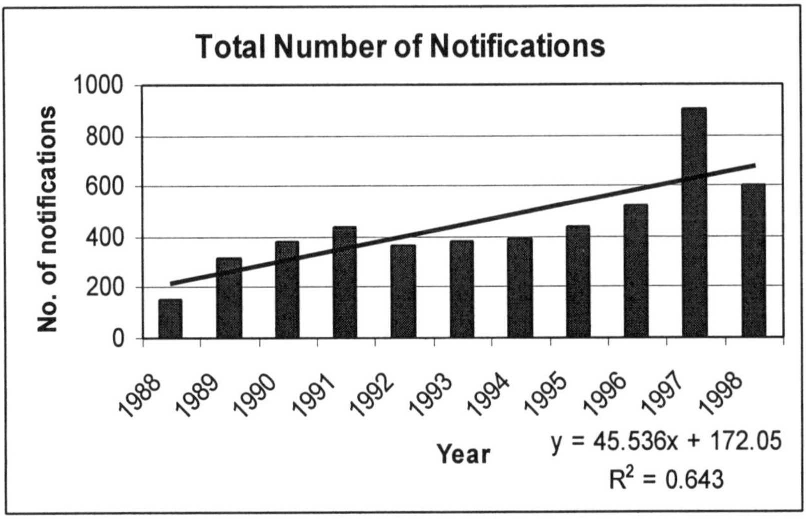

$y = 45.536x + 172.05$

$R^2 = 0.643$

Source: Elaboration on data from DGIII Directive 98/34 database.

A first tentative conclusion therefore is that EU member states exhibit a *steadily increasing activity in product regulation*, even if the trend increase is weaker (due to qualifications) than that depicted in Figure 7.2. Prima facie this is a worrying trend. After all, this is not what one would expect once one considers the following. The scope of national product regulation is significantly narrowed because of approximation at EU level and – in agricultural products benefiting from price support – because of EC product regulations. Such EU rules either preempt national product regulation (in this case, for agricultural product quality levels supported at different prices) or lead to transposition of EC directives, but they are not part of the notification under the Mutual Information Directive. The Atkins (1997) study for the *Single Market Review* estimates that no less than 50 per cent of intra-EC trade in manufacturers and 55 per cent of the share of EU manufacturing value-added are covered by approximation under the old and new approaches together. If notifications are in this huge area, they must represent additional requirements or other forms of 'goldplating,' which makes one wonder whether and to what extent such additions are justified in terms of costs and benefits. If not justified, they imply extra regulatory burdens, hindering the exploitation of the full potential of the internal product market (see below). Mutual recognition has also become important in the internal product market. Atkins (1997) estimates that this covers 28 per cent of intra-EU trade of manufactures and 21 per cent of EU manufacturing value added. In this area, member states are subject to three constraints: the case law following *Cassis de Dijon*, the disciplines under Directive 98/34 (and its Committee) and regulatory competition. If mutual recognition were effective, it is hard to understand why member states would be eager to adopt new regulations in so many instances, and over so many years, A fortiori, if regulatory competition occurs, One would expect fewer extra requirements or none at all, as long as equivalence is not undermined.

Let us inspect the data in greater detail. This should contribute to a better understanding of the nature and sources of national regulatory pressures. A first query is whether there are indications about inimical effects the proposed regulations might have. Proxy answers to the question can be distilled from Figure 7.3, giving the number of comments and detailed opinions of the member states and the Commission. Since there are 15 (before 1995, 12) member states, the total numbers for the member states are likely to comprise double-counting, in the sense that, often, more than one member state will comment, or provide a detailed opinions, on a draft law of another member state. Since disaggregated data for 1992-1994 are not available, inferences have to be drawn with caution. In the years 1988-1991, the Commission was apparently very alert, with the number of detailed opinions being as high as or higher than those of all the member states.

In the period 1995-1998, it would seem that a learning effect had taken place: detailed opinions number, annually, a little over 100 or even much less, and there is no trend increase (even though the notifications kept on going up). This means that the Commission spotted fewer potential barriers to free movement. The comments reflect more or less the trend increase of the notifications. As noted, the comments might relate to the quality of regulation, and hence might reduce the regulatory burden, but there is no public information about this.[62] It is also not clear whether and to what extent member states have subsequently altered draft laws, following the comments. It seems safe to conclude that the peer-review of national regulations has intensified, but its impact cannot be measured.

Figure 7.3 Trend in total number of comments and detailed opinions

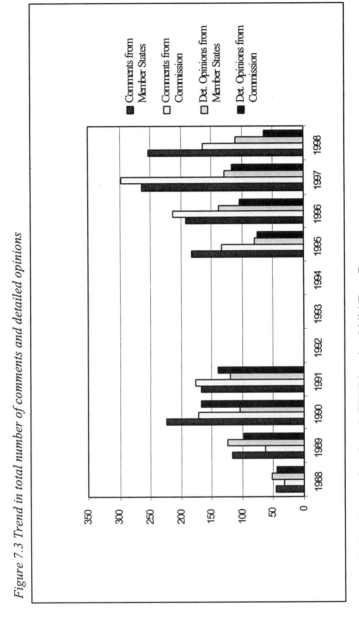

Source: Elaboration on data from DGIII Directive 98/34 Data Base.

Figure 7.4 Trend in total number of notifications in France

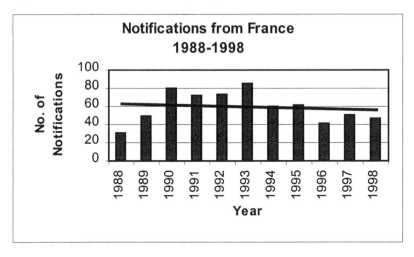

Source: Elaboration on data from DGIII Directive 98/34 database.

Figure 7.5 Trend in total number of notifications in Italy

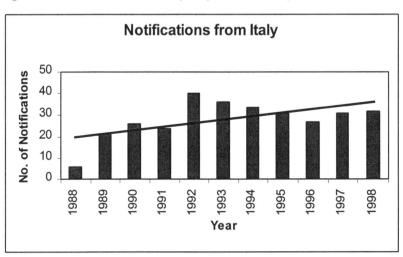

Source: Elaboration on data from DGIII Directive 98/34 database.

A second query is whether the trend is due only to some member states, or is evenly distributed. The answer is that regulatory styles differ markedly between member states, as reflected in great differences in notifications. Over the four years 1995-98, the Netherlands, Germany, Austria and the UK accounted for 58 per cent of total notifications (if one takes out the extra notifications of the Netherlands in 1997, it still remains in the top four). France has reduced its notifications recently but was in the top four in the early 1990s. Countries like Germany and the UK both show trend increases over the period 1988-98. Figures 7.4 and 7.5 illustrate the cases of Italy and France, which deviate from this pattern, in that France shows a slight trend decrease (the only member state to do so), while Italy exhibits a trend increase but at a much lower level of notifications throughout. Given the emerging case law on the notification duties, the Commission's strenuous efforts to detect non-notification via third sources, and the increasing awareness trickling down from the 98/34 Committee to national administrations, it is possible that some part of the notifications is due merely to the better functioning of the reporting procedures. It is impossible to know how well the national systems work (until a revealing crisis breaks out), but we submit that a learning effect has led to improved reporting in the 1990s, and even more so after the CIA-Security (or Securitel) case of 1996. It is improbable, however, that this learning effect would explain the entire trend increase of 11 years, still less that it would compensate for what, ceteris paribus, might have been expected to be a significant decrease.[63]

The third query is whether sectoral aspects may help to explain the trends. Table 7.4 gives the total number of notifications over 15 years, right from the beginning of the notification system. The sectoral share in the total is compared to sector (EU) industrial output and intra-EU trade shares. This simple exercise is only aimed at finding 'outliers', on the assumption that these three shares should not be very different. This assumption can be defended by the association of sector size with the range of different or differentiated products to which regulations may apply.

Of course this association is only to be expected within fairly wide margins of variation.[64] Of the eleven categories distinguished, and ignoring 'other products' for which notifications are only 2 per cent, one can identify four 'sectors' as outliers. In energy, minerals and wood, 2 per cent of notifications compares with large multiples in output and trade shares. Apparently, the *products* in this area are lightly regulated (although entry in gas and electricity production, transmission and distribution was then still under exclusive rights). With respect to chemicals such a conclusion would clearly be mistaken (see, e.g. Maglia and Sassoon, in Volume II of this study). We submit that in this sector detailed old-approach directives have reduced the regulatory autonomy of the member states so much that national notifications remain relatively modest (and probably comprise in many cases amendments rather than major new requirements). Different again is the health, medical equipment, environment, packaging group, where one would expect significant regulatory activity, despite the low 'economic' shares. It is interesting, however, to observe that the general category of 'environment' (included here) is not the cause of an upsurge of overall notifications. One reason could be that EU directives are numerous in this field (over 200) and have wide coverage, thereby pre-empting a good deal of 'domestic' regulation.

Table 7.4 Total number of notifications by sector, 1984-98

Sector	No. of notifications	Share of sector in EU-15 output (industry)	Share of sector in intra-EU industry trade
Machinery and engineering	1114 (20%)	18.8%	25.4%
Building and construction	629 (12%)	10.0 %	n.a.
Energy, minerals and wood	104 (2%)	11.4%	18.0%
Products for household and leisure	149 (3%)	5.8%	3.4%
Agriculture and food products	842 (16%)	17.1%	10.6%
Chemicals	308 (6%)	12.2%	3.9%
Health, medical equipment, environment, packaging	269 (5%)	0.4 %	2.6%
Transport	796 (15%)	13.3%	15.7%
Telecommunications	862 (16%)	3.5%	7.8%
Pharmaceuticals	155 (3%)	2.9%	1.9%
Other products	125 (2%)	4.6%	10.7%
TOTAL	5353 (100%)	100.0%	100.0%

Source: Elaboration on data from DGIII Directive 98/34 database and from the EC, *Panorama of European Industry,* 1997.

Finally, telecoms equipment is conspicuously high (16 percent). This is largely explained by the need for new re-regulation as a result of liberalisation and the heavy-handed (type-approval) licensing directive 91/263. Meanwhile, this directive has been replaced by a less demanding one, based on new-approach procedures and self-certification (module A) of the global approach. In future, one should expect this sector to induce fewer notifications, despite its rapid growth in economic importance. Indeed, the increasing trend in this sector over 1988-98 becomes 'flat' if one considers only the period 1994-98.

A second tentative conclusion is, therefore, that a closer inspection of the data can, at best, only provide partial explanations of the trend increase. There are indirect indications that peer-review in the 98/34 Committee seems to have intensified. This has led to draft laws that pass the mutual recognition test more easily. However, there is no evidence that the regulatory burden of all those new national regulations is justified, other than for allowing free movement. Moreover, all member states except France, contribute to the trend increase; and France's decrease is only slight. In the sectoral profiles, only the telecoms equipment sector gives reason to expect a decline. All in all, based on the flow data available, the second hypothesis cannot be rejected. The data set does not establish whether the presumably enthusiastic use of remaining national autonomy by the member states is due to the fewer and weaker mechanisms (than at EU level) which check the quantity and improve the quality of regulatory initiatives, still less whether this is indispensable in view of the validity of the first hypothesis. Nevertheless, one can hardly fail to be impressed by the sheer quantity of national regulation outside the direct transposition of EC directives and the trend increase in it. The crucial point is the cumulative costs of adapting to such laws, statutes and decrees, the net benefits to society of which are assured neither at national nor at EU level (in the latter case, this is because – outside EC directives – they fall under subsidiarity, albeit in some cases with proportionality). Such decentralised pressures cannot possibly be expected to take into account the EC-wide cumulative problems for, e.g. businesses having to operate in the internal market with so many different – and continuously changing – legal requirements.

Could one come up with other rationales to explain why no significant decline of national product regulation has taken place, even though such rationales might not be easy to verify empirically? One suggestion could be that 'gold-plating' is often justified, in the sense that the new approach only refers to objectives and effects (usually of SHEC), purposefully leaving scope for national regulation. As long as free movement is guaranteed, and cross-border competition works well, the costs of such national regulation would tend to fall on the residents of the member states involved, who retain the option of importing goods produced elsewhere in the Community. However, 'gold-plating' may lead to de facto 'standards' influencing distribution and consumer behaviour, in which case formal mutual recognition does not translate into genuine choice: the foreign supplier will have to adapt. Another suggestion could be that the many changes in products, processing, and technology nowadays prompt far more frequent changes in legislation, especially technical annexes. But this argument presumes that member states use a rather intrusive regulatory style. One can also easily introduce New Approach-style laws at national level, with a focus on objectives and effect, while referring to standards so that re-regulation is not (often) needed. Finally, it is quite possible that the decline of national product regulation is still to come. New Approach directives have only been in force anywhere for up to ten years or so, and often the envisaged European standards are so numerous that their full range is only available after a lag of half a decade or more (e.g. for machines). In food, the full consequences of mutual recognition (most of the case law is actually in food) have only begun to trickle down in revised national laws in the course of the 1990s. This is because many specifications in the old laws were unenforceable for imports, or struck consumers as unnecessary. In telecoms equipment, we saw that a decline can be expected.

6. CONCLUSIONS

This paper has been prompted by the paradox that considerable liberalisation and regulatory reform in the EU since the mid-1980s has led insistent demands for further regulatory reform. Although there has been an understandable emphasis on reforms of network industries and services (as six chapters in Volume II testify), the paradox is greatest in product markets, because it was precisely there that the reform and liberalisation efforts were initially concentrated.

We have examined the four reform tracks in EU product markets: mutual recognition of existing national product regulation; the prevention of new regulatory barriers from arising by the submission of national draft laws to an EC-test (including the obligation of an equivalence clause); the new approach to approximation of national regulation; and competitive, high-quality conformity assessment under the global approach. We conclude that EU reforms have been significant for the better functioning of the internal product market. Exactly how effective these reforms are is exceedingly difficult to access. For instance, are the numerous European standards subjected to a cost-benefit test or other ways of evaluating their economic optimality? There is, in many instances, ample scope for a wide range of economic gains, depending on the technical and legal details of the reforms. This might explain in part why the paradox has arisen: the gains have remained at the low end of the range.

However, the remainder of the paper has considered two other reasons why the economic gains from reforms which are, in and by themselves, widely appreciated are reduced if not entirely neutralised. These two weaknesses in the EC product regime are the considerable practical problems of making mutual recognition work (and the consequent weakening of competitive pressures); and the steadily increasing flow of new national product regulation. The central problem with mutual recognition is how to make it work in day-to-day practice in trade and sales, for businesses and consumers who do not know (and should not need to know) the intricacies of EC case law and procedures. A painstaking drive, led by the Commission but broadly supported by member states for new regulations, has gradually improved acceptance in the market place. The Europeanisation of standards helps, too, of course. Yet, in sectors like foodstuffs and medicines, and in some areas of chemicals (e.g. pesticides) neither approximation nor mutual recognition works satisfactory because of disagreements or lack of trust among the member states. It is quite possible that the slowly improving acceptance of mutual recognition will eventually reduce current problems, but, at present, business is not convinced that the principle is effective in exploiting the potential of the single market. There are still too many instances where pan-EU business strategies might prove to be too costly when delayed or derailed by difficulties (or extra costs) caused by evading or refusing mutual recognition.

The authors would strongly encourage the Commission to pursue its strategy of: a) improving the information regarding what mutual recognition implies in practice, (the Commission should avoid trying to explain all the legal technicalities in documents for businesses and consumers, and produce instead simple guides, perhaps even different ones for different sectors, with plenty of practical examples, distributed via trade associations and information offices); and b) 'cooperative federalism' with the, thus far successful, package meetings with member states and through intensifying the networks of responsible national officials.[65] Absent success on this score, businesses and possibly consumers might begin to press for further centralisation (presumably via directives), which might well reduce the flexibility and innovativeness of the economic operators without compensating justification.

The second weakness is the worrying trend toward ever increasing national product regulation. Based on a single data set, and despite some qualifications that we discuss at some length, the upward trend would appear quite robust. It is worrying for two reasons. One is that, other things being equal, one should expect a significant *decline* in national product regulation since the late 1980s due to approximation, mutual recognition and the general treaty prohibition on regulatory product barriers (Art. 28, EC). We have attempted to come up with various explanations for the trend, based on the data available, but these yield, at best, a partial explanation. Therefore, the second hypothesis, formulated in Section 2.1, cannot be rejected. This hypothesis postulates that member states will use their remaining regulatory autonomy in an enthusiastic fashion, constrained by the single market and globalisation, but sheltered by 'subsidiarity' in other ways. This expectation is based on the fact that the member states, unlike the EU as a whole, are not subjected to 'federal' pressures and discipline (such as proportionality or, better still, cost-benefit assessment) on national regulation outside EC directives. A possible explanation for this national regulatory drive is the political economy of regulation: regulation justified by societal benefits and without unnecessary regulatory 'burdens' (i.e., maximising the net benefits over costs) is very demanding in terms of principles and procedures which prevent private interests in markets, public administration, and domestic politics from exerting effective influence, beyond mere information (see the first hypothesis in Section 2.1). The authors have not attempted to verify the actual determinants of national product regulatory output, as this would require a massive research effort with many contributors. Our suggested explanation is merely put forward for consideration. We do suggest, however, a few alternative 'rationales' for the great regulatory activity in member states, but without offering further empirical analysis.

The second reason why the upward trend in national product regulation is worrying has to do with the sheer quantities involved. At the end of the 1990s, the annual number of notifications hovered around 600 a year, not counting national laws directly transposing EC directives. Even a constant rate of notification for the next decade would yield no fewer than 6,000 notifications; extrapolating a trend increase of 10 per cent per year (which might slow down, see Section 4.2.3) would yield a ten-year total of some 15,000! There is no obvious way of verifying whether, and to what extent, such a huge regulatory output at the national level actually inhibits the exploitation of the full potential of the internal market. Nonetheless, such decentralised pressures cannot possibly be expected to take into account the EC-wide cumulative problems for, e.g. businesses having to operate in the entire internal market, facing so many different – and continuously changing – legal requirements, just in product markets. This is not to suggest that this national regulatory drive is bound to continue unabated. But it does amount to a strong prima facie case for paying much more attention to the Community-wide economic impact of regulatory activities which, legally, are beyond scrutiny under subsidiarity.

NOTES

1. European Commission (1985), especially the Annex.
2. Molitor et al. (1995); UNICE (1995).
3. See European Economy (1996).
4. See Council Recommendations of 12 July 1999 on the Economic Policies of the Member States and the Community, *Official Journal EC,* 1999/570 of 17 August 1999, pp. 34-61.
5. For instance, OECD (1997) and Björndal and Pilat (1997).
6. McKinsey Global Institute (1997).
7. Longrove et al. (1998).
8. European Commission (1993b), 7.
9. See also Galli and Pelkmans (Introducory chapter) and OECD (1997).
10. If equity rather than efficiency is the public policy goal, regulation should be avoided, and transfers should be used in ways that minimise administrative costs and complexity.
11. See also Labory and Malgarini, in this volume.
12. E.g. Peltzman (1989).
13. Note that Nieuwenhuis (1997), works with two models, both modelling wages implying rent-sharing. The first model also allows for X-inefficiency.
14. European Commission (1997), p. 25.
15. A price comparison with the US shows for higher prices in Europe, e.g.: oil for heating (70 per cent higher), natural gas (10 per cent higher), diesel (90 per cent higher) and electricity (40 per cent higher) for large users (see European Commission, 1998, p. 14). See also Riechmann and Schulz as well as Prosperetti, both in Volume II.
16. See in this context the Council Resolution on the quality of the drafting of Community legislation, (1993) OJ C 166/1. For more details on the

regulatory quality of EU legislation, see Pelkmans, Labory and Majone, in this volume.

17. Under Directive 98/34, formerly Directive 83/189 (and subsequent revisions). See also Section 4.3.

18. Directives under Art. 95, EC (formerly Art 100A, EC). Thus far there has been no systematic reform of regulations; where it has been undertaken, it has mostly been done by the Commission, in the few areas where powers have been assigned exclusively to the EU, or the Commission specifically (e.g. competition policy, aspects of agriculture and trade policy).

19. For extensive analyses of the numerous details and technicalities of the four tracks and their economic, legal, institutional and political aspects see, e.g. Vos (1999), Joerges (1992), Pelkmans (1987), Pelkmans and Costello (1991), CEPS (1992), Egan (1998), Weatherill (1996), Machado Jorge (1995).

20. Case 120/78, *Rewe-Zentrale AG* v *Bundesmonopolverwaltung für Branntwein* [1979] ECR 649, although this principle was only explicitly developed in Case 113/80, *Commission* v *Ireland* [1981] ECR 1625.

21. Case 8/74, *Procureur du Roi* v *Dassonville* [1974] ECR 837.

22. See, more recently, for instance, Cases C-238/89, *Pall-Dahlhausen* [1990] ECR I-4827; C-362/88, *GB-INNO-BM* v *Confédération du Commerce Luxembourgeois* [1990] ECR I-667, C-126/91, *Schutzverband gegen Unwesen in der Wirtschaft* v *Yves Rocher* [1993] ECR I-2361. See, however, the ECJ's more restrictive approach in cases C-267 & 268/91, *Keck and Mithouard* [1993] ECR I-6126.

23. Case 120/78, *Rewe-Zentrale AG* v *Bundesmonopolverwaltung für Branntwein* [1979] ECR 649.

24. Communication of the Commission concerning the consequences of the judgment given by the Court of Justice on 20 February 1979 in Case 120/78 ('*Cassis de Dijon*'), (1980) OJ C 256/2. The reference in the text to SHEC refers to safety, health, environment and consumer protection, the main objectives of practically all product regulation.

25. See Case C-184/96 *Commission* v *France (Foie Gras)* [1998] ECR I-6197.

26. Consolidating the 83/189 Directive and its subsequent amendments; we shall henceforth speak of the 98/34 Ctee and no longer of the 83/189 Ctee. See Official Journal EC L 204 of 21 July 1998.

27. Official Journal EC L 321 of 30 Dec. 1995.

28. Adopted on 28 May 1969, (1969) OJ C 76/1.
29. See Joerges et al. (1988) and, more generally, Pelkmans (1987).
30. For a discussion and an attempt to restate the delegation problem, see Joerges et al. (1999).
31. Global Approach, Council Decision 93/465/EEC of 22 July 1993, OJ L220, 30 September 1993.
32. See Vos (1999).
33. Case 188/84, *Commission* v *France ('Woodworking machines')* [1986] ECR 419.
34. Majone (1990).
35. Joerges (1992), p. 45.
36. See European Commission (1999).
37. For instance, Council Decision on the adoption of an action plan for the exchange between Member State administrations of national officials who are engaged in the implementation of Community legislation required to achieve the internal market, (1992) OJ L 286/65.
38. The need for administrative cooperation was underlined by Sutherland (1992). See European Commission (1993a and 1992).
39. European Commission (1999a).
40. As suggested in Weatherhill (1996).
41. Atkins (1997).
42. Preparatory work was under way in CEMBUREAU, a cement trade association in Brussels. Note also that ENV-197-2 exists, a 1994 CEN Cement Conformity Evaluation pre-standard, setting the requirements for attestation of conformity to the ENV-197-1.
43. In 1994 the cement industry was punished by a record fine totalling 248 million ecu (!), after the Commission discovered that CEMBUREAU operated as a cartel at least since 1983, partitioning the single market into protected national markets, a flagrant violation of Art. 81, EC (antitrust) (formerly Art. 85, EC).
44. The 15 EU member states plus Switzerland. Hungary applied in 1996.
45. See the Commission in its *Communication on the management of the mutual recognition of national rules after 1992. Operational conclusions reached in the light of the inventory drawn up pursuant to Article 100b of the EC Treaty*, (1993) OJ C 353/4.
46. (1995) OJ L 321/1. See also Weatherill (1996).
47. See, inter alia, European Commission (1996a).

48. Between 1992 to 1994, the Committee met 16 times. See COM(96) 286 final, 29.
49. COM(96) 286 final. In general, see Joerges and Vos (eds.) (1999).
50. See Weatherhill (1996).
51. Dehousse (1989).
52. COM(96) 286 final, 27.
53. For instance, 12th Annual Report, (1995) OJ C 254, at 16.
54. Case C-317/92, Commission v Germany [1994] ECR I-2039; Cases C-52/93 and C-61/93, Commission v Netherlands [1994] ECR I-3591; Case C-289/94 Commission v Italy [1996] ECR I-4405.
55. Weatherill, (1996), p. 183.
56. See European Commission (1993c), sections I and II.
57. The inventory did not bring to light many cases which would not be solved by insisting on mutual recognition, according to case law or, alternatively, by approximation. Moreover, the data collection under Art. 100b EC proved slow and cumbersome – member states administrations were not organised in a way to facilitate the identification of such special provisions over an extremely wide regulatory spectrum.
58. See Decision 3052/95 of 13 December 1995, (1995) OJ L 321/1.
59. The General Product Safety Directive is 92/59/EEC,in Official Journal EC L 288 of 11 August 1992. For other examples and legal details, see E. Gippini Fournier and S. La Pergola (1996).
60. The authors are indebted to the Commission for supplying the data.
61. Ongoing work in the OECD aims to develop methodologies applicable to measuring qualitative date. At the same time a huge dataset for national regulation (stock data) has been collected from OECD members. Elsewhere in this volume, Boeri, Nicoletti and Scarpetta work with the early results of this research.
62. The bi-annual report, due for 1995-96 (or even for 1997-98) was not published by the Commission as late as December 1999.
63. This seems to be confirmed by the thrust and the details of the DG III paper (III/2185-EN) of 28 February 1996, as quoted in note 47.
64. In preparing Table 7.3, the authors had to rework the data set because Commission reporting over the entire period is not consistent in grouping sectors. And, as noted, Directive 88/182 widened the coverage of the notifications.
65. The following quotation from the 16th Annual Report on Monitoring the Application of Community Law (1998), COM (199)301 of 9 July 1999,

pp. 20-21 illustrates the relevance of our suggestion:

66. While Community secondary legislation and the Commission's action on the basis of Article 30 of the Treaty have gradually introduced the principle of free movement into national laws and national administrative practices, this means that cases of barriers with which operators are faced relate less and less to a Member State's acceptance of the principle of mutual recognition, say, but more to the actual way in which the principle is applied in specific cases where certain products are not accepted in the Member State of destination. For the Commission, this involved often in-depth technical analyses of these products, their health or safety implications, and a corresponding analysis of the national rules which prevent them being accepted. The technical and legal complexity of the cases means that the Commission is continuing to emphasise methods of solving these problems that are based on close collaboration with the national authorities. Meaningful dialogue allows the two sides to reconcile the various interests at stake as much as possible, balancing the legitimate concerns of the Member States in protecting health and safety with the requirement to ensure uniform and effective application of Community rules. In this spirit, the Community is focusing on package meetings as a framework where an open, informal discussion can achieve rapid solutions to the barriers exposed by operators. In 1998, these meetings took place with all the Member States except Luxembourg. In general, the success rate of these meeting is high: of all the cases examined, more than 50% have been settled, either during the meeting or by the adoption of a measure by the Member State following a commitment made during the meeting. Disputed cases represent on average only just over 10% of the cases discussed.

REFERENCES

Atkins, W.S. (1997), *Technical barriers to trade*, Study for the Review of the Internal Market 1996, Brussels/Luxembourg, Office for Official Publications of the EC.

CEPS (1992), *The EC without technical barriers*, Centre for European Policy Studies, CEPS Working Party Report No. 5, Brussels.

Dehousse, R. (1989), 'The Institutional Dimension of the Internal Market Programme', *Legal Issues of European Integration*, pp. 109-136.

Egan, M. (1998), 'Regulatory strategies, delegation and European market integration', *Journal of European public policy*, Vol. 5 No. 3, September.

European Commission (1985), White Paper COM(85) 314, 13 June.

European Commission (1992), *The operation of the Community's internal market after 1992. Follow up to the Sutherland report*, Commission's Communication to the Council and the European Parliament, SEC(92) 2277 final.

European Commission (1993a), *Reinforcing the effectiveness of the internal market*, Commission's Communication to the Council and the European Parliament, COM(93) 256 final, 26-30.

European Commission (1993b), *Making the most of the internal market: strategic programme*, Commission's Communication to the Council, COM(93) 632 final.

European Commission (1993c), *Management of the mutual recognition of national rules after 1992,* Operational conclusions reached in the light of the inventory drawn up pursuant to Article 100b of the EC Treaty, COM(93) 669, 15 December.

European Commission (1996a), *National Regulations affecting products in the internal market – a cause for concern. Experience gained on the application of Directive 83/189/EEC 1992-4*, III/2185-EN final, Brussels, 28 February.

European Commission (1996b), *Report of the Commission about the functioning of Directive 83/189 in 1992, 1993 and 1994*, COM(96) 298, 26 June.

European Commission (1997), *The competitiveness of European industry*.

European Commission (1998), *The competitiveness of European industry*.

European Commission (1999), *Mutual recognition in the context of the follow-up to the Action Plan for the Internal Market*, COM(99) 299, 16 June.

European Economy (1996), *Economic evaluation of the single market*, Reports & Studies, 1196/4 , December 1996

Gippini Fournier, E. and S. La Pergola (1996), *La nouvelle procedure d' information mutuelle sur les mesures nationales derogeant au principe de libre circulation des marchandises à l'interieur de la Communinauté*, Revue du Marché Europeen Unique, 1996-4

Joerges, Chr. (1992), 'Social regulation and the legal structure of the EEC', in B. Stauder (ed.), *La securité des produits de consommation*, Zürich: 1992, pp. 31-47.

Joerges, Chr. and E. Vos (eds) (1999), *EU committees: social regulation, law and politics*, Oxford: Hart Publishing.

Joerges; Chr., J. Folke, H.W. Micklitz and G. Brüggemeier, (1988), *Die Sichereit von Konsumgütern und die Entwicklung der europäischen Gemeinschaften Nomos*, Baden-baden. English version published as EUI Working Papers LAW 91/10-14, Florence, 1991.

Joerges, Chr., H. Schepel and E. Vos (1999), *The Law's problems with the Involvement of Non-governmental Actors in Europe's Legislative Processes: the Case of Standardisation under the New Approach*, EUI Working Paper Law No. 99/9, forthcoming.

Longrove, N. et al. (1998), 'Why is labour productivity in the UK so low?', *McKinsey Quarterly*, 1998/4, pp. 44 ff.

Machado, Jorge H. (1995), *Assured performance: The role of conformity assessment in supporting the internal market*, CEPS Paper No. 60, Brussels.

Majone, G. (ed.) (1990), *Deregulation or Re-regulation? Regulatory Reform in Europe and the United States*, London.

McKinsey Global Institute (1997), *Removing barriers to growth and employment in France and Germany*, Frankfurt/Paris/Washington D.C., March.

Molitor, B. et al. (1995), *Report of the Group of independent experts on legislation and administrative simplification*, Brussels, COM(95)288, May.

Nieuwenhuis, A. van (1997), *Assessing the economy-wide effects of deregulation*, CPB Report, 1997-4, The Hague.

OECD (1997), *The OECD Report on Regulatory Reform*.

Pelkmans, J. (1987), 'The new approach to technical harmonisation and standardisation', *Journal of Common Market Studies*, Vol. 25, March.

Pelkmans, J. and D. Costello (1991), *International Product Standards*, UNIDO Working Paper, Vienna.

Peltzman, J. (1989), 'The economic theory of regulation after a decade of deregulation', *Brookings Papers on Economic Activity*, Microeconomics Series.

Sutherland, Peter (1992), *The internal market after 1992. Meeting the challenge*, Report to the EEC Commission by the High Level Group on the operation of the Internal Market of 26 October.

UNICE (1995), *Releasing Europe's potential through targeted regulatory reform*, Brussels, November.

Vos, E. (1999), *Institutional frameworks of community health and safety regulation: Committees, agencies and private bodies*, Oxford: Hart Publishing.

Weatherill, S. (1996), 'Compulsory notification of draft technical regulations: the contribution of directive 83/189 to the management of the internal market', *Yearbook for European Law*, Vol. 16, pp. 129-204.

8. The Economic Impact of Product Liability: Lessons from the US and the EU Experience

Francesco Silva and Alberto Cavaliere

1. INTRODUCTION

Despite the general trend towards deregulation and liberalisation of markets, the production of rules concerning product safety has continued to increase in the European Union in the last 20 years. Product liability concerns led to the introduction in 1985 of the EC Directive 85/374, which established a strict liability regime in all member countries. The aim of standardisation of product safety rules led to the introduction of a directive about general product safety in 1992 (92/59/CEE). In addition to these general directives, specific EC safety directives have been issued with respect to food safety, toys, telecommunications equipment, motor vehicles, tractors, hydraulic diggers, household appliances and tower cranes.

The increasing regulation of product quality at the European level is linked to the completion of the internal market, requiring uniform legislation in all countries in order to assure the same level of consumer protection to all European citizens and to eliminate in the meantime any non-tariff barriers to intra-Community trade. The great impetus that has been given to consumer protection is typical of advanced industrial economies to the extent that an increased demand for safety is linked to growing incomes. This impetus is reducing the differences with the American economy, whose attention to consumer welfare led to the introduction of a strict liability regime for defective products as early as 1960s to the continuous extension of product safety regulations.

However the US also experienced a crisis of its product liability system during the 1980s, giving rise to a debate concerning the impact of product liability rules on market efficiency. This debate, as we shall see, has probably conditioned the formulation of the EC directive that was introduced in that period. In fact the introduction of the EC directive on product liability has been accompanied by opposition from some portions of the business community, based on fears about the high liability burden that fell on American firms as a result of court decisions. The directive on product safety seems to have encountered less opposition and, to our knowledge, did not give rise to much debate. This is probably due to the fact that it appears to be suited to the internal evolution of firms towards the introduction of total quality control systems as a response to growing needs about product safety expressed by consumers.

Even though not many years have passed since the introduction of these laws, an assessment about their economic impact can now be attempted. This paper focuses on the efficiency of product liability rules both from the point of view of theory and of the general impact on the American and European economy. We shall also deal with product safety regulation especially concerning its relationship with product liability. This will lead us to a discussion of the impact of the directive on general product safety (92/59/CEE).

In Section 2, we present a survey of the main theoretical results about the efficiency foundations of product liability as an instrument for accident prevention and compensation, emphasising those cases in which additional regulation is necessary. We then compare the enforcement of liability laws in the US and the EU to account for the wide differences between the two systems. In Section 3, we analyse the economic impact of strict liability for defective products in the US experience. In particular we try to discuss to what extent the inefficiencies resulting from a reduced supply both of products and liability insurance can be ascribed to strict liability per se or to the interaction between it and some typical features of the American legal system. In the fourth section we deal with the economic impact of the EC directive. Despite the restricted empirical evidence with respect to the US, the comparatively limited role played by liability laws in implementing product safety in Europe will appear very clearly. As costly access to justice is frequently invoked as a possible explanation we deal with this issue by presenting some evidence about the legal costs of cross-border transactions and further comparing the American and European legal systems in this respect. Given the restricted role played by product liability in Europe, safety regulations should have been comparatively more important in guaranteeing safer products. This has led us to explore the institutional and market interactions between product liability and product safety regulation in Section 5. The economic impact both on manufacturing and insurance industries of the directive of general product safety is analysed in this respect. Some conclusions follow in Section 6.

2. THE INTERNALISATION OF SAFETY RISKS THROUGH PRODUCT LIABILITY: THEORETICAL RESULTS

Product quality can have multiple dimensions. For analytical purposes we distinguish between those aspects of product quality that can cause injuries to consumers or damage their health, and those aspects of quality that merely affect consumers' satisfaction in connection with their expectations and the promises of sellers. In the first category we consider product safety. Examples of characteristics that fall into the second category are product durability, proper working, energy consumption, after sales services, etc.

In the first case, we have a problem of negative externalities that can be internalised both with product liability and product safety regulation. In the second case consumers are exposed to the risk of non-performance of products in relation to the price-quality combination that was expected. This kind of risk can then be assured with guarantees, but also regulating information by mandated disclosure or imposing standards of performance.

2.1 The theory of liability assignment with perfect information

The existence of safety risks due to the consumption of products raises an externality issue. Economic efficiency requires that consumption benefits should be properly diminished to account for expected damaged. The socially optimal quantity to be consumed should then correspond to the equality between marginal benefits and marginal production costs plus the marginal expected damages representing the social costs of safe production. Of course, the question is how to internalise the externality. Product liability can be useful in this respect.

From the theoretical point of view, we can distinguish three abstract liability regimes: strict liability, negligence and no liability. With strict liability (also known as liability without fault), the producer is liable for any accident caused by the product, independently of his care. Once the relationship between the injury suffered by the accident victim and the defective product is proved, the producer is held liable. The burden of proof falls upon the producer, who must show the absence of a product defect in order to be exempted form liability. With negligence, lack of care on the part of producers must be shown in order to hold the manufacturer liable for product accidents. This is a fault-based liability regime. The burden of proof falls upon the consumer who must show in a lawsuit the negligence of manufacturer to take adequate care. With no liability, the consumer is entirely responsible for any product accident.

Given full and symmetrical information, no transaction costs and risk-neutral consumers and firms, the Coase theorem assures that in a competitive market the social optimum can be attained independently of the assignment of the liability rule (Polinsky, 1983). With strict liability producers are completely responsible for any accidents that may occur to consumers. Therefore they are induced to bear the cost of care that adds to production costs, increasing the final price paid by consumers. Consumers will treat the product as completely safe and will purchase the optimal quantity since the price already incorporates the cost of care. Under the negligence rule, producers will be liable only if they do not respect a standard of care and sell risky products. Consumers who are informed about the risk incurred by purchasing and consuming the products will take account of expected damages in their decision. So, even if prices are lower than under the strict liability rule, only the socially optimal quantity will be consumed. In the absence of any liability assignment, consumers will entirely bear the losses due to accidents caused by faulty products and will add the cost of care to the final price of products. Less risky products will cost less to consumers and will be purchased in greater amounts.

When the care taken by victims can play a significant impact on accidents, strict liability no longer will be optimal and one should add a defence of contributory negligence in order to create incentives also for consumers to take the socially optimal level of care. With heterogeneous consumers and firms, however, the negligence rule is no longer optimal, because given differences among firms in the ability to comply with safety risks, it is inefficient to constrain every firm to supply the same standard of care. The same is true also for consumers. (Why should the standard of care taken by car drivers be equal to that of truck drivers?) On the other hand, given the cost of obtaining information on the appropriate care levels, the courts will probably adopt arbitrary standards.

Imperfect incentives to take the proper level of care may be due to the absence of perfect competition. Market power implies a reduction of output with respect to the socially optimal quantity. The degree of care one is led to observe depends on the cross-effects of care and outputs on the costs of the imperfectly competitive firm. From the social point of view, production of a more hazardous product by a monopolist is better with respect to the supply of this same product under perfect competition. On the other hand, one can show that introducing potential competition creates incentives for improvements in product safety (Spulber, 1989).

If consumers misperceive product risks, the attainment of a social optimum will be dependent on the liability regime. Actually, the rule of strict liability continues to be efficient even when consumers have imperfect information about safety risks. Consumers know that they will be completely compensated for any loss caused by products and will treat the product itself as if it were perfectly safe, regardless of their information about risks. However, they will be constrained to take account of the actual risks in their purchase decisions, because final prices will include the cost of care taken by producers, and the quantity purchased will be adjusted accordingly. With a negligence rule, social inefficiencies arise. In fact, firms can continue to take a proper standard of care to avoid liability from product accidents, but consumer misperceptions will not lead buyers to purchase the optimal quantity as their decisions will not take account of expected losses from product damages. With any liability assignment, even firms won't take account of safety risks, so that not only output will exceed the optimal quantity but also the level of care will not be adjusted to actual safety risks. Then with consumers' misperceptions strict liability is optimal because it can work as a substitute for perfect information about safety risks (Shavell, 1980 and Polinsky, 1983).

The assumption of risk neutrality on which the neutrality of liability assignment is based, may be inadequate given the kinds of risk that consumers may face while using products (injuries, health damages, etc.). It would seem more reasonable to assume that consumers are risk-averse while firms are risk-neutral. Then it is optimal to completely shift risks from consumers to firms. The assignment of liability will not be neutral in this respect due to its implication for risk allocation. Strict liability remains optimal even with risk-averse consumers because it implies that firms are completely responsible for product accidents, while negligence and no liability cannot be optimal. Negligence with a care standard implies that firms are simply incited to respect the standard while the remaining portion of risk is borne by consumers. With no liability assignment, consumers bear all the safety risks. In this last case, inefficiencies could be amended by an additional contract implying risk-sharing agreements between firms and consumers.[1] However, given that contract contingencies are costly to implement and given contract incompleteness, this contract may not be optimal. If the safety risk is not completely shifted to firms, consumers may directly adjust their purchase to reduce the risk of product failures. Producers may provide both an insufficient level of care or even excessive care if reductions in safety risks are required to sell the product.

We can than conclude that with risk-averse consumers only strict liability assures that the socially optimal level of care will be chosen. But even strict liability cannot be sufficient if legal limits on liability are imposed. This is the case when an accident causes very large injuries and a firm does not dispose of the resources that are necessary to compensate very large damages. Actual liability may be limited to firm assets or a limit *(liability cap)* may be imposed by national civil law (as implied by the European Directive, see Section 4).[2] In these cases only direct product regulation can impose a remedy to the failure of the liability system (Posner, 1986 and Shavell, 1984). Another argument for direct regulation comes into play in the opposite case: when expected damage is so small that consumers will not file a lawsuit. But in these cases *class action suits* can provide a useful tool to aggregate small claims.

Concerning risk-allocation issues, one must then consider the opportunity of liability insurance for producers. The existence of such an opportunity may create negative effects on producer incentives to take care as liability insurance 'isolates' insured firms from the tort liability system. Damage payments compensate victims but their deterrence effect is highly diminished. Only insurance pricing accurately reflecting expected damages from product accidents can lead to an efficient level of care.[3]

2.2 Asymmetric information, liability failures and regulation

Thus far we have explicitly or implicitly assumed symmetrical information between consumers and firms about care levels. Now let us suppose that care levels and/or the likelihood of product accidents are private information of both parties[4] and assume for simplicity that both consumers and firms are risk-neutral. A double-adverse selection issue arises in this case, as each party will be incited to overestimate the cost of care thereby reducing the quantity of output exchanged in the market with respect to the socially optimal quantity. Economic analysis concerned with this issue have shown that with private information the efficient allocation depends on the prior assignment of liability (Spulber, 1985). In fact, given private information about the cost of care, both parties enjoy information rents and non-appropriated gains from trade materialised in output reductions. In order to restore optimality, rents from additional exchanges must cover information rents for the consumer and the firm. Since it can be shown that information rents of both agents are increasing in the assigned share of liability, the choice of the liability regime itself affects efficiency. However, theoretical analysis establishes that liability rules will not be sufficient to guarantee the attainment of social optimality in these cases.[5]

If care levels can vary, efforts by consumers and firms to reduce safety risks may not be directly observable by the other party. To the extent that this effort is a hidden action on both sides of the contractual relationship, we have to deal with a double moral hazard issue. Even if there is a joint interest of producers and consumers in minimising both the sum of losses from product accidents and the total cost of care, this aim cannot be achieved because each party has an incentive to shirk in taking care by free-riding on other party's care. The problem is further complicated by assuming risk-averse consumers because optimality require complete shifting of risks to producers, but unobservable efforts of consumers to reduce safety risks requires that at least some portion of total risk be borne directly by them in order not to eliminate their incentive to take care. Given the legal interests that are protected (human life and health), one can assume that moral hazard on the part of consumers is not an issue. Of course most consumers would not be less careful with their life simply because they would be compensated in the event of damage. But consumers' misperceptions about product risks can nevertheless affect their level of care.

This trade-off between risk sharing and incentives prevents the attainment of first-best optimality. Obviously this problem extends to the contractual relationship between an insurance company and a firm seeking product liability insurance. Economic models that have subjected this problem to careful analysis conclude that a transfer payment may not exist such that consumers' and producers' care are optimally chosen. To the extent that liability regimes can be considered equivalent to transfer functions between firms and consumers, even the rule of strict liability cannot assure efficiency when moral hazard is considered.

Given the failure of liability rules under adverse selection and moral hazard,[6] we have again a case for regulatory action. To the extent that government agencies have superior information about technical issues such as the cost of care or the likelihood of product accidents, they can mandate specific actions to reduce safety risks to the optimal level. However, problems due to asymmetrical information can also persist between firms and regulatory agencies. In this case, not only may efforts to avoid accidents be reduced but efforts may instead be devoted to the avoidance of regulation. Therefore some standards may also impose additional costs on consumers and firms without yielding commensurate reductions in expected losses.

What seems to be needed is additional communication between contracting parties to reduce the asymmetry of information. This aim has been pursued in the US by reducing regulation focused on standards and increasing the role played by hazard warnings and regulation of consumer information (Beales et al., 1981). There are, in fact, failures in the market for information that require state intervention. Information is a public good (non-rival and only incompletely excludable) and this can explain why the market for risk information is so tiny. Moreover firms have no incentive to provide hazard warnings voluntarily because any competitor may profit from the difficulty of processing technical information and confused consumers beliefs which give rise to losses to the disclosing firms. Public programmes of hazard warnings have proved successful in some cases, such as cigarettes. The evidence provided by Viscusi et al. (1995) show that hazard warning for cigarettes have been so successful in reducing smoking that a level of safety has been obtained that is probably greater than the socially optimal level. Quite interestingly this is due to the development of 'moral suasion' against smoking, that is viewed as socially unacceptable from a moral point of view. This seems to be in accordance with the statement by K. Arrow that 'non-market controls, whether internalised as moral principles or externally imposed, are to some extent essential for efficiency'.[7]

3. THE IMPACT OF PRODUCT LIABILITY ON MARKET FUNCTIONING: THE US EXPERIENCE

The most recent OECD report about product liability states that 'The goal for a liability system should be to maximise consumer welfare by efficiently providing just compensation for injuries incurred and deterring future injuries without unreasonably impeding the supply of goods and services to consumers'.[8] This sentence highlights the two main functions of a liability system: compensation and deterrence. Compensation of victims should be fair and deterrence of accidents should be optimal. Moreover compensation and deterrence are intimately linked one to another. If damages awarded by courts are punitive, victims are more than compensated for their economic losses and accidents are deterred below the optimal level because firms may consider reducing the supply of products in order to reduce liability costs. Even if it is difficult to define the optimal level of safety of an industrial system, one can evaluate if different product liability systems perform efficiently with respect to the two main goals of compensation and deterrence.

3.1 The crisis of the liability systems and its impact on the supply side

In the US, given the great attention to consumer welfare and the decentralised nature of society, the liability system has been extensively used as an instrument to provide product safety, although during the 1970s regulation of product standards and product recalls have also increased. During the mid-1980s, however, the liability system experienced a crisis that induced both social scientists and policy-makers to reconsider some of its main features and to make proposals for reform.[9]

Since the 1970s there has been a continuous increase in the recourse to tort liability as illustrated in Figure 8.1. Liability payments have increased enormously, even considering the decreasing accident rate, and some markets have been dislocated by the very high liability burden and legal uncertainty that the system placed on firms.

The insurance system has been primarily affected by the increasing demand of third-party insurance by firms. Insurance rates rose enormously from 1984 to 1986, even if this trend has been reversed in the subsequent periods.[10] The rise of premiums in the mid-1980s has been paralleled by the increase in firm self-insurance. In some extreme cases, insurance coverage has also been refused, and this has resulted in parks and swimming pools not being opened because of lack of insurance. Some products such as diving boards in hotel swimming pools and amusement park rides have literally disappeared.[11]

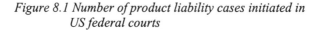

*Figure 8.1 Number of product liability cases initiated in
US federal courts*

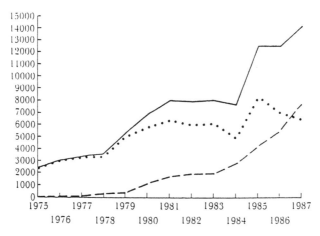

_____ Personal injury product liability cases.
. . . . . Personal injury product liability cases, excluding asbestos.
_ _ _ Asbestos cases.

Source: Viscusi (1991), p. 24.

According to Priest (1991), the inefficiencies of the US liability system
are rooted in its economic foundations. The diffusion of tort liability was due
not only to the Pigouvian principle of cost internalisation fostered by
Calabresi (1970) but also to the idea of using strict liability as a sort of
insurance to provide compensation to the victims of product accidents. The
first issue is concerned with efficiency: strict liability was important because
firms were in a better position than consumers to control product safety. The
second principle is more concerned with equity, to the extent that liability has
been conceived as a system to provide insurance to all consumers, even to the
poorest who could not afford to buy insurance coverage. In some sense, it
was conceived as a welfare provision. Manufacturers could buy insurance
more easily and then transfer its cost to consumers through the price system.

However there are differences between first-party and third-party
insurance delivery in terms of risk aggregation and control of adverse
selection and moral hazard that could explain the reduction of availability of
liability insurance in the mid-1980s.

With the increasing liability costs, low-risk firms have self-insured
directly. As a reaction, insurance companies have reduced insurance coverage
to high-risk firms either by increasing deductibles, reducing the level of
aggregate coverage or even refusing coverage. Moreover manufacturers

withdrew products because third-party insurance is more costly than first-party insurance (three to five times) and in some cases the impact on final prices was such that consumers were no longer willing to buy the product.

The continuous extension of tort liability and the award of more than compensatory damages did not necessarily increase the investment in precautions by firms, because the availability of insurance isolated firms from economic losses due to product accidents. Moreover safety can be enhanced through the extension of tort liability only if additional firms' precautions do not substitute investments in safety by victims.[12] As we have outlined in Section 2 there is a significant double moral hazard issue if we assume that safety precautions are hidden actions.

A survey of manufacturers reported that in 1986 47 per cent had withdrawn products, 39 per cent had decided against introducing new products, and 25 per cent had discontinued new product research because of expanded liability.[13] The cost structure of some industries has also changed because of liability costs, due not only to insurance premiums and self-insurance costs but also to the addition of legal fees. As a result, in 1991, 15-25 per cent of the price of a new ladder were liability costs. Due to product liability insurance, the Hepatitis vaccine, in 1995, cost \$160 in the US compared to \$12 in Taiwan. In the US about \$500 in the cost of a car is directly linked to product liability costs while only \$50 of the cost of an imported car account for the same kind of expenses (OECD, 1995).

A controversial issue concerns the effect of strict liability on innovation. Strict liability seems to have a chilling effect on R&D because new products attract tort lawsuits. Actually new products may be misused by consumers, increasing then the probability of accidents. To the extent that the American courts did not recognise the *state of the art defence*, the introduction of new products became more and more risky.

The *state-of-the-art defence* or *development risk defence* protects the manufacturer from liability if the company was unaware of the product defect at the time the product was sold. Nowadays the majority of US courts permit this defence, as a result of the restatement of liability laws that followed the liability crisis of the mid-1980s. In the past, claims involving long-term product effects, especially on health, have been treated differently. A doctrine of *retroactive liability* has been applied to firms that probably could not anticipate the extent of risk they imposed on consumers on the basis of the state of scientific knowledge. The result was the explosion of what Viscusi (1991 and 1997) calls *toxic torts*. Cases involving asbestos hazards fall into this category of claims. Viscusi points out that this kind of hazard was not completely understood at the time of exposure. Consequently firms could not anticipate that they would be held liable in the future for damages related to asbestos. Toxic torts[14] represent then a case where awards have little deterrent effect on accidents.

Nevertheless, this is also a typical case in which there could be private information and/or hidden actions that cause inefficiencies due to adverse selection and moral hazard as reported in Section 2. Actually, in the case of toxic tort, a presumption seemed to operate that firms could have suspected the negative impact on human health of these products, before the subsequent mass diffusion of scientific knowledge about this impact.[15]

More evidence on the relationship between innovation and product liability is provided by Viscusi (1991) showing that firms introducing new products are characterised by an higher liability burden. Actually the average ratio between product liability insurance premiums and a firm's sales appears to be 5 per cent greater for firms with significant product patents. However, the reverse is true for process patents: firms in industries without process patents have a 15 per cent higher product liability cost rate. The reason may be that safety-oriented innovation in the manufacturing process can reduce manufacturing defects and liability costs. Deeper statistical analysis concludes that overall product liability also positively affects product innovation, except at very high levels of liability where on balance, there is a net discouraging effect.

3.2 The implementation of strict liability in courts and access to justice in the US

The US liability system has been considered inefficient to the extent that transaction costs are higher with respect to compensations awarded to victims. According to a research report quoted by OECD (1995) in 1988, only $16.9 to $19.3 billion (of the $34.7 to $40.5 billion spent on tort litigation) was paid to the plaintiffs. Approximately 52 per cent of the total amount represented legal fees, litigation expenses of both the plaintiff and defendant, insurance company processing costs, the value of the litigant's time, and the cost of operating the court system.[16] However the opponents of a radical reform of the system point out that the growing amount of data shows that the system itself is working well to the extent that the number of liability cases (excluding asbestos claims) is coming down, punitive damages are more and more rare and awards are proportional to the amount of harms.[17]

The inefficiencies of the American liability system have been ascribed to the existence of a strict liability regime. However strict liability was introduced in the legal system of the US well before the crisis of the 1980s and precisely in 1963.[18] Moreover there is evidence showing that a negligence-based system can also be very inefficient as well.[19]

The 'real' liability standards that prevail also depend on other features of the system, besides the existence of strict liability per se. As stated by Rogers, 'strictness of the liability varies considerably along a spectrum from near-absolute liability to little more than a reversed burden of proof'[20] and the various liability regimes found in each system will find a place at some point or another along the continuum.

Some important features of the American liability system relate to the *state-of-the-art defence*, the responsibility of the product user and the character of damage awards. We have already dealt with the *state-of-the-art defence* in last section. Concerning the responsibility of the product user, the doctrine of comparative fault prevails on the doctrine of contributory negligence.[21] Under the first, if a plaintiff is partially responsible for the accident, the liability of the producer is reduced accordingly, while under contributory negligence the manufacturer is completely exempted. Damages are crucial not only to provide compensation to victims, but also to determine the cost of liability insurance. We can distinguish between compensatory damages and punitive damages. In the US, compensatory damages not only cover economic losses but extend also to non economic losses such as 'pain and suffering' and, more recently to 'Hedonic' awards, justified in order to compensate victims for the loss of pleasure to enjoy life. Punitive damages, not allowed in most OECD countries, increased dramatically in the US up until the mid-1980s,[22] when the idea was proposed to put a cap on them in order to reform product liability.

Producer liability can also be reduced by including in liability laws statutes of repose, that establish time limits to file a claim, and collateral source rules, preventing plaintiffs from obtaining a multiple recovery of damages (both from courts and from medical insurance, for example). Viscusi (1991) finds that liability insurance turned out to be more profitable in those states in which statutes of limitations and collateral source rule were included in liability laws. This result could then explain the crisis in insurance availability in those states characterised by unpredictable liability regimes, because no statutes are provided to control claims and damage awards.

In our opinion the features of the strict liability regime we have just described have interacted with some other typical features of the US legal system to produce the liability crisis of the mid-1980s. We mainly refer to the respective role of juries and judges in lawsuits and to the contingent fee system with regard to attorney's compensation.

With the exception of Ireland, the US is the only country where liability lawsuits are decided by juries. The jury system certainly plays a role in allowing for disproportionate awards to victims of product accidents, thereby contributing to the unpredictability of the liability system. Decisions related to non-economic damages (pain and suffering and punitive damages) are largely subjective and under the rule of strict liability the actions of producers are irrelevant. Therefore 'strict liability tends to pit technology or a specific product against an injured or deceased plaintiff. In such a contest jurors often can find it easier to rule in favour of the plaintiff'.[23]

Attorney compensation has an impact on the number of lawsuits tried, the number of lawsuits settled prior to trial and the level of damages awarded. In the US, attorney compensation is based on contingency fee arrangements: lawyers are paid for their service only if the plaintiff is successful, and the amount due depends on the size of the award.[24] This kind of arrangement and the opportunity of US attorneys to advertise their services makes it very easy for consumers to have access to compensation[25] but can also increase litigation over the amount that can be considered optimal from the point of view of the internalisation of the cost of accidents. In the UK, another legal system based on common law but where contingency fee arrangements are considered unethical, attorneys are much more likely to recommend abandonment or pre-trial settlements to injured consumers than in the United States (OECD, 1995).

Empirical evidence about the US shows that claims dropped are about 20 per cent and that among the remaining claims, about 95 per cent are settled out-of-court. The rate of plaintiff success in court is only about one-third. Economic models represent the litigation process as a bargaining game in which plaintiffs and defendants are engaged as rational decision-makers.[26] The likelihood of dropping a case is reduced as the expected pay-off to the plaintiff increases. Actually, the diffusion of non-economic and punitive damage awards increases the stakes while the features of the strict liability system of the US increase the probability of plaintiff success. But also the rate of out-of-court settlements is positively affected. Evidence suggests that parties anticipate the impact of court outcomes and incorporate these expectations in earlier bargaining decisions. When negotiating an out-of-court settlement, parties split the economic rents corresponding to the difference between the defendant's maximum offer and the plaintiff's minimum asking amount. Lillard and Viscusi find that the bargaining power is evenly divided.[27]

American scholars are probably so familiar with their system of access to tort law to undermine its role in the liability crisis. They have been more concerned with the application of liability laws in courts. The timing of the crisis suggests to Viscusi that strict liability per se cannot be the cause and that 'two likely candidates are the extension of the concepts of a design defect and the increased role of hazard warnings'.[28] While manufacturing defects are single items deviations from a broader production run (the *odd* unit), design defects imply that a single product is excessively unsafe. However this is established through 'risk-utility tests' on the basis of which a producer is to be held liable for the accident if the risk of injuries given current product design exceeds the product's utility. This kind of procedure raises some methodological issues: does not product risk itself affect consumer utility?[29] Moreover this kind of test is applied by juries who cannot be very familiar with a subject that resembles cost-benefit analysis.

Concerning hazard warnings, as we have seen in Section 2 they can be useful to reduce consumers' misperceptions of risk, by increasing consumer information. Liability is presumed if it can be shown that the injury would have been prevented had the manufacturer warned the user of the product's dangerous characteristics. The presumptions adopted[30] have been such that when a consumer is injured despite the existence of a warning, the warning is supposed to have been inadequate. Warning law seems then to be closer to absolute liability than to strict liability.

5. THE ECONOMIC IMPACT OF THE EC DIRECTIVE ON PRODUCT LIABILITY

The EC directive on product liability was introduced with the aim of standardising different national legislation existing in this field and to guarantee a minimum level of product safety to all consumers of the European Union. Directive 85/374 aimed at implementing a common scheme of strict product liability in European countries just when the US was experiencing the crisis of its liability system as described in the last section. Therefore, the business community feared the increase of insurance rates and the rise of claims and lawsuits that have characterised the American experience.

Fifteen years after the introduction of this directive, it is possible to state that these worries were not justified and that the European experience is completely the opposite of that faced by the United States. Given the reduced concern about product liability and the limited experience with the implementation of the directive, there is less empirical evidence about European countries than there is with respect to the United States. However, even the reduced evidence at our disposal enables us to state that there was neither a significant increase of insurance costs due to the directive nor the rise of claims and lawsuits feared by the manufacturing and insurance industries. We are less able to trace the impact of the directive on the growth of accidents and product injuries. A study for the European Commission estimated that the accidents caused by consumer goods in the EC have led to 30,000 fatalities and 40 million injuries per annum.[31] Of course this evidence suggests that the social cost of accidents remains a problem of considerable magnitude in the European Union.

4.1 Optional provisions to limit strict liability in Europe

Although the EC directive was inspired by the idea of extending the strict liability regime to all European countries, the most substantial innovation has been the inversion of the burden of proof in liability lawsuits, as victims of a product injury are not required to prove that the manufacturer was negligent. They just have to prove the harm, the defect and the causal relationship between the injury and the defective product. The defendant must then prove the absence of a causal relationship between the product and the injury. However, the recent Green Paper of the European Commission devoted to product liability,[32] points out that in some cases it is even difficult for the consumer to prove that the injury is actually due to the product. The asymmetrical information between consumer and producer again benefits the latter, giving him easier access to the technical knowledge that is necessary to prove that the accident was not due to a defective product. In view of this fact the European Commission wonders if some presumption about the causal relationship should be included in the directive in order to overcome these problems.

The directive allows national legislation to introduce limitations and defences that practically dilute the economic impact of strict liability. Actually even if liability based on negligence (fault-based liability) can be distinguished in theory from strict liability (liability not based on fault), in practice the distinction between the two is very fluid and also depends on procedural aspects. Originally the directive offered the option to exclude primarily agricultural products and game (i.e. foods not being processed) from strict liability. The logic of this exclusion seems to be unclear to the extent that one cannot presume that consumers are well informed about risk associated with consumption of hormone enriched, conserved, dyed and radiated foodstuff. The large economic losses following the impact of the mad cow disease and more recently the scandal concerning chicken-breeding in Belgium, has led the European Union to take a different attitude towards this kind of product, extending also to them the product liability regime contained in the EC directive of 1985.[33]

Another option concerned the adoption of a state-of-the-art defence (or developmental risk defence) as stated in Art. 7 of the directive. Under this defence the producer must show that the state of scientific and technological knowledge was at such a level at the time the product was put into circulation that it was not possible to discover the existence of the defect. The inclusion of such a defence can be justified in order not to weaken the incentive of firms to introduce new products because of unpredictable liability consequences, as was discussed in Section 3.1 concerning the American experience. The introduction of the state-of-the-art defence can also be seen as a weakening of the strict liability regime that the directive aimed to impose.

However the formulation of Art. 7 is such that the defence would be hard to establish: if knowledge existed somewhere, then defendants could be held responsible even if they did not know it themselves. But the same principle can be formulated differently in national legislation. For example, concerning the UK implementation case, Burrows (1994) states that the formulation included in the Consumer Protection Act seems to place liability only upon producers who cannot show that the defect could not 'reasonably' have been discovered. Such a formulation can lead the courts to a negligence evaluation of the net benefits of producer efforts to discover defects in product design. In such a legal environment, producers will be induced to keep private any information about product risks in order to avoid the liability burden.[34]

In Germany national legislation concerning product liability before the directive was such that the producer could only be exempted by showing either that the defective unit was the odd unit that escaped all controls or that the defect depended on a risk that the producer could not foresee at the time of manufacture. The German implementation of the European directive on product liability with the *Produkthaftungsgesetz* of 15 December 1989 removed the *odd unit defence* and maintained the *product development risk defence*.[35] Depending also on the interpretation of such a defence, one can classify the European liability regime as one based on fault or not.

The European Commission challenged the UK implementation of Directive 85/374, and the ECJ (European Court of Justice) held that in order to be exonerated from liability 'the producer must prove that the objective state of scientific and technical knowledge, including the most advanced level of such knowledge, at the time when the product in question was put into circulation was not such as to enable the existence of the defect to be discovered. Further, that knowledge must have been accessible at the time when the product in question was put into circulation'.[36] So under the interpretation of the ECJ, the *state-of-the-art defence* is much narrower than under national laws, as the test concerning knowledge is objective and the only subjective leeway lies on the issue of accessibility.

It is claimed that under strict liability, without a development risk defence, the producer will have greater incentive to reduce product risk. However our theoretical survey of Section 2 shows that with private information there are adverse selection issues that are difficult to face even with a strict liability regime. If the development risk is also difficult to insure, once it is removed from the exemptions from liability, one wonders if the creation of a public fund to compensate the victims is a better solution for these cases.

The third optional provision is the adoption of a limit on the total liability for damage resulting from death or personal injury caused by identical items with the same defect. If this option is adopted the directive establishes a minimum liability limit of 70 million ecu. Germany, Greece, Portugal and Spain have adopted total liability limits.

Any claim must be brought within three years of the date upon which the injured person became aware of the damage. A claim under the directive is lost if not brought within ten years from the date on which the producer put the product into circulation. Such a long statute of repose should force producers of durable goods such as household appliances and cars to improve product safety with respect to the past.

4.2 Main differences with respect to the US experience

Major differences with respect to the US system exist with regard to damage awards and attorney compensation. Non-economic damages (such as pain and suffering) are not recognised by the EC directive – but member states are allowed to include such damages in their national laws – and punitive damages are unknown in the European liability system.

A very important difference between the two systems concerns the fact that physical injuries in Europe are compensated through the social security system, while in the US appeals to the liability system is much more widespread because welfare state provisions are much more restricted than in European countries. This fact is now also recognised in the recent Green Paper of the European Commission about product liability, pointing out also that in some countries (Belgium) compensation via the product liability regime is justified when welfare state provisions are not sufficient.[37]

Concerning attorney compensation, what is important to notice is that in the European Union the loser of a lawsuit pays both his own and the opponent's legal costs. As the opponents of consumers are often big companies incurring high legal costs, generally a single consumer cannot afford the cost of legal action and consumer associations in Europe generally lack the level of resources that is necessary to sponsor injured victims of product accidents.

The idea of the liability system as a public insurance device to provide compensation to every consumer, which typifies the US experience, seems to be very distant from the implementation of product liability in Europe where some institutions of the welfare state operate with this same aim but are directed to the citizen as such and not only to him as a consumer. It is interesting to verify to what extent this difference negatively affects the other important function of tort liability: the internalisation of the cost of accidents in order to improve product safety. In order for a liability system to correctly perform its deterrence function, a certain amount of liability claims (and lawsuits) should be in place. However the evidence at our disposal is very poor in this respect.

The first study carried out by the European Commission on the implementation of the EC directive, dated 1995, clearly reported that only three lawsuits had been filed since 1985 based on the directive[38]. Of course most actions are settled out-of-court but accounting for the fact that, according to a leading insurance company, only 5 per cent of total liability claims reach the European courts,[39] we can estimate that there has been about 60 liability claims based on the EC directive filed between 1988 and 1995. A lot of claims continue to be based upon national laws. Interpreting this evidence, one must recall that the EC directive cannot be invoked for products sold before 1988 and that product liability lawsuits require very detailed technical assessments.

Concerning the impact on insurance rates, the explosion of growth rates that was feared by the business community has not taken place. Insurance rates have increased, but the growth rates are lower than expected. Moreover, the picture is not uniform in the single national markets of the European Union.[40] What is more important to remark is the persistence of a very big difference between the European and the US market. In fact insurance rates imposed on European firms exporting in North America can be from 10 to 20 times greater with respect to those imposed on firms that limit their activity to the European market.

The level of insurance that firms disposed of before the introduction of the directive has been evaluated as not sufficient, given the new regime. But according to the report on the implementation of the EC directive, the growth of insurance rates is not only due to the introduction of the directive but to the increasing attention being paid to product quality issues. To the extent that a reduction of insurance availability has been observed, it should be seen as a consequence of increasing competition in the insurance markets (some major risks are excluded from insurance in order to avoid competition in insurance rates) or of the macroeconomic cycle (some firms reacted to the recession by choosing self-insurance).[41]

Even accounting for this evidence there could also be other factors peculiar to the directive in itself that have been invoked to explain its modest impact. For example, Larouche (1999) points out that while the directive requires full harmonisation (with the exceptions we have already discussed) it leaves national laws untouched. According to his view, in one way or another the directive is less protective than national laws in almost every state and this explains both the political difficulty of implementing it in lieu of them and the fact that plaintiffs would continue to prefer national laws as a mean of redress.[42]

4.3 The impact of costly access to justice

One cause that has frequently been invoked for the reduced impact of the directive on the number of claims and lawsuits has been the cost of justice in the European Union. According to Hodges (1995), the directive per se should have reduced the cost of justice to the extent that consumers have only to show the existence of product defects whereas previously they had to prove the negligence of manufacturers (a much more difficult task). However in many countries legislation already placed the burden of proof on producers, so that the EC directive did not represent a major change in their liability regime.

Some studies have been commissioned by the 'Directorate General XXIV' of the European Commission to evaluate the cost of justice in the single market. These reports are mainly concerned with cross-border transactions, but we think that their results have a more general significance. The most recent of these reports clearly states that 'the cost which the parties have to pay in obtaining justice are high and the duration [of civil proceedings] is long'.[43] The legal expenses are such that in most member states of the European Union only a dispute valued at 50,000 ecu might be sufficiently large to justify the pursuit of a cross-border claim. Actually, legal costs in all member states very quickly exceed the value of the claim for all amounts of claim below 2,000 ECU. Even at a dispute value of 50,000 ecu, the total legal fees are far more than half the value of the claim. Remembering that the European legal system imposes the obligation on the loser to pay also the legal expenses of his opponent (cost-shifting rule) each party is basically at risk to lose 75,000 for potentially winning 50,000 ecu.

Moreover, some other comparisons between the US and the European legal systems can give further insights into the costly access to justice that European consumers experience. Given that procedural norms and standards are oriented towards aiding the party that is presumed to be weaker, under European legal concepts the weaker party is the defendant. Therefore the defendant should be given the right of forum at his place of residence or business and should be afforded the time necessary to be heard and defend himself. In the American legal culture, as the defendant is a company deriving income from the place where the plaintiff resides, this is sufficient grounds to provide for jurisdiction at the plaintiff's residence. In the US the plaintiff is held to be the party aggrieved by the defendant, which is the reason to seek redress from the courts. Therefore court fees are particularly low and there is no cost-shifting against the plaintiff in the event that he loses the case.

Cost-shifting rules not only double the risk for each individual party but work differently for consumers and for firms. Firms are *multiple players* in court proceedings and can make a general litigation strategy.[44] Consumers are typically *one-shot* players and the cost-shifting rule makes litigation so risky that they must be very sure to win before going to court, as they cannot recover their legal fees in another case. One can then conclude that 'cost shifting does serve as a barrier for consumers to courts'. Improving consumer access to justice should enhance the compensation function of tort liability for product defects (litigation would increase). In the meantime if any offence or breach of contract can be easily taken to court there would be also a deterrence effect (litigation would decrease).[45] Moreover, if the result of civil proceedings can be easily foreseen, legal security will be improved and this will have a positive impact on economic growth.[46] In fact, it has been estimated that within the context of cross border transactions, and considering all the economies of the EU, the current lack of legal security creates annual losses of 100 billion ecu.

Finally the first period of implementation of the EC directive shows that there is an increasing concern across European firms for product safety and product quality in general. This concern is not seen as a specific result of the introduction of the directive on product liability. The directive should be seen as only one of a set of policy measures that are aimed to increase the quality level of European products. During the last 20 years, not only there has been an increasing consciousness of consumers concerning their right to use safer products, but there has been a significant development of safety regulations both at the national and at the community level. The relationship between product liability and safety regulations represents then a relevant issue to deal with.

5. PRODUCT LIABILITY AND PRODUCT SAFETY REGULATION: COMPLEMENTS OR SUBSTITUTES?

We have already discussed in Section 2 the existence of liability failures that call upon the intervention of safety regulations, to avoid the social cost of accidents. These failures occur in three main cases: 1) compensation for damages that exceed a firm's assets; 2) losses, considered from the point of view of a single individual, that are so small that the injured party does not file a claim; and 3) asymmetrical information about the cost of care, product risks and care efforts. The third case is so widespread that it can justify per se the use of regulation rather than tort liability to address market failures. It is also then clear why one cannot rely exclusively on tort liability instead of regulation to reach this objective.

In economic reality the two institutions interact to control product safety risk. It would then be interesting to see the nature of institutional interactions that take place in the two systems on which our discussion focuses: the US and the EU.

Concerning the US, the 'appropriate division of labour' between regulation and product liability has been discussed by Viscusi (1988) showing the inefficiencies that arise because of overlap between the two policies. Actually regulatory agencies in the US do not make specific allowances for the role played by tort liability. But in practice tort liability prompts additional regulation,[47] and the result may be a more than optimal level of safety. The most important issue discussed by Viscusi is the different consequences of regulatory compliance and regulatory violations for what concerns the attribution of liability in lawsuits. In fact, regulatory compliance is admissible as a defence but does not assure that the product will not be subject to product liability lawsuits.[48] Regulatory violations instead have much more impact in showing that the producer was negligent.[49] With the aid of empirical evidence Viscusi demonstrates that 'Regulatory violations reduce the probability that a claim will be dropped, increase the likelihood of an out-of-court settlement, increase the size of such settlements, and enhance the claimant's prospects in court actions'.

The liability crisis of the mid-1980s (see Section 3) together with the expanded scope of government regulation have caused the institutional overlap to be particularly felt in the US. Considering the asymmetrical effects of regulatory compliance and regulatory violations, Viscusi proposes to exempt firms from potential liability if they can demonstrate compliance with government regulation. The proposal was based on the assumption that most government regulation is more stringent than the economically efficient risk level, so that the liability system creates inefficient safety incentives for firms already complying with regulation. For firms not complying with product liability, regulation represents an additional incentive. However, the proposal of Viscusi is less convincing from the point of view of the efficient insurance of accident victims. Although it is true that third party insurance has caused the problems we have described in Section 3, one cannot exclude compensation on the grounds of the existence of health insurance programme or because of high transaction costs that comprise a much greater percentage of compensation itself.

Of course the picture is quite different in Europe. As we have already outlined in Section 4, the number of claims and lawsuits is so small in the EU that regulation should have been the main instrument to assure consumers an optimal level of product safety. An analysis of product safety regulation in Europe would require a separate work. However a few words are needed to explain the evolution from a command-and-control approach to a market-oriented attitude of this branch of regulation.

European regulation of product safety has always been concerned with two main aims: 1) to guarantee a minimum level of safety to all European consumers and 2) to harmonise the different national legislation in order to prevent the erection of non-tariff barriers to free trade among European countries. The Community wanted to avoid the introduction of very detailed directives focused on single products and has preferred to regulate wide classes of products. Pharmaceuticals and food have been a very important exception to this general rule of conduct. To impose the general principle of product safety and to fill any existing gap in the European regulation concerning this issue, a directive about general product safety (92/59/CEE) was introduced in 1992. We deal later in this chapter with the interaction between this directive and product liability.

To ensure standardisation it was necessary for bodies in charge of controlling product conformity to adopt homogeneous criteria and to earn an international reputation. Europe reached this aim by adopting the quality control standard ISO (International Standardisation Institute) 9000 and ensuring in addition that private certification and testing institutes were credited and rated following the ISO 45000 standard. The conformity of products to EU directives is now also certified by the use of the trademark CE (93/465/CEE).

It has been remarked (Marchetti, 1999) that the distinction between regulatory compliance voluntary adoption of a system of total quality control is less and less significant, given the main features of product safety regulation as embodied for example in the directive for general product safety. The analysis of this directive actually reveals that voluntary certification along the ISO 9000 standard practically follows from the necessity to comply with its contents. In the meantime the increasing market concerns for product safety naturally leads many firms to adopt quality control in order to satisfy customers, resist competition and/or improve market positioning.

For example, if a dangerous product is discovered, the authorities in charge can impose its withdrawal from circulation (Art. 3 of the directive). If the firm is unable to trace it, the same authorities can impose withdrawal from circulation of all items and then forbid temporarily or permanently the marketing of this same product. A product is traceable and can be easily recalled (and modified if necessary) when firms are organised along the ISO 9004 standard. Voluntarily adopting this standard is then convenient in order to avoid product withdrawal from the market when only some items are found to be defective. Quality control and especially the fact that lots of products are traceable under the ISO 9000 standard could show that only a few items are defective and avoid a public ban on product deliveries being imposed on the firm. It is quite important to note that the threat of product withdrawal is credible as it is the strategy of those producers that actually decided to recall their defective products from the market after the implementation of the directive.[50]

The adoption of a system of quality control can help firms reduce their exposure to product liability to the extent that product safety is increased and any defective product can be easily withdrawn and/or recalled without any impact on the firm's reputation. In fact behind the credible threat of product withdrawal deriving from enforcement of the directive (92/59/CEE), any firm risks the even larger losses associated with a tarnished reputation when a product accident is heavily advertised in the media.[51] In fact, it has been shown that consumer misconceptions are such that even very small risks give rise to an overreaction by consumers when these risks are highly publicised by the media (Viscusi, 1997). The final result is a collapse of sales and even a drop in the value of the firm's assets.[52]

So even if product liability claims are not frequently filed in Europe, there is always the possibility that a product accident could impose significant losses to firms either because the EU directive on general product safety requires product withdrawal or because of the impact of negative advertisements. The best solution is actually accident prevention through the adoption of total quality control. The reduction of product risk will have a further impact on production costs because insurance costs should also diminish.

The results of research projection about the economic impact of Directive 92/59/CEE on insurance companies operating on the Italian insurance market are presented below.[53] To carry out this research, 24 firms were selected, belonging to the top ten firms operating in the Italian insurance market or to multinational companies. The answers come from 12 firms representing at least 60 per cent of the market, evaluated as the flow of new insurance contracts in the field of product liability. These results show an increase in the ratio between damage awards and cashed premiums, which can be ascribed both to an increased awareness on the part of consumers and a greater vulnerability of firms with respect to the information about product accidents disseminated by the media. This vulnerability requires safety campaigns consisting of costly product recalls that can form the object of insurance contracts as product liability does in lawsuits. Another important result in this respect is the increasing burden for insurance companies due to these safety campaigns at the same time that the burden linked to consumer losses decreases. Insurers are of the opinion that the directive 92/59/CEE will actually be successful in improving product safety to the benefit of consumers. They also believe that the CE trademark and the voluntary certification of quality will reduce risks. In fact, insurers place a lot of weight on the codification and traceability of product lots because damages are proportional to the quantity of defective products and to their geographical spread.

Another part of the same research has tried to estimate the impact of quality certification on the economic performance of Italian firms adopting the ISO 9000 standards. Generally the adoption of quality control standards is voluntary, depending more on the decisions of far-sighted entrepreneurs, and market requests than on deep knowledge of safety regulations. The trend of the ratio of sales over employees demonstrates the productivity gains of these firms. Quality certification increases their competitiveness by improving the firms' positioning within their sector. Short-run economic results are closely related to the improvement of a firm's reputation and exports, but also to better control on internal organisation. Big companies can benefit immediately from economies of scale due to improvements in their internal organisation. Small and medium firms generally experience an immediate an increase in production costs especially due to the increased cost of skilled labour necessary to implement quality control inside the firm. Afterwards, they experience marginal increases in sales and, above all, stabilisation of their market shares. The impact on internal organisation is partly connected to an increase of bureaucratic activities and partly to more management activity. The results seem then to envisage concrete occupational opportunities for skilled labour to be involved in quality control, especially in small- and medium-sized firms.

6. CONCLUSIONS

Economic activities are risky. The use of products and services may cause accidents that cannot be accounted for in firm choices without some public intervention. Product liability has been conceived as an appropriate tool to internalise the cost of accidents in those activities that can prevent them. Theoretical analysis has shown that strict liability regimes can be considered socially optimal given consumers' misconceptions and risk-aversion. However, there are liability failures arising from private information about the cost of care and care efforts, both on the part of firms and consumers. Therefore, even strict liability cannot assure social optimality because of double-adverse selection and double moral hazard problems due to asymmetrical information. Safety regulation should be then necessary to eliminate inefficiencies. Unfortunately, there are also regulatory failures that require responses from society.

Historical experience seems to confirm the predictions of theory, at least in some respects. In the US after the shift to strict liability at the beginning of the 1960s there has been a continuous extension of the concept to economic activities, especially since the mid-1970s. This fact has been ascribed to the extensive use of the compensation function of the liability system as a sort of distributive tool in the hand of juries. The shift of liability to insurers has produced adverse selection and moral hazard problems in the insurance market. These problems materialised in a continuous increase of insurance rates, an increase in the incidence of self-insurance and reduced availability of insurance. The product market has also been affected as shown by product and service withdrawals and the exceptional increase in the price of some risky products.

On the other side of these inefficiencies are the economic rents that must have been created. Certainly, consumers and firms had to share a great part of them with their attorneys. Practically more than one-half of total compensation awards seem in fact to have benefited the legal system. Easy access to the courts, the contingency fee system of attorney compensation and, probably, also the opportunity of lawyers to advertise their services should have fostered the diffusion of product liability in the US.

The European experience is very different. Even after the introduction of EC Directive 85/374 establishing a strict liability regime, there are wide differences among the various countries. But overall in Europe, the liability burden on firms is greatly reduced compared to the US. The rise of insurance rates and the impact on the cost structure of firms seems not to have dislocated either the product or service market or the insurance market. The empirical evidence at our disposal was not very current and the new study that is going to be completed for the European Commission by the year 2000 could shed new light on this issue. But as a matter of fact, European consumers are not accustomed to turn to product liability, as shown by the reduced number of claims and lawsuits, even after the introduction of strict liability. Uncompensated damages have not been felt to be an issue in European countries, probably because social security usually provides insurance coverage for the victims of injuries. So it is the difference of welfare state provisions between Europe and the US that could also explain the different impact of product liability on the economic system. This could be a matter for further research concerning product liability and welfare state reforms in Europe.

Moreover, there are more technical issues connected to Directive 85/373 in itself that can help to explain the fact that consumers in Europe continue to appeal to national legislation. The directive has been conceived in such a way to enable each country to keep national legislation that probably continues to be more favourable to consumers, at least in some features. That is why in practice there is less harmonisation than expected. The imposition of a minimal harmonisation, apart from national legislation, could probably have produced more convergence at least on some basic principles.

However, there could be also more substantial reasons for the lower number of claims. One of these is costly access to justice that is fostered by cost-shifting rules that still prevail in European courts. A foray into the European legal system is generally more risky for consumers than for firms. Transaction costs are also considerable and lawyers, not operating on a contingency fee basis, can extract rents only from the duration of lawsuits. One cannot then be surprised at consumers' habits with respect to tort liability. In fact, these habits seem to be at odds with respect to the increased consumer consciousness and demand for quality and safety that has been registered in all studies.

Given the reduced appeal to product liability in European countries, one wonders about the internalisation of the cost of accidents. Safety regulation in

European countries should have worked in this respect, but only a deeper analysis of the data on product accidents could confirm this presumption. Moreover one could also question the fact that many claims and lawsuits are necessary to make product liability a serious deterrent for risky products. In fact, in the event of an accident nowadays, corporate reputation can be badly damaged, especially if newspapers and television give the incident extensive coverage. This could be a credible threat that works for deterrence even if no claims are filed in court.

A further question concerns the impact of product liability on dynamic efficiency through the rate of innovation. Basically a trade-off has been presumed to exist between a strict liability system and product innovation, to the extent that this liability regime imposes a sort of tax on products that are revealed to be dangerous per se, independently of the negligence of manufacturers. The development of new products may be discouraged to the extent that they have unpredictable liability effects. To avoid just such an undesirable result, a *state of the art defence* has been introduced in the EC directive, in order to protect producers from liability in the case that product defects were unknown when the product was put into circulation, given the state of scientific and technological knowledge at that time. However empirical evidence concerning the US has shown that product liability can discourage product innovation but it is an incentive for process innovation so that it can generally be stated that product liability fosters innovation, except at very high levels of liability.

The provision of the *state of the art defence* has been seen as sort of exemption from strict liability and as a way to drive the European system towards a fault-based liability regime. However the interpretation given by the ECJ seems much narrower with respect to defences allowed by national legislation, thereby supporting the conception of the regime introduced by the directive as a non-fault one.

In any event, there are very tricky issues that are connected to this feature of product liability. Firms can possess private information about both the cost of care and care efforts they have no interest to reveal, and unsafe products can be put into circulation unless a serious accident is publicised by the media and sales collapse. In other cases, firms really do not know that the product may be dangerous and may discover product defects afterwards, when the product is already on the market. Moreover, consumers can overreact to information about product risks and discourage firms from revealing any information at all. That is why public programmes of hazard warning may be useful in this respect.

From our analysis we are led to conclude that while internalisation of the cost of accidents in the US has proven to be too costly for the economic system, cost internalisation is not yet at a sufficient level in Europe. However such a conclusion would be incomplete without considering both the impact of safety regulation and the issues linked to the definition of an optimal level of safety from the economic point of view.

As far as regulation is concerned recent research has shown the positive impact of the EC directive on the general safety of products (92/59/CEE), to the extent that it seems to be consistent with market evolution and informational constraints. The directive works on the basis of the threat of product withdrawal from the market in case of defects and implicitly induces firms to adopt quality control. Firms adopting ISO 9000 standards can rapidly organise product recalls if a defect is discovered after sale, thereby avoiding both negative advertisement and a product liability suit. As confirmed by insurers, the directive may be really successful in accident prevention enhancing product safety. In many cases, the approach seems to be completely voluntary to the extent that quality control results from demand push and it is completely independent of the knowledge of the EC directives. Regulation works here as a credible threat, and we doubt that product liability could work as well in the framework of the European legal system. It would thus be risky to think of a reduction in the role played by regulation in order to promote product liability coupled with firms' voluntary action fostered by their need to develop a reputation for high quality in the products market.

Finally economic theory, to our knowledge, has not yet given a satisfactory answer to the problem of defining the optimal level of safety. This is a subject for further research. Unfortunately, public policy proposals cannot avoid facing a cost-benefit analysis even in this field.

NOTES

1. In principle, with no transaction costs it could be optimal to subscribe to a complete contingent contract whereby risk is optimally allocated. For example, the consumer could buy product insurance from the firm in the form of a guarantee or product warranty. Given competition among sellers the consumer will purchase from the producer that offers the best deal considering also producers' care and the best product insurance contract. See Spulber (1989).
2. Examples include the asbestos case in the US: losses exceeded firm assets recognised by the court as the firm's maximum liability.
3. Public authorities can play a useful role in this respect by collecting and supplying information about products that increase public knowledge of safety risks.
4. To make this statement clearer, we can adduce the following example concerning a contract for medical care between a patient and a physician. The patient may have private information about his propensity to follow a prescription, his tolerance of particular drugs or the result of previous treatments. The physician may possess detailed technical knowledge that is unavailable to the patient. The

private information known to the patient and physician may bear on the estimated success of the treatment. See Spulber (1989), p. 433. Or suppose that a firm operating in the telecommunication s sector possesses detailed technical knowledge about the impact on human health of the use of mobile phones while consumers are informed about their frequency of use of the same product, the propensity to use it inside cars or to let children make use of this same product. Also in this case the private information of both parties affects the extent to which individual health is really at risk.

5.   See Spulber (1989), p. 440.
6.   One must also remember that in economic reality both problems jointly affect private contracting.
7.   See Arrow (1968).
8.   See OECD (1995), p. 44.
9.   The principle of *liability without fault* was established in 1963 by the American Law Institute (Section 402A of the Second Restatement of Torts) and adopted by the majority of the American states. After 30 years of experience, there was a review in May 1997 by the American Law Institute (Restatement of the Law Third, Torts: Product Liability, xxxi, 382 pp., 1998). However no attempt to pass a federal law in this field has been successful to date.
10. From 1987 to 1993, insurance costs fell from $4 billion to $2.6 billion. Current rates amount to 26 cents for each $100 of damages. See Commissione delle Comunità Europee (1999), p. 11.
11. See Priest (1991).
12. A famous example from regulation is the increase in the ingestion of medicines by children following the FDA compulsory insistence on child-proof bottle caps, presumably because parents became more likely to leave the 'child-proof' bottles within reach or less likely to secure the tops.
13. See McGuire, E. Patrick (1998), *The Impact of Product Liability*, New York: Conference Board. Quoted in Priest (1991), p. 46.
14. The scale of this litigation has been enormous as described by Viscusi: 275,000 asbestos claimants and 335,000 claims related to other toxic substances. See Viscusi (1991) p. 273.
15. There are nowadays some fears about the impact that cellular phones could have on the human brain. But who can guess the amount of knowledge that is related to this kind of hazard directly owned by the telecommunications industry with respect to insurance companies and consumers?
16. A study carried out by the insurance sector in 1989 (the Tillinghast study) estimated the yearly cost of the US tort system as being even greater and amounting to $117 billion! (See Commissione delle Comunità Europee, 1999, p. 15).
17. US Senate, report no. 105-32, pp. 2, 44, 71, 75. Quoted in Commissione delle Comunità Europee (1999), p. 16.
18. As reported by Priest (1991), the California Supreme Court, announced in 1963 in Greenman v. Yuba Power Products Inc., the standard of strict tort liability for personal injuries caused by products. Then in 1964 the American Law Institute

announced its acceptance and recommendation of the standard of strict liability for defective products (see also note 9).

19. In the UK, the Pearson Report estimated that the cost of operating the tort law system was equivalent to 85 per cent of the value of the compensation paid (Report of Royal Commission on Civil Liability and Compensation for Personal Injury, Cmnd.7054 (1978). Quoted in Larouche (1999), p. 3.

20. See Larouche (1999), p. 1.

21. Nowadays only six states retain the doctrine of contributory negligence.

22. For example, in Cook County the number cases involving the award of punitive damages were three in 1960-64, and grew to 75 in 1980-84. In San Francisco, these same cases passed from 14 in 1960-64 to 51 in 1980-84. An extraordinary growth in the size of punitive damage awards has also been noticed in a short period of time. See OECD (1995).

23. See OECD (1995), p. 32.

24. A typical contract calls for the attorney to receive 33.3 per cent of the judgement, although the amount can range from 20 to 50 per cent. See OECD (1995).

25. As a matter of fact, attorney advertisement has been allowed since 1977, and one can observe that the significant growth of product liability cases in federal courts starts in 1978.

26. The game is sequential: plaintiffs must choose whether to drop a case at various stages, and both parties must decide whether to settle a case out-of-court, the amount they will ask or offer for any out-of-court settlement, and whether to litigate the case.

27. See Lee Lillard Lee and W. Kip Viscusi, 'The Bargaining Structure of the Litigation Process', working paper, RAND Corporation Institute for Civil Justice, 1990, quoted in Viscusi (1991), p. 90.

28. See Viscusi et al. (1995), p. 75.

29. See Priest (1991).

30. According to Priest the presumptions are that the manufacturer possesses complete knowledge about product dangers, that warnings of these dangers are easily and cheaply given, and that all consumers will read, comprehend and act on them. See Priest (1991).

31. See Burrows (1994), p. 68.

32. See Commissione delle Communità Europee (1999), p. 18.

33. Directive 1999/34/CE (Journal Officiel No L 141, 4.06.99).

34. Actually there are a number of cases where the dangers of products were known by producers long before serious harm occurred. See Burrows (1994), p. 75.

35. See Larouche (1999), pp. 2-3.

36. ECJ judgement of 29 May 1997. Case C –300/95, Commission v. UK (1997) ECR I-2649. The UK had implemented Directive 85/374 in Part I of the Consumer Protection Act 1997, p. 43. See Larouche (1999).

37. See Commissione delle Comunità Europee (1999), p. 14.

38. For example, there is no major case involving the Consumer Protection Act of 1987 in the UK, while in Germany only one case on the *Produkthaftungsgesetz* has reached the Courts so far. See Larouche (1999), p. 5.

39. See Swiss Re (1996), p. 38. Surprisingly this percentage is practically identical to that estimated by Viscusi for the US. See Viscusi (1991).
40. A trade association grouping the mechanical industry in Germany reported a growth rate between 10 and 15 per cent after the introduction of the directive. Some other firms quoted growth rates no larger than 7.5 per cent.
41. See Hodges (1994).
42. On the contrary if the Community had opted for minimal harmonisation without leaving national laws untouched, it could have produced more convergence among national laws as a result.
43. See Von Freyhold (1998), p. 275.
44. For example, if after a number of litigations the company has recovered one ecu more in judgements than it has spent on legal fees, its litigation strategy is profitable.
45. One would not necessarily observe a decrease in the number of disputes. There could be instead an increase of settlements at an earlier stage or of out-of-court settlements (as one can discern from the evidence concerning the US experience).
46. Estimating the macroeconomic impact of the cost of judicial barriers, Wagner has shown that legal security is a major factor in economic growth and the absence of legal security leads to economic slow-down. See H. Wagner "Macroeconomic Analysis of the Cost of Judicial Barriers for consumers in the Single Market," in von Freyhold, Gessner, Vial and Wagner (eds.), *"The Cost of Judicial Barriers for Consumers in the Single Market,"* Report for the European Commission, Brussels, 1995. Quoted in von Freyhold, Vial & Partner Consultants (1998), p. 276.
47. This result appears clearly in the case of asbestos. Asbestos litigation was followed firstly by occupational regulation on the part of OSHA (Occupational Safety and Health Administration) and environmental regulation on the part of the Environmental Protection Agency (EPA) subsequently. Product liability lawsuits then added practically additional regulation. See Viscusi (1988), p. 300.
48. However companies may use compliance to show that the risk utility test (see Section 3) is favourable and the product cannot be considered defective.
49. With the aid of empirical evidence, Viscusi demonstrates that 'Regulatory violations reduce the probability that a claim will be dropped, increase the likelihood of an out-of-court settlement, increase the size of such settlements, and enhance the claimant's prospects in court actions'. See Viscusi (1988), p. 303.
50. Some examples are given by the Opel and Heineken companies. During 1996 Opel started to recall all its Astra models that were marketed until 1994 (about 2,5 million cars) in order to substitute two components that proved to be defective. In 1993, the Heineken company had to withdraw from the market some lots of bottles because of the use of defective glass that could release splinters during transport or final use. The operation has been carried out in five European countries, Israel, Hong Kong and Canada. See Marchetti (1996), p. 53.

51. Concerning Italy, the case of the Moulinex centrifuge, dating to May 1997, can be cited. Some items of this product exploded because of a defect and consumers reported some injuries because of the accident. This event was reported by several newspapers on their front page and commented during television news in at least two occasions. The company decided to conduct a safety campaign recalling some items and supplying some items without defects freely to consumers. See Marchetti (1998), p. 272.

52. Losses can also extend to the stock market to the extent that the reduction of demand affects the value of a firm's shares. Viscusi (1991) reports the case of Agent Orange litigation in the US. Thousands of Vietnam veterans were exposed to the potent herbicide Agent Orange and filed claims against the producers of this chemical. The leading one was Dow Chemical. The original announcement of the Agent Orange class action suit in the Wall Street Journal led to a 10-day loss for Dow Chemical of $221 million. Three subsequent adverse events in the case imposed additional losses of almost $400 million to the company. A judge in the case decided that the plaintiffs had not established causality conclusively and in spite of the fact that plaintiffs won the case, the amount awarded was far below the level originally anticipated, resulting in an increase the value of Dow Chemical Company by over $300 million. See Viscusi (1991), p. 88.

53. We thank E. Marchetti, CER and IRS for allowing us to publish these results.

REFERENCES

Arrow, K. (1968), 'The Economics of Moral Hazard: Further Comment", *American Economic Review*, Vol. 58, June, pp. 537-539.

Beales, H., R. Craswell and S. Salop (1981), 'The Efficient Regulation of Consumer Information', *Journal of Law and Economics*, Vol. 24, No. 3, pp. 491-539.

Burrows, P. (1994), 'Product Liability and the Control of Risk in the European Community', *Oxford Review of Economic Policy*, Vol. 10, No. 1, pp. 68-83.

Commissione delle Comunità Europee (1999), Libro Verde, *La responsabilità civile per danno da prodotti difettosi,* Brussels, COM (1999) 396.def.

Hodges, C.J.S. (1994), *Relazione destinata alla Commissione Europea e concernente l'applicazione della direttiva 85/374/CEE in materia di responsabilità per danno da prodotti difettosi.* Contratto di studio N. ETD/93/B5-3000/MI/06.

Larouche, P. (1999), 'Directive 85/374 and Product Liability in the EU', Paper presented at the Workshop on Regulatory Reform and Market Functioning, CEPS, Brussels, 30 May-1 June.

Marchetti, E. (1996), 'La Valutazione dei rischi nella Responsabilità Civile da Prodotti Difettosi', *Economia e Politica Industriale*, No. 46.

Marchetti, E. (1999), 'Qualità dei Prodotti, Responsabilità dei Produttori ed Assicurazioni: un'indagine sul campo', in CER/IRS, *Competitività e Regolazione*, Bologna: Il Mulino.

OECD (1995), *Product Liability Rules in OECD Countries*, OECD, Paris.

Polinsky (1983), *An Introduction to Law and Economics*, Boston: Little Brown and Co.

Posner, R. A. (1986), *The Economic Analysis of Law*, Boston: Little Brown.

Priest, G.L (1991), 'The Modern Expansion of Tort Liability: Its Sources, Its Effects and Its Reform', *The Journal of Economic Perspectives*, Vol. 5, No. 3, pp. 31-50.

Shavell, S. (1980), 'Strict Liability versus Negligence', *Journal of Legal Studies*, Vol. 9, January, pp. 1-25.

Shavell, S. (1984), Liability for Harm versus Regulation of Safety', *Journal of Legal Studies*, Vol. 13, June, pp. 357-374.

Spulber (1989), *Regulation and Markets,* Cambridge, MA: The MIT Press.

Swiss Re (1996), *Product Liability Claims in Europe*, Swiss Reinsurance Company, Zurich.

Viscusi, W.K. (1988), 'Product Liability and Regulation: Establishing the Appropriate Institutional Division of Labour', *American Economic Review*, Vol. 77, pp. 300-304.

Viscusi, W.K. (1991), 'Product and Occupational Liability', *The Journal of Economic Perspectives*, Vol. 5, Number 3, pp. 71-92.

Viscusi, W.K. (1997), *Rational Risk Policy*, Oxford: Clarendon Press.

Viscusi, W.K., Vernon, J.M. and J.E. Harrington (1995), *Economics of Regulation and Antitrust*, Cambridge, MA: The MIT Press.

Von Freyhold, Vial & Partner Consultants (1998), *The Cost of Legal Obstacles to the Disadvantage of Consumers in the Single Market*, European Commission, DG XXIV.

9. Regulation and Labour Market Performance

Tito Boeri, Giuseppe Nicolètti and Stefano Scarpetta[1]

INTRODUCTION

The increasing literature on the interaction between liberalisation-integration of product markets and labour market reforms is often highly speculative and draws on a rather weak empirical base. Cross-country indicators of regulatory frameworks are often lacking, which makes it difficult to identify the linkages with observed outcomes in the labour and product markets. Moreover, empirical studies have often focused exclusively on the impact of certain labour market regulations, largely ignoring the role of product market regulations and the interaction between regulatory interventions in the two markets. As a result, while there are convincing theoretical arguments pointing to a potentially positive effect of product market liberalisation on labour market performance, empirical investigations of this issue are lacking. This paper aims at providing some preliminary evidence on these issues (for additional evidence see Nicoletti et al., 2000). In particular, the cross-country patterns and changing profile of product and labour market regulations are identified. Evidence on the relationships between product and labour market regulations is discussed in the context of other policies and institutional factors affecting the labour market; and the clustering and convergence of institutions across countries are characterised. More importantly, the paper reports evidence of a potentially significant impact of product and labour market regulations on employment and its composition. The evidence presented draws heavily on a novel set of cross-country indicators of regulation in the product and labour markets assembled at the OECD. It should be stressed at the outset that these indicators are preliminary estimates preliminary estimates and should be taken only as rough approximations of the regulatory stance across OECD countries.[2]

The plan of the paper is as follows. Section 1 reviews the theoretical and empirical evidence concerning the effects of regulations in the product and labour markets on the labour market. This section also sheds some light on the possible interaction between regulatory regimes in the two markets. Section 2 presents the quantitative indicators of the strictness of the labour market and product market regulations, while Section 3 discusses the cross-country co-variations between indicators of labour and product market regulations. This section also identifies some clusters of countries that share similar features in these two domains. Section 4 analyses the interactions between, on the one hand, product market and labour market regulations, and, on the other hand, labour market performance with particular emphasis on the level and composition of employment. Finally, Section 5 evaluates the convergence of labour market institutions within and across the clusters identified in Section 3, which provides a preliminary test of the convergence and/or race-to-the-bottom hypothesis.

1. LABOUR AND PRODUCT MARKET REGULATIONS AND THEIR EFFECTS ON THE LABOUR MARKET

Economic regulation can be broadly defined as the use of the coercive power of the government to restrict the decisions of economic agents.[3] It may include restrictions on firm decisions over entry, exit, the use of inputs, the quantities and the types of output produced as well as prices. These restrictions are likely to affect significantly (in intended or unintended ways) the functioning of labour and product markets. Moreover, since market forces will continue to act even under the most stringent regulatory conditions, outcomes in the labour and product markets will generally be driven by the interplay of those forces with the existing regulatory framework. As a result, regulation can be expected to have important repercussions on overall allocative and productive efficiency.[4]

In the following, the focus is set on a subset of government-imposed restrictions that may affect the level and composition of employment. These include: i) labour market regulations disciplining hiring and firing decisions of firms; ii) product market regulations restricting firm decisions over entry and output; and iii) direct interventions of the state in resource allocation, especially through public ownership and control of business enterprises. Conceptually, these regulatory interventions may all have both direct and indirect effects on labour market equilibrium, either in isolation or interacting among them and with other public policies.

1.1 Employment protection legislation: rationale and effects on the level and the dynamics of employment

1.1.1 The rationale and potential effects of employment protection legislation

In all OECD countries, there are rules and regulations that govern the employment relationship between workers and firms. Those referring to hiring and firing practices are often referred to as 'employment protection' legislation (EPL). These rules and regulations govern unfair dismissals, restrictions on lay-offs for economic reasons, compulsory severance payments, minimum notice periods and administrative authorisations.

The EPL regulations may affect the equilibrium level of employment – as well as its dynamics over the business cycle – in different ways:

- By reinforcing job security, EPL may enhance productivity performance, as workers will be more willing to cooperate with employers in the development of the production process (Akerlof, 1984).
- To the extent that EPL leads to long-lasting work relationships, it may encourage employers to provide training to workers with potentially beneficial effects on human capital and labour productivity. A better skilled workforce may also increase internal flexibility and thus lead to a better functioning of production activity (Piore, 1986).
- EPL may also be a way to internalise the social costs of dismissals by moving the social burden of re-allocating a worker to another job closer to the firm's profitability criteria (Lindbeck and Snower, 1988).
- However, if these regulations are very strict, as in many European countries, firms may become more cautious about adjusting their workforce with the ultimate effect of reducing labour turnover, e.g. movements from employment to unemployment and from unemployment back to employment (Bertola, 1990).
- In addition, if hiring and firing costs are not transferred into lower wages, total labour costs for the firms increase and this may lead to a lower level of employment, other things being equal.
- The effective coverage or implementation of standard employment protection provisions influences the overall strictness of EPL regulations. For example, in many countries employment protection provisions for workers with regular contracts are often extended to those with fixed-term contracts after a given tenure or number of renewals has been reached. In addition, in some countries, the judicial system appears

to have interpreted legislation more strictly than was intended by the law.

- A different degree of strictness of regulation governing permanent versus temporary employment (fixed-term contracts and contracts through temporary work agencies) may affect the structure of employment. Stricter regulations for permanent contracts relative to those for temporary contracts are likely to promote a shift from permanent to temporary employment (as is occurring in a number of European countries). This has the potential effect of distorting the optimal composition of employment between temporary and permanent contracts. Moreover, those who are able to maintain a permanent contract (often the insiders) will enjoy an even higher level of job security, bringing about an increase in wage pressure (Bentolila and Dolado, 1994). In contrast, those under temporary contracts (often youths and other workers with little work experience or low skills) will bear the brunt of employment adjustment (Saint Paul, 1996).

1.1.2 What do previous empirical studies suggest about the impact of EPL on the labour market?

Empirical evidence on the impact of employment protection legislation is mixed, not least because of the lack of suitable data on the enforcement and evolution of regulations over time (Bertola et al., 1999). A clear distinction exists between the potential effects of EPL on employment turnover as distinguished from the equilibrium level of employment (unemployment) and its composition (temporary/permanent; youth/prime-age workers, etc.).

- *Employment turnover.* There is consistent empirical evidence that strict employment protection legislation reduces unemployment turnover. Under strict EPL provisions, the unemployment pool is more stagnant, with fewer people being laid off, but also fewer unemployed people getting a new job. (Bentolila and Bertola, 1990; and Nickell and Layard, 1998). The effects on employment turnover are less clear cut: Bertola and Rogerson (1997) and Boeri (1999) found similar job creation and job destruction rates across countries with different EPL regimes but lower unemployment inflows in flexible labour markets). As stressed in Boeri (1999) and OECD (1999), a possible explanation is that strict EPL may foster job-to-job shifts rather than overall employment turnover because insofar employers and workers will seek direct shifts from one job to another without intervening unemployment spells, in order to avoid the associated dismissal and search costs.

- *The level of employment.* Some studies (e.g. Scarpetta, 1996) suggest a detrimental effect of strict EPL on the level of employment to working-age population ratios. Nickell and Layard (1998) indicate that this may be partially due to the low participation rates in southern European countries, which also have strict EPL. Participation rates may be low, however, especially amongst youth, precisely because employment prospects are lower when the EPL system is stricter.
- *Overall unemployment rate.* There is also no consensus as to the overall impact of EPL on unemployment. Part of the disagreement stems from the use of different models. However, disagreement persists even amongst papers using the same indicator (the OECD summary index, see OECD Jobs Study, 1994a and b). While a recent study (Elmeskov et al., 1998) suggests a somewhat more robust effect on unemployment if changes in EPL over the past two decades are taken into account, OECD (1999a) could not find a statistically significant effect of EPL on aggregate employment.
- *Composition of employment and unemployment.* Nickell and Layard (1998), Scarpetta (1996) and OECD (1999a) suggest a stronger effect of strict EPL on youth unemployment. Moreover, Grubb and Wells (1993) indicate that strict EPL for permanent workers may encourage firms to shift to temporary workers and more generally foster self-employment.
- *Persistence of unemployment.* By reducing unemployment turnover, strict EPL is also found to slow down the labour market adjustment after an exogenous shock (Jackman et al., 1996; Scarpetta, 1996). Unemployed workers may lose human capital over time and they may exert a lower moderating impact on wages (Blanchard, 1998; Bertola, 1990).
- *Dualism.* Countries with stronger employment protection for regular contracts tend to display a bimodal tenure distribution with either very short or very long tenures (Boeri, 1999). In countries where fixed-term contracts are liberalised, a large share of employees with fixed-term contracts tend to insulate permanent workers from adjustment (Bentolila and Dolado, 1994), thereby increasing their bargaining power and the corresponding wage pressures.

1.2 Product market regulation and the labour market

In the product market too, regulatory provisions are generally motivated on public interest grounds. The main rationales for product market regulations include natural monopoly conditions, externalities, asymmetric information and other types of market failures. However, economic theory also suggests that regulations are generally implemented as a response to pressures of interest groups acting to maximise their (broadly defined) incomes. As a result, regulation may be biased towards benefiting interest groups that are better organised and gain more from regulatory interventions. A detailed analysis of these issues is outside the scope of this paper.[5] It should be noted, however, that existing regulatory frameworks may be flawed by several (possibly concurring) factors:

- The effects of some regulatory provisions often drift away from the original public interest aims, resulting in the protection of special interest groups.[6]
- Regulations and their implementation are sometimes likely to involve costs that exceed their expected benefits.[7]
- Technical progress and the evolution of demand can render obsolete in a number of instances the design of existing regulations.
- The progress in regulatory techniques may make it easier than in the past to fine-tune regulation, e.g. by separating potentially competitive and inherently imperfect markets.

As a result, in the absence of regulatory reform, existing regulations are often likely to be ineffective and unnecessarily restrictive of market mechanisms in both the product and labour markets, potentially bringing about static and dynamic inefficiencies and losses in social welfare.[8]

The effects of product market regulations on labour market outcomes are complex because they are mediated by market behaviour, industry structure, governance issues and labour market institutions. In general, entry restrictions may originate from explicit legal impediments or limitations on the number of competitors allowed in certain markets as well as from the lack of administrative transparency and/or heavy administrative burdens (so-called administrative regulation). Entry restrictions are also associated with international trade and investment policies that deter competition by non-resident firms either through explicit measures (such as tariffs and legal limitations on foreign ownership) or implicit measures (such as non-tariff barriers and administrative obstacles to the establishment and operation of foreign firms in the domestic market).

Entry restrictions in (otherwise) competitive markets cause production inefficiencies by reducing equilibrium output, moving firm size away from the minimum efficient scale of operation and sheltering inefficient firms from competition by new entrants. Ill-designed entry regulations may cause similar inefficiencies in imperfectly competitive markets by reducing or eliminating actual or potential competition. In addition, entry restrictions constrain the supply of a particular type of capital and entrepreneurial ability (Krueger and Pischke, 1997). Finally, by reducing product market competition and international technology spillovers, restrictions on foreign competitors are likely to result in lower output and employment growth – negatively affecting long-run employment levels.[9]

The inhibition of product market competition has immediate consequences for labour demand both at the firm level and in the aggregate. In general, the wage elasticity of demand will be reduced and the labour demand schedule will shift inwards (Hicks, 1935). In addition, the existence of rents induced by the lack of competition will generally prompt employees to ask for wage premia, especially if they are unionised.[10] Ceteris paribus, this will induce firms to choose capital-labour ratios higher than in a competitive situation, causing lower employment and additional productive inefficiencies.[11] Therefore, except in some cases of natural monopoly, entry restrictions will generally negatively affect economic efficiency and labour market equilibrium relative to a perfectly competitive benchmark, having important effects on both the overall level of employment and its composition. The level may be negatively affected by distortions in labour demand, upward pressures in wage rates and reduced rates of enterprise creation and survival, the composition by the differential effects of regulatory and administrative provisions on different kinds of enterprises (e.g. sole proprietor vs corporate firms). While the nature and the intensity of these effects will depend also on the features of labour market institutions (e.g. degree of unionisation and centralisation of bargaining mechanisms), their sign will generally remain the same across different institutional settings (Nickell, 1999).

State control over business enterprises, through either ownership or administrative guidance, is a well known potential source of inefficiency.[12] State ownership generally provides shelter from the market discipline exercised by private shareholders as well as from the threat of takeover or bankruptcy. Corporate control and monitoring is made more complex than in private enterprises by the supplementary hierarchy of principal-agent relationships involving the interests of politicians and bureaucrats. In addition, the incentives and objectives of public managers are different from those of managers of private firms, often deviating from pure profit maximisation. Searching for political support rather than for support from shareholders, the public manager will generally have a tendency to overuse capital and/or labour, practice less price discrimination (when endowed with market power) and satisfy the non-economic goals imposed (implicitly or explicitly) by the government. These distortions are often favoured by the presence of soft budget constraints, due to the availability of state aid and debt guarantees. To the extent that state control shelters inefficient firms from competitive pressures and creates or preserves market power, it can be expected to have the same effects on labour market equilibrium as entry restrictions.

Clearly, in some sectors, such as non-tradeables and/or public utilities, protection from domestic and foreign competitors and labour hoarding by state-controlled firms can maintain employment at artificially high levels for some time, but the related productive inefficiencies are likely to spill over to the entire economy, reducing equilibrium output and employment elsewhere. Moreover, the implied budgetary costs are likely to result in an increased tax burden, which reins in economic growth. In any case, the increasing integration of OECD economies (both de facto and de jure, through international treaties and agreements) makes it practically impossible to pursue such policies even in the relatively short run.

1.3 Policy interactions

Labour market outcomes may also be affected by the interaction of EPL with other policies and labour market institutions as well as with product market regulations. The first type of interactions has only recently been analysed in the empirical literature. Bertola and Rogerson (1997) and Elmeskov et al. (1998) suggest that higher employment turnover costs due to more stringent employment protection legislation are associated with higher unemployment in countries with intermediate bargaining systems where wages do not fully adjust. Moreover, Buti et al. (1998) point out that stringent EPL may act as a substitute for unemployment insurance benefits. Under this hypothesis, countries might opt for either generous unemployment benefits with lax EPL or vice versa. They argue that a combination of very generous benefits with strict EPL would lead to higher structural unemployment. However, the authors use simple bivariate correlation in their analysis, and Elmeskov et al. (1998) found no significant evidence of this interaction in an econometric analysis of the determinants of structural unemployment for a large sample of OECD countries.

Potential interactions between EPL and product market regulations are manifold and may have significant effects on labour market outcomes. For instance, the possibility that lower employment levels in monopolistic sectors is compensated by higher employment in other more competitive sectors depends on the flexibility of wages in these other sectors to accommodate higher employment of 'released' workers. If wages do not fully adjust because of high reservation wages, high wage floors and/or nation-wide wage agreements, then lower aggregate employment is likely to result.

Moreover, the insider power of workers employed in firms sheltered from competitive pressures (either by legal, administrative and trade restrictions or public ownership) can be compounded by the presence of unduly restrictive EPL, pushing up wage premia and lowering equilibrium employment. Similarly, the existence of thresholds for the application of EPL to collective or individual dismissals may affect the minimum efficient scale of firms (after accounting for the cost of regulations) and favour particular kinds of company structures (such as sole proprietor firms). This effect can be reinforced (or weakened) by a profile of administrative burdens favouring (or discouraging) the creation of individual firms. Therefore, on the whole, different combinations of the regulatory regimes in the labour and product market can be expected to result in different labour market equilibrium configurations, potentially distorting the optimal level and composition of employment (e.g. between dependent and self-employment). At the same time, the effects of regulatory reform are likely to be different depending on the initial combination of regimes and on the sequencing of the reforms in the two markets. To date, empirical evidence on the relationship between labour and product market regulations across countries and on their effects on labour market outcomes has been lacking.[13] The next sections of this paper provide an initial attempt in this direction.

2. ASSESSING DIFFERENCES IN REGULATORY REGIMES ACROSS COUNTRIES

From a theoretical standpoint, there is a strong presumption that ill-designed regulatory regimes, which unduly restrict labour and product market competition and distort governance mechanisms may reduce equilibrium employment and affect its composition. However, since regulations are usually introduced in second-best situations related to purported market failures, their actual impact on labour market outcomes can only be ascertained empirically, attempting to relate differences in regulatory regimes over time and/or across countries to the observed patterns of employment.

The analysis of the linkage between regulation and labour market performance has generally stumbled on the lack of synthetic and comparable measures of the stance of regulation across countries. In this paper, a large set of information on product and labour market regulations at the economy-wide and sectoral levels was used to establish cross-country patterns of regulation and to construct internationally-comparable indicators of regulation (see below). Information on labour and product market regulations consists of a multitude of sector-specific or general-purpose provisions.

Although, in principle, cross-country comparisons of individual provisions are possible, the analysis of the linkages between regulation and labour market performance is meaningful only after some aggregation has been made. Therefore, information that was essentially scattered and qualitative had to be measured in quantitative terms and summarised in a uniform and, as much as possible, objective way across countries.

Cross-country comparisons of regulatory regimes were performed using a multi-dimensional approach. The focus was set on summary indicators synthesising several dimensions of labour or product market regulation. These indicators were obtained (using a data-based aggregation methodology) as a combination of first level, more detailed, indicators of individual regulatory provisions. The main advantage of this approach is that the relative positions of countries evaluated along multiple dimensions are unlikely to be as sensitive to data problems as those positions established on the basis of multiple comparisons of uni-dimensional indicators.

The overall regulatory environment was analysed along four main axes, distinguishing between a) the control of resources and market behaviour by the state; b) barriers to entrepreneurial activity; c) barriers to trade and investment; and d) employment protection legislation for permanent and temporary workers. In order to organise and simplify the data, a multiple-tier structure of indicators was established, featuring at the bottom the individual provisions, at the first level the aggregation of these provisions into indicators of single dimensions of regulation (first-level indicators), at the next level the aggregation of these first-level indicators into the four axes of regulatory intervention (summary indicators) and at the top the two indicators of overall regulation in the product and labour markets.[14]

In order to reduce discretion, multi-variate data analysis techniques were used to identify regulatory regimes and to aggregate first-level indicators into the summary measures of product and labour market regulation. Cluster analysis made it possible to group countries sharing similar regulatory environments. Starting from the values of the indicators, this technique builds similarity matrices whose entries are the (Euclidean) distances resulting from pair-wise comparisons of the individual indicators across countries. An algorithm based on the sequential minimisation of these pair-wise distances progressively reduces the dimension of the matrix by clustering together countries with minimum distances (so-called single linkage clustering). The results of this clustering algorithm can be inspected by means of a variety of graphical representations, such as tree-like diagrams called 'dendrograms'. Factor analysis made it possible to aggregate the first-level indicators according to an 'objective' weighting procedure that maximises in a parsimonious way the proportion of the total variance in the data explained by the resulting indicators.[15] This approach yields a minimal set of indicators that best summarises the variance of regulation across countries, with no priors as to which regulatory provisions may be most influential on performance and no arbitrary weights involved in the aggregation of the first-level indicators. Nonetheless, given the qualitative nature of most of the basic information on regulation, some degree of subjectivity was inescapable in the construction of the first-level regulatory indicators. A precise description of the data sources and methodologies used in the construction of first-level and summary indicators is in Nicoletti et al. (1999).

Prior to describing differences in product and labour market regulation across countries, a few cautionary notes are in order. First, the indicators of product market regulation are based on a very preliminary set of data. Second, they only cover formal regulations, leaving out other kinds of regulatory interventions such as administrative guidance or self-disciplinary measures of professional associations. Third, no attempt was made to measure the quality of product market regulations and the extent to which they are actually enforced. As a result, the ranking of countries provided by the summary indicators should be considered only as an approximation of the strictness of product market regulations across the OECD.

2.1 Indicators of labour market regulation

As a step ahead in the analysis of the effect of EPL on labour market performance, this study uses a set of indicators of employment protection legislation concerning both regular and temporary workers.[16]

2.1.1 Regulation of permanent employment

We focus on the strictness of the following individual dismissal protections for workers with permanent contracts: i) procedural inconveniences that employers face when trying to dismiss a worker; ii) notice and severance payments; and iii) prevailing standards of and penalties for 'unfair' dismissals. Table 9.1 presents the different aspects that have been considered within these three broad categories.

Procedural requirements refer to the process that has to be followed from the decision to lay off a worker to the actual termination of the contract. They include: the delay before the notice of dismissal can start (for example, because there has to be a series of previous warnings); whether a written statement of the reasons for dismissal must be supplied; whether a third party (such as a works council or the competent labour authority) must be notified or consulted; and whether dismissal cannot proceed without the approval of a third party.

Notice and *severance pay* may differ for blue-collar and white-collar workers, or for dismissals for personal reasons and for economic redundancy (see OECD, 1999a). In general both notice and severance payments tend to be higher for white-collar workers and for redundancies than for blue-collar workers. In this study we consider an average of regulations affecting the two categories of workers.

Under *difficulty of dismissal,* the analysis includes the length of the *trial period* because during this period a dismissal cannot be contested for its unfairness: the shorter the trial period the stricter is the regulation on unfair dismissal. Moreover, account is taken of cases where the employer cannot demonstrate appropriate previous efforts to avoid the dismissal, or when social, age or job tenure factors have not been considered. Finally, account is taken of the fact that, in some cases, labour courts may require employers to *reinstate* a worker affected by an unfair dismissal, or award high compensation payments in excess of regular severance pay.

Table 9.1 EPL indicators for permanent workers

Regular procedural	Procedures	
inconveniences	Delay to start a notice	
Notice and severance pay for	Notice period after	9 months
		4 years
no-fault individual dismissals		20 years
	Severance pay after	9 months
		4 years
		20 years
	Definition of unfair dismissal	
Difficulty of dismissal	Trial period	
	at 20 years	
	Reinstatement	

2.1.2 Regulation of temporary forms of employment

As discussed below, many OECD countries have reformed regulations for temporary employment, by either allowing fixed-term or TWA (temporary work agency) contracts, or by liberalising their use. Indicators of the stringency of EPL for temporary contracts are reported in Table 9.2. They refer to: i) the 'objective' reasons under which they could be offered; ii) the maximum number of successive renewals; and iii) the maximum cumulated duration of the contract. Most Anglo-Saxon countries have always allowed the use of temporary contracts without any significant restrictions. Currently, some countries continue to list specific situations that may, however, go beyond 'objective', time-limited tasks (e.g. business start-ups or workers in search of their first job). There are also significant differences on the maximum duration of fixed-term contracts. There are no limitations on the number of renewals in Canada, Ireland, the United Kingdom and the United States, but this is only the case in a number of other countries if separate, valid 'objective' reasons can be given for each new contract. In these cases, after successive renewals labour courts may be asked to examine the validity of the request for a further contract. In this respect, a number of countries facilitate the use of fixed-term contracts by setting by law the maximum number of renewals (e.g. Belgium, France, Germany and the Netherlands).

Table 9.2 EPL indicators for temporary workers

Temporary contracts	Fixed-term contracts	Valid cases other than the usual 'objective'
		Maximum number of successive contracts
		Maximum cumulated duration
	Temporary work agency (TWA) employment	Types of work which are legal
		Restrictions on number of renewals
		Maximum cumulated duration

2.1.3 Summary indicators of employment protection legislation over the past decade

Figure 9.1 plots the summary indicators of EPL for permanent and temporary workers for 1990 and 1998. In countries along the diagonal, the summary EPL indicator did not change over the 1990s; in those above the diagonal, regulations became tighter in the past decade; and in those below the diagonal, regulations were relaxed.

Broadly speaking, there has been a tendency for a significant deregulation of temporary contracts, while only modest changes have been recorded for permanent contracts. Only Finland, Portugal and Spain have significantly eased regulations for permanent workers. In Finland both the delay to the start of notice and the notice period itself were reduced; Portugal tightened its regulation by increasing the amount of mandated severance payments; and in Spain new permanent contracts were introduced with lower (albeit still high) severance payments. The Netherlands eased restrictions on dismissals,

Figure 9.1 Indicators of the strictness of employment protection legislation,
   1990-98

Panel A. Regular and temporary contracts

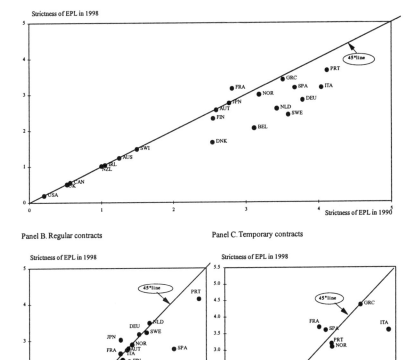

Panel B. Regular contracts   Panel C. Temporary contracts

Note:
The indicator is the weighted sum of indicators referring to several aspects of employment protection legislation for regular contracts as well as for fixed-term and TWA contracts. The original indicators range from 0 (least restrictive) to 6 (most restrictive). The weights are extracted from a factor analysis of original indicators.
Source: The summary indicators are from Nicoletti et al.(1999).

widening exemptions from general dismissal law but increased the minimum notice period and decreased the maximum periods. In the process of harmonising notice periods for blue-collar and white-collar workers,

Germany increased the length of notice for long-tenure workers. By contrast, mandated notice periods seem to have decreased somewhat in Spain, Sweden and Finland.

In a number of countries (e.g. Japan, Germany, Italy, Belgium, Finland, New Zealand and Sweden), fixed-term contracts can now be used in a wider range of situations than at the beginning of the 1990s. The maximum number of successive renewals has been extended in Germany, Italy, Belgium, the Netherlands and Sweden. Increases in the maximum cumulative duration of successive contracts have been legislated in Germany, Italy, Belgium, the Netherlands, Portugal and Sweden. In Spain, fixed-term contracts were liberalised in the late 1980s, and, following the dramatic increases in their use, some restrictions have recently been re-imposed. In Denmark and Sweden, all restrictions on the types of work for which TWA employment is legal have been removed, and in Italy and Spain, TWAs have become legal for certain types of work whereas previously they were illegal in all circumstances. Other relaxations on the range of jobs for which TWAs are allowed have taken place in Denmark, Germany, the Netherlands, Norway and Japan. In Denmark, restrictions on the number of renewals have been removed; and the maximum duration of successive contracts has been increased in Germany, Belgium, Denmark, Portugal and the Netherlands. Other countries took limited or no action to reform this kind of labour market regulation.

2.2 Indicators of product market regulation

Product market regulation was analysed along three main axes: a) direct state control of economic activities, through state shareholdings or other types of interference in the decisions of enterprises and the use of command and control regulations; b) barriers to private entrepreneurial activity, through legal limitations on access to markets or administrative burdens and opacities hampering the creation of businesses; and c) regulatory barriers to international trade and investment, through explicit legal and tariff provisions or regulatory and administrative obstacles. The country rankings resulting from the corresponding summary indicators are shown in Figure 9.2.

The analysis of direct state control was based on five first-level indicators concerning i) the presence of state-controlled enterprises in business (two and three digit) industries, ii) the presence of special voting rights in private enterprises, iii) the degree of control exercised by legislative bodies over state-owned business sector enterprises, iv) the propensity to resort to command and control, rather than incentive-based, regulatory provisions and v) the extent of public ownership in the non-agricultural business sector.[17]

Figure 9.2 Summary indicators of product market regulation

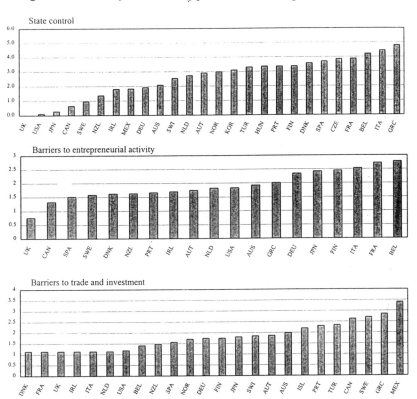

Note: Country scores reflect the results of factor analysis. Summary indicators are obtained weighting factors by their relative contributions in explaining the total variance of the factors. Factor analysis was applied to basic indicators. All variables were cast in 0-6 scale from least to most regulated. The data and estimation methodology are described in Nicoletti, Scarpetta and Boylaud (1999)

Based on these indicators, hierarchical cluster analysis identified two large groups of countries. A group of 'incentive-based' countries, including most common-law countries, Japan, Germany and Sweden, characterised by a below-average degree of state control and a group of 'command-based' countries, including the other OECD countries. Within these groups, countries differ mainly by the extent of government interference in the operation of private businesses (e.g. special voting rights and use of command and control regulations). Correspondingly, two main underlying factors were identified in the data, clearly separating out government interference in private business operation from the other indicators of state control. The summary indicator of direct state control shows considerable variation across countries and identifies the US, the UK, Canada, Sweden, Japan and New Zealand as the countries with relatively low state control. At the other extreme, Greece, Italy and Belgium are identified as the countries with the highest state control.

The analysis of regulatory barriers to entrepreneurial activity was also based on six first-level indicators concerning i) the features of the licensing and permit system, ii) initiatives to reduce administrative burdens, iii) administrative transparency, iv) legal limitations to entry in (two and three digit) business industries, and administrative burdens on the creation of v) corporations and vi) sole proprietor businesses.[18] Countries proved to be relatively dispersed along the various dimensions of this axis of regulatory intervention and no readily interpretable groupings could be established by means of cluster analysis. Three main factors could be identified relating to legal barriers, administrative burdens on the creation of businesses and more general barriers created by administrative procedures. The summary indicator suggests that, overall, barriers to entrepreneurship are less variable than state control across countries. According to this indicator, countries with the lowest barriers include the UK, Canada and Spain, while the highest barriers are found in Belgium, France and Italy. The average ranking of the United States reflects low legal barriers but relatively heavy administrative procedures.

The analysis of barriers to international trade and investment was based on five first-level indicators: i) legal and administrative barriers to foreign ownership of businesses, ii) the existence of explicit provisions discriminating business activity on the basis of nationality, iii) nationality discrimination implied by regulatory and administrative procedures, iv) average trade tariffs and v) the incidence of non-tariff barriers to trade.[19] Due to the limited coverage of some of these indicators, the focus had to be restricted to a few issues, which are not necessarily fully representative of the countries' trade and investment policies.[20] Cluster analysis classified countries in two broad groups: a highly homogeneous group comprising the majority of European countries and the United States; and an idiosyncratic group of countries, partly characterised by less open trade policies, including five European countries (Norway, Sweden, Greece, Switzerland and Portugal), the Australasia countries (New Zealand and Australia), Japan and Turkey. Two main discriminating factors were identified: tariff and regulating barriers, including indicators ii, iii and iv, and other barriers, including indicators i and v. The resulting summary indicator ranks France, Italy, the UK, Denmark, Ireland, the Netherlands and the United States as being the most open, while Canada, Sweden, Greece and Mexico appear to have a relatively high level of barriers.

Using these summary indicators three patterns of overall product market regulation could be established: a mostly common-law group, characterised by a combination of relatively liberal inward and outward-oriented regulatory policies; a mostly continental European group (including also Australia), characterised by relatively liberal outward-oriented policies, but more interventionist and restrictive inward-oriented policies; and an idiosyncratic group composed of countries with widely different inward-oriented policies but sharing relatively closed outward policies (including Canada, Sweden, Portugal and Greece). The summary indicator of product market regulation suggests that the countries having the most liberal regulatory approaches are the United Kingdom, the United States and, to a lesser extent, New Zealand Ireland and Japan, while the most restrictive approaches are found in Greece and, to a lesser extent, Italy and Belgium (Figure 9.3). In order to interpret these results correctly, it should be reminded that only formal and explicit regulations have been taken into account, leaving out all other informal procedures through which the government or trade associations can influence economic behaviour as well as possible differences in enforcement.

Figure 9.3 Overall indicator of product market regulation

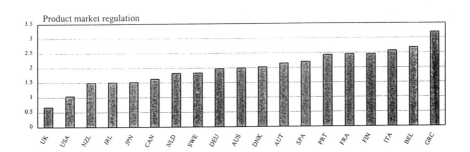

Note: Factor analysis applied to summary indicators of state control, barriers to entrepreneurial activity and barriers to trade and investment. The data and estimataion methodology are described in Nicoletti, Scarpetta and Boylaud (1999).

3. THE RELATIONSHIPS BETWEEN REGULATIONS IN THE LABOUR AND PRODUCT MARKETS

The analysis of the various dimensions of regulation in the product and labour markets can be combined to investigate the features of the overall regulatory environment across OECD countries. Employment protection regulations and product market regulations may be correlated across countries and contribute to an overall regulatory framework which influences labour market performance. Interestingly, the overall indicators of product and labour markets suggest that, in general, restrictive product market regulations are matched by analogous EPL restrictions. There is a strong statistical correlation between the two overall indices of regulation across countries (correlation = 0.76, significant at the 1% level).

To shed further light on this issue, we use *cluster analysis* to construct groups of countries that share common patterns across the two sets of regulations and try to interpret these groups. The analysis was performed using as basic data the aggregations of the first-level indicators (summary indicators) obtained by means of factor analysis. For the product market we included the summary indicators of i) state control, ii) barriers to entrepreneurial activity and iii) barriers to trade and investment. For the labour market we included the summary indicators of i) EPL for permanent workers and ii) EPL for temporary workers.

The dendrogram in Figure 9.4 identifies patterns of behaviour among the OECD countries.[21] Four clusters can be identified:

- The first includes most Southern European countries (France, Italy, Greece and Spain) which combine strict regulation on both the labour and product markets.
- The second includes continental European countries, which share relatively restrictive product market regulations, but can be further split in two sub-groups according to the EPL stance: Belgium and Denmark being less restrictive than Germany, Austria, the Netherlands, Finland and especially Portugal.
- The third group includes common-law countries, which are characterised by a relatively liberal approach in both the labour and product markets (the United States, the United Kingdom, Canada, Ireland, Australia and New Zealand).
- Finally, Japan and Sweden are outliers in the sense that they combine relatively restrictive labour market regulations with relatively few (formal) restrictions in the product market.

Figure 9.4 Dendrogram of product market regulation and EPL[1,2]

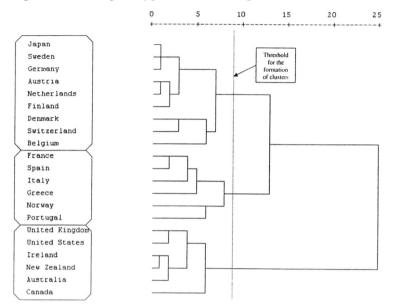

[1] Clustering based on the indicators of state control, barriers to entrepreneurship, barriers to trade and investment and EPL for temporary and regular workers
[2] Figure should be read from left to right. The top index measures the similarity between countries belonging to the same cluster (from the most to the least similar).

4. REGULATIONS IN THE PRODUCT AND LABOUR MARKETS AND LABOUR MARKET PERFORMANCE

As stressed in the introduction, the OECD countries display large differences in labour market performance despite underlying market forces that have led to increasing economic integration. To some extent, differences in performance may be due to macroeconomic factors, such as differences in cyclical developments and the inertia deriving from the historical divergence of economic policies across countries, which resulted in different equilibrium configurations. However, the widespread implementation of policies aimed at ensuring macroeconomic stability for sustainable growth, in Europe and in other OECD countries, suggests that part of the performance gaps must be related to other factors. These may include policies, regulations and institutions directly affecting the labour market as well as the regulatory environment characterising the product market. In this section we focus on three aspects of labour market performance that seem to be particularly sensitive to regulations: 1) the overall employment rate in the business sector (business sector employment divided by the working age population); 2) the incidence of self-employment in total business sector employment; and 3) the incidence of temporary in total employment.

4.1 Bivariate correlations between regulations and employment patterns

Figure 9.5 plots the business sector employment rates in the OECD countries (average of the 1990-95 period), while Figure 9.6 shows their evolution over the past two decades. There are clearly significant differences in the share of working age population which is employed in the business sector across the OECD countries: it ranges from about 40 per cent in Spain to up to 70 per cent in Switzerland. These differences are related to overall labour market conditions in different countries, which also affect the decision of certain groups (youths, women in particular) to enter in the labour market, as well as to the role of the state as an employer in the economy. Figure 9.6 also suggests very different trends over time. North American countries, Japan, the UK, the Netherlands and some other smaller countries in Europe have shown a positive trend over the past two decades. In contrast, some of the Nordic countries have shown a significant fall in the early 1990s (due to the sharp economic crisis there), and most European countries have shown stable or slightly declining trends.

Figure 9.5 Employment rate in the business sector, 1990-95

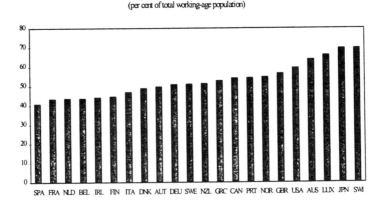

(per cent of total working-age population)

Source: OECD database

Figure 9.6 Trends in employment rates across the OECD countries, 1982-95

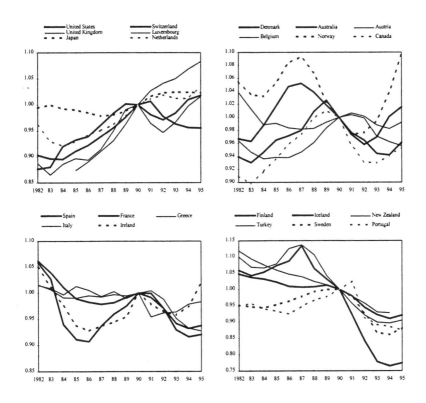

Source: OECD database

The OECD countries also show marked differences in the composition of employment. Figure 9.7 plots the share of self-employment in total employment across countries and across the main sectors of the economy. Despite significant cross-sectoral differences, some common patterns can be identified. There is a clear tendency for Mediterranean countries to have a higher incidence of self-employment in all sectors of the economy, and particularly so in the service sector, while the proportion of self-employment is much lower in continental Europe and in most English-speaking countries. The agricultural sector stands apart in this respect insofar as a larger-than-average proportion of self-employed is found in countries with a relatively lower overall degree of development (Turkey, Greece and Ireland).

Figure 9.7 Share of self-employment, 1995

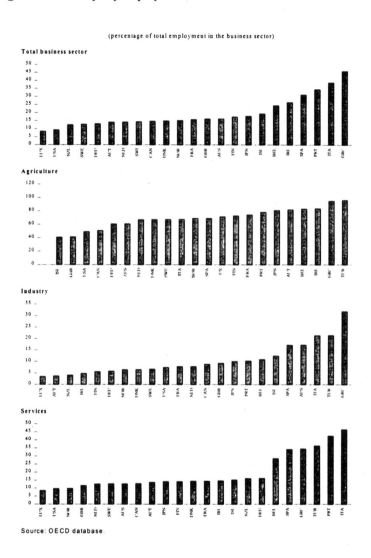

(percentage of total employment in the business sector)

Source: OECD database.

The proportion of temporary employment also varies a great deal across countries and over time. Figure 9.8 plots the incidence of temporary employment in total employment in 1985 and 1997.

Figure 9.8 Share of temporary employment. 1985 and 1997

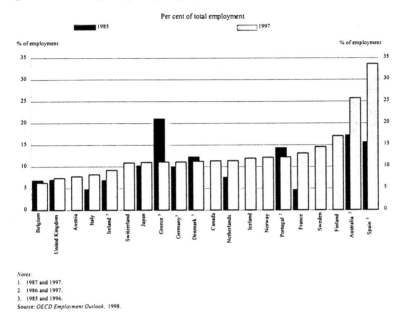

Notes:
1. 1987 and 1997.
2. 1986 and 1997.
3. 1985 and 1996.
Source: *OECD Employment Outlook.* 1998.

There has been a tendency in the majority of OECD countries to increase the proportion of temporary employment in total employment, particularly in Spain where almost one-third of total employment was under temporary contract in 1997. It is more difficult to find clear geographical divides as the incidence of temporary employment is relatively high in some European countries as well as in Australia.[22] Table 9.3 also reveals significant differences in the evolution of employment over the current recovery period. In contrast with patterns recorded in previous recovery, the growth in temporary employment has played a major role in total employment developments, compensating falling (or stable) permanent employment in a number of European countries such as Austria, France, Germany, Italy, Portugal and Sweden. In the other countries a more balanced combination of employment has been observed with both permanent and temporary jobs being created.

How do these patterns of employment relate to regulations in the product and labour markets? As mentioned in the previous section, empirical evidence on the labour market effects of regulations is mixed and often altogether lacking. Below we relate the indicators of product and labour market regulations to the three main indicators of employment patterns.

Table 9.3 Changes in permanent and temporary employment, 1993-97 (average annual change as a percentage of total employment)

	Total employees	Permanent	Temporary[a]	Share of temporary in employment 1997	Share of temporary in total employment growth
Australia	2.6	1.1	1.4	25.8	55.6
Austria[b]	-0.7	-1.5	0.8	7.8	
Belgium	0.9	0.5	0.3	6.3	41.0
Czech Republic[b]	-0.2	0.0	-0.2	7.9	
Denmark[c]	1.3	0.9	0.3	11.2	27.6
Finland[b]	3.0	2.2	0.8	17.1	26.7
France	0.8	0.1	0.7	13.1	87.5
Germany[c]	-0.4	-0.6	0.2	11.1	
Greece[c]	2.1	1.6	0.5	11.1	22.8
Iceland	1.1	1.3	-0.2	12.0	
Ireland[c]	5.7	5.1	0.6	9.2	10.7
Italy	-0.6	-1.1	0.4	7.5	
Japan	0.9	0.6	0.3	11.0	29.3
Luxembourg[c]	0.9	0.7	0.2	3.3	25.0
Mexico[b]	6.2	2.5	3.7	54.2	60.1
Netherlands	1.8	1.3	0.6	11.4	30.6
Portugal	-0.6	-1.2	0.6	12.2	
Spain	2.7	1.4	1.3	33.6	47.6
Sweden[b]	-1.8	-2.6	0.8	14.6	
Switzerland	-0.5	0.2	-0.7	10.9	
United Kingdom	1.4	1.0	0.5	7.4	34.0

Notes:

a. In most countries temporary workers are distinguished from permanent workers as being individuals with a work contract of fixed duration. The date on the numbers of temporary workers are not fully comparable across countries as specific definitions vary; for example, the data may or may not include certain groups such as those working for employment agencies, apprentices, trainees and seasonal workers. See OECD Employment Outlook, 1996 for further details on the definition of temporary work.

b. 1995-97.

c. 1993-96.

Source: OECD Employment outlook, several issues.

Figure 9.9 focuses on business-sector employment rates. Agricultural employment is omitted given the large proportion of self-employed in that sector who are only marginally affected by the regulations examined in this paper. The bottom panel suggests that a significant correlation exists between the employment rate and the stance of EPL: tight regimes tending to be associated with a lower proportion of employment in the non-agricultural business sector. The relationship between product market regulation and business sector employment is even stronger, although the country sample is somewhat smaller than that for EPL regulations.

Figure 9.9 Employment rate in the non-agricultural business sector and regulations, 1995

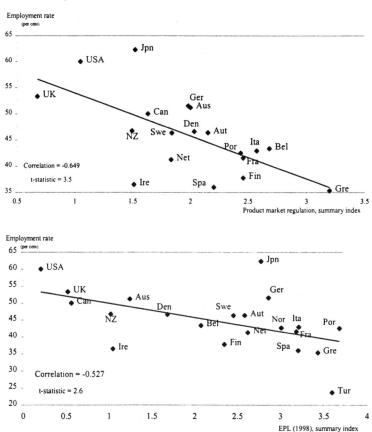

There is also a significant correlation between the share of self-employed and a measure of excess regulation for the creation of corporate firms versus the creation of sole proprietor enterprises (Figure 9.10): in countries where regulations for corporations are stricter than those for sole proprietor firms, there is a higher incidence of self-employed.[23] The rationale for the use of a measure of excess regulation instead of a simple indicator of regulation for sole proprietorship is that ceteris paribus, within a country, the choice between the type of firm to create does not necessarily depend upon the absolute degree of stringency of regulations but rather on the relative degree of stringency vis-à-vis the alternative.

Figure 9.10 Share of self-employed and product market regulations

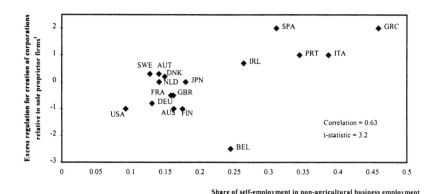

1. The difference between the indicators of administrative burdens on the creation of corporations and sole proprietor firms.

Figure 9.11 sheds light on the potential effects of EPL regulation on temporary employment. As in the previous case we have used a concept of excess regulation: the difference in the stringency of EPL regulations for permanent versus temporary employment. The figure gives only partial support to the idea that stricter regulations for permanent employment relative to those for temporary employment lead to a higher share of temporary employment in the economy. There is indeed a positive association between the excess regulation and the incidence of temporary employment, but it is not statistically significant. There are two clear outliers: Spain and to some extent Australia. In the latter case, we have already stressed that the interpretation of temporary employment is somewhat different than that of most European countries. In the case of Spain the excess regulation for permanent workers has had a disproportionate impact on the development of temporary employment. Spain has very tight regulations on both permanent and temporary employment and the difference in stringency between the two has de facto produced a very strong impact on employers' preference for temporary employment. This may suggest the existence of non-linear effects stemming from regulations: in countries with very stringent EPL, a relative small difference in EPL between temporary and permanent employment may lead to more significant shifts towards one or the other than in countries with less restrictive overall regulatory stances.

Figure 9.11 Employment protection legislation and temporary employment,
        1995

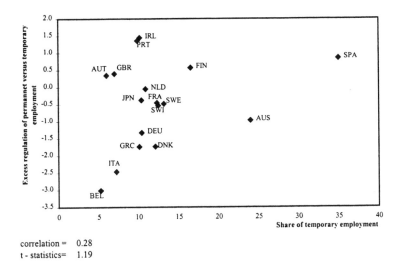

correlation = 0.28
t - statistics= 1.19

4.2 An empirical investigation of the determinants of the non-agricultural employment rate

The analysis in the previous section suggests that regulations on product and labour markets can play a significant role in the level and composition of employment. However, many other factors are likely to affect employment over and above regulations. In this section, we move away from simple bivariate correlations and estimate a structural model of employment including a number of explanatory variables in addition to EPL and product market regulations. In particular, we focus on the structural determinants of the non-agricultural business sector employment rate across countries and over time.

4.2.1 The reduced-form model
The theoretical framework for the analysis follows the familiar Layard-Nickell-Jackman (1991) bargaining model. The essential features of this model are an upward sloping *wage-setting* schedule, based on the assumption that real wages are the results of a bargaining process between employers and employees, who are able to exert some market power, combined with a

downward sloping *labour demand* schedule. The labour demand schedule is influenced by product market conditions, while the wage-setting schedule is influenced by wage push factors, including labour market policies, the strength of workers in the wage-bargaining process and, more generally, the institutional framework of the labour market. This simple model leads to the identification of a reduced-form employment rate equation.

A number of structural elements have been identified in the literature (for an exhaustive review, see OECD Jobs Study, 1994a and b, and Nickell and Layard, 1998) as contributing to the equilibrium level of employment (unemployment). Here we consider those for which data exist for a significant number of countries over time: i) an indicator of the average unemployment benefit replacement rate (average of different duration and family conditions of the unemployed person); ii) the system of wage bargaining including the union density (the proportion of workers who are members of trade unions) and the form of bargaining; iii) the level of taxes on the use of labour;[24] and iv) the summary indicator of EPL.[25]

The summary indicator of the *bargaining system* combines two aspects: the level of bargaining, being centralised, intermediate (at sector or regional) or decentralised (firm level); and the degree of coordination amongst, on the one hand, employers' associations and, on the other hand, trade unions. This combined variable allows considering cases where cooperation between employers and unions in an industry bargaining setting (e.g. Germany and Austria and, more recently, Italy, Ireland and the Netherlands with the income policy agreements) may be an alternative, or functional equivalent, to centralised systems, thereby mimicking their outcomes.

We include the public employment rate as an additional explanatory variable in the equation to test for the hypothesis that only the business sector employment rate is affected by policy institutions and labour and product market regulations. In other words, a unitary coefficient on the public employment rate would fully justify the focus on the business sector employment rate for the study of the effects of institutions and regulations on employment.

The high correlation between the summary indicator of product market regulation and that of labour market regulation makes it difficult to identify their respective contribution to employment outcomes. In addition, for the former we only have one observation (referring to 1997-98) which limits its use in a panel data estimation procedure. Thus, we opted for a two-stage approach whereby we first estimate a reduced-form equation using a panel of cross-country, time-series variables and then correlate the estimated country-specific fixed effects with the indicator of product market regulation. The country-specific effects are already purged of the effects of EPL on employment rates, and thus the correlation with PM regulations should be considered as an additional effect of these regulations to that due to the high collinearity between the two regulatory regimes.

4.2.2 The empirical results

Table 9.4 presents the results of our reduced-form non-agricultural employment rate equation, which was estimated using a panel of 19 OECD countries over the 1982-95 period.[26] More details on the econometric results presented in the table are found in Nicoletti and Scarpetta (1999).

The F-test at the bottom of Table 9.4 suggests that the null hypothesis of a unitary coefficient for the public sector employment rate is rejected at the 5 per cent level. Put another way, there is some evidence that, over the period of time considered in the analysis, public employment crowded out private employment, but the estimated effect is rather modest. It should be stressed that this is only a partial analysis: to the extent that public employment is financed by increased tax rates – whose coefficient is negative and statistically significant – the detrimental effect of public employment on business-sector employment may become larger.

Table 9.4 also suggests that income support systems affect employment outcomes. In particular, higher average replacement rates lead to lower employment rates (and higher unemployment rates; see Scarpetta, 1996). These findings corroborate the idea that the effects of overly generous benefits on the reservation wage of unemployed job-seekers may dominate the positive impact on search effectiveness through income support, thereby leading to lower equilibrium employment rates. Moreover, different collective bargaining arrangements affect labour market outcomes. The estimated coefficients for the measures of centralisation/coordination (decentralised countries are the reference group) give some support to the hump-shaped hypothesis (Calmfors and Driffill, 1988), whereby both highly centralised/coordinated systems and fully decentralised systems help to restrain the wage claims of insiders and raise employment.[27] It is also interesting to note that the tax wedge effect appears to be statistically significant. These results confirm recent findings by Nickell and Layard (1998) and Elmeskov et al. (1998). The table also suggests a significant impact of stringent employment protection regulations on employment rates. This result reinforces the evidence discussed above on the basis of bivariate correlations.

*Table 9.4 Reduced-form employment rate equations, 1982-95 (non-
          agricultural employment/working age population, fixed effects)*

Independent variables			
	Coeff.	St-err.	T-stat.
Government sector employment	0.71	0.12	6.03
Unemployment benefits replacement rate	-0.11	0.03	-4.22
Union density	-0.07	0.03	-2.67
Corporatism (intermediate)	-1.77	0.44	-4.05
Corporatism (high)	0.74	0.41	1.81
Employment protection legislation	-1.35	0.71	-1.91
Tax wedge	-0.09	0.05	-1.73
Output gap	0.61	0.04	17.1
No. of observations	223		
No. of countries	19		
F-test (fixed effects)	129.1[c]		
F-test (gov.sect.empl.=1)[a]	6.1[b]		

Notes: Each coefficient represents the expected change in the employment rate by an unitary change in the independent variable.
a. The null hypothesis is that the coefficient of the government sector employment rate is equal to 1. The test does not reject the null hypothesis at the 1 per cent level. See Nicoletti and Scarpetta (1999) for more details.
b. Statistically significant at the 5 per cent level; at the 10 per cent level.
c. Statistically significant at the 1 per cent level

4.2.3 Explaining differences in employment to population ratios

How do these results help to explain cross-country differences in employment to population ratios? To address this question, Table 9.5 breaks down the difference between each country's non-cyclical employment rate[28] and the OECD average into its determinants, namely differences in unemployment benefits, the tax wedge, employment protection regulations and the wage bargaining system. The last column in the table shows the unexplained part of the cross-country time-series variability accounting for unobserved country-specific factors.[29] The parameters referring to the wage bargaining system include the combined effects of union density and the centralisation/coordination of wage bargaining.

Table 9.5 Explaining cross-country differences in non-agricultural business sector employment rates

	Difference $Er_i\text{-}er_{OEC}$	UB	Institutional factors[b]	EPL	TWEDGE	Country-specific effect[c]
Australia	4.2	0.5	-0.3	0.9	1.5	1.7
Austria	-0.7	0.2	0.6	-0.1	-0.1	-1.2
Belgium	-4.8	-1.4	-2.2	-0.4	-1.4	0.5
Canada	4.7	0.1	0.8	1.4	1.0	1.5
Denmark	3.9	-3.0	-1.4	0.0	-0.8	9.0
Finland	-0.2	-0.6	-3.0	-0.1	0.1	3.3
France	-4.2	-0.7	0.8	-0.4	-0.6	-3.2
West Germany	2.1	0.2	1.7	-1.0	-0.7	1.9
Ireland	-11.3	0.3	0.0	1.0	-0.2	-12.3
Italy	-6.2	2.7	1.6	-1.2	-1.1	-8.2
Japan	10.0	2.2	1.4	-0.3	1.7	5.0
Netherlands	-7.4	-2.3	2.2	-0.6	-0.9	-5.7
New Zealand	0.1	-0.1	-0.7	1.0	1.3	-1.5
Norway	2.9	-0.9	-0.1	-0.6	-0.2	4.7
Portugal	-4.7	0.2	-1.4	-1.2	0.5	-2.9
Spain	-12.3	-0.4	1.0	-0.9	0.1	-12.1
Sweden	6.8	0.1	-2.8	-0.7	-1.1	11.2
UK	6.1	1.2	-0.4	1.4	0.4	3.6
US	11.0	2.0	2.1	1.6	0.7	4.6

Notes:
a. Actual non-agricultural employment rate minus government employment and minus the cyclical component estimated from the coefficient of the output gap.
b. Union density (UDENS) and the degree of centralisation/coordination.
c. The country-specific effect is calculated as a residual.

The table confirms that a limited number of policy and institutional factors can explain a significant proportion of the observed differences in non-cyclical employment rates. However, in a number of cases, other omitted factors contribute to explain their employment rates over and above those that we could include in our model (as shown by the relatively large country-specific factors). The table suggests that overly generous unemployment benefits could account for as much 2-3 percentage points lower non-agricultural business sector employment rates in some countries.

Likewise, a wage bargaining characterised by uncoordinated sectoral agreements may lead to 3 percentage points lower employment rates (at the maximum). Likewise, excessive taxes on labour use in Belgium, Italy and Sweden could be considered responsible for more than 1 percentage point lower employment rates. Turning to EPL, the table suggests that these regulations significantly affect employment rates, other things being equal. While countries with relatively lax systems (Canada, the United Kingdom and the United States) enjoy higher employment rates (around 1.5 percentage points higher), those with very strict systems (e.g. Portugal and Italy) may have 1.2 percentage points lower employment rates.

4.2.4 The role of product market regulations

As stressed above, the index of regulations on the product market cannot be included in the regression analysis due to the lack of time dimension and, more importantly, because of the high correlation with the index of employment protection regulations. However, the bivariate correlation between the unexplained country-specific effects (Table 9.5) and the PM index may shed some light on the role of strict regulations in the product market over and above those stemming from the combined effect with labour market regulations (Table 9.6). As expected, the significant correlations found in the previous bivariate analysis are weakened once the several factors affecting cross-country differences in employment are controlled for. However, correlations generally remain correctly signed and a few of them retain significance, especially when outliers are eliminated (second column of Table 9.6). As mentioned above, due to lags in the effects of structural policies on market outcomes, in countries (such as Ireland) where radical product market reforms were implemented towards the end of the sample period, the end-of-period measure of regulation necessarily bears little relationship with the average employment rate even if a strong causal link between regulations and employment were to exist. Therefore, bivariate correlations have been computed both with and without this country.

Despite the fact that there is only a weak correlation between the overall indicator of product market regulation and the country-specific effects, several aspects of PM regulations seem to be more closely related with it. For example, the presence of a high degree of state control in business sector activities seem to exert a strong negative effect on business sector employment rates, especially through regulations interfering in the activity of private (or privatised) business enterprises and administrative burdens on business start-ups. In particular, entry restrictions due to costly and opaque administrative practices and the distortion of market mechanisms associated with the excessive presence of the state in the business sector would appear to explain the pattern of employment rates across OECD countries over and above the policy, regulatory and institutional factors specific to the labour market. While considering these results we should, however, keep in mind the strong positive correlation between the summary measures of EPL and product market regulation, which makes it difficult to identify their separate contribution to the explanation of cross-country differences in employment rates.

Table 9.6 The employment rate: country-specific effects and regulation (non-agricultural, 1982-1995)

Regulatory indicators	Including outliers	Excluding outliers
Product market regulation	-0.16	-0.30
Inward-oriented policies	-0.30	-0.40
Outward-oriented policies	0.38	0.31
State control	-0.32	-0.42*
Public ownership	-0.21	-0.24
Interference in private firms	-0.34	-0.49*
Size of public enterprise sector	0.05	0.01
Scope of public enterprise sector	-0.33	-0.39
Special voting rights	-0.60*	-0.67*
Use of command and control regulation	-0.17	-0.33
Barriers to entrepreneurship	-0.02	-0.08
Administrative transparency	0.24	0.28
Adm. burdens on business start-ups	-0.36	-0.53*
Legal barriers to entry	0.26	0.35
Adm. burdens for corporations	-0.54*	-0.72*
Adm. burdens for sole proprietor firms	-0.17	-0.42
Barriers to trade and investment	0.38	0.31
Regulatory and tariff barriers	0.31	0.28
Other trade barriers	0.22	0.14
Regulatory barriers	0.10	0.04
Non-tariff barriers	-0.12	-0.08

Notes:

* Indicates significance at 10 per cent levels.

Outlier country is Ireland.

5. THE CHANGING PROFILE OF REGULATIONS

The above analysis suggests that the stance of product and labour market regulations is highly correlated across countries. Moreover, both the overall regulatory environment and some institutional features of labour markets, notably the presence of overly generous unemployment benefits, sectoral and uncoordinated wage bargaining institutions, strict employment protection and high labour taxation, negatively affect employment rates, that is, the capacity of economies to mobilise labour supply. However, our findings should be qualified in several ways.

First, our results rely on measures that, albeit significantly improved from previous studies, are still an approximation of actual regulatory policies, especially since it is difficult to gather information on the actual enforcement of the various regulations. Data constraints also prevent us from estimating the structural relationships, and unfortunately, economic theory provides little guidance in imposing those restrictions that would allow recovering from reduced form estimates the underlying structural parameters, which could be better interpreted and used in the context of policy simulation exercises.

Second, and perhaps more importantly, our findings provide only partial indications as to which institutional features would need to be reformed in order to increase employment rates. This is because the various parameter estimates summarise the impact of ceteris paribus changes in some institutional features, while the analysis in Sections 2 and 3 pointed to potentially significant interactions and complementarity among the various institutions.

Moreover, the results presented in Section 4 refer to the effects of policy and institutions in the 1982-95 period. It is difficult to extrapolate from these results the effect of policy reforms in the future insofar as reforms in one area may be nullified by contrary reforms in other areas. Put another way, reducing unemployment benefit generosity by 10 percentage points may not lead to an increase of 1.1 percentage points in the employment rate, as suggested in the previous section (Table 9.4), if this reduction is obtained at the cost of stricter employment protection legislation.[30] The existence of this and other trade-offs (partly, but not only, dictated by political economy factors) in the design of labour market and social welfare institutions suggests that piecemeal reforms may be offset by countervailing changes in other institutional features.

Third, there are important dynamic effects of changes in institutions that are not captured by our estimates. Once more data limitations, namely the short and discontinued time-series on labour market institutions, do not allow us to estimate a richer set of parameters capturing partial adjustment to long-run equilibria. However, we have every reason to suspect that the adjustment to institutional changes takes time, and that reforms themselves are a long-term process. Some evidence on the sluggishness of institutional adjustment is provided below.

The slow adjustment of institutions suggests that the impact of reforms is crucially dependent on the expectations that agents have on the ultimate purpose of regulatory changes, hence on the longer-term design of institutions. These dynamic and expectational effects of reforms are likely to be very important. If reforms are perceived as temporary, it is highly unlikely that they would work in the direction (and magnitude) implied by our parameter estimates.

Thus, the best way to interpret our findings is as indications of the fact that some regulatory and institutional environments are more conducive to low employment rates than others. Rather than using these estimates to advocate some reforms and predict their impact, we prefer to adopt here a more cautious (and positive) approach. First, we will try to identify which changes are occurring in policies, regulations and institutions across countries. The focus will be mainly on policies, regulations and institutions concerning the European labour markets. Next, based on our previous employment estimates, we will try to assess whether the observed pattern of changes is likely to lead to higher or lower employment rates. Finally, we will try to verify whether different regulatory regimes (over time and across countries) are associated with different attitudes towards social and welfare policies.

5.1 The institutions, 'they are a'changing'

The first question to ask is whether institutions are changing at all. According to popular wisdom, institutions, notably social welfare institutions, are something static, unmodifiable and indeed unmodified over long periods of time. Is this true?

We collected information enabling us to assess two dimensions of institutional dynamism. The first is the degree of persistence of those institutional features for which reliable measures can be obtained for sufficiently long periods of time. The second is the number and nature of reforms that have occurred in this area, as can be grasped by qualitative information on economic and policy developments in the various countries.

5.1.2 Persistence of institutional features
Table 9.7 displays Spearman rank-correlation as well as simple-correlation coefficients of various measures of the stance of social policy and employment protection in OECD countries over time. A simple-correlation coefficient close to unity for an institutional feature points to a high degree of persistence of this feature while a rank-correlation coefficient approaching zero is an indication of a low persistence in the ranking. Both correlation coefficients are displayed as rank correlations which can be more reliable than simple correlations when available measures are deemed to mainly provide an ordering of countries.

Table 9.7 Persistence of institutions, 1980-90 (correlation coefficients)

	Unemployment benefits	Employment Protection Legislation	Public pensions	Social assistance
Simple correlation	0.94**	0.93**	0.98**	0.58*
Spearman rank correlation	0.93**	0.90**	0.98**	0.75*
Number of observations	19	14	13	14

* *Denotes significance at 95% confidence.*
** *Denotes significance at 99% confidence.*

The first measure captures the generosity of unemployment benefits. In Table 9.7, we have used a summary measure of generosity that focuses on the first two years of unemployment (in any event, in most countries individuals with unemployment durations longer than 24 months are eligible only for means-tested social assistance, whose coverage and level are assessed below). Second, we have weighted replacement rates for the second year of unemployment by the incidence of long-term unemployment.[31] This means that, in a country where 50 per cent of unemployment is long-term (lasts more than 12 months), a weight of 0.5 is given to replacement rates offered in the second year of joblessness.[32] The correlation coefficients point to a relatively high degree of persistence in the way in which countries differ in the provision of income support to the unemployed individuals.

The second measure considered in Table 9.7 deals with employment protection regulations. As discussed in Section 2, there is indication also in this case of a high persistence in the relative position of the various countries as far as employment protection is concerned. The third institutional feature is a measure of the generosity of public pensions, namely the ratio between the (public) pensions received by persons aged 65 to 74 and the disposable income of individuals aged 55 to 64. This is a summary measure of the actual contribution offered by public pensions to the replacement of pre-retirement earnings. Pensions are relevant also in this context because of the role played by early retirement schemes as non-employment benefits. Data come from national sources, which have been assembled (in a way to satisfy cross-country comparability purposes) by the OECD. This seems to be the most persistent institutional feature of the four: both correlation coefficients are indeed close to unity.

The fourth measure captures social assistance provisions, namely those cash transfer schemes aimed at guaranteeing subsistence to people in need. In this case, the generosity measures are provided by the ratio of social assistance expenditure[33] to the number of persons having income lower than or equal to 50 per cent of the average wage. We have in this case a rather low persistence in the levels of social assistance, and some indication that rank reversals have occurred in the generosity and coverage of income support schemes of the last resort.

Overall, institutional asymmetries across countries would seem to be highly persistent: evolutions in the 1990s did not significantly affect the country rankings that prevailed in the mid-1980s. The only exception is social assistance where there is evidence of rank reversals and more broadly significant changes in the levels and coverage of provisions.

5.1.2 Taking stock of institutional reforms

Table 9.8 summarises the number and nature of both marginal and radical reforms carried out in the EU over the 1986-97 period in three domains: employment protection, unemployment benefits and pensions. Information as to the broad direction of reforms (more or less employment security, more or less generous non-employment benefit systems, more or less encompassing public pensions) is also provided. A variety of sources (including country economic reviews carried out by the OECD, Income Data Source studies, EC-MISSOC reports, etc.) were used to take stock of reforms carried out in Europe.

The inventory of reforms is organised along two main dimensions. On the one hand, we distinguish reforms on the basis of their broad orientation, that is, whether they tend to reduce or increase the generosity of public pensions and non-employment benefits and make employment protection more or less strict. This is, after all, the same dimension along which the figures commented upon so far have been organised here and therefore we believe that it is not necessary to add more information.

On the other hand, we distinguish reforms depending on whether they are *marginal* or *radical*. This procedure is done in two stages. At first, we rely on qualitative assessment, which is based on an evaluation of the scope of the various reforms. In particular, we preliminarily classify as radical those reforms that satisfy at least one of the following criteria: reduce replacement rates by at least 10 per cent; are comprehensive, that is, do not address just minor features of the cash transfer schemes but rather reform their broader design; and involve existing entitlements rather than being simply phased-in for the new beneficiaries of the various schemes (e.g. reforms of employment protection should also concern workers under permanent contracts). In the second stage we look at the actual behaviour of the series which should be most affected by the reforms and only if we observe a change in the underlying trend of these series do we judge that our qualitative assessment is confirmed. Clearly, the second stage of the procedure can only be implemented for the reforms carried out before 1993, as we need a minimum number of observations in order to establish whether a change in the underlying trend has occurred. Sometimes even in the case of reforms done before 1993, the second-stage validation procedure cannot be implemented as some reforms are followed just a few years later by regulatory changes moving in the opposite direction and therefore undoing part of the initial institutional changes. In all the cases where the second-stage procedure cannot be implemented, only the first-stage assessment is used. The first-stage assessment was validated in 85 per cent of the cases.

Table 9.8 Reforms of employment protection legislation (EPL), non-employment benefits and pension systems in Europe(1986-97)

		Decreasing generosity and regulations	Increasing generosity and regulations	Total per row
Employment Protection Legislation	Marginal	20	16	36
	Radical	6	2	8
Non-employment benefits	Marginal	37	32	69
	Radical	7	2	9
Public pensions	Marginal	30	37	67
	Radical	7	2	9
Total per column		107	91	198

Note: See the text for details on how reforms are classified (e.g. the distinction between marginal and radical reforms).

Source: Fondazione Rodolfo Debenedetti.

Which series are we using in the empirical validation procedures? In the case of employment protection we look at labour market flows, notably unemployment inflows, because previous work has found a strong negative correlation between employment protection and the incidence of unemployment[34] In the case of pension reforms, we look at the dynamics of pension expenditures and revenues earmarked for public pension funds: we expect radical reforms to significantly affect at least one of the two. Finally, in the case of non-employment benefits, we use proxy outflows from unemployment[35] (or outflows from the live registers to jobs in the countries for which such data are available): we expect radical reforms to significantly affect exit flows from unemployment. (Unfortunately, we have no data on exit flows from non-employment.)

The most striking fact highlighted by the table is the large number of reforms: one can count 198 reforms, more than one every two years for each institutional feature. Significantly, reforms often seem to move in opposite directions. For instance, there is almost the same number of reforms increasing the generosity of public pensions as those reducing them and often such mutually offsetting changes occur within the same country within a short period of time. Moreover, most of the reforms are of the incremental and marginal type, which means that old regulations were often not removed and that new ones were simply added. As stressed above, in the field of employment protection, for instance, many reforms were confined to the introduction of new types of contracts, leaving the 'regular' ones untouched. Similarly, cuts to non-employment benefits were rarely discrete, as they involved reductions, at most, of 5-10 per cent of replacement rates.

Albeit reforms were mainly marginal and often inconsistent, there is little doubt that institutions were and are changing. The obvious question to pursue is: in which direction did these changes occur?

5.2 Reform patterns and employment outcomes

There is not a common pattern of reform that can be discerned across countries as, after all, initial conditions were significantly different from country to country. Yet, some characteristics of reform are shared across quite a wide range of countries.

The dominant tendency in the field of unemployment benefit systems and, more broadly, in measures dealing with redundancies, has been towards a tightening of the system, in terms of stricter eligibility criteria, shorter maximum duration of benefits, and, in some cases, lower replacement rates. This is the route taken by Austria, Canada, Iceland, Ireland, the Netherlands,

Boeri, Nicoletti and Scarpetta

Norway, Spain and the UK. However, in some of the countries where these programmes were initially undersized by OECD standards – e.g. southern European countries such as Greece and Italy – the tendency has been instead towards the introduction of new schemes (e.g. the so-called 'Liste di Mobilità' in Italy) which provide a larger replacement of earnings in the case of job loss. Access to early retirement schemes, invalidity or sick benefits has been restricted in those countries, such as Austria, Italy, Germany, the Netherlands, Norway and Spain, which had in the past made large use of these (rather expensive) schemes to cushion the social costs of redundancies.

As already stressed in Section 1, reform of employment protection schemes has generally involved the liberalisation of fixed-term contracts and the introduction of a wider range of non-standard forms of employment (e.g. temporary agency work). This dominant trend towards increasing flexibility in the adjustment of employment has been coupled with reforms aimed at more flexible working-time arrangements in a number of countries. There are, however, a few exceptions such as in France where EPL for permanent workers has been tightened and the normal working week of 35 hours has been adopted.

Industrial relations have generally evolved by assigning greater importance to decentralised wage bargaining institutions or better coordination amongst social partners at the different levels of negotiation (national, sectoral, firm) (see OECD, 1999b). The most radical reforms in this context occurred in New Zealand, Australia and the UK. In continental Europe, reforms have been more gradual and have typically resulted in the establishment of a two-tier bargaining structure in which nation-wide or sectoral wage agreements are supplemented by firm-level collective bargaining structures. The scope for exemptions from contractual minima set in the context of national agreements has also been expanded in countries such as Germany and Italy, mainly as a recognition of the fact that these floors were crowding-out employment in the new Länder or in the Mezzogiorno. In the midst of reforms, coordination of decentralised wage agreements is difficult and was indeed hardly achieved. Most frequently, the adding of a second bargaining tier resulted in 'summatory' effects, whereby wage increases agreed at the firm level were simply added to those reached at the national or sectoral level.

There are also indications that some easing of product market regulations occurred in a number of countries (see OECD, 1999b). In particular, licensing requirements were simplified in the Netherlands, more competition in professional services (e.g., lawyers) was granted in Germany, Finland, Spain and Switzerland; and shop opening hours were relaxed in Austria, Belgium, Denmark, Finland, Germany, Greece and Italy. EU-wide liberalisation is taking place in telecommunications, airlines and, much more slowly, in the electricity industry, and steps allowing for more competition in financial services have been taken or are envisaged in a wide range of countries. As shown in Section 2, however, even at the EU level cross-country differences in product market regulations remain significant, especially in the areas of state control and barriers to entrepreneurship.

Overall, these reforms are largely oriented in a direction which – according to the results of the multivariate analysis in Section 2 – should enhance employment rates. However, a number of conditions will have to be met before the reforms fully display their effects. First, as most reforms are marginal and our parameter estimates point to rather small effects of the various institutional features on employment to population ratios, reforms should gain in scope in order to have some a sizeable impact on the labour market. Second, given the role played by expectations and the fact that reversals of liberalisation episodes have occurred in some countries, reforms will have to gain momentum in order to be credible and we believe that they need to be credible in order to be effective. Thirdly, reforms will have to be encompassing rather than piecemeal, thereby avoiding that substitutions of policy instruments occur which jeopardise the ultimate purpose of reforms.

In a nutshell, predictions as to the likely impact of ongoing reforms can only be made based on some understanding of what lies behind these reform efforts. Are they just episodes, and governments are bound, sooner or later, to be punished by voters for their bravery? Are the policy changes simply devices to comply with recommendations of international organisations exerting structural surveillance and imposing their conditionality (if any) on economic policies? Or are these reforms the by-product of a long-term process, e.g. the result of stricter regional integration and capital mobility putting competitive pressure on national welfare systems and domestic regulations obstructing business? These questions are particularly relevant for understanding the likely evolution of institutional reforms in the EMU area.

5.3 Regulatory reform, economic integration and the convergence/ divergence of social policies

Product market liberalisation has been implemented in Europe mainly within the framework of the EU directives, which provide precise guidelines for countries (including administrative and judicial ways to impose compliance). By contrast, reforms in the labour market have been more disparate and not necessarily coherent across countries, since they remain largely within the domain of national policies. However, EMU may impress a change in the labour market reform effort of the member countries.

There are, at least, two schools of thought on the effects of EMU on structural reforms. For illustrative purposes it is useful to characterise these schools by taking their most extreme positions. We are fully aware that there are many other speculations in the forefront, which offer a much more balanced view than those proposed below.

On the one hand, there are those who argue that EMU will force governments to necessarily deal with structural issues, as there is hardly anything else to do. According to the so-called 'there-is-no-alternative' or TINA argument – as labelled by Calmfors (1998), governments in the monetary union will have to concentrate their efforts on structural policies. With monetary policy decided elsewhere and tight conditions for fiscal policy within the framework of the Stability and Growth Pact, countries will be able to cope with (asymmetric) shocks only if they increase the flexibility of their product and labour markets. Other scholars argue that the removal of remaining barriers to the mobility of goods and services and the greater price transparency involved in the adoption of a common currency (in the context of the EMU) will increase competitive pressures on national fiscal systems. This will create stronger and stronger pressures to dismantle the welfare state (Sinn, 1998), set in motion a *race-to-the-bottom* in social welfare provision and possibly phase-out employment protection in an attempt to attract FDI. Depending on whether this tendency towards more structural reforms and smaller social welfare systems is deemed desirable or not, arguments are made for a harmonisation of social and labour policies at the EU level or simply their coordination.

On the other hand, there are those who argue that EMU will hardly make any difference in terms of institutional reform, except those that are intrinsic to the creation of a monetary union. For instance, there is little doubt that monetary union will de facto decentralise even the most centralised national wage bargaining system. Besides these initial effects of EMU on institutions, monetary union will play in favour of the status quo for a number of reasons. First, it is suggested that incentives to reform labour markets in order to cope with the inflation bias associated with structural unemployment will be reduced under EMU because, with the ECB determining monetary policy in the whole currency union, labour market reforms in a given country will have only a small effect on the common rate of inflation. Second, in the light of the heterogeneity of institutions across countries (and of the substitutability and complementarity of these), the way in which competitive pressures will act to reduce social welfare provisions is not at all self-evident. Put another way, there are many arbitrage conditions to be met and just one factor, namely capital, moving around. It should be stressed that the findings of the analysis above on the incremental and marginal nature of reforms ultimately suggest that the complexity of social welfare and labour institutions is almost everywhere increasing rather than decreasing over time. This supports the case for a lack of transparency and persistent country-specific institutional design.

If theorists are divided as to the likely impact of EMU on institutional reform, empiricism offers only modest guidance to clarify these issues. Lucas' critique implies that making inferences on future trends based on past observations may be highly misleading when structural breaks, such as the advent of EMU, occur. Nevertheless, this should not sound like a justification to avoid spending time looking at data available on the convergence and divergence of institutions in the last fifteen years. At the worst, this exercise will tell us something about the effects of economic integration in broad terms rather than the effects of EMU.

Table 9.9 provides information on social spending over GDP by main expenditure item. In addition to looking at convergence within the OECD area, we also look at convergence within the EU as well as the three country clusters (southern Europe, continental Europe and common-law countries) discussed in Section 2. The latter were obtained while tracking similarities in regulatory frameworks. Yet, they are also associated with characteristics of welfare states. For instance, the strong employment protection provided in southern European countries was historically associated with the provision of low insurance against the risk of job loss, and relatively small welfare states.

In the table, we draw on data from the OECD Social Expenditure Database and build groups of expenditure items.[36] In particular, we put together old-age, survivor pensions and care for the elderly services; we include in the same group health, occupational injury and sickness benefits and we put early retirement and active policies in the broader class of measures for the unemployed. While some of these groupings may be challenged on grounds that they mix rather different policy instruments, they are nonetheless essential for assessing convergence in terms of the categories of beneficiaries of social spending. We are interested in verifying the convergence in social welfare institutions. Therefore, we tabulate not only the (un-weighted) averages, but also the (un-weighted) standard deviations of expenditure shares over GDP across and within country groups. These measures of dispersion can be used to broadly assess the degree of 'sigma convergence' within and across the various country groups.

Table 9.9 Convergence in social policy expenditure (as a % of GDP)

	Total 1980	Total 1985	Total 1995	Old age 1980	Old age 1985	Old age 1995	Disability 1980	Disability 1985	Disability 1995	Health 1980	Health 1985	Health 1995
Unweighted Averages												
Group A	17.17	20.01	22.30	6.67	7.48	8.52	1.08	1.24	1.27	6.60	6.35	6.88
Group B	21.13	22.67	26.38	7.96	8.16	9.25	1.90	1.92	2.15	6.82	6.83	7.37
Group C	15.79	18.18	18.94	5.79	6.18	5.85	0.59	0.68	1.12	6.00	6.02	6.70
European Union	21.09	23.29	24.45	8.30	9.03	9.41	1.69	1.84	1.86	6.94	6.71	6.64
Unweighted standard deviations												
Between countries	6.67	6.69	8.12	2.62	2.72	3.47	1.02	0.99	1.05	2.20	1.90	2.02
Within Group A	5.04	6.45	4.99	2.73	3.25	2.88	0.28	0.31	0.31	1.29	1.60	1.46
Within Group B	5.78	5.29	5.16	2.38	2.38	2.56	1.18	1.11	1.10	1.52	0.99	1.19
Within Group C	2.40	3.92	2.43	1.71	1.56	1.45	0.21	0.31	0.86	1.80	1.33	0.58
Between groups	2.77	2.26	3.72	1.09	1.01	1.79	0.66	0.62	0.55	0.43	0.41	0.35
Within the EU	5.78	5.03	8.14	2.17	2.06	3.56	1.05	0.94	1.06	2.08	1.78	2.16

	Family 1980	Family 1985	Family 1995	Unemployment 1980	Unemployment 1985	Unemployment 1995	Housing and Social Asst. 1980	Housing and Social Asst. 1985	Housing and Social Asst. 1995	Other 1980	Other 1985	Other 1995
Unweighted Averages												
Group A	1.25	1.34	1.42	1.22	3.07	3.48	0.35	0.51	0.70	0.01	0.01	0.04
Group B	2.23	2.12	2.63	1.73	2.95	3.97	0.45	0.62	0.82	0.04	0.07	0.12
Group C	1.41	1.48	1.53	1.10	2.52	2.17	0.89	1.30	1.50	0.01	0.01	0.03
European Union	2.07	2.00	2.11	1.62	3.01	3.49	0.44	0.67	0.79	0.03	0.03	0.07
Unweighted standard deviations												
Between countries	1.04	1.04	1.29	1.21	1.72	2.02	0.48	0.66	0.81	0.08	0.09	0.13
Within Group A	0.89	1.10	1.02	0.94	1.37	0.93	0.21	0.34	0.67	0.02	0.02	0.02
Within group B	0.84	0.67	1.13	1.65	1.81	1.96	0.30	0.44	0.57	0.09	0.11	0.17
Within group C	0.73	0.81	0.78	0.47	1.93	1.79	0.66	0.95	1.01	0.01	0.02	0.06
Between groups	0.53	0.42	0.67	0.33	0.29	0.93	0.29	0.43	0.43	0.02	0.03	0.05
Within EU	1.09	1.10	1.31	1.33	1.67	2.08	0.40	0.63	0.75	0.07	0.09	0.14

Source: OECD Social Expenditure Database (1980-1996).

Note: Group A (Southern Europe): France, Italy, Portugal and Spain. Group B (continental Europe) Australia, Austria, Denmark, Finland, Germany, Belgium, the Netherlands, Norway, and Switzerland. Group C (common law countries): United States, United Kingdom, Canada, Ireland and New Zealand.

The first fact highlighted by the table is that there does not seem to be a tendency towards decreased social spending in any of the four groups of countries. If anything, expenditure increases as a share of GDP. This is important as it suggests that regulatory reform, economic integration and freer mobility of capital so far does not seem to have involved a race-to-the-bottom in welfare provision. Neither are there indications of a tendency towards convergence in the size and composition of social spending across countries. Surprisingly, diverging levels of social spending and social expenditure structures emerge within the EU: the standard deviations are almost always increasing (and this holds even accounting for scale effects, that is, using coefficients of variation rather than standard deviations). Some convergence would seem to occur within some regional blocks, notably the southern Europe group, but this holds only in terms of overall social spending rather than for each expenditure item.

Data on social expenditure are deeply affected by differences in the efficiency of social welfare administrations and cannot capture qualitative institutional differences across countries. Thus, we looked at convergence also in terms of characteristics of the various institutions. In particular Table 9.10 looks at collective bargaining institutions, and Table 9.11 at unemployment benefit systems. The former are described in terms of the degree of unionisation, centralisation and coordination and the latter in terms of generosity (replacement rates) and coverage. All these terms and measures should by now be familiar to the reader as they have been discussed in Sections 1 and 2.

The tables support some of the observations made above about the direction of reforms. In particular, there seems to be some tendency towards a decline in the degree of unionisation of the workforce and in the generosity of unemployment benefit systems (replacement rates, if not necessarily coverage, decline in most country groups[37]). However, on the whole, there seems to be little support for the idea that a process of institutional convergence is at work. The overall and between groups standard deviations are increasing. Only within specific groups (e.g., the southern European cluster) would some tendency towards convergence seem to emerge.

Table 9.10 Convergence in bargaining institutions

	Coverage			Unionisation			Centralisation			Coordination		
	1980	1985	1995	1980	1985	1995	1980	1985	1995	1980	1985	1995
Australia	88	80	80	48	41	35	2.2	1.5	1.5	2.2	2.2	1.5
Austria	98	98	98	56	46	42	2.2	2.2	2.2	3.0	3.0	3.0
Belgium	90	90	90	56	51	53	2.2	2.2	2.2	2.0	2.0	2.0
Canada	37	38	36	35	34	33	1.0	1.0	1.0	1.0	1.0	1.0
Denmark	69	69	69	76	71	76	2.2	2.0	2.0	2.5	2.2	2.2
Finland	95	95	95	70	72	81	2.5	2.2	2.2	2.2	2.2	2.2
France	85	92	92	17	10	9	2.0	2.0	2.0	1.8	2.0	2.0
Germany	91	90	92	36	33	29	2.0	2.0	2.0	3.0	3.0	3.0
Italy	85	83	82	57	50	50	1.0	1.0	1.0	1.0	1.0	3.0
Japan	28	23	21	31	25	24	1.8	1.8	2.0	1.5	1.5	2.5
Netherlands	76	71	81	31	25	24	2.0	2.0	2.0	3.0	3.0	3.0
New Zealand	67	67	31	31	25	26	2.0	1.5	1.1	2.0	2.0	2.0
Norway	75	75	74	56	45	24	2.0	2.2	2.2	1.5	1.0	1.0
Portugal	70	79	71	57	56	58	1.8	2.2	2.0	2.5	2.5	2.5
Spain	76	76	78	61	30	25	2.2	2.0	2.0	1.8	2.0	2.0
Sweden	86	86	89	13	16	21	3.0	2.2	2.0	2.0	2.0	2.0
United Kingdom	70	47	47	80	83	91	2.2	2.2	2.0	2.5	2.2	2.0
United States	26	18	18	50	39	34	2.0	1.8	1.6	1.5	1.2	1.0
Unweighted averages												
Overall	73	71	69	48	42	41	2	2	2	2	2	2
Group A	79	83	82	48	36	35	2	2	2	2	2	2
Group B	85	84	85	54	48	46	2	2	2	2	2	2
Group C	50	43	33	49	45	46	2	2	2	2	2	2
European Union	83	81	82	51	45	47	2	2	2	2	2	2
Unweighted std dev.												
Overall	21.7	24.0	26.6	19.1	19.8	22.8	0.5	0.4	0.5	0.6	0.7	0.7
Group A	7.3	7.0	10.1	20.5	21.0	22.5	0.5	0.6	0.5	0.6	0.6	0.6
Group B	10.5	11.2	10.4	15.3	16.6	22.5	0.4	0.4	0.5	0.6	0.7	0.7
Group C	21.9	20.3	12.0	22.2	25.7	30.1	0.8	0.5	0.5	0.6	0.6	0.6
European Union	9.7	13.3	13.7	20.2	21.3	25.4	0.5	0.4	0.5	0.6	0.7	0.7
Between groups A,B,C	18.8	23.4	29.0	3.0	6.1	6.0	0.2	0.1	0.1	0.4	0.4	0.4

Note: Group A (Southern Europe): France, Italy, Portugal and Spain. Group B (continental Europe) Australia, Austria, Denmark, Finland, Germany, Belgium, the Netherlands, Norway and Switzerland. Group C (common law countries): United Kingdom, Canada, Ireland and New Zealand.

Table 9.11 Convergence in unemployment benefit systems

Country	UB generosity		UB coverage	
	1991	1995	1990	1995
Austria	31.0	25.8	89	90
Belgium	42.3	41.6	89	94
Denmark	51.9	70.3	100	100
Finland	38.8	43.2	101	100
France	37.2	37.5	81	77
Germany	28.1	26.4	64	76
Greece	17.1	22.1	5.3	50
Ireland	29.3	26.1	95	95
Netherlands	51.3	45.9	145	144
Portugal	34.4	35.2	22	43
Spain	33.5	31.7	54	40
Sweden	29.4	27.3	66	73
United Kingdom	17.5	18.1	86	97
Unweighted average				
Overall	24.3	22.0	87.5	93.5
Group A	30.6	31.6	52.5	52.5
Group B	40.6	42.2	98.0	100.7
Group C	23.4	22.1	90.5	96.0
European Union	34.0	34.7	80.4	83.0
Unweighted standard deviation				
Overall	10.67	13.67	29.87	28.18
Group A	9.10	6.78	24.12	16..86
Group B	9.97	16.27	26.61	23
Group C	23.40	22.10	90.50	96
European Union	10.67	13.67	29.87	28.18
Between groups (A,B,C)	*8.62*	*10.05*	*24.39*	*26.56*

Notes:
Group A (Southern countries): France, Italy, Portugal, Spain.
Group B (Continental Europe): Austria, Denmark, Finland, Germany, Belgium, the Netherlands.
Group C (Common-law countries): United Kingdom, Ireland.

6. TENTATIVE CONCLUSIONS

This paper uses a novel set of indicators of regulation in product and labour markets to shed some light on cross-country differences in the level and composition of employment and to discuss the likely effect of regulatory reforms on OECD labour markets. In addition, comparing differences in regulatory policies with the changing patterns of social policies has allowed a preliminary investigation of the possible linkages between regulatory environments, different degrees of economic integration and the characteristics of the welfare systems in European countries.

Indicators of employment protection legislation (EPL) and of various dimensions of product market regulation suggest that, despite the widespread regulatory reforms, OECD countries remain characterised by widely different approaches to regulating product and labour markets. Overall, countries tend to adopt similar approaches in the two markets: where product markets are adverse to competition and state interference in the business sector is high, labour markets tend as well to have tight legislation protecting the employed pool. Therefore, clear country clusters can be identified according to the degree of strictness of regulations in the two markets.

Even controlling for a number of policy and institutional factors affecting the labour market, it is possible to detect significant effects of the summary indicators of both EPL and product market regulation on the level and the composition of employment rates of OECD countries. In particular, countries with tight EPL and restrictive product market regulation tend to have lower employment rates in the non-agricultural business sector. At the same time, biases in the regulatory environment will tend to distort the composition of employment. For instance, a more restrictive EPL for regular workers relative to temporary employment tends to increase the proportion of workers moving from one temporary contract to another. Similarly, higher regulatory and administrative burdens for corporations relative to sole proprietor companies tend to increase the proportion of self-employed in the non-agricultural business sector.

A widespread (but often slow-moving) tendency to reform product market regulation can be observed in European countries, mainly as a result of EC initiatives. By contrast, policies, institutions and regulations affecting the labour market move in largely idiosyncratic ways, with most countries implementing largely marginal reforms. In this context, one could ask whether OECD institutions are acquiring those features that are most conducive to foster employment rates. Our analysis suggests that the answer should be a timid yes. Institutions are changing and much more than usually thought, and generally in a direction that one can consider rather desirable in the light of our econometric results. Yet, much ground remains to be covered, most reforms are marginal and piecemeal in scope, and there is nothing irreversible in them. The expectation of reversals in reform strategies may seriously jeopardise reform efforts because regulatory changes lacking credibility may be ineffective. Contrary to claims commonly made that stricter economic integration should foster competition across national systems – and hence stimulate institutional reforms converging to the best practices – stronger integration in the EU area does not seem to have been associated so far with convergence in a number of labour market institutional features, such as employment protection, collective bargaining, as well as the size and structure of social expenditure. The extent to which EMU will feed into this process is highly uncertain and theorists are divided in assessing the role that monetary union will play in the deepening and furthering of structural reforms. While a careful 'wait and see' behaviour should be recommended to those researchers who do not want to enter a highly speculative debate, those involved in policy-making should be aware of the fact that economic convergence does not necessarily exert competitive pressures on national institutions that require increased efficiency in social welfare and employment protection provisions. Hence, if they deem that social welfare reforms are necessary, they should not spare any energy in trying to support them.

NOTES

1. We thank Giampaolo Galli, Jacques Pelkmans and Paolo Sestito as well as participants in the Workshop on 'Regulatory Reform, Competitiveness and Market Functioning' for helpful comments on a previous draft of this paper.
2. The indicators are used in this paper under the exclusive responsibility of the authors and do not engage the OECD or its member countries. They report the situation in OECD countries in 1997 or 1998, depending on the country and the indicator, and are based on the information available and country submissions as of June 1999. Nicoletti et al. (1999) revised and extended the indicators based on more recent data and provided a detailed description of the database and the methodology followed in their construction.
3. For a discussion of the concept of economic regulation, see Viscusi et al. (1997).
4. For instance, the cost of US federal regulations were estimated to range from 4 to 10% of GDP (Office of Management and Budget, 1998), while the costs of regulation for the Dutch economy were estimated to range from 11 to 14% of Net National Income (van Bergeijk and Haffner, 1996).
5. For a discussion of theories of regulation and the related empirical evidence, see for instance, Noll (1989a and b), Winston (1993) and Winston and Crandall (1994).
6. Special interest groups are usually composed of a relatively small number of producers whose individual marginal gains from regulatory interventions are large as opposed to the large audience of consumers,

who are typically dispersed and ill-organised and whose marginal gains are individually small. See Peltzman (1989).

7. On the balance of costs and benefits of regulation, see Office of Management and Budget (1998).

8. For a review of the rationale, the status and the potential effects of regulatory reform in OECD countries, see OECD (1997b).

9. On the effects of international openness on growth, see for instance Edwards (1998).

10. For a survey of theory and evidence of the effects of product market competition on wages, see Nickell (1998).

11. The ratio would not be optimal from a social perspective because the cost of labour to the firm would exceed the opportunity cost of labour to society.

12. For a survey of the relationship between ownership structure and economic efficiency and the related empirical evidence, see World Bank (1995) and Vickers and Yarrow (1991).

13. For a somewhat crude attempt to study the combined effects of labour and product market regulations on economic growth in European countries, see Koedjik and Kremers (1996).

14. The first-level indicators were obtained by turning qualitative information into numerical format using a system of codes (e.g. the presence or the absence of a regulatory provision were assigned different codes) and by ranking the resulting data on individual regulatory provisions on an identical 0-6 scale reflecting the implied degree of restrictiveness of the provisions (from least to most restrictive). Around 70 first-level indicators have been used to construct the two summary indicators of product and labour market regulation.

15. For a similar application of factor analysis in economic research, see Berlage and Terweduwe (1988).

16. Basic indicators of EPL can be found in (OECD, 1999).

17. Indicators i-iv are based on national sources (see Nicoletti et al., 1999); indicators v-vi drew on Centre Européen des Entreprises à Participation Publique, CEEP (1997); and those for non-European countries on Gwartney and Lawson (1997).

18. Indicators i-iv are based on national sources (see Nicoletti et al., 1999); indicators v and vi drew on Logotech (1997) and Bureau of Industry Economics (1996).

19. Indicators i-iii are based on national sources (see Nicoletti and Scarpetta, 1999); indicators iv-v drew on OECD (1997a).

20. In order to increase the coverage, missing values for some of the EU countries were set equal to the values suggested by EC provisions.

21. The dendrogram is a graphical representation of all the possible groups of similar observations that can be obtained from cluster analysis. The graph is tree-structured and should be read left to right (roots to top). In the beginning, the number of groups is equal to the number (N) of observations (the roots). Then the country pair with the lowest distance forms the first group. In the following steps, pairwise comparisons between all remaining countries and between these and the first group are performed and new groups are formed. The points at which two countries (or groups of countries) join are called knots and are numbered progressively from N to (N + K), where (N + K) is the total number of groups and the (N + K)th knot corresponds to the group containing all observations (the top of the tree). As hierarchical clustering unfolds, an index of inter-group similarity is calculated at each juncture. The higher the index the more dissimilar are the observations contained in the groups being joined. Since eventually all countries are grouped together, at some knot rather disparate groups will be forced to join, implying a large jump in the index. The optimal number of groups is often situated at such junctures.

22. It should be stressed, however, that the nature of temporary contracts in the latter is different from most of those in Europe: temporary contracts in Australia are 'casual' jobs offered to young workers who prefer to bargain the non-coverage of pension and health insurance for higher pay.

23. Belgium is a clear outlier in this figure, combining relatively more strict regulations for the creation of sole proprietor enterprises with a fairly large share of self-employment in the business sector.

24. The tax wedge on the use of labour is the ratio of (employers' and employees') social security contributions and income taxes over total labour costs (employers' social security contributions plus gross wages). It should be stressed that the taxes on labour may have an impact on equilibrium employment only in the presence of market imperfections. For example, workers may be able to resist offsetting wage cuts in a collective bargaining framework; unemployment benefits are in some cases fixed or subject to floors and ceilings which weaken their relationship with earnings; and non-labour income effects may be important (Phelps, 1994; Pissarides, 1996).

25. The summary indicator of EPL refers to 1990 and to 1998. The raw indicators of regulations referring to 1990 (on which the summary indicators have been constructed) are from the OECD Jobs Study (1994a,b). The methodology used to construct the time-varying EPL indicator is described in Nicoletti and Scarpetta (1999).

26. In the table, the two variables referring to the centralisation/coordination of the wage bargaining indicate the effects of intermediate or high centralisation/coordination with respect to that of decentralised systems. The distribution of countries according to the different aspects of collective bargaining and changes over time is presented in Elmeskov et al. (1998).

27. The coefficient for intermediate level of bargaining is even larger and more significant if time-varying groupings of centralisation/coordination are replaced by fixed groupings (late 1980s). This can be explained by the fact that moves towards higher centralisation/coordination occurred in the 1980s, while moves towards further decentralisation occurred only in the late 1980s/early 1990s and, consequently, there has been less time for their beneficial effects to surface in the labour market.

28. The non-cyclical, non-agricultural business sector employment rate is calculated as follows: the actual non-agricultural business sector employment rate is calculated from the estimated parameters; then the effect of the cycle is defined on the basis of the coefficient on the output gap as follows: non-cyclical employment rate = actual employment rate – (bgap)*gap, where bgap is the coefficient for the gap in Table 9.4.

29. A positive value of the country-specific effect means that the included explanatory variables would predict a lower-than-observed employment rate, and that other missing variables are needed to explain the residual employment and vice versa.

30. Buti, Pench and Sestito (1998) nicely characterise the presence of an inverse relationship between, on the one hand, 'on-the-job protection', that is, various kind of obstacles to dismissals, and, on the other, 'in-the-market' workers' protection, that is, non-employment benefits.

31. These replacement rates are from the OECD database. The overall summary measure of the generosity of unemployment benefits done by the OECD is based on simple averages of nominal replacement rates over the first five years of unemployment. However, the replacement rates offered in the first year of joblessness may be more important than, say, the benefits provided in the fifth year. Likewise, it may be important to consider actual coverage of benefits.

32. We are aware of the fact that the duration of unemployment may be affected by the duration of benefits. Yet, this 'endogeneity' problem of our measure seems to us to pose less serious problems than giving the same weight to all years of unemployment.

33. Social assistance expenditure is measured according to the OECD Social Expenditure Database.

34. See, for instance, Boeri (1999).

35. Proxy outflow rates are computed as follows: $O_{t,t+1} = I_{t,t+1} - (U_{t+1} - U_t)$ where O denotes proxy outflows, I inflows and U unemployment levels. All primary data come from the OECD Unemployment Duration Database.
36. Eurostat has recently revised classifications of social spending in the context of the ESSPROS (European System of Integrated Social Protection Statistics)
37. We have deliberately excluded Italy from Table 9.10 since replacement rates computed after the introduction of the Mobility Lists are not comparable to those available before 1992, which covered only 'ordinary' unemployment benefits.

REFERENCES

Akerlof, G. (1984), *An Economist's Book of Tales,* Cambridge: Cambridge University Press.

Bentolila, S. and G. Bertola (1990), 'Firing Costs and Labour Demand: How Bad is Eurosclerosis?', *Review of Economic Studies,* No. 57, pp. 381-402.

Bentolila, S. and J.J. Dolado (1994), 'Labour flexibility and wages: Lessons from Spain', *Economic Policy*, No. 18, April.

Bergeijk, P.A.G. Van and R.C.G. Haffner (1996), *Privatisation, Deregulation and the Macroeconomy*, Cheltenham, UK: Edward Elgar.

Berlage, L. and D. Terweduwe (1988), 'The Classification of Countries by Cluster and Factor Analysis', *World Development*, Vol. 16, No. 12, pp. 1527-1545.

Bertola, G. (1990), 'Job Security, Employment and Wages', *European Economic Review,* Vol. 34, North Holland, pp. 851-886.

Bertola, G. (1992), 'Labour turnover costs and average labour demand', *Journal of Labour Economics,* No. 4.

Bertola, G. (1999), 'Microeconomic Perspectives on Aggregated Labour Markets', mimeo. Forthcoming in the *Handbook of Labor Economics,* Vol. 3.

Bertola, G. T. Boeri and S. Cazes (1999), 'Employment Protection and Adjustment: Evolving Institutions and Variable Enforcement in OECD Countries', *ILO Working Papers*, forthcoming.

Bertola, G. and R. Rogerson (1997), 'Institutions and Labor Reallocation', *European Economic Review,* Vol. 41, pp. 1147-1171.

Blanchard, O. (1998), 'Thinking about Unemployment', mimeo.

Blanchard, O. and P. Portugal, (1998), *What Hides Behind an Unemployment Rate: Comparing Portuguese and US Unemployment*, National Bureau of Economic Research, Working Paper No. 6636.

Boeri, T. (1999), 'Enforcement of Employment Security Regulations, On-the-Job Search and Unemployment Duration', *European Economic Review,* Vol. 43, pp. 65-89.

Bureau of Industry Economics (1996), *Business Licenses. International Benchmarking Report 96/9*, Canberra.

Buti, M., L.R. Pench and P. Sestito (1998), 'European unemployment: Contending theories and institutional complexities', *Economic and Financial Reports*, BEI/EIB, Report 98/01.

Calmfors, L. (1998) 'Macroeconomic Policy, Wage Setting and Employment: What Difference Does the EMU Make?', Institute for International Economic Studies, Seminar Paper No. 657.

Calmfors, L. and J. Driffill (1988), 'Bargaining Structure, Corporatism and Macroeconomic Performance', *Economic Policy,* No. 6

Centre Européen des Entreprises à Participation Publique (CEEP) (1997), Annales Statistiques.

Edwards, S. (1998), 'Openness, productivity and growth: what do we really know?', *The Economic Journal*, No. 108, March.

Elmeskov, J., J.P. Martin. and S. Scarpetta. (1998), 'Key Lessons for Labour Market Reforms: Evidence from OECD Countries' Experience', *Swedish Economic Policy Review,* Vol. 5, No. 2, 1998.

Grubb, D. and W. Wells (1993), 'Employment Regulation and Patterns of Work in EC Countries', *OECD Economic Studies,* No. 21, Winter, pp. 7-58.

Gwartney, J. and R. Lawson (1997), *Economic Freedom of the World 1997, Annual Report,* Fraser Institute, Vancouver, B.C.

Hicks, J. (1935), 'Annual survey of economic theory: the theory of monopoly', *Econometrica* Vol. 3, 20.

Jackman, R., R. Layard and S. Nickell, (1996), *Combating Unemployment: Is Flexibility Enough*, Centre for Economic Performance Discussion Paper No. 293.

Koedjik, K. and J. Kremers (1996), 'Market opening, regulation and growth in Europe', *Economic Policy.*

Krueger, A. and J.-S. Pischke (1997), 'Observations and Conjectures on the U.S. Employment Miracle', *Comparative Labor and Politics Journal*, No. 2.

Layard, R., S. Nickell and R. Jackman (1991), *Unemployment, Macroeconomic Performance and the Labour Market*, Oxford: Oxford University Press.

Lazear, E.P. (1990), 'Job Security Provisions and Employment', *The Quarterly Journal of Economics*, August, pp. 699-726.

Lindbeck, A. and D.J. Snower, (1988), *The Insider-Outsider Theory of Employment and Unemployment*, Cambridge, MA: MIT Press.

Logotech (1997), 'Etude comparative internationale des dispositions légales et administratives pour la formation de petites et moyennes entreprises aux pays de l'Union Européenne, les Etats-Unis et le Japon', Projet EIMS 96/142, April.

Nickell, S. (1997), 'Unemployment and Labor Market Rigidities: Europe versus North America', *Journal of Economic Perspectives*, Vol. 11, No. 3, Summer, pp. 55-74.

Nickell, S. (1999), 'Product Markets and Labour Markets', *Labour Economics*, Vol. 6.

Nickell, S. and R. Layard (1998), 'Labour Market Institutions and Economic Performance', Centre for Economic Performance, Discussion Paper No. 407, September. Forthcoming in the *Handbook of Labor Economics*, Vol. 3.

Nicoletti, G., R.C.G. Haffner, S. Nickell, S. Scarpetta and G. Zoega (2000), 'European integration, liberalisation and labour market performance', in G.Bertola, T. Boeri and G. Nicoletti (eds*), Welfare and employment in a united Europe*, Boston, MA: MIT Press.

Nicoletti, G. and S. Scarpetta (1999), *Product and labour market regulations and performance in the OECD labour markets*, OECD, Economics Department Working Paper, forthcoming.

Nicoletti, G., S. Scarpetta and O. Boylaud (1999), *Summary indicators of employment protection legislation and product market regulations for the purpose of international comparisons*, OECD Working Paper, Economics Department.

Noll, R. (1989a), 'Economic Perspectives on the Politics of Regulation' in R. Schmalensee and R.D. Willig (eds), *Handbook of Industrial Organization*, Vol. 2, Amsterdam: North-Holland, pp. 1253-87.

Noll, R. (1989b), 'The Economic Theory of Regulation after a Decade of Deregulation: Comments', *Brookings Papers on Economic Activity: Microeconomics*, pp. 48-58.

OECD (1994*a*), *The OECD Jobs Study: Facts, Analysis, and Strategies*, Paris.

OECD (1994*b*), *The OECD Jobs Study, Evidence and Explorations, Part II*, Paris.

OECD (1997*a*) *Indicators of Tariff and Non-tariff Trade Barriers*, Paris.

OECD (1997*b*), *The OECD Report on Regulatory Reform*, Paris.

OECD (1999*a*), *Employment Outlook*, Paris.

OECD (1999*b*), *Implementing the OECD Jobs Strategy: Assessing Performance and Policy*, Paris.

Office of Management and Budget (1998) US Office of Information and Regulatory Affairs, Draft Report to Congress on the Cost and Benefits of Federal Regulations.

Peltzman, S. (1989), 'The Economic Theory of Regulation after a Decade of Deregulation', *Brookings Papers on Economic Activity: Microeconomics*, pp. 1-41.

Phelps, E. S. (1994), *Structural Slumps: The Modern Equilibrium Theory of Unemployment, Interest and Assets*, Cambridge, MA: Harvard University Press.

Piore, M. (1986), *Labor Market Flexibility*, Berkeley, CA: University of California.

Pissarides, C.A. (1996), 'Unemployment and vacancies in Britain', *Economic Policy*, October.

Saint Paul, G. (1996), *Dual Labour Markets*, Cambridge, MA: The MIT Press.

Scarpetta, S. (1996), 'Assessing the Role of Labour Market Policies and Institutional Settings on Unemployment: A Cross-Country Study', *OECD Economic Studies*, No. 26, 1996/1.

Sinn, H. (1998), *European Integration and the Future of the Welfare State*, CEPR Discussion Papers, No. 1871.

Vickers, J. and G. Yarrow (1991), 'Economic Perspectives on Privatization', *Journal of Economic Perspectives*, Vol. 5, No. 2, pp. 111-132.

Viscusi, W. K., J. M. Vernon and J. E. Harrington, Jr. (1997), *Economics of Regulation and Antitrust*, Cambridge, MA: The MIT Press, pp. 307-311.

Winston, C. (1993), 'Economic Deregulation: Days of Reckoning for Microeconomists', *Journal of Economic Literature*, Vol. XXXI, No. 3, pp. 1263-89.

Winston, C. and R.W. Crandall (1994), 'Explaining Regulatory Policy', *Brookings Papers on Economic Activity: Microeconomics*, Brookings Institution, Washington, D.C., pp. 1-49.

World Bank (1995), *Bureaucrats in Business: The Economics and Politics of Government Ownership*, World Bank Policy Research Reports, World Bank, Washington, D.C.

10. Deregulation and Labour Market Reforms: The Role of the Social Partners

George Gelauff and Marc Pomp[1]

1. INTRODUCTION

Flexible labour markets are often seen as part of the solution to the European unemployment problem, and as a way to adjust to asymmetric shocks in an integrating Europe. Therefore, deregulation and reform of labour market institutions are high on the policy agenda. In this paper we focus not on the desirability of such reforms, but on how labour market reform is achieved, an issue that has received relatively little attention in the literature (an exception is Saint Paul, 1996). In particular, we look at the role of the social partners (organised labour and employers' organisations) in the reform process. In some countries, e.g. the UK, conflicts with organised labour accompanied policies aimed at increasing flexibility. In other countries unions and employers' organisations cooperated in making labour market institutions more flexible.

This raises the question of how the involvement of social partners affects the reform process. We address this question through a case study of the Dutch experience with involving social partners in labour market reforms. To this end we use a broad definition of labour market reforms, encompassing reforms of wage-bargaining institutions, social security reforms and reforms of labour market regulations. The reason for choosing the Netherlands is not just that we are both familiar with this country, but also that in recent years the Netherlands is seen as a case of successful involvement of the social partners in policy-making. From this case study we draw a number of tentative lessons which we then apply to the experiences in four other countries (UK, Italy, Austria and Germany). This allows us to assess in what respects the Dutch experience was special and in what respects other countries have had similar experiences. The ultimate aim of this comparative analysis is to assess when involving the social partners in the reform process is a feasible option.

The paper is organised as follows. To start with, Section 2 briefly reviews the debate on labour market flexibility. Section 3 presents a case study of the Dutch reforms since 1982, focusing on the role of the social partners. The section concludes with a number of tentative lessons. Section 4 compares the Dutch experience with reforms undertaken in four other European countries. Through this comparison we attempt to 'test' the conclusions drawn from the Dutch case study. This allows us to assess whether other countries were confronted with similar challenges as the Netherlands, and if so whether they responded in similar ways. Again, our focus in this comparison is on the involvement of social partners in the reform process. Section 5 presents the conclusions.

2. LABOUR MARKET FLEXIBILITY: A BRIEF REVIEW OF THE DEBATE

The causal link between unemployment (or, more broadly, economic performance) and labour market flexibility is subject to much debate. In this section we very briefly summarise the theoretical and empirical literature on the benefits of flexibility. The main message is one of substantial disagreement over the benefits of increased flexibility.

By a flexible labour market we mean a labour market in which wages and employment respond quickly to changing circumstances.[2] With respect to wage flexibility a distinction may be drawn between nominal and real flexibility. Similarly, with respect to employment flexibility a distinction may be drawn between internal flexibility (flexibility in the number of hours per worker or in the distribution of hours worked over the days in a week) and external flexibility (flexibility in hiring and firing).

According to a widely shared view, increased labour market flexibility leads to lower unemployment: 'Policies to reduce labour market rigidities and improve flexibility are likely to reduce the size and duration of adverse movements in unemployment associated with exogenous disturbances and make it easier to close output gaps'. (OECD, 1994, p. 69). Empirical evidence indicating that flexibility leads to higher employment is presented in Di Tella and MacCulloch (1998), using a subjective flexibility index based on interviews.

Others are skeptical about the importance of at least some types of labour market rigidities. For example, Nickell (1997) argues that strict employment protection legislation and general legislation on labour market standards do not appear to have serious implications for average levels of unemployment (p. 72). This conclusion is based on econometric work using proxies for employment restrictions.

Abraham and Houseman (1995) go beyond one-dimensional flexibility indicators and argue that internal flexibility (i.e. varying working hours per worker) is relatively easy in Germany because of short-time arrangements, whereas in the US flexibility is mainly external, taking the form of hiring and firing. They conclude that 'strong worker job security can be compatible with employers' need for flexibility in staffing levels.' (Abraham and Houseman, 1995, p. 308).

Since the subject of this paper is the role of the social partners in labour market flexibility, an obvious question is: what determines unions' attitudes towards flexibility? The literature puts forward three main determinants: insider-outsider considerations, internalisation of externalities and vulnerability to hold-up situations. Firstly, insider-outsider theories (Lindbeck and Snower, 1988) suggest that there is no unambiguous answer to this question, and that the answer is likely to differ across types of flexibility. For example, one would expect that unions are especially opposed to flexibility-enhancing measures that undermine the bargaining position of insiders such as lowering firing restrictions of permanent workers. But some flexibility-increasing measures may reinforce the position of insiders. For example, Coe and Snower (1997) present evidence that in Spain the introduction of fixed-term contracts (in itself a flexibility-increasing measure) reduced the risk of lay-offs for staff on permanent contracts. This raised their bargaining power, and reduced flexibility of insider wages.

A second important determinant of union attitudes towards flexibility is likely to be the bargaining level. In a seminal paper Calmfors and Driffill (1988) argue that centralised unions have an incentive to internalise externalities in wage bargaining. In their model both completely decentralised and highly centralised wage bargaining lead to wage flexibility. Under decentralised bargaining workers have little bargaining power. As a result, the wage bargain is close to the market-clearing outcome. With a high degree of centralisation trade unions internalise the effects of higher wages on job opportunities. This leads to wage moderation.

These ideas may be extended to bargaining over employment regulations. Applying the same reasoning as above, we would expect that under centralised bargaining unions would be more willing to abolish flexibility-reducing regulations if this leads to lower unemployment.

In a third line of reasoning, recent analysis of bargaining regimes indicates that centralised bargaining may even outperform decentralised bargaining in important respects (Teulings and Hartog, 1998). The key insight of their analysis is that centralised bargaining reduces the hold-up problem which arises when ex-post renegotiation opens the possibility for a party to attract a larger share of the rents from relationship-specific investments than ex-ante agreed upon (see Box 1 below).

Box 1. The hold-up problem

The hold-up problem arises if contracting parties substantially invest in relationship-specific assets, characterised by sunk costs, and if in addition contracts are incomplete. Sunk costs are costs that are irrecoverable once made. Once the relationship-specific investment has been made, the investing party can be forced to accept a worsening in the terms of the relationship, because the investment cannot be put to an alternative use without substantial losses. As a consequence, the investing party has been held up (Milgrom and Roberts, 1992, pp. 136 and 307; Armstrong et al., 1994, p. 138). Of course the investing party is aware of the possibility of ex-post opportunism. Therefore, if the party that benefits from the investment cannot convince the investing party of its commitment to keep to the initial agreement, the fear of becoming vulnerable to ex-post opportunism can induce the investing party to abstain from profitable investments. As a consequence, welfare-improving value creation has been curbed.

In the context of a firm-worker relationship, hold-up problems arise because labour contracts do not fully specify the division of rents from relationship-specific investments. Relationship-specific investments only pay off when a relationship continues (Teulings and Hartog, 1998, p. 66). Examples of relationship-specific investments by workers are training and on-the-job learning to operate the firm's equipment, or buying a house close to the workplace. In addition, appropriate utilisation of a firm's investments in equipment often also depends on good labour relationships. It is not feasible to determine the productivity and pay rises that should result from every type of investment in all future circumstances. Hence, employers and employees are vulnerable to possible exploitation by the other party once they have invested in their mutual labour relationship. They fear that the other party grasps the fruits of their cooperative stance (Marsden, 1995), since they have little means to enforce commitment. For instance, once employers have invested in equipment, workers may threaten to quit or shirk on the job unless they receive higher wages. Likewise, employers may threaten to fire workers who have invested in relationship-specific assets in order to lower their wages. As a result of incomplete contracts, a lack of commitment discourages shared investments in firm-specific quality. Since these investments raise productivity, the hold-up problem curtails welfare.

Hence, preventing renegotiation solves the hold-up problem. Nominal wage contracts that a priori specify future wages, for instance in the form of indexation, reduce the hold-up problem, because they reduce the likelihood of future renegotiation (Malcomson, 1997). An example to which we shall return in Section 4 was the 'scala mobile' in Italy. However, indexation is an imperfect solution. External shocks may require renegotiation of the contract, which again raises the risk of a hold-up situation. Under centralised bargaining, central interest organisations renegotiate the contract, independent from the specific circumstances in particular firms. For the actors at the firm level renegotiation is outside their control and therefore they are unable to adjust the terms of the agreement to their ex post bargaining strength. As a result, centralised bargaining limits the hold-up risk while at the same time enhancing wage flexibility in response to aggregate shocks.

A decentralised bargaining system lacks this type of flexibility. Therefore under decentralised bargaining individual workers and employers have no alternative but to stick to their ex ante nominal wage contract until the outside option becomes binding, in other words until one of the parties terminates the contract. For example, a large negative shock may lead the employer to end the labour contract by dismissing the workers. Consequently, under a decentralised bargaining system, like in the United States, flexibility mainly follows from separation, migration of employees and lower wages for new hires. This type of micro-flexibility may be a second-best response to a lack of aggregate flexibility (Teulings and Hartog, 1998, p. 6).

From the perspective of the government, a potential advantage of involving social partners in the policy-making process is that such involvement may help in policy implementation. There are two reasons for this. First, social partners have superior information about their members' situation and preferences compared to the government. Moreover, they are better able to communicate proposals to their members by taking recourse to a common set of values and perceptions. Second, because social partners are accountable to their members it is more credible that their actions (compared to those of the government) serve the interests of their members (Streeck and Schmitter, 1991; CEPR, 1993). Therefore, if the government tries to implement a policy without involving unions and employers' organisations, it will be less successful than if it implements the same policy with social partners' involvement.

3. LESSONS FROM THE NETHERLANDS?

3.1 Introduction

What does the Dutch experience teach us about the involvement of social partners in the reform of institutions that relate to the labour market? This is a relevant question since it is widely perceived that the impressive employment performance of the Netherlands over the past 15 years is somehow related to the role played by the social partners. In this connection the so-called Wassenaar agreement of 1982 between the social partners is often seen as a watershed. However, involvement of the social partners has not always been beneficial. During the stagflationary 1970s and early 1980s, involvement of the social partners in economic policy-making impeded the adjustment process leading to a deep crisis of the Dutch 'consultation economy'. The way social partners supervised and implemented social security caused a second crisis in the early 1990s. These two crises initiated a reform process, which substantially altered the role and position of the social partners in socio-economic policy.

The reform process revitalised the Dutch consultation economy through a stronger separation of responsibilities between the government and the social partners. At the same time the consultation process shifted towards general recommendations on institutions relevant to employees and employers such as flexible contracts or minimum wages. Because of these characteristics, current Dutch labour market institutions may match demands towards flexibility, experimentation and diversity raised by social, technological and international trends.

The aim of this section is to draw lessons from the shifts in the Dutch consultation economy. The following section summarises the institutional setting. Section 3.3 reviews the performance of the Dutch economy since the 1970s (for more extensive discussion see Van Ark et al., 1996; Bovenberg, 1997; CPB, 1997; Visser and Hemerijck, 1997). Section 3.4 turns to the crises in the consultation economy and social security. Section 3.5 derives lessons from the Dutch experience.

3.2 Institutional setting

The Netherlands presents a clear example of a socio-economic order based on cooperative exchange. Cooperative exchange involves bargained consultation and cooperation between a limited number of otherwise independent agents with different preferences. In the Netherlands sectoral bargaining prevails, yet tripartite coordination on a national level increases the extent of centralisation. Dutch trade unions usually follow the recommendations of their confederations as a starting point for negotiations, although these guidelines allow some freedom for variations in bargaining positions across sectoral trade unions to take account of sector-specific conditions (de Kam et al., 1995). As a counterbalance, employer confederations decide upon a common position vis-à-vis trade unions as well, although this common position is not binding (IDS, 1995). Based on the general positions of confederations, consultation and discussion at an economy-wide level between employers' and unions' confederations takes place in the bipartite Foundation of Labour (Stichting van de Arbeid). The government is also involved in this process. The discussions in the Foundation of Labour occasionally lead to economy-wide recommendations that serve as guidelines for negotiations the sectoral level.

Until 1982, the Dutch government was strongly involved in wage formation. Government influence evolved from direct wage determination by the government until 1963 to collective bargaining between trade unions and employers' associations, influenced by the government through wage interventions and consensus-building. Tripartite wage debates between the government and confederations in order to reach consensus on 'sensible wage growth' were common practice. Persuasion was usually directed at the Foundation of Labour, the meeting place of employer and worker representatives at the economy-wide level (Korver, 1993). Between 1963 and 1982, direct wage interventions regularly took place. The 1982 agreement of the Foundation of Labour (the Wassenaar agreement) made social partners more independent and coincided with the end of direct wage interventions.

In addition, discussions and consultations over socio-economic policy take place in the tripartite Social and Economic Council. The Social and Economic Council consists of three equal-sized groups of representatives of unions, employers' organisations and independent experts. Until 1995 a legal obligation existed for the government to consult the Social and Economic Council on issues of socio-economic policy.

Central coordination and tripartite concertation make the Netherlands a prototype of a socio-economic order based on cooperative exchange. Lehmbruch's scale of corporatism – the best of several such scales according to Teulings and Hartog (1998, p. 29) – ranks the Netherlands second after Austria (see Table 10.1).

A final important feature of Dutch labour market institutions is mandatory extension of collective agreements to the entire industry (Hartog and Theeuwes, 1997, p. 162). Extension is not automatic, but requires the consent of the Minister of Social Affairs and Employment. Through mandatory extension, unions have much more influence than would be concluded on the basis of union membership alone. This is illustrated by the fact that although only about 25 per cent of all workers belong to a union, almost 75 per cent are covered by a collectively bargained agreement.

Table 10.1 Lehmbruch's ranking of corporatism

1	Austria	7	Finland	13	Italy
2	Netherlands	8	Ireland	14	United States
3	Sweden	9	Switzerland	15	Canada
4	Norway	10	Japan	16	Australia
5	Denmark	11	France	17	New Zealand
6	Germany	12	United Kingdom		

Source: Teulings and Hartog (1998, p. 30).

3.3 Performance: deep fall and gradual recovery

Throughout the OECD, stagflation characterised 1973-82, yet the Dutch economy was particularly hard hit. Already during the 1960s and early 1970s, Dutch real wages surged ahead of the northwest European average (van Ark et al., 1996, p. 296). Wage increases led to a sharp increase of real labour costs. Export prices only partially followed wage increases in order to prevent a loss of world market shares. As a consequence, profitability in exposed sectors fell. The first hike in oil prices further depressed profitability. Inactivity rose, not only in terms of unemployment but also in terms of disability benefit recipients (see Figure 10.1). Expansionary government policies and higher social benefits raised public expenditure.

The second oil crisis together with the restrictive worldwide monetary policy of the early 1980s led to a deep recession. The Netherlands got caught in a vicious circle. The growth in the number of benefit recipients raised public expenditure on social security, which required increases in taxes and social security contributions. This led to an increase in labour costs, declining labour demand, and a further increase in inactivity. To a certain degree rising public deficits limited the increase of taxes and contributions, but at the price of an accelerating government debt.

In the early 1980s all alarm bells were ringing. Unemployment had reached 12 per cent of the labour force in 1983. This is shown in Figure 10.2, which also depicts the unemployment histories for the countries discussed in Section 4 of the paper.

Figure 10.1 Number of benefit recipients below 65 years in the Netherlands, 1970-95

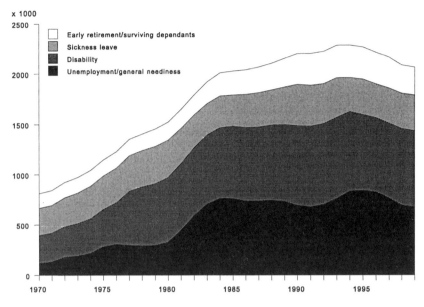

Figure 10.2 Unemployment, 1975-98

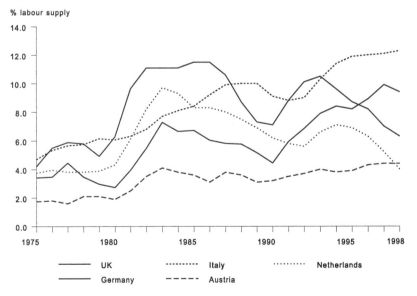

The number of disability benefit recipients had quadrupled over 1970-85 (van Ark et al., 1996, p. 319). Public expenditure had soared from 31 per cent of GDP in 1960 to 60 per cent in the early 1980s, largely caused by rising income transfers and interest payments. The public deficit approached 7 per cent of GDP in 1982.

The new centre-right government that came into office in November 1982 broke the vicious circle. It initiated a policy of budgetary restraint, unlinked public sector wages and social security benefits from wages in the private sector, and cut statutory unemployment benefit levels from 80 per cent to 70 per cent of gross wages (see Figure 10.3). Moreover, it exerted considerable pressure on the social partners to reach an agreement to moderate wages. With almost 10 per cent of the labour force unemployed, and expectations diminished by some ten years' experience with crisis, the bargaining position of the unions had become very weak. This led to the above mentioned bipartite 'Wassenaar' agreement that abolished automatic cost-of-living wage indexation in exchange for working-time reduction. An explicit aim of the agreement was to restore profitability.

Figure 10.3 Minimum wage and modal wage, 1970-95

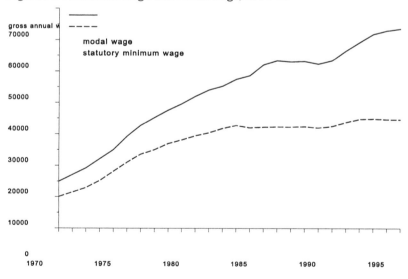

In the following years these developments resulted in substantial wage moderation, which contributed to an improvement in the labour market. In addition, an attempt was made to break the vicious circle of rising inactivity and rising public expenditure through far-reaching reforms of social security regulation. Employment growth gradually picked up and unemployment fell. Budgetary restraint controlled the public sector deficit. Public spending fell by some 10 percentage points over 1983-96. Once the public deficit had approached acceptable levels in the 1990s, the government could support wage moderation with tax reduction.

A strong increase in labour supply made extra demands on the Dutch labour market. Over 1969-98, the growth rate of Dutch labour supply (in persons) averaged 1 per cent per year, much higher than in most other OECD countries. This was due to a rapid growth in the population in the relevant age brackets and an increase in female participation rates. Employment growth not only had to be sufficient to reduce unemployment but also had to absorb the large number of people that entered the labour market.

A considerable part of the increase in employment after 1982 consists of part-time and flexible labour contracts. Part-time work has become a key feature of the Dutch labour market (OECD, 1995, p.61). It accounts for three- quarters of the growth of employment since 1983. Currently 30 per cent of Dutch workers have a part-time contract and 9 per cent a flexible contract (the two categories partially overlap) (Bovenberg, 1997, p. 20). The share of part-time work is some 10 to 15 percentage points lower in other OECD countries (CPB, 1997, p. 296).

Worker preferences are a dominant reason for part-time work (Delsen, 1995). Part-time work is characterised by a fixed number of working hours and a contract that is usually of unlimited duration. It enhances working-time flexibility in response to predictable fluctuations in work loads, in particular if part-time workers can be employed at more busy hours (OECD, 1994, p. 93). The growth of part-time employment in the Netherlands is strongly related to the increase of female labour force participation (Delsen, 1995).

Temporary contracts through a temporary work agency (TWA) are also relatively widely used. A flexible contract is characterised by a limited duration or a variable number of contractual working hours. The share of temporary worker increased towards approximately 3 per cent of total employment in 1995 (CPB, 1997). The predominant motivation to hire this type of flexible workers is to deal with fluctuations, temporary assignments or to replace absent workers (Van Bolhuis, 1996). This type of contract provides employment or working-hour flexibility.

3.4 The other side of the coin: What went wrong in the Netherlands?

If, as argued in Section 2, cooperative exchange is strong in dealing with aggregate shocks, then what explains the dismal performance of the Dutch economy during the stagflationary 1970s and early 1980s when the country was hit by large macro-economic shocks? We believe that at least part of the answer must be sought in institutional flaws. Two main sets of institutions failed during the 1970s and 1980s: firstly the consultation economy, i.e. the system of cooperative exchange itself, and secondly social security. Both failures directly involved the unions and employers' organisations. What lessons do these failures provide?

Failure of the consultation economy

During the stagflationary period of the 1970s and early 1980s, the Dutch socio-economic and political order failed as an effective device for crisis management (Hemerijck, 1993; Visser and Hemerijck, 1997). In the period 1973-82, unions and employers' organisations failed to reach successful agreements in the Foundation of Labour and disagreed in the Social and Economic Council on the goals of economic policy, while economic growth stagnated and unemployment surged.

This failure to deal with macro-shocks can be traced to three fundamental causes: insider power, a macro hold-up problem and government involvement in cooperative exchange. Insider power inhibits internalisation of external effects. As noted in Section 2, centralised unions may internalise the effects of the bargaining outcome on outsiders, but there is no guarantee that they will do so completely. The weight attached to the interests of outsiders is likely to depend on several factors, including the labour market situation. The tightening of the labour market in the 1960s had created union member militancy and had shifted power away from central trade union confederations towards their member unions. This reduced the encompassing character of corporatist associations. As a result they were less able to internalise the external effects of their actions.

The second cause concerns a hold-up problem at the aggregate level. Centralised bargaining to a certain degree replaces the hold-up problem at the firm level by a hold-up problem at the aggregate level. Like firm-level relationships, centralised relationships may suffer from commitment and coordination problems. Eichengreen (1996) presents the basic argument. At the central level, capital and labour enter into an agreement to finance investment and thus economic growth through wage moderation. For various reasons the agreement is an incomplete contract. If this were a one-shot game, then both parties would have an incentive to renege on the contract after the ex-ante agreed investment had been made. Workers may demand high wages to extract quasi-rents, capitalists may pay out profits in the form of dividends and refuse to reinvest. Recognition of this risk leads to underinvestment: the hold-up problem. However, since capital and labour expect to continue to play subsequent rounds of this game in the future, they are playing a dynamic rather than a one-shot game. In this dynamic game, both parties may under certain conditions have an incentive to stick to their promises. Recognition of this may avoid the hold-up problem. Whether it is beneficial to stick to promises depends inter alia on the expected returns to investment (part of which accrues to labour in the form of higher wages). If the expected returns to investment are high, then the high investment-cum-wage moderation scenario unfolds. If on the other hand the expected returns from investment are low, then the low investment-cum-excessive wage claims scenario unfolds.

In particular during the stagflationary period, the Dutch consultation economy (along with other economies) may have suffered from this central-level hold-up situation. During the 1950s and 1960s, the expansion of institutions such as social security or employment protection strengthened the position of labour in the intertemporal bargain with capital. However, labour did not exploit its improved bargaining position because it expected to benefit from moderate wage demands in the expectation that profits would be invested in projects yielding high rates of return. In a time of high economic growth and a situation of labour shortage this met little resistance from the side of capital (see Caballero and Hammour, 1998, for a formal analysis). When economic growth fell, amongst others due to less room for technological catching up with the US, the benefits of a joint relationship fell and labour changed its bargaining behaviour. As a consequence, capital refused to invest. Unemployment restored general equilibrium, because it weakened the bargaining position of labour.

The third reason for the failing consultation economy concerned the involvement of the government in the consultation and bargaining process. The way in which the government was involved in this process, rather than government involvement per se, seriously complicated decision-making. Deliberation and consultation took much time and the government tried to influence behaviour of the social partners with measures that with hindsight turned out to be misdirected. For instance, in 1974 the government established the full linkage of public-sector wages and social security benefits to private-sector wages (Hemerijck, 1993, p. 169). The aim was to induce voluntary wage restraint of unions by establishing institutional solidarity between wage earners and people depending on social security. Prime minister Den Uyl and Social Affairs Minister Boersma believed that the linking mechanism, guaranteeing a parallel development of earnings and benefits, combined with progressive fiscal policies would help to contain social spending costs because it would induce the unions to limit wage rises (Toirkens, 1988; Hemerijck, 1995). In addition, it was argued that these linking mechanisms would act as automatic stabilisers in an economic downturn.

Of course, according to current insights a high replacement rate is not exactly conducive to wage moderation. Moreover, when real wage increases exceeded productivity growth these automatic stabilisers turned into automatic de-stabilisers: inactivity and rising benefit levels called for higher social security premiums, which fed back into higher wage demands because of shifting forward of tax and premium incidence.

Through its involvement in the social contract the government limited the incentive for social partners to internalise the external effects of their bargaining agreements. Employees and employers did not fully pay for the increase in social security benefits, since social security outlays were partly financed out of taxes on pensioners and through a considerable increase in government debt.

Failure of social security
The Dutch social security system in the mid-1980s was very vulnerable to economic crisis. Several institutional aspects of the system contributed to this vulnerability: high benefit levels, limited monitoring of benefit claimants, imperfect supervision and a lack of financial incentives. From an international perspective benefit levels in the Netherlands were relatively generous, in particular for unemployment and disability insurance. In addition, generous extra-statutory arrangements supplementing the statutory scheme protected Dutch employees from income loss during illness.

The Dutch social security system was also weak in monitoring claimants. Sickness absenteeism in the Netherlands has traditionally been assessed only on the basis of random checks by so-called 'lay controllers' (see Prins, 1990). This monitoring device, while protecting privacy, is less effective in fighting moral hazard. The Dutch integrated disability insurance system, which is unique in the world, does not distinguish between disability due to occupational risks and social risks. Disability insurance due to occupational risks lends itself well to a detailed description of the insured risk, facilitating direct regulation of the inflow into the scheme. However, disability due to social risk is difficult to verify especially if subjective complaints are a sufficient ground for claiming benefits. Finally, in the Netherlands, the privacy of the unemployment insurance benefit recipients was relatively well protected. For instance, no cross-check of computer records took place against other social insurance funds. This complicated the verification of information.

Independent supervision of the benefit administration has long been lacking in the Netherlands. The social partners, who were strongly involved on the operational side, were also responsible for supervision. Already before WWII, social security was administered by a broad range of administrative organisations. In 1945 proposals for reform met with strong opposition from the social partners united in the Foundation of Labour and failed. For 18 branches of industry separately, industry insurance associations (Bedrijfsverenigingen) administered unemployment, sickness and disability insurance. These were representative organisations of employees and employers. Formal supervision was in the hands of the tripartite Social Insurance Council.[3] However, social partners preferred to arrange organisational issues in the bipartite Federation of Industry Insurance Associations, which made the Social Insurance Council largely ineffective. Mixed and unclear responsibilities hampered the efficacy of the tripartite Social Insurance Council. Also the Social and Economic Council, the tripartite body that advised on socio-economic policy (see above), was hardly an example of decisiveness. In 1967 the Minister of Social Affairs asked the Social and Economic Council to advise on simplification of the organisation and supervision of social security. After 17 years, the council published its advice: 'Involvement of the social partners in the execution and supervision of social security was indispensable for the proper functioning of the Dutch welfare state' (Visser and Hemerijck, 1997, p. 144).

Cooperative exchange in the organisation and supervision of social security led to large-scale shirking of responsibilities. All parties involved had an interest in a generous administration, in particular for disability benefits. Employers used disability insurance to lay off workers 'in a social way'. The workers involved gained from a high disability benefit until the end of their working life. The interest of the government was to keep official unemployment figures low. Eventually, quickly and generously granting a benefit became synonymous with an efficient benefit administration.

Finally, the Netherlands did not use any financial incentives in the administration of social security. For instance, until 1994, most Dutch employers faced little financial incentive to combat sickness absenteeism because benefits for most firms were paid by a sectoral fund. In contrast, German employers were financially responsible for the sickness payments during the first six weeks of illness of an employee. German absenteeism rates due to illness were around 30 per cent lower than Dutch rates until the end of 1993.

In conclusion, the Netherlands provided not only high benefits but also did not seriously monitor the eligibility of claimants for benefits. Regulation and supervision of the benefit administration were inadequate. Financial incentives to encourage decentralised administrators to reduce the inflow and increase the outflow were lacking. Hence, the Dutch system invited moral hazard of benefit recipients, employers and the benefit administration. This set the stage for failure of the system, failure which became apparent only gradually in the late 1970s and the beginning of the 1980s when the Dutch economy was hit by adverse macroeconomic shocks and a vicious circle of rising inactivity and rising labour costs set in. Since the problems were concentrated among the unskilled, a paradoxical result was that the welfare state failed to promote social cohesion. High taxes and premiums raised labour costs while high replacement rates at the lower income levels implied high reservation wages, low search intensity and a compressed wage structure. These factors combined to reduce demand for low-productivity workers. Hence, the loss of employment was concentrated among low-skilled workers. Prolonged periods of inactivity eroded their human capital and working habits, making unemployment for these groups difficult to reverse.

3.5 Reform

Reform of the consultation economy

The dismal economic performance and the failure of the consultation economy initiated a reform process. As indicated in Section 3.3, from the end of 1982 onwards the new Dutch government broke the deadlock by taking a more independent position in cooperative exchange (see also Hemerijck, 1993, Visser and Hemerijck, 1997). In this way, stagflation led to a major internal reform process of the Dutch socio-economic order. Existing institutions were not abolished but given a new interpretation. The more independent position of the government changed the bargaining position of the social partners and increased flexibility in decision-making. At the same time, because the institutional framework had not been abolished, some degree of commitment remained. Once agreement had been reached on the longer-term common goal of restoring profitability and employment in the Foundation of Labour agreement of November 1982, the institutional framework and the participants' experience with consultation facilitated a joint approach to address economic and social issues. The 1980s and 1990s witnessed a number of successful bilateral agreements between the social partners.

The 1992 agreement in the Social and Economic Council (SER, 1992) codifies the internal reform of the consultation economy that had taken place during the 1980s (see also Rinnooy Kan, 1993, p. 45). It identified three cornerstones: a clear division of responsibilities between government and social partners, consultation to identify areas that require policy action, and application of specific policy instruments to implement these actions by each of the actors in their specific area of responsibility.

As to the first cornerstone, SER (1992, p. 119) specifies the following division of responsibilities. Wage negotiations and agreements concerning conditions of employment are primarily responsibilities of the social partners. Fiscal and monetary policies are primarily responsibilities of the government and the central bank. Employment and labour market policies are a joint responsibility of the government and the social partners.

The second cornerstone, consultation, remains an essential element of the model, but it has changed considerably. The character of consultation shifted from result-oriented bargaining to 'enabling agreements' that identify common policy interests, specify general guiding lines or define boundary conditions. The government and social partners no longer bargain over mutual concessions, like trading tax reduction for wage moderation, or aim at reaching consensus over 'sensible wage growth'. As a consequence, agreements no longer specify a detailed outcome for which the parties involved should strive, such as a specific level of wages and taxes. Instead the purpose of consultation is to develop common policy orientations. Agreements contain non-binding qualitative recommendations on specific topics like training, youth unemployment or minimum wages.

As a third cornerstone, each of the three parties, i.e. employers' organisations, unions and the government, applies its specific policy instruments to implement the general enabling agreements. The phrase 'policy instruments' should be seen in a broad perspective. Generally, central organisations only recommend or try to convince sectoral organisations or individual companies to implement certain measures.

The 1996 'flexicurity' agreement in the Foundation of Labour is an example of the operation of the consultation economy after reform. Before taking policy measures to enhance labour market flexibility, Dutch policy-makers consulted the Foundation of Labour. The advice of the employers' and employees' representatives in the Foundation traded more security for workers through temporary work agencies (TWAs) against more flexibility in hiring and firing regulations (see Box 2). In the following years the 'flexicurity' agreement formed the basis of new legislation, which largely followed the recommendations of the Foundation of Labour. As of January 1 1999, the law has been operational. The first results are mixed. Cases have been reported in the press where temporary workers lost their job because employers refused to give them a permanent position. In other cases the law fits in the tendency of TWAs to invest in their employees.

Box 2. Flexibility advice of the social partners, 1996

In 1996, the social partners in the Foundation of Labour agreed upon the so-called 'flexicurity' advice. This advice combined security for workers at Temporary Work Agencies (TWAs) with flexibility in employment regulation. It comprises the following main elements:

More security
With respect to temporary work through TWAs:
• Flexible workers through TWAs can get a fixed-term labour relation with the TWA for the duration of their assignment, but after three assignments and a minimum total tenure with the TWA, they finally get a contract for unlimited duration.

More flexibility
With respect to firing rules:
• The maximum period of notice can be reduced to 4 months.
• The period of authorisation and the period of notice can partly overlap.
With respect to temporary work through TWAs:
• Abolish the legal maximum on the duration of the temporary assignments.
• TWAs do not need a licence.
With respect to fixed-term contracts:
• The introduction of a (short) probationary period for fixed-term contracts.
• More scope to renew a fixed-term contract (without the previously required period of 31 days in between).

Source: STAR Foundation of Labour (1996).

Social security reforms

In the mid-1980s the number of social security recipients had reached a level where every working person had to support almost one benefit recipient. Consensus emerged that reform of the social security system was called for. The system had become counterproductive in achieving the objectives for which it was set up. Rather than stabilising shocks and protecting solidarity, it had resulted in the persistence of employment losses, reduced access of vulnerable groups to the labour market, and a vicious circle eroding the economic base for providing generous benefits.

In the mid-1980s, reforms aimed primarily at fighting moral hazard of workers and benefit recipients by reducing the level of benefits. Minimum benefits fell compared to the average wage level by freezing the minimum wage, to which these benefits are linked, in nominal terms during most years and even lowering it by 3 per cent in 1984. As described above, in 1982 the government unilaterally, and against union opposition, took the decision to cut the link between benefits and private wages. The government used a strategy of small steps, which year after year cut back slightly on the welfare state, to prevent major social conflict. Thus, unemployment benefits and statutory disability and sickness benefits were cut in several steps from 80 per cent to 70 per cent of final pay during the 1984-86 period, once more against union opposition. The unions even offered a wage freeze if the government would withdraw the proposed cut in social security benefit levels. But the government declined the offer. The 1984 policy proposal to cut public sector wages, minimum wages and benefits by 3 per cent encountered strong union opposition. Public sector unions 'organised their largest ever postwar strike, only to find out that they had become isolated' (Visser and Hemerijck, 1997, p. 101).

These reductions in statutory benefit levels were not very successful in substantially reducing the number of recipients of social insurance benefits, in part because supplementary arrangements negotiated by social partners offset some of the cuts in disability and sickness benefits. The deeper problem was that the social partners did not fully internalise the adverse effects of higher benefits on moral hazard because the public statutory scheme paid most of the benefits. This combination of public and supplementary private insurance gives rise to over-insurance (see Teulings and Van der Ploeg, 1993, and Lindbeck, 1994). Social partners have few incentives to introduce measures or arrangements to prevent the insured event, because the public insurance fund would reap most of the gains.

In 1987 measures were introduced to combat moral hazard of workers and benefit recipients. In particular, eligibility conditions and screening of benefit recipients were tightened by introducing waiting periods before being entitled to benefits, tightening the disability and unemployment criteria, and introducing more insurance elements in unemployment insurance by linking benefits more closely to work history. However, these measures did not change the role of social partners in the administration and supervision of social security.

This step was finally taken in the 1990s, when social insurance was reformed more fundamentally by affecting the behaviour of employers, benefit administrations and supervisory bodies. The discretionary room of benefit administrators was reduced through new regulation so as to cut the inflows into the various schemes. Later on, financial incentives were introduced to reconcile discretionary decision-making with spending control and an active policy of returning claimants back to work. Other recent reforms aim at reducing the role of the public sector in executing sickness and disability schemes by relying more on competition between private insurance companies and public agencies.

The reforms of the early 1990s, and in particular the 1991 measures to reform disability insurance, caused severe social turmoil. Employers and employees in the Social and Economic Council could not agree on disability reform (Visser and Hemerijck, 1997, p. 141). The government took its own responsibility and announced measures to reform disability and sickness insurance, reducing the level of protection. 'On 17 September 1991, on the invitation of the entire union movement, nearly one million people marched the streets of The Hague in what was probably the largest such demonstration in Dutch history.' (Visser and Hemerijck, 1997, p. 117). The Social Democrats, who took part in the government that took the reform measures, lost a third of their members and a quarter of their electorate during the 1994 elections. Relationships with the unions were at an all-time low (Visser and Hemerijck, 1997, p. 142).

Subsequent measures removed the social partners from the supervision of social security administration. After the Public Audit Office concluded, and a Parliamentary inquiry later confirmed, that the absence of independent supervision had contributed to the unbridled growth of social security outlays, supervision of employee insurance was delegated to an independent body, the Social Insurance Supervisory Commission (CTSV). This body, set up in 1995, was established to introduce more checks and balances and to clarify and separate responsibilities in the governance structure of social insurance.

3.6   Lessons

Over the past decade centralised bargaining and consultation seems to deliver quite good results. However, during the 1970s and early 1980s, this was not the case. What, then, has changed? We draw a number of lessons:

Dealing with macroeconomic shocks
1.   The first lesson from the Dutch reform process emphasises the need for a quick response to a crisis. The Dutch reforms only took place after the country reached a desperate socio-economic situation and taking action

became inevitable. However, by then it had become very difficult to reduce inactivity levels.

Three fundamental causes may be identified behind these time lags: insider power, a macro-hold up problem, and government involvement. Institutional reform has partly solved the first and last problem. The extent to which the second problem has been solved remains uncertain. On the one hand the decline in unemployment during the past few years has strengthened the bargaining position of labour. On the other hand, globalisation and EMU have strengthened the bargaining position of capital (since the threat of capital flight has become more credible). This should help in moderating wage demands.

Institutional reform
2. Institutional reform may entail deregulation to enhance flexibility, but may also entail regulation. In particular social security requires a sufficient degree of regulation to guarantee that benefits accrue to those who really need them. It also requires a large degree of government policy discretion to take necessary reform measures. This does not comply with strong involvement of social partners in the implementation and regulation of social security. Reforms undertaken during the past 20 years indicate that this lesson has been learned. Thus reform of the social security system established a larger degree of government control and diminished the role of the social partners. However, further reforms that are currently under discussion will once again strengthen the involvement of the social partners in social security. It remains to be seen whether sufficient checks and balances have been introduced to avoid the unfavourable effects of social partners involvement.
3. Reforms do not always require a change in regulations. Informal reforms in which parties find new roles within existing institutions do not require a long process of institutions building.
4. Centralised consultation together with decentralised implementation may strengthen labour market flexibility. Consultation between government and social partners over general guiding lines and tailor-made decentralised implementation forms a useful way to deal with social, technological and international trends that require flexibility.

Involvement of social partners in institutional reform
5. There have been very few reforms that affected the position of insiders. Exceptions were the de-linking of public sector wages from wages in

the market sector and the reduction of replacement rates. These reforms were fiercely opposed by the unions.

6. An important aspect of the reform process in The Netherlands consisted of social security reform. These reforms were fiercely opposed by the unions. Again this may be due to the perceived impact of social security reform on insider power. At any rate, the implication is that it is rather pointless to try to enlist the unions in social security reform.

4. Testing the Dutch lessons: experiences in four other countries

4. 1 Introduction

In this section we compare the Dutch experience with developments in four other countries: the UK, Austria, Germany and Italy. These four countries represent a broad spectrum of labour market institutions. The aim of this comparison is two-fold. First, to identify in what respects the Dutch experience was special and in what respect it shared features with other countries. Second, to assess whether the lessons drawn in the previous section hold up against the evidence from other countries. The discussion focuses on the following questions:

- What were the major reforms in labour market institutions and social security arrangements over the past 20 to 30 years?
- Were the social partners involved in these reforms?
- What were the effects of the reforms on the position of insiders?

Before describing individual country experiences, the following section presents a brief overview of institutions and of key economic indicators. Section 4.3 presents answers to the questions listed above for each of the four comparison countries. Finally, Section 4.4 summarises and draws some conclusions.

4.2   Institutions and key economic indicators

The UK has one of the least regulated labour markets in the OECD. In terms of bargaining level, Austria is at the other extreme, whose labour market institutions in many respects are similar to those of the Netherlands. Somewhere in between (still in terms of bargaining level) are Italy and Germany. Table 10.2 summarises labour market institutions in the Netherlands and in the four comparison countries. Table 10.3 presents comparative data on labour market outcomes, income distribution and GDP per capita.

Table 10.2 Labour market institutions in five countries

	Netherlands	UK	Italy	Austria	Germany
Employment protection	Intermediate	Low	High	High	Intermediate/ high
Bargaining level	Industry level, informally coordinated at the national level	Mostly firm level	Industry level, informally coordinated at the national level	Industry level, informally coordinated at the national level	Industry level, weak coordination at the national level
Extension of collective agreements	Yes	No	Yes, as far as wages are concerned	Yes	No (agreements are binding for members of the employers' organisation)
Tripartite institutions	Yes	No	No	Yes	No: tariff-autonomie
Replacement rate (early 1990s)	79	61	42	63	72
Statutory minimum wage*	Yes	Yes (until 1993; reintro-duction in April 1999)	No	No	No

*In Italy, Austria and Germany, collective agreements frequently stipulate minimum wage levels.

Sources: Country studies, Grubb and Wells (1993), OECD (1994), replacement rates from Salomaki and Munzi, (1999).

Table 10.3 Labour market outcomes

	Netherlands	UK	Italy	Austria	Germany
Employment/ population ratio, 1997 (%)	68	71	51	67	64
Labour supply growth 1985-1995 (per cent/year)*	1.4	0.3	0.7	1.5	-0.1
Employment growth 1985-95 (per cent/year)*	1.5	0.6	0.5	1.5	-0.7
GDP per head 1998 (US$ PPP, x 1000)	23.1	21.2	21.7	24	22.8
Income distribution: D9/D5, 1994	1.66	1.86	1.6	1.82	1.61
Income distribution: D5/D1, 1994	1.56	1.78	1.75	2.01	1.44
Unemployment rate, 1997	5.5	7.1	12.2	4.2	9.8
Working hours per employee	1321	1498	1482	1576	1529

*Italy: 1985-1992; Germany (total): 1991-95.

Sources: Employment/population ratio, labour supply growth and employment growth: OECD 1997, p. 191; GDP per head: OECD, Main Economic Indicators, April 1999; Income distribution: OECD, Employment Outlook 1996; working hours per employee: CPB 1998.

4.3 An overview of labour market reforms in the UK, Italy, Austria and Germany

4.3.1 United Kingdom

What were the major reforms in labour market institutions and social security arrangements over the past 20 years?

Starting in 1979, successive conservative governments introduced far-reaching reforms in UK labour market institutions. In order to put these reforms into perspective, and to understand the non-consensus approach of the Thatcher governments towards labour market reform, we must say something about institutional developments prior to 1979 (when the first Thatcher government came into power). An important general conclusion from this period is that attempts at reform largely failed. A good illustration of this general conclusion is the attempt (by a conservative government) in 1971 to make collectively bargained agreements legally binding. This was motivated by developments during the 1960s when industry-wide agreements were losing their regulatory effectiveness. So-called 'shop stewards' (firm-level representatives of the union) increasingly negotiated additional benefits over and above what had already been bargained collectively. They were able to do this because collectively bargained agreements were not legally binding. This explains the 1971 policy decision: making collective agreements binding would have curtailed the power of the shop stewards.

The new law was fiercely opposed by the unions. Booth (1995, p. 25) explains this by pointing to the complexity of the new law, but her account leaves room for an alternative explanation for union opposition. The act contained a number of other provisions besides making collective agreements binding: it made pre-strike ballots compulsory, it abolished compulsory union membership (the so-called 'closed shop') and it prescribed a conciliation pause before any strike that might endanger the national interest. Perhaps the unions' opposition was directed at these aspects of the act, rather than at its complexity, although we admit that this is hard to judge for outsiders.

The subsequent Labour government which came into power in 1974 returned to the old situation of non-binding collective agreements in return for voluntary incomes policy. As a result, the incentives for employers to conclude (non-binding) collective agreements diminished. The percentage of the workforce covered by collective agreements fell from 70 per cent in 1970 to less than half of all employees now. In some sectors, notably the public sector, national agreements remained important until the 1980s, when the

Thatcher government took steps to abolish collective bargaining also in the public sector.

The main objective of the 'Thatcher reforms' was to reduce union strength. An important step in this direction was the abolishment of the closed shop. In 1978, just prior to the reforms, about 23 per cent of all workers were employed in closed shop firms. Union power was also reduced by a variety of other measures: restricting picketing (henceforth only allowed at one's own place of work); the requirement of secret pre-strike ballots; union responsibility for strikes called by union officials; abolishing the automatic deduction of union dues from wages; and withdrawal of collective bargaining rights for teachers.

Blanchflower and Freeman (1994) argue that the Thatcher reforms led to a marginal increase in responsiveness of employment and nominal wages to market conditions but to no improvement in the responsiveness of real wages to unemployment. It remains unclear whether the Thatcher reforms resulted in a better functioning of the labour market.

As will be clear from the above discussion, many of the Thatcher reforms involved changes in legal procedures. Informal institutional change of the Dutch type, where following the Wassenaar agreement of 1982 the government changed its negotiating stance, has also been important. Government involvement in wage-setting was very limited in the Thatcher era, whereas in the 1960s and 1970s, price and incomes policies where repeatedly used in an attempt to moderate inflation. For example, the Labour governments in 1974-79 achieved wage moderation by concluding a Social Contract with the TUC, trading pro-union legislation (including the return to non-legally binding collective agreements) and a promise of Keynesian policies for wage restraint. Initially this was quite successful: social contracts succeeded temporarily in wage restraint. In order to achieve this the government put a lot of moral pressure on local bargaining unions under the slogan 'give a year to Britain'. The government also stressed solidarity of the labour movement with the Labour government. For a while this strategy of wage moderation through moral suasion, without any fundamental institutional reform, seemed to work. But in the end the Social Contract was unsustainable: "[I]t was always clear that the social contract was not institutionally viable as a longer-term strategy and that the inevitable return to 'free collective bargaining' would again release the pent-up pressures of wage competition. The only question was whether the break-up had to occur under the dramatic circumstances of 1978, or whether a more sensitive management of government-union relations and better timing could have facilitated a more orderly retreat that might have allowed Jim Callaghan to survive another general election". (Scharpf, 1997, p. 236). What followed was a wave of strikes culminating in 'the winter of discontent' of 1978-79, resulting in high wage settlements and high inflation. This provided the basis for the conservative election triumph under Mrs. Thatcher in 1979.

Did the government seek consensus with the social partners before implementing the reforms?

Labour market reforms under Thatcher and previous Conservative governments were undertaken without trying to achieve consensus with the unions. In view of the type of reforms enacted under Thatcher, which drastically reduced union power, this should perhaps not be surprising. With respect to the 1971 reform (the attempt to make collectively bargained agreements legally binding), things are less clear cut. To outsiders like us it would seem that under certain circumstances unions might have agreed, but that the attempt failed because of other union-unfriendly features of the act.

Labour governments usually did seek active support from the unions. However, support was sought on wage moderation, not on reforming labour market institutions. Indeed, as already indicated, in one case (1974) wage moderation was obtained in exchange for rolling back the reforms introduced by the previous Conservative government.

What was the effect of the reforms on the position of insiders?

It would seem that reducing union power from a setting in which wage bargaining was already decentralised must have reduced the power of insiders. If the UK had started from a highly centralised bargaining regime, it is conceivable that insiders would have become more able to increase their wages above market-clearing levels by extracting rents, but this does not seem an adequate description of the UK labour market in the years prior to the Thatcher era. Blanchflower and Freeman (1994) reach a different conclusion. In their view, '[t]he reforms failed to recognise the power of insider pressures for rent-sharing and related policies that segment decentralised labour markets in periods of less than full employment.' (p. 75) Apparently, they view the pre-Thatcher period as characterised by centralised bargaining. As argued above, central agreements may have worked for a brief period prior to the winter of discontent of 1978-79, but according to Bean and Crafts (1996) they did not constitute a viable option for the longer term. In their view, the 'social contracts' were counterproductive and the 'Thatcher approach' of undertaking major reforms, if needed against fierce union opposition, should have been embraced much earlier.

Concluding remarks on the UK

The UK labour market is now one of the least regulated in the OECD. Formal firing restrictions have never been very strict in the UK (Blanchflower and Freeman, 1994), but before 1979 de facto employment protection was probably quite restrictive since unions were very powerful at the firm level. This illustrates the general point that formal labour market regulations provide an incomplete picture of actual labour market flexibility.

A second conclusion is that nation-wide agreements between unions and the government may sometimes serve short-term objectives, but at the cost of longer-term objectives. Thus Bean and Crafts (1996) argue that post-war governments should have had more courage in dealing with the unions (compare the Netherlands in the late 1970s/early 1980s). The fact that the current Labour government does not intend to roll back most Conservative reforms supports this view. Of course, lack of courage is not the only possible explanation for the behaviour of pre-Thatcher Labour governments: perhaps their policy views really did differ from those of the present Labour government.

4.3.2 Italy

What were the major reforms in labour market institutions and social security arrangements over the past 20 years?

Italian labour market institutions underwent substantial change over the past decades. Before summarising these changes, it is instructive to cite two insiders' summary judgement of these changes: 'Efforts at labour market reform, particularly stimulated by centralised tripartite agreements from the early 1980s onwards, have produced a few significant results, but in general have not been capable of reversing the slide towards labour market ossification' (Garonna and Sica, 1998, p. 71). Later we come back to the assessment of the recent reforms.

Reforms and changes in Italian labour market institutions over the past 20-odd years can be grouped under three headings: wage indexation, bargaining level and employment protection.

Wage indexation: a unique institutional feature of the Italian labour market was the 'scala mobile', a mechanism for linking wages to increases in the cost of living. Introduced through negotiations between social partners in 1951, it was (after many modifications) abolished in 1992. An important consequence of the 'scala mobile' was that it removed to a large extent wages from the bargaining table (Pellegrini, 1998, p. 158). Unions bargained mainly over other aspects of the labour contract such as hours, holidays and training.

In addition, unions' federations sometimes bargained (with employers but also between themselves) over the extent of indexation and over wage differentiation across types of workers. Between 1975 and 1985, the 'scala mobile' was based on equal nominal pay rises for everyone, irrespective of the individual wage rate (Bertola and Ichino, 1995, p. 387). Erickson and Ichino (1995, p. 270) argue that "the slogan 'equal pay for equal work' would have been subscribed to by most union leaders during this period, and it is difficult to doubt that a large part of the compression of wage differentials observed in the 1970s was caused by the unions' successful pursuit of egalitarian pay policies." Perhaps not surprisingly, many high-skilled union members disagreed with this egalitarian strategy. In 1980, 40,000 high-level white-collar workers marched against the unions in protest against this strategy. At around the same time, a process of heavy plant restructuring led to mass layoffs in the industrialised regions. As a result, the unions lost large numbers of members and public support (Erickson and Ichino, 1995, p. 270).

Bargaining level: The importance of centralised bargaining has undergone important changes in the post-war period. National agreements between the social partners were important during the 1950s. Between 1965 and 1975, bargaining shifted from the industry level to the enterprise and firm level. In 1985 attempts at centralised agreements collapsed over disagreement on changing the 'scala mobile' from nominally fixed wage adjustments towards a system based on proportionality. In the early 1990s the pendulum swung back to national agreements.

Employment protection: following widespread social unrest, culminating in the 'autunno caldo' (hot autumn) of 1969, strong employment protection laws were introduced in 1970, with the Charter of Workers' Rights (Bertola and Ichino, 1995, p. 386). Despite several attempts at reform, formal employment protection is still very strict in Italy. Moreover, not all changes are in the direction of greater flexibility: at the beginning of the 1990s stringent firing regulations were extended to small firms (albeit in an attenuated form; Garonna and Sica, 1998, p. 72). However, formal employment protection may not give an adequate impression of the flexibility of the Italian labour market. Anecdotal evidence suggests that in Italy rules frequently are applied rather loosely: 'outwork, moonlighting, self-employment and the informal economy provide a great deal of flexibility' (ibid., p. 69). Furthermore, small, unincorporated family firms are important as sources of employment and innovation. There is some reason to believe that this flexible belt of small family firms has shrunk during the

1990s (ibid., p. 71). If this latter view is correct, then informal flexibility may have diminished.

Did the government seek consensus with social partners before implementing the reforms?

In the early 1990s a severe fraud-related political crisis and a monetary crisis which pushed the lira out of the EMS created a national sense of urgency, and made possible a number of important central agreements between the government and the social partners. We briefly describe these reforms. As already indicated, in 1992 the 'scala mobile' was abolished through a collective agreement. This was a very painful process, summarised by Visser (1996, pp. 293-4): 'The elections of April 1992 and alarm over the size of the public finance crisis helped the new government create an atmosphere of emergency, allowing it to propose drastic cuts in public expenditure, wage restraint and substantial tax increases. The centrepiece of the agreement was wage restraint through the abolition of the automatic cost-of-living adjustments ('scala mobile'), this time with none of the usual tax and welfare side-deals. The unions were finally brought around by the prime minister's threat to resign, causing a near split in the GCIL'. (CGIL is one of the three major union federations.)

The 1992 agreement was followed by a spate of opposition and worker unrest. This experience placed the reform of bargaining institutions high on the agenda (Visser, 1996, p. 294) and a new tripartite agreement in 1993 clarified the division of responsibilities between the different bargaining levels. Until 1993 the division of bargaining authority between the national level and the industry or firm level was not always clear. As a result, agreements reached at a higher level were often not considered final by worker representatives at lower levels (compare UK). Some inside observers are as yet unconvinced that the new system will work (Garonna and Sica, 1998, p. 75).

The short-lived Berlusconi government which came into power in 1994 took a non-cooperative stance towards the social partners, and no central agreement was reached during this period. But in 1995 a new government reached agreement on pension reform. The agreement of 1996 stipulated that there would no longer be an automatic transformation of fixed-term contracts into permanent contracts.

An often-heard criticism of tripartite reform agreements in Italy is that unions were 'bribed' into these agreements by compensating workers who are affected by these reforms (Garonna and Sica, 1998, p. 72). This took the form of offering attractive early retirement plans and public employment for redundant workers. In recent agreements, the government bought (limited) flexibility through fiscal incentives, mostly social security rebates (compare the Netherlands in the 1970s).

Concluding remarks on Italy
One of the most salient institutional features of Italy's post-war labour market history was the 'scala mobile', which to some extent removed wages from the bargaining table. But was this a good thing? The 'scala mobile' may have diminished the need for renegotiating labour contracts, and may thus have contributed to alleviating certain hold-up problems at the firm level. However, because wage adjustments were automatic, the system led to real wage rigidity. As a result, external shocks requiring a decline in real wages (such as a decline in the terms of trade) could not be accommodated by the system. In addition a possible disadvantage of the system is that because wages were already taken care of through the 'scala mobile', unions focused on other issues such as worker protection. To what extent this explains the restrictiveness of firing rules in Italy is unclear, but it cannot be ruled out.

The reforms leading to the abolishment of the 'scala mobile' provide a second conclusion: a major institutional reform that affects the position of insiders requires a sense of urgency, brought about by economic or political crises (compare the Netherlands).

Finally, there is an interesting parallel between the 1993 agreement clarifying the division of responsibilities between the social partners and the Dutch 1992 agreement of the Social and Economic Council (see Section 3.5).

4.3.3 Austria
What were the major reforms in labour market institutions and social security arrangements over the past 20 years?

Austrian labour market institutions have changed very little over the period 1960-95. Highly centralised bargaining has been characteristic of Austrian labour market institutions at least since the 1950s. Almost all workers (98 per cent; Guger, 1998, p. 52) are covered by collective agreements. Formal wage bargaining takes place at the industry level, but in practice the bargaining process is highly coordinated through preparatory talks in the Austrian Trade Union Federation (ÖGB) which also controls the finances of individual unions and fixes the dates at which individual unions may start a new round of negotiations. Coordination is further enhanced by the wage leadership of the metal unions.[4]

Some tentative labour market reforms have been introduced in recent years, especially in the area of working time arrangements. These used to be very restrictive in Austria, and had been reported in company surveys as a

major disadvantage of doing business there (Aiginger and Peneder, cited in
European Economy, 1998 No. 2, p. 118). Working-time regulations were
substantially deregulated in May 1997 when a new law (the
Arbeitszeitsgesetz) was passed which increased from eight weeks to one year
or more the period during which the maximum allowable working time
would be calculated. The recent collective agreement (1997-78) in the
important metal industry was based on this law, and introduced 'working-
time accounts' which allow companies to vary working time between 32 and
45 hour per week (subject to daily and annual limits).

Employment protection laws, which were already relatively restrictive,
have become more restrictive for older workers with the introduction in 1996
of a bonus-malus system which provides a penalty to the employer in case of
a dismissal of a worker aged 50 or more (on the other hand, hiring a worker
aged 50 or more is now subsidised). Introducing more flexibility in hiring
and firing is being discussed between the social partners but no agreement
has yet been reached.[5]

Finally, the government and the social partners reached consensus on
pensions reforms in 1997. Whether these reforms solve the problem of rising
pension liabilities is subject to debate (OECD, 1998, p. 49).

All in all, labour market reforms are of very recent date and do not seem
to be very fundamental. Nevertheless, an Austrian observer argues that
'corporatism and its institutions have generally been losing influence.'
(Guger 1998, p. 55). He attributes this trend to globalisation and EU
regulation (Austria joined the EU in 1995). One sign of the declining
influence of central agreements is that they are increasingly given a flexible
interpretation at the decentralised level. Thus works councils sometimes
agree to changes to centrally negotiated agreements at plant level to promote
flexibility and preserve jobs. Strictly speaking this is illegal, suggesting that
collective agreements are not (always) rigidly interpreted.

Did the government seek consensus with social partners before
implementing the reforms? The governments' basic institutional philosophy
has always been and continues to be consensus-seeking. The recent reforms
discussed above were achieved through agreements reached between the
government and the social partners. Much like in the Netherlands, consensus
seeking is supported by institutions that enhance consultation between the
government and the social partners. All the major unions are members of the
ÖGB, founded in 1945, while employers are compulsory members of the
Chambers of Agriculture, Commerce, and Labour. Both the ÖGB and the
Chambers have seats in the Parity Commission for Wages and Prices, which
was founded in 1957. The Federal Chancellor and relevant ministers are also

represented in the Parity Commission. Although the Commission has no legal authority nor any means of applying sanctions, the Commission is seen as an important vehicle for coordinating wage negotiations. The Commission has formed a number of subcommittees, of which the three most important are the committees on prices, on wages and the Economic and Social Advisory Board (a close parallel to the Dutch social and Economic Council).

What was the effect of the reforms on the position of insiders? The recent reforms have not reduced the power of insiders. For some groups, notably older workers, insider power has even increased through the reforms.

Concluding remarks on Austria
The institutional setting in Austria is quite similar to the Netherlands, both in terms of institutions that support consensus-seeking as well as in terms of the division of tasks between actors at the central level and at the decentralised level. Thus, as in the Netherlands, central agreements are coupled with flexible implementation at lower levels.

Of course, there are also differences between the two countries. Internal flexibility (flexible work and part-time work) is much less in Austria (although this is changing under influence of recent reforms). Austria has no legal minimum wage and replacement rates are much lower (Table 10.2). Furthermore, the role of foreign workers in both economies differs. In Austria restrictions on the use of foreign labour introduced in the 1970s led to a fall in the number of foreign workers from 6 per cent of the labour force in 1973 to 4.5 per cent of the labour force in the mid-1980s. This provided a partial buffer to unemployment. In the Netherlands the number of foreign workers has been rising uninterruptedly since the 1960s.

In many respects the outcomes in the two countries are quite different also: Austria did not experience a severe economic crisis during the early 1980s (see Figure 10.2), and its income distribution is much more skewed (Table 10.3). Lower replacement rates may be one of the causes for both outcomes. Thus, although bargaining and consultation institutions in the two countries were similar, it seems that Austria was much better able to deal with aggregate shocks.

4.3.4 Germany
What were the major reforms in labour market institutions and social security arrangements over the past 20 years?

Although there had been some minor reforms in the German labour market in the 1980s, such as the 1985 Employment Promotion Act which eased firing restrictions and increased the probationary period for new workers from six months to one year and the Working Time Act of 1987 which introduced greater flexibility in working hours, the main impetus for reform was provided by German re-unification in 1989. In March 1990 unions and employers' organisations proposed to transfer the Western model of industrial relations to the east. Subsequently they advocated modernisation of East German industry and succeeded in quickly raising East German wages in order to prevent low-wage competition by eastern firms (Sinn and Sinn, 1992, p. 166). This transfer of institutions prevented a lengthy process of institution-building that currently requires much effort in other transition countries. Against these advantages, the rigidities of the Western socio-economic order constituted a major disadvantage (Giersch et al., 1992, p. 268). The extensive framework of regulations and lengthy administrative procedures limited flexible reallocation of labour, physical capital and finance, which was required for East German restructuring.

After the initial boom unification put severe strain on the German model (Lehmbruch, 1996). High negotiated wage increases in 1995 led to a crisis in the metal employers' organisation, with member firms leaving the organisation. This weakening of employers' organisations made it more difficult to arrive at a peak-level agreement to tackle the problems associated with unification (Lehmbruch, 1996). The unions' 'Bündnis für Arbeit' proposal failed and the government initiated a reform process with its 'Programme for growth and employment' and subsequent proposals for tax reform. However, political and social opposition made implementation very difficult.

Especially in the new Länder, employers increasingly withdrew their membership from employer associations, or succeeded in paying wages below the agreed wage bargain: (... there has been a tendency for companies to conclude wide-ranging agreements, often at plant level, which guarantee employment security and investment for several years in return for lower labour costs and improved flexibility' (OECD, 1998, p. 103). Increasingly, opening clauses in sectoral agreements explicitly allow firm-level wages to fall short of agreed wages. The textile and clothing industry agreement allows lower wages to be paid by firms facing financial difficulties. In the chemical industry, the agreement allows lower wages for previously long-term unemployed.

Unification also necessitated social security reform. In the 1970s and early 1980s, German social security arrangements seemed to perform quite well. In contrast to the Netherlands, Germany was able to contain its social spending as a percentage of GDP despite the oil shocks, helped by the various checks and balances built into the governance structure of social insurance. Although the social partners administer social insurance (except for unemployment insurance), the German government either supervises the administration of social insurance directly or delegates this to independent bodies: the Federal Insurance Office (Bundesversicherungsamt) or Federal Audit Office (Bundesrechnungshof). Unemployment insurance is administered by the Federal Labour Office, which is supervised by the social partners and representations from various levels of government.

However, after German unification social security spending rose dramatically: between 1989-94, the total bill increased by the equivalent of 3.5 per cent of GDP. Unemployment benefits and old-age pensions accounted for most of this recent increase in social security spending. In the absence of social consensus about how this heavy burden of unification was to be shared, it set in motion a vicious circle (reminiscent of the Dutch vicious circle in the 1970s and early 1980s) of tax increases wage increases and employment reductions in Germany as a whole. The increasing number of recipients of public transfers in combination with a weak employment performance have contributed to increasing concerns about the sustainability of the present German social security system.

Several measures to reform social security have been taken during the second half of the 1990s, largely without the involvement of the social partners or social consensus. Some of these measures, such as stricter criteria for receiving unemployment benefits, have met opposition in labour courts and prove difficult to implement (OECD, 1998, p. 107). In addition, measures such as a higher minimum age for receiving unemployment benefits are subject to generous transition arrangements (OECD, 1997, p. 125).

The government's attempt to reform sickness benefits has been largely offset by the social partners. Sickness pay is particularly generous in Germany, and even overtime pay is compensated during illness. In 1996 the German government reduced statutory sick pay to 80 percent of the reference wage, but supplementary provisions negotiated by employers and unions continue to supplement benefits to 100 percent (OECD, 1997, p. 125). However, overtime pay is no longer compensated. Moreover, in the negotiation process a price may have been paid in the form of lower wage increases.

In addition to adjustments in social security, measures have been introduced to enhance labour market flexibility. In 1996 employment protection has been eased by raising the threshold for company size from 5 to 10 employees (the new government has lowered the threshold back to 5). The maximum duration of fixed-term contracts was extended from 18 to 24 months. Regulations on part-time work have been reduced and private employment agencies were allowed (OECD, 1998, p. 105). Beside these legal measures, social partners introduced time accounts in wage agreements, which enhance working-time flexibility.

Did the government seek consensus with social partners before implementing the reforms?

The German constitution contains a provision known as 'Tarifautonomie' which constrains government involvement in industrial relations. Wage formation is autonomous (hence 'Tarifautonomie'), which means that unions and employers' organisations bargain over wages without any intervention from the government (Lampert, 1992, p. 240). This unique institutional feature is partly explained by a general distrust in government caused by the traumatic experience of the war: 'The state was regarded as a possible danger to society and democracy rather than as a partner in bargaining. It was better, many agreed, to keep the state at a distance' (Slomp, 1990, p. 129). Another reason is that past experience with government involvement in bargaining had been very unfavourable (Paqué, 1996). During the Weimar Republic compulsory arbitration by the Federal Ministry of Labour was intended as a procedure of last resort to settle industrial disputes, but instead induced the parties to strongly hold on to their bargaining positions and speculate on a favourable outcome of arbitration. The arbitration process created lengthy procedures and worsened industrial relations, since generally at least one party disapproved the compulsory agreements.

Within the limits set by Tarifautonomie there have been short-lived attempts at informal coordination between government and representatives of labour and capital. In 1967 the Minister of Economics Schiller initiated the Concerted Action: regular meetings between representatives of government, the Bundesbank, the social partners and economists (Giersch et al., 1992, p. 148; Smyser, 1993, p. 19). The aim of the Concerted Action meetings was to guide the participants on the level of wages, prices and investment that were most suited from an economic perspective. Coordination concerned only the provision of information; parties did not conclude any formal agreements and the meetings were not institutionalised in a specific organisational model like the Dutch Foundation of Labour or the Social and Economic Council. These meetings were not very successful. Already in 1970 and 1971 representatives of labour and capital hardly responded to the guidance given and in 1977 unions quit Concerted Action.

Developments since reunification have led to a new search for tripartite agreements. After the failed attempts in 1995 and 1996, the recent change of government has initiated a tendency towards more central coordination. The

'Bündnis für Arbeit, Ausbildung and Wettbewerbs-fähigkeit', as it is now called, ranks high among the policy objectives of the new government that took office in November 1998. However, until now progress has been modest. The first round of discussion identified a broad range of topics for further deliberation: tax reform, social security reform, flexible working time, innovation and competitiveness of companies, access of small companies to capital market, reduction of barriers to start a company, schooling and active labour market policy aimed at young and long-term unemployed (Bundesregierung, 1998). On wages only 'wage policy that supports employment growth' is mentioned, mainly because unions oppose wage moderation, emphasise 'Tarifautonomie' and want to keep wages a full responsibility of the social partners. But this is like Hamlet without the prince: it seems pointless to seek consensus on measures to improve economic performance and reduce unemployment without being more specific on wages.

What was the effect of the reforms on the position of insiders? The limited (and temporary) easing of employment protection and the stricter criteria for receiving unemployment benefits may in theory have weakened the bargaining position of insiders. Nevertheless insider pressure remains strong in Germany. A case in point is the relatively high recent wage bargain struck in the metal industry (4 per cent in nominal terms).

Concluding remarks on Germany
An overall conclusion from this brief review is that the German social market economy encountered severe problems in coping with reunification. This may be partly due to the formal separation of government and the social partners in the socio-economic order. Arguably, this strict separation hampers attempts to establish support and commitment for addressing nation-wide challenges. We hasten to add that too much involvement of the government may not be a good thing either, witness the Weimar experience and the Dutch experience in the 1980s. The recent steps towards a social dialogue in the 'Bündnis für Arbeit, Ausbildung and Wettbewerbsfähigkeit' may strike the right balance, if the parties succeed in bringing up wages for discussion.

Another conclusion from the German experience is that the social market economy was probably well suited for dealing with small shocks – hence its success prior to unification – but that the large shock brought about by unification required far-reaching reforms that were beyond the reach of the social market economy, such as a substantial easing of employment protection and a lowering of replacement rates. This explains why the limited reforms undertaken since unification have been implemented largely without involvement or support of the social partners.

4.4 Conclusions

Table 10.4 summarises the reform histories of the five countries discussed in this paper. Although the table is not complete in that not every reform is mentioned, we have made an attempt to include all the major reforms. Columns one and two require no explanation. The third column indicates whether social partners cooperated in designing and/or implementing the reform. The final column indicates the effect of the reforms on insiders. This column is based on our own informal assessment, but in most cases we believe that the impact of a given measure on the position of insiders is fairly clear cut. The main exceptions are reforms that facilitate part-time contracts and flexible contracts. On the one hand, these reforms raise effective labour supply which will weaken the power of insiders. On the other hand such reforms lead to a kind of dual labour market with a group of core workers and a flexible belt of temporary workers and workers on flexible contracts. Because the flexible belt bears the brunt of any recession, this reinforces the position of insiders. As argued in Section 2, the example of Spain indicates that this is more than just a theoretical possibility.

The conclusion that we draw from this table is that social partners never cooperate in reforms that diminish insider power, e.g. by reducing employment protection, curtailing union power, or lowering replacement rates. There is only one exception: the abolition of the 'scala mobile' in Italy in 1992. This implies that it is pointless to try to involve the social partners in reforms affecting the position of insiders.

A second conclusion from the table is that in only one country have social partners been bystanders during the whole period, namely in the UK. Closer inspection of the table shows that this is probably explained by the type of reforms undertaken in the UK, which were very much aimed at reducing insider power. Coupled with the first conclusion (that unions never agree to cut insider power) this suggests that given the reforms undertaken in the UK, involving the unions in a cooperative way was not a feasible option. As argued in the country section on the UK, unfavourable previous experience with involving the social partners in a reform process probably also played a role.

Table 10.4 Summary of country experiences since 1980

Country and year	Description of reform measure	Involvement of the social partners	Impact on the position of insiders
UK			
1980	Increased employment duration required for unfair dismissal protection	no	Long-term employees weakened
1980	Weakened closed shop and other measures that reduce union power	no	Insiders weakened
1980	Reduced unemployment benefits	no	Insiders weakened
1982	Further weakened closed shop and other measures that reduce union power	no	Insiders weakened
1984	Further reduced union power	no	Insiders weakened
1985	Increased employment duration required for unfair dismissal protection	no	Long-term employees weakened
1988	Further reduced union power	no	Insiders weakened
1993	Extended employment protection rules to part-time workers	no	Full-time employees weakened
1993	Abolished wage councils (minimum wage)	no	Insiders weakened
Italy			
1983	Reduced indexation	no	Insiders weakened
1984	Introduced temporary contracts for youth workers	no	Permanent workers strengthened

1985	Extended coverage of unemployment benefit schemes	no	Insiders strengthened
1986	Allowed lay-offs for economic reasons	no	Insiders weakened
1986	Made wage indexation proportional	mixed	Mixed
1987	Liberalised restrictions surrounding temporary contracts	no	Permanent workers strengthened
1989	Extended employment protection rules to small firms	no	Permanent workers strengthened
1990	Extended unfair dismissal legislation to small firms	no	Permanent workers strengthened
1991	Relaxed firing restrictions for large firms	no	Insiders weakened
1992	Eliminated 'scala mobile'	yes	Weakening
1993	Rolled back 1991 reforms (counter-reform)	yes	Insiders strengthened
1993	Clarified bargaining process	yes	Neutral
1996	Widened use of atypical work contracts, increased opportunities for part-time work	yes	Mixed
1996	Allowed set up of private agencies for temporary work	yes	Mixed
1996	Stopped automatic transformation of fixed-term contact into permanent contracts	yes	Mixed

Netherlands			
1982	New coalition government changes bargaining game	no	Insiders weakened
1982	Wassenaar agreement between social partners	yes	No impact
1983	Delinked public sector wages and social security benefits from wages in market sector	no	Insiders weakened
1985	Sped up administrative firing authorisation	no	Insiders weakened
1985/6	Reduced unemployment benefits and disability benefits	no	Insiders weakened
1987	Reduced minimum length of labour contracts from two years to six month	no	Permanent workers strengthened
1993	Further reduced disability benefits	no	Insiders weakened
1995	Automatic conversion of temporary contracts into permanent contracts after three renewals	yes	Mixed
1998	Flexicurity agreement	yes	Mixed
Germany			
1984	Liberalised restrictions surrounding temporary contracts	no	Permanent workers strengthened
1985	Eased firing restriction, longer probation period	no	Insiders weakened
1987	Greater flexibility in working hours	no	No impact

1994	Further liberalised restrictions surrounding temporary contracts	no	Permanent workers strengthened
1996	Reform of dismissal protection for small firms by raising threshold for company size	no	Insiders weakened
1997-1998	Social partners conclude wide-ranging agreements on employment security in exchange for lower wage demands and (internal?) flexibility	yes	Permanent workers strengthened
Austria			
1997	Increased internal flexibility by extending the period over which maximum allowable working time should be calculated	yes	No impact
1997-1998	Social partners conclude wide-ranging agreements on employment security in exchange for lower wage demands and internal flexibility	yes	Permanent workers strengthened

Sources: Country Sections (see above) and Saint Paul (1996), Bertola and Ichino (1995), Blanchflower and Freeman (1994).

5. CONCLUSIONS

It is now time to ask whether the lessons drawn from the Dutch experience (see Section 3.6) are confirmed or contradicted by experiences elsewhere. We answer this for each of the seven lessons drawn in Section 3.6.

Dealing with macroeconomic shocks

1. The first lesson – the need for a quick response to economic crises – is confirmed by experiences in the UK, Germany and Italy. In each of these countries fundamental institutional reform was only undertaken when the crisis had become very serious. This suggests that there are powerful forces that stand in the way of a quick response. Although we have no hard evidence on this, it is at least plausible that the three fundamental causes behind these time lags in the Netherlands (insider power, a macro-hold up problem, and government involvement: see Section 3.4) also applied in the other three countries. Institutional reform in the Netherlands, the UK, Germany and Italy has partly solved the first and last problem. The extent to which the second problem has been solved remains uncertain. In the Netherlands, the decline in unemployment during the past few years has strengthened the bargaining position of labour. On the other hand, globalisation and EMU have strengthened the bargaining position of capital (since the threat of capital flight has become more credible).

Institutional reform

2. The second lesson that we drew from the Dutch experience referred to the need for independent regulation and supervision of social security. This finds confirmation in the German experience, where such institutional arrangements have long succeeded in containing social spending. It remains to be seen whether recently proposed reforms in the Netherlands, which will enhance the role of the social partners in social security, will succeed in avoiding the pitfalls of previous involvement of the social partners.

3. With respect to the nature of institutional change we concluded from the Dutch experience that an important role was played by informal institutional change (i.e. changes in bargaining behaviour not based on changes in laws and regulations). This is confirmed by the reform experiences in Germany, the UK and Italy. In these countries also, institutional reform to some extent involved parties finding new roles within existing institutions.

4. We argued that the role of centralised consultation has changed in The Netherlands, from binding central agreements to broad guidelines that can be implemented in a flexible manner at the sectoral level. Similar changes are taking place in the three

comparison countries where centralised consultation plays an important role, namely Germany, Austria, and Italy. In these countries also, flexible interpretation of central agreements at the local level is becoming more common.

Involvement of social partners in institutional reform

5. We found that in the Netherlands reforms that weaken the position of insiders were opposed by the unions. This is confirmed in all four countries included in the comparison. This suggests that it is pointless to try to lure the social partners into cooperating in such reforms. Indeed, such attempts may be time-consuming leading to costly delays in the reform process (see also the first lesson).
6. With respect to social security reforms, the Dutch experience suggests that such reforms will be opposed by the unions. This fits in with the experience in the comparison countries where we have found few examples of involvement of the unions in reform of the social security system. Again this suggests low expected payoffs to (possibly time-consuming) attempts at enlisting the unions in such reforms.

NOTES

1. We are grateful to Paul Besseling, Jan Donders, Rocus van Opstal and Fiorella Padoa Schioppa Kostoris for helpful comments.
2. We mainly focus on the national labour market, because most labour market institutions operate on a national level and generally regional wage coordination is strong. This implies, however, that we do not deal with issues such as the extent to which regional wage differences or labour mobility may reduce differences in regional unemployment rates.
3. One-third of the members of the Social Insurance Council consisted of union representatives, one-third of employer organisations' representatives and one-third was appointed by the Minister of Social Affairs.
4. Nonetheless, there is some disagreement over the extent to which the ÖGB succeeds in coordinating the bargaining strategies of individual unions. Guger argues that the degree of coordination is often overestimated (Guger 1998, p. 46). In support he points to large and growing wage differentials. However Rowthorn offers an historical

'explanation' for these differentials. In his view, the Austrian labour movement 'has pursued a bargaining strategy which favours certain historically powerful groups of male workers'. (Rowthorn, 1992, p. 125). In this connection, it is also relevant to note that Austria has no official minimum wage.

5. The social partners have recently agreed to a report which was 'guardedly positive about the potential benefits from increased flexibility' (OECD, 1998, p. 115). This does not suggest much enthusiasm for greater flexibility on behalf of the social partners.

REFERENCES

Abraham, K.G. and S.N. Houseman (1994), 'Does Employment Protection Inhibit Labor Market Flexibility? Lessons from Germany, France, and Belgium', in R.M. Blank (ed.), *Social Protection versus Economic Flexibility. Is There a Trade-off?*, Chicago: The University of Chicago Press, pp. 59-93.

Albeda, W. (1993), 'De toekomst van de overlegeconomie', in N.A. Hofstra and P.W.M. Nobelen (eds), *De Toekomst van de Overlegeconomie*, Assen/Maastricht: Van Gorcum.

Ark, B. van, J. de Haan and H.J. de Jong (1996), 'Characteristics of economic growth in the Netherlands during the postwar period', in N. Crafts and G. Toniolo (eds), *Economic Growth in Europe Since 1945*, Cambridge: Cambridge University Press.

Armstrong, M., S. Cowan and J. Vickers (1994), *Regulatory Reform: Economic Analysis and British Experience*, Cambridge MA.: MIT Press.

Bean, C. and N. Crafts (1996), 'British economic growth since 1945: relative economic decline...and renaissance?', in N. Crafts and G. Toniolo (eds), *Economic growth in Europe since 1945*, Cambridge: Cambridge University Press, pp. 131-172.

Bertola, G. and A. Ichino (1995), 'Crossing the River: A Comparative Perspective on Italian Employment Dynamics', *Economic Policy*, October, pp. 361-420.

Blanchflower, D.G. and R. B. Freeman (1994), 'Did the Thatcher reforms change British labour market performance?', in R. Barrell (ed.), *The UK Labour Market: Comparative aspects and institutional developments*, Cambridge: Cambridge University Press, pp. 51-92.

Bolhuis, M. van (1996), *Externe Flexibilisering, een Onderzoek bij Bedrijven*, Ministry of Social Affairs and Employment, Inspectiedienst SZW, The Hague.

Booth, A.L. (1995), *The economics of the trade union*, Cambridge: Cambridge University Press.

Bovenberg, L. (1997), 'Dutch Employment Growth: an Analysis', *CPB Report* 1997/2, pp. 16-24.

Bundesregierung (1998), http://www.bundesregierung.de.

Caballero, R.J. and M.L. Hammour (1998), 'The Macroeconomics of Specificity', *Journal of Political Economy*, 106(4), August, pp. 724-767.

Calmfors, L. and J. Driffill (1988), 'Centralisation of Wage Bargaining and Economic Performance', *Economic Policy*, April, pp. 13-61.

CEPR (1993), *Making Sense of Subsidiarity: How Much Centralisation for Europe?*, CEPR Annual Report 1993, London.

CPB (Netherlands Bureau for Economic Policy Analysis) (1997), *Challenging Neighbours, Rethinking German and Dutch Economic Institutions*, Berlin: Springer Verlag.

CPB (1998), *Recent Trends in Dutch Labor Productivity: The Role of Changes in the Composition of Employment*, Working Paper No. 98, The Hague.

Coe, D.T. and D.J. Snower (1997), 'Policy Complementarities: The Case for Fundamental Labour Market Reform', CEPR Discussion Paper No. 1585, Centre for Economic Policy Research, London.

Delsen, L. (1995), *Atypical Employment: an International Perspective, Causes, Consequences and Policy*, Groningen: Wolters-Noordhoff.

Di Tella, R. and R. MacCulloch (1998), 'The Consequences of Labour Market Flexibility: Panel Evidence Based on Survey Data', mimeo, Harvard University.

Eichengreen, B. (1996), 'Institutions and Economic Growth: after World War II', in N. Crafts and G. Toniolo (eds.), *Economics growth in Europe since 1945*, Cambridge: Cambridge University Press, pp. 38-72.

Erickson, C.L. and A.C. Ichino (1995), 'Wage Differentials in Italy: Market Forces, Institutions, and Inflation', in R.B. Freeman and Lawrence Katz (eds.), *Differences and Changes in Wage Structures*, Chicago: The University of Chicago Press, pp. 265-305.

European Economy, (1998), No. 2, The Economic and Financial Situation in Austria.

Garonna, P. and F.G.M. Sica (1997), 'Intersectoral Labour Reallocations and Flexibility Mechanisms in Post-War Italy', in H. Siebert (ed.), *Structural*

Change and Labor Market Flexibility, Experience in Selected OECD Economies, Tübingen: J.C.B. Mohr (P. Siebeck).

Giersch, H., K.-H. Paqué and H. Schmieding (1992), *The Fading Miracle: Four Decades of Market Economy in Germany*, Cambridge: Cambridge University Press.

Grubb, D. and W. Wells (1993), 'Employment Regulation and Patterns of Work in EC Countries', *OECD Economic Studies*, 21.

Guger, A. (1998), 'Economic Policy and Social Democracy: The Austrian Experience', *Oxford Review of Economic Policy*, Vol. 14, No. 1, pp. 40-58.

Hartog, J. and J. Theeuwes (1997), 'The Dutch Response to Dynamic Challenges in the Labour Market, in H. Siebert, (eds), Structural Change and Labour Market flexibility: Expierience in Selected OECD Economics, Tubingen: Mohr (Siebeck).

Hemerijck, A.C. (1993), *The Historical Contingencies of Dutch Corporatism*, Oxford: Balliol College, University of Oxford.

Hemerijck, A.C. (1995), 'Corporatist Immobility in the Netherlands', in C. Crouch and F. Traxler (eds), *Organized Industrial Relations in Europe: What Future?*, Avebury: Aldershot:, pp. 183-226.

IDS (1995), *Pay and Conditions in the Netherlands 1995*, IDS International Documents.

Jackman R., R. Layard and S. Nickell (1991), *Unemployment, Macroeconomic Performance and the Labour Market*, Oxford: Oxford University Press.

De Kam, C.A., W. van Drimmelen and N. van Hulst (1995), *Loonvorming en Loonpolitiek in Nederland*, Groningen: Wolters-Noordhoff.

Korver, T. (1993), 'Labour market, labour contracts and collective bargaining, the Netherlands' in J. Hartog and J. Theeuwes (eds), *Labour Market Contracts and Institutions, a Cross-National Comparison*, Amsterdam: Elseviers Science Publishers B.V.

Lampert, H. (1992), Die Wirtschafts- und Sozialordnung der Bundesrepublik Deutschland, 11th Edition, München: Olzog Verlag.

Lehmbruch G. (1996), 'Crisis and institutional resilience in German corporatism', paper presented at the 8th International Conference on Socio-Economics, Genève.

Lindbeck, A. and D.J. Snower (1988), *The Insider-Outsider Theory of Employment and Unemployment*, London: The MIT Press Cambridge.

Lindbeck, A. (1994), 'Uncertainty under the Welfare State, Policy-Induced Risk', OCFEB Research Centre for Economic Policy, Research Memorandum No. 9403, Erasmus University Rotterdam.

Malcomson, J.M. (1997), Contracts, Hold-Up, and Labor Markets, in J. Pencavel (ed.), *The Journal of Economic Literature*, Vol. XXXV, No. 4, pp. 1916-1957.

Marsden, D. (1995), 'Deregulation or Cooperation? The Future of Europe's Labour Markets', *Labour*, Special Issue 1995, pp. 67-91.

Milgrom, P. and J. Roberts (1992), *Economics, Organization and Management*, New Jersey: Prentice Hall.

Nickell, S. (1997), 'Unemployment and Labor Market Rigidities: Europe versus North America' *Journal of Economic Perspectives*, Vol. 11, No. 3, pp. 55-74.

OECD (1994), *The OECD Jobs Study, Evidence and Explanations, Part II, The Adjustment Potential of the Labour Market, Paris.*

OECD (1995), OECD Economic Surveys, the Netherlands, Paris.

OECD (1997), OECD Economic Surveys, Germany, Paris.

OECD (1998), Labour Force Statistics 1977-1997, 1998 edition, Paris.

Paqué, K.-H. (1996), 'Why the 1950s and not the 1920s? Olsonian and non-Olsonian interpretations of two decades of German economic history', in N. Crafts and G. Toniolo (eds.), *Economic Growth in Europe since 1945*, Cambridge: Cambridge University Press, pp. 95-106.

Pellegrini C. (1998), 'Employment relations in Italy', in G.J. Bamber and R.D. Lansbury (eds.), *International & Comparative Employment Relations, A study of Industrialised Market Economies*, London, Thousand Oaks, New Delhi: SAGE Publications pp.144-168.

Prins, R., (1990), 'Sickness Absence in Belgium, Germany, FR and The Netherlands, A comparative study', Nederlands Instituut voor Arbeidsomstandigheden, Amsterdam.

Rinnooy Kan, A.H.G., (1993), 'De Nederlandse overlegeconomie in de jaren negentig: een kritische balans', in N.A. Hofstra and P.W.M. Nobelen (eds), *De Toekomst van de Overlegeconomie*, Assen/Maastricht: Van Gorcum.

Rowthorn, B. (1992), 'Corporatism and Labour Market Performance', in J. Pekkarinen, M. Pohjola and B. Rowthorn (eds.), *Corporatism: a superior economic system?*, Oxford: Clarendon.

Saint-Paul, G. (1996), 'Exploring the political economy of labour market institutions', *Economic Policy*, Vol. 23, pp. 265-315.

Salomäki, A. and T. Munzi (1999), 'Net Replacement Rates of the Unemployed: Comparisons of Various Approaches', *Economic Papers*, European Commission.

Scharpf, F.W. (1997), *Games Real Actors Play, Actor-Centered Institutionalism in Policy Research*, Boulder and Oxford: WestviewPress.

SER (1992), *Convergentie en Overlegeconomie*, Advies 92/15, The Hague.

Sinn, G., and H.-W. Sinn (1992), *Jumpstart: the Economic Unification of Germany*, Cambridge, MA: MIT Press.

Slomp, J.F.W. (1990), Labor Relations in Europe: A History of Issues and Developments, New York: Greenwood Press.

Smyser, W.R. (1993), *The German Economy: Colossus at the Crossroads*, 2nd ed., Harlow: Longman.

STAR Foundation of Labour (1996), 'Nota Flexibiliteit en Zekerheid', No. 2/96, The Hague.

Streeck, W. and P.C. Schmitter (1991), 'Community, Market, State - and Associations? The Prospective Contribution of Interest Governance to Social Order', in G. Thompson, J. Frances, R. Levaci and J. Mitchell (eds), *Markets, Hierarchies and Networks*, London: Sage Publications, pp. 227-241.

Teulings, C.N., and F. van der Ploeg (1993), 'De Vermoedelijke Ineffectiviteit van de WAO-Maatregelen', *Economisch Statistische Berichten*, Vol. 78, pp. 576-579.

Teulings, C.N. (1996), *De Plaats van de Vakbeweging in de Toekomst*, The Hague: Welboom, Scientific Publications Series.

Teulings, C.N., and J. Hartog (1998), *Corporatism or competition: Labour contracts, institutions, and wage structures in international comparison*, Cambridge: Cambridge University Press.

Toirkens, J. (1988), Schijn en werkelijkheid van het bezuinigingsbeleid 1975-1986, Kluwer: Deventer.

Visser J. (1996), 'A truly mixed case: industrial relations in Italy', in J. van Ruysseveldt and J. Visser, *Industrial Relations in Europe, Traditions and Transitions,* in association with the Open University of the Netherlands, SAGE Publications, London, Thousand Oaks, New Delhi, pp. 265-309.

Visser, J., and A. Hemerijck (1997), *A Dutch miracle: Job growth, welfare reform and corporatism in the Netherlands*, Amsterdam: Amsterdam University Press.

11. Market Structure Dynamics and Economic Growth

Martin Carree and Roy Thurik[1]

1. INTRODUCTION

Giant corporations were seen as the sole and most powerful engine of economic and technological progress in the early post-war period. Schumpeter (1950) provides an image of large corporations gaining the competitive advantage over small and new enterprises and of giant corporations ultimately dominating the entire economic landscape. This advantage would be due to scale economies in the production of new economic and technological knowledge. These scale economies would result from the organisation of teams of highly trained specialists working on technological progress in a routinised fashion. The large corporation was thought to have both superior production efficiency and superior innovative efficacy. Galbraith (1956) points out that in his world of countervailing power, large corporations are superior to small ones in nearly every aspect of economic behaviour such as productivity, technological advance, compensation and job security. In his world all major societal institutions contributed to the maintenance of the stability and predictability needed for mass production. In the worlds of Schumpeter and Galbraith, there is no room for small-scale, experimenting firms thriving on the uncertainty of technological advance, whimsical markets and the individual energy of an obstinate entrepreneur. Only large industrial units were thought to be able to compete on global markets producing global products.

The continuous decline in the number of small firms in the Western economies and the alleged successes of the East European centrally led economies and the successes of the American corporate giants like IBM, US Steel and General Motors contributed to this image. In this era of mass production, the US dominated world trade in industries where it could reap the fruits of its enormous endowments of physical capital. The efficacy of large firms was the main incentive of policy-makers when they tried to set up new regional economic entities like the European Union. Economic policy-making was aimed at maintaining stable domestic markets accommodating the mass-production technologies of these large units. Concern was growing whether the smaller European corporations in their fragmented markets could cope with their American competitors (Servan-Schreiber, 1969). The field of industrial economics was preoccupied by the virtues and the evils of large firms. See White (1982) and Lucas (1967) for two early exceptions dealing with the determinants of the share of smallness and the co-existence of large and small firms, respectively.

Also more recently, this world of ever-growing largeness and declining smallness has intrigued economists. The exploitation of economies of scale and scope was thought to be at the heart of modern economies (Teece, 1993). Chandler (1990) stresses the importance of investment in production, distribution and management needed to exploit economies of scale and scope. Audretsch stresses the influence the image of the East European economies and the perceived Soviet threat had on Western policy-makers: 'The fear in the West was not only that the accumulation of economic assets would lead to unprecedented productivity in the Soviet Union and Eastern Europe; of even greater concern was the assumed leaps and bounds in technological progress that would emerge from the huge and concentrated research and development programs being assembled. From the vantage point of the late 1950s and the early 1960s, the West seemed not only on the verge of losing the space race, but perhaps even more important, the economic growth race' (Audretsch, 1995, p. 2). It was a period of relatively well defined technological trajectories, of a stable demand and of seemingly clear advantages of diversification. Audretsch and Thurik (1997) characterise this period as one where stability, continuity and homogeneity were the cornerstones and label it the managed economy. Small businesses were considered to be a vanishing breed.

Times have changed for the centrally led economies that proved to be a failure and disappeared. They have changed also for the Western economies where large firms have been downsizing and restructuring and where entrepreneurship has been rediscovered (Carree, 1997 and Wennekers and Thurik, 1999). Birch was the first to supplement or even oppose the conventional wisdom of the late 1970s displaying evidence that most new jobs were emanating from small firms (Birch, 1981). Scanning the literature Gold (1981) finds little support for scale. Also casual evidence was starting to become available that small firms were outperforming some of their larger counterparts. Acs (1984) shows that small-firm employment is expanding in the American steel industry at the cost of that of large, incumbent companies facing divestiture and laying off people. Already in 1984, Acs surmises that microeconomic forces such as choice of technology and organisation are at the heart of the ongoing transformation of markets and not macroeconomic disequilibria.

Slowly, more and more substantial evidence became available that economic activity moved away from large firms to small, predominantly young firms in the 1970s and 1980s. Brock and Evans (1986) provide an extensive documentation of the changing role of small business in the US economy. They are the first to attempt to understand these new developments filling the void of economic research concerning formation, dissolution and growth of businesses and concerning the differential impact of regulations across business-size classes. The new role of small firms and their new interaction with large ones is described in Nooteboom (1987b). Blau (1987) shows that the proportion of self-employed in the US labour force starts to rise in the late 1970s. Acs and Audretsch (1993) and Carlsson (1992) provide a survey of evidence concerning manufacturing industries in countries in varying stages of economic development. Acs (1996) shows that the self-employment rate in OECD countries declined until 1977 and increased between then and 1987. See also Loveman and Sengenberger (1991) and Carree et al. (1999). Carlsson (1989) provides data on the share of the Fortune 500 industrial companies in total manufacturing. He shows that this share in total manufacturing employment dropped from 79 per cent in 1975 to 73 per cent in 1985. In the same period the share of these firms in total manufacturing shipments dropped from 83 per cent to 78 per cent. More recently, he shows that the former share dropped to 58 per cent in 1996 and the latter to 75 per cent (Carlsson, 1999).

Considerable data material is available showing that the size class structure of American firms is changing. European data documenting the size distribution of firms was not available until recently in a systematic manner. However, Eurostat has begun to publish yearly summaries of the firm size distribution of EU members at the two-digit level for the entire business sector. Below we will use data from the third edition of this summary, entitled *Enterprises in Europe* (Eurostat, 1994). The efforts of Eurostat are currently being supplemented by the European Network of SME Research (ENSR), a cooperation of 16 European institutes. This organisation publishes a yearly report of the structure and the developments of the small business sectors in the countries of the European Union. See the various editions of *European Observatory* which provide an account of the state of small business in Europe such as, for instance, EIM (1997).

Table 11.1 shows the development of the share of large business (firms with more than 500 employees) in total employment in some European countries, Canada, Japan and the US in the late 1980s and early 1990s. On average, European countries have experienced a decreasing share, but the most pronounced decreases are found for Canada and the US It is striking that large-firm presence rose in Japan and Germany, two economic powers that have not performed very well recently. One has to admit, however, that the decline of smallness in these two countries has been only moderate and that the reasons for their economies to slow down differ considerably. The table does not show whether the decreases of the large firm employment share are due to sectoral shifts or whether they are due to downscaling within industries. They are probably due to a combination of downscaling in the manufacturing sector and a decreasing share of this sector in the total economy.

Table 11.1 The employment share of large firms, LFP

Country	LFP (1988)	LFP (1991)
Belgium	36	35
Denmark	23	21
Finland	39	37
France	35	34
West Germany	36	37
Portugal	24	21
United Kingdom	35	34
Canada	39	35
Japan	27	28
United States	50	43

Note: Beginning of period is 1989 for Finland and end of period is 1990 for France and West Germany and 1992 for Japan.

Source: OECD (1994).

Carlsson (1992) mentions two explanations for the shift away from a managed economy and towards an entrepreneurial economy. The *first* deals with fundamental changes occurring in the world economy from the 1970s onwards. These changes relate to the intensification of global competition, the increase in the degree of uncertainty and the growth in market fragmentation. The *second* deals with changes in the character of technological progress. He shows that flexible automation has had various effects resulting in a shift from large to smaller firms. The pervasiveness of changes in the environment – that is in the world economy – and in the direction of technological progress results in a structural shift affecting the economies of all industrialised countries. The shift in the nature of technological change particularly involving flexible automation facilitated product differentiation and led to a new division of labour involving more cooperation and less competition between large and small firms. Piore and Sable (1984) argue that in the 1970s firms and policy-makers were unable to maintain the conditions necessary to preserve mass production. Mass production was based upon the input of special-purpose machines and of semi-skilled workers and the output of standardised products. A fundamental change in the path of technological development led to the occurrence of vast diseconomies of scale. This market instability resulted in the demise of mass production and promoted flexible specialisation. Piore and Sable (1984) use the term Industrial Divide for the 'reversal of the trend' from that towards more large firms to that towards more small ones. Jensen (1993) refers to the Third Industrial Revolution when describing the same phenomenon. Meredith (1987) discusses the advantages of a range of recently developed flexible production techniques for small-scaled enterprises. Audretsch and Thurik (1998) point to the role knowledge plays when explaining the shift from the managed economy to the entrepreneurial economy.

This shift away from large firms is not confined to manufacturing industries. Brock and Evans (1989) show that this trend has been economy-wide at least for the United States. They provide us with four more reasons as to why this shift has occurred: the increase of labour supply; changes in consumer tastes; relaxation of (entry) regulations and the fact that we are in a period of creative destruction. Loveman and Sengenberger (1991) stress the influence of two trends of industrial restructuring: that of decentralisation and vertical disintegration of large companies and that of the formation of new business communities. Furthermore they emphasise the role of public and private policies promoting the small business sector. See also Carree (1997) and Carree et al. (1999) for literature surveys of the determinants of the shift away from a managed economy and towards an entrepreneurial economy.

The question whether this change of the size class structure of industries has influenced the economic performance of these industries has received limited attention. This has to do with a persistent lack in knowledge of market structure dynamics (Audretsch, 1995). In other words, there is a lack in knowledge concerning questions such as who enters and exits, what determines this mobility and what are its effects, in particular on economic performance. Here we are concerned with one of the most important questions in economics: why do industries or economies grow? The link between industrial organisation and economic growth has always been the subject of considerable debate. As exposed earlier, traditionally, the prevalent assumption was that giant companies are at the heart of the process of innovation and creation of welfare. This assumption is generally referred to as the Schumpeterian hypothesis. Recently, the debate centres on the question whether the process of decentralisation and deconcentration, which virtually every industrialised country has experienced in the last two decades, has had positive welfare implications. Audretsch (1995) calls this shift in orientation of our social-economic thinking 'the new learning'.

The question of the link between the shift in the industrial structure and subsequent growth can be answered in two ways. *First*, by investigating the many consequences of the shift in the locus of economic activity. For instance, one may study whether this shift has been favourable to the process of innovation and rejuvenation of industries. See Acs and Audretsch (1990), Audretsch (1995) and Cohen and Klepper (1992 and 1996). Alternatively, one may focus on the discussion of the relation between the role of small firms and competition and industry dynamics. See Audretsch (1993, 1995) and You (1995). Moreover, the role of small firms in the job-creation process, usually treated as a controversial topic despite countless studies showing that small firms are a major engine in this process, may be dealt with. Davis, Haltiwanger and Schuh (1996) and Carree and Klomp (1996) provide some insights in this topic. Lastly, the role of small firms as a vehicle for entrepreneurship may be the focal point of our attention. Baumol (1990) provides an extensive account of the role of entrepreneurial activities and their consequence for prosperity throughout history. Acs (1992) brings it all together in a short descriptive manner and surveys some consequences of the shift of economic activity from large to smaller businesses. His claims are that small firms play an important role in the economy serving as agents of change by their entrepreneurial activity, being the source of considerable innovative activity, stimulating industry evolution and creating an important share of the newly generated jobs. The evaluation of the various consequences of this shift is difficult but necessary to establish whether it is desirable and to be promoted by economic policy. It is difficult because none of these consequences is, in fact, independent of the other three and because the evaluation offers something of a series of trade-offs. See also Audretsch and Thurik (1997) who contrast the most fundamental elements of the newly emerging entrepreneurial economy with those of the managed economy identifying 15 trade-offs that are essential for these two polar worlds. For instance, small businesses may contribute to higher growth because of their contribution to the selection process due to their variety. On the other hand, the selection process may lead to a lower level of stability and, hence, to welfare losses. Or, while employment levels may rise as firm size declines, the lower average wages small firms pay may at least partly offset the welfare effect induced by the employment growth.

A *second* way to answer the question is to go around the intermediary variables between the shift in the industrial structure and growth such as technological change, entrepreneurship, competitiveness and job generation. The question then becomes whether there is a direct empirical link between this shift and performance measures such as employment, growth or productivity. Some preliminary empirical results of the relation between changes in the firm size distribution and economic growth are presented in Thurik (1996). The analysis shows a positive effect of an increase in the economy-wide share of small firms on growth in gross domestic product for some European countries. The interpretation of this result is somewhat difficult because it is not clear whether changes in the economy-wide share of small firms result mainly from changes in the sectoral composition or from downscaling in the specific industries. Schmitz (1989) presents an endogenous growth model relating entrepreneurial activity and economic growth. He shows that an increase of the proportion of entrepreneurs in the working force leads to an increase in long-run economic growth. His model also implies that the equilibrium fraction of entrepreneurs is lower than the social optimal level, providing a rationale for policies stimulating entrepreneurial activity. Holmes and Schmitz (1990) develop a model of entrepreneurship in the spirit of T.W. Schultz. They show how specialisation in managerial tasks and entrepreneurship – responding to opportunities for creating new products and production processes – may affect economic development. Some evidence of a well established historical (long-term) relationship between fluctuations in entrepreneurship and the rise and fall of nations is assembled by Wennekers and Thurik (1999). In this respect also the work of Eliasson (1995) on economic growth through competitive selection is of relevance. Such a relation is characterised by significant time lags. There is more evidence on the relation between size class distributions and economic performance. For instance, see Nickell (1996), Nickell et al. (1997) and Lever and Nieuwenhuijsen (1999) who present evidence that competition, as measured by an increased number of competitors, has a positive effect on the rate of total factor productivity growth. Acs et al. (1999) point to differences in competition and entrepreneurship when comparing the more successful US economy to that of Europe and Japan.

The present paper follows the second way. It investigates the link between smallness and growth bypassing the analysis of all the intermediary variables. It presents two models linking performance and firm size distribution. As a prelude to the formal models the relative virtues of large as well as small firms are dealt with in a descriptive way.

This contribution is organised as follows. In Section 2 reasons are discussed why large firms may outperform small firms. This is followed by a discussion of reasons for the opposite phenomenon of small firms outperforming their larger counterparts. The question which effects dominate is interpreted as an empirical one. For this empirical discussion two models are used. The *first* model uses a sample of European manufacturing industries for the period 1990 through 1994. By dealing with data at a relatively low industry level the disturbing influence of changes in sectoral composition is eliminated. In Section 3 these data are described and the extent of 'smallness' in these industries is documented. Data are used of 14 manufacturing industries in 13 countries (Belgium, Denmark, Finland, France, Germany, Italy, the Netherlands, Norway, Portugal, Spain, Sweden, Switzerland and the United Kingdom). This description is followed by an analysis of the effect of the share of small firms on the growth of output in these manufacturing industries. The *second* model uses a cross-section of member countries of the European Union over a time period in the early 1990. Both data and an analysis of the effects of the growth differential between small and large firms on aggregate growth are reported upon in Section 4. Section 5 concludes with general policy recommendations. Section 2 benefited from Thurik (1996) and Carree and Thurik (1999), Section 3 from Carree and Thurik (1998) and Section 4 from Audretsch and Thurik (1997).

2. ELEVEN EFFECTS STIMULATING LARGENESS OR SMALLNESS

The debate about the causes and consequences of firm size, that is about the firm size distribution, is as old as economics itself. See Audretsch (1993). This debate received continuous academic interest but fails to have been conspicuous. Until some 15 years ago its outcome was more or less unanimous: small firms would either disappear or be allowed to lead a marginal life. There have been isolated dissidents. The early Schumpeter accentuated the role of smallness in economic restructuring and Schumacher talked about the virtues of smallness in the darkest of the mass-production times. See Schumpeter (1934) and Schumacher (1973), respectively. Santarelli and Pesciarelli (1990) elaborate on Schumpeter's ideas of entrepreneurship being the underlying force of economic development, presented in his German edition of *The Theory of Economic Development*

(1911), but partly excluded from the translated American edition of 1934. In his pioneering empirical study, Birch (1981) claimed to have discovered that most new jobs emanated from small firms. This finding contradicted the prevailing body of knowledge and intuition of that time. Mainstream economists, however, kept thinking that small firms would lead a fading life. It was not readily apparent how Birch's finding had to be reconciled with the empirical evidence showing the ongoing concentration of economic activity that had prevailed for decades. The inherent potential of scale economies was already brought forward by Adam Smith's famous pin factory example. Karl Marx advanced his image of an ever-decreasing number of giant organisations based upon a huge concentration of capital and usurping the labouring masses. Moreover, there are some theoretically powerful and empirically often corroborated mechanisms supporting the shift away from new and small firms and towards large and incumbent ones. See Thurik (1997) and Carree and Thurik (1999).

First, there is the effect of *scale*, usually interpreted as the fall of average costs with increasing volume of output. This mechanism occurs in many business functions from productive to administrative and on different levels of aggregation: in business units, in establishments and in enterprises. The sources of scale economies are well known. One is that fixed set-up or threshold costs do not vary with the level of output. For instance, the costs of setting up a scientific gathering are fixed to a large extent. The costs of the organisation and the preparation of the presentations and the presentations themselves become more effective if the number of attendants to the meeting increases.

Second, there is the effect of *scope*, usually observed as the fall of average costs of a product if the number of different but related products increases. See Nooteboom (1993). Its sources can range from the use of indivisible resources (the room where a scientific meeting is held can be used for various purposes), to complementarity (presentations at scientific meetings can also be used as material for prospective articles in journals) and interaction (discussion during and between the presentations).

Third, there is the effect of *experience*, defined as the decline of average costs with increasing production volume accumulated over time. The best-documented examples of unit costs falling over time as a result of past experience are those of the Liberty freighters and B-29 bombers during WW II. See Scherer and Ross (1990) and Lucas (1993).

It is clear that these three cost effects are detrimental to the survival of small firms. Small firms may try to compensate for these cost disadvantages by creating networks or other inter-firm relations (Oughton and Whittam, 1997). From Williamson's contribution to the economic sciences we know that the organisers of productive output can choose between two basic governance structures: that of integration of input within the hierarchy of the firm and that of purchase of input on the market. See Williamson (1975). The *advantage* of the latter structure lies in the economy of scale resulting from specialisation. For example, the consultant gains from specialisation doing similar consultancy work for many firms for which it does not pay to employ a specialist for solving similar problems occurring only with intervals. The *disadvantage* lies in the occurrence of transaction costs. Three stages of a transaction define three different sources of costs. The stage of contact involves search and marketing costs: search costs for the firm to be consulted and marketing costs for the firm supplying consultancy inputs. The stage of contract involves information, negotiation and definition costs. The stage of control involves costs of monitoring, discussion, feedback, redesign, arbitration, etc. Nooteboom (1993) argues that smaller firms face higher transaction costs per unit of transaction than large ones because *first*, there are threshold costs in all three stages of the transaction. The relative contribution of these threshold costs disappears the larger the transaction becomes; *second*, small firms suffer more from the cost of acquiring and processing information. They are more sensitive to uncertainty, discontinuity, opportunism and specificity.

So, the *fourth* effect, the effect of *organisation* defined as using outside production for one's inputs instead of inside production, boils down to the occurrence of more scale effects and to the appearance of transaction effects of both which are damaging to the level of unit costs of small production kernels.

So far, these four effects provide the rationale for the success of large firms. There must be more factors to explain the existence and success of small ones.

The *fifth* effect is the *transportation* effect. Production and organisation costs discussed above are only part of the total cost structure. There is also the cost of delivering output to customers or bringing customers to the place where service is provided. See Scherer and Ross (1990). Many studies predict and report significant scale economies on the level of establishments in the retail industry. See Nooteboom (1982 and 1987a) and Frenk et al. (1991). Still there is a considerable number of small retail stores. Customers take into account their transportation costs when looking for supplies. This is why a geographic dispersion of demand goes together with a geographic dispersion of supply. And then smallness, at least at the establishment, plant, or in the retail case, store level has manifest advantages.

The *sixth* effect is that of the *market size*. Small firms are often well equipped to be successful in small markets. In many markets scale economies have no meaning because they cannot be obtained. For example, it is easy to check that all participants of some scientific gathering wear a different shirt.

Variety is a significant customer requirement. The market for a singular piece of apparel is small when compared to the entire textiles market. There is no apparent bonus for large firms in markets that are fragmented in size. Bradburd and Ross (1989) provide empirical evidence that small firms may prosper in market niches.

The *seventh* effect is that of *adjustment*. There is a trade-off between efficiency – production costs given some output level – and adjustability – the cost of adjusting a certain level of output. Large firms can often produce at lower unit costs than small firms can. But small firms can usually adjust their output level at lower costs than large firms, because they are either more labour-intensive or use different equipment. See Mills and Schumann (1985), Brock and Evans (1989) and Das, Chappell and Shughart II (1993). Small firms survive and even prosper in this world of flexible specialisation. See Fiegenbaum and Karnani (1991). It is the story of the two transportation firms: one firm using large lorries, thriving in a market with a persisting high demand for shipment, the other firm using small ones, thriving in a turbulent market with a varying demand for lorries. It is the story of many firms in the post-mass-consumption age: they produce exactly what the customer wants. They pay little attention to questions whether anyone else wants the product, whether the firm has made the product before or whether there will be follow-up demand for the product. See *The Economist* (1994). It is also the story of the firms in the so-called industrial districts, competing and cooperating at the same time. There is no apparent bonus for large firms in markets that are fragmented in time.

The *eighth* effect is that of *effectiveness*. The essence of this effect is that different goods and services have different meanings for different people. See Brock and Evans (1986). A shirt that fits the average attendant of a scientific meeting is not the same good as a shirt tailored to fit a specific individual and bought for showing off at a specific occasion. A shirt factory can make shirts of the first type cheaper than a tailor can. But one receives more effective units of shirt from a tailor. At least someone, who is sensitive to the satisfaction of knowing the uniqueness of his shirt or the gains of showing it off to others, will experience the effectiveness of a unique shirt. The rationale being that the existence of both the factory and the tailor in the shirt market can only be explained if output is measured in terms of effective units of shirts instead of just shirts. This not only explains the co-existence of clothing giants and tailors, but also that of supermarket chains and speciality stores, of the McDonald chain and three-star restaurants. Jackson (1984) shows in a utility maximisation context how an increase in wealth leads to the consumption of a larger variety of products. Acs, Audretsch and Carlsson (1990) suggest that international competition has increased exposure to foreign products, which would also enlarge the demand for variety.

The *ninth* effect is that of *compensating factor differentials*. This effect becomes evident when answering the question why small firms in industries where scale economies play an important role or firms that have been termed in the industrial organization literature as sub-optimal scale firms, are able to exist? One answer provided by a now rather large literature linking firm size and age to survival rates is that they are not – at least, not with the same likelihood as their larger and more mature counterparts. It is exactly this literature identifying the positive relationship between firm size (and age) and the likelihood of survival that confirms the suspicion that, at least some small firms are confronted by a size-related disadvantage. Audretsch (1995) and Audretsch et al. (1999) suggest a different answer: small firms are able to compensate for any size-related disadvantage by pursuing a strategy of compensating factor differentials, where factors of production are deployed differently and compensated differently. Probably, smaller scale firms pursue a strategy of seeking product niches and therefore do not compete directly against the larger firms included in a rather broadly defined industry classified by a national statistical office. They do not compete on the market of outputs or on that of inputs. This is certainly consistent with the findings in Audretsch et al. (1999) that firms operating in an industry where the small firms have the innovative advantage rely less on reducing employee compensation. That is, innovative activity and pursuing niches is clearly a type of compensating strategy deployed by smaller competitors to offset what would otherwise be an inherent size disadvantage.

The *tenth* effect is that of *control*. Nooteboom (1987b) claims that this is one of the least documented. The discussion of what defines a small firm is probably as everlasting as the discussion of where small firms stem from. A challenging definition of a small firm is that of a firm where one person or a small group of persons is in control, or which bears the personal stamp of one person. Though imprecise, this definition at least stimulates the investigation of behavioural advantages like entrepreneurial energy, motivated and effective labour due to the mutual proximity of customers, suppliers, production floor, management and ownership, etc. Entrepreneurial and organisational energy may flourish and be well controlled and guided in a small environment. Many management gurus earn big money hammering this down. The best evidence of this entrepreneurial energy is that many entrepreneurs convince themselves to work below the minimum wage and convince their employees to work below market prices, i.e. at a price lower than what a large firm would offer for a similar job. See Evans and Leighton (1989) and Oosterbeek and Van Praag (1995). The higher levels of control, commitment, motivation, perseverance and energy prevailing in small units easily explain this wage differential. That is why the effect of control is important. Wiggins (1995) discusses the related subject of ownership. He claims that ownership is the key advantage to explain why entrepreneurial activities are carried out in small enterprises rather than in large firms where the entrepreneur is an employee. It is straightforward that the effect of control is not futile in an environment where the effect of adjustment (and hence flexibility and manoeuvrability) plays a role. They reinforce each other in their struggle to outperform the advantages of scale.

The *eleventh* and final effect we would like to mention is that of entrepreneurial rewards. Since William Baumol's essay showed us that entrepreneurship cannot only be productive as well as unproductive, but even destructive, we should start thinking of ways to grab the essence of how societies reward entrepreneurial activities. See Baumol (1990). Baumol's basic hypothesis is that, while the supply of entrepreneurship varies across societies, its productive contribution varies even more. The reason is that the societal perspective determines to what degree entrepreneurial activities are used for productive achievements such as innovation or unproductive ventures such as rent-seeking or organised crime. Murphy, Shleifer and Vishny (1991) provide some empirical evidence showing that countries with a relatively high number of graduates from law schools, educated mainly to redistribute income, grow slower, ceteris paribus, than countries that have a relatively high number of graduates in technical disciplines.

Probably, there are many institutional factors influencing the size distribution of firms. Fiscal regulations may strongly affect the propensity of people to start firms. They may stimulate people to combine their main job in a large firm with forms of self-employment. Also, the influence of the trade unions and worker participation may drop if firms stay small. Technical requirements may be circumvented if firms stay small because small firms are often exempt from many legal, technical, organisational and environmental regulations to a certain degree.

Like the effects stimulating largeness, those stimulating smallness are not independent in their influence. The effects of market size and adjustment are mutually reinforcing when explaining smallness in many markets of producer goods and services. The supplier producing a specific car part in a given year is likely to produce a different but evenly specific part the next year. This supplier operates in a market that is fragmented both in size and time. The effects of market size, adjustment and effectiveness are mutually reinforcing when explaining smallness in many markets of consumer goods and services. The small firm producing a unique shirt this year is likely to produce a different unique shirt next year, particularly if the shirt has a high fashion value. This market is fragmented in size, in time and in taste.

3. LARGE FIRM PRESENCE AND MANUFACTURING PRODUCTION

This section investigates the effects of differences in the size class structure of firms on industrial performance in a sample of 14 industries in 13 countries for the period 1990-94. The share of large firms is calculated from Eurostat (1994). Not all data of industries and countries in this Eurostat report are used. Some countries are not incorporated because they provide establishment data instead of enterprise data. Furthermore, industries are not taken into consideration whose the total number of employees is below 10,000. Finally, Eurostat sometimes does not provide employment data due to reasons of confidentiality. Two measures of the share of large firms are calculated. The first is the employment share of enterprises with 100 or more employees, MFP (Medium-sized and large Firm Presence). For this variable there is a total of 144 observations. The second is the employment share of enterprises with 500 or more employees, LFP (Large Firm Presence). For this variable there are 130 observations. The correlation between the two measures MFP and LFP for the 130 observations is 0.93. Total production growth from 1990-93 and from 1990-94 is measured by the production indices of the industry in 1993 and 1994 with 1990 as the base year. The primary sources for the indices are Eurostat (1996) and OECD (1996).

Data are available for 13 countries (number of industries incorporated): Belgium (11), Denmark (10), Finland (7), France (14), Germany (13), Italy (14), the Netherlands (13), Norway (6), Portugal (12), Spain (14), Sweden (8), Switzerland (8) and the United Kingdom (14). All data refer to the year 1990 except for Italy (1989) and Switzerland (1991). The five countries where total employment in the industries incorporated is in excess of one million persons are Germany (7.6 million), United Kingdom (4.9 million), Italy (4.2 million), France (4.0 million) and Spain (2.4 million). Total employment in the 144 industries equals 27.3 million persons. Table 11.2 shows how these are distributed across the 14 two-digit level manufacturing industries. The next four columns of the table show the average medium-sized and large firm presence, MFP, and the average production indices of 1993 and 1994, respectively. The right hand column shows the average correlation between MFP and the production indices of 1993 and 1994. The non-weighted average of these correlations is -0.07. On average medium-sized and large firm presence and growth of production appear to be negatively related but the differences across industries are considerable. The correlations range between -0.55 for the Paper, publishing and printing industry (NACE 47) and +0.66 for Instrument engineering (NACE 37).

Table 11.2 Some statistics of 14 European industries

NACE	Description	OBS	EMPL	MFP	P93	P94	COR
21/22	Basic metals	8	907	0.87	91.6	99.4	-0.48
24	Non-metallic mineral Products	10	1,081	0.55	88.0	94.0	-0.18
25/26	Chemicals	12	2,047	0.82	100.5	107.7	0.41
31	Metal articles	9	2,972	0.39	89.0	93.8	-0.07
32	Mechanical engineering	11	3,146	0.58	87.5	93.1	0.02
34	Electrical engineering	10	2,949	0.74	99.1	107.4	0.09
35	Motor vehicles	8	1,885	0.89	85.9	96.5	0.10
37	Instrument engineering	7	492	0.54	92.0	95.7	0.66
41/42	Food, drink and tobacco	13	3,177	0.58	102.5	104.1	-0.11
43	Textiles	10	1,410	0.61	87.0	91.5	-0.48
45	Footwear and clothing	11	1,872	0.38	87.2	87.7	-0.49
46	Wood and wooden products	13	1,759	0.27	95.8	102.0	-0.09
47	Paper, publishing and printing	11	2,381	0.57	100.4	105.9	-0.55
48	Rubber and plastics	11	1,269	0.56	95.7	101.8	0.15
All		144	27,348	0.59	93.5	99.0	

Note: OBS stands for the number of countries for which data are available on MFP and production indices for both 1993 and 1994. EMPL stands for the total employment in the industries for the countries for which data are available (in thousands). MFP stands for average medium and large firm presence (the share of firms with more than 100 employees in total employment). P93 and P94 are the average production indices in 1993 and 1994, respectively. The production index in base year 1990 is equal to 100. COR is the average correlation between MFP and P93 and between MFP and P94.

Source: Carree and Thurik (1998).

To test for the existence of the effect of the share of (medium-sized and) large firms on growth of production, we use the following equations:

$$(1) \quad P_{ij} = a_i + b_j + c \, MFP_{ij} + e_{ij}$$
$$\text{and}$$
$$(2) \quad P_{ij} = a_i + b_j + c \, LFP_{ij} + e_{ij},$$

where i refers to industry and j to country. The variable P_{ij} is the production index of industry i in country j in 1993 or 1994 (1990=100). The variables a_i and b_j are industry and country dummies, respectively. The variables e_{ij} and f_{ij} are mean zero disturbances assumed to be i.i.d. It is necessary to incorporate industry dummies because a level of large firm presence considered relatively high in one industry may be considered relatively low in another. Choosing a specific period for which to evaluate economic growth is crucial. If the period is too long then the size class structure of the industry may change considerably during the period of observation. If the period is too short then the effect of the size class structure may be overshadowed by the business cycle influence on industry output. We consider two periods, 1990-93 and 1990-94. In 1993 most European manufacturing industries experienced a period of recession. The average production index in our sample in that year was 93.5. The year 1994 disclosed a recovery for most industries and the average production index rose again to almost the same level as in 1990.

In Table 11.3, least squares estimation results are presented of equations (1) and (2) in case only industry dummies are incorporated, i.e. $b_j=0$ for all j. The results weighed with industry employment are presented as well. This implies that countries and/or industries with a large number of employees have a stronger impact on the regression results. Table 11.3 shows that the effect of MFP or LFP on growth of production is significant only in case weighted least squares results are considered. There is little difference between equations (1) and (2) in the percentage of variance explained. The interpretation of the coefficients in the table is straightforward. For example, the weighted least squares results in the first two rows of Table 11.3 imply that an increase in MFP by 0.1 leads to a decrease in output growth by 1 per cent for the 1990-93 period and 2 per cent for the 1990-94 period. That is, industries not only appear to be more affected by the recession in case medium-sized and large firms had a larger employment share, they also tend to recover more slowly from this recession.

Spain and Portugal are two countries in a stage of economic development different from the other countries. The GDP per capita in the two countries is about two-thirds of that in the other countries and the large firm presence in industries is considerably lower than in the same industries in the other countries. Probably many firms in Spanish and Portuguese manufacturing suffer from sub-optimal scale. Small firm presence may only have a positive effect on output growth in a certain stage of organisational and technological development in which scale economies have become less important. Spain and Portugal joined the European Union in a later phase than the other countries of the sample and probably have not yet reached this stage. See Carree and Thurik (1998) for some results showing that the effect of MFP and LFP on the growth of output is stronger when Spain and Portugal are left out.

Table 11.3 Estimation results with industry dummies (t-values in parentheses)

Measure	Year	Countries	Obs.	Unweighted	R^2	Weighted	R^2
MFP	1993	All	144	-6.66 (1.2)	0.35	-12.34 (3.5)	0.30
MFP	1994	All	144	-7.81 (1.1)	0.29	-21.23 (4.5)	0.19
LFP	1993	All	130	-0.18 (0.0)	0.34	-11.77 (3.1)	0.27
LFP	1994	All	130	-1.01 (0.1)	0.27	-19.08 (3.8)	0.16

Note: MFP is medium and large firm presence and LFP is large firm presence. Industry dummies are incorporated in all regressions.

Source: Carree and Thurik (1998).

In Table 11.4 least squares estimation results are presented when country dummies are incorporated. Only the results for MFP are presented because they do not differ considerably from those for LFP. The reason for incorporating country dummies is to correct for country-specific events in the 1990-93 and 1990-94 periods. One such event was the collapse of the Finnish-Russian trade relationship leading to a strong recession in the Finnish economy. The general conclusion remains that industries with a higher medium and large firm share in 1990 have shown less growth of output in the subsequent years. This conclusion is valid for manufacturing industries in more highly developed European countries.

Table 11.4 Estimation results with country and industry dummies (t-values in parentheses)

Measure	Year	Countries	Obs.	Unweighted	R^2	Weighted	R^2
MFP	1993	All	144	-5.85 (0.7)	0.43	-14.74 (2.6)	0.35
MFP	1994	All	144	-3.50 (0.3)	0.42	-18.58 (2.4)	0.30

Note: MFP is medium firm presence and LFP is large firm presence. Country and industry dummies are incorporated in all regressions.

Source: Carree and Thurik (1998).

4. SMALL FIRM PRESENCE AND AGGREGATE GROWTH

There are many consequences of the shift from a managed economy to the entrepreneurial one such as alterations in innovative activity, employment, wage rate, market dynamics and a propensity to export. Probably, there are many more consequences than the ones mentioned in the Introduction to the present contribution. For instance, a qualitative change in the demand for consultancy inputs will occur as a consequence of this shift. The basic question is whether, at the end of the day, the entrepreneurial economy leads to more economic growth than the managed one. In the previous section an attempt was made to answer the question using data material for the manufacturing industry only. In the present section we will go one step further and present some results as to what happens to economies as a whole. Clearly, as in the previous section no analysis will be made of all the effects this shift has on the economy, such as alterations in innovative activity, employment, wage rate, market dynamics, propensity to export, a qualitative change in the demand for consultancy inputs, etc. which themselves can be growth determinants. By looking at the economy as a whole, we are able to also take into consideration the shift from manufacturing towards services. Many manufacturing firms have downsized and concentrated on core business. This has led to an accelerated process of new firm formation in the producer services sector (Piergiovanni and Santarelli, 1995).

We observe different patterns in the economic growth of European countries. One part of these differences is due to countries being in different stages of the business cycle. Another part is due to specific institutional, historical, political and social circumstances. The question is whether there is a third part due to the stage of their transition from the managed form to the entrepreneurial form of their economy.

In order to test whether we are able to decompose economic growth into these three components, we have to define the entrepreneurial stage of the economy as well as growth. For growth the real gross national product is taken as indicator. The definition of the entrepreneurial stage of the economy is less straightforward. It is tempting to use the growth of the number of entrepreneurs. The number of entrepreneurs, however, is a notoriously difficult variable (Wennekers and Thurik, 1999), since the definitions throughout the European countries vary widely and attempts to synchronise lack a convincing status. Moreover, it is not available for a large enough number of European countries. See Audretsch and Thurik (1998) and Carree et al. (1999) for some recent investigations using number of entrepreneurs in

OECD countries. That is why an attempt is made to capture the stage of the transition using the annual percentage growth of value-of-shipments of small- and medium-sized firms minus the annual percentage growth of value-of-shipments of large firms.

Apart from data limitations there are other drawbacks for using entrepreneurship as a prime variable. Small firms are certainly a vehicle in which entrepreneurship thrives. There are more such vehicles such as business units within large corporations. We realise that there are more ways for entrepreneurship to contribute to growth than through smallness. Entrepreneurship, in the form of new firms, and 'intrapreneurship', in the form of new ideas and responsibilities implemented in existing organisations, are essential to creating new economic activity. Entrepreneurial energy is not limited to small business owners, self-employed individuals, etc. Large companies promote 'intrapreneurship' within business units to achieve more flexibility and innovativeness. Recent studies on the role of competition (Nickell, 1996), of deregulation (Koedijk and Kremers, 1996) of intrapreneurship (Stopford and Baden-Fuller 1994) and of the nature of innovation (Cohen and Klepper, 1996 and Hagedoorn, 1996) support this view. There may be something like an entrepreneurial climate affecting also large firms and governmental institutions (Wennekers and Thurik, 1999). But since what happens within these latter contexts is bound to correlate with the world of smallness, it seems justified to use the smallness indicator introduced above.

In order to link the stage of transition from the managed to entrepreneurial economy to economic growth, data are used provided by the European Observatory (EIM, 1993, Table 2.13, 1994, Table 2.18 and EIM, 1995, various tables) and by the OECD (1994). Three variables are used: the annual percentage growth of real gross national product, the annual percentage growth of value-of-shipments of small- and medium-sized firms (with employment less than 500 employees), and the annual percentage growth of value-of-shipments of large firms (with employment of at least 500 employees). They are measured for three distinct time periods: 1988-90, 1989-92 and 1990-93 for the then 12 member countries of the European Union (EU-12), i.e. excluding, Finland, and Sweden. The country-year observations are divided into six groups on the basis of the degree to which value-of-shipments has shifted from large to small firms. Group 6 has the strongest shift. For each group, the average percentage growth of GNP is computed. Figure 11.1 relates these percentage growth rates to the relative shift in economic activity from large to small firms for each of the six groups. Those groups experiencing a greater shift in economic activity towards small firms have also achieved higher growth rates.

Figure 11.1 Growth and the relative shift towards small firms

Average Percentage GNP Growth

Grouped observations of shift towards small firms

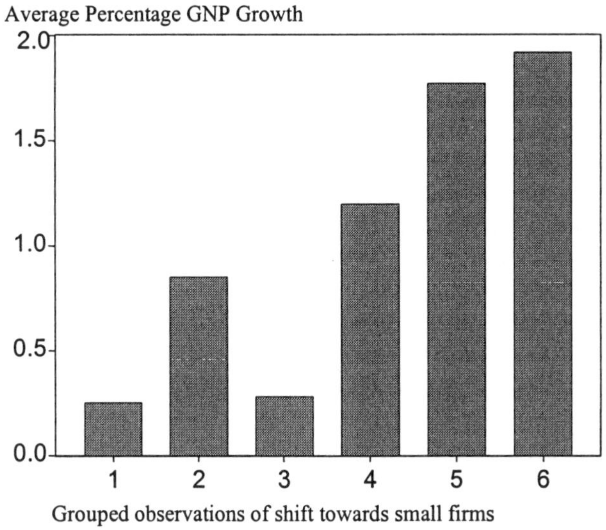

A disadvantage of using figures like the one presented here is that the causality problem cannot be solved. One cannot infer from the figure whether aggregate growth influences the excess growth of small firms or whether excess growth of small firms influences aggregate growth. An indication of the separate influences can only be given using regression relations with an adequate correction for both effects. This will be the subject of the remainder of this section. See also Audretsch and Thurik (1997).

The percentage change in gross national product of each country, ΔGNP, is linked to the stage of the transition from a managed economy to a entrepreneurial one, as represented by the percentage change in the value-of-shipments accounted for by small firms, ΔSF, minus the percentage change in the value-of-shipments accounted for by large firms, ΔLF, so that

(3)

$$\Delta GNP_{cp} = \sum_{c=1}^{C} \alpha_c D_c + \sum_{p=1}^{P} \beta_p D_p + \gamma(\Delta SF_{c,p-1} - \Delta LF_{c,p-1}) + \delta\Delta GNP_{c,p-1},$$

where D_c and D_p denote two vectors of dummy variables referring to countries $c = 1,...,C$ and periods $p = 1,...,P$. These dummy variables are used because countries experience different stages of the business cycle at different points in time, and because country specific institutional, historical, political, and social factors are bound to influence economic growth. Clearly, one less than $C + P$ dummy variables are used while computing the regression statistics to avoid full multicollinearity. The contribution of the shift of the size class structure of firms to the percentage growth of GNP is represented by γ. The influence of this shift on GNP growth is supposed to be lagged. The data used for GNP growth refer to the 'succeeding' years 1991, 1993 and 1994.

Equation (3) also includes lagged GNP growth in order to correct for the autocorrelation of GNP growth over time. Moreover, small firms' turnover is probably more procyclical than large firms' turnover. The small firm's part of the economy has a different sectoral composition, a higher domestic orientation and a lower strategic orientation than the large firm sector. If GNP increases (decreases), lagged GNP will increase (decrease) and small firms are more (less) likely to grow than large firms. If $\delta \Delta GNP_{c,p-1}$ is left out of the regression equation, coefficient γ will become positive because of this cyclical effect. This has nothing to do with the structural effect of the size class shift influencing GNP growth we are looking for. That is why lagged GNP growth is used in the regression equation and δ can be interpreted as the 'mean' degree of autocorrelation of GNP growth in the countries of the European countries. Factors specific to each country influencing economic growth, other than the shift in economic activity between large and small firms, are reflected by α, while factors specific to each time period are reflected by β.

The data set consists of a total of 36 (12 countries times three periods) observations covering an early period. However, two outliers had to be omitted in the period 1988-90. The growth in value-of-shipments exhibited by large firms in Spain was exceptionally high and that in Denmark exceptionally low. In *Enterprises in Europe* (Eurostat, 1994) it is reported that data for these two countries should not be used for this period. The remaining 34 observations are used for computing the regression coefficients. The only dummy variable with a significant contribution is D_{1994}. This is easy to understand in view of the unexpectedly high jump in GNP growth in 1994. Weighting with the number of active population and using dummy variable D_{1994} only, we find that γ equals 0.308 with a standard error of 0.166 and that δ equals 0.448 with a standard error of 0.167.

A limitation of the calculations is that the data include a number of estimates. Moreover, the regression results are sensitive to modification of specification. Follow-up studies are required for corroboration of these results. These studies would profit from the use of longer time series, the use of models where the reverse causality is taken into account in an explicit fashion and the use of data sets including the number of self-employed. Reverse causality can occur in various situations: growing industries may give opportunities for new and small firms using new technologies because growth may endanger the market position of incumbent firms. Furthermore, reversed causality may occur if there is a 'refugee' effect when the economy slows down. An increase in the unemployment level will probably affect the propensity of people to start firms. The latter mechanism occurs most notably in periods of downturns in the business cycle. See Audretsch and Thurik (1998) and Carree et al. (1999) for analyses using longer time series and set-ups explicitly modelling the reversed causality. See Carree et al. (1999) and Wennekers and Thurik (1999) for a more thorough treatment of the consequences of the use of various definitions of the concept of entrepreneurship. In the present study, γ representing the effect of excess smallness on aggregate growth is found to be positive. It has a t-value of 1.9 in the period 1991-94 for EU-12. We have to conclude that, based on the findings of this exercise, there is evidence suggesting that a shift in economic activity away from large firms and towardss small enterprises is a catalyst for economic growth, at least for member countries of the European Union over a recent time period.

The evidence provided by Schmitz (1989) and Nickell (1996) can be considered complementary to the investigations presented here. Schmitz presents a theoretical endogenous growth model relating entrepreneurial activity and economic growth. He shows that an increase of the proportion of entrepreneurs in the working force leads to an increase in long-run economic growth. Nickell studies the effect of competition on the development of productivity of firms. He finds that an increased number of competitors is associated with higher rates of total factor productivity growth. There are several other studies that are complementary also. Audretsch and Thurik (1998) provide an analysis showing the consequence of lagging behind in the transition process. Using a sample of 23 OECD countries they find that, on average, increasing entrepreneurship leads to initially decreasing unemployment for the period 1974 through 1994. Carree et al. (1999) use the same data set but an entirely different model. They apply the concept of an equilibrium relation between the number of entrepreneurs and the stage of economic development. This relation is hypothesised to be a decreasing function of economic development in that the number of entrepreneurs per labour force is high in low-developed economies whereas there is a later phase where mass production and scale economies thrive. A vast literature points at a still later phase of economic development where the entrepreneurship rate is increasing again. This phase is characterised by 'the reversal of the trend' (Brock and Evans, 1989, Loveman and Sengenberger, 1991, and Carree, 1997) towards decreasing economies of scale and scope. Therefore a U-shaped equilibrium relation is tested in their set-up. They present evidence that such a relation exists and that deviating from the equilibrium rate of entrepreneurship leads to lower economic growth. Out-of-equilibrium situations can occur due to exogenous shocks and institutional divergences, for instance, because government regulation of market activity might obstruct and frustrate the spontaneous, corrective forces of entrepreneurial adjustments.

5. SMALLNESS AND ECONOMIC GROWTH

Causes and consequences of the shift in economic activity from large to small firms have been on top of the research agenda since the early 1980s. In the present contribution it is investigated whether a higher share of small business at the start of the 1990s has led to higher output growth in the subsequent years in European manufacturing. Second, an analysis is made whether excess growth of small firms over their larger counterparts has led to additional macroeconomic growth for member countries of the European Union in the early 1990's. The results of both investigations are meant to supplement the intuition of many policy-makers that the changes in industrial structure have had some real effects on economic performance. Indeed, the results indicate that a manufacturing industry with a low large firm presence relative to the same industries in other countries has performed better in terms of growth of output. This suggests that lagging behind in the industrial restructuring process has come at a cost of lower economic growth. The results also indicate that on the macroeconomic level additional growth may be expected if small firms grow faster than their larger counterparts. Countries that have been most active in stimulating the small business sector in the 1980s may very well have reaped the fruits of this policy. Regression calculations such as the ones presented in the present contribution are a powerful instrument but have shortcomings. They refer to a certain period, to certain countries and depend upon the implicit assumptions of the underlying model. The results become more powerful if the findings are in line with related work in this area using other data and other methodologies. There is a growing body of related work producing similar results such as that of the endogenous growth model of

Schmitz (1989), of Nickell (1996) studying the effect of competition on the development of productivity of firms, of Audretsch and Thurik (1998) on the relation between the number of entrepreneurs ˙per labour force and unemployment and of Carree et al. (1999) on the equilibrium relation between the number of entrepreneurs per labour force and the stage of economic development.

European politicians and representatives of social and institutional groups fear for a further rise of the already unacceptably high level of unemployment. The endless series of efficiency and cost-cutting operations of the public and large business sectors cause this high level. They hope that unemployment can be fought by stimulating smallness. Probably, this is true for various reasons. *First*, stimulating smallness lifts the dependency on possibly sluggish and transient resources like scale, scope and experience, and intensifies the dependency on resources such as adjustment and effectiveness. The latter resources are likely to be more robust against uncertainty and change than the former. Stimulating small firms means stimulating new and hence young firms. This implies stimulating newness and diversity. Both are indispensable ingredients for prosperous modern economies. Diversity is the starting phase for selecting, and selection breeds the next generation's products and markets. *Second*, stimulation of smallness means stimulation of labour-intensity and hence employment by definition. See Loveman and Sengenberger (1991). *Third*, stimulating small firms is a means of stimulating entrepreneurship, in the form of new firms and in the form of new ideas and responsibilities implemented in existing organisations. This is essential to knowledge-based economic activity because the potential value of new ideas and knowledge are inherently uncertain (Audretsch and Thurik, 1998). The existing firms will not pursue many new ideas because they have different agendas or simply do not recognise their potential value. If a new firm is not started to pursue such ideas they will simply remain untapped.

The industrial structure of a knowledge-based entrepreneurial economy is very different from one based on the mass-production of relatively known products using established processes. It is a much more fluid and turbulent economy, where people are quick to move into situations where their ideas are valued. It is an economy where failure loses much of its pejorative connotation because it is recognised that trial and error and experimentation are essential to innovation and the creation of new ideas. A knowledge-based entrepreneurial economy also promotes human fulfilment. Just as creativity, autonomy and independence become not only important characteristics for personal growth and development (Lumpkin and Dess, 1996), but also for economic growth and development, managerial and organisational structures of hierarchy and authoritarianism give way to teamwork, networks and interdependence. *Finally*, stimulation of smallness implies an increase in the variety of the range of products and services offered. This paves the way for a process with different innovative approaches (Cohen and Klepper, 1992) and also satisfies a fragmented and differentiated demand.

We do not claim that each new and small firm is an agent of change, representing the new entrepreneurial economy. In fact, our analysis in Section 3 has shown that the effect of small business presence on economic progress depends upon the industry and stage of economic development. Many of the traditional small firms (mom-and-pop businesses) in less developed countries can be characterised rather as obstacles to change than as agents of change. Also, many of the small start-ups in highly developed countries play only a limited role as agents of change and many of them disappear after a short time period. Policies providing incentive schemes for new and small firms in general may therefore suffer from ·decreased probabilities of new firm survival without achieving much transformation towards an entrepreneurial economy. However, there is room for at least two types of policy intervention. The first type is policy aimed at promoting the creation of new technology-based firms in selected industries. The second type is policy aimed at providing newly created firms, irrespective of their industrial classification, with the financial, organisational and technological resources needed to grow in both domestic and foreign markets. This type of generic policy in particular promotes variation among new businesses. This creates the basis for a selection process that may result in new products and approaches. This selection process may not be hampered by incumbent firms striving to maintain their competitive position.

In the United States small firms replaced large firms not just in terms of generating the large majority of the 18 million new jobs created in the 1980s, but also in terms of much of the innovative activity that has driven the growth of new industries and renewed international competitiveness (Audretsch, 1995). Meanwhile, throughout Europe, job layoffs and downsizing of large enterprises, often in traditional moderate-technology industries, have been common phenomena.

The industrial transformation is shaping the development of Western capitalism and should trigger a shift in government policies away from constraining the freedom of business to contract through regulation, public ownership and antitrust. It should be geared towards a new set of enabling policies fostering small and new firms, entrepreneurship and the creation and commercialisation of new knowledge. What specific policy measures have to be taken is the object of a different study. De Koning and Snijders (1992) provide a survey of the various public policies introduced during the 1980s in the countries of the European Union. See also Storey and Tether (1998) and OECD (1998). Embracing the resolutions of the 1997 Luxembourg summit on unemployment would be a wise first step. These resolutions dealt with the stimulation of new and young firms in areas such as tax deregulation, administrative measures, loan guarantee programmes, venture capital, joint venturing, enterprise culture, training programmes, access to technology and R&D and impact reports. The empirical results obtained in this paper and supported by findings in the recent literature suggest that a policy of stimulating small firms, or more generally entrepreneurship, may be one of the most effective ways of combating the current alleged weakness in competitiveness, growth potential and employment generation of European industry.

NOTES

1. The authors would like to thank David Audretsch for comments and for allowing the use of material we have worked on recently. They would also like to thank Enrico Galli, Jacques Pelkmans, Enrico Santarelli and other participants of the workshop on Regulatory Reform, Market Functioning and Competitiveness held at CEPS in Brussels, 31st May and 1st June 1999. Martin Carree is also affiliated to the Faculty of Economics and Business Administration, Maastricht University, the Netherlands.

REFERENCES

Acs, Z.J. (1984), *The Changing Structure of the US Economy*, New York: Praeger.
Acs, Z.J. (1992), Small business economics: A global perspective, *Challenge,* Vol. 35, November/December, pp. 38-44.
Acs, Z.J. (1996), 'Small firms and economic growth', in P.H. Admiraal (ed.), *Small Business in the Modern Economy*, De Vries Lectures in Economics, Oxford: Blackwell Publishers.
Acs, Z.J. and D.B. Audretsch (1990), *Innovation and Small Firms*, Cambridge, MA: MIT Press.
Acs, Z.J. and D.B. Audretsch (1993), 'Conclusion', in Z.J. Acs and D.B. Audretsch (eds), *Small Firms and Entrepreneurship: An East-West Perspective*, Cambridge: Cambridge University Press.
Acs, Z.J., D.B. Audretsch and B. Carlsson (1990), 'Flexibility, plant size and industrial restructuring', in Z.J. Acs and D.B. Audretsch (eds), *The*

Economics of Small Firms: a European Challenge, Dordrecht, NL: Kluwer Academic Publishers.

Acs, Z.J., B. Carlsson and Ch. Karlsson (1999), 'The linkages among entrepreneurship, SMEs and the macroeconomy', in Z.J. Acs, B. Carlsson and Ch. Karlsson (eds), *Entrepreneurship, Small and Medium-Sized Enterprises and the Macroeconomy*, Cambridge: Cambridge University Press.

Audretsch, D.B. (1993), *Kleinunternehmen in der Industrieökonomiek: ein neuer Ansatz*, Discussion paper FS IV 93-26, Wissenschaftszentrum Berlin.

Audretsch, D.B., 1995, *Innovation and Industry Evolution*, Cambridge, MA: MIT Press.

Audretsch, D.B., G. van Leeuwen, B. Menkveld and A.R. Thurik (1999), *Are small firms really sub-optimal?: Compensating factor differentials in small Dutch manufacturing firms*, Research Report 9901/E, EIM Small Business Research and Consultancy, Zoetermeer, NL.

Audretsch, D.B. and A.R. Thurik (1997), *Sources of growth: The entrepreneurial versus the managed economy*, Discussion Paper 1710, Centre for Economic Policy Research, London.

Audretsch, D.B. and A.R. Thurik (1998), *The knowledge society, entrepreneurship and unemployment*, Research report 9801/E, EIM Small Business Research and Consultancy, Zoetermeer, NL.

Baumol, W.J. (1990), 'Entrepreneurship: productive, unproductive and destructive', *Journal of Political Economy*, Vol. 98, pp. 893-921.

Birch, D.L. (1981), 'Who creates jobs?', *Public Interest*, Vol. 65, pp. 3-14.

Blau, D. (1987), 'A time series analysis of self-employment', *Journal of Political Economy*, Vol. 95, pp. 445-467.

Bradburd, R.M. and D.R. Ross (1989), 'Can small firms find and defend strategic niches?', *Review of Economics and Statistics*, Vol. 71, pp. 258-262.

Brock, W.A. and D.S. Evans (1986), *The Economics of Small Businesses*, New York: Holmes and Meier.

Brock, W.A. and D.S. Evans (1989), 'Small business economics', *Small Business Economics*, Vol. 1, pp. 7-20.

Carlsson, B. (1989), 'The evolution of manufacturing technology and its impact on industrial structure: An international study', *Small Business Economics*, Vol. 1, pp. 21-37.

Carlsson, B. (1992), 'The rise of small business: Causes and consequences', in W.J. Adams (ed.), *Singular Europe, Economy and Policy of the European Community after 1992*, Ann Arbor, MI: University of Michigan Press, pp. 145-169.

Carlsson, B. (1999), 'Small business, entrepreneurship, and industrial dynamics' in Z. Acs (ed.), *Are Small Firms Important?*, Dordrecht, NL: Kluwer Academic Publishers, forthcoming.

Carree, M.A. (1997), *Market Dynamics, Evolution and Smallness*, Amsterdam: Thesis Publishers.

Carree, M.A. and L. Klomp (1996), 'Small business and job creation: A comment', *Small Business Economics,* Vol. 8, pp. 317-322.

Carree, M.A. and A.R. Thurik (1998), 'Small firms and economic growth in Europe', *Atlantic Economic Journal,* Vol. 26, pp. 137-146.

Carree, M.A. and A.R. Thurik (1999), 'Industrial structure and economic growth', in D.B. Audretsch and A. R. Thurik (eds), *Innovation, Industry Evolution and Employment*, Cambridge. Cambridge University Press.

Carree, M.A., A. van Stel, A.R. Thurik and A. Wennekers (1999), *Business ownership and economic growth*, Research Report 9804/E, EIM Small Business Research and Consultancy Zoetermeer, NL.

Chandler, A.D. Jr., 1990, *Scale and Scope: The Dynamics of Industrial Capitalism*, Cambridge MA: Harvard University.

Cohen, W.M. and S. Klepper (1992), 'The trade-off between firm size and diversity in the pursuit of technological progress', *Small Business Economics,* Vol. 4, pp. 1-14.

Cohen, W.M. and S. Klepper (1996), 'A reprise of size and R&D', *Economic Journal,* Vol. 106, pp. 925-951.

Das, B.J., W.F. Chappell and W.F. Shughart II (1993), 'Demand fluctuations and firm heterogeneity', *Journal of Industrial Economics,* Vol. 41, pp. 51-60.

Davis, S.J., J. Haltiwanger and S. Schuh (1996), 'Small business and job creation: dissecting the myth and reassessing the facts', *Small Business Economics,* Vol. 8, pp. 297-315.

(The) Economist (1994), Between two worlds: A survey of manufacturing technology, 5 March.

EIM (1993), *European Observatory: First annual report*, Zoetermeer, NL.

EIM (1994), *European Observatory: Second annual report*, Zoetermeer, NL.

EIM (1995), *European Observatory: Third annual report*, Zoetermeer, NL.

EIM (1997), *European Observatory: Fifth annual report*, Zoetermeer, NL.

Eliasson, G. (1995), 'Economic growth through competitive selection', paper presented at the 22nd Annual EARIE Conference, Juan les Pins, 3-6 September 1995.

Eurostat (1994), *Enterprises in Europe, third edition*, Luxembourg.

Eurostat (1996), *Industrial Trends Monthly Statistics 1996/6*, Luxembourg.

Evans, D.S. and L. Leighton (1989), 'Why do smaller firms pay less?',

Journal of Human Resources, Vol. 24, pp. 299-318.

Fiegenbaum, A. and A. Karnani (1991), 'Output flexibility- a competitive advantage for small firms', *Strategic Management Journal,* Vol. 12, pp. 101-114.

Frenk, J.B.G., A.R. Thurik and C.A. Bout (1991), 'Labour costs and queueing theory in retailing', *European Journal of Operations Research,* Vol. 55, pp. 260-267.

Galbraith, J.K. (1956), *American Capitalism: the Concept of Countervailing Power,* Boston, MA: Houghton Mifflin.

Gold, B. (1981), 'Changing perspectives on size, scale and returns: An interpretive survey', *Journal of Economic Literature,* Vol. 19, pp. 5-33.

Hagedoorn, J. (1996), 'Innovation and entrepreneurship: Schumpeter revisited', *Industrial and Corporate Change,* Vol. 5, pp. 883-896.

Holmes, T.J. and J.A. Schmitz Jr. (1990), 'A Theory of Entrepreneurship and its Application to the Study of Business Transfers', *Journal of Political Economy,* Vol. 98, pp. 265-294.

Jackson, L.F. (1984), 'Hierarchic demand and the Engle curve for variety', *Review of Economics and Statistics,* Vol. 66, pp. 8-15.

Jensen, M.C. (1993), 'The modern industrial revolution, exit, and the failure of internal control systems', *Journal of Finance,* Vol. 48, pp. 831-880.

Koedijk, K and J.J.M. Kremers (1996), 'Market opening, regulation and growth in Europe', *Economic policy: A European forum,* pp. 443-460.

Koning, A. de and J. Snijders (1992), 'Policy on small and medium-sized enterprises in countries of the European Community', *International Small Business Journal,* Vol. 10, pp. 25-39.

Lever, M.H.C. and H.R. Nieuwenhuijsen (1999), 'The impact of competition on productivity in Dutch manufacturing', in D.B. Audretsch and A.R. Thurik (eds), *Innovation, Industry Evolution and Employment,* Cambridge: Cambridge University Press.

Loveman, G. and W. Sengenberger (1991), 'The re-emergence of small-scale production: An international comparison', *Small Business Economics,* Vol. 3, pp. 1-37.

Lucas, R.E. (1967), 'Adjustment costs and the theory of supply', *Journal of Political Economy,* Vol. 75, pp. 321-334.

Lucas, R.E. (1993), 'Making a miracle', *Econometrica,* Vol. 61, pp. 251-272.

Lumpkin, G.T. and G.G. Dess (1996), 'Clarifying the entrepreneurial orientation construct and linking it to performance', *Academy of Management Review,* Vol. 21, pp. 135-172.

Meredith, J. (1987), 'The strategic advantages of new manufacturing technologies for small firms', *Strategic Management Journal,* Vol. 8, pp. 249-258.

Mills, D.E. and L. Schumann (1985), 'Industry structure with fluctuating demand', *American Economic Review*, Vol. 77, pp. 184-193.

Murphy, K.M., A. Shleifer and R.W. Vishny (1991), 'The allocation of talent: Implications for growth', *Quarterly Journal of Economics*, Vol. 106, pp. 503-530.

Nickell, S.J. (1996), 'Competition and corporate performance', *Journal of Political Economy*, Vol. 104, pp. 724-746.

Nickell, S., P. Nicolitsas and N. Dryden (1997), 'What makes firms perform well?' *European Economic Review*, Vol. 41, pp. 783-796.

Nooteboom, B. (1982), 'A new theory of retailing costs', *European Economic Review*, Vol. 17, pp. 163-186.

Nooteboom, B. (1987a), 'Threshold costs in service industries', *Service Industries Journal*, Vol. 6, pp. 65-76.

Nooteboom, B. (1987b), 'Doen en laten van het MKB', in A.F.M. Nijsen, B. Nooteboom, C.W. Kroesen, J.J. Godschalk and J. Buursink (eds), *Op Maat van het MKB*, The Hague: Staatsuitgeverij.

Nooteboom, B. (1993), 'Firm size effects on transaction costs', *Small Business Economics*, Vol. 5, pp. 283-295.

OECD (1994), *Economic Outlook*, July, Paris.

OECD (1996), *Indicators of Industrial Activity*, No. 2, Paris.

OECD (1998), *Fostering Entrepreneurship*, Paris.

Oosterbeek, H. and M. van Praag (1995), 'Firm size wage differentials in the Netherlands', *Small Business Economics*, Vol. 7, pp. 173-182.

Oughton, C. and G. Whittam (1997), 'Competition and cooperation in the small firm sector', *Scottish Journal of Political Economy*, Vol. 44, pp. 1-30.

Piergiovanni, R. and E. Santarelli (1995), 'The determinants of firm start-up and entry in Italian producer services', *Small Business Economics*, Vol. 7, pp. 221-230.

Piore, M. and C. Sable (1984), *The Second Industrial Divide: Possibilities for Prosperity*, New York: Basic Books.

Santarelli, E. and E. Pesciarelli (1990), 'The emergence of a vision: The development of Schumpeter's theory of entrepreneurship', *History of Political Economy*, Vol. 22, pp. 677-696.

Scherer, F.M. and D. Ross (1990), *Industrial Market Structure and Economic Performance*, Boston, MA: Houghton Mifflin Company.

Schmitz, Jr., J.A. (1989), 'Imitation, entrepreneurship, and long-run growth', *Journal of Political Economy*, Vol. 97, pp. 721-739.

Schumacher, E.F. (1973), *Small is Beautiful*, New York: Harper and Row.

Schumpeter, J.A. (1934), *The Theory of Economic Development*, Cambridge,

MA: Harvard University Press.

Schumpeter, J.A. (1950), *Capitalism, Socialism and Democracy*, New York: Harper and Row.

Servan-Schreiber, J.-J. (1969), *The American Challenge*, London: Hamish Hamilton.

Stopford, J.M. and C.W.F. Baden-Fuller (1994), 'Creating corporate entrepreneurship', *Strategic Management Journal*, Vol. 15, pp. 521-536.

Storey, D.J. and B.S. Tether (1998), 'Public policy measures to support new technology-based firms in the European Union', *Research Policy*, Vol. 26, pp. 1037-1057.

Teece, D.J. (1993), 'The dynamics of industrial capitalism: Perspectives on Alfred Chandler's scale and scope', *Journal of Economic Literature*, Vol. 31, pp. 199-225.

Thurik, A.R. (1996), 'Small firms, entrepreneurship and economic growth', in P.H. Admiraal (ed.), *Small Business in the Modern Economy*, De Vries Lectures in Economics, Oxford: Blackwell Publishers.

Wennekers, S. and A.R. Thurik (1999), 'Linking entrepreneurship and economic growth', *Small Business Economics*, Vol. 13, pp. 27-55.

Wiggins, S.N. (1995), 'Entrepreneurial enterprises, endogenous ownership, and the limits to firm size', *Economic Inquiry*, Vol. 33, pp. 54-69.

White, L.J. (1982), 'The determinants of the relative importance of small business', *Review of Economics and Statistics*, Vol. 64, pp. 42-49.

Williamson, O.E. (1975), *Markets and Hierarchies: Analysis and Antitrust Implications*, New York: The Free Press.

You, J.I. (1995), 'Small firms in economic theory', *Cambridge Journal of Economics*, Vol. 19, pp. 441-462.

12. Better EU Regulatory Quality: Assessing Current Initiatives and New Proposals

Jacques Pelkmans, Sandrine Labory and Giandomenico Majone

---

1. INTRODUCTION AND STRUCTURE

Since the early 1980s, the EU, business and other interest groups in Europe and many observers have woken up to regulatory reform as a major economic, political and legal issue. Initially, an impressive agenda of introducing competition and facilitating intra-EU market access was addressed, mainly under the 'EC-1992' programme and a range of complementary initiatives. This phase of reform can be labelled 'regulation for liberalisation'. There can be little doubt that the implementation of this agenda has greatly improved the functioning of the EU's single market, with positive effects on growth and, particularly, on the competitiveness of European companies.

With EC-1992 largely accomplished and follow-up action further improving it, the debate in the 1990s began to emphasise *the justification and proper nature of EU regulation in a single market*. It is this meaning of regulatory reform that is the subject of the present chapter. For short, we call it 'regulatory quality'. Chapter 3 in this volume (by Sandrine Labory and Marco Malgarini) briefly introduces the notion of regulatory quality and identifies some major problems at the interface between the EU and its member states. They point out, as also do we, that regulatory quality is ultimately a matter of the credibility of intervention. This present chapter focuses on regulatory quality at EU level and assesses all the EU initiatives in the 1990s with a view towards putting forward a range of institutional and policy proposals.

The EU regulatory system operates at two (or, in federal countries, three) levels of government: the EU and member states' level, but the latter is confined to implementation and enforcement. This implies that the two EU level reform processes, referred to above, might not necessarily be mirrored at the member states level. From an economic point of view, the growth and job-creating potential of the single market cannot be segregated from how national markets function. While there is room for regional and national differentiation, the economic interdependence is too great to ignore the EU-national interplay when assessing reforms. In order to get the most out of the single market, national reforms for liberalisation as well as national improvements of regulatory quality are essential, too. *Where appropriate, coordination or agreed parallelism between these two-level reform processes would be desirable.* It is in this perspective that we focus on EU regulatory quality.

In studying EU regulatory quality, we are interested in the effectiveness of such reforms for the (better) functioning of the single market, and, as a result, the improvement of the competitiveness of the EU's industry and services. The Union prides itself that it has undertaken an array of complementary initiatives in order to improve EU regulatory quality. We shall survey these initiatives, present (where possible) the results so far, and assess the accomplishments where evidence allows. We conclude that these reforms are not without merit, but the actual impact on the single market functioning and competitiveness is likely to be modest at best. Permanent pressures to regulate (more) can be identified and the disciplines or incentives to raise quality are too weak. Hence, deeper reforms are needed. Therefore the second part of the paper presents a menu of proposals to intensify regulatory reforms at EU level for the benefit of the single market and business competitiveness performance.

The structure of the paper is as follows. Section 2 recalls the main features of 'regulation for liberalisation' at EU level and the increasingly coordinated structural reforms at member state level, via the Cardiff process. It is only against this backdrop that one can meaningfully address the EU reforms for the realisation of 'regulatory quality'. Section 3 distils an emerging EU vision of regulatory quality from the initiatives undertaken from 1991 until today. Section 4 briefly assesses, qualitatively, three elements of this vision with respect to the better functioning of markets in the EU: these three are subsidiarity and proportionality; cost/benefit assessment (and other impact assessments including the Business Test Panel); guidelines for regulation in EU institutions and other initiatives to raise the 'legislative quality' of EC regulation. Section 5 provides a critical analysis of another element – simplification – in particular the results of the SLIM programme, operational since 1996. Section 6 attempts to understand where the Community stands today with respect to regulatory quality reform. It is here that the conclusions of the first half of the chapter can be found – the remainder consists of suggestions for deeper reforms. The main inference from Sections 2-5 is that regulatory quality has improved in a number of technical ways, and in some specialised areas, but has failed to impact noticeably on market functioning and competitiveness. We also take notice of recent trends to co-opt business directly in the reform process, not only in SLIM and BEST (or even in the Molitor report) but also via the Trans-Atlantic Business Dialogue. Nevertheless, permanent pressures to produce more EU regulation have been identified and, if not carefully justified, such pressures might affect market functioning even negatively. For all these reasons the paper discusses a range of reform proposals. Section 7 makes the case for greater regulatory competition under proper conditions which is strictly speaking a matter between member states, but it pre-empts EU regulation and can be facilitated at EU level. Section 8 returns to the fundamentals of regulatory credibility and identifies a number of threats to such credibility. Section 9 addresses four 'internal' threats to regulatory credibility ('internal' refers to the regulatory system itself) and possible solutions, i.e. regulation by information, the EU analogue of the US state implementation plan (with variable federal funding), a central EU regulatory unit with the Commission President, and the EU regulatory 'budget' based on systematic (compliance) cost/benefit assessment. Section 10 discusses the (legitimate) politicisation of the Commission (also due to EP powers) and the (autonomous or independent) agencies as a way to raise regulatory credibility, without losing accountability.

2. THE REGULATORY FRAMEWORK FOR EU LIBERALISATION OF MARKETS

Before analysing EU reforms for greater regulatory quality, it is useful to comprehend the overall regulatory framework of the Union after EC-1992 and the link with market performance. We distinguish two levels – EU and national – but emphasise their strong interdependence.

2.1 EU market reforms

The hard core of EU regulation is that related to the free movement of agricultural and industrial products, services (including those provided by network industries or former utilities) and factors of production such as labour, financial capital and technology. Besides the fundamental principles of free movement in the EC Treaty, this 'regulation for liberalisation' consists of the following elements:

- a range of prohibitions (to regulate) for member states;
- the obligation, imposed by case-law, of mutual recognition;
- approximation of national regulation by means of directives;
- regulation (by the Commission directly, or by Council and Parliament) in the framework of common policies, such as:
  - competition policy (which addresses the market failure of market power, and hence deals with the proper functioning of the single market)
  - agricultural policy (where intrusive price and market regulations constrain market functioning, as a condition for free agricultural trade in the EU)
  - trade policy (which regulates the terms for market access of third countries' exporters and ensures that external competitive pressures are uniform over the EU insofar as this depends on market access); and
- other regulation at EU level where competences are mainly exercised by member states (e.g. social policy or social security) or where approximation is the usual means (e.g. environment), or where there is little or no direct impact on market functioning (e.g. structural funds).

Regulatory reform could in principle deal with all of these categories. However, the level of ambition of such reforms would differ greatly and comprehensive reform for all aspects would be impossible to achieve simultaneously. Focus is therefore required. For the same reason, even the present paper with its wide scope excludes some areas of possible regulatory reform. First, it can be argued that there are important flaws in the EC Treaty, which unduly restrict the range of prohibitions (to regulate) for member states. Two flaws of great importance to market functioning, and indeed to the competitiveness of enterprises, are the inconsistent and conditional fashion in which the treaty deals with the free movement of labour,[1] and exclusive competence for member states in matters of ownership, without any facilitation or provision for patents and other intellectual property rights.[2] However, such *constitutional reforms* or ingenious second-best solutions are not the subject of this paper.

Second, regulation as part of the common policies could be assessed with different degrees of ambition. Thus, we do not deal with the regulatory aspects of EC competition policy. In agricultural and trade policy, the most important impact of regulatory intervention is on relative and absolute prices.

Again, this is not the subject of the present paper. Where trade policy is related to product or services regulation, it has no independent function, but merely one of control and enforcement. In agricultural policy, however, the fact that intervention prices or so-called restitutions (export subsidies) are paid to farmers for specific agricultural products, forces the EU to classify different quality levels of e.g. potatoes, onions, grains, etc. (since the market will generate different prices for different qualities). One additional benefit of agricultural reform away from price support to income support (preferably decoupled from output) would be that this intrusive type of EC regulation could henceforth be left to market forces and private certification bodies. The present paper will not discuss this area of regulation.

The scope of regulatory activity of the present paper is therefore 'limited' to the vast areas of a) mutual recognition in goods and services,[3] b) approximation (the bulk of the so-called 'acquis') and c) a few cases of other regulations (e.g. social, environment and company law).

2.2 National reforms in the Economic Union: the Cardiff process

The advent and the actual arrival of monetary union had has a significant impact on the economic policy coordination and consultation between the member states. Of course, a good deal of this intense activity is macroeconomic. However, given the subject of the present paper – regulatory reform and EU regulatory quality – it is interesting to appreciate that microeconomic aspects are also dealt with at both EU and member state level, and indeed at the interface between the two.

The roots of this development are clear: the EU has pursued EMU, not just MU. In other words, it has always been firm policy, indeed a treaty obligation, to build an economic union as the foundation for Monetary Union. Unlike the latter, economic union has not been defined in the treaty, but, following the 1989 Delors Committee report, it has been widely accepted to comprise:

- a competitive (i.e. 'properly functioning') single market,
- economic and social cohesion (to be pursued via appropriate policies as well as conditional grants-in-aid or transfers), and
- budgetary discipline of the member states.

Clearly, the first two elements are microeconomic in nature and have actual or potential linkages with regulatory reforms at EU level.

But the growth and job-creation capacity of the European economy is but partially promoted by building economic union in this sense. The interdependence between relatively 'sheltered' parts of national economies and the 'exposed' economic activities in the single market, as well as the interdependence between all the national economies in the EU, make it economically very difficult, and undesirable, to strictly separate 'domestic' and EU-driven economic regulation and policies. The inability to reform and to adjust in member state will inevitably imply negative externalities for other member states. They may take the form of lower export and investment opportunities, a lesser dynamism in growth and employment, a tendency to resist pro-market policies (if not liberalisation) at EU level and perhaps a reticence to pursue external openness and exploit globalisation. In addition, insufficient restructuring and adjustment may hinder the proper functioning of the monetary union in the case of shocks.

Therefore, it might be self-defeating for the Union to take a legalistic view of the limits of EU competences, if this would result in a neglect of regulatory reform at the member state level and the impact on the EU national economic interdependence. This fundamental conclusion was accepted in the European Council in Cardiff in June 1998. As a result the 'Cardiff process' has led to annual reports about regulatory reform *both* at the EU and member state level[4] and, subsequently, to recommendations about the nature and speed of regulatory reform for *individual* member states in the so-called Broad Economic Guidelines (surveillance obligation based on Art.. 99, EC (formerly Art. 103, EC) in the framework of EMU), traditionally adopted in June.[5]

The Cardiff process represents a breakthrough. Whereas it is important to respect a degree of autonomy for member states' policy-making and regulation under subsidiarity, so as to avoid undue centralisation of the Union, it is crucial to interpret this autonomy in a functional manner and not in a narrow legalistic sense. The Cardiff process in effect recognises that national regulatory reforms are a crucial issue of common concern, if the pursuit of a well functioning EMU – permitting higher growth and a higher job content of that growth – is to be achieved. A major step in the generation of such quality growth is the induced competitiveness of industry and services, more exposed to competition and seeking restructuring and innovation to improve productivity and value-added, while lowering input costs and other costs.

The Cardiff process should be helped by the so-called Luxembourg process on the formulation of policy guidelines for boosting national employment. Although the Luxembourg process has a much wider scope than regulation (e.g. retraining, skill formation, employability, active policies for the long-run unemployed), it does refer to regulatory reforms in the labour markets via peer pressure, benchmarking and agreements with the social partners.

Since the focus of the present paper is on regulatory quality *at the EU level*, efforts of EU liberalisation (see Section 2.1 above) and national regulatory reforms not directly resulting from EU decisions cannot be studied. It is indispensable, however, to appreciate the entire area of EU regulatory quality in this broader EU-national context, shaping the economic potential for EMU.

3. AN EMERGING EU VISION OF REGULATORY QUALITY

The great strides in liberalisation for the various free movements brought with it a significant increase in EU level regulation. Nevertheless, this increase was *circumscribed* by new principles and regulatory techniques which (ceteris paribus) reduced the costs of regulation for the functioning of markets, without losing the double benefit of intra-EC liberalisation and overcoming the market failure. They included:

- Mutual recognition of national regulation, as long as regulatory objectives are 'equivalent' (and indeed justified;[6] where this applies, EU regulation does *not* increase, since no EU regulation is adopted).
- The new approach to approximation, with its focus on objectives and effect, and no longer on detail (less intrusive EU regulation).
- Reference to standards, European rather than national (and the European ones should be aligned with world standards where available), based on the regulatory objectives of the directive(s). This has increased flexibility of specifications, where specifications are helpful for certainty or clarity, while providing room for innovation. Besides, the combination of the new approach and European standards has created equivalent national regulation in many product markets, so the 'extra' EC layer does not add to, but reduces costs.
- The 'global approach' to conformity assessment, creating a uniform set of risk-based requirements for testing and certification; again, this 'extra' EC layer does not add to costs, but should reduce them.
- Home-country control in several service sectors such as banking, insurance, road and air transport. This principle is a corollary to the 'global approach' in product markets; the national bodies supervising and inspecting financial institutions and/or health and safety of transport equipment and the maintenance procedures of the service providers are themselves subject to quality rules and demanding obligations to exchange information so as to build and retain trust; based on this trust, this 'home-country control' is mutually recognised, so that service

providers can operate throughout the internal market without a serious risk of market failure; clearly, this 'light' form of EU regulation adds only a minimum of an extra regulatory layer and this is justified by the major benefits of service liberalisation in the single market

The strategy to regulate, where justified, the newly liberalised single market is therefore quite well designed in terms of principles and regulatory techniques.[7]

The concerns that gradually began to emerge in the early 1990s represented a further shift of regulatory ambition. member states and business in Europe increasingly questioned whether this (broadly) well received regulatory strategy for liberalisation should not be complemented by approaches ensuring *'regulatory quality'*. The preoccupations vary from a) the actual implementation, case by case, of the 'regulation for liberalisation' strategy, b) the danger that the EU level would develop habits of excessive centralisation in areas where regulatory powers are shared between the EU level and the member states (e.g. environment; social) but which would not necessarily fall under issues of 'liberalisation', to c) a host of technical and legal features which cause excessive complexity, lack of transparency and at times, inconsistencies in EU regulation.

We shall not write the history of this debate, and limit ourselves to a few highlights and references. The highlights are depicted in Figure 12.1. It is clear from this picture that the recent debate on EU regulatory quality has been intense and productive. Not counting independent reports in various member states, four major reports were commissioned. The 1992 Sutherland report[8] suggested five criteria for the adoption of new EC regulations and emphasised consolidation of existing regulations. The 1995 Molitor report[9] produced 18 recommendations that should reduce the undue regulatory burden for business in Europe and promote simplification. The 1995 UNICE report[10] stressed the problem of the cumulative nature of the regulatory burden (i.e. regional, national and EU regulation) and showed how concerned business in Europe was that the regulatory burdens impinged upon their competitiveness. The 1998 BEST report[11] – which has a scope far wider than regulation only – argues for a 'better regulation unit' directly under the Commission President, mirrored by a similar unit in the Council's General Secretariat, and a 'think small first' principle for regulatory reform.

Both the Maastricht and the Amsterdam Treaties have stimulated the debate and produced some tangible reforms. Art. 5, EC (in Maastricht still, Art. 3b, EC) introduced the principles of subsidiarity and proportionality. In December 1992, this led to an agreement in the Edinburgh European Council

Figure 12.1 EU regulatory quality: highlights of the debate

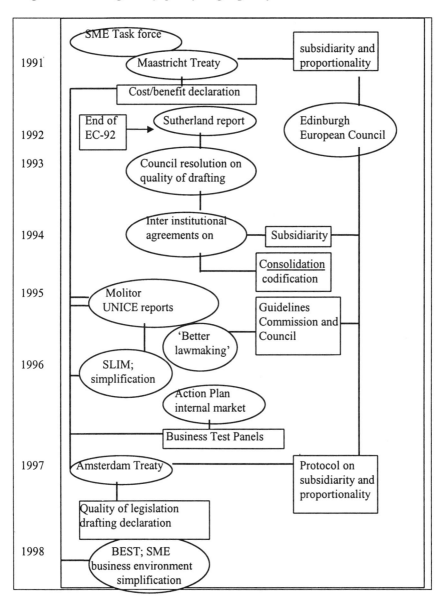

that every new proposal of the Commission (and amendments by the EP and Council) would be subjected to a test. This agreement was codified in a Protocol attached to the 1997 Amsterdam Treaty, which went into force on 1 May 1999. An inter-institutional agreement about subsidiarity procedures (in 1994) facilitates the working of these ideas. The member states attached the (18th) Declaration on costs and benefits of EU regulation to the Maastricht Treaty, which is echoed in the guidelines of the Commission (1996) and of the Council (1995) on how-to-regulate as well as in the Molitor, UNICE and BEST reports.

The Sutherland report and other pressures also led to a more systematic review of the legal aspects of regulatory quality. Stimulated by a 1993 Council resolution on the quality of drafting, these concerns were addressed in the 1995-96 Council and Commission guidelines as well as annual reports on 'Better Law-making' by the Commission. Further impetus might be expected from the 39 Declaration of the member states attached to the Amsterdam Treaty.[12]

We submit that one can distil from this complicated and ongoing debate an *emerging vision of EU regulatory quality*, complementing the EU regulatory strategy for liberalisation. The emerging vision is summarised in Figure 12.2. It is striking that only parts of two elements date from the 1980s; essentially, the 'vision' has emerged during the 1990s. The 'older' parts include risk-assessment (e.g. for chemicals regulation), much refined and standardised in the 1990s; the 'fiche d'impact' (on business, including SMEs) which was of little significance at first, and some manuals on drafting EC legislation.

Figure 12.2 Emerging vision on EU regulatory quality

<u>Quality issues</u>   <u>EU approach</u>

- At EU level, only if
  - ◆ justified
  - ◆ no more than necessary

Subsidiarity and proportionality

- Impact analysis
  risk

Cost and benefit test, including (proper) assessment possible cost effectiveness

Selective impact assessments (by definition, partial)
  - business impact (including SMEs)
  - environmental impact

- Simplification

Simplification of the regulatory acquis

- The craft of drafting

Regulatory guidelines, for Commission proposals and Council review + amendments (EP?)
legal quality of drafting (e.g. clarity, consistency, enforceability, low risk of fraud); consolidation; transparency

- Non-central
  implementation

Decentralisation (to member states) and delegation of executive tasks (to autonomous EU agencies)

4. IMPROVING EU REGULATORY QUALITY: WILL MARKETS BENEFIT?

This section provides basic guidance for understanding the nature and scope of three quality issues of Figure 12.2: justification of (how much) regulation at EU level (in 4.1); impact analysis (in 4.2); and the 'craft of drafting' (in 4.3). Section 5 will single out the SLIM programme for closer scrutiny. The issue of non-central implementation will not be addressed here. Insofar as member state implementation of EC law is concerned, Section 9 will make some suggestions to improve the unsatisfactory record thus far.

4.1 Subsidiarity and proportionality

EU regulatory quality hinges on a proper and consistent application of the principles of 'subsidiarity' and 'proportionality'. It is important to appreciate why this is so, and what impact this has on market functioning.

Subsidiarity is a principle guiding the assignment of powers, including regulatory power, to the appropriate level of government. By nature it is a functional principle. Unfortunately, it is not always employed functionally. Two important instances of dysfunctional application in EU practice come to mind. First, the assignment of powers in the treaties themselves is not systematically subjected to a subsidiarity test. The implications are of great importance for the proper functioning of the internal market. Thus, the example in Section 1 (and note 2) about the lack of a Community patent is mainly due to a flaw in the treaty, that would never have passed a subsidiarity test. Nevertheless, there is a compelling justification for not subjecting treaties to subsidiarity, because it would by-pass the ratification process of the member states, which is the best-available revelation of preferences.

Constitutionally and in diplomacy, such a by-pass is of course unacceptable. Interestingly, it is also at odds with the economic theory (of multi-tier government) underlying the principle of subsidiarity. This theory is based on the fundamental idea that public policy, executed by governments mandated by voters, can only be efficient if it properly reflects the preferences of those voters. Efficiency, here, is defined as the greatest possible satisfaction of preferences. Since preferences differ and, to some extent, differ more between regions, and between countries, than within regions or within countries, a close correspondence of public policy with voters' preferences will often require the assignment of (regulatory) powers to regional and/or national governments rather than to higher tiers. Assigning public economic functions to higher tiers of government should only be done whenever, and to the extent that, criteria are fulfilled which ensure benefits of centralisation over and above those of decentralisation. These criteria are negative and positive cross-border spillovers ('externalities') and scale. In only slightly different wording, these criteria are in the Treaty text of Art. 5, EC (formerly Art. 3B, EC). But it is obvious that a generally applicable subsidiarity principle cannot override a specific (and constitutionally rather careful) expression of preferences via a ratification of treaties. So, if the EU treaty is ratified (even with 'flaws' insofar as the internal market is concerned), it must be viewed as the conscious acceptance of (costly) decentralisation preferences.

Second, subsidiarity is often used politically in the EU Council and in national debates on the EU. It is asserted that powers should remain with or 'return' to the member states. As a general statement of the principle of subsidiarity, this is simply wrong. Subsidiarity is a two-way principle: if the benefits of centralisation – as expressed in the criteria of spillovers and scale – can be substantiated, the assignment to a higher tier, often the EU level, is the functional outcome. This is just as much 'subsidiarity' as opting for decentralisation is when the criteria do not apply. Too many politicians, and others, *confuse the point of departure* of the subsidiarity test – a national or regional assignment is closer to the voters and hence is preferable, unless proven too costly – *with the test itself.*

The subsidiarity test (see Table 12.1) in the Community has four steps. This perhaps somewhat abstract test is easily brought to life when applied to examples. Take the market for medicines. Introducing a new medicine on the market is subject to strict approvals for purposes of health and safety. Such regulation falls under shared powers (step 1). Doing these approvals on a national basis in the internal market causes serious negative externalities (see e.g. the EAG study by Burstall and Reuben, 1988, for the Cecchini report). So, there was a 'need-to-act' in common (step 2). Given some degree of uncertainty about the sufficient commonality of (strict) health and safety objectives between the member states – including the rigour of testing and certification – member states experimented with complicated variants of step3. This did not prove credible, although it helped – gradually – to overcome a lack of trust between the member states. In 1995, the European Medicinal Agency began operating on the basis of several procedures, with a centralised option and central arbitration as the main innovations (step 4), which have meanwhile proven to be highly successful. Clearly, this lowers the costs of introducing medicines in the internal market – without lowering health and safety – while significantly reducing uncertainty, which in turn stimulates innovation.

Table 12.1 The EU subsidiarity test

<u>Step 1</u>: Verify whether the issue at stake falls under shared or (EU) exclusive powers	If exclusive, the treaty rule cannot be undone by the test. If shared, the test can be applied.
<u>Step 2</u>: The 'need-to-act' in common; is regulation at national level ineffective or too costly because of scale or externalities (the two criteria)?	If one criterion (or both) applies (apply), there is a 'need-to-act' in common
<u>Step 3:</u> Can the common action avoid centralisation at EU level? For example, by cooperative action among some or all member states, or by coordination, or by jointly accepting constraints on national regulation.	Non-centralised common action retains some national powers, hence is preferred, provided it is - Feasible - Adequate - Durable. If not, non-centralisation is <u>not credible</u> to market players and will not solve the issue, while inducing costs (e.g. Uncertainty)
Step 4: Centralisation at EU level is justified if step 3 is not credible.	

Proportionality is a sequel to the subsidiarity test. Once step 4 is reached, that is, the *benefits of centralisation* can be reaped, the *costs of centralisation* ought to be minimised. These costs are the subject of the 'how-to-regulate' test. This test verifies three principles:

Proportionality:	The EU[13] should regulate no more than is necessary to attain the objective.
Differentiation:	The EU should differentiate EU level regulation (whenever this does not induce distortions or barriers) so as to respond to diverse national preferences.
Different degrees of binding:	Between an EC regulation, directive, decision, or recommendation (without affecting legal certainty and non-discrimination).

As noted, the Amsterdam Treaty has incorporated a Protocol on Subsidiarity and Proportionality that essentially covers the exposition above. It should serve as a guardian against *undue* centralisation, which might unnecessarily suppress national preferences. The open question is whether the Council applies the test functionally rather than politically. If member states cling too much to the preservation of national regulation, the internal market will function sub-optimally. The 1996-97 Single Market Review[14] has identified a considerable number of areas where member states resist justified centralisation, whether in the simple form of fully fledged liberalisation (e.g. giving up unjustified exceptions) or in the form of approximation or joint regulation. The Protocol on Subsidiarity (already in use since 1993) is therefore a necessary but by no means sufficient condition to achieve optimal (de-)centralisation, so that markets work better.

It is also interesting to consider 'mutual recognition' in goods markets. In terms of subsidiarity, mutual recognition (MR) is an innovative solution: under equivalence of (national) health or safety objectives, MR ensures the removal of the market failure, without introducing another one (namely, regulatory barriers in the internal market). In so doing, a common constraint on national regulatory (and enforcement) power is accepted, but no (other) 'need-to-act' in common arises. That is if it actually works at the very moment that economic agents in the market – in the first instance, typically business – exploit the opportunities MR gives rise to. Jacques Pelkmans, Ellen Vos and Luca Di Mauro, (Chapter 7 of Volume I) and Atkins, 1997 (for the Single Market Review of 1996-1997) show that mutual recognition cannot be taken for granted, however. Quite the contrary, elaborate mechanisms at EU level (preventive, under Directive 98-34; cooperative, in bilateral meetings between member states and the Commission; and many infringement procedures) are required to make MR work, and even then not without costs. Still, there are lingering doubts in business and among experts, whether MR serves as a reliable guide to do business in the internal market. This is costly for business, for example in the form of heightened uncertainty.

In the subsidiarity test, these elaborate mechanisms can be interpreted as a modest degree of centralisation, namely, for the most part as (intense!) forms of cooperation under step 3, besides the usual Commission role as 'guardian of the treaty'. The test is clear, however, about the shift to step 4, once the cooperative mechanisms are not credible to the market players. If member states attach great value to their regulatory powers, they have to accept fully and uncompromisingly the cooperative mechanisms so that they are credible in the market place. If member states do not do that, approximation (under qualified majority voting) becomes superior to MR.

Proportionality may also have important practical implications for the better functioning of markets. The European Court of Justice has shown the way in cases where a national regulatory means (e.g. an import ban for beers, not made according to the Reinheitsgebot) was considered far too restrictive for achieving the purpose (health; possibly, proper information to consumers about the ingredients of beer). As a result, the unrestrictive means of labelling was opted for. At the EU level, the Court has insisted on proportionality, not for reasons of better market functioning, but as a protection against undue centralisation of powers – the EU level should use the powers assigned for the agreed purposes but no more than necessary. Clearly, there is scope for interpretation here. Is the 'old' approach of harmonisation of almost every technical detail not 'disproportional'? Yet, even in the SLIM project on fertilisers (see Section 5), a group of user experts (business) and civil servants from the Commission and member states recommended to maintain the old approach in 16 fertilisers directives, while consolidating it into one superdirective. In the case of motor vehicles, interviews confirmed, informally, that the costs (including long periods of uncertainty) of switching to the 'new' approach are considered close to prohibitive.

Proportionality forces the consideration of least-restrictive alternatives and their feasibility and (other) costs. Its explicit appearance in the Treaty of Maastricht is not as great a 'reform' as one might think, however, because the European Court of Justice has already developed case law. More important, still, the 'new' approach to approximation, the global approach to conformity assessment, and 'home country control' coupled with MR in services have all greatly helped to improve market functioning compared to the 'uncommon market' of the early 1980s, and these breakthroughs pre-date the Maastricht Treaty. All of these breakthroughs accord well with proportionality. There is, however, one change in the process of adopting EU regulation that has long been called for by European business, namely careful and timely *consultation* prior to writing draft directives. Art. 9 of the Protocol explicitly instructs the Commission to do this. In the course of the 1990s, Green Papers and other open forms of consultation have become routine and this is perceived as highly beneficial. Art. 9 also stipulates that Commission proposals should duly take into account 'the need for any burden' (e.g. to business and citizens) 'to be minimised and proportionate to the objective'. In other words, the practical significance of the Protocol for EU regulatory quality is considerable.

The proper application of subsidiarity and proportionality may also be of importance to a regulatory problem that is increasingly identified by European business as costly: that of 'cumulation'. A political rather than functional application of subsidiarity and proportionality is likely to allow too much discretion for member states to regulate. There are many pressures that might prompt member states to utilise this discretion by more regulation. The upshot would be a cumulation of national and EU requirements – not properly justified – which inflicts an undue regulatory burden on business. If regions and even local authorities would have such discretion, too, there is a serious risk that the 'cumulative' regulatory burden *in the EU* is very high for business, even though the *EU level regulation_* properly complies with least-cost principles, such as the new approach, etc. Indeed, both the Molitor report and the UNICE report of 1995 identify 'cumulation' as a problem for business. There is no systematic mechanism in the EU to prevent, let alone, rectify, undue cumulation, and in so doing reduce compliance costs for business.

4.2 Cost/benefit and impact assessments

During the 1990s, evaluations, impact and effect assessments and cost/benefit analysis (CBA) as well as imperfect substitutes of CBA have been called for throughout the OECD, at EU level and in many member states. The EU level attention to CBA and impact assessments of various kinds is therefore part of a wider trend. But, as this subsection will try to show, it is anything but clear what effective change of conduct of regulators and (EU) decision-makers the debate has brought about, and hence, what cost reduction or net increase of benefits it has generated for markets. To the authors it would seem that there is a) confusion about CBA and other assessments applied to EU level regulation, b) little clarity about the actual use of such evaluations and c) hesitation, if not inhibitions in the Commission to apply assessments according to minimum standards (but we readily admit that it is exceedingly hard to base this perception on observable facts). If these inferences are correct, one should not expect such 'virtual' reforms to have a positive impact on market functioning. Indeed, the expected costs of a negative impact on competitiveness of business in Europe cannot be fully and properly considered by decision-makers if mere lip service is paid to evaluations.

We shall first remind the reader what the proper economic framework is for the assessment of European regulation. Subsection 4.2.1. should be read together with chapter 3 in volume I (Sandrine Labory and Marco Malgarini). *Any* regulatory initiative should be assessed within this framework. CBA and other assessments are tools to sharpen, and sometimes to quantify, the answers, only after doing full justice to this framework. We proceed by a comparative exposition of the various types of (economic) assessment used at

EU level. The various tools are not equivalent and the choice of one tool rather than another may lead to different conclusions as to the desirability of a particular EU regulation for the EU public interest. Subsequently, we recall the official EU policy on assessments and its possible ambiguities, and end with several tentative proposals to use assessments systematically, according to certain standards of quality and transparency.

4.2.1   The basic economic framework

Box 1 summarises the main questions to be asked and answered whenever a regulatory problem is raised at EU level (based on Jacques Pelkmans and Sandrine Labory, 1998; see also Sandrine Labory and Marco Malgarini, Chapter 3 of Volume I).

Box 1. Basic Economic Framework for European Regulation

Why intervene?
-    market failures
-    if effects are non-trivial and
-    if market-based incentives or cooperative solutions are impossible.

At what level?
-    subsidiarity test
-    explicitly consider cooperative (but credible) solution among member states
-    consider two-levels solutions, if appropriate.

What instruments are available?
-    constraints at EU level
-    national or EU subsidies sometimes; or taxes at national level
-    usually regulation, including economic instruments.

Least-cost regulation
-    minimise costs of centralisation
-    minimise degree of binding, where possible
-    consider different types of regulatory solutions.

Maximise net benefits
-    assess options as to effectiveness
-    use appropriate analytical tool (e.g. various models, cost-benefit analysis, etc.)

The first question is: why regulate? It should identify the market failure(s). One should avoid regulation when there are no market failures – in such cases, markets function properly. If equity problems arise (although this is usually dealt with at national rather than EC level), they should not be addressed by distorting or throttling market incentives but via targeted subsidies, social security or tax breaks. It is not always easy to properly identify a market failure. In any event, the actual regulatory activities (and EC case law) accompanying the establishment and the improvement of the functioning of the internal market have shown that EC law can accommodate the core issues. Thus, in product markets[15] safety, health, environment and consumer protection (SHEC) can be and have been addressed. They can be justified, under proper conditions, as internalities[16] and/or externalities[17] that hinder or undermine the proper functioning of markets, or, sometimes, prevent markets from emerging in the first place. Mutatus mutandis, the same is true for services markets.

The second question to ask is: at what level of government? This point has been discussed in Section 4.1 with a subsidiarity test (Table 12.1). The third question to ask is: What are the instruments available, and whether regulation is the appropriate instrument. When considering instruments, it is good to think of the following sequence:

i. Can the markets be helped to overcome the failure by new market institutions and/or better (and reliable) information?

ii. If not, can so-called economic instruments be utilised? (These are instruments that induce market players to alter their conduct by market-compatible mechanisms or by creating markets for certain rights – e.g. taxation, subsidies, user-charges, markets in quotas or pollution permits, insurable liabilities, etc. Their great economic advantage is that, for a given policy objective, market agents can vary their conduct according to price, and respond by adjustments, including innovation, etc., thereby preventing any unnecessary 'regulatory burden'.)[18]

iii. If not or not adequately, regulation should be considered as the main or complementary solution.

However, the choice of instruments at EU level is severely constrained. Most EU level regulation consists of approximation precisely where the (non-agricultural) internal market of goods and services is concerned. The subsidiarity test discourages direct EU level regulation as highly centralist [19] and the legal basis in the treaty would often be absent. The recommendation of the 1995 Molitor report to substitute regulations for directives to increase legal security for European business would not accord well with the treaty (and even then, ought to be subjected to a subsidiarity test). EU level subsidies are few (mainly R&D), thus far. The logic of approximation leads the EU to provide a regulatory basis for subsidies at the national level, in order to accomplish policy objectives in the EU public interest. Taxation at EU level is not possible – the EC has no right to tax. Hence, tax exemptions are not feasible, so that the only option is to allow specific tax exemptions at national level, so as to accomplish policy objectives in the EU public interest. Liability (at least for products) is subject to an EC directive (see the paper by Silva and Calvaliere, Chapter 8 in Volume I) but little attention has been paid to exploiting this market-based approach to the full in the EU.

The fourth question concerns the regulation at EU level at least-cost. This essentially amounts to the application of proportionality (see Section 4.1), supplemented by a search for all alternative regulatory solutions. The fifth question, finally, takes up the challenge of maximising, for the EU public interest, the *net benefits* (that is, the benefits of overcoming the market failure, netted by the costs of the least-cost solution). CBA, and other more limited assessments, can only be properly performed under this fifth question, once the previous four questions have been carefully addressed.

4.2.2.   Cost-benefit analysis and other assessments

No less than six different types of economic or 'impact' assessments are used by policy-makers or in advisory reports. And other labels are sometimes used, sowing even more confusion without adding value.

Consider Table 12.2 below. Before commenting on that table, however, we wish to emphasise that the assessment of (European) *regulation* is a variant of traditional assessments of projects or (infrastructural) investments. Whereas projects or the construction of a large bridge or tunnel tend to have fairly well identifiable effects of a regional character and upon limited groups of actual or potential users, service providers, etc., the assessment of regulatory initiatives tends to be more difficult. Reasons include the difficulties in identifying all (indirect) effects and the diffuse ways, and the extent to which various groups or areas might be affected. A central problem with assessing regulation is the required information, a good deal of which may be asymmetrical or difficult to verify. This crucial issue cannot be elaborated here (see e.g. Pelkmans and Labory, 1998, pp. 33-35, and the new economics of regulation).

Shifting CBA and other assessment methods from projects or (public) investments to regulation may explain the proliferation of labels and methods.

The ideal method for properly assessing (European) regulation is no undoubtedly cost/benefit analysis (see the last two rows of Table 12.2). The interesting question is whether it can be done, given the demanding information requirements to conduct CBA properly. There are at least three considerable problems with information. First, for many specific, highly targeted instances of regulation (e.g. a directive on the safety of buses) the collection of all the needed information may prove difficult, because much of it might not be available in the public domain as it might be too specific – it may also be time-consuming, to collect. Second, information may be 'private' – hence, not observable or obtainable – and its acquisition may be partial, biased or manipulated, without sufficient possibilities to verify this. Regulatory games 'played' between authorities and (potential) regulatees are largely based on the strategic use of information (besides lobbying skills and the power of numbers and size).

Table 12.2 Assessment methods of European regulation

Method	Costs		Benefit		Scope	EU
	Social	Private	Social	Private		Public interest
Cost-minimisation	Yes	Yes	Given	--	All affected areas/groups	OK, when benefits uncontroversial
Cost-effectiveness (costs per measurable unit of the desired effect minimised)	Yes	Yes	Given	--	Idem	Good for comparison of measures, when benefits are uncontroversial
Business impact analysis 'fiche d'impact'	?	Yes	?	Yes	Impact on business, or often SMEs, only	Only acceptable, if clearly part of wider assessment framework
Competitiveness analysis (adds the analysis of the business impact on competitiveness)	?	Yes	?	Yes	Widens 'impact' to competitiveness of firms	Idem; however, dubious if 'competitiveness' is not carefully defined and only at firm level
Environmental impact analysis	Yes	Yes	Yes	Yes	CBA, but only applied to EU environmental regulation	Desirable
Cost-benefit analysis	Yes	Yes	Yes	Yes	Comprehensive and generally applicable	Desirable

Third, a special difficulty exists with the benefits of regulation. Benefits can be well understood and uncontroversial (e.g. in specific instances of health services, such as ambulance services based on minimum standards).

More often than not, however, benefits are diffuse, and they can also be elusive, and hence hard to measure. The subsequent valuation of the benefits – already problematic, and frequently hard to accept for those holding extreme preferences – then becomes impossible. Yet, if benefits cannot even be proxied, the most important advantage of CBA – perhaps its raison d'être – falls away. Policy-makers will understandably shift to cost-effectiveness or cost minimisation analysis.

For these reasons, CBA is discredited by some and seen as arbitrary by others precisely for the elements where it should add value over cost-based approaches. This criticism – although justified in and by itself – *is not a reason to dismiss CBA*; rather, it serves as a warning to harbour realistic expectations of what it can deliver. Subjecting a regulatory initiative to CBA has two formidable advantages which are independent from all the difficulties about information: i) it is the most systematic and comprehensive methodology, forcing all those involved to trace all indirect and perhaps unexpected (side-) effects, whether quantifiable or not (so, non-economists can participate in all stages[20] and can help to define the model questions asked from economic consultants, if necessary); and ii) it forces regulators, (potential) regulatees (usually, business) and experts to reflect on the benefits, collect the available information and to get as clear and understandable a picture of differential benefits, depending on various regulatory options, even when no formal valuation is attempted. Let us now look at other methods in Table 12.2.

Cost minimisation simply compares measures according to the costs they entail, ignoring the *effects* of different measures. For example, different measures to reduce emissions from road vehicles, such as fuel tax, performance requirements for engine technology, inspection and maintenance programmes, etc., would be compared according to the costs they each entail, regardless of the level of emissions reductions they generate (therefore assuming they all lead to the same level of emissions reductions). In contrast, cost-effectiveness analyses compare measures according to the cost per unit of emissions reduction. This requires assessing the amount of emissions reductions generated by each measure, as well as their cost. This method chooses a measure according to whether it achieves the objective and whether it entails the least cost compared with other measures.

Ideally, in order to assess a measure, the total costs would be compared with the total benefits generated by the measure, looking at all possible effects of the measure, not just the effect on the stated goal. This is what a cost-benefit analysis does. Concerning measures to reduce emissions, benefits may include not only the benefits of reducing emissions (improved air quality, human health, ecosystems, and so on), but also benefits in terms of productivity improvements (e.g. due to changes in production processes to manufacture environmentally friendly products), and business developments (e.g. new businesses created following the measure, such as private test centres that check the conformity of vehicles in circulation).

The *difference between cost-benefit and cost-effectiveness analyses* lies in the fact that the latter concentrates on one type of benefit: the effect of the measure on the stated objective. For example, a cost-effectiveness analysis of a regulation to reduce emissions from road vehicles will assess costs relative to one effect: the reduction of emissions. The measure is cost-effective if the cost per unit of emissions reduction is judged low. This approach often *results in the collapse of the goal and the instrument into a single entity.* For instance, a regulation (the policy instrument) which puts a limit on emissions from vehicles is just merged with the goal (reducing emissions). However, a systematic approach would look at all the effects and the way in which the measure takes effect.

As noted, the difficulty of measuring benefits does not mean that a proposed policy option should be assessed only according to cost-effectiveness criteria, because ignoring benefits might lead to the wrong decision. A cost-benefit analysis is the most reliable of all types of analysis, since it accounts for all (negative and positive) effects.[21]

Table 12.2 also mentions the business impact analysis (especially for SMEs) and competitiveness analysis. Such approaches are partial and hence it is essential for the EU public interest that they are not produced outside the framework of Box 1 and are not used in isolation. With these conditions fulfilled, these analyses are legitimate tools if properly utilised. We would like to add two points. First, we have not found an analytical study or other systematic information about the 'fiche d'impact', used in draft directives since the late 1980s (for a description, see Schulte-Braucks, 1998). It might be the case that these 'fiches' are not based on a rigorously justified methodology, and, as a consequence, comprise variable information of unclear relevance to decision-makers. Is it, for instance, a mere reflection of highly informal 'consultation' processes that are required anyway with potential regulatees (in the Commission Guidelines of 1996)? Second, of course the costs to European business matter as well as the implications for competitiveness. In a properly conducted CBA this would be analysed. However, *a sole focus* on the costs to business or the impact on competitiveness can be misused. Business is right to be in the forefront in resisting and preventing over-regulation, but it should frame this in the EU public interest, short of being counterproductive. The same goes for environmental and consumer groups – it is misleading to argue for the 'benefits' of ever-greater environmental protection or the security of ever-lower risk exposure, without having proper regard to their costs and – in the relevant case – to diverse risk-preferences of individuals (at least, if these preferences do not lead to externalities to be paid by society).

4.2.3 Improving regulatory assessment at EU level

The use of cost-benefit analysis (CBA) to improve EU regulation has been widely called for recently. First of all, the 18th Declaration of the member states, annexed to the Maastricht Treaty, states that:

> '...the Commission undertakes, by basing itself where appropriate on any consultation it considers necessary and by strengthening its system for evaluating Community legislation, to take account in its legislative proposals of costs and benefits to the member states' public authorities and all the parties concerned'.[22]

The June 1996 Report of the Competitiveness Advisory Group (Ciampi Group) to the Florence European Council recommends the use of CBA in the field of social regulation. The 1995 Molitor Report, the 1995 UNICE report and the European Round Table of Industrialists (1996), all claim that systematic CBA of proposed regulations is needed for more efficient EU regulation, and the list is not exhaustive.[23] The 39th Declaration adopted by the IGC concluding the Amsterdam Treaty is about the 'quality' of Community legislation, presumably out of concern for the costs of EC regulation.

The authors have not been able to verify whether and to what extent the Commission systematically utilises CBA or elaborate cost-effectiveness studies, and reports on them publicly, in ways that allow a minimum degree of independent verification. We are not aware of any report on the actual policy of the Commission in this regard, whether the Guidelines on this point are implemented differently by different DGs, who decides, on what basis, whether economic assessment will be done, whether there are sufficient funds to subcontract, whether Council members demand such preparatory work and discuss it carefully. We should also be interested in the actual role of the 'fiche d'impact' (on business, including SMEs).

According to Schulte-Braucks (1998), the Business Impact Assessment (BIA) is being reconsidered, especially with a view to SMEs. The pressures are mentioned but the substantive reasons are not specified "... its (the BIA) objectives are not well understood, either by the Directorates General proposing legislation or by outside interests, including business. Its operation has also been criticised by both the Council and the European Parliament" (p. 208). The BIA typically investigates at four levels: economy-wide; business impact per sector (to be indicated by the regulating DG); the 'specific compliance costs and administrative burdens 'and' '(R)eporting, monitoring and enforcement costs', as well as 'the appropriateness of conformity assessment'(where it concerns product legislation); and the impact on SMEs ('can the draft legislation be designed in a way which would be compatible with SME's needs'?). The envisaged improvements will emphasise that 'more comprehensive evaluations are necessary, particularly in relation to the more complex legislative proposals. These will increasingly draw on cost-benefit or cost-effectiveness analysis, where appropriate'.

In the annual Commission Report on Better Lawmaking in 1998,[24] there is no mention of any reform, activity or accomplished improvement in regulatory assessment.[25] We have also not been able to find a common framework or Commission manual, nor any indication of movement in this direction, with one possible exception – DGXI. According to Rubinnaci (1998, p. 239), an 'important effort is being made...to improve the way in which the cost and benefits of draft environmental legislation are assessed'. In one highly specific area, that of 'risk assessment', the Commission (in cooperation with the member states) is in the process of producing very detailed guidelines, procedures and technical recommendations in a kind of manual.[26]

Two improvements would seem to be needed, even on the basis of casual empiricism and given the lack of information. First, there are few, if any, indications that the implementation of the 18th Declaration of the Member States is monitored and reported. Even though certain efforts seem to be undertaken in environmentally sensitive product sectors (e.g. chemicals), what about numerous other product directives, let alone directives in services such as road, maritime, rail, bus and air transport, financial services, telecoms and postal? It is not at all clear whether traditional cost-benefit analysis is suitable for services. One should also reflect on the enormous difference between specific old-approach directives and (very wide) new-approach directives. How can one proceed with an economic assessment of the toy directive, based on six complicated CEN standards, and referring to perhaps as many or 50,000 to 60,000 differentiated products, with thousands of new or amended ones every year? Similarly, the machines directive is said to cover more than 40,000 highly differentiated products. Yet another area is health and safety in the workplace (Baldwin and Daintith, 1992), where approximation directives of a highly specific nature were legislated after the Single Act at an extraordinary speed, with little if any systematic reliance on CBA. What then does the 18th Declaration mean, if there is no agreed basis of what to do in which regulatory areas, and if there is no monitoring and reporting? General Commission and Council Guidelines on draft legislation are of limited help.[27] *Does this mean that the reform is merely virtual*, except in some specific areas of product regulation?

Second, it is thus far unclear whether the requirement of CBA or other suitable assessments is *actually used by the European decision-makers*. To be sure, CBA should not and cannot replace political decision-making. Nevertheless, there is great scope to influence the positioning of decision-makers and the rationale provided, if a) risk assessment and CBA are placed much earlier in the process [28] (reducing excessive biases prompted by NGOs and 'incidents') and b) decision-makers are presented the summaries of risk-assessment, CBA and some basic guidelines in simplified terms. Thus they will be forced to explain publicly why they deviated from well established principles and/or to accept higher regulatory costs. Thus, Desarnauts (1998) shows, for three regulatory initiatives (two draft directives and one decision) that the three core principles of the UK Regulatory Appraisal Process[29] are violated.

A final point is the cost of assessment itself. It is unclear whether all DGs with regulatory assignments devote sufficient (or any) budgetary resources to assessment. Informally, the authors have been told repeatedly that such funds are often tiny or simply absent. Lacking data for the EU, the following might be instructive. According to the US Congressional Budget Office in 1997, the median cost of carrying out 85 regulatory impact analyses in transport and the environment was 240,000 euro, ranging from 12,500 euro to 5.3 million euro. It is also instructive to note that, on average, each took three years of effort by 2.2 government (FTE, full-time equivalent) staff members along with outside consultants (quoted in Hopkins, 1998).

4.2.4 The Business Test Panel

As a complement to the insistence by European business that the costs and benefits of EU regulation should be properly assessed, the Commission proposed in 1998 to set up a pilot project of impact assessment by business itself.[30] According to the proposal 'the ultimate objective of each initiative is to improve the Commission's regulatory impact analysis procedures and in this way adopt better quality proposals' (p. 3). The Business Test Panel does not replace the normal consultation but is a supplement to it in the final phase of preparing legislative proposals. However, the objective and merits of the draft directive should not be assessed; the aim is to quantify the compliance costs and assess the administrative burdens for business; alternative solutions can be identified. The panels should be representative (SMEs and larger size), participating firms should be ready to undertake the necessary work, participation should be voluntary and confidentiality is assured. The idea is that member states set up the panels and 'correspondents' liaise with the

Commission. Time limits are strict because the panels 'must not hold up the legislative process' (p. 5). On the choice of the draft directives, the proposal is vague: not much more is specified than 'a significant impact on business' and 'affect a wider range of sectors'. One can understand that a pilot phase does not include narrower draft directive. Nevertheless, drafts that concern a small number of sectors can also be burdensome.

It is too early to assess the utility of the Business Test Panel. From interviews it would seem that the implementation of the pilot projects suffered from teething problems such as i) the first two pilot projects were small and did not assess a (new) regulatory 'burden' for business but rather measures which would imply a relief; ii) the Commission services turned out not to be very keen to submit a draft directive to the Panel's scrutiny (if correct, this might signal more than an initial resistance and actually reveal a preference to regulate, without the 'nuisance' of outside assessment); and iii) it took the member states quite a while before the national panels became operational.

The third consultation of the panel would seem to be a much better example of what was intended.[31] The subject was the draft directive on waste from electrical and electronic equipment. The idea of this draft directive is that producers would have to assume strict responsibility for the management of electrical and electronic products at the end-of-life stage. In this third consultation coverage is fairly wide (611 businesses from ten member states) and the assessment of business – both quantitative, in terms of compliance costs, and qualitative – is fairly detailed. Alternative options are proposed (e.g. shared responsibility; banning certain materials only when risk assessment about alternatives is available). The nature of the burdens for business is specified in considerable detail and firms are classified as to size and sectors. Remarkably, there are very large differences in average compliance costs for firms, as classified per member state, and between producers, retailers and recyclers.

Very tentatively, it seems useful to conduct consultation with business about draft directives that are suspected to considerably affect the costs of business in this organised and detailed fashion. Early in the year 2000, the Commission is expected to evaluate the pilot project and make proposals how to forward.

4.3 Legal quality and regulatory guidelines

The authors do not pretend to be capable of adding value to the legal aspects of the debate on EU regulatory quality. We merely raise two queries. First, is there sufficient clarity about what exactly the desired, or perhaps minimum, legal quality ought to be? We have our doubts, but the improvements seem to be heading in the right direction. Second, can one expect the impact of the legal quality reforms as conducted in the EU throughout the 1990s to be perceptible in markets, if not, help competitiveness?

As to what exactly the desired legal quality is, a proliferation of checklists, principles, manuals and recommendations is supposed to contain the answer. And, of course, the European Court of Justice remains the final watchdog for procedural safeguards, some of which directly concern legislative quality. The volume about the conference by the Dutch Presidency (Kellerman et. al., 1998) shows how widespread and intense concerns about quality have become throughout the EU (and the OECD). On a number of principles there is agreement and ways are being explored to render their application effective in the drafting process. The complications and legal and institutional detail go beyond the scope of this paper. We merely wish to query how much of all this is truly effective, and how much is only 'virtual'.

Consider Table 12.3. It contains four sets of checklists, presented only in terms of simple slogans. The table therefore cannot do justice to the useful work underlying these checklists. Indeed, the purpose of Table 12.3 is different, namely, to merely show that confusion may win over clarity, causing drafting processes to take up even more time without yielding much advantage for market functioning.[32]

It would seem that the main virtue of the explicit checklist is a combination of awareness and discipline. Table 12.3 shows that this applies to the OECD level, the EU level and the member state specified here.[33] It is likely that these checklists could be standardised to a considerable degree, because the overlap is appreciable. The sequence of checks differs, however. Some of the differences relate to the level of government whereas some are institution-specific. Without standardisation, it is very hard to verify how 'quality control' can be systematically exercised in the EU, that is, systematically between all drafts and systematically over time.

Many of the principles specified are appealing, and some of them border on the obvious. Clearly, regulatory reform for the better functioning of the internal market, and ultimately competitiveness and growth, should (ideally) take for granted that the legal quality of (EU) regulation is properly scrutinised and guaranteed. Regulatory reform must assume that the EU is capable of solving this basic quality issue.

In this light it is surprising that both high Commission and Council officials resist an external body made up of *independent* lawyers, verifying EU legal quality. In most member states this is routine (e.g. Council of State in the Netherlands, etc.). Such a body would end the confusion over quality and serve as a permanent guarantee for quality, in a transparent fashion.

Table 12.3 Checklists for regulatory quality

OECD	Commission	Council*	The Netherlands
Correct problem definition	Justification and objective	Clear, simple, concise, unambiguous	Necessity (justification) and proportionality
Justification	Legal basis	Strict discipline on cross-references	Consistency with higher (e.g. EC) law
Is regulation preferable above alternatives?	Reader-friendly and user-friendly	Internal consistency	Respect the primacy of parliament
Legal basis	Subsidiarity and proportionality	Clear definition of rights and obligations	Stable and predictable
Appropriate level of government	Simplification	A standard structure	Compliance should be feasible
Benefits justifying the costs	Consistency with other EC policies	Preamble should justify in simple terms	Effectiveness
A transparent distribution of costs over society	External consultation	No wishes or political statements	Consistency and coherence vis-à-vis existing laws
Clarity, consistency, comprehension, accessibility	Assessment, cost and benefit, etc.	Consistency with existing legislation; avoid repetitions	Simple, clear, transparent
Full, open consultation	Assessment of fraud risks	Amendments without any further provisions	Assessment (also of alternatives)
Effective compliance	Financial statement	Time-tables clear	Accessibility, and non-specialist explanations

* For drafting only (Council Resolution 8 June 1993, OJ EC 93/C 166).

Probably its greatest merit would be that the search for greater legal quality does not remain 'virtual', in a jungle of largely invisible legal exchanges, but is and remains effective. In preventing 'low' quality, the costs of regulation would be lowered compared to past practices.

The second question is more pertinent, however. Do the reforms of the 1990s that were intended to improve legal quality impact on market functioning, and in so doing, do they induce greater competitiveness? It would seem that, on the basis of a narrow definition of legal quality, this is only accidentally the case. One can argue, with justification, that many of the 'checks' in Table 12.3 are no more than necessary conditions for good law-making. If one accepts this position, then regulatory reform should merely take these efforts for granted, and be concerned solely with the *substance* of regulation, affecting conduct (perhaps even structure) and performance in markets. The narrow perspective is best expressed in the Council's 'ten commandments' for proper drafting.

A wider perspective emerges if one has closer look at checks such as 'simplification', 'proportionality' and 'accessibility'. Apart from SLIM (see Section 5), specific simplifications (e.g. the infamous chocolate directive) and so-called 'recasting' have been undertaken. One can query whether there is much 'new' here. For instance, proposals to simplify the chocolate directive have been submitted during a period of more than two decades (!) whereas, in fact, it can be withdrawn, while ensuring proper labelling (perhaps with a good system of private certification for quality chocolates), letting mutual recognition prevail.[34] On proportionality, the Better Law-making report of 1996 (European Commission, 1996) specifies two forms, namely the greater use of framework directives and the establishment of common minimum standards where e.g. codes of conduct did not work.[35] Under 'accessibility' it suggests recasting and formal and informal consolidation. This is to be applauded as it reduces the search costs for business, consumers and citizens, in attempting to understand Community law. Nonetheless, all these laudable efforts will barely be noticeable in product and services markets and risk being sold as substitutes for far-deeper regulatory reform affecting markets in their competitive functioning and incentive structures.

5. THE COMPLICATIONS OF SIMPLIFICATIONS: LESSONS FROM SLIM

Regulatory complexity increases costs for business (and sometimes consumers too) and has a discouraging effect on entrepreneurial activity in general, and on market entry and trade in particular. It is entirely possible that complexity might have the effect of (what is called in industrial economics) 'raising rivals' costs', that is, making it harder for potential or fringe competitors to exercise rivalry and challenge. The sensitivity for complexity, although widespread, would seem to be greatest among SMEs.

No wonder that the 1995 Molitor and UNICE reports strongly emphasised simplification. Indeed, simplification was the 'mission' for the Molitor group, although in the course of the group's deliberations and during the ensuing debate on its report, some degree of disenchantment was expressed about the undue extension of simplification to deregulation. Since

1995, the intense EU debate on the need for simplification has led to two distinct lines of simplification activities at the EU level: specific simplification and recasting initiatives, and the SLIM programme. In the 1996 Better Lawmaking report (European Commission, 1996, Annex II/1), nine specific simplification initiatives are listed, some of which refer to groups of Directives or Commission Regulations. In the 1998 report (European Commission, 1998) another 15 new proposals are announced without any specification. The latter report contains a graph showing that over 60 specific simplification measures have been proposed by the Commission since the Edinburgh European Council in December 1992, and that nearly 30 have been adopted by the European Parliament/Council. Because some of these proposals refer to groups of directives,[36] this might refer to a noticeable improvement of market functioning. However, the incredible diversity of the initiatives makes it very difficult to evaluate, even roughly, the merits of specific simplification. To our knowledge, there is no systematic reporting on these initiatives, and on what they could imply for business or other market agents.

Therefore, we will focus on the SLIM programme. The initiative was launched in May 1996, motivated by business calls to lower the regulatory burden, as expressed for instance in the UNICE and Molitor reports.[37] Contrary to the Molitor report, SLIM attempts to focus attention on specific issues and is not meant to advocate deregulation: recognising that complicated regulations can reduce the competitiveness of business, and especially small businesses, SLIM aims at analysing the state of regulation in a number of areas and coming up with proposals for simplification. The link with the main focus of the present research project is clear: '(SLIM)... forms part of the Commission's Confidence Pact for Employment. Simplifying legislation can contribute to the Pact's objectives of enhancing the competitiveness and employment-creating potential of business'.[38] No doubt, it *can*. The question is: does it actually do so?

The idea behind SLIM is that the criteria for selecting cases and the work method should increase the likelihood that the regulatory burden for business would decrease, and flexibility – where relevant – would be promoted. There are four *criteria* selecting topics:

- An excessive administrative burden on business (as indicated by business and the Internal Market. Advisory Committee consisting of member sates)
- The SLIM method should bring added value
- Feasible for the small SLIM teams, working against tight deadlines (e.g. 4-6 months only)
- Sufficient resources within the Commission services.[39]

Whereas the latter two are mere constraints, the second one is highly subjective and elusive. One might suspect that it is circumspect language for avoiding controversial cases, but the actual results show that such cases have not been avoided.

The *working method* is based on the co-optation of 'users' (that is, business and the member states), and the limitation to small groups (teams of five business experts and five national experts are typical, plus Commission officials). The work is extremely targeted and focused on making precise recommendations.

EU institutions take the view that SLIM is a success. The Commission's reports and the continuation of successive phases are evidence of this. The Council has provided strong political backing, at least in resolutions. The European Parliament has complimented SLIM in the Crowley report.[40] It is not so clear whether this institutional satisfaction goes far beyond rhetoric and wishful thinking. After all, who would be willing to advocate complexity as a virtue? Simplification under strict constraints and without altering the objectives (e.g. overcoming market failures) is almost too good to be true, and cannot be other than desirable. However, the SLIM process does not incorporate a methodology or even a rough indicative measure of the 'added value' expected to be achieved. The recommendations are merely listed, without any signal of how (much) they would reduce the regulatory burden.

We shall proceed as follows. First, a survey table will be presented on the SLIM activities thus far. Second, the limits of SLIM will be sketched insofar as this becomes clear from the available documentation and literature. Third, a relatively simple case dealt with in Phase II (fertilisers) will be inspected a little more closely, for purposes of illustration.

Table 12.4 shows four phases with a total of 14 initiatives, undertaken in a period of three years. It allows the following nine conclusions.

1. The work method is relatively effective, in the restrictive sense that small teams of experts with a well defined and limited mission, can *operate quickly and produce results* (i.e. recommendations).

2. The work method is largely apolitical, and this *artificially facilitates* the work of experts; some conflicts of interests prevent consensus, and this is reported, but there is a fruitful search of where consensus on simplification can be found.

3. The subjects chosen are neither *marginal areas, for the most part, nor are they uncontroversial*; subjects such as VAT, banking, insurance, and EMC are important elements of the acquis; areas such as intra-stat, construction products, coordinating (aspects of) national social security and pre-packaging legislation, and no doubt VAT are controversial.

4. Simplification is inherently limited in results, when the difficulties which may derive from 'using' EU regulation in a particular area are *due to reasons, other than (avoidable) complexity*, but are for example technical (e.g. many distinct products or services or institutions), procedural (e.g. the market innovations go faster than the EU), and/or political (e.g. compromises between member states holding different views). The reports on banking and on insurance mention these points explicitly, but to some extent they can be found in several other reports. This point is fundamental: simplification (at EU level) is too constrained an exercise to yield an impact that is economically of much importance. *Lifting the constraints might help but would alter the nature of the exercise* - it also risks to be followed more critically (while reducing the rhetoric, presumably).

5. Although the Commission often embraces all, or many, of the recommendations (in the first three phases, at least), this is perhaps not so surprising as it is an active contributor to the SLIM groups; nevertheless, there are informal signals that criterion no. 4 (resources within the services of the Commission) actually reduces the possibilities for SLIM. The Commission services consider a SLIM activity an extra burden (note that only the specialists can usefully participate – and those specialists are usually few) .

6. As noted, there are *no yardsticks to measure* the 'effectiveness' or 'success', or for that matter, the impact on costs, innovation or competitiveness. One ultimate measuring rod is the *actual* change in rules and procedures. Reporting here is not systematic and, at least for this obvious yardstick, this should be done, for observers to be able to assess results. It would seem that one (simplified) directive (on ornamental plants, a relatively 'easy' and limited case) has been adopted; seven draft directives (on statistics, diplomas and VAT) have been tabled and some administrative, procedural or Commission-controlled regulatory changes were also accomplished. There is also some progress on CEN/Commission cooperation in construction products (e.g. mandates are completed). There seems to be no way of knowing how important (e.g. for markets) these accomplishments really are. It seems fair to say that these actual accomplishments are modest.

7. Council, or at least different coalitions of a few member states (and, in VAT, 'the' member states), *does not seem to follow what it preaches.* Several SLIM-phase reports make diplomatic statements about 'a certain contradiction' (COM(97)618, p. 4) between the political determination to simplify and the reluctance to actually accept specific recommendations.

8. It is not obvious from the reports whether business itself is behind Council resistance, except in the case of Intra-stat.[41]
9. On the work method, it would seem that *the nimble-footed process* - in some sense, a benefit – also *has costs*. One is that there is no cost/benefit approach, even in the most elementary fashion of asking (all) the right questions in a purposeful sequence. The upshot is that one gropes in the dark about the meaning of the recommendations; another is that, although business is co-opted, regulators (i.e. member states and Commission) dominate numerically and consultation of other member states (sensible, in view of the Council work later) tends to strengthen this bias: the 'case' discussed below seems to confirm these reservations.

*Table 12.4 Work and progress under SLIM**

No. and phase	Regulatory area	Agreement in groups	Commission acceptance	COM proposals	Council/EP adoption
I/1	Intra-stat	Less than full	Largely	Some, in 1997	Partly not needed (2 COM regulations); simple nomenclature procedure blocked in Council; conciliation between EP and Council on fewer data requirements
II/1	Construction products	Unanimous (also, 3 options)	Accepts combination	Draft amendment of directive under preparation; CEN mandates completed	
III/1	Seven sectoral directives of diploma recognition	Unanimous	Yes	Substitution of 6 Council decisions by one COM decision expected and one draft directive in 1997 on automatic recognition	EP amendments to draft directive unacceptable to COM
IV/1	Ornamental plants	Less than full; growers doubted the need for any directive	Accepts combination of options	Yes	Dir. 98/56; OJL226 of 13.8.98

V/2	VAT	Less than full; member states often separate	Largely	Three draft directives in 1998 i.a. to simplify VAT issues for cross-border sales; studies	
VI/2	Fertilisers (now 16 directives, old approach)	Unanimous	Fully	Overall single recasting draft directive promised	
VII/2	External Trade combined nomenclature (2nd phase Intra-stat, see above)	Unanimous	Fully	Can be done within present Council Reg. (deletes many 8-digit lines) Cmte progress very slow	
VIII/2	Banking services	Less than full	For the most part	Will propose or alter procedures; reporting requirements; amendment	(Codification will get priority over SLIM)
IX/3	Insurance services	Less than full	For the most part	Codification of life and non-life directives promised; COM interpretative communication on 'general good' in 1999	
X/3	EMC-directive (electro-magnetic compatibility)	Less than full	For the most part	Broad consultation in 1999 on possible amendments	
XI/3	Coordinating social security (of member states)	Less than full; considerable differences on some issues	Accepted the 'broad thrust'	Incorporated in wider proposal for new legal framework in Dec. 1998	
XII/4	Company law	(no report yet)			
XIII/4	Pre-packaging legislative	(no report yet)			
XIV/4	Dangerous substances	(no report yet)			

* This table includes information until May 1999 (report on SLIM results of third phase of February 1999 is the latest; COM (1999)88).

We illustrate the work method of SLIM by inspecting the case of fertilisers (VI/2). We wish to stress that this illustration is not meant to undermine any appreciation of the swift work against a tight deadline; rather, it is meant to show the drawbacks of the method. This group was started in order to simplify a very complex legislation, made up of 16 directives, in order to establish the single market for fertilisers and improve the protection of health and the environment.

Without going into the details of the scope and nature of the directives, the SLIM group identified different changes in the legislation that could result in simplification. Three main points were considered:
1. Would it be preferable to combine together the 16 directives together into a single directive, just pasting them together, or to rewrite the legislation in a modernised form?
2. Should the legislation follow the Old Approach, or the New Approach?
3. Should there be partial harmonisation or total harmonisation?

In order to find the answers to the three questions above, the SLIM group organised a consultation with the users: member states (agricultural and industry ministries) and organisations representing producers and consumers interests. Two questionnaires, a first questionnaire and a follow-up questionnaire were sent to 21 interested users. Different meetings and discussions took place, and the SLIM group then drew conclusions. Its recommendations were to:
• Put together and modernise the 16 directives into one directive, following the old approach; and
• Simplify the procedure for approval of new fertilisers by reducing the size of the groups of fertilisers defined in the directive's classification.

In order to illustrate the lack of systematic analysis, we report here the main steps and discussions of the working group. A first questionnaire was sent and drew very few respondents. Given the limited number of responses, a follow-up questionnaire had to be sent to confirm preferences. The follow-up questionnaire was sent in the course of the summer 1997, and results were discussed at the second meeting of the group, on 15 September 1997. However, some inconsistencies arose. For instance, in the first questionnaire, respondents were asked whether there had been any reports of health problems. Since that question was answered negatively, the follow-up questionnaire asked for confirmation that there were no report of health problems. However, only 10 out of 36 polled members of the group had replied to the first questionnaire. The conclusion is therefore based on a very limited sample.

The overall conclusion is that SLIM is probably a useful, although severely limited exercise. It is useful as an ex-post review of a highly targeted nature, basically on *avoidable compliance costs.* It is severely limited due to a host of reasons including the fact that complexity is often unavoidable; that isolation from political decision-making may be an illusion; that there is no way to appreciate the merit of the recommendations; that conflicts of interest among private 'users' colour one's view of what is 'avoidable'; and that resources and time constrain the work. It is in this context that one may welcome the direct involvement of business – it helps, as far as it goes. As far as the Council is concerned, SLIM proposals should ideally be voted only by *simple* majority, as they purely and only concern 'simplification'!

6. WHY DEEPER REFORMS?

The 1990s have witnessed greater attention being paid on the part of EU policy-makers as well as European business 'EU regulatory quality'. EC-1992 of course consisted mainly of 'regulation for liberalisation'. The follow-up of EC-1992 only pursued selected instances of liberalisation throughout the decade, because a large degree of formal market integration had already been accomplished by the end of 1992. The greater attention to regulatory quality is understandable in the context of these developments. Thus initially, member states and European business were concerned that perhaps too much regulation was going to be generated at EU level, and that there were few if any systematic procedures or assessments for ensuring that the net benefits of such rules to the EU would be maximised. In the course of the decade, the debate became far richer and the roots of the concerns more fundamental. Figure 12.1 in Section 3 and various chapters in these two volumes testify to the pervasiveness and breath of the scope of the debate at the turn of the decade. The introductory chapter (Galli and Pelkmans) as well as Chapter 3 (Labory and Malgarini), establish that, the regulatory climate in the EU today is considered a major determinant of the performance of the EU economy in general, and of business in Europe in particular. The focus on the (relative) economic performance of the EU vis-à-vis the US, and sometimes vis-à-vis Japan or other OECD countries, is often labelled the 'competitiveness debate'. The increased sensitivity to improved economic (and business) performance, compared to benchmark performers, is the result of concerns about the Union's record in economic growth and (net) job creation, in a context of intensifying globalisation. As a consequence, the demand for higher regulatory quality at both EU and national level has greatly increased, and the actual and perceived implications of failure to pursue regulatory reform tend to be ever more severely criticised.

It is in this policy and market contexts that the search for better EU regulatory quality should be evaluated. Sections 2-5 of the present paper leave little doubt that the Union has responded to the rising demand for better EU regulatory quality. In Figure 12.2 we have stylised an emerging vision on EU regulatory quality. All five elements of this vision have been addressed. For this reason alone, the policy response at EU level is undoubtedly in the right direction. This response has led to a much better appreciation of the costs of 'low quality' regulation. This has been achieved by:

- Subjecting all draft legislation to subsidiarity and proportionality tests;
- Taking greater care to organise prior consultation with business (specifically SMEs as well) in traditional and innovative ways (e.g. the Business Test Panel);
- Adopting formal declarations about the need for cost-benefit assessment and improved 'legal quality';
- An attempt to lower compliance and transaction costs by 'simplification' of existing EC directives and procedures;
- A host of legal activities to actually improve 'legal quality';
- Policy action to improve the decentralised implementation of Community law[42]) by the member states; and
- Initiatives to delegate executive tasks to autonomous EU agencies and (e.g. in competition policy) to member states authorities.[43]

It is exceedingly difficult to 'measure', with any degree of confidence, the effectiveness of all these initiatives. The evidence provided in Sections 2.5 of the present paper, however, would seem to support the following conclusions:

1. Until 1999, there was no mechanism to consider the combined ('cumulative') impact of EU level and national regulatory reforms. For the concerns which EC-1992 gave rise to (e.g. fear of undue centralisation; too hasty drafting without due consultation at EU level; etc.), this is largely irrelevant. But with the demand for regulatory quality becoming central to the improvement of economic performance in the EU, the failure to address 'cumulation' would be serious. Therefore, the Cardiff process (see Section 2.2) is an important breakthrough. After one round of Cardiff, it is premature to draw conclusions. In any event, the mechanism is not based on legal (EC) competences but on a blend of peer review and OECD-type country evaluations. Knowing how deep and pervasive public and private resistance against (genuine) regulatory

reform can be, also in the member states, the expectations about the Cardiff process should not be set too high. There is also an economic reason for that. If the (regulatory) determinants for better economic performance would be clearly identifiable, the results of benchmarking could directly suggest 'success formula' or policy packages to improve performance. Unfortunately, the manifold complexities of regulation and the structural differences between the member states together make it very difficult to 'write recipes' for regulatory reform, including elusive aspects such as the efficiency of public administration (etc.), which guarantee increased growth or job creation. In 1999 the Broad Economic Guidelines contain reform recommendations for individual member states, but they tend to be limited to aspects of the acquis that help reforms (e.g. Belgium should speed up telecoms liberalisation; etc.) or to excesses. The issue of cumulation, which business complains is an undue burden and which may hinder the EU's economic performance, is neither directly nor other than selectively addressed.

2. The subsidiarity and proportionality test has probably prevented or suppressed undue centralist impulses in the circuit of EU institutions. But otherwise, especially subsidiarity is, more often than not, politically interpreted by member states. This is dysfunctional for the internal market, because fully-fledged liberalisation with competitive markets and cross-border access may well require stronger powers at EU level, in specific cases.

3. The increasing emphasis on regulatory impact analyses has almost certainly led to 'virtual reforms' only, except in the case of selected environmental issues where CBA has been used. The authors have no systematic information on the frequency and effectiveness of CBA or cost-effectiveness analysis in environmental EU regulation. In any event, we have been unable to find any report or other evidence that the cost-benefit (18th) Declaration of the member states of 1991 is monitored, promoted via funding, training or is implemented otherwise. This is worrying. Indeed, we have received signals that CBA or other systematic impact assessments are seen as a nuisance, as disturbing, as too 'technical' or as useless.

4. The simplification pursued via the SLIM programme results in very modest improvements at best, and with a low speed, for only a few areas. At times, even these modest improvements get blocked in the ensuing decision-making, following the SLIM proposals. SLIM is designed in such a way that genuine reform is avoided.

5. Insofar as legal quality and legislative procedures are concerned, a great deal has been done to improve the 'craft of drafting' according to explicit

principles, procedures and manuals, both for Commission and the legislature (Council and EP). Yet, Table 12.3 and some other signals raise considerable doubt about the effective impact on the regulatory process and its fruits.

Altogether, the conclusion is that the EU search for regulatory quality has failed – thus far – to impact noticeably on market functioning and hence competitiveness. Attempts to increase the effectiveness and practical relevance of the initiatives to achieve greater regulatory quality have included *the co-optation of business*. This has been done in essentially two ways. First, business has played a prominent role in various committees and other awareness work. Important examples include the 1995 Molitor Committee, the 1995 UNICE report (based on business questionnaires as well as meetings with companies in many member states, and funded by the Commission), the 1998 BEST report (on the business climate for SMEs) and the strong and systematic cooperation between the TABD and the US-EC authorities as well as the emerging cooperation between the ASEM Business Council and the authorities of ASEM countries in East Asian and the EU. In some respects, the role of business leaders in the Competitiveness Advisory Group (reporting to the Council and the President of the Commission between 1995 and 1999) could also be mentioned here. Business is under increasing pressure given the context of intensified competition and globalisation, and hence they want results. Probably the clearest case in demanding results explicitly and every time, is the TABD, which focuses almost entirely on 'regulatory cooperation' across the Atlantic. Simplification, mutual recognition and regulatory reform with a view to market access and a lower regulatory burden for business is pursued vigorously, with detailed proposals. But also the insistence from UNICE and the ERT (European Round Table of Industrialists) is incessant. Given this relatively new method of prompting better regulatory quality, it is unlikely that the modest impact on market functioning and competitiveness will be easily accepted.

Second, business has come to be directly involved in the regulatory reform process. In SLIM business experts help formulate simplification proposals, which – if accepted by the Commission – go to Council and EP for adoption. As has been shown (Section 5), SLIM is too severely constrained to make much of an impact, and political difficulties behind existing directives often resurface once simplification is suggested. In the Business Test Panels (Section 4.2.4), a direct, firm-based impact assessment of draft directives is conducted and alternative options can be included in the report. This potentially promising approach – which has only just started –

can only work effectively if Commission services embrace such assessments as a good way to get better regulatory quality (there are signs that the services do not) and if member states actively invest in this process.

In the new millennium the pursuit of EU regulatory quality cannot be expected to remain as fragmented, selective and noncommittal as it has been during the 1990s. It will require regulatory reform that bites, that is, in markets but prior to that, in the regulatory process. The remainder of this paper consists of a series of suggestions how to go down the route of reform for better regulatory quality, for the purpose of getting the most from the functioning of the single market and the Economic Union.

It is good to point out that the source of regulatory pressures is usually found in the EU and national regulatory process itself! It is therefore indispensable to have regard to the regulatory process and approaches in order to accomplish effective reform. A revealing note from the 1998 Better Law-making report[44] distinguishes five categories of proposals for regulation the Commission has proposed over four years. I is interesting to note that this analysis reveals *strong and permanent* pressures to regulate more at EU level. The categories are:

1. Direct result of international agreements (35%!);
2. Amendments of existing EU regulation (25-30%);
3. Proposals at the express request of other Community institutions (Council, EP), the member states and business (sic) (20%);
4. Non-discretionary acts, required by existing Community legislation (10%); and
5. Commission-originated proposals after consultation, green papers, etc. (10%).

Under item (3) alone, the European Council asked the Commission 80 times to carry out new studies and/or take new initiatives between 1995 and 1998. All this is not a priori 'wrong'. What matters is whether such regulatory pressures are justified and indispensable in terms of costs and benefits in the EU public interest.

7. FACILITATING REGULATORY COMPETITION

Regulatory competition forms a dynamic consequence of mutual recognition and is therefore possible in many sectors in the EU, both in product and services markets. Under certain conditions, it would improve regulatory quality while intensifying competition. Pursuing regulatory competition is in

Pelkmans, Labory and Majone

the domain of member states, although the EU level can facilitate it in the EU public interest.

The starting point is mutual recognition. Under mutual recognition, free movement (of goods or services) prevails, even though the relevant product or services laws are different between member states, as long as the objective(s) and effect of the relevant laws are 'equivalent'. It will expose national regulation to the forces of arbitrage: consumers may choose between (products or services produced under) domestic regulation or that of any other member state, by importing the relevant products or services. To the extent that production factors find it profitable to respond to regulatory differences, mutual recognition and free movement may induce cross-border factor flows. All this should improve welfare on account of greater variety and additional output in the EU. But, since mutual recognition is a static notion, no more than a one-time adjustment would take place.

Regulatory competition is dynamic and takes this process further. It is defined as the alteration of national regulation in response to the actual or expected impact of cross-border mobility of goods, services or factors on national economic activity (see Jeanne-May Sun and Jacques Pelkmans, 1995). Behind this alteration are complex business-government interactions. Jurisdictions with costly regulations may find business pressing to reduce their regulatory burden, when faced with import competition from jurisdictions with 'light' regimes. Alternatively, local business and government may agree on strategic deregulation so as to boost certain activities in the internal market. Since this may also be practised, or responded to, by other member states, iterative processes of regulatory competition may develop. Where member states would keep ambitious regulation, the costs will fall on that member state's economy – this can be interpreted as meaning that the (local) benefits of satisfying these preferences are more than worth the (local) costs. Quality or other non-price determinants induced by this regulation would make products from other jurisdictions poor substitutes; hence, they would prevent local business from suffering too much from import competition. When factor mobility is at issue, location benefits would apparently outweigh the benefits of relocation at the margin. The upshot would be that where regulatory differences remain large, despite exposure to arbitrage, this would be economically justified.

As a rule, however, one would expect a process of regulatory competition to induce a 'market-driven' regulatory convergence in the EC. The condition is that this should not be allowed where a negative externality is the relevant market failure since it would lead to fragmentation of the internal market or insufficient regulation (e.g. environment, discriminatory measures), but it would be suitable if information asymmetries or other 'internalities' are the problem. At the end of a process of regulatory competition, the market-driven convergence could be codified as essential requirements in EC approximation. It is unlikely that, in the absence of mutual recognition, the Council would be capable of knowing the preferences of consumers and other economic agents. Worse still, approximation may be abused by Council precisely to *prevent* regulatory competition by ruling out or limiting mutual recognition (or their analogues such as home country control, or the origin principles in taxation).

As long as 'equivalence' of objective(s) and effect relates to a justified and proportional solution for a market failure, regulatory competition may be a good alternative to 'benchmarking'. Indeed, it might well be superior because it will less likely be influenced, let alone controlled, by civil servants supervising or having designed the regulation (and tending to resist alternative solutions) and by businesses or conformity assessment service providers who enjoy higher sales under more costly options.

The fear for fiercer competition has, in actual practice, hindered the full application of mutual recognition (see Pelkmans, Vos and Di Mauro, in Chapter 7 of this volume). Although this is sometimes understandable given the difficulties of exactly establishing the extent of a market failure, the Single Market Review has unveiled numerous instances where vested interests resisted market access out of fear of eroding rents or losing market share. In increasing the vigilance of the Commission in monitoring mutual recognition, not only would free movement be permitted, but the possibilities for regulatory competition would greatly increase. And this is likely to be beneficial precisely in the instances and countries where this has recently been most heavily resisted. Regulatory competition, under the proper conditions, is therefore attractive as an option for regulatory reform in the EU. Such regulatory competition would amount to a kind of automatic, market-driven regulatory reform, without a 'race to the (regulatory) bottom'. The race to the bottom is prevented by the equivalence principle, coupled with the overcoming of the relevant market failure.

8. THE PROBLEM OF REGULATORY CREDIBILITY IN THE EU

Credibility is the single most important indicator of regulatory quality; in fact, of good public policy in general (see also Labory and Malgarini in Chapter 3 of this volume). Current economic, technological and political development, in the EU and worldwide tend to drastically reduce the effectiveness of the traditional command-and-control approach to policy-making and, correspondingly, to increase the significance of policy-credibility. Because of growing economic, financial, ecological and political interdependence, national policies are increasingly projected outside the national borders but they can achieve their objectives there only if they are credible. Thus, the traditional trade-off between persuasion and command – a policy lacking credibility could be enforced by coercive means, just as a nearly worthless currency could be made legal tender by legislative fiat – is being radically altered by the permeability of national borders. What is true at the national level is a fortiori true at EU level, where coercive means are few and costly to use.

Also the growing complexity of public policy continues to erode the effectiveness of the old command-and-control methods. The most important characteristic of the newer forms of economic and social regulation is that their success depends on affecting the attitudes, consumption habits or production patterns of millions of individuals and hundreds of thousands of firms. The new tasks are difficult, not only because they deal with technologically complicated matters, but even more because they aim ultimately at modifying individual expectations and behaviour. Credibility and persuasion are much more likely to achieve such complex policy objectives than commands and controls.

The major reforms of EC rule-making undertaken since the 1980s – the shift from total to minimum harmonisation, the New Approach to technical standardisation, the increasing reliance on mutual recognition as a key regulatory principle and the extension of qualified majority voting – may be seen as attempts to increase the credibility of EC regulations. However, as the various contributions to this project testify, much remains to be done.

To understand the nature of the problem of regulatory credibility in the EU, it is useful to distinguish between *internal and external threats to credibility*. Internal threats arise from the way the regulatory system has been designed and is operated, while external threats originate in the social, economic or political environment in which the system is embedded. This is, of course, an analytical distinction; in practice, internal and external threats often interact. Thus, the risk of regulatory capture is an external threat, but it may be made more serious by the way the regulatory institutions have been designed. For example, the advantage of agencies or commissions regulating all the public utilities, as in the United States, over different agencies separately regulating each utility, as in Europe, is their greater resistance to capture by any single industry.

Despite such complications, the distinction between internal and external threats to credibility is useful to understand the different dimensions of the problem, and the nature of the proposed solutions. In the four parts of

Section 9 we discuss a group of proposals dealing with serious internal threats to the credibility of European regulation: excessive reliance on command-and-control; poor implementation; insufficient attention to the costs of regulation and poor coordination within and across regulatory programmes.

Among the external threats to credibility, the most serious one today is, arguably, the growing politicisation, or, more precisely, the parliamentarisation of the European Commission. This is probably a positive development from the point of view of democratic legitimacy, but it does raise a credibility problem analogous to the 'time inconsistency' problem studied by monetary economists. Just as an independent central bank is the institutional solution to the problem of achieving a credible commitment to monetary stability, so, we argue in the last Section, independent European agencies may be an appropriate solution to the credibility problem raised by the increasing dependence of EC regulators on the variable preferences of shifting majorities in the European Parliament.

According to his biographers, John Maynard Keynes always followed a dual reform strategy, proposing reforms that were feasible within the given constraints, while at the same time trying to change the constraints themselves. This excellent strategy has inspired the following pages. The reforms proposed in the Section 9 could be carried out under the existing institutional constraints, while the establishment of truly independent European agencies may require treaty revision. It seems to us that the potential benefits are large enough to justify such revisions.

9. INTERNAL THREATS TO REGULATORY CREDIBILITY

9. 1 Regulation by information

Public policy depends, of course, on relevant, timely and especially credible information. Nowhere is such dependence stronger than in the area of social regulation – environmental and consumer protection, risk regulation, occupational health and safety – where the policy-maker often faces problems at the frontier of scientific and technical knowledge. In addition to this instrumental view of information as an important input into the regulatory process, however, another view is emerging, according to which information can actually *constitute* policy, even if only on a contingent or provisional basis: regulation by information.

An important justification for public regulation is the existence of information failures – the fact that the market does not always provide the type and amount of information that consumers, workers or investors need in order to make rational choices. However, public regulation does not have to take the form of binding rules. One important alternative strategy is to provide reliable information to people exposed to particular types of risk. Health and environmental hazards, in particular, often lend themselves quite well to interventions of this type. Information concerning levels of exposure to particular risks, and the level of disease associated with that exposure, can facilitate relatively efficient risk-reduction measures. The extent to which information strategies can supplement or even supplant formal rule-making is a question that is actively debated in the United States.

Thus, it has been suggested that the US Occupational Safety and Health Administration (OSHA) should devote fewer resources to the development of mandatory standards and more to information development. Standards would be reserved for emergency situations, particularly intractable problems, and areas that demand a uniform approach (Mendeloff, 1988).

Another well known specialist in risk analysis, Kip Viscusi, argues that most mandatory standards should be replaced by risk information. He admits that a more direct regulatory approach has to be considered when workers find it difficult to appreciate information pertaining to very low probability hazards. However, justification for such intervention should be required on a case-by-case basis; the existence of a workplace risk should no longer be taken as a self-evident reason for direct regulation. Rather, substance-by-substance regulation would be permitted only if it can be shown that an information alternative is unworkable (Viscusi, 1983).

Also in the European Union there are indications of a growing preference for non-coercive, information-rich strategies, as shown by the current popularity of 'tertiary rules' or soft law. The rules of European soft law provide a less formal alternative to binding acts, or 'secondary rules', such as regulations, directives and decisions. They are particularly attractive when secondary legislation proves politically contentious or difficult to implement. Soft law appears in a number of guises: resolutions, declarations, action programmes, deliberations, memoranda and guidelines.

Robert Baldwin (1995) discusses different cases where the devices constituting the soft law of the Community represent useful alternatives or complements to formal legislation. Thus, in a number of policy fields, including the environment and health and safety at work, action programmes provide a useful framework for negotiation between member states and the Commission, and for deliberation for specific actions. Also, tertiary rules are particularly attractive from the point of view of subsidiarity since they offer member states a higher level of flexibility in implementation than would be offered even by a directive.

Some of the European agencies established in the early 1990s, in particular the European Environment Agency (EEA), could be seen as further examples of a general shift to modes of regulation based on information and persuasion rather than on command and control. These new agencies do not have the power of rule-making, adjudication, and enforcement normally granted to American regulators, and even lack the more limited powers enjoyed, for instance, by the Regulatory Offices in Britain. Council Regulation No. 1210/90 of 7 May 1990, for example, specifies the tasks of the EEA as follows: to provide the member states and the Community with information; to collect records and assess data on the state of environment; to encourage harmonisation of the methods of measurement; and to promote the incorporation of European environmental information into international monitoring programmes.

There are political and legal reasons why the new European agencies have been denied powers that regulatory bodies normally possess outside the EU or in some EU countries (Majone, 1996). This limitation seems to condemn the agencies to play only an ancillary role in the European regulatory process. It is possible, however, that the constraint may turn into an opportunity: with knowledge and persuasion as the principal means of influence at their disposal, agencies such as the EEA could develop indirect, information-based modes of regulation that are actually more in tune with current economic and technological conditions than the coercive instruments that have been denied to them. However, a policy based on information can affect expectations and behaviour only if it is credible, and credibility requires a certain measure of political independence. Indeed, the willingness of an increasing number of countries to delegate powers to agencies operating at arm's length from government is best understood as a means *whereby politicians can commit themselves to regulatory policies* that would not be credible in the absence of such delegation.

If credibility is important to policy-makers, it is even more important to bodies such as the new European agencies, whose main task is to provide objective information, and opinions based on the best-available evidence rather than on political expedience. We come back to the issue of the political independence of existing and future European agencies in the final Section, after completing the discussion of internal threats to the credibility of the current EC regulatory system.

9.2 The implementation deficit

The seriousness of the problem of poor and/or uneven implementation of EC regulation by member states has been recognised by successive European

Councils since the early 1990s. The fact that EC directives are implemented by national authorities that differ widely in efficiency, expertise and resources necessarily creates a good deal of uncertainty for economic agents. Where EC rules are not implemented evenly, there is the additional danger that national regulators may become frustrated and lose any incentive to enforce the rules generally.

For these reasons it may be interesting to examine how American regulatory federalism has attempted to improve cooperation between state and federal agencies in order to enhance the quality of enforcement. One of the most interesting techniques to improve federal-state partnership are the *state implementation plans* (SIPs), which allow the states to develop and implement their own regulation, under federal oversight, as long as they meet precise quality standards. This approach is used extensively in the regulation of occupational health and safety, and also in some areas of environmental regulation.

In 1970, when the Occupational Safety and Health Act (OSH Act) was passed, few American states had comprehensive laws dealing with safety and health at work, and fewer still had adequate programmes to enforce them. Sponsors of federal legislation criticised the lack of uniformity among state programmes, which created competitive disadvantages and discouraged nation-wide progress in this important area of social regulation. However, the OSH Act does not provide for the complete federalisation of the field. The objective of assuring safe and healthy conditions at the workplace was to be reached, in part, by 'encouraging the States to assume the fullest responsibility for the administration and enforcement of State occupation safety and health laws', by means of federal grants and approved state plans (OSH Act. Section 2(b)(11)). The provisions for SIPs are contained in Section 18(b) through (g) of the Act. Section 18(b) provides that states desiring to regain responsibility for the development and enforcement of safety and health standards under state law, may do so by submitting and obtaining federal approval of a state plan which meets the strict requirements set fourth in Section 18(c) (see below). Approval of a state plan by the Occupational Safety and Health Administration (OSHA) permits the state to re-enter the field of occupational health and safety regulation.

The requirements set forth in Section 18(c) are, first, that a state must provide for the development of state standards 'at least as effective' as corresponding federal standards. Second, Section 18(c)(2) requires state plans to provide enforcement of state standards at least as effective as federal enforcement. Section 18(c)(3), moreover, requires state inspection rights to be at least as effective as those available to OSHA.

Sections 18(c)(4) and (5) are perhaps the most relevant ones from an EC perspective. They state that the Secretary of Labor (in whose Department OSHA is located) is to approve a state plan only if it provides 'necessary' qualified personnel and 'adequate' funds to carry out enforcement functions. For the first three years after initial approval, the state plans are considered to be 'developmental'. The most important feature of the developmental stage is that during this period the federal and state governments have concurrent jurisdiction. The Secretary of Labor evaluates, monitors and audits the state plan at least every six months. States with approved plans must submit annual activity reports and inform the public of its right to file written complaints during this three-year period. During this same period, the federal government may contribute up to 90 per cent of the costs of developing the SIPs. When all developmental steps are completed, OSHA issues and publishes in the Federal Register, a formal *notice of certification*. This action signifies the beginning of the 'operational' stage of the state plan. Theoretically lasting one to two years, the operational stage usually involves no federal compliance activity, but OSHA retains discretionary concurrent jurisdiction. During this stage there is still intensive monitoring of the state plan by OSHA. Maximum federal operational grants drop to 50 per cent of state implementation costs.

In sum, implementation plans provide a mechanism to reconcile two apparently conflicting objectives: the desire to have high standards applied in a uniform manner throughout the country, and the desire of the states to retain their regulatory sovereignty. Could such a model be transported to the EC level?

The setting is of course radically different in the Community, where decentralised implementation, far from being the exception, tends to be the rule. Yet, to require member states to draw up an implementation plan and to set up the means that are necessary to make it operational would force them to address the implementation issue more systematically than is currently the case. National governments would need to identify the resources – both human and financial – which will require mobilisation if the objective set at Community level is to be reached.

In this connection, it is important to keep in mind that a significant proportion of Commission legislative proposals are a response to specific requests of the other European institutions (specially Council and Parliament), the member states themselves, and economic actors (as noted in Section 6, above). In particular, as a recent Commission Report on Better Law-making (European Commission, 1998) points out, 'The proliferation of specialised Council compositions...has led to a very significant increase in the number of requests to the Commission to initiate legislation. In each of its compositions the Council tends to want to extend the scope of Community action in the fields it covers' p.12).

If all such requests were to be accompanied by an implementation plan, this would impose greater discipline on all sides, forcing the other institutions to be 'far more discriminating when they ask the Commission to present proposals and avoid making proposals more complex by burdening them with details...' (ibid.).

A system like the one proposed here can work only if the Commission is technically equipped to assess the adequacy of implementation plans, to monitor the activity of national administrations and to provide guidance – all tasks that the Commission is currently not in a position to carry out satisfactorily, but which *could be entrusted to agencies* organised along the lines indicated in Section 10, below.

9.3 Improving executive oversight

Among the major shortcomings of the EC regulatory system are the lack of rational procedures for selecting regulatory priorities, the absence of central coordination and oversight leading to serious inconsistencies across and within regulatory programmes, and the insufficient attention paid to the cost-effectiveness or, better still, the net benefit, of individual rules.

The patchwork character of Community regulation and the lack of incentives to search for economically efficient solutions are due in large part to political and institutional factors such as the complexity of EC policy-making, disagreements among member states concerning priorities, and the need for the Commission to respond to national initiatives, and to requests by other European institutions. However, the shortcomings of Community regulation also have causes that are intrinsic to the regulatory process as such. We discuss the structural problems of the regulatory process in Section 9.4. Here it is sufficient to point out that even a country such as the United States, with its century-old experience of statutory regulation at state and federal level, had no executive-branch oversight of regulatory agencies until the 1970s. After the emergence of the health, safety and environment regulatory agencies in the 1970s, however, it became important to verify that these regulations were in society's best interest and, in particular, that the costs they imposed were justified by the benefits they were expected to produce.

Traditionally, American agencies were constrained by little other than their legislative mandate and potential judicial review as to whether they were adhering to the mandate. Congress can, of course, pass legislation requiring that an agency take a particular type of action, but routine regulatory actions seldom receive congressional scrutiny. Most important, there is no need for congressional approval for a regulatory agency to take action provided that it can survive judicial review. Hence the need for executive oversight of the agencies. Such oversight is the responsibility of a specialised unit within the Executive Office of the President, the Office of Management and Budget (OMB).

A central regulatory clearinghouse is needed also in the EU in order to ensure that actions taken by different Directorates General (and, in the future, by different European Agencies) meet basic standards of consistency and efficiency. Moreover, such a centralised unit would help the President of the Commission to fulfil his responsibility of providing political guidance to the Commission's work under Art. 219, EC (formerly 163, first para.). Notice that a European OMB could be established within the framework of the present treaties. It would systematise and generalise what the Commission is already doing, for example, in the case of the European Agency for the Evaluation of Medicinal Products (EMEA).

Hence, it is interesting to review in some detail the role of the American OMB in controlling and coordinating the work of federal agencies. The first stage of the development of a federal regulation occurs at the time when an agency decides to regulate a particular area of economic activity. Once a topic is on the agency's regulatory agenda, it must be listed as part of its regulatory programme, where the purpose of this review is to identify potential overlap among agencies, to become aware of particularly controversial regulatory policies that are being developed, and to screen out regulation that appears to be particularly undesirable. These reviews have essentially an informational function, alerting OMB to potential inter-agency conflicts.

The next stage in the development of a regulation is to prepare a Regulatory Impact Analysis (RIA). This requires the agency to calculate benefits and costs and to determine whether the benefits of the regulation are in excess of the costs it imposes on the regulated activities. The agency is also required to consider potentially more desirable policy alternatives, such as information strategies instead of a command-and-control approach. After completing the RIA, the agency must send the analysis to OMB for its review, which must take place 60 days before the agency issues a Notice of Proposed Rulemaking (NPRM) in the *Federal Register*. During this period OMB reviews the proposed regulation in its current form. In some instances, OMB negotiates with the agency to obtain improvements in the regulation, and in a few instances OMB rejects the regulation as being undesirable. At that point, the agency has the choice either to revise the regulation or too withdraw it.

This OMB review is generally a secret process. The secretive nature of the review process is intended to enable the regulatory agency to alter its position without having to admit publicly that it has made an error in terms of the regulation it has proposed. Keeping the debate out of the public arena prevents the parties from becoming locked into positions for the purpose of a public image. The disadvantage of secrecy is, of course, that it excludes Congress and the public from the regulatory policy debate. For this reason, under the Clinton administration, OMB has made a major effort to open up more aspects of this review process to public scrutiny.

If the proposal does not receive OMB approval, the agency can make an appeal to the President or to the Vice President if the latter has been delegated authority for this class of regulatory issues.

After receiving OMB approval, the agency can publish the NPRM in the *Federal Register*. Typically included in the material inserted in the official journal is a detailed justification for the regulation, which often includes an assessment of the benefits and costs of the regulatory measure. Once the proposal has been published in the *Federal Register*, it is open to public debate. There is a 30- to 90- day period for public notice and comment. After receiving and processing these public comments, the agency must then put the regulation in its final form. In doing so, it finalises its regulatory impact analysis and submits both the regulation and the accompanying analysis to OMB 30 days before publishing the final regulation in the *Federal Register*. OMB has roughly one month to review the regulation in its final form and decide whether to approve it. The overwhelming majority of regulations are approved and published as final rules in the official journal. Generally speaking, one can say that the OMB review process alters regulations in minor ways, such as introducing alternative methods of compliance that will be less costly but equally effective as those proposed by the agency. The main function of the OMB review is to force the agencies to support their proposals by well developed analyses, something the EU is lacking despite all the calls to do it (see Section 4.2.3 above). OMB has also been successful in screening out some of the most inefficient regulations, such as those with costs per life saved, well in excess of $100 million (Viscusi, et al., 1997)

9.4 The regulatory budget

In addition to monitoring the quality of individual agency proposals, a regulatory clearinghouse located at a sufficiently high level in the Community bureaucracy, preferably in the office of the President, could also coordinate all regulatory activities by imposing a novel type of budgetary discipline.

Coordination is a serious problem in any complex organisation, but it is especially acute in the case of regulatory activities. While the size and priorities of non-regulatory, direct-expenditure programmes are determined by political executives through the normal budgetary process, budgetary constraints have a limited impact on regulatory activities. This is because the real cost of regulations is borne not by the regulators, but by the individuals and organisations that have to comply with the regulations. The result is a serious lack of coordination both within and across regulatory programmes and agencies.

Regulatory issues tend to be dealt with sector by sector, and even within the same sector, it is often difficult to see that regulatory priorities are set in a way that explicitly takes into consideration either the urgency of the problem or the benefits and costs of different proposals. For example, the imbalance between water and air pollution control existing in the EC can hardly be explained by differences in the seriousness of the relevant problems. Also, the marginal health benefits produced by certain environmental directives, such as the one on the quality of drinking water, appear to many analysts to be out of proportion with the very substantial costs imposed on the water industry and, ultimately, on all citizens. Again, the piecemeal procedure of the Commission in proposing new regulations has resulted in directives in areas where harmonisation is a low priority, while neglecting other areas that need a considerable amount of harmonisation. Such problems are compounded whenever previously centralised responsibilities are allocated to various decentralised agencies.

If a lack of budgetary discipline is a serious defect of the regulatory process, one can attempt to create coordination and control mechanisms similar to those traditionally used for direct public expenditures. This is the idea of a *regulatory budget*. In its basic outline, the regulatory budget – as proposed by several distinguished American economists – would be established jointly by Congress and the President for each agency, starting with a budget constraint on total private expenditures mandated by regulation, and then allocating the budget among the different agencies. Simultaneous consideration by OMB of all major regulatory proposals would permit an assessment of their joint impact on particular industries and on the economy as a whole.

Thus, the administrative procedure for implementing a regulatory budget would mirror that of a fiscal budget. In addition to the traditional budget submissions, the President would send to Congress a budget limiting the regulatory costs that could be imposed on the national economy. After enactment by both houses, the regulatory budget would be forwarded to the President to sign into law. Like the fiscal budget, the regulatory budget would be open to political debate. In fact, the actual level of the regulatory budget can only be determined through the political process, as in the case of the fiscal budget.

Again like the fiscal budget, the regulatory budget focuses on the costs rather than the benefits of regulation. However, since each regulatory agency would face a constraint that limits its total mandated spending, it would have an incentive to allocate its resources in the most efficient manner to achieve its policy objectives. If forced to choose between programmes, agencies would be encouraged to choose those that provide the greatest benefit per unit of cost. By formalising this portion of the budget allocation process, Congress and the President would have an added interest in ensuring that regulatory funds are allocated to the agencies that produce the most substantial benefits for society. They would also assume responsibility for the overall magnitude and priorities of regulation, and for inter-agency coordination.

The primary difficulty in implementing a regulatory budget is cost estimation. Without a reliable, consistent estimate of costs (broken down by agency and by regulatory programme), it is impossible for a budgetary authority to make sensible allocations of resources across different agencies and regulatory programmes.

Regulatory costs fall into three distinct categories:

1. Operations of the regulatory agencies. These costs are represented by salaries, administrative costs and capital expenditures needed to operate the agency.
2. Compliance by firms, consumers and government organisations. This category includes the direct expenditures that are needed to comply with a given regulation. So-called process costs – the costs of filling out paperwork and dealing with administrative requirements – also fall into this category of direct costs.
3. Indirect economic costs in the form of reduced output and efficiency loss. For example, if a regulatory agency mandates a new safety device on a product, then the price of that product will almost certainly rise because of higher production costs. As a consequence, some consumers who would have bought the product at the old price will now find themselves priced out of the market. In addition, producers will earn lower profits, and some marginal firms may go out of business. These combined effects are often termed 'dead-weight loss' to reflect unrecoverable costs to society of reduced production due to regulation.

Now, operating costs are relatively easy to quantify, as they are already reported as part of the fiscal budget; they are by far the smallest part of the cost of regulation. Compliance costs are generally obtained through surveys or audits of affected firms, or through engineering studies. Indirect economic costs would have to be calculated by means of general equilibrium models simultaneously examining the interactions of all consumers, all firms and all markets. Whatever the theoretical interest of such general equilibrium analysis, its usefulness in a policy structure such as the regulatory budget is probably limited. In practical terms, the most important inputs into the regulatory budgetary process are estimates of compliance costs.

Sophisticated techniques of compliance costs assessment (CCA) have been developed in recent years, not only in the US, but also in Europe. In the US, for example, the Environmental Protection Agency has carried out extensive analyses to estimate the cost of recent amendments to the Clean Air Act (CAA) and to the Safe Drinking Water Act (SDWA). Estimates of pollution control expenditure mandated by the CAA amendments indicate a 'budget' of $79 billion in compliance costs borne by economic agents between 1993 and 2000. Similarly, private expenditures resulting from new regulations for water treatment have been budgeted at $1.5 billion to $2.4 billion a year, or $20 billion for the entire 1993-2000 period.

In the UK, all government departments must prepare a CCA when evaluating policy proposals likely to affect business. Similarly, all papers for cabinet and cabinet committees, and minutes to the Prime Minister's Office for collective discussion, that deal with proposals that may have an impact on business, must clearly spell out likely compliance costs.

Departments are also asked to prepare a CCA for all EC regulations and directives likely to be burdensome to business, whether or not the Commission is preparing an impact assessment. A CCA should also be prepared for all UK legislation to implement agreed EC directives, as well as for Communities acts, which, although not binding on member states, may lead to burdensome regulations (Froude, et al., 1994).

In 1986, the European Commission introduced a system that weakly echoed the UK CCA system for EC legislative proposals. Originally, every draft legislative proposal being considered for adoption by the Commission was to be accompanied by an impact assessment ('fiche d'impact') outlining the impact of the proposed measure on small- and medium-sized enterprises. Since 1990, however, assessments have only been completed on the most burdensome legislative proposals contained in the Commission's Work Programme. DG XXIII, at the beginning of each year, identifies those measures on which impact assessments should be completed. Others may be added to the list during the course of the year. Section 3 above has discussed at length the problems and practice of regulatory impact assessment in the Commission.

Thus, some basic elements of a regulatory budget are already available at the EC level and at least in some member states. This mechanism could be developed further in selected policy areas such as water pollution control. A Community OMB would provide the necessary focus for such efforts. In fact, the experience of the United States – where a regulatory budget has been introduced in some policy areas on an experimental basis – shows that the success of this reform depends crucially on the existence of a regulatory unit at the highest level in the Executive Branch.[45]

10. EXTERNAL THREAT TO REGULATORY CREDIBILITY: THE PERILS OF POLITICISATION

The increasing level of politicisation of the Commission arguably represents the most serious external threat to the credibility of EC regulation. The appointment procedure defined by Art. 214, EC introduces some radical changes. If, under the old Art. 158, EC, the national governments could nominate a new Commission President only after consulting the European Parliament, now, under the new Art. 214, EC, their nomination must be approved by the EP. Moreover, the President and other members of the Commission remain subject to a vote of approval by the EP, as in classical parliamentary systems.

A further institutional innovation is provided by the link between Parliament's terms of office and that of the Commission. Since a newly elected Parliament takes part in nominating the Commission, any significant changes in the EP's composition are now reflected at Commission level.

These developments augur a deep transformation in the relationship between the EP and the Commission. The Commission will, henceforth, be fully responsible to the EP, whose influence will be felt in all its activities, whether administrative or legislative. Thus, the right already given to the EP in the Maastricht Treaty to request the Commission to 'submit any appropriate proposal on matters in which it considers that a Community act is required' (Art. 192, EC, formerly 138B, EC), may be seen as coming close to a true right of legislative initiative.

Of course, an increasing level of politicisation of Community policy-making becomes unavoidable as more and more tasks involving the use of political discretion are shifted to the European level. These developments and the problems connected with the next enlargement not only increase the administrative tasks of the Commission, but also emphasise the Commission's political responsibilities. In this context, the demand for a greater role of the EP becomes understandable.

At the same time, we should not be blind to the risks which politicisation entails for the process of EC regulatory policy-making. One of the most frequently cited reasons for governments to delegate policy-making powers to 'non-majoritarian' (i.e. politically independent) institutions, such as central banks and regulatory commissions, is the need to preserve policy continuity against the changing preferences of variable parliamentary majorities. In turn, policy continuity is seen as a necessary condition of policy credibility.

Thus, in most countries, regulatory policy-making is now delegated to specialised agencies or commissions operating at arm's length from government. The point of insulating regulators from the political process is to *enhance the credibility* of regulatory commitments. The assumption is that the head of an independent agency attaches more importance to the agency's statutory objectives than do politicians, who are influenced by electoral considerations. Agency heads generally expect, and are expected by others, to have a well defined agenda, and to measure their success by the amount of the agenda they accomplish. They are also aware that courts can review their decisions and can overturn them if they seem to depart too greatly from the language and the aims of the enabling statute. Hence, they have an additional incentive to pursue the statutory objectives of the agency, even when those objectives no longer enjoy political support. For these reasons, the growing politicisation of the Commission – a process which is both inevitable and, perhaps, positive in terms of perceived legitimacy – is the strongest argument in favour of an increased recourse to regulatory agencies operating at arm's length from the Commission and the other European institutions.

It should be noted that the term 'agency' covers a variety of organisational forms – commissions, directorates, inspectorates, authorities, services, offices, and so on – which perform functions of a governmental nature, and which often exist outside the normal departmental framework of government. The most comprehensive definition is probably provided by the US Administrative Procedure Act (APA). According to this important statute which regulates the decision-making processes of all agencies of the federal government, an agency is a part of government that is generally independent in the exercise of its functions and that by law has authority to take a final and binding action affecting the rights and obligations of individuals, particularly by the characteristic procedure of rule-making and adjudication.

Agency status does not require that an agency exercise its powers with complete independence, either vertically (in terms of being subject to administrative review), or horizontally (in terms of being required to act in concert with others). If an authority is in complete charge of a programme, it is an agency with regard to that programme, despite its subordinate position in other respects.

To exemplify, the American independent regulatory commissions, such as the Interstate Commerce Commission or the Securities and Exchange Commission, are agencies, but so are the Occupational Safety and Health Administration (located within the Department of Labor), the Food and Drug Administration (part of the Department of Health and Human Services), and the Environmental Protection Agency (which is independent by law, but whose chief administrator serves at the pleasure of the President).

In the EU context, most of the new European agencies, as well as Eurostat, are de facto agencies in the same sense. The European Central Bank is, of course, independent both de jure and de facto. An interesting feature of the new European agencies is that they have not been designed to operate in isolation, or to replace national regulators. Rather, they are expected to become the central nodes of networks including national agencies as well as international organisations.

National and EU representatives sit in the management boards and the scientific committees of the new agencies. These committees formulate the scientific opinion of the agency and may perform other important functions. Thus the two scientific committees of the Agency for the Evaluation of Medicines (EMEA) – one for medicinal products for human use and one for veterinary medicines – also arbitrate disputes between pharmaceutical firms and national authorities. Each of the two committees consists of two members nominated by each member state, while the Commission is not represented in the committees, no doubt in order to emphasise their functional independence.

The committee members represent the national regulatory authorities, but it would be wrong to assume that, through their power of appointment, the national governments effectively control EMEA's authorisation process. In fact, both committees – which already played a significant role in the old multi-state drug application procedure – have not only become more important, but also more independent since the creation of EMEA. This is because it is in their interest to establish an international reputation for good scientific work, and for this purpose the degree to which they reflect the views of the national governments is irrelevant (Gardner, 1996).

This change in the incentive structures of regulators operating in a transnational network deserves to be emphasised by making use of sociologist Alvin Gouldner's terminology. In his work on the professions, Gouldner introduced the distinction between 'cosmopolitans' and 'locals'. Cosmopolitans are likely to adopt an international reference-group orientation, while locals tend to have a national or sub-national (e.g. organisational) orientation. Hence, local experts tend to be more submissive to the institutional and hierarchical structures in which they operate than do cosmopolitan experts, who can appeal to the standards and criteria of an international body of scientific peers. Using this terminology, we may say that EMEA is pioneering in the transformation of national regulators from 'locals' to 'cosmopolitans'. It does this by providing a stable institutional focus at European level and important links to extra-European regulatory bodies such as the US Food and Drug Administration.

In addition, EMEA (which has exclusive competence only for the approval of 'high-tech' drugs) permits real regulatory competition between agencies for authorisation business. This type of *competition among agencies* should help to keep EMEA more flexible and less bureaucratic than it might otherwise become (Gardner, 1996).

As already noted, EMEA is an agency only de facto, and the same is true of all the new European agencies with the possible exception of the Office for Harmonisation of the Internal Market (Trade Mark Office), which is funded from user fees. The reason why EMEA is not an agency de jure is that its determinations concerning the safety and efficacy of new drugs must be approved by the Commission. The Commission, not the agency that has done all the necessary scientific work, bears the final responsibility for drug approval. This anomalous situation has not created serious problems, so far. However, the growing politicisation of the Commission, and the likelihood that more agencies will be created in areas ranging from telecommunications and food safety to energy and other public utilities, suggests that such anomalies should be removed as soon as possible.

The legal barrier to the delegation of decision-making powers to independent agencies is, allegedly, the 'Meroni doctrine' of the European Court of Justice – which dates from the 1950s. Even present members of the ECJ hold the doctrine to be outdated, since it relies on a very traditional view of administrative control, ignoring the many procedural and substantive mechanisms by which agency independence and public accountability can be reconciled.

Theoretical considerations and the century-old experience of the American regulatory state show *that independence and accountability can be reconciled* by a combination of control mechanisms, rather than by oversight exercised from any fixed place in the political spectrum: clear and limited statutory objectives to provide unambiguous performance standards; reason-giving and transparency requirements to facilitate judicial review and public participation; due process procedures to ensure fairness among the inevitable winners and losers from regulatory decisions; and professionalism to withstand external interference and reduce the risk of an arbitrary use of agency discretion (Majone, 1996). In the words of an American scholar

(Moe, 1987), when such a system of multiple controls works properly, no one controls an agency, yet the agency is 'under control'.

In terms of both efficiency and legitimacy, independent and publicly accountable agencies provide a superior answer to the regulatory challenges of the internal market, and of globalisation, than the cumbersome and opaque comitology system. Regulatory credibility depends crucially on a clear allocation of responsibilities. The consensual, bargaining approach that has characterised regulatory policy-making in the EC for almost four decades, is no longer viable.

NOTES

1. Art. 3 sub. c, EC (same numbering in Amsterdam Treaty as before) speaks about 'persons', as does Art. 14, EC (formerly 7A, EC); yet Arts. 39-42, EC (formerly, 48-51, EC) speak about securing the 'freedom of movement for workers', which – unsurprisingly, given this purposeful inconsistency – is highly conditioned. A *single* market should of course stipulate, in Art. 3 sub. c, EC, the free movement of workers, unconditionally. This flaw has prevented the removal of serious distortions in the EU (common?) labour market

2. Art. 295, EC (formally Art. 222, EC) assigns ownership issues exclusively to Member States. This has prevented a Community patent ever since the first proposal in 1962! Other IPRs have become regulated at EC level, but only recently. This flaw has been extremely costly.

3. In labour markets there is next to no mutual recognition, due to either 'host-country control' principles (which invariably increase rigidities) or very detailed regulation of the 'old-approach' type (e.g. some cases of diploma recognition). A general obligation to allow free movement of workers in Art. 3, EC would prompt great improvement here.

4. In the so-called Cardiff I process the Commission wrote a report on the functioning of the EC product and Capital markets (COM(1999) of 10 of January 1999), complemented by national reports. Under an initiative of the Commission ('welcomed' by the Cardiff European Council), a so-called Cardiff II report was presented (COM (1999)61 of 17 February 1999) which is broader (includes also labour and public finance). In the year 2000 the latter will be replaced by an implementation report about Cardiff I and the reform recommendations in the Broad Economic Guidelines.

5. The Commission recommendations for the Broad Economic Guidelines for 1999 are in COM (1999) 143 of 30 March 1999.

6. By derogations (of free movement, under Art. 30, EC, formerly Art.. 36; EC, or the rule of reason under Art. 28, EC, formerly Art. 30, EC, for goods; somewhat similar case law has developed for services under Art. 43, EC, formerly Art. 52, in combination with Arts. 45/46, formerly Arts. 55/56, EC)

7. See also the chapter by Pelkmans, Vos and Di Mauro in Volume I, and Pelkmans and Sun (1994).

8. Sutherland et al. (1992).

9. Molitor et al., (1995).

10. UNICE (1995).

11. BEST Task Force (1998), Volume I, April; see also COM(98)550 of 30 September 1998, which comprises the Commission's response to the BEST report.

12. Excellent surveys of the legal aspects of EU regulatory quality are Piris (1998) and Timmermans (1998), as well as some other essays in A. Kellerman et al. (1998).

13. Note that in specific cases (e.g. where derogations of the free movement of goods and services are concerned, or where universal or public service obligations are regulated for utilities) the European Court imposes proportionality on national regulation, too.

14. European Commission (1996). See Monti (1996); special issue of *European Economy*, Reports and Studies, 1996/4 (December 1996); and the 38 background studies having been published by the OOPEC in Luxembourg under the heading: *Single Market Review*, during 1997 and 1998.

15. Excluding, for the most part, regulatory activities in agricultural market organisations, and to some extent, fisheries.

16. Costs or benefits of a transaction that the parties to the transaction have not accounted for in the exchange. Such extra transaction costs can arise from imperfectly observable information (possibly leading to moral hazard and selection solution), asymmetric information and from contingencies in the case of long-term contracts.

17. Costs or benefits transmitted between agents, in the absence of any related economic transaction between those agents (e.g. pollution, contamination, etc.).

18. For some theoretical economic considerations about the optimal choice between command-and-control and economic instruments, under different assumptions about information (etc.), see Labory and Malgarini, in Chapter 3 of Volume I, Section 2.1.

19. Other than in agriculture, competition policy and trade policy (the latter two being 'exclusive' EU level powers), it is little used.

20. As the non-expert methodology of Pelkmans and Labory (1998) shows.
21. In Pelkmans and Labory (1998, case study no. 1, in the Appendix) the drawbacks of using cost-effectiveness compared to CBA are illustrated for the study done for the Auto-Oil-I programme.
22. We assume that the 18th Declaration of the Member States, refers to the costs and benefits *for the EU*, when it speaks of '..costs and benefits to the Member States' public authorities and all the parties concerned'. Otherwise, we would have to infer from this formulation that the specific mentioning of the Member States' public authorities (and not the public interest they are expected to stand for) suggests some degree of self-interest. This would be consistent with the so-called 'positive theory of regulation' and with 'public choice' approaches. Of course, also European regulation, or the lack of it, can be biased by self-interest of regulators (be they national, or at the EU level), or by so-called 'capture' of regulators by the regulatees. *Enhancing transparency by permanent attention to the costs and benefits of regulation is no doubt helpful to reduce the importance of self-interest or capture.*
23. A collection of other appeals and resolutions can be found in European Policy Centre (1996).
24. European Commission (1998).
25. Also, in a survey by Ciavarinni Azzi (1998), Columbia Journal of European Law, Vol. 4/3, summer), the issue of regulatory assessment, its actual use or reform is not mentioned.
26. Thus, in November 1997, DG III (chemicals unit) organised a workshop with specialists from the member states, based on an elaborate draft of such a manual.
27. It all depends on the level of ambition one has. The Commission's guidelines begin by quoting the 18th Declaration and comprise useful (and correct) statements about CBA for regulation. But they remain overly general.
28. As Desarnauts (1998, p. 256) notes, too. The hormones-in-beef case in WTO is an extreme instance in which the EU position was fixed – legally based on the precautionary principle – without ever having gone through a rigorous risk assessment before WTO in 1998 instructed the EU to do so.
29. Namely, think small first; proportionality; focus on the goal.
30. See COM (1998) 197 of 30 March 1998, The Business Test Panel, a pilot project.
31. Third consultation of the Business Test Panel – the proposal for a directive on waste from electrical equipment (WEEE), 6 August 1999 (meanwhile published on the website of DG XV of the Commission).

32. That this also worries leading lawyers, is evident from the following remark Chris Timmermans (1998, p. 44): 'A quick look into the literature...aimed at ensuring an acceptable quality of (Community) law suffices to demonstrate how diverse this notion of quality is being used and how many facets it may include'.

33. See Muller-Graf (1998) and other comments for the experiences or debates in some other member states.

34. Given that the EC has horizontal directives for labelling, hygiene in food, etc.

35. Interestingly, under 'subsidiarity' and 'alternatives to legislation' codes of conduct are advocated (as well as self-regulation and voluntary agreements).

36. Three examples from the 1996 report: a) six old-approach food directives (so-called recipe law); b) a single directive for diploma recognition in crafts and trades, leading to the repeal of no less than 35 directives; and c) recasting the tractor framework directive and its 23 specific old approach directives.

37. COM 96 (204) of 8 May 1996, SLIM, a pilot project.

38. COM(97)618 of 24 November 1997, p. 3 (Report on the results of the second phase of SLIM).

39. The second report on SLIM (phase 2) adds the desire not to interfere with exercises of legislative revision or consolidation already underway. COM(97)618 of 24 November 1997, p. 3.

40. A4-0108/97 adopted on 9 April 1997.

41. See the detailed accounts by Heinemann (1998) and Dondelinger (1998) in Kellerman et al. (1998). Note that '(B)etween the conflicting interests of users and providers (of statistics, the authors) there is no path which may satisfy all parties'. (Heinemann, 1998 p. 181).

42. Not specifically analysed in this paper, as this has been well-covered in the literature and by EU sources. See for instance, the 16th Annual Report on Monitoring the Application of Community Law, COM 1999(301) of 9 July 1999 (and earlier annual reports), the Score Board of DG XV on implementation, the Single Market Review of 1996-1997, etc.

43. Again, not analysed in the present paper. On the agencies, however, see Section 10. On delegation of competition policy, see the White Paper, COM (1999)132, on the modernisation of the rules implementing Arts. 85 and 86 of the EC Treaty, White Paper.

44. COM(1998)715 of 4 December 1998.

45. The current state of the American debate is documented by the Special Issue on regulatory budgeting of the December 1998 issue of the journal *Policy Sciences.*

REFERENCES

Atkins, W.S. (1997), 'Technical Barriers to Trade', in *The Single Market Review Series, Sub-series III*, Vol. 1, Luxembourg: OOPEC.

Baldwin, Robert (1995), *Rules and Government*, Oxford: Clarendon Press.

Baldwin, Robert and T. Daintith, (eds), (1992), *Harmonisation and hazard – regulating workplace health and safety in the EC*, London: Graham and Trotman.

BEST Task Force (1998), *Report of the Business Environment Simplification Task Force,* 2 volumes European Commission, DG XXIII, Brussels.

Burstall, M. and B. Reuben (1988), *The cost of non-Europe in the pharmaceutical industry*, Background documents of the Cecchini report, Research on the cost of non-Europe, Basic Findings, Volume 15, OOPEC, Luxembourg.

Ciavarinni Azzi, G. (1998), *Columbia Journal of European Law*, Vol. 4, No. 3, (summer).

Competitiveness Advisory Group, 1996, *Second report*, Brussels, June.

Desarnauts, J. (1998), 'Comments' (On Risks), in A.E. Kellerman et al., (eds), (1998), *Improving the Quality of Legislation in Europe*, The Hague/Boston/London: Kluwer Law International.

Dondelinger, J. (1998), 'Comments' (On Intra-state) in A.E. Kellerman et al., (eds), (1998), *Improving the Quality of Legislation in Europe*, The Hague/Boston/London: Kluwer Law International.

European Commission (1998), *Better Law-Making 1998, A Shared Responsibility*, COM(1998)715 final, December 1998.

European Commission (1996b, *The Impact and Effectiveness of the Single Market*, COM(96)520, 30 October.

European Commission (1996b), *Better Law-Making 1996*, CSE(96)7, 27 November.

European Policy Centre, 1996, *The need for cost-benefit analysis*, EPC, Brussels.

European Round Table (1996), *Bench-marking for policy-makers: the way to competitiveness, growth and job- creation*, ERT, Brussels.

Froude, Julie, Rebecca Boden, Anthony Ogus and Peter Stubbs (1994) 'Toeing the line: compliance cost assessment in Britain', *Policy and Politics*, Vol. 22, No. 4, pp. 313-322.

Gardner, John S. (1996), 'The European Agency for the Evaluation of Medicines and European Regulation of Pharmaceuticals', *European Law Journal*, Vol. 2, No. 1, pp. 48-82.

Heinemann, J. (1998), 'Simplification in statistics: the Intra-State case', in A.E. Kellermann et al., (eds), (1998), *Improving the Quality of Legislation in Europe*, The Hague/Boston/London: Kluwer Law International.

Hopkins, T. (1998), 'Comments' (On Risks), in A.E. Kellermann et al, (eds), (1998), *Improving the Quality of Legislation in Europe*, The Hague/Boston/London: Kluwer Law International.

Kellermann A.E., Ciaviarini Azzi G., Jacobs S. and Deighton-Smith R., (eds), (1998), *Improving the Quality of Legislation in Europe*, The Hague/Boston/London: Kluwer Law International.

Majone, Giandomenico (1996), *Regulating Europe*, London: Routledge.

Mendeloff, John (1988), *The Dilemma of Toxic Substance Regulation,* Cambridge, MA: The MIT Press.

Moe, Terry (1987), 'Interests, Institutions and Positive Theory: the Politics of the NLRB', *Studies in American Political Development*, Vol. 2, pp. 236-299.

Molitor, B. et al., (1995), *Report of the Group of independent experts on legislative and administrative simplification*, COM (95)288 of 21 May.

Monti, M. (1996), *The single market and tomorrow's Europe*, Luxembourg, OOPEC.

Mueller-Graf, P-C. (1998), The quality of European and national legislation; the German experiences and initiatives, in A.E. Kellermann et al. (eds), (1998), *Improving the Quality of Legislation in Europe*, The Hague/Boston/London: Kluwer Law International.

OECD (1997), *The OECD report on regulatory reform*, 2 volumes, OECD, Paris.

Pelkmans, J. and J.M. Sun, (1994), 'Towards an EC regulatory strategy: Lessons from learning-by-doing', in OECD, *Regulatory cooperation for an interdependent world,* OECD, Paris.

Pelkmans, J. and S. Labory, 1998, *European regulation and cost-benefit analysis: a methodological guide for non-specialists*, unpublished study for DG III, CEPS.

Pelkmans, J., E. Vos and L. Di Mauro, (2000), 'Reforming Product Regulation in the EU: A Painstaking, Iterative Two-Level Game', Chapter 7 in this volume.

Piris, J.C. (1998), 'The quality of Community legislation: the viewpoint of the Council Legal Service', in A.E. Kellermann et al., (1998), *Improving the Quality of Legislation in Europe*, The Hague/Boston/London: Kluwer Law International.

Rubinacci, L. (1998), 'Comments' (On the Use of CBA), in A.E. Kellermann, et al., (eds), (1998) *Improving the Quality of Legislation in Europe,* The Hague/Boston/London: Kluwer Law International.

Schulte-Braucks, R. (1998), 'The European Commission's Business Impact Assessment System' in A.E. Kellermann, et al., (eds), (1998) *Improving the Quality of Legislation in Europe,* The Hague/Boston/London: Kluwer Law International.

Silva, F. and Cavaliere (2000), 'The economic impact of product liability: Lessons from the US and the EU experience', Chapter 8 in this volume.

Sun, J.M. and J. Pelkmans (1995), 'Regulatory competition in the internal market', *Journal of Common Market Studies*, Vol. 33, No. 1 (March).

Sutherland, P. et al. (1992), *The internal market after 1992-meeting the challenge,* SEC (92) 2044, Brussels, October.

Timmermans, C. (1998), How to improve the quality of Community legislation: the viewpoint of the European Commission, in A.E. Kellermann et al., (eds), (1998*), Improving the Quality of Legislation in Europe*, The Hague/Boston/London: Kluwer Law International.

UNICE (1995), *Releasing Europe's potential: through targeted regulatory reform*, Brussels, November.

Viscusi, Kip W. (1983) *Risk by Choice; Regulating Health and Safety in the Workplace,* Cambridge, MA: Harvard University Press.

Viscusi, Kip W., John M. Vernon and Joseph E. Harrington, Jr. (1997), *Economics of Regulation and Antitrust*, Cambridge, MA: The MIT Press, 2nd edition.